City, Marriage, Tournament

Margaret Tudor and the Duke of Albany. Portrait from a private Scottish collection.

City, Marriage, Tournament

Arts of Rule in Late Medieval Scotland

LOUISE OLGA FRADENBURG

The University of Wisconsin Press

The University of Wisconsin Press
114 North Murray Street
Madison, Wisconsin 53715

3 Henrietta Street
London WC2E 8LU, England

5   4   3   2   1

Printed in the United States of America

Library of Congress Cataloging-in-Publication Data
Fradenburg, Louise Olga, 1953–   .
    City, marriage, tournament: arts of rule in late medival
  Scotland / Louise Fradenburg.
     406 pp.   cm.
    Includes bibliographical references and index.
    ISBN 0-299-12950-0   ISBN 0-299-12954-3
    1. Scotland – Politics and government – 1371-1707.   2. James IV,
  King of Scotland, 1473-1513.   3. James III, King of Scotland,
  1451-1488.   4. Marriages of royalty and nobility – Scotland – History.
  5. Scottish literature – To 1700 – History and criticism.
  6. Edinburgh (Scotland) – Intellectual life.   7. Scotland –
  Civilization – 15th century.   8. Kings and rulers in literature.
  9. Tournaments – Scotland – History.   10. Monarchy – Scotland – History.
  11. Stuart, House of.   I. Title.
  DA784.5.F74   1991
  941.104 – dc20   91-12976
                    CIP

To my mother, Inni Louise Varga Fradenburg
and my father, William Joseph Fradenburg
with love and thanks

Contents

Illustrations

Acknowledgments

City, Marriage, Tournament began in Scotland, where my research was supported by a Junior Faculty Fellowship from Dartmouth College and by an Honorary Fellowship at the Edinburgh University Institute for Advanced Studies in the Humanities. I benefited enormously in those days from the knowledge and good counsel of Emily Lyle, School of Scottish Studies, Edinburgh University; Rosalind Marshall, Scottish National Portrait Gallery; and Michael Lynch, Department of Scottish History, Edinburgh University. Roger Mason, of the Department of Scottish History at St. Andrews University, was my patient interlocutor; he and his colleague, Norman T. Macdougall, kindly read and commented on various parts of the manuscript. Lee W. Patterson of Duke University also helped to shape "City" when I wrote a version of it for his anthology *Literary Practice and Social Change in Britain, 1380–1530*. Peter Stallybrass, Peter Travis, and David Kastan read early drafts of the manuscript and cheered me on. My research assistants, especially Margaret Pappano, Maura Nolan, and Christopher Sciglitano, were generous with their thoughts as well as with their labor. And many thanks go to the University of Wisconsin Press for its painstaking attention to the development of this book: Barbara Hanrahan and Raphael Kadushin were ideal editors; and my readers, Leah Marcus, John Ganim, Carolyn Dinshaw, and John Fyler wrote marvelously detailed and thoughtful reports.

I also want to acknowledge Glending Olson and Giles Gamble, who introduced me to Middle Scots poetry; my friends at the University of Virginia, Laurene McKillop, Kathryn Lynch, Dennis Tosh, Jim Kee and Craig Davis, who shared ideas with me about literary theory and about medieval literature, as did, more formally but equally generously, Leo Damrosch, Hoyt Duggan, Wally Kerrigan, and Tony Spearing; and I owe very special thanks to the wisdom and deep tact of Del Kolve. My love and thanks go to the friends and family who provided so many of the pleasures, and helped me through the pains, of the book years: Michael, Elaine, and Nicholas Aitken, Alastair Aitken, Joan and Tom Irvine, and Olive Rutherford, who made a home for me in Edinburgh; my astonishing friends Carla Carr, Carla Freccero, Horace Porter, Julia Rowe, Matthew Rowlinson, Ivy Schweitzer, Brenda Silver, Melissa P. Zeiger, and my funny Valentine Barbara Cunningham; my invariably perceptive sister Jan; my wonderful stepsons Casey and Morgan. Finally I want to thank my husband Richard Corum, for giving me the courage many years ago to change my work, and for continuing to help me.

Thanks to the University of California Press for permission to reprint parts of "Narrative and Capital in Late Medieval Scotland," in Lee W. Patterson, ed. *Literary Practice and Social Change in Britain, 1380–1530;* and to Duke University Press for permission to reprint parts of "Spectacular Fictions: The Body Politic in Chaucer and Dunbar," *Poetics Today* 5 (1984): 493–517. Some of the material in "Tournament" was first presented as a paper entitled "James IV and Tournament Pageantry" to the Traditional Cosmology Society's conference on Kingship, Edinburgh 1985.

Introduction

In *The Aristocrat as Art*, Domna C. Stanton writes that "aristocracy, like play, contains an underlying esthetic impulse. It involves, it is *poiesis*. Unlike the artist who works with materials external to himself — and for this reason is potentially productive or utilitarian — the aristocrat uses the self as his raw material."[1] My exploration of arts of rule in late medieval Scotland — of the city of Edinburgh as an imaginative figure; of royal marriage as an occasion for the celebration of bonds between king and queen, sovereign and nation; of the tournament as a site for the phenomenalization of the aristocratic self of honor — begins with a premise very like that of Stanton's. Arts of rule are, in part, works of imagination, without which the bonds on which sovereignty depends could not be effected. But while the aristocrat Stanton describes "uses the self as his raw material," the aristocracy of the later Middle Ages — and particularly that form of the aristocracy which is sovereignty — must depend upon the recognition of others for the difference that defines its distinction. In enacting himself, then, the sovereign uses the selves of other people as well as his own, and over those other selves, as well as his own, he tries to exert a power of change.

It is a mistake to think of power as force designed merely to conserve or to maximize itself, to preserve its identity, and therefore as force that resists change; it is a mistake even to think of power as force that resists change but, in doing so unwittingly, brings about change. While conservation (or containment) and maximization are important activities of power, the assumption that power will tolerate no radical alterations in its identity, no mutilation or death, hypostatizes the very conception of an identifiable self, desirous of preserving itself, that speaking of "power" rather than of people might seem to be trying to dislocate. Since it is difficult to resist sentimentalizing concepts of creativity and of change — since it is, for example, not always easy to consider that some changes, some inventions, can destroy the power of those who need change most to reinvent their world — it can become difficult, in turn, to theorize as historically significant those changes wrought and perhaps even sought by the powerful, without seeming thereby to valorize them.

But power is as much power of action as of inaction, though the distinction between action and inaction is difficult to sustain. The chapters that follow try to show, in the context of sovereignty in late medieval Scotland, how resistance to change often produces change and equally how change itself captivates and pacifies. Desires for historical difference, for discontinuity, often produce regressive identifications with an even earlier past, or futurism, as in the case of James IV of Scotland; desires for continuity sometimes take the form of an inactivity forceful enough to compel crisis, as in the case of James III. The ensuing discussion speaks of sovereigns because, while their power to make history has been greatly exaggerated, it has also been misperceived: while sovereigns must come to believe with a special intensity in their power to make changes or prevent them, their subjects must also believe in a sovereign power of change if they are to believe in a sovereign at all. This interchange has its own history—the history of the art of rule.

While, then, sovereigns will at times be seen trying to absorb all possible differences and resistances, I will not be arguing that they accomplish this goal; and I show how sovereigns are the effect of interactions with their subjects—that sovereignty is the effect of dialectic, of a relationality, between sovereign and subject, imagined sometimes as the relation of creator and creature, or of courtship, or of rivalry. There is no secure borderline between sovereign and subject—the subject, for example, must identify to some degree with the sovereign, the sovereign with the subject—and while this permeability of sovereign and subject can produce severe anxiety, it is also in part how the experience of rule is produced. This book thus attempts to reconsider the difference between the sovereign and the subject, by showing how sovereignty depends both on the making and the unmaking of such distinction. This book also tries to explore the permeability of one king's reign with respect to another, in the form of the relation between James III and James IV. Distinctions between town and Crown, Scotland and England, the Lowlands and the Highlands, come under similar scrutiny. Lastly, it will be noticed that this book concerns a period of time often thought of as "transitional." No effort has been made to define the fifteenth and earlier sixteenth centuries in Scotland as either medieval or Renaissance or to posit the categorical difference of "transitional" eras from other kinds of eras.

The sovereign is created in and through the inventive activity of his subjects; he depends upon their willingness to "produce" him as unique, both through works of imagination and works of labor. But the sovereign must also be representative—must be linked, by extensive and important bonds, to the entire community. And he, too, must play a creative role: he must negotiate the difficult complex of similarities and differences that constitute him as the unique exemplar of his country. He may accomplish this by force and by a variety of material interventions in the lives of his subjects; his arts of rule, like the arts of the subject, must be "productive" and "utilitarian" as well as purely imaginative. But the createdness of sovereignty—the sovereign's dependence on the productivity of his subjects—must be concealed as well as, at times, revealed, if the sovereign is to lay claim to the specialness of being which will authenticate his privilege. Thus one of the chief techniques in the sovereign's art of rule will be the constitution of himself as uniquely and supremely creative, in contradistinction to the createdness which will be ascribed to his subjects. There is a "familial" art of rule, which exploits relations between creator and creature, parent and child, in order to effect the bonds of rule—to effect belief in the special reality of the monarch, hence to transform the interiority of the subject into that special form of imaginative love which is devotion.[2] The king lays claim to a special substantiality—to being, as creator, the source of all substance—in order to authenticate himself, so that he can, at the same time, distance himself from the subjection to mortality, necessity, "nature," which must characterize the body of the creature. But at those times when his commonality with his subjects is of greatest importance, his very mortality may make him loved.

Even though the sovereign "must" be recognized, believed in, as king, father, creator, he must be loved as king and therefore, in a sense, "chosen" by his subjects. Had they a choice, it would be he: it is crucial to many arts of rule that the sovereign appear both as a choice and as a necessity. In offering himself as choice, the sovereign must be both accessible and inaccessible, embodied and disembodied; in choosing, it perhaps goes without saying that the subject must be understood as fully capable of choice, free of any constraint upon the will, perfect in his or her capacity for consent. This transforms the subject into a "sovereign" subject—a perilous development, but one which, treated with care, can produce the strongest of bonds.[3] The bond between subject and sovereign is at times imagined as a love between "equals" made so by their love, hence it is at times imagined as marriage.

I will be concerned with the ways in which sovereignty solicits the experience of the difficult, fragile bond of likeness and difference that constitutes the sovereign's relation to the subject. The first section of the book, "City," explores the creation of Edinburgh, in the late fifteenth century, as capital of Scotland. In particular, it explores the ways in which James III (r. 1460–88) tried to produce Edinburgh as his "creature," but it also explores, through the poetry of James Foullis and William Dunbar, how the consequences of Edinburgh's growing preeminence were experienced by at least some of the Crown's subjects. The imaginative style of James III is studied partly in contrast with that of his son, James IV (r. 1488–1513) — the former consistently vilified in historical representation, the latter just as consistently glorified.

The second part of this book, "Marriage," is devoted to an analysis of the close connection between marriage and sovereignty; it is also devoted to an analysis of queenship, which is, unlike kingship, often dependent on marriage. The relation between king and consort exacerbates the difficulties and opportunities of the relation between sovereign and subject: the queen, like the king, must be unique, but if she is a consort, she must in turn not endanger the king's uniqueness. Because of the complexities of queenship, queens can model the intersections of sovereign and subject, the subject made "sovereign" by love and the sovereign made subject to love. Marriage, like sovereignty, has as its chief purpose the production of communion between differences; marriage, moreover, is a powerful way of imagining the transformation of inequality into equality and thus assists sovereignty in the production of the experience of choice rather than of coercion.[4] This experience of choice was particularly important at a time when James's marriage to an English princess might have seemed to threaten both the integrity and the honor of his realm. If the Scots were to make peace with England, might the choice of peace with the enemy come to seem as risky, as adventurous, hence as productive of honor, as enmity?

"Tournament," the third part of this book, is devoted to an analysis of James IV's tournament of the wild knight and the black lady and to an analysis of the arts of honor — honor being the ethical form of the conflict between ficticity and being through which privilege seeks its way. The honorable subject must appear as such and is thereby constituted through a special intensity of appearance, but the honorable subject must thereby reconstitute his essence in order not to seem purely fictitious. Moreover, the image to which he aspires seems to demand a certain renunciation of the unruled body. The king, in soliciting identifications with his nobility, uses the tournament of the wild knight and the black lady to argue for and celebrate such renunciation, as well as to enjoy his special power to revel in the unruled body. Ambition becomes his theme, at a time when James IV begins to think seriously of crusade, just after his "pacification" of Gaelic Scotland. The subject of "Tournament" is thus intimate violence — the problem of division within Scotland, rather than between Scotland and England — and how it might, in turn, be turned to account for expansionism on the seas and through crusade, by presenting the king as wild, civilized, and legendary.

The later Middle Ages was a time of rich, rapidly changing, and confusing opportunities for the structuration of sovereignty — a time when arts of rule and of embodiment (tournament, peripatetic kingship) were being reimagined, in coexistence with newer forms (capital, elaborate nuptial pageantry) that tried to lay claim to the past and thereby to conceal their historicity and consequently their vulnerability. Late medieval Scotland is of particular interest to a study of arts of rule both because of its comparative "decentralization" and because of the comparative flexibility which that decentralization gave to monarchical imaginings: the Scottish "estates," for example, did not have the historical and institutional solidity of the English Parliament, a difference perhaps reflected in the divergent treatments given to the estates in Chaucer's *Parliament of Fowls* and Dunbar's *The Thrissill and the Rois.* But Scottish kings shared Europe's dreams of power, however limited their capacity to pursue those dreams may have been. In Scotland, as elsewhere at this time, there was considerable anxiety about the risks involved in the art of rule; and often such anxiety produces urgent idealizations of rule. The idealizations made risks of their own, as is suggested by the prophetic aestheticizations of Dunbar's *The Thrissill and the Rois,* the distantiations of Jonsonian masque, and the ultimate fate of the Stewart dynasty on English soil. And within these sketchy parameters, there are differences of desire, style, and timing, differences that are important to explore not least because they reveal that sometimes authority constitutes itself through the very embrace of historicity that might seem to set us free.

City

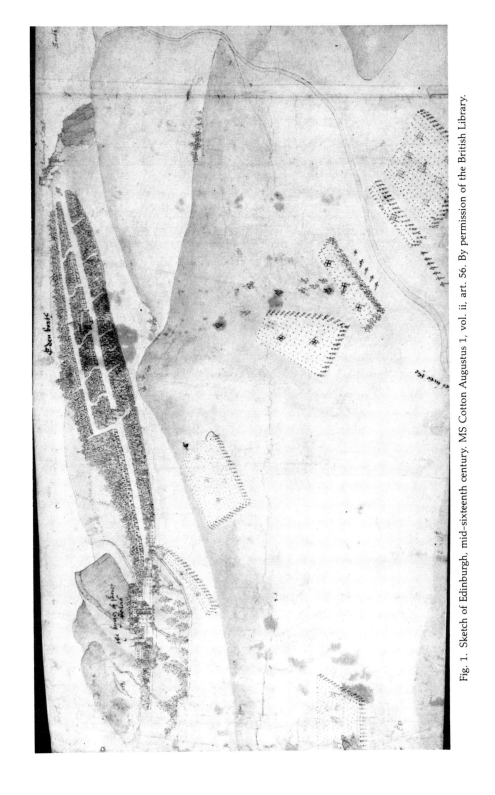

Fig. 1. Sketch of Edinburgh, mid-sixteenth century. MS Cotton Augustus 1, vol. ii, art. 56. By permission of the British Library.

1

Imagining the City

> Then a mighty angel took up a stone like a great millstone and hurled it into the sea and said, "Thus shall Babylon, the great city, be sent hurtling down, never to be seen again! No more shall the sound of harpers and minstrels, of flute-players and trumpeters, be heard in you; no more shall craftsmen of any trade be found in you; no more shall the sound of the mill be heard in you; no more shall the light of the lamp be seen in you; no more shall the voice of the bride and bridegroom be heard in you! Your traders were once the merchant princes of the world, and with your sorcery you deceived all the nations."
>
> — Revelation 18:21–23

THE following chapters explore how late medieval Edinburgh — at that time, newly preeminent among the royal burghs of Scotland — functioned as an imaginative figure in the political culture of the late fifteenth and early sixteenth centuries.[1] In trying to understand the role of the city in late medieval imagining, it is necessary that we recognize how, in different texts and at different times, figurations of the city have often involved a problematic of origins. The idea of the city seems so often to raise the specter of ontological crisis. It provokes us to ask what we mean when we say that something *begins* and to ask about the values we attach to the concept of *beginning*. Does *beginning* mean continuity or rupture?[2] Modern scholarship on the development of the Scottish burghs, for example, has long participated in the discourse of origins exemplified by Henri Pirenne's work and pursued by Marxist theorists concerned with the transition from feudalism to capitalism.[3] Modern historians want to know who or what gave rise to the medieval city; who or what sustained it; whether it was part of the country surrounding it or whether it was different. Their questions are framed most often in economic terms, particularly in terms of a discourse of production. In a number of modern texts, the discourse of production proceeds by way of a return to the authority of theoretical categories, hence by way, on the level of method, of a return to preoccu-

3

pation with legitimacy and illegitimacy. These texts ask: Is the medieval city the product of forces "internal" or "external" to feudalism? Is the medieval city part of the feudal or the capitalist "mode of production"?

That the interests of medieval monarchy and burgh were particularly closely identified in Scotland is suggested by the sudden irruption of the burghs into documentary life toward the middle of the twelfth century — a time when David I (r. 1124–53) was proceeding to remodel Scotland, insofar as circumstances permitted, on the basis of Anglo-Norman feudalism, a project which in turn seems to have involved the fostering or outright creation of urban settlements.[4] Historians have been impressed not only by the sudden appearance of the burgh charters but also by the suggestion, given by the burghs' often strikingly similar layouts, of deliberate planning. Rodger has argued that, though the layouts of the burghs "were governed by natural features, for example, the dominant position of the castle," and by the need for transportation links, "within such constraints these new towns were also planned. . . . there is clear evidence of a coherent over-view stamped upon the initial developments."[5] One study of St. Andrews concludes that the town was "planned from its foundation on . . . [an] ambitious two-street pattern" perhaps sited on a preburghal vill or "clochin" mentioned in a late twelfth-century charter.[6] The situation of Edinburgh just before the period of the royal burgh (1100–1296) is described in "The Growth of Edinburgh" as follows: "The summit of the Rock was crowned by a fort, hardly yet a castle in the mediæval sense, with an outer settlement close below it on the western part of the Rock. . . . At a bow-shot distance down the ridge there was a little suburb spreading out to the east."[7] With these antecedents, the burgh is imagined to have been erected and planned in accordance both with topographical considerations and "Scottish custom."[8] McWilliam believes that the burghs were planned by the "first burgesses"; Rodger goes so far in the direction of royal inspiration as to propose that "it is difficult to see who other than the king's nominees would have initiated the original demarcation of burgages."[9] For Rodger, then, the burghs were in a quite literal sense the creations of the king; he is one of the most enthusiastic recent participants in the view that Scottish burghs "were the newly founded creations of David I in the twelfth century."[10]

How, then, to tell the story of the appearance of the burghs? To Mackenzie, the burghs seem not "native" to a rural economy "and therefore in their origin suggest something of method or artifice."[11] Numerous writers speak of the burghs as "plantation towns," creations *ex nihilo* by the word (charter) of the Crown (to be compared with the towns established by the English on the Welsh borders and in Ireland), populated by strangers —

perhaps even Flemings — imported for the purpose. Through these towns the kings would pacify and domesticate the unruly natives. But "The Growth of Edinburgh" vacillates, as its title suggests; it speaks not only of a "series of great efforts" but also of "organic development."[12] It is as clear to Dicks — who painstakingly undertakes the tracing of centuries-old patterns of native settlement — that David I "favoured what must already have been established centres" as it is to Rodger that the burghs were the king's "newly founded creations."[13] Perhaps, Dicks argues, the problem is one of nomenclature: the "burgh," with its chartered privileges, was a *legal* creation, but not necessarily a creation *ex nihilo* (from "greenfields"); "pre-urban nuclei" go back to the Dark Age capitals, the Roman occupation, the Iron Age, and beyond.[14] How (once again) to tell the story of burgh origins? The city appears in these narratives as a construct — in this regard it matters little whether a legal or physical construct is at issue — whose character as construct both lures and challenges practices of historical narration. Verbal fiat or evolution? The "active star" of David I or the most ancient of patterns? "Beginning" as continuity or as break? "Native" inspiration or foreign (English) models?[15]

It does at least seem to be agreed that the legal status and privileges granted by David I and his successors were responsible either for the birth or growth of the burghs and that the interests of Crown and town were closely meshed from the beginning — tolls, rents, judicial profits, and ultimately loans, intermittent taxation, extraordinary contributions to royal ransoms and marriage deals, and, last but not least, the Great Customs being significant sources of royal revenue.[16] Indeed, tolls and rents from the burghs were, according to Duncan, the sources from which "the whole of David I's known revenue in money is derived. It is not surprising therefore that so active a ruler, with many projects costly in capital on hand, should have actively promoted the growth of burghs."[17] The conferment of burghal status and its attendant privileges was linked to royal revenues from the burgh. But difference arose from identity. The burghs were originally conceived and treated like feudal vassals, but they were "unable to function smoothly under seigneurial jurisdiction and manorial rule."[18] Their self-containment was the result of a protectionism that sought to protect fledgling commerce — in other words, to permit the accumulation of mercantile capital — and thus to guarantee royal exploitation of the towns' wealth. But this self-containment exacerbated the difference of the burghs from other aspects of medieval society. The history of relations between royal burgh and Crown can indeed be described as the history of the former's efforts to separate itself from the judicial and administrative machinery of the latter; but in so doing the burghs turned increasingly inward — in this regard no more interested in unleashing the "flows" of capitalism than medieval kings or tribal elders — thus participating, ironically, in their own containment.[19] The burghs' struggles to acquire monopolies and regulate trade, to gain legal privileges and autonomy, might seem to have done little to alter their status as enclaves of commercial exchange within an aristocratic order largely devoted to other methods of enrichment and to the joys of the gift.

Rodney Hilton has written of medieval merchants in general that "they had close financial associations with the leading feudalists; they were so enmeshed in the political and social relationships of European feudalism that no breakthrough to a new form of society was to be expected under their leadership."[20] Marxist historians have also argued over the origins of medieval towns and their place within the feudal "mode of production"; Hilton supports the view that extrinsic theories — towns and trade arose within an otherwise agrarian society because of the opening-up of far-distant trade routes — have the pernicious effect of making commerce and capital into the sole "mover" of change in human history. The transition from feudalism to capitalism is then to be explained by forces intrinsic to the feudal mode of production, namely the peasants' struggles to retain an ever-larger share of the surplus. Medieval merchants participated in the economic exploitation of the peasantry. They thus acquire the distinction of being members of a class (the middle one) whose ultimate hegemony was ensured not by their own efforts but by those of other actants. The medieval towns were more like blocking figures than protagonists of history.

The position, thus rudely sketched, finds considerable support in the later history of the burghs. Gibb and Paddison, in their study of burghal monopolies, "spatially-defined trading privileges," "overconcentration of exchange," and the striking rise of nonroyal burghs in the early modern period, conclude that

From the late-medieval period onwards trade generally, and long-distance trade particularly, increased in importance, and the privileges and monopolies of the royal burghs were seen increasingly as obstacles to the free development of commerce. The expansion of trade was accompanied by the demise of the decentralised feudal state and its replacement by the more centralised, absolutist state. The privileges of the royal burgh were to come under attack from two sides, from the need to encourage trade and liberalise the arrangements by which it was conducted, and from the demand to shift powers of economic regulation away from the burghs and centralise them within the state.[21]

Mackenzie, too — not a Marxist historian — conceives of the seventeenth century in particular as a time when the medieval "burghal" economy was

displaced by a "national" economy, a change succinctly exemplified by an
enactment of 1663 laying down that "'the ordering and disposal of trade
with foreign countries' was a prerogative of the Crown."[22]

Rather more complicated conceptualizations of the historical efficacy of
merchant capital than the one described above appear in John Merrington's notion of an "internal externality" — "feudalism was the first mode of
production in history to allow, by its very absence of sovereignty, an autonomous structural place to urban production and merchant capital" —
and in Perry Anderson's argument that the structure of the centralized state
was "fundamentally determined by the feudal regroupment against the
peasantry, after the dissolution of serfdom; but it was secondarily *overdetermined* by the rise of an urban bourgeoisie."[23] Hindess and Hirst argue
that "while certain elements of the capitalist mode of production may be
present in feudal society the capitalist mode of production itself cannot."[24]
Despite the ingenuity of these formulations, the concept of a "mode of production" remains categorical in them, and both merchant capital and urban
production are to remain contained within the bounds of feudalism thus
conceived. The challenge posed by the city to linear historical narration
is thus as evident in the Marxist accounts here discussed as in the non-
Marxist ones; the difference of the city is read either as merely apparent
or as continuous with a feudal form of sovereignty, not as a radical break.

But even in the fifteenth century, James III of Scotland (r. 1460–88) was
interested in commerce on his own account, as were some of his nobles;
and though the act of Parliament of his reign that stated for the record the
rights of the first and second estates to pursue trade said nothing about
the Crown's prerogative to manage foreign trade generally, it stands nevertheless as a reminder that kings were interested in imitating as well as
exploiting burgesses — a situation more traditionally discussed in the context of later "mercantilism."[25] And if the burghs functioned as an "internal
externality," their externality to the interests of the Crown was nonetheless "haunting." If the medieval merchants were unwilling to lead a "breakthrough to a new form of society," the "old" form of society could nevertheless read contradiction in the burghs' perforations of Crown control,
just as much as the notorious insecurity of land tenure in Scotland might
have been a means of repressing the unthinkable in another sphere. There
are evidences that in the fifteenth century relations between Crown and
burgh were "uneasy":

Internal factionalism was revealed in an act of 1458 which declared that no bands
or leagues were to be made within the burghs; there was to be "na commotioun
nor rysing of commownys in hindering of the common lawe"; no inhabitant of
a burgh was to "be fundyn in manrent nor ride nor rowt in feir of weir witht na

man bot witht the king or his officiaris or witht the lorde of the burghe"; nor was any inhabitant to "purches ony lordschipe in oppressione of his nychtburis." . . .

In other respects the relationship between king and burghs was also uneasy. It is remarkable that in the general council of 1456 "The universale burowys of the realme" complained that the poor commons were greatly oppressed by the king's sheriffs and constables.[26]

The act of 1454 that confirmed the annual meeting of the Court of the Parliament of the Four Burghs in Edinburgh shows signs of an attempt to "prune" the Parliament, which in 1405 had apparently been "free to discuss all matters of common concern, . . . into the shape of the fourteenth-century court of the four burghs, useful to the king as a source of judicial profits."[27]

Other signs of a "self-interested antiquarianism in James II's dealings with the burghs" involved the galvanizing of the chamberlain ayres — which traditionally had been the chief instrument of Crown control over burgh justice — into repressive and exploitive action, by fining burgesses "who offended against pristine burghal custom by dwelling outside the burgh. . . . It is not surprising that in the parliament of March 1458 reference was made to chamberlain ayres 'be the quhilkis all the estatis, and specialy the pure commownis, ar fairly grevyt.'"[28] And James II revived direct taxation. James III's enthusiasm for the economic register meant a different and perhaps more complicated picture of relations between town and Crown in the succeeding reign; in James IV's reign, however, "the burghs lost something of their independence," while Edinburgh's own interdependence with the Crown continued unabated.[29] I have cited these details not to purvey a portrait of the medieval merchant as revolutionary nor to propose a complexity and multiplicity of detail that would defeat attempts at conceptualization; the account I will try to give of the shaping of Edinburgh in the fifteenth century will, I hope, set at rest any fears to the contrary. But I do wish to give force to the towns' perforations and resistances — to allow that the difference they made, made some difference. Jameson proposes to read periods of "transition" as "the passage to the surface of a permanent . . . struggle between . . . various *coexisting* [my emphasis] modes of production"; and if we are to retain the concept of a mode of production at all, it can only be by way of a conceptualization that allows us to retain, insofar as is possible, a sense both of the particularity and the multiplicity of historical "moments."[30] Otherwise we cannot conceive of historical agents — whether classes, individuals, groups associated by kinship or interests or gender — as acting both "for" and "against" themselves, and as beginning as well as continuing.

If the city functions as an ontological problem in historical narrative, then we need to try to understand why this is so. First, the city poses the problem of change — of the changes giving rise to the city as well as the changes for which the city is often held responsible (sophistication, aliena-tion, the devaluing of rural and familial experience, the making of money from money, the making of new things).[31] Change brings newness into being; the imagination is as much at work in our economic life as it is in our poetry. For this reason, the city — not exclusively, but with a par-ticular kind of power — poses the problem of how human beings construct and produce their world. The artisanal or fictive economic activities pur-sued within the city are figured in the very construction of the cityscape itself. It is possible — though still a profound misrecognition — to forget the extent to which nature, the country outside the city walls, has been con-structed by human curiosity, presumption, intervention, labor. It seems to be more difficult to forget the fact of the city's construction, a fact which implies human creativity and a decentered human responsibility for the shape of the world. Indeed, forgetting this fact will often require, in one historical form or another, the fantasy of a city plan that reinscribes the superreal in the form of royal or divine creativity.[32] It is not surprising, then, that the figure of the city has so often been "split" in two: the city must either locate its origins in superreality or become the site of abjec-tion, even of plague. It becomes a figure either of the upholding or dissolu-tion of boundaries.[33] And as that which threatens to reveal and therefore undo the createdness of cultural constructs, the city can become a figure for crises of belief — for crises in our ascription of superreality to various privileged cultural constructs.

In his analysis of the ontological implications of the "primal scene," Ned Lukacher foregrounds the problem of memory: the "ontological self" de-pends upon "the notion of a subject for whom 'reality' inheres only in the self-presence of perception and recollection."[34] Lukacher's critique of the ontological self suggests that remembering can become a way of attempt-ing to repair the relation of the human creature to superreality, a way, for example, of recovering an external origin — the agency of the creator — within the interiority of the creature. Thus, the ideal city of St. Augustine — who was writing at a time of extreme cultural crisis — is imagined in much the same way as is Augustine's own memory. In Augustine's *Confessions,* the memory is called both *sinus* and *aula.* Kenneth Burke, in *The Rhetoric of Religion,* writes that "in the Latin dictionaries the range of the meanings for the word [*sinus*] is given as: curve, fold, hollow, coil, bosom, lap, purse, money, bay, gulf, basin, valley; figuratively: love, affection, protection, intimacy, innermost part, heart, hiding-place."[35] The memory is closely associated in Burke's reading of the *Confessions* with strongly maternal and "infantile" strands of meanings and images, with "plenitude" and "manifoldness."[36] But the memory, through its identification as *aula*, is also to be associated with the paternal strand of meanings in Augustine, with the separations and discriminations of order celebrated most explicitly in *The City of God*.[37] The range of meanings for *aula* is "court, forecourt, inner court, yard, hall, palace, royal court, residence, courtiers, princely power, royalty."[38] The notions of protection, domesticity, recess, secrecy, are thus linked with the plenitude of Augustine's "free maternal city" of God and with the architecture (and architectonics) of *potestas*.[39] The idyll that Augustine discovers hidden away within himself is imagined as a princely palace, an inner temple of grandiosity.

Augustine's identification of *aula* with memory takes place within the context of a profound meditation on the simultaneous proximity and mystery of the inner self; estrangement and restoration are imagined in terms of place. For Augustine, the perfect place is the free maternal city of peace, imagined as indistinguishable from the court of the absolute judge and ruler; the city of God, in its absolute form, is the result at once of an eternally nurturing, loving proximity and of the severity of righteous discrimination—for the city of man lies far below it, split off, projected, separated. On earth, only the ignorant fail to see where the city of man ends and the city of God begins.

Augustine thus tries to make one and make good plenitude and discrimination; at stake in this process of atonement and reparation is, for Augustine, the nature of the relations between maternity and paternity, love and aggression, nurturance and punishment. His texts suggest a felt discordance between the maternal strand of meanings and the paternal strand, and they suggest how this discordance may be eased by the appropriation of the maternal strand for the paternal strand, whereby plenitude becomes associated with a peaceful city that is nonetheless the product of warfare and repudiation. Augustine's texts, in short, suggest some further ways in which the concept of the primal scene might be useful in our exploration of the figure of the city. As William Kerrigan has argued, the primal scene is a way of encountering one's own createdness, mortality, and finitude—the finitude, too, of one's creators; it is, at least potentially, an uncovering of the createdness of superreality.[40] The concept of the primal scene finally speaks to the experience of loss in relation to maturation and familiality—to the project of growing up, of situating oneself in a generational chain; to one's sense of the "times" one lives in and the changing ways in which those times are to be lived in.

The rendering in familial terms of traumatic confrontation with the contingency of origins is not, however, exclusive to modern psychoanalysis (though psychoanalysis, in contradistinction to many earlier myths of origin, orients itself toward the dissolution of the "subject's" dependence and the analysis of his resistance to such dissolution). We have seen the importance of familial images to Augustine's treatment of historical crisis; the later Middle Ages was also a critical time in which the difficult relation of creature to creator was imagined in strongly familial terms. The later Middle Ages increasingly recognized, both in theory and in practice, the secularity—the human reality—of the grounds, purposes, and practices of production. At the same time, theology located the Creator at an increasing distance from human creation, and brought Him back through the corporeal excesses of affective piety. Belief in the Real Presence was attacked and was resubstantiated not only through the bodily pain of tortured heretics but also through the emphasis, in late medieval communion ritual as well as Corpus Christi spectacle, on the beholding of the sacrament.[41] The intensification of monarchical spectacularity—of visual representation of the king's magnificence—was also part of the attempt, in the later Middle Ages, to remake belief in medieval icons of superreality.

We have said that, in modern historical narratives, the question of production—of which economic forces produced the city and were in turn produced by it—has been uppermost. But in a number of medieval narratives of the city—partly because, as Philippe Ariès has put it, the "idea of childhood was bound up with the idea of dependence"—the paramount question was one of reproduction, which could be treated figuratively and which brought in its train questions of nurturance, loyalty, gift, debt, fertility, and discord.[42] The authority of the sovereign is linked with the role of sovereign as provider. Central, in particular, to the courtly fictions of the later Middle Ages is the representation of magnificence—of the sovereign's power to create a splendid, indeed a paradisal, court; of the court's reflection of the splendor of its sovereign creator. Through the representation of magnificence, the courtly text proclaims the paternity of the sovereign. And it seeks to locate, in the sovereign, maternal love as well as paternal power, each conceived, as Burke might put it, in the "register" of rule. The sovereign's rule is imagined as enabling the fertility of the land; maternity is seen to depend on the monarchical phallus; human production and reproduction are dependent on sovereign agency. The confluence of relations of domination and nurturance in the "family" of the princely or baronial household constitutes the place wherein problems of creation are experienced and imagined. The problem of the city, in turn, is imagined as the problem of its relation to the court.

In late fifteenth- and early sixteenth-century Scotland, Edinburgh became the imaginative site of apparently contradictory ideas of the city: on the one hand, a royal creature, dependent on Crown patronage for its privileges and therefore its life, owing services to its lord in return; on the other, a possible source of disorder, a threat (though, ideally, not a lasting or true one) to the good life of its creator and its country. Insofar as the king "creates" the city by granting its privileges — by giving it life — he is its originator, and this kind of identity exists between them.[43] Yet the gift given to the city by the king is the gift of difference: the city is demarcated, contained, and inside it special activities are pursued. The creation of the city is thus an act of divisiveness; it sets up different categories of things, a fall from Edenic simplicity into things equal and unequal.[44] As a dependent whose dependence is undependable, the city is imagined as a site of change, of passings-away, of a narrativity of limit and loss. Though contained within the aristocratic order, the city — in Gilles Deleuze and Félix Guattari's terms — "haunts" that order, as a "nightmare" and "anxious foreboding."[45] Included, it may be the "free maternal city" of plenitude, at once *sinus* and *aula;* repudiated, it may be Babylon, the city of earth — site of sexuality, ungovernable women, beautiful clothing, trade, crafts, and, in the end, grief.

A discussion of William Dunbar's poems on Edinburgh will help to extend further our understanding of the ways in which the late medieval courtly text imagined the city. A poet in the court of James IV of Scotland, Dunbar wrote "The Dregy of Dunbar Maid to King James the Fowrth being in Strivilling," a poem apparently associated with one of the king's penitential retreats to the Franciscan house at Stirling. The poem contrasts the purgatorial deprivations of the Stirling retreat with the glorious plenty of "parradyis / In Edinburcht," and if the poem is any indication, Dunbar himself may have presented the poem at Stirling.[46]

> And I that dois ȝour panis discryve
> Thinkis for to vissy ȝow belyve —
> Nocht in desert with ȝow to dwell,
> Bot as the angell Sanct Gabriell
> Dois go betwene fra hevinis glory
> To thame that ar in purgatory
> And in thair tribulatioun
> To gif thame consolatioun
> And schaw thame quhen thair panis ar past
> Thay sall till hevin cum at last.
>
> (ll. 71–80)

The poet and company are described as singing "Ane dirige devoit and meik," a parody of the office for the dead that invokes God and St. Giles — the patron saint of Edinburgh — in its prayers for the release of the penitents into the solace and joy of the "mirry toun."

> Out of ȝour panefull purgatory
> To bring ȝow to the blis and glory
> Off Edinburgh, the mirry toun,
> We sall begyn ane cairfull soun,
> Ane dirige devoit and meik.
>   (ll. 19–23)

The poem thus, as Joanne Norman has argued, makes ironic use of the *contemptus mundi* expressed in the office for the dead – a liturgy devoted to separation from the world, to the work of leave-taking – to affirm the "joys of the earth which lie in Edinburgh."[47] These joys are presented chiefly through images of feasting, reminiscent of the parodic and carnivalesque tradition of the feast of fools.[48] The poem itself is felt by Norman to embody a "discrepancy . . . between man's preferred ideals and his instincts," a "moral paradox" concretely exemplified by the "psychological complexity" of James IV – the sensuality and promiscuity, the taste for mortification that led him not only to the discipline of the Stirling retreat but also to the wearing of an iron belt under his clothing, in penance, so the legend goes, for the murder of his father.[49] But while the poem is dialogic in a number of ways, the purpose of its discursive multiplicity is inclusive. The poem attempts the identification of the Edinburgh court with the paradisal space of the heavenly court; its purpose is to effect a relation between mortification and communion, between privation and bodily transfiguration.

Dunbar styles himself as resembling a heavenly messenger, a mouthpiece bearing divine consolation, a link between two worlds and hence a traveler across limits and limitations. The spatial positioning of the poet, then, marks out his role as the servant of inclusion, whose words will bring the alienated children of the court back to the *sinus* (and *aula*) of plenitude. The poet's words are an instrument of mediation: they speak for, by, and through the court. Both poet and poem are imitators; the difference between them and their exemplars provides the humor which, through its jollying of the superego, permits the metaphorical identifications of Stirling with purgatory and Edinburgh with the bliss of the heavenly court. Parody is an art of the creature. In this poem humor is apotropaic; the guardian of grandiosity, it wards off punishment and humiliation. It is the role of the poet as entertainer to get ideality and pleasure on the same side – by turning the penitential life at Stirling into a narrative for which the bliss of courtly heaven shall be the closure, hence by turning separation and frustration into the promise of union, the work of separation into a process of restitution, of reinclusion of the idyll. The maternal body is thus recomposed. Penitence is only a temporary privation, a temporary alienation from plenitude. The mortification of the body is thus "presented in terms of the ultimate rewards in store for those of good will who subject themselves to the principle of governance. That is, . . . the logical contrast between sovereignty and subjection is resolved by translation into terms of narrative sequence whereby the principle of subjection, of mortification, first prevails, but is finally followed by the sovereign principle of boundless rejoicing."⁵⁰ Neither James IV's displays of penitence nor his displays of excess are at odds with the principle of sovereignty thus conceived. Both the desire for judgment and the desire for plenitude are promised satisfaction, the one seeming to lead to the other. The poem thus affirms a future, as against the trauma of loss; it affirms the possibility of rapprochement, of leaving and refinding the source of plenty. Dunbar urges the exiled court to "Cum hame and dwell no moir in Strivilling," which is a "hiddous hell" (ll. 93–94). We are reminded, once again, of the coincidence of *sinus* and *aula*, of "protection," "intimacy," the "heart" with the architecture of *potestas*.

And, as we have indicated, "home" is chiefly imagined as oral plenty. The hermits in Stirling

> takis 30ur pennance at 30ur tablis
> And eitis nocht meit restorative
> Nor drynkis no wyn confortative
> Bot aill, and that is thyn and small,
> With few coursis into 30ur hall,
> But cumpany of lordis and knychtis
> Or ony uder gudly wichtis
> Solitar walkand 30ur allone
> Seing no thing bot stok and stone.
>   (ll. 10–18)

The Edinburgh court, however, is envisioned as dwelling in "hevins glory", feasting on

> swan, cran, pertrik and plever
> And every fische that swymis in rever;
> . . . the new fresche wyne
> That grew upoun the rever of Ryne,
> Fresche fragrant clairettis out of France,
> Of Angers and of Orliance,
> With mony ane cours of grit dyntie:
> Say ye amen for cheritie.
>   (ll. 51–58)

Oral poetry — the poetry of courtly plenitude — is conjunctive, paratactic. It serves up its treats in rapid succession or, better yet, spreads them out side by side; and it includes every variety. The eagerness of Dunbar's verse is the prosodic manifestation of a kind of circularity of communion to be associated with the Edinburgh court, as against the verticality of ascent from purgatory to "hevinis glory." And manifoldness — variety — figures the exfoliation of a (divine) unity, so that the poem brings together the movement inward, to "home," with the creative movement outward to a recuperated diversity.

Moreover, the "Solitar walkand" of Stirling is contrasted with the richness of the Edinburgh banquets; the assurance of presence, of company, that is concomitant with the idea of plenitude, is celebrated in Dunbar's vision of a community of consumption and in the insistently plural and choral forms of his poem. In the "Dregy," language and vision are both incorporative: the eyes are used "orally," to "take in" food; one sings as part of a larger body, a larger voice. The courtiers both take in and are taken in by something greater.

In the "Dregy," then, mouth-watering description evokes a paradise seemingly beyond dependence. The court itself is the source of plenty; the role of Edinburgh's merchants in the importation of luxury foods, of laborers in producing the fruits of the earth, is imaginable only as the court's power to serve up and consume the best wines from faraway places. Dearth is likewise imaginable only as a willed penitence, an aspect of order. In Stirling, fish is bought and sold: "Quhair fische to sell is non bot spirling" (l. 95). But the fish of the Edinburgh feast swim in rivers, and its wines simply grow on the Rhine. The heavenly court of Edinburgh has no economy save that of spectacular display and consumption; all is surplus, to be given away to itself in communal feasting. The court thereby materializes its communal honor. No rivalries fracture it; eating does not mean being eaten; it is neither dependent on supplies from elsewhere nor conceived as a "class" or "estate" divisible from others. Having caught up all "flows" into its own circularities, whatever might be haunting it — of which purgatorial dearth is a pale reminder — remains unseen.

It is therefore unsurprising that, in the "Dregy," Edinburgh itself seems to have no existence apart from the court. That the city is somehow present in the poem's sense of the court is, however, indicated by references to the "mirry toun" and to its patron saint. The references serve to mark the poem's identification of city and castle. There is no vantage point from which to see Edinburgh as separate — as, say, the object of a masterful vision. There is no difference between court and city, or, put another way, the difference of the city makes no difference to the court. Insofar as difference is not fully folded into the *sinus* of the court, it is depicted as a landscape of absence, a scene of privation — a "desert." Only in Stirling

is fish — and only one kind of fish — for sale; Dunbar's line "Quhair fische
to sell is non bot spirling" evokes the frustration of an articulated taste
that must have "manifoldness" if it is to approach the satiety of the breast
"conceived in the absolute." Frustration is brought together with the de-
ferrals of what is conventionally thought of as economic life, with the need
to earn and search out food. It is only in Stirling that one sees "no thing
bot stok and stone" (l. 18), matter that cannot be incorporated. "Nature"
in Stirling is resistant, excluding. Only there is the threat of separation
from the physical world great enough for Dunbar to include a seeing subject *in* the poem. The "autonomization" of sight marks the distance from
plenitude; sight, once again, is the register of our exclusion, just as, in visual
orality, it becomes a means of our reinclusion. In the "Dregy," however,
exclusion is only a prelude; the poem tells the story of reinclusion by the
all. Narrative is present (in the optative mood) as the promise of home-
coming, the movement from the outside in. It is a means whereby difference can be imagined as making no difference. The "Dregy" narrates a wish
for a courtly future.

In Dunbar's "To the Merchantis of Edinburgh," as in *The City of God*,
the paternal strand is uppermost; difference does make a difference. The
difference between the "Dregy" and the "Merchantis" is, indeed, strongly
reminiscent of the split between the emphasis in Augustine's *Confessions*
on maternal plenitude and the emphasis in *The City of God* on paternal
discretion and punishment. The "Merchantis" represents the otherness of
the earthly city, and that otherness is what founds the hortatory stance
of the poem — a single, isolated, prophetic stance, speaking its alienation
from what it sees to those in view, a stance identified with the principle
of judgment, of discrimination. It is itself the stance of one who has been
set apart and is therefore inseparable from a particular visual structure,
a panoramic view from which the poet is able to see all aspects of city
life (the "hie croce," the "stinkand scull," "craftis vyll," "beggeris"). In contrast with the choral circularities of the "Dregy," this visual structure is
vertical, as though the poet were looking down at the city from the vantage point of the court — that is, from the castle, the architecture of *potestas*.
In this poem, vision — the antiurban space of Revelation — is identified with
the exposing gaze of the paternal strand; description is projective, repudiating. Hence the poem's refrain, addressed to the "merchantis of renoun":

> Think ȝe not schame,
> Sen as the world sayis that ilk
> In hurt and sclander of ȝour name?
> (ll. 26–28)

The poet—a man, apparently, of honor—speaks for the world; all eyes are trained on Edinburgh.

The city is a space that swallows up the light:

> ʒour stinkand scull that standis dirk
> Haldis the lycht fra ʒour parroche kirk;
> ʒour foirstair makis ʒour housis mirk
> Lyk na cuntray bot heir at hame.
>
> (ll. 15-18)

The inbuilding characteristic of the severely constricted space of late medieval and early modern Edinburgh evokes in the poet a claustrophobia which itself bespeaks the urgency of his need to separate from the city, to get away from the constriction (as opposed to the communal expansion) of the body: the merchants are "hamperit in ane hony came" (l. 39).[51] As Dunbar sees it, the city is so far from being an image of the "edible"— from being a work of desire—that it is closing in on itself, indeed swallowing itself up. There is, therefore, a strong tone of disgust:

> May nane pas throw ʒour principall gaittis
> For stink of haddockis and of scaittis,
> For cryis of carlingis and debaittis,
> For fensum flyttingis of defame.
>
> (ll. 8-11)

One cannot enter the city without being assailed through the orifices of one's body. The food, moreover, is poor: "And at ʒour trone bot cokill and wilk, / Pansches, pudingis of Jok and Jame" (ll. 24-25). Food itself has become a signifier of lack rather than of plenty: "At ʒour hie croce quhar gold and silk / Sould be, thair is bot crudis and milk" (ll. 22-23). In going from the "Dregy" to the "Merchantis" (there is no way of knowing which poem was written first), in going from the poetics of inclusion to exclusion, the poet has gone from the joys of cuisine to the outraged elimination of waste.

The repudiated city is not the "free maternal city" of plenitude, but rather a "hiddous hell." Beyond the "Dregy's" identification of city with castle lurks a world of formlessness and bodily passion, full of noise rather than language, a choked rather than an articulated space. It is "innerness" gone mad and hence thrown off. The poem sees in the earthly city a world in which the masses are not patterned; it uses language to wall in chaos.

The blame for this phenomenological catastrophe belongs, according to Dunbar, to the merchants, whose desire for "Singular proffeit" blinds them to their responsibility for common profit. The merchants of renown do nothing for the poor, nothing to set this not-so-"mirry" town in order: "3our proffeit daylie dois incres, / 3our godlie workis les and les" (ll. 50–51). The chaotic rapacity of a "dishonorable" form of exchange, one conducted without generosity in the spirit of immediate gain, undoes political organicism, dirtying and fracturing the body of the realm. Central to the poetics of exclusion is the fear of losing "possessions," of losing the contents of the body; the merchants try to withhold their profits, and the wall that keeps their madness out of the poet is the wall that keeps the surface of the body intact.

Money is, as Fenichel puts it, a departicularized and hence "loseable" possession; it is not capable of being stamped with "subject-quality" (I am imagining both collective and individual subjects), does not seem, like the valuables described by Marcel Mauss, to bear the spirit of its giver and its homeland with it.[52] Mauss writes that "there is money only when precious objects, condensed wealth or tokens of wealth are made into money—when they are . . . impersonalized, detached from any relationships with moral, collective, or individual persons other than the authority of the state which mints them."[53] The valuables used as means of exchange and payment by nonminting societies have, beyond their "economic" nature, "a mystical nature and are talismans or 'life-givers'. . . . they have a very general circulation . . . but they are still attached to persons or clans (the first Roman coins were struck by *gentes*), to the individuality of their former possessors and to contracts made between moral beings. There [*sic*] value is still subjective."[54] By threatening the ascription to objects of subject-quality, money—defined in the narrow sense—threatens the capacity of the object for symbolic introjection, hence threatens to separate subject from object. In psychoanalytic terms, money sets a limit to narcissism; it marks where the subject ends and where the world of alienated "objects," which it must seek to "acquire," begins. Money cannot phenomenalize honor; it is the token of exchange peculiar to creatures rather than to creators.

Feasting is not without its dangers, and Dunbar's poem repudiates the destructive greed of orality—the desire to scoop out, to suck out, to exhaust (greed is sometimes pictured with gaping mouth in medieval iconography)—by projecting it onto the merchants, in accord with the conventions of estates satire. The solution to the problem of greed is not structural change but moral reform: the merchants should eschew fraud and distortion, keep order, and relieve the poor. They must, in other words, display distributive justice; they must give generous gifts of alms. The solution is, in Mauss's terms, an "aristocratic" one.

Dunbar, moreover, threatens reprisals if the merchants fail to reform the town:

> Sen for the court and the sessioun
> The great repair of this regioun
> Is in ȝour burgh, thairfoir be boun
> To mend all faultis that ar to blame,
>   And eschew schame;
> Gif thai pas to ane uther toun
> Ȝe will decay, and ȝour great name.
>
> (ll. 57–63)

He thus evokes the punitive narrativity of *The City of God:* the city that does not mend its faults will decay. Mortification sent from above makes a kind of order out of the disorders of the earthly city. The city is reminded of its transience, its creatureliness; it is read against the absolute. Moreover, the view that Edinburgh's problems result solely from internal corruption demands that the city continue to look inward rather than outward. The isolation of "Singular proffeit" as a mercantile sin underscores the isolation of the city and distinguishes its forms of exchange from the wide variety of economic processes in which it participates; it thus upholds the court's fantasies of magical surplus and its preference for modes of giving and receiving rather than buying and selling. The court's fantasies of surplus might be said to encode its desire for and its partial dependence on the commercial power of the city; at the same time greed is confined to the city and banished from the idyll of the court. Dunbar's poem, therefore, draws an ideological boundary that confines the city to a difference tolerable within limits; its disorders uphold the principle of order. When the poet looks at the "great repair of this regioun," he sees only visitors, not inhabitants. The city has not (yet) swallowed up the court, and the court need not fear constriction by the city.

2

Edinburgh's Story

THE two poems by William Dunbar discussed in the previous chapter deal, by way of splitting, with accords and discords that had for centuries characterized relations between Crown and city. In fifteenth- and early sixteenth-century Edinburgh, both the identification of Crown and city and the difference between them were foregrounded and made problematic by the city's emergence as the effective capital of Scotland. Edinburgh's notorious congestion was itself partly the result of the "great repair" of which Dunbar writes. Whereas the royal burghs had earlier functioned as a group of more or less self-contained siblings — some with more privileges than others, but broadly similar in their powers and practices — in the later Middle Ages Edinburgh's claim to be first among equals grew increasingly strong. Its claim was based partly on its greater wealth, partly on the pressure of monarchical centralization, which — though a more halting and experimental process by far than in England or France of the same date — had by the early sixteenth century located nearly every important judicial, administrative, and military machine in Edinburgh.[1]

Distinguished visitors and ambassadors from other countries were frequently lodged in the tightly nestled houses of the city. In 1474, for example, the bishop of Durham and Lord Scrope arrived in Edinburgh as ambassadors to the negotiations for the marriage of Prince James with the Princess Cecilia. They were lodged in the townhouse of the bishop of Dunkeld, and Thomas of Yare (a merchant and burgess of Edinburgh, treasurer of the burgh in 1480) was paid more than four hundred pounds for their expenses.[2] Windsor Herald had come to Edinburgh to pursue the same business, and the wife of Snowdon Herald was reimbursed for his expenses; "Snawdonis wife" was also paid twenty pounds for like expenses on another occasion.[3] It is not clear whether these occasions were financially or otherwise profitable for the town residents, whether they represented an exploitation of or a contribution to the town's resources; but they do indicate quite clearly that at least the prominent members of the town had frequently to participate in the affairs of the castle. Diplomacy was not a business conducted exclusively in a physically isolated royal enclave. In 1464 one distinguished visitor, Henry VI of England—in exile in Scotland because of "certain rebellious traitors"—conferred upon Edinburgh "full and free liberty to traffic in England as the natives thereof, and to pay no other duties for their merchandise than his subjects the citizens of London did." (He presented this charter as thanks for the honorable reception he had received from the provost and community of Edinburgh during his long residence there.)[4] Edinburgh's chances of profiting from this charter were, to say the least, dubious, but the charter is nonetheless a reminder of Edinburgh's involvement with the monarchical vicissitudes even of England.[5]

The betrothal of Prince James and Princess Cecilia was solemnized in the Blackfriars of Edinburgh on 26 October 1474.[6] The first installment of Cecilia's dowry—two thousand English marks—was paid at St. Giles, the parish church of Edinburgh. St. Giles itself was one of the few burgh churches in Scotland to be erected to the dignity of collegiate status—"the ultimate symbol of prestige," achieved "in 1468 after an unsuccessful attempt earlier in the century."[7] Stell notes that nowhere in Scotland do chapels and chantries survive in greater profusion than in St. Giles; the "dramatic expansion" of the church in the fifteenth and sixteenth centuries attests not only the strength of Edinburgh's civic pride at the time but its wealth as well. One of these chapels, the Preston aisle, "was added after 1455 by the magistrates and community of Edinburgh to commemorate the acquisition of the arm-bone of the patron saint by Sir William Preston of Gourton, who had unconditionally bequeathed it to the 'mother kirke.'"[8] A bond, dated 11 January 1454/55, by the officers and community of the town to William Preston, praises his father of the same name for his diligence in acquiring the relic; it promises the building of the aisle, with a splendid tomb for Preston's father that would display his arms and a brass tablet crediting him with bringing the arm-bone to Edinburgh. The bond also gave Preston's "nerrest of blude" the right to bear the relic in civic processions.[9] The crafts also made it a matter of civic pride to share in the adornment and upkeep of the church: in 1451 the Skinners established and provided support for the altar of St. Christopher, and in 1475 the aisle and chapel of St. John the Baptist was granted to the Wrights and Masons.[10] Mention of such foundations is frequently found in the crafts' Seals of Cause, documents—which appear in profusion in the town records of the later fifteenth century—attesting the crafts' desire for official recognition and some measure of self-government. During the feast of St. Giles, the crafts went in procession along with the merchants of the town and the arm-bone of its patron saint; they were allowed to group themselves together and to display banners, as an order of 1509 enjoined the Weavers, Walkers, and Shearers.[11]

James III, in his supplication to the pope for the erection of St. Giles to collegiate status, describes the town as among the most populous, famous, and splendid towns of the realm of Scotland and refers to the many prelates and other magnates, and to the great multitude from various parts of the world, residing in or visiting the town in which the king himself "resided much." The pope, in his reply, was pleased to agree that Edinburgh was a place sufficiently "distinguished and celebrated for population" to qualify for the exaltation of its church.[12] When the city makes its appearance in the refulgent eloquence of papal diplomacy, its excess population — its "multitude" — makes it seem a silk purse rather than a sow's ear. That James III should have thus worked on behalf of Edinburgh's chief symbol of civic pride is itself an indication of the importance of the city to the style and practices of his checkered rule.

Evidences of centralization come before the reign of James III: Edinburgh had, for example, long been the usual meeting place of the Court of the Parliament of the Four Burghs, a body that "decided questions involving the usages of Burghs, and the rights and privileges of burgesses" and legislated regarding "such matters as the principles of moveable succession."[13] At the beginning of the fifteenth century, James I "ordained" that the Court of the Four Burghs should meet in Edinburgh, which was confirmed by James II in 1454.[14] But the policies of James III were of crucial importance in assuring the preeminence of Edinburgh. Norman Macdougall has described James III "as an innovator in that, to a greater extent than any previous king, he ran his administration from Edinburgh." Under James III, all parliaments (with one exception) were held in Edinburgh, as were the sessions of the Lords of Council. And "from 1469 onwards — apart from five isolated charters, . . . all traceable royal charters under the great seal — some 650 — were granted at Edinburgh. . . . it seems likely that the royal administrative seals were kept permanently in Edinburgh, at least during the [1480s]."[15] The same story is told by the innumerable payments, recorded in the Treasurer's Accounts for 1473–74, to messengers summoning people to come to Edinburgh on Crown business.[16] Though James IV and James V took up once again the peripatetic administration of civil justice — James IV's notorious restlessness meant that government had, at times, to be conducted outside of Edinburgh, and he was vigorous in attending justice ayres — there was really to be no turning back from the course set by James III. The exchequer was held most frequently in Edinburgh; the king's treasure and the records of the royal administration were housed in Edinburgh Castle; the king's artillery was likewise made and stored there; James IV's naval ambitions, "typified in the *Great St. Michael*," were partly executed there; there, too, coins were minted.[17]

Macdougall has also suggested that James's policy of centralization was reflected in his "preoccupation," during his last years, "with the building and endowment of his new collegiate church at Restalrig, which he may have planned to replace St. Mary of the Rock, St. Andrews as the Chapel Royal."[18] Despite his "hoarding" and "frugality" (for James III, the role of "source of plenty" meant "guardian of plenty" and a whole host of defenses against the designs he imagined his subjects to have on his person), James III seems to have been somewhat concerned to patronize theologians and churchmen and to adorn various ecclesiastical foundations, however limited his interest in the kind of secular poetry and spectacle more traditionally associated with the reign of James IV.[19] This is a feature of James III's severe and paternalistic style of rule that has been inadequately stressed by Macdougall's account of the king's "miserly nature" and failure to provide "court life and its perquisites," though Macdougall's description of the king as "aloof, overbearing and vindictive," lacking "any sense of justice," displaying delusions of imperial grandeur and an "alarming belief in the sanctity of his office," is not in fact at odds with James's apparent conviction that God was on his side and that actions of the most arbitrary character could thereby be justified.[20]

To James III's patronage of ecclesiastical institutions in Edinburgh should be added his continuing support of Trinity Collegiate Church, founded by his mother, Mary of Gueldres, the work of which was carried on by James after her death.[21] During his reign Pope Pius II granted plenary indulgences to visitants to Trinity; in 1466 or 1467 James allocated ten pounds from the Edinburgh customs to be given to the church's provost, Edward Bonkil (himself a member of a prominent Edinburgh family), for an organ; and Lorne Campbell has suggested the likelihood that James had some part in the commission of the magnificent Trinity Altarpiece, painted for the church by Hugo van der Goes.[22] The altarpiece links the royal family and the loyal provost with the Trinity as Holy Family; it features portraits of the king (fig. 2), Prince James, Queen Margaret (fig. 7), Edward Bonkil, and an icon of the Trinity (fig. 3), and Colin Thompson speculates that the central panel missing on one side may have been an "enthroned Virgin."[23] The relation between Father (represented, in "archaic" fashion, with bare head) and Son (the crucified Christ, painted with shocking "realism") is the emotional center of the icon.[24] The icon is a striking image of the relation between subjection and sovereignty, and is, moreover, bizarre in its ironic relevance to the themes of James's reign: his son was "ultimately

Fig. 2. King James III of Scotland with the Princes of Scotland. Trinity Altarpiece, attributed to Hugo Van der Goes. Reproduced by permission of Her Majesty the Queen. (On loan to the National Gallery of Scotland. Photograph provided by the National Gallery of Scotland.)

THE HOLY TRINITY

Fig. 3. Trinity, from the Trinity Altarpiece, attributed to Hugo Van der Goes. Reproduced by permission of Her Majesty the Queen. (On loan to the National Gallery of Scotland. Photograph provided by the National Gallery of Scotland.)

so afraid of his father's actions that he became the indirect instrument of James III's death." Macdougall describes James's relations with his family as "an appalling catalogue of internecine treachery and mistrust which may be explained mainly in terms of the neurotic suspicions of an exceedingly unpleasant king."[25] The "archaic" use of gold leaf in the treatment of the Father's throne is also featured in the treatment of the church organ in the Bonkil panel, perhaps meant to represent the organ donated by James III.[26] Thus the panels, in their own way, try to bring together the paternal and maternal strands: a *pieta* of father and son rather than of mother and son; the throne of the father – the seat of *potestas* – nonetheless present and linked to James's gift to Trinity, the church founded by his mother; perhaps a throned Virgin, moved, we might say, from her place in *pieta* to the register of *potestas*.

To what extent James III was involved in the artistic conception of the panels – if, indeed, he had anything to do with them at all – is impossible to say; but the portrait seems to be from life, and Bonkil may have traveled to the Netherlands on this commission.[27] The portrait bears, in fact, a "marked resemblance" to the likeness of James imprinted on the silver groat of 1485, "the earliest Renaissance coin portrait outside Italy," which shows, as Macdougall notes, the imperial crown rather than the coronet.[28] The motif on the patterned brocade behind the queen is the thistle, the royal badge of the kings of Scotland, first known to have been used during James's reign.[29] The broken tressure (of fleurs-de-lys) on the royal arms depicted in the king's panel may have been connected with an act of Parliament of 1472, "by which the tressure was to be abolished altogether," and thereby any implication that Scotland was subject to France.[30] Thus the panels also bear the marks of James III's partiality for chivalric manifestations of his claims to greatness. What may, then, have been one of the most remarkable works of art and ideology to grace the Scotland of the later fifteenth century was enshrined in the king's favorite town of Edinburgh.

Our sketch begins to suggest that James III wished to make Edinburgh into a site for the display of his grandiose ambitions, of which his fixity in Edinburgh, his fantasies of foreign (rather than domestic) travel, his membership in a number of chivalric orders, his interest in European diplomacy, his taste for stamping his image on coins and portraits, his hoarding of treasure, and his designs on the incomes of the Church and of his nobles are all manifestations. Where Scotland was concerned, to James III – and, therefore, to Edinburgh – all things would come. His relation to Edinburgh may be described as one of identification; if Edinburgh had once been one of a group of "sibling" burghs, it was now to be distinguished as the city

Fig. 4. Trinity, from Margaret Tudor's Book of Hours. Photo from the Picture Archives of the Austrian National Library, Vienna. Codex Vindobonensis 1897, fol. 43 verso.

Fig. 5. King James IV of Scotland, from Margaret Tudor's Book of Hours. The arms on the altar are those of his father, James III of Scotland. Photo from the Picture Archives of the Austrian National Library, Vienna. Codex Vindobonensis 1897, fol. 24 verso.

in which the king "resided much." The city, in a sense, was one of James's "familiars"; his relation to it and his cathexis of the economic register were "innovations" not always understood by his contemporaries. Edinburgh's centrality in the crisis of 1482 — when the king was imprisoned by his uncles, and his brother, the duke of Albany, attempted to gain control of the king and his kingdom — is thus strikingly appropriate.

And indeed, in the later fifteenth and early sixteenth centuries, Edinburgh became the pattern for many things. To cite just a few examples: when the rebuilding of Dunbar Castle was undertaken in 1497, the king's chamber was patterned after his chamber in Edinburgh, "a man being specially sent to take measurements."[31] In 1468, Aberdeen wrote to Edinburgh for advice on a legal question.[32] In 1511 the town council of Aberdeen decided to receive Queen Margaret "als honorablie as ony burgh of scotland except edinburgh allanerlie."[33] To be recognized as preeminent in the matter of royal welcomes — those symbolic enactments of the Crown's relationship to the city — was no small thing. The Crown enjoyed municipal spectacle in other ways as well: James IV attended the city's Corpus Christi pageant and was "visited yearly by two boy bishops, one from the collegiate church of St. Giles . . . — 'the Sanct Nicholas, bischop of the toune,' — the other from the Abbey Church of Holyrood."[34] Edinburgh was also the site of spectacular executions. Andrew Adamsoune, who was convicted of murdering Thomas Peblis in Edinburgh Castle (and who tried to escape while imprisoned there) was beheaded, "His head to be put upon the West Port and his hands and feet fixed upon the Ports of the four Burghs nearest to Edinburgh."[35]

To what extent James III influenced affairs in Edinburgh itself is difficult to assess. We might note, however, that during his reign there was an "appreciable development" in the number of burgesses attending Parliament and in the number of burghs represented; he seems to have been interested in encouraging their participation.[36] Legend has it that it was James who gave to the crafts the Blue Blanket, their official banner, and the Seals of Cause appear frequently during his reign.[37] Nicholson notes that it is "striking" that the craft organizations, "which attracted suspicion in the reign of James I" and were not to fare well under James IV, "acquired respectability in the second half of the fifteenth century."[38] The burgh records contain one letter, with James III and William Scheves as signatories, that demonstrates the extent to which James took a personal interest in the particulars of burgh life. It details where the markets should be held, "for the honoure proffit and honestes of our saide burgh and plennesing of voide placis within the samyn, that the merkettis to be haldin in tyme tocum . . . salbe haldin and set on this wise as eftir followis, that is to say: In the first the merket of haye, stra, gers, and hors mete to be vsit and haldin in the Cowgate, fra Forestaris Wynd doun to Peblis Wynd."[39]

James III's own activities as well as his deliberate policies regarding Edinburgh were closely involved with burgh life. The wealth of the city — particularly the health of its wool exports in comparison with those of other burghs — may have provided a "powerful practical motive" for James III's decision to locate in Edinburgh: "Because of its continuing prosperity, Edinburgh was the only place in Scotland where there were any financiers, and common sense would therefore suggest the burgh as a permanent home for the royal administration."[40] James III was borrowing from a number of prominent Edinburgh merchants in 1482 and in 1488 (the two most critical years of his reign, the latter year fatal) — Richard Lawson among them, who became a provost of Edinburgh and served on the Lords of Council from 1483.[41] The *sederunt* list for the trial of William Douglas for treason and *lese majeste*, held at Edinburgh in 1512, includes Sir Alexander Lauder, at that time provost of Edinburgh; the poet Gavin Douglas, provost of St. Giles; and Patrick Paniter, secretary to the king, as well as the usual powerful earls and bishops.[42] The city thus also became importantly involved in royal justice.

James III's household bought extensively from Edinburgh merchants, and it may be assumed that at least this aspect of his continual residence was profitable to the town. Among the merchants he patronized most frequently were Isabel Williamson and David Whitehead. Rosalind Marshall has summarized Isabel Williamson's contributions to the material splendor of the court: "She sold them linen for the royal shirts, black cloth for the King's hose and a variety of velvets, satins and rich silk stuffs to make into gowns and doublets. She could likewise provide velvet and damask for the Queen's cloaks and kirtles and could even produce forty squirrel skins to trim a gown. When the Queen gave birth to a prince it was Mrs Williamson who supplied the velvet for his coat, the cloth for his shirts and sheets and the brown material to cover his cradle."[43] David Whitehead sold the king velvets, satins, and ginger; the records indicate that he traded with Bruges, that he had the tack of the common mills, that he was a town officer in 1475 — when he appended the seal to the aforementioned grant of the Isle and Chapel of St. John in St. Giles to the Wrights and Masons — and that by 1481 he was a member of the "greitt dusane," the town's central governing body.[44]

The interdependence of town and Crown is also manifest in the career of Andrew Wood of Leith, who on 18 March 1483 was granted a feu-charter of Largo "for his services and losses during the war on land and sea."[45] Wood had become a trusted servant of James III, remaining loyal to him

throughout the crisis of 1488.[46] Wood survived the fall of the king and
the rise of the rebel party by becoming in turn the trusted servant of James
IV; he was the king's "familiar knight" by 1495 and by 1513 was "just as
concerned as any noble that his surname and arms be preserved to posterity."[47] Wood was also made a burgess of Edinburgh on 8 January 1490,
"ad requestum magistrorum hospitii et eorum prepositi et datur gratis"—
"gratis at the request of the masters of the hospital and their provost."[48]
In 1475 John Barton, the "senior member of a seafaring family of Leith,"
captained James III's carvel, and the family was later prominent in James
IV's interests as well.[49]

The Crown's desire for maritime power clearly served local careerism
and bound Edinburgh's castle, town, and ports together in an increasingly
tight mesh of interests. These developments served the expansion of Edinburgh's privileges as much as they served the Crown. During the course
of the fifteenth century Edinburgh acquired a "stranglehold" on its neighboring port; a charter of James III in 1482 confirmed Edinburgh's control
of Leith, which was reconfirmed by a charter of James IV, granting also
the recently built port of Newhaven to Edinburgh, along with executive
and judicial powers and profits, and maintenance responsibilities, for both
Leith and Newhaven.[50] Nicholson writes that "if the economic interests of
burgesses, barons, and king had once been distinct they were no longer
so in the reign of James III"—one consequence of which was "the increased
involvement of king and parliament in commercial diplomacy."[51] And there
is evidence of an "increased interest in trade shown by the barons and the
king" at this time.[52] In addition to importing luxuries from the Low Countries through his Scottish merchants, "in 1476 [the king] . . . . tried to
establish a direct connection with Italy by granting" a safe-conduct to Flor-
entine merchants, so that they "might be unimpeded by acts of parliament
in selling their goods to the lords of the council and the king's 'familiars.'
. . . the king's hides were sent to France and Flanders for wine, his woollen
cloth [was] exported for saltpetre and for wine"; his ships also went to Denmark.[53] Early in his reign an act of Parliament, largely concerned with re-
stricting overseas commerce to the already-powerful and prosperous merchants of the realm, reminded Scotland "that it salbe leful to prelatis, Lordis,
barouns, clerkis, to send thar propre gudis with thar seruandis and to by
agane thingis nedeful to thar propre vse."[54] Lythe also remarks on the special buoyancy of royal trading and farming in the Crown revenues for
James III.[55] Lady Hamilton, James III's sister, was exporting hides; her husband was engaged in salt production.[56] Margaret Crichton, James III's niece,
married William Todrik, a merchant and burgess of Edinburgh who had
on 8 February 1506 "a grant under the Great Seal of certain exemptions

from custom for his goods and merchandise, in consideration of his marriage" with James IV's cousin.[57] She later married George Halkerston, a
custumar of Edinburgh, and on 21 October 1516 she herself appears for
one month as sole custumar of Edinburgh.[58] Thus, by the early sixteenth
century a woman of royal blood was accounting to the Crown for the export duties of its chief city.

Edinburgh became, in the fifteenth century, the chief burgh of Scotland
and the single most important site for the display and practice of royal
power. As Margaret Crichton's career suggests, the interests of town and
Crown might at times become so intermeshed as to be practically indistinguishable. Wedged on its high ridge between the castle on one side and
the aristocratic suburbs and Holyrood on the other, Edinburgh was constricted by the ideology and geography of medieval *potestas;* but its boundaries were pressed from within as well as without by churchmen and court
servants as well as by its own citizens and the dispossessed. It is clear,
too, that by the fifteenth century the distinction between burgess and court
servant would not always have been an easy one to maintain. Dunbar's
poem "To the Merchantis of Edinburgh" does not suggest that aristocrats
or prelates or monarchs might take a hand in contributing to the town's
reformation; he does not, at least in that poem, "see" that members of the
first or second estates lived there. Nor does he suggest that Edinburgh
might relieve the hideous welter of its streets by expanding and rebuilding: his vision is simultaneously isolating and containing. The city is to
stay within its bounds, and indeed Edinburgh was slow enough to break
bounds. By the mid–sixteenth century, the burgh was scarcely 400 yards
wide (from north to south – its axis ran east from the castle to Holyrood),
and the "total area within its walls" was only 140 acres. Michael Lynch
writes that, at this time, "Edinburgh was fast in process of becoming a
prosperous, thriving, and bustling metropolis while yet retaining many
of the restrictive habits and most of the dimensions of the old medieval
burgh. The town's walls serve as a reminder that the reformation took
place within the context of the closeted thinking of a medieval burgh."[59]
Constriction, overcrowding, inbuilding – and an incapacity to break,
though not to struggle against, imaginative bounds – appear in Dunbar's
poem and the records of the burgh. The "closeted thinking of a medieval
burgh" was not, however, alone responsible for these conditions; the King's
Wall

cut in two the whole of the gardens on the south side of the High Street, and from
the regularity of surviving close lines to this day taken along with [a] . . . letter
of James III [enjoining the burgesses to maintain the wall] and entries in the Coun-

cil Records, we can see that the burgesses had little or no use for it, and constantly made openings to suit themselves with the object of keeping connection between the upper and lower parts of their plots. It is in fact so clearly connected with military needs and not civic defense, that one may be tempted to speculate on the possibility that it was erected by the English. . . .

The King's Wall had disastrous effects on the life of the burgh, for here we have a main cause of a tradition of overcrowding and high building.[60]

The King's Wall symbolizes both the willingness of Edinburgh's citizens to work within the bounds — literal and imaginative — prescribed for them by the castle and the town's growing need, at the same time, to redefine its relation to the architecture of *potestas* (in this case, by making holes in it). James III's supplication to the pope regarding the collegiate status of St. Giles indicates how much the Crown might imaginatively or rhetorically invest in the grandeur of its cities. But it is important to stress that the grandeur of the city was to be a borrowed one; the city was to depend upon the Crown and to serve its interests. The ideology of isolation and containment expressed both the desire that the town be kept within bounds — that its interdependence with the Crown rest ultimately on its dependence — and the fear that the town might break those bounds. At the same time the strength of the Crown depended at least to some extent on the strength of the city. Though the creation of a strong capital seems to have been one of the chief projects of James III's reign — whether or not he knew it — the obverse of his description of Edinburgh as the town in which he resided much is the hope, present also in Dunbar's poem, that if the city did not behave itself the Crown might "reside" elsewhere and take its privileges with it. The act of Parliament of 1487 that tried to move the Court of the Parliament of the Four Burghs to Inverkeithing may be an illustration both of this hope and of its futility.[61] Fourteen hundred eighty-seven was the year before James's defeat and death at Sauchieburn, and his support was comparatively strong in the north.

The burgh's welfare had in fact depended for centuries on the patronage of the monarch; the charters that recorded the Crown's granting of privileges to the burghs were the effects of grace. This was most obviously true of the royal burghs, held directly by the Crown; but even the burghs of barony were conceived, at least theoretically, as being held for the Crown by an intermediate lord. In this sense the courtly fantasy of the monarch's endless power to patronize was indeed "productive." But of course the monarch patronizes his burghs because they seem politically and economically advantageous, and he comes to depend upon the services of those he calls his "lovits" — his "beloveds" — the merchants and burgesses of the town. The king is thus "haunted" by the possibility that his progeny might become monstrous. Thus relations between king and capital must be represented with special care, as the effect of the king's grace. The fate of the capital city is identified with the will of the court at a time when the king's vulnerability to the city is perhaps first beginning to be imagined.

3

Exchanges of Faith: James III and the Crisis of 1482

In his study of James III, Macdougall remarks that "the seizure of James III at Lauder in July 1482 was an event without parallel in fifteenth century Scottish political history."[1] While trying to muster an army at Lauder to meet an English advance on Berwick, the king was seized by two of his uncles — the earls of Atholl and Buchan — and subsequently imprisoned in Edinburgh Castle. Some of the members of his household were hanged by the rebels at Lauder.

Two factors that helped bring about the king's seizure and imprisonment will interest us particularly in this discussion. The first is the "black money": in need of money for defense against the English (and unwilling to drain his growing treasure-hoard for the purpose), James III seems to have "indulged in a drastic debasement of the coinage over a period from about 1480 until 1482, producing very base billon coins and a large quantity of copper ones."[2] The issue of the black money was, to put it very mildly, unpopular; it was held responsible for great hunger and dearth and hit the merchants and the peasantry particularly hard. By the summer of 1482, "the debased money had been in circulation long enough for the king to have lost the support, not so much of the nobility, but rather of the merchant class and those lower in the social scale." This gave the nobles a "popular cause to make their own."[3]

The second factor is what Macdougall refers to as "the breakdown of normal relationships amongst the royal Stewart kin." The later part of 1479, or early 1480, saw the "imprisonment, death and forfeiture" of the king's brother John, the earl of Mar; the king's brother Alexander, duke of Albany, was also summonsed for treason, and he fled to England.[4] Perhaps understandably within this context, a remission — issued in March 1482 — for seizure of Edinburgh Castle during the king's minority seems to have

alarmed rather than appeased the king's uncles, the earls of Buchan and
Atholl.[5] In 1482 the possession of Edinburgh Castle was, as Macdougall explains, the "key factor in the Stewart half-uncles' bid for political power"; thus in the summer of 1482 they repeated their earlier treasons
by again taking custody of the castle and overreached themselves by imprisoning the king to boot. It would have been particularly galling to James
that Buchan, in particular, owed his prominence largely to the king's previous patronage.[6] Meanwhile, Albany had signed a treaty with the English
that would make him a vassal king of Edward IV in exchange for English
military support in seizing the crown.[7] Shortly after the king was removed
to Edinburgh Castle by Atholl and Buchan, then, Albany and the duke
of Gloucester (later Richard III) arrived at the head of a large English army
to find the king whom they had hoped to coerce in quite other hands.
James's relations with his kin were disastrous; by the early 1480s the royal
family lay almost in ruins, and James's reign looked likely to follow.

James's "high-flown view of royal authority" seems, then, to have meant
that no rivals could be brooked.[8] Nearly everything that has been known
or written about James III's style of rule (its rigidities, its deceptions, its
avarice, its intolerance of disloyalty) suggests that James identified monarchy with omnipotence and that his style was accordingly omnivorous:
to be all things meant, for James, to have all things. He feared replacement and robbery equally. Treason — always a concern for the medieval
monarch — was nothing short of an obsession during his reign.[9] And his
obsession with treason was unsurprisingly the obverse of his own designs
on everything everybody else had.[10] What seems, above all, to have provoked the crises of James's reign was specifically James's inability to give,
his investment of *potestas* at the expense of plenitude. His subjects came
to view him as dangerous, not merely because he had fantasies of imperial
grandeur but also because the stringencies of his rule threatened to undo
the fiction of *cura*, to provoke ideological crisis by making *potestas* appear
as atrocity.

The king was thus unable to maintain cordial relations with anyone not
his "creature" — with anyone not willing to signify a creaturely, rather than
a rivalrous, identity and difference. He could not have "similars"; this is,
I think, why his "familiars" became such an important theme in his legend
and in his reign.[11] The king's relation to Edinburgh itself — as simultaneously a center which he might fully occupy, a way of feeling himself to
fill all available space, and a docile creature, more dependent, at least in
fantasy, upon his patronage than any powerful magnate could have been —
is something like a relation to a familiar. James liked to create things, but
apparently it was to him unthinkable that his creations should grow up.[12]

Because James created his capital by ruling almost exclusively from it, however, ironically — and perhaps inevitably — its castle became his prison.[13] By the later fifteenth century, control of Edinburgh was beginning to mean control of the nation — at least in the minds of some of Scotland's most powerful actors, perhaps in the minds of Edinburgh's own citizens. Not least among the striking features of the crisis of 1482 was that the burgesses of Edinburgh were partly responsible for liberating the king from the consequences of their city's preferment.

Soon after Albany and Gloucester arrived in Edinburgh, it became clear to them that the pursuit of their own designs was impossible under the circumstances of the king's imprisonment by the uncles. Gloucester settled for money. On 4 August 1482 the provost and community of Edinburgh bound and obliged themselves to repay Edward IV "certain and diuers gret sommes of money" that he had sent to Scotland for the dowry of his daughter Cecilia — should the monarch decide not to pursue further a projected marriage between Cecilia and Prince James.[14] The price of Gloucester's departure was considerable — eight thousand English marks. The bond was produced to Edinburgh by Garter King at Arms on 27 October.[15] If the capture and imprisonment of the king was "an event without parallel" in fifteenth-century Scotland, then the turning-back of the largest English army to invade Scotland in eighty years by the sole expedient of Edinburgh's money was perhaps almost as striking.

Albany, casting about for some way of regaining his inheritance, decided to make a show of loyalty to the king. Accordingly, at the end of September — the king had now been imprisoned for two months — Albany laid siege to the castle, along with the officers and community of Edinburgh.[16] The king was released from the castle on 29 September, and since the castle itself had not been provisioned, it was surrendered by mid-October. This in turn may imply that the town had been provisioning the castle all along, though not necessarily with enthusiasm.

Meanwhile, Edinburgh was coping with further financial demands. Andrew Stewart (another uncle), bishop-elect of Moray, in league with Buchan and Atholl in their imprisonment of the king, aspired to the archbishopric of St. Andrews, and by 8 November the burgesses of Edinburgh had pledged six thousand gold ducats to further his promotion at the papal *curia* in exchange for a bond obliging the king's uncles to pay them back.[17] By this time the king's uncles were still largely in control of the government, and James was a long way from regaining power.

That Edinburgh played an active role in any of the various conspiracies against the king seems unlikely. It is true that Archibald Crawfurd, the abbot of Holyrood (near Edinburgh), appears as treasurer of the uncles' regime, but this need not indicate disaffection or complicity on the part of Holyrood's neighboring town.[18] It may, however, indicate that Holyrood — perhaps for reasons more personal to Crawfurd than pertaining to the abbey itself — did not find James a congenial neighbor. Signs of strain in the burgh itself are evident in the fact that Edinburgh had three provosts in 1482. In the terms of an indenture drawn up at Edinburgh on 16 March 1483 — signed three days later by Albany, now fled to Dunbar, as capitulation to the again-powerful James — it is specified that Albany's supporter, the master of Morton, was to surrender the sheriffship of Edinburgh.[19] Whether Morton had any popular support or had been thrust upon the burgh by Albany is impossible to say; by this time Edinburgh had been granted the right to choose its own sheriff, and Morton may have been the result of, the exploitation of, or an obstacle to the execution of this new privilege.

It is safe to say, however, that the tradition of factional exploitation of Edinburgh offices — evident in the troubles of James V's minority — had begun, to be continued in 1487 by the striking appearance of Patrick Hepburn, Lord Hailes, as "Lord Provost" of Edinburgh.[20] The compiler of the list of Edinburgh's provosts notes that "the minute of the election of Lord Hailes is curious, as containing the first known application of the title of 'Lord Provost' [a title taken up again by Lord Home in 1514 and by Arran in 1518], and also as empowering him to elect deputes and presidents."[21] Hepburn's election occurred the year before the king's fall at Sauchieburn at the hands of rebels led, nominally at least, by Prince James. Hepburn was instrumental in that fall; he was to profit from the rise of James IV perhaps more completely than any other of the young king's supporters, and the list of offices he received shows clearly that Edinburgh was one of his chief interests.[22] Macdougall notes that Hepburn was "the man who had been forced to surrender Berwick castle to the English in 1482, and who may have been mistrusted by James III as a result"; he was also a neighbor of the Humes, with whom James by 1487 had been feuding for quite some time over Coldingham Priory.[23] James would likely have noticed Hepburn's move on Edinburgh; it is therefore possible that Hepburn had some popular support, for the move might have been a risky one otherwise. And Patrick's uncle, Alexander Hepburn, who served as provost in 1490, was also sheriff of Edinburgh in 1482 and for some years following, until Patrick Hepburn himself became sheriff "in fee and heritage" in 1488.[24] If by 1488 Hepburn and his allies had cause to fear "growing royal interference in the south-east," perhaps Edinburgh — or at least some elements therein — was likewise wearying of the king's constant attentions.[25]

Perhaps most significant for Edinburgh's role in the crisis of 1482, however, is the following complaint from the Seal of Cause of Edinburgh's Hammermen, dated 2 May 1483: "In the first thair complaint buir and specifyit that thay war rycht havely hurt and put to greit poverty throw the doun cumming of the blak money, walking [and] warding, and in the payment of ʒeldis and extentis quhilkis thay war compellit to do be vse, and to be compellit thairto be our Lordis authoritie mandimentis and chargis."[26] There is evidence, then, that Edinburgh was hard hit—and unhappily so—by some of the king's policies. And its sense of economic outrage would have been exacerbated further by the bleak possibility of having to pay eight thousand marks to the English and six thousand ducats to the uncles—all this following hard upon the heels of a devastating currency devaluation and the expensive demands of warfare. It seems, again, unlikely that the town had sufficient grievances against the king actually to seek his overthrow. Its behavior during the crisis is that of a town beset by factional politics, doing its best to play both sides against the middle and thereby at least to minimize the damage. Though there is evidence that Edinburgh was beset by factional difficulties earlier in the fifteenth century, it must be emphasized that nothing like the crisis of 1482 had ever happened to Edinburgh before (nor, for that matter, to any other burgh in Scotland); never before had it been thrust into the center of a national crisis as complex as this one, and the town proved itself in the art of exchange. For Edinburgh did have sufficient grievance to exploit the king's weakness in order to gain greater independence from royal domination. Its role in liberating the king may have meant that the town could not afford to refuse its aid; it may have meant that the town had nothing to gain from the uncles; it may have meant a desire to rescue the king who had made it his capital. It is likely that all these motives were in play at different times on the part of different actors. But in any case, two charters of James III dated 16 November 1482—one week after the bond of obligation by the uncles—grant Edinburgh a wealth of new privileges, and it is to these charters that we now need to turn our attention.

The two charters in question—one "granting the office of Sheriffship" to Edinburgh and authorizing it to hold "a Peremptory Court of twenty-one days when necessary; and to make ordinances for the good government of the Burgh"; the other granting to Edinburgh the "customs from the harbour and road of Leith"—carefully list the names of the burgh officers involved in the siege of Edinburgh Castle and give an equally careful and complete list of Albany's newly restored titles.[27] This gives the charter almost the flavor of an unofficial pardon. It records the efforts made by Albany and the burgh on the king's behalf, perhaps in order to clear the parties concerned from blame, but certainly to try to establish their entitlement to reward.[28] That one of the privileges granted by the first charter should be a reconfirmation of the burgh's ancient right to legislate for its own welfare may suggest that the citizens of Edinburgh were seeking to guard against future retaliation by the king, should he have any suspicions about their actions. On the one hand, then, we have Edinburgh recording its assistance to Albany in liberating the king from the clutches of the uncles. On the other hand, we have a list of witnesses: "the reverend fathers in Christ, John Bishop of Glasgow, our chancellor, James bishop of Dunkeld; our beloved uncles, Andrew elect of Moray, keeper of our privy seal, John earl of Athol lord Baluany; . . . the venerable father in Christ, Archibald abbot of our monastery of Holy Rood of Edinburgh, our treasurer," and so forth. In short (with the exception of Buchan, who seems not to have been present), we have the uncles and their principal supporters.[29] The spectacle of the uncles witnessing, in full detail and panoply, charters rewarding Edinburgh for acting with Albany to release the king from the prison they put him in is to be wondered at; it generously illustrates the byzantine nature of national and city politics at this time. The uncles were still largely in control of the royal government, which means that they kept its seals; for the king, therefore, to have issued any sort of charter, he would likely have had to do so in the presence of at least some of the uncles' men. The uncles, then, must have approved of the charters; but the pomp and completeness of the witness-list suggests something beyond the pragmatics of doing Crown business at Edinburgh Castle in the autumn of 1482.

The charters follow by just over one week the bond whereby the uncles pledged repayment of the six thousand gold ducats for Andrew Stewart's promotion as archbishop of St. Andrews. Macdougall is probably right, then, to propose that the charters were a further quid pro quo in the same business: "a benevolence to the uncles, in Albany's name, at the king's expense!"[30] The charters signify more, however, than just a matchless piece of convolution. They attest Edinburgh's willingness to deal with all the parties concerned in the crisis — its willingness, that is, openly to pressure the king with support from the uncles, in order to make good their losses — and the uncles' willingness, in turn, to appease the town's financiers with more than a paper IOU. (The king may have seemed to the burgesses an unlikely candidate for survival; the uncles would surely have wanted to avoid, so far as was possible, the town's hostility.) Moreover, to have given away rights of shrieval jurisdiction to a town so mixed up in current events was a proposition the uncles might have slept on, even if Edinburgh's chances of exploiting the privilege to the uncles' detriment would have seemed slim. They might, too, have thought twice about making the privileges granted by the charter an apparent quid pro quo for liberating the king—even if their action as witnesses might have seemed to record their disassociation from the agents who imprisoned him. Charters do not customarily go into such detail about the history behind and reasons for their issuance. Edinburgh may indeed have made the charters a condition of their pledge of the six thousand gold ducats. And the idea for at least the substance of the charters must have come from Edinburgh. The privileges granted are substantial and specific to Edinburgh's situation and desires.

The charters, in essence, confer upon Edinburgh greater independence from the techniques and structures of royal domination. The officers and community of the burgh receive the "honor" of having the office of sheriff "within themselves" (infra se), meaning not only that the profits of feudal justice would now enrich the burgh but also that the burgh would now exercise the lord's traditional rights over the body of the criminal. In a sense, then, the privilege of sheriffship "embodies" the burgh by empowering the relations among bodies within the burgh; it grants to the burgh the power of alteration, of injury. The charter thus provides for the elaboration and intensification of the autonomy and the innerness of the city, its sense of itself as a particular "world." The burgh was also granted the right to hold a peremptory court of twenty-one days, because the procedures of the Court of the Parliament of the Four Burghs had become so tedious and slow.[31] And by acquiring the customs of Leith and the provost's right to be sheriff within its bounds, Edinburgh's "stranglehold over its unfortunate port" was guaranteed.[32]

Thus not only did the privileges reinforce, as burgh privileges had always done, the extent to which the burghs were set apart from the rest of the population, they also enhanced Edinburgh's special difference from the other burghs of Scotland (its exemption from the process of the Court of the Parliament of the Four Burghs) and enabled expansionism (its designs on Leith) as well as autonomy. The "worldness" of the city—its separation from the authority of its creator—is produced in part by drawing an even thicker line around it. The "worldness" of the capital city is produced by allowing it to engulf the resources of other regions, which it accomplishes by internalizing certain feudal forms of extraction of surplus value (justice, tolls). The extent to which the charters distinguish Edinburgh from other burghs and cater to its economic expansionism bespeaks and reproduces precisely the unique prominence that led to the granting of the charters in the first place.

By internalizing lordship, however, the merchants and burgesses of the town do little to transform lordship. Insofar as the town appropriates rather than changes the techniques of feudal power — by, for example, treating Leith as a "vassal" port, rather than combining with it or engaging in some kind of economic reciprocity with it — the town will seem, in its difference, to mirror the king rather than to present him with a face unrecognizable as such. The creature will resemble its creator. But through its growing preeminence — the special difference of the capital, which in its specialness resembles the special difference of the sovereign — the city may seem to threaten a "capacity for self-transformation into a separate verbal or material form." The charter's linking of Albany and town might suggest that the creature has become a rival.[33] And the rulers of the city — the merchants and burgesses — as well as their own ruler may be "haunted" by the difference capitalism makes to feudalism — by the "flow" (however reluctant) of Edinburgh's credit, and by the power (however fledgling and repressed) of the crafts. Finance and artisanal production were two severely codified aspects of burghal economic life whose access to privileged representation was, when not precluded altogether, carefully controlled. The repression of the "knowledge" that the world is produced by human creativity, labor, and desire is frequently at stake not only in aristocratic representations of the late medieval burgh but also in the practices of power within the burgh itself — to the extent, at least, that those practices reveal an identification with aristocratic forms of power.

James III's charters assert the resemblance between town and Crown by presenting bourgeois difference as a repetition of the feudal "same." The narrative in James III's charter treats Edinburgh not as a disaffected financier or a town full of angry craftspeople, but as — like Albany — a feudal vassal.[34] A story is told that describes the

faith, loyalty, love, benevolence and cordial service which our beloved and faithful the present office-bearers of our Burgh of Edinburgh, underwritten . . . with our dearest brother Alexander duke of Albany earl of March and of Mar and Garviauch, lord of Annandale and Man, have already providently rendered to us in liberating our person from imprisonment in our Castle of Edinburgh, in which against the pleasure of our will we were held captive, exposing their persons to great peril of life, while besieging the said Castle with our said brother, in consequence of which attack our royal person now rejoices in liberty.[35]

The charter does not choose to tell a story of the English king's extortion of a promise of eight thousand marks out of the Scottish king's own subjects, nor does it tell a story of the merchants' ability (at least in theory) to buy the security of their country — a story that would feature the power of alteration of merchant capital rather than of aristocratic war, and might work as a tale of the merchants' good deeds in parting with their goods.

Nor does it tell the kind of story we have told earlier in this chapter—the story of political plague—of factional rivalry, payoffs, intrigue, and manipulation. These stories are encoded in various ways in the charter—by its very existence, by its lists of witnesses and donees—but we do not have, for our story's heroes, either generous or canny merchants. We do not have, for our story's plot, the loss and reparation of capital.

Instead of economic loss and reparation, we have risk and triumph—the romance story of the rescue and liberation of an imprisoned king. The romancing of James's imprisonment projects a closure in which he will be present, at the end, to distribute rewards to the faithful, to those willing to fulfill the feudal obligations of warfare and the demands of honor. Between James III and his subjects there has been no broken faith, no false love, but the real thing—what the charter refers to as "fidem legalitatem amorem et beneuolenciam cordialeque servicium." This is the idyll that conceals the trauma of loss, that repairs the damage done by the primal scene of betrayal and greed. The charter's conferral of aristocratic virtues on the merchants and burgesses of Edinburgh—nothing quite like this language is to be found in earlier burgh charters—is the remaking, as against betrayal, of the community of honor, which is a community founded on fidelity. Treason threatens to dissolve the difference between sovereign and servant on which the very idea of sovereignty is founded; but James's charter repairs the communion of sovereign with servant and in doing so reconstitutes both. The charter accomplishes this not only through the story it tells but also through the very fact of its being a charter—an instance of royal patronage.

The language of the charter may be "deceptive." It may have been extorted from an unwilling king, whose favorite emotion was not gratitude. But the language of the charter is also a restoration of voice and hence a symbolic act—a way of making one and making good. Because it is split off from the sphere of Machiavellian politics, it allows the king—threatened with the loss of his kingship—to re-create himself as king, by symbolizing his own magnanimity and his capacity to produce community through the *fides* of his servants (who act, not independently, but dependently, through the dedication of the servant to the sovereign). The charter narrates a liberation; it is also, in the sense we have just outlined, the scope of the king's own freedom from dependence. The charter is presented as the effect, not of the contrivances of servants, but of the patronage of the sovereign. Thus his voice is not to be represented as bound by physical constraint; the charter enacts the transformation of imprisonment—a threatening form of embodiment, insofar as it limits the king's power to the space of his own body and hence radically limits his capacity for self-extension – into a powerful form of the royal word. Nor is the king to be seen as bound by the terms of payoff or bargain; the charter, again, is a gift. The clauses that introduce the narrative read as follows: "Since no act of duty between man and man is recognized as more necessarily belonging to the obligation of benevolence than that we should bestow most on those by whom we are most beloved: Hence it is that we, considering with thoughtful mind [*alta mente*] the faith, loyalty, love. . . ."[36] And it is specified that the "labours" of the town were "free" ("et pro suis gratuitis laboribus et serviciis nobis impensis et exhibitis").[37] Services are rendered freely (and rewarded freely) because of a relation of loyalty and love. As Pierre Bourdieu might put it, *credit* is replaced, in this charter, by *trust* – like fidelity, a special form of belief.[38] The services and rewards thus exchanged are not ends in themselves – not the purpose of exchange – but, again, phenomenalizations and productions of community.

At the moment that the charter takes up the question of the nature of this exchange – and it is very clearly concerned to do so – the power of alteration conferred upon the giver by the gift makes its presence felt. The presence of this power of alteration is marked in part by the use of the phrase *alta mente:* from his lofty station, the king "considers" the services of those who love him, as though he had been watching history take place below. The place of the king in the architecture of *potestas* – which, ironically, had become his prison – is thus recuperated: his verticality, his transcendence, is reasserted against his circumscription, through his possession of the high mind of Jove. One aspect of the gift – an aspect exploited in the charter for the purposes of asserting James's own freedom from coercion – is its apparent gratuitousness, its suggestion of the possibility of unearned love and endless plenty. The sovereign, as we have noted, must identify himself as the source of this endless plenty. But the sovereign's gift nonetheless is coercive, because it (re)makes the person to whom it is given; in the remaking of the person, the repossession of the servant's interior, the gift is returned by way of loyalty, which is the aristocratic form of religious belief. The gift is thus double; it duplicates within itself the doubleness of the power of alteration, which is both the power to unmake and the power to make. In James's charter, no less than in the works of Augustine and, as we shall see, of James Foullis, this doubleness is experienced as a difference, often as a division: *sinus* and *aula,* the maternal and paternal strands, love and aggression, peace and war, paradise and plague. And yet this contradictoriness is somehow made one and made good, in the person of the sovereign or the creator: the pain of being altered is reappropriated for the intensity and certainty of belief. It is the very fictiveness of the superreal – its requirement that a "construct" be re-presented as the constructor — that demands, in the figure of the creator, the copresence of unmaking with making. Thus if it is the remaking of the Creator Himself that is really at stake in Foullis's *Calamitose*, in James III's charter it is the remaking of the sovereign, through the reconstitution of fidelity and loyalty, that is at stake.

The problem of loyalty pressures the shape of James's charter enough to produce the words *Tenebuntur tamen*. Nevertheless, says the charter, the officers and community of the burgh *shall be bound* "to cause to be celebrated yearly for ever a funeral Mass of Requiem Placebo Dirige with chanting, in the Collegiate Church of St. Giles of the said Burgh on the third and fourth days of the month of August, for the weal of the soul of our late progenitor, and of our soul, and of the souls of our own ancestors and successors, with suffrages of prayers for our prosperity [*pro nostro prospero statu*]."[39] *Status* has meanings of "condition" or "state" but also of "position" or "standing posture" (in English, too, one can have *a* status of any sort, but to have status means to be high up). *Prosper* has meanings of "fortunate," "favorable," "lucky," as well as "prosperous." The phrasing, in short, brings together once again *sinus* and *aula* — appropriate to a stipulation that asserts both the power of the *gift*, and the *power* of the gift. For it is not only that the power of the king's gift of privileges to the burgh has produced the rupture of the *Tenebuntur tamen* in the otherwise unrelieved stylistic benevolence of this charter; it is also that the city, through its communal prayers, will dedicate itself to the eternal prosperity of the Stewart dynasty. The king has reminded the citizens of the earthly city of the ambiguity of the gift and the power of obligation to reproduce itself; the king's gift to the city will be returned in the form of the city's efforts on behalf of the king's eternal enjoyment of "a realm of unremitting plenty."

The response solicited by James from Edinburgh is one of perpetual mourning. Whereas, as we shall see, James Foullis's *Strena* puts plenitude in the place of loss, James III will turn loss into plenitude by way of purgatorial mortification. The diminishment of the king's wealth and power through the privileges granted in the charters is here replenished by the demand that the king be forever memorialized, forever encrypted, that he and his gift live on *in* the devotional practices of his favorite city and the parish church which James himself had patronized.[40] Thus, once again, the interior of the servant is penetrated and remade for fidelity. The gift turns into a perpetual possession, in both senses of the word; this gift truly bears with it the spirit of its giver and its homeland.[41] Such was James's response to the designs of his creature upon his person: he would be remembered. In James III's charter the restoration of the sovereign's possession of the community will be enacted through memorialization. The damage done to sovereignty by the primal scene of trouble in the city will be repaired by the willingness of the servant perpetually to remake the sovereign in his memory. The transformation of human imagining into remembering is one of the most fundamental operations of power.

James might have wished the story of his relations with his preeminent city to have ended with its dedication to the worship of the ancestral blood, and the dynastic future, of the Stewarts. His own story ended not with his possession of a community, but with the fragmentation and loss of community. The year 1488, as we have indicated, brought another rebellion — caused, in part, by his designs on Coldingham Priory and the subsequent alienation of Humes, Hepburns, and many more; in part by his preferential treatment of his second son, whose marriage he had been pursuing with greater assiduity than that of his first son and whom he raised to the dignity of the duke of Ross on 29 January 1488.[42] Evidence of his first son's disaffection may be found in Rothesay's apparent willingness to fall into the hands of the rebel party. And the Aberdeen Articles — a pact drawn up between the rebels and the loyalists, "casually" broken by the king — reveal the prince's "dissatisfaction with the household and living" permitted him by the king.[43] The creature had finally become a monster.

Whether James III's other creature — Edinburgh — had become a monster is less clear. James's preference for Edinburgh was so marked that we can only assume it must have been a serious crisis indeed to induce him to leave. Patrick Hepburn's role as lord provost of Edinburgh in 1487, Alexander Hepburn's control of the sheriffship from 1482 onward, the attempt in 1487 to move the Court of the Four Burghs to Inverkeithing, and the disappearance of the burgh customs during the period March–May 1488 remain troubling and enigmatic.[44] But the castle was held for the king; he returned to visit the "royal jewel house" once again, to make elaborate dispositions for his treasure, and to try to rally support, before leaving to meet his death at Sauchieburn in a battle described thus by Pitscottie:

> The ciuill weir, the battell intestine,
> Nou that the sone with baner bred displayit
> Aganis the fader in battell come arreyit.[45]

In a sense, Pitscottie was right to see James III as a kind of Laius. For it was, in large part, James's inability to tolerate his creatures that led him to his defeat at Sauchieburn; and everything he did to repress rivalry — his refusal, in particular, to empower his eldest son — seems to have brought him closer to his end.

4

God's Own Hand:
The Poetry of James Foullis

> Then I saw a new heaven and a new earth, for the first heaven and the first earth
> had vanished, and there was no longer any sea. I saw the holy city, New Jerusalem,
> coming down out of heaven from God, made ready like a bride adorned for her
> husband. I heard a loud voice proclaiming from the throne: "Now at last God has
> his dwelling among men! He will dwell among them and they shall be his people,
> and God himself will be with them. He will wipe every tear from their eyes; there
> shall be an end to death, and to mourning and crying and pain; for the old order
> has passed away!"
>
> — Revelation 21:1–4

THIS chapter considers the poetry of James Foullis, a burgess of Edinburgh and a prominent advocate and courtier during the reign of James
V of Scotland (1513–42). Thanks largely to the work of John Durkan,
Foullis's poetry is now known to scholars of Scottish humanism and has
recently begun to receive serious textual and editorial treatment. This chapter studies Foullis as a poet of the city and in particular as a poet whose
figurations of infantile and parental strands of meaning are worked out
through his identification with Edinburgh. Foullis wrote at a time when
Edinburgh, Scotland, and Scotland's kings had suffered much from calamity: from continuing economic depression, plague, disastrous battles, the
death of James IV, the disorders of the fragile minority of James V and
his virtual imprisonment in Edinburgh. In Foullis's poetry, the recovery —
the re-membering — of childhood, city, and monarchy are mutually implicit. We will begin with a brief survey of the material and discursive circumstances in which Foullis's poetry was produced.

Thomas Davidson, burgess and guild-brother of Edinburgh, seems to
have become the favored royal printer during the reign of James V. Instances, at least, of Davidson's patronage by the Crown date from the time

of his greatest activity as printer of government documents and "croniklis."[1] Davidson printed *The hystory and croniklis of Scotland* (Bellenden's translation of Hector Boece's Latin work) and the *Actis* of Parliament of James V. Colophons in both the *Croniklis* and the *Actis* style Davidson as "prentar to the Kingis nobyll grace"; for the latter job he was apparently chosen by Sir James Foullis, clerk register.[2] Davidson was also responsible for printing a Latin poem known as the *Strena* and addressed to James V on taking up the kingship of the country.[3] Since the poem alludes to James V's assumption of power in 1528, it is likely that the poem was printed in that year, perhaps commissioned for a royal welcome.[4] It is possible, too, that the poem represents an early collaboration of Sir James Foullis with the Davidson press; for, though the *Strena* is anonymous, John Durkan has suggested that James Foullis is the most likely candidate for its authorship.[5] Foullis's connections with Edinburgh and with printing, his interest in Latin poetry, and the thematic and rhetorical resemblances between the *Strena* and his other poetry strongly support this attribution.

James Foullis was a burgess of Edinburgh; his father may have been a member of the guild of Skinners, and his mother was the daughter of Sir James Henderson, or Henryson, of Fordell, an advocate to James IV.[6] Foullis himself became king's advocate in 1527; held the post of secretary to the king in 1529, one year after the probable publication of the *Strena;* served as clerk register from 1532 to 1549; and was in 1542 a member of the privy council.[7] He was also a neo-Latin poet. His *Calamitose pestis Elega deploratio* was published in Paris ca. 1511 and dedicated to Alexander Stewart (the illegitimate son of James IV, who became archbishop of St. Andrews), to whom he wrote that "his object in publishing was to entice students at home to take up the study of polite letters."[8] Foullis seems to have worked at a pitch of nationalist, royalist, and belletristic fervor for most of his life. After his stay in Paris Foullis studied at Orléans, famed for its instruction in law and host of a vigorous Scottish "nation" for which Foullis was a "specially active and zealous" procurator.[9]

Foullis's *Calamitose* is a nightmarish vision of disasters that have befallen Edinburgh. In the letter to Stewart, Foullis explains that plague had driven many students from Paris to Orléans, and he recalls the terrible plague that had ravaged Scotland some years before. Written, then, "under the influence" of the later plague in Paris ("suppressa memor bissenos fata per annos, / Horrende repeto tela cruenta necis," ll. 45–46) the *Calamitose* memorializes the plague of the late 1490s, during which Foullis lost his entire family. The poem tells the story of how, while Foullis himself lay seriously ill with the plague, his small sister and brother died, and finally his parents. Personal loss and municipal and national catastrophe intertwine in Foullis's *Calamitose.*

Nature is represented as demonic. Scotland is a white land clothed with Thracian snows and rivers formed of marble ice (ll. 11–12). Into this landscape Death rushes, a wolf, an archer, shooting arrows of plague whose poisoned iron crushes the innermost limbs, destroys bone marrow, and stiffens the body with ulcers (ll. 20–40). In the *Calamitose*, the human body is dismembered and decomposed; the body of the world, too, is dead or dying. The *Calamitose* is an attempt to give voice to the tortured body of whose isolation, exposure, and voicelessness Elaine Scarry so movingly writes. According to Scarry, it is the destruction of community — the destruction both of the community's beliefs about itself and of the victim's capacity to experience community — that is at stake in acts of torture and of war. Great pain is both "language-destroying" and "world-destroying."[10] Plague is, in the register of disease, the apocalyptic form of the world- and word-destroying power of pain. In the plague, says Girard, "All life, finally, is turned into death, which is the supreme undifferentiation"; plague "symbolizes desymbolization itself."[11] The destruction of the body and of the human world which has been made for and by the body is also linked, in the *Calamitose*, to the destruction of temporal community: time, too, is full of horrors. Foullis repeatedly alludes to previous catastrophes (Niobe, l. 65; the fall of Troy, l. 350), creating a dynamic of remembering in which the experience of loss serves perpetually to recall earlier losses. Memory is an instrument of self-extension, of struggle against the reduction of world and self to the painful body; it links Foullis's, and Scotland's, injuries to a history of catastrophe. But memory thereby becomes, at the same time, an instrument of further torture: the suffering memory finds, in history, no resting place. Losses are displaced only to reappear at every turn; continuities bespeak only the experience of discontinuity.

The narrator of the *Calamitose* chooses to end his complaint simply by appealing to the Muse to cease her lamentations; if one were to weep for the living — for creatures subject to decay — this would be a task for more tongues than there are stars in the sky and fish in the sea. Lamentation would be endless. The moment of the poem's most ambitious attempt to speak the unspeakable, to resymbolize that which has been desymbolized, is also the moment at which the human voice breaks down. Nearly all writers on mourning remind us of how grief impoverishes the subject's world; grief is that negation of desire, that disappearance of the object, which participates most closely in the world-destroying character of physical pain. The *Calamitose* treads the borderline moment at which language begins to break down from grief and pain, the moment at which the radical embodiment of death makes its appearance. Foullis's vision of the impoverishment of the human voice by mourning, of the need for an infinitude of voice in order to speak unendurable loss, thus gives way to an invocation of divinity. Recognition of the limits of the human voice — recognition of creatureliness — paves the way for reparation of the relation to the Creator.[12] The poem concludes: "Pone igitur questus gemebundi pectoris altos, / Et sit pacato purior aura Deo" (ll. 495–96).[13]

The *Calamitose*, then, is at once a protest against persecution and an acceptance of its terms and structure. Foullis describes the traumatic and ominous outbreak of fire in St. Giles as the impiety responsible for the scourge of the plague (l. 149); terror is explicated as an effect of divine wrath and punishment. The obverse of healing miracle, plague instances the immateriality of the Creator in the form of arbitrary power, because it signifies God's transcendence of all conceivable limits on the extension and creative power of the human body. As a manifestation of that force which emanates unilaterally from God, plague contrasts with, bypasses, and indeed puts an end to the historical processes by which human production and reproduction make the world. It is a response to failure of belief or of worship; it is the demand that human materiality be sacrificed in resubstantiation of the immateriality of God, that human interiority be sacrificed to an exteriorized Creator.[14] Thus the failure of municipal vigilance and worship which leads to the outbreak of fire in St. Giles will be atoned for through a "shattering" of the city. The blankness within an interior that has forgotten what is due to the Creator — the blankness of carelessness — is, moreover, projected onto and temporarily reflected in the blankness of the Creator's gaze. Jupiter looks down, with no apparent concern for the future of the human race (l. 435). The possibility of absolute ending is envisaged as an inability to see care (*cura*, l. 436) in the gaze of the Judge. In the place of an icon of belief, Foullis registers a moment of frightening emptiness. Forgetfulness unmakes the relation between creature and Creator, which is — since the Creator must be imagined by the creature — a relation of belief. Pain re-members that relation through dismemberment.

In keeping with the spectacular qualities of this poem — in which the absolute Judge ("Tu, criminis ultor / Et iudex, nulli sceptra secunda tenes" [You, punisher of guilt, and judge, you hold a kingdom second to none], ll. 439–40) marks his power on the bodies of the guilty and the guilty city — Foullis's poem materializes figural narrative links, so that everything, however apparently insignificant, threatens to become a matter of life and death, of absolute proportions. Plague means that one death not only prefigures but causes another, provoking images both of earlier devastation and apocalypse. Contagion turns particular losses into universal destruction. The impious breakdown of the boundary, hence of the relation, between Creator and creature, issues in universal breakdown—the dissolution of all boundaries, including, again, the boundary between life and death.[15] In other words, the remaking of belief through pain must be total, for there is no space—no interior—that can remain obdurate or careless. Edinburgh's impieties thus threaten the well-being of the entire nation. The power of the city's fortunes to affect those of the land depends upon the poem's sense—its fear—of the impossibility of inconsequence. Narrative inexorability—the horrifying significance of a nonevent, an absence of care or activity—narrows the space of human life to a pinpoint, overwhelms it with the revenge of the sacred.[16] Apparently local events lead rapidly to, and, indeed, are, enormities. The city's absolute connectedness to the fortunes of the realm is a principle inculcated by the poem's demand for vigilance, for acceptance of responsibility. In Foullis's poem, the city finds its relation to its judge and to its country by locating itself as criminal. Its reinclusion in the community, indeed the reconstitution of the community of the realm, is predicated upon its temporary exclusion—an exclusion which, once again, mirrors the creature's own forgetful exclusion of the Creator.[17]

It is within this context that we can best understand the *Calamitose*'s lamentation over the blindness of youth ("Sed ruit in cecas fragilis natura tenebras" [But fragile nature rushes into blind shadows], l. 55), which is understood as the capacity of youth for suppressing deadly things ("Quid suppressa memor bissenos fata per annos, / Horrende repeto tela cruenta necis" [What doom I remember, suppressed for twelve years; horribly I remember the weapons of slaughter], ll. 45–46). Foullis's lament links his own forgetfulness with the guilt of the community; at the same time it is a plea for the forgivability of youthful error, for the possibility of inconsequence ("Omnia, ceu veniunt, stulta iuventa facit. / Et licet expertis novit resipiscere damnis" [All things, just as they come, youth makes foolish. And, losses having been endured, youth may learn to come to its senses], ll. 58–59). In the *Calamitose*, remembering what has been suppressed is thus figured as reparation for wrongs; it is a re-membering of the interior, a restoration of past to present through a newly heightened consciousness and vigilance. Remembering thus seems, in the *Calamitose*, to offer recovery of continuity with one's youth; and it expresses a wish for the chance to grow up, to survive failures of vigilance. For growing up poses a threat to the boundary between Creator and creature; having a life threatens to push back the poles of the sacred, to reduce narrative inexorability. It is for this threat that Foullis wishes to atone.

Linked to this form of reparation is the shift from the displayed, carnal, marked, suffering body of the city to its obverse, the gaze of the monarch.

The poem turns from "Aspicis, augende non ulla propaginis extat / Cura; timent homines conciliare pares" (You look down, but no care for the increase of children is visible [in your face]; people are afraid to unite, ll. 435–36) — where the uncaring gaze seems to neglect not only a particular *iuventus* but the entire progeny of humankind — to the assertion of belief in God's concern for men, a concern shown through his stern instruction.

> Tu, criminis ultor
> Et iudex, nulli sceptra secunda tenes.
> Regia sit, quamvis rigida, pro lege voluntas
> Et rata sunt verbo condita cuncta suo.
> . . . .
> Imperio celum et terram regis omnia lato,
> Cunctaque iudicii sunt rata verba tui.
> Tu gemitus miserare pios, per quinque precamur
> Vulnera, sis nostris prompta medela malis!
> Cura tibi sit quanta hominum, tua seva docet mors.
>   (ll. 439–51)

(You, punisher of guilt, and judge, you hold a kingdom second to none. There will be royal will, however stern, according to the law; all things have been established by your word. . . . You rule all things of land and sky with vast power; your words have established courts of justice. You pity pious groans; through wounds we pray that you may be a prompt remedy for our evils! Your cruel death tells us how great, for you, is the care of men.)

Cura has been recovered for the paternal gaze through the latter's very harshness. The turn from absent to present *cura* is, moreover, mediated through the creature's plea to the Creator for guidance: "O genitor, moderare manum" (l. 439). The acceptance of creatureliness, once again, permits reparation of the parent and of his relation to the child. The poem's belief in the reparation of the threatened progeny of the Creator — the reparation of the body of mankind and its relation to its Creator — depends upon the creature's ability to decipher *cura* in the downward glance of the *genitor*. *Potestas* — the absolute power of the Creator, symbolized by his "distance from the body," his capacity to injure and not be injured — is similarly recovered for the purposes of the kind of love that makes, and lets, creatures grow, through the figure of Foullis's uncle James Henryson, who, after the death of Foullis's family, supports the stricken orphan like a big tree (*magna . . . arbore*, l. 273) and who is thanked in the *Calamitose* for thereby preserving the fortunes of the Foullis family and its future progeny.[18]

Foullis's response to the primal scene of plague is, finally, a theodicy — a registration of the agony produced by disruption in the creature's love for the Creator and a reinvestment in the powerful love of the Creator for His creature. Difference — the sense of particularity, autonomy, even isolation produced by the crisis of origins — is viewed by Foullis either as illegitimate rupture or as reparable through reunions that restore fullness of presence. The *Calamitose*, like Augustine's *City of God*, is finally a sublimation of the terror of discovering one's own particularity and contingency, of the terror of being a creature the nature of whose relation to the Creator is radically in question. And, again like *The City of God*, Foullis's poem thus becomes a reading of human history *against* the absolute, an inhabiting of exclusion (an acceptance of creatureliness) as the only means of reinclusion in the peace of God's heaven: "Pone igitur questus gemebundi pectoris altos, / Et sit pacato purior aura Deo" (Put aside, therefore, profound complaints of the heart's lamenting, and may heaven be purer, with a peaceful God, ll. 495–96).

The Edinburgh of Foullis's youth was indeed ravaged by calamity. Grandgore — venereal disease — had arrived in 1497.[19] Plague came the following year: the burgh records for the period 1498–1500 contain a number of provisions for trying to contain "the daynger of perilous seknes of pestilence now rissin in the eist pairts and lairgelie spreid."[20] The crowded space of the burgh — Edinburgh was, as we have noted, notorious for its constriction even among medieval burghs — meant rapid spread of infection. In Foullis's *Carmen elegum*, however — a poem written after the *Calamitose*, when Foullis was a student at Orléans — Edinburgh is young, happy, flourishing, an idyll of plenitude rather than a city of earth struck down by misfortune and chaos. The poem is a patriotic one: it opens with "Scotorum eterna nomen cum laude triumphet." Scotland is warlike but brief in wrath, loves truth and hates broken faith:

> Precipuus celi cultus, magnique Tonantis;
> Debita huic pietas, non simulata, placet.
> Duratura diu crescat sub sidere fausto
> Scotia, cristicolis terra beata viris,
> Augeat ut nostri longevos principis annos
> Juppiter, huic patri stemmata longa trahat
> Candida protelent fatales pensa Sorores,
> Immemor officii sit soror aspra sui!
> O sua semper ames Iacobum Scotia quartum,
> Quo duce te celo fama secunda feret.
> Vivat Edinburgi felix, generosa iuventus,
> Gaudeat, et veris floreat aucta bonis.
>
> (ll. 15–26)

(Triumph, O name of Scots, with threefold praise!
Ennobled be thy race by noble deeds!

.   .   .   .

She [Scotland] loves to serve heaven's mighty Thunderer,
And worship Him with piety unfeigned.
Long, under favouring stars, may Scotland thrive,
And long be blest with worshippers of Christ,
That Jupiter may then be pleased to grant
Our king long life and scions in long line!
Long may the Fates defer their righteous tasks,
Long may the cruel Sister stay her hand!
Love James the Fourth, O Scotland, with whose aid,
Auspicious fame will thee to heaven exalt!
Long live Edina's happy, generous youth,
Rejoice and flourish, dowered with every good!)[21]

The conclusion of the *Carmen elegum* transforms Edinburgh from a scene of plague into the happy youth, blessed with every good, whom Foullis might have wished himself to be. The *Carmen elegum* is the idyll that displaces the trauma both of the city's and the poet's loss, and its wishes for Scotland's triumph are inseparable from its wish for the longevity of the monarch and his scions — for the superreality of enduring dynasty. Thus the *Carmen elegum* reconstitutes the body and future history of a nation. The shift from the *Calamitose* to the *Carmen elegum* repeats, on an intertextual scale, the split within the *Calamitose* itself between the nothing of an abandonment so devastating that it cannot be adequately mourned and the all of reunion with the Creator. The split thus makes possible Foullis's belated identification with the figure of the protected and flourishing child; it protects the ideality of the relation between Creator and creature. And it thereby enables the reappropriation, for Foullis's icons — Scotland, James IV, Jupiter — what Scarry speaks of as the "vibrancy," the "certainty," of pain.

The *Carmen elegum*'s revision of privation, disease, and death proceeds through images of vitality, images that recover life from death and thereby assert, for Foullis, the invulnerability of the borderline. Life, moreover, is made urgent and compelling through the use of imperatives. The jussive subjunctives *vivat*, *gaudeat*, and *floreat* evoke the obverse of absolute unmaking, of plague: they command vitality.[22] In contrast with the belatedness of hope in the *Calamitose* — the despair, figured by contagion, over the powerlessness of human intervention — the jussive subjunctives of the *Carmen elegum* evoke the power to command desire into existence, to transcend the limitations of human making.[23] Narrative in the *Carmen elegum* is thus overwhelmed, not by the radical limits set by plague to human intervention, but by a kind of purposiveness of imagination. The coalescence of imperative and optative becomes, after the despair of the *Calamitose*, the primary "mood" of narrative in Foullis's poetry. Thus in the *Strena*, Foullis foresees (like Jupiter), prophesies, casts his glance backward on a history of calamity made tiny by the view: history is read as omen.

The subjunctives of the *Carmen elegum* are appropriate, moreover, to a poem suffused with reminiscences of the diction and motifs of Virgil's imperial *Aeneid* (*pietas, fama, fatales*, a Jupiter who directs the destiny of empire from on high, the fantasy of a protective fate in which narrative becomes, not a contingent or open-ended process of change, but rather a spinning-out of sacral anteriority). These reminiscences of a poem that takes as its subject the struggle to undo catastrophic loss — the devastation of Troy, the cruelty of Juno, Aeneas's loss (and abandonment) of Creusa and Dido, his ultimate founding of an empire that was to be identified with the name of its great city, Rome — are in turn appropriate to the *Carmen elegum* in its culminating celebration of a city happy in its youth.[24] The threat posed to youth — to the chance to grow up — by jealous divinity is present, too, in the *Carmen elegum*, in Foullis's wish to defer the *Soror aspra*, the "cruel sister." As Edinburgh is imagined — a happy youth — through tropes of plenitude, death and loss are imagined as the disappearance of the maternal strand: woman appears, in the *Carmen elegum*, in her capacity not as giver of life but as destroyer, the overseer of the timing of men's lives, of human narrativity. And yet her cruel dictates may be overturned by a truly loving God. Fruitfulness — here in the form of the fullness of a life — is appropriated for, and dependent on, the intervention of the Creator.

The study of Latin poetry — and Foullis's surviving poetry is in Latin, not in what Gavin Douglas called "Scottis" — gave Foullis a language, a poetics, and a tradition whereby he could write and rewrite calamity, isolate fortune from misfortune, true *cura* from its mere appearance.[25] The *Carmen elegum* is Foullis's reinscription of himself and his city — both products of human making, refigured as wayward but repossessible creatures — into a scene of inclusion. Hence Foullis's fervor in pursuing the well-being of the Scottish "nation," in exile at Orléans; hence his encouragement of students "at home" in the pursuit of letters. In the *Carmen elegum* poetry is, for Foullis, a means to innocence. The imperative mood and the tropes of Latin imperialism are ways of wishing calamity away. Foullis's humanism, his Latinity, his studies abroad, constitute an "imperial" way of including, at the periphery of Europe, all of Western culture and history — and thus a way of making one and making good the world, of struggling against exclusion from the world. The elision of Foullis's own pain — of the pains, too, of city and nation — serves, once again, a dream of "self-extension," of vastness, of the unlimited imagination.[26]

The wish expressed by Foullis at the end of the *Carmen elegum* for James IV's long life was not, however, to be fulfilled. James IV — along with James Henryson, Foullis's uncle and patron — met his death at Flodden in 1513, the year after Foullis entered the *Carmen elegum* into "The Book of the Scottish Nation."[27] James IV's death seems to have abandoned Scotland to a crisis of confidence in the capacity of *potestas* to protect its creatures, a crisis exacerbated by the fragile infancy of the new king.[28] James V was crowned at Stirling on 21 September 1513; he was seventeen months old. In the struggles for power that ensued, Edinburgh played a critical role, and we should at this point remind ourselves of Edinburgh's economic and political centrality in late fifteenth- and early sixteenth-century Scotland.

Gordon Donaldson's account of the troubles of James V's minority amply illustrates the importance of the role played by Edinburgh in national politics in the early sixteenth century. He notes that the earl of Angus exploited, in his struggles with the earl of Arran's government, "the popularity which he and his Douglas kinsmen enjoyed in Edinburgh. In July 1517 there had been 'ane inordinat motioun of the people' in that town; there was an 'actioun and debait betuix my lord of Arane and the toun' in November 1519; and in March 1520 Arran declared that 'he sould nocht cum within the toun quhill my Lord Chancellar [Beaton] maid ane finall concord betuix him and the nychbouris thairof.' . . . [In] April 1520 . . . the Hamiltons were driven out of Edinburgh by the Douglases."[29] Scotland's and Edinburgh's fortunes continued to be hectic: twice James was "erected" to power by those who controlled him; in February 1524/25 Arran and Margaret Tudor, the Queen Mother, held Edinburgh Castle, while Angus held the town.[30] It was arranged in July of that year that the leading nobles should hold custody of the king in turn, but in November Angus declined to give up the king and kept him, in effect, a prisoner. Efforts were made to liberate him, but none succeeded until, between 27 and 30 May 1528, the king escaped from Edinburgh to Stirling Castle after reaching a "secret agreement with his mother." He returned to Edinburgh to begin his rule of the country on 6 July, Angus having fled the town.[31]

Clearly Edinburgh was both participant in and chief locus of a long, complex, and volatile struggle for national power. Those living in Edinburgh at the time could scarcely have failed to be affected in some way by the events of the day; in 1528, the year of James's assumption of power, the question of burgess loyalty to the king would likely have been a critical one. This is the "background" to the *Strena* — a poem probably written

by a burgess of Edinburgh and printed by a burgess of Edinburgh.[32] It is
not possible, given the extent of our present knowledge, to say what part,
if any, Foullis played during the time of the troubles or exactly where his
loyalties lay. But since in James V's early years Edinburgh had been the
scene of the king's imprisonment and since the king's wardens had been
"popular" in Edinburgh, we may be sure that any burgess of Edinburgh
hoping to advance himself through future royal patronage — and certainly
any burgess whose royalist identification was as powerful as that of James
Foullis — would be happy to signify his loyalty to the king. It is clear, in
any case, that the *Strena* is in thoroughgoing fashion a poem and a production of Edinburgh and its vicissitudes.

Both the title page and the opening lines of the poem declare its status
as prophecy of happier days: "Tempora magnanimo que nunc felicia Regi /
Sydera portendunt, dicere Musa cupit" (The stars foretell a fruitful time
for the great-souled King, [a prophecy] which the Muse now longs to
sing").[33] The stars themselves foretell both this great-souled king and the
fruitful or fortunate time (*tempora felicia*) that is thus, from the inception
of the *Strena*, linked to the destiny of James V. The beloved of the Muses,
James V is appealed to for guidance, then the narrative begins. Jupiter sends
a message to Phebus lamenting Scotland's disorders and demanding that
reformation be effected. The message bids Phebus shine brightly upon Scotland; he obeys without delay, and the fertility of the land is renewed. The
poem ends with a vision of James V ruling justly over a tranquil land.
In the *Strena*, foresight, fortune, and kingship are joined together in a wish
for protection. If one can look into the future, one will see, not a helpless
child imprisoned in the toils of political plague — of, in Girard's terms, "sterile
rivalries," "reciprocal violence" — but rather a great king (*magnanimo Regi*).[34]
By bringing together anticipation with memory, hindsight with foresight,
the *Strena* subjects the story of James's growing-up to a radical compres-
sion. It is a poem in flight from historical narration, from chronicling the
oppressive changefulness of the preceding era.

After invoking the Muse's desire for a prophecy of fortunate times, the
poet says that he will undertake this hazardous enterprise only if supported
by James, dear to the Muses:

> Ausus ob hec nimium tenui cantare Camena,
> Incipiam auspiciis, rex Iacobe, tuis.
> Pieridum tu dulce decus, concede favorem
> Edere Iudicio metra legenda bono.
> Torpentes fracto repares cum pectine nervos,
> Et moveas docilem per tua fila manum.
>
> (ll. 3–8)

(Therefore, having dared to sing with too-weak verse, by your auspices, King James, I will begin. You, the sweet honor of the Muses, grant me the support to bring forth strains to be decorously sung. May you repair the strings, listless, [the] plectrum broken, and may you move my easily led hand across your strings.)

The poet's earlier poems — perhaps he refers to the *Calamitose* — have been feeble (*tenui* has the sense of physical enfeeblement, and can be used of a sound too low to hear as well as of an inability to hold on or to hold course). The poet's voice is thus styled from the outset as the kind of voice appropriate to a creature: no rival to the voice of the Creator (whose voice signifies His transcendence of the limits of the human body), the voice of the poet is imagined simultaneously as physically weak and as physical, as barely emergent from the body.[35] The threat of ambition, presumption — of "any capacity for self-transformation into a separate verbal or material form" — is immediately defused: like the paradise which it will describe, the *Strena* is itself a gift, a favor — the effect, rather than the cause, of royal patronage.[36] It is the king himself, the "sweet honor" of the Muses, who grants the poet's strains, who moves the poet's docile hand over the strings. The poet's gift to the king — as the *Strena* was perhaps intended to be — is really the king's gift to the poet. The king's body is in him, moving the strings, the poet's hands. The poem marks its own paternity, its origin; the hazard of beginning — of the radical break — is wishfully made secure by the poem's affirmation of its creatureliness, of its status as the new creation of the sovereign. The previous enfeeblement of the poet is thereby revivified, given "vibrancy." The possibility of new life thus depends upon the permeability of the human surface, its willingness to open itself to possession by the sovereign. And by including greatness, Foullis becomes part of something greater: the repaired communion of servant and sovereign.

Not only, then, is the language of the poem rescued from the enfeebled body, but the possibility of "self-extension" into the world, of a community of language, is likewise restored through the elaborateness of communication that follows the invocation: Jupiter, considering all things in his lofty mind (*alta mente*, l. 11, a phrase that appears in royal charters of the later fifteenth century, including the 1482 charters of privileges to Edinburgh), immediately (*Protinus*, l. 11) commands his winged servant to come before him. He gives his *Nuncius* (l. 16) writings to bear to the shining god, Phebus, and the messenger flies below and announces to Phebus that the immeasurably great ruler of Olympus has sent him a letter. Phebus quickly halts his horses, reads the subscript without delay (*Nec mora*, l. 21), splits the seal, and reads, in golden letters (*auratis . . . notis*, l. 22) the text I have described. Considering James V's need to smuggle secret messages out of Edinburgh in order to secure his release from the clutches of the Douglases, Foullis's vision of the rapidity of the messenger and the efficacy of the sovereign word is both especially pointed and poignant. The immediacy of textual transmission is an image of the royal word's ideal power of immediate penetration and of the trust that can therefore be reposed in an obedient servant, for whom the royal word is the only word. Letters are golden; Foullis was a good choice for the secretariat.

The opening invocation is followed by an allusion to Janus *bifrons*, who has begun the year — "Principium bifrons anni Iam Ianus apertum / Fecerit" (ll. 9–10) — and to *Phebus celsius*, who shines loftier in the sky. Time begins, in the poem, with a figure of the year's capacity to look backward or forward, and with the introduction of Phebus we are plunged into forward motion. Here, as in the invocation, the poem is occupied with the hope of *renovatio*, of making a new beginning; the break from the past will reveal its disorders to have been themselves but a momentary break, capable of reform, in the design of order. As Scarry writes of the chapters in Genesis, "there is a sense of erasing, . . . beginning again, starting over," which "re-enacts the idea of original world creation"; at the same time, a continuity is asserted, the interior sameness of history. The Creator's "power of alteration" — which is also the power to maintain and multiply his children in life — will work, in the *Strena*, on the human body and voice, on the body of the land, and on time.[37]

Accordingly, we move from Phebus and from time to the potent Father himself, who contains all things in his deep and lofty mind ("Ipse potens rerum pater alta mente reponens / Omnia," ll. 11–12) and who foresees all destined changes. As in the *Calamitose*, the ability to see all things from this lofty height is linked with the Creator's "power of alteration." In the *Strena*, though, there is no frightening blankness in the gaze of the Creator; the primal scene becomes a reunion. Jupiter is fully present, protective, propitiated, as is suggested by the opening lines of Jupiter's letter:

> Nos qui celestes positis digessimus orbes
> Legibus; et certis volvimus astra modis,
> Cura hominum nonnulla tenet: terrena potestas
> Summa nisi faveant numina, nulla foret.
>
> (ll. 23–26)

(We who arranged the swift planets with fixed laws, and maintained the stars in their sure boundaries, the many cares of men occupy us: the greatest earthly power would be nothing if the gods did not favor it.)

Jupiter takes care of man. Without his blessing, we would be nothing.

It is significant, then, that Jupiter himself chronicles Scotland's calamities, transforming the Douglases and their ilk into haughty Catilines and scheming Lycurguses; spoken by the voice of the Creator, historical narration records the ultimate powerlessness of human violence. Jupiter explains that James IV was struck down by the power of fortune — the personification of meaningless change — and the malignity of the stars:

Ut regem aversata fuit Fortuna potentem,
Dira sub infausto sydere fata tulit.
Nam desperatis languet pessundata rebus
Scotia, que miseros ducere visa dies.

(ll. 31–34)

(As Fortune rejected the powerful king, she bore harsh fates beneath an ill-omened star. For Scotland was weak and ruined by hopeless circumstances, [and] seemed to protract its wretched days.)

Scotland is cast into a mourning which threatens, from the perspective of the creature, to be endless.

In Scotland's troubled times, *Pax, amor, sine cede manus* (hands without bloodshed), *Gloria, iustitie, concordia,* are gone from the land (l. 37). They leave in their place only *rupta fides, pax simulata, falsus amor,* bloodshed and rebellion (l. 35). In grief-stricken Scotland, everything is broken, bloody, deceptive. Human violence — the wrongful appropriation of the Creator's (and the sovereign's) power of injury — dismembers; yet it is strangely insubstantial. It is linked to dissimulation, to the idea of a nothingness behind appearances, to bodiless words and smiles — hence, to a failure of the relation between origin and end. Human violence becomes, in the *Strena,* a parody of the Creator's "power of alteration." Thus, without the sovereign, only rupture and betrayal are possible; the sovereign is the true source of peace, faith, loyalty, honor, love, and justice, in contrast with his rivals, who only seem, but are not. Behind the seeming chaos of the troubles, the creature will be able, finally, to decipher *cura;* chronicle is thus the story of a superficiality. The internal violence which threatens to engulf the community is split off, at once demonized and derealized; the ideality of the sovereign creator's power of alteration is thereby protected.

Jupiter, immediately after his narration of Scotland's calamities, declares the need for reformation, lest anyone think that no Jupiter rules above ("Cogimur errores tandem componere tantos, / Ne quis regnantem non putat esse Iovem" [We must finally right such great wrongs, lest it seem that no Jove rules], ll. 49–50). Jupiter sends to Phebus a message written in golden letters, which contrasts the insubstantiality of unauthorized human violence with the sovereign's power of injury. The letter foretells

James V's valor and prowess in war, his strength to subdue the prideful and the perjured: Scotland will rejoice more in him than Troy would have rejoiced in the survival of Hector — who was for so long Troy's stay, Troy's wall, against utter destruction ("Hectore nec tantum sua Troia superstite gaudens," l. 61). Under James's rule falsehood itself will be expelled from the land. The power to uncreate has been recovered from irreality by super-reality. It will be James V who restores the threatened symmetry of earthly and divine governance by reasserting the power of the Creator to inter-vene in the affairs of men through the agency of his sovereign child. At the end of the poem, James V is described as *puer Jovis*. Here, the likeness, rather than the unlikeness, of Creator and creature is affirmed: their link is sovereignty, a special form of difference from all other creatures. The *Strena's* recovery of Scotland from political plague proceeds through a re-covery of the sovereign creator's total presence within the interiority of the world.

Jupiter's letter then moves on to order the remaking of the land. Phebus is sent to make Scotland feel the stroke of his heat ("stroke" is *plaga*, the root, interestingly, of "plague" and hence a primal word in Foullis's poetry).[38]

> Temperiem diffunde bonam, sic grata colonis
> Ut veniat messis semine digna suo.
> Nos quoque pro nostre prolis faciemus honore
> Quod bene susceptum, secula cuncta canent.
>
> (ll. 69–72)

(For the honor of our progeny we also will produce something which, supported well, all generations will sing of.)

Honore has the sense of public honor, office, preferment, as well as of honorary gift, boon, favor; *susceptum* has meanings of esteem and ad-miration, but can also have the sense of sustaining, supporting, bringing up a child as one's own. The *Strena* itself fulfills Jupiter's prediction that his descendants shall celebrate in song both the god's power to produce and his magnanimity in giving honor. The rejuvenation of Scotland is thus the result neither of natural processes nor of human production; it is a miracle — a gift, a boon, from Jupiter to his children, his creatures. The restoration of paternity and genealogy — the acceptance of creatureliness — results in the gift of love, conceived as the fertility of the land. The Crea-tor — and the sovereign through him — is the only source of plenty. This having been established, the poet is allowed to narrate directly the revivi-fication of the land, his voice now the voice of the Creator.

Phebus obeys Jupiter's behest, dispelling the clouds so that "natura suas varie et subtiliter artes / Perque astra exercet, viscera perque soli" (Variously and finely, nature works her arts over the stars, and through the very heart of the country, ll. 79–80). There follow adverbs of expectancy, of an end of waiting (*Mox*); the world is being re-created. There are images of fauns in the woods, of Priapus tending gardens, of Flora clothing the countryside with flowers, of murmuring streams and clear-sounding rivers: Scotland is alive, sentient. And labor is but impotent compared to this magical fertility: "Seminibus paleata Ceres fecundat opimis / Iugera, que nullo culta labore forent" (With plentiful seeds Ceres fertilizes acreages mixed with chaff, which will be cultivated with no labor, ll. 95–96). Peasants need struggle no longer — rule is what ensures abundance. And the economic power of the city is nowhere to be seen. The guilty city — chief site of Scotland's troubles during the minority of James V— is displaced altogether by the scene of plenitude, which closes with the following: "Maiori redeunt spumantia mulctra colostro, / Et solito pecudes grandius uber habent" (The beasts give back foaming milkpails from a greater milking, and have udders more swollen than is usual, ll. 101–2). Foaming milkpails and heavy udders (*uber,* etymologically related to *ubertatis,* the word used by Augustine to describe the "realm of unremitting plenty" that he and his mother discovered during their shared mystical experience) are the final images in Foullis's catalog of plenitude.[39] The gift appears again as the form of exchange appropriate to the rejuvenated world; but since the relation to the transcendent and unmade Creator has been recovered, the gift may now be perceived as immanent within the world (*redeunt* has the primary sense of "giving back"). With the restoration and hypervaluation of the everyday world, of the domestic — as opposed to the calamitous — the "maternal strand" has been recomposed into the fertile and lactating body of the land; and the flow of milk is associated, in the lines that follow, with the notion of favor, with the clemency (*clementia*) of the gods (*divum*): "Res ita disposuit nostras clementia divum: / Propitios meminit quis magis ante deos?" (Thus the clemency of the gods has set our affairs in order; who was mindful more than the propitious gods? ll. 103–4). And lest this recomposed maternity slip away from its relation to paternity, the notion of discrimination is invoked (*disposuit*). Moreover, the following and final lines of the *Strena* remind us that the son of Jupiter — James V— wields his scepter over the calmest of lands and gives good laws to his people: "Interea Iovis ipse puer placidissima regni / Sceptra gerens, populo dat bona Iura suo" (Meanwhile the boy of Jove, bearing the most gentle scepter of the kingdom, gives virtuous laws to his people, ll. 105–6). The maternal strand (*placidissima*) is indeed well ruled in Foullis's poem. Thus the calamity of the creature is made good through a making one of the paternal and maternal strands in the principle of sovereignty; the losses of Scotland are re-membered. In Augustine's terms, *sinus* coincides with *aula*.

Let us speculate once again, then, that the *Strena* was designed to rehabilitate Edinburgh and its citizens in James's eyes by voiding a history of treason and putting in its place a narrative of *renovatio* and of the eternity of the Stewart dynasty. Let Flodden and the Douglases — Scotland's antimasque — be banished from discourse like the clouds and winds expelled from Scotland by Phebus's warmth. Then finally what this story of expulsion and reparation suggests is that relations between king and capital need to be represented very carefully indeed — if the capital has become a prison for the king. The reparation of the strained relations obtaining between Crown and capital in the early sixteenth century — a reparation imagined as a restoration of magical fertility, so that the king seems to reproduce the city rather than to have been produced by its power and strife — constitutes, finally, the ideological project of the *Strena*. The *Strena* is Foullis's most ambitious poetic attempt to repair the damage done to his belief in *potestas* by his "knowledge" of the *human* production of super-reality — his knowledge of the primal scene.

The primal scene can help us to conceptualize the field of historical possibility in which the burgh, and its citizens, existed in Scotland during the late fifteenth and early sixteenth centuries. For the primal scene brings out not only the doubleness inevitable to all beginnings — the choice, presented by Foullis's image of Janus *bifrons*, of looking backward or forward — but also the openness of defining and theorizing anew both *origin* and *break*, *creator* and *creature*, in historical rather than theological terms. The primal scene makes clear how the fear of starting over on one's own can produce regressive positions — like that of Foullis — whose "backwardness" might conceal the strength of the challenge that produced them. It makes clear how, in the case of James III, the desire to create and the fear of having one's creatures start over on their own can produce a kind of tragedy of innovation. The primal scene also makes clear how the wish to start over on one's own might produce the historical concept of a multiple and decentered creativity that has itself been created. In the fifteenth and early sixteenth centuries, Edinburgh experienced something like a primal scene — a revisionist reading of its own status as creature. The texts that present this experience pose, in turn, sharp challenges to historical narration: to what extent was Edinburgh's charter "progressive," to what extent "regressive"? Does Foullis's poetry encode, in however infantile a fashion, the loss of one sense of beginning and the desperate need to formulate another? The difficulties of these questions insist upon the changeful character of the late medieval Scottish city. They insist, too, upon the danger of mobilizing secularizations of the "prime mover" or categorical ingenuities like Merrington's "internal externality" against the contingency and irreducibility of event. Thus they suggest, finally, the importance of embracing a decentered historical practice that gives to the project of beginning both the horror and the futurity of ending.

Marriage

5

Sovereign Love

What is your beloved more than any other,
O fairest of women?

—The Song of Songs 5:9

In 1503 James IV concluded an alliance with Scotland's old enemy, England, by marrying Margaret Tudor. His choice was an ambitious one, and it inaugurated a newly expansionist era for Crown activities, one which was to continue until the end of James's reign. In 1507 and then again in 1508 James IV staged a tournament of the wild knight and the black lady, in which James himself appears to have jousted as the wild knight. This pageant too spoke to James's ambitions: it addressed the impatience that led him to disrupt the succession and rebel against his father; it celebrated the king's pacification campaigns in Gaelic Scotland, pursued with particular zeal in the years following his marriage; it pointed toward James's dreams of naval power and crusade. The issues addressed by the marriage differed in some ways from those addressed by the tournament: the arts of James's wedding were largely preoccupied with the alliance's break from the past, with the danger posed to national identity by a foreign queen and by the "ignoble arts of peace"; the arts of the tournament were largely preoccupied with the question of internal fragmentation and with the legitimacy of violence as a response to domestic unrest. Marriage and tournament share nonetheless a concern with the historical agency of sovereignty—with the power of sovereignty to create discontinuity, whether in the name of peace or war. The tournament of the wild knight and the black lady will be discussed at length in the section "Tournament." The present section explores James's alliance with England; Margaret's bridal journey; the Edinburgh pageants for Margaret's royal entry; and *The Thrissill and the Rois*, a poem written by William Dunbar apparently for the occasion of the wedding. But in exploring the concepts of sovereignty—of queenship as well as kingship — and of marriage which James and Margaret shaped and were shaped by, "Marriage" raises questions which will remain important to discussion of the tournament of the wild knight and the black lady. The present chapter advances theoretical considerations about the nature of sovereignty — its interest in blackness, disguise, love — that will help us to appreciate, in subsequent chapters, the intricacies of the arts of marriage and of tournament in late medieval Scotland.

In *Literary Fortifications,* Joan DeJean recalls the legends of the Sun King's black sister, who was said to be "locked away in a convent," and of Louis's twin brother *au masque du fer,* likewise kept hidden away from public view; she argues that these stories expressed "political anxieties."[1] Louis XIV, then, was rumored to have hidden away terrible secrets. One secret, his twinship, had to be hidden away because it would call into question the monarch's exclusiveness — in Bataille's terms, his "heterogeneity."[2] The other secret, his dark sister, had to be hidden away because it would call into question the king's "homogeneity," his identity with the French people. There is an uncanny likeness between the legend of Louis XIV's twin brother and black sister and James IV's tournament of the wild knight and the black lady.[3] There are also important differences between these representations. In the case of Louis XIV's twin brother and black sister, we are presented with repudiated and captivated "natural" bodies, kept hidden, made public only by the mouth of rumor, enjoyable only when split off from sovereignty.[4] James IV's tournament of the wild knight and the black lady presents us on the other hand with a knight who, because he is both a *wild* knight and a wild *knight,* publicly enacts within his own person a relation between wildness and civilization, repeating this doubleness by turning out to be the king. And the black lady is spectacular. Though both the Enlightenment legend and the sixteenth-century tournament made use of the "heterogeneous" — of danger, wildness, mystery — in putting sovereignty into play, there is an important difference between a sovereign who chooses to embody his relation to difference — who dramatizes his own heterogeneity — and a sovereign whose split-off dubiety is only permitted to be spoken of by the comparatively disembodied voice of rumor.

Still, Louis XIV's secrets suggest that sovereignty, though it takes different historical and individual forms, is often a difficult negotiation: the king is an effect of paradox. He is the most representative of people, but this makes him unique. On the one hand, he exemplifies reasonableness, the "natural," everyday certitudes, regular exchange, propriety; on the other hand he is uncommon, excessive. He is the fount of virtue, but he is also entitled to sensuality, luxury. He is characterized by a special richness both

of bodily experience and of theatricality, and hence by a sovereign capacity
for metaphor which allows him to move between embodiment and disembodiment in a way not available to the ordinary citizen. Because the king
"is" all things, he becomes the privileged site of a surplus of being, of superreality. But he is also an equally privileged site of loss, because his capacity for metaphor — his "power of predication" — can make him a threat
to boundaries, person and number. This relation to excess imperils and
vivifies his purity.

The king decomposes easily. He cannot be too much like his subjects,
in part because this would reveal that sovereignty is an artifact; the scandalousness of the possibility that the king is just like other men is registered by the legend of Louis XIV's twin. But the king also cannot be too
different from his subjects. If there is not enough ordinariness in him — if
his link to the everyday and the merely real is cut altogether — he will seem
to be too much, not like us, and therefore foreign. Hence the anxiety exists
that he might have blackness in his blood. But it is also true that the legends
of the twin and the black sister offer a kind of transgressive, mystifying
energy: on the one hand, the pleasure of undoing hierarchy, of discovering
in the king a common humanity that can glamorize ordinariness itself;
on the other, the pleasure of mingling gender and race, of discovering in
one's exemplar the very allure of difference. The legends about Louis XIV
may, then, have been circulated by desire as well as by anxiety — whether
we conceive this as a desire of some of Louis XIV's subjects for a more
materialized and immediate sovereignty or a desire of the monarchy to
signify a very particular relation to immediacy and materiality.

James IV's interest in the motif of the "king-in-disguise" is indicated by
his tournament of the wild knight and the black lady.[5] We also have Pitscottie's probably unreliable testimony about the king's predilection for this
motif:

[H]e had sic perfyte fauour and hope withtin his realme that he wald ryde out
throw the haill realme him allone, wnknawin that he was king of ony man, and
wald oftymeis ludge in poore mens houssis as he had bene ane travelland man
throw the contrie; and in the meane tyme wald requyre of them that he was ludgit
quhair was the king or how the king wssit him self towartis his barrouns or quhat
they spak of him throw the contrie sa they wald ansuer him as they thocht goode,
so the king be this way knew quhat was spokin of him throw the contrie.[6]

In this story, the king seems to lay down the distance that separates him
from the ordinary man, the "private" subject. What is being tested is, in
part, whether the king both is and is not a member of common humanity.
The king remains king, despite the fact that he has taken off his crown;

"plain speech" has not revealed him to be ordinary. And yet his willingness to endure plain speaking shows that at some level he recognizes that he is a man like other men; the sovereign's need, at least at times, to make himself accessible to his people is represented as the sovereign's consent to accessibility. But though these journeys are freely undertaken and have the quality of exploit, they are supposedly accomplished for the sake of the people. Hence they have about them an air of sacrifice, embedded as they are in an understanding of the king's difference from the people as a (potentially tragic) alienation: he can only be intimate with people when his grand and exacting identity is unknown. The motif of the king-in-disguise makes homogeneity work for sovereignty; it solicits an identification between kingship and common humanity by heroizing them both. The king becomes an adventurer; the subject becomes an outlaw or is at least specially courageous and outspoken, as in the medieval Scottish story of Rauf Coilȝear. Not just any common man can signify the king's bond with common humanity. But the heart, the interior, of the subject is being tested for its "truth" by stories of disguised kings; the king's (potentially tragic) alienation glorifies a situation of scrutiny. Stories of disguised kings suggest how the private and plain character of the subject is simultaneously solicited and feared by sovereignty; the king's disguise is a benign — rather than an openly authoritarian — means of possessing the hearts, and bodies, of his subjects. Identity and difference of sovereign and subject are both recuperated through such transformations.[7]

They are also redeemed in the story of the Shulammite's love for Solomon in the Song of Songs, a story of great importance to representations of the bond between subject and sovereign in general and to James IV's arts of rule in particular.[8] The potential of darkness for sovereignty is suggested by the link made in the Song of Songs between the Shulammite's blackness ("I am dark but lovely") and the richness of metaphor that makes the "set-apartness" of her beauty—and of her poetry, her "song of all songs"—an effect of its expansiveness, its power to include the body of the world ("your hair like a flock of goats streaming down Mount Gilead," "Your neck is like David's tower"). Such simultaneities of identity and difference, of delicate specificity and vast reference, are the stuff of metaphor; and metaphor is essential to the paradoxical art of sovereignty. By such means the king composes himself as a difference with which his subjects can nonetheless identify.

Sovereignty is to an important extent a matter of the creation of bonds. And the creation of transcendent bonds will be interdependent with the vibrancy and certainty of bodily experience. As Kristeva writes: "Supreme authority, be it royal or divine, can be loved as flesh while remaining essentially inaccessible; the intensity of love comes precisely from that combination of received jouissance and taboo, from a basic separation that nevertheless unites."⁹ "Basic separation," distance, absence, the disembodied quality of our objects of belief — lack or loss — is not necessarily given, nor is it a liability for a king. The sovereign is created as distant, and the distance allows him to be desired in a particular way, as ideal, as disembodied ("With my own hands I opened to my love, / but my love had turned away and gone by"). And yet, if the sovereign is not to vaporize altogether, if he is to maintain a reality beyond question, the distance of the ideal nonetheless requires embodiment ("your name like perfume poured out"). Thus sovereignty promises a fantastic, a perfect but imaginary closure to the very yearning it brings into being: this is "sovereign love." Sovereign love surrounds, helps to create, the subject's experience of loss; hence the subject's need to be bonded to the sovereign other, to remake his or her inner heart for that other. Thus sovereign love is a means of shaping desire so that its creativity may be captured. The mutuality of lack and fulfillment that characterizes sovereign love allows the subject to feel simultaneously at one with and free of power and thus assists the experiential transformation of what Pierre Bourdieu calls "coerced relations" into "elective" and "reciprocal" ones.¹⁰

Love, then, seems to have the power to make as well as unmake being. The sovereign's power to alter is often understood as the power of creativity: the Word ("your name like perfume poured out") is both bodied and disembodied. The intensification of existence that promises to close off the yearning that impels sovereign love is, in absolute form, Being Itself — the source of all being, the Creator, who is absolutely loving, who falls out of oneness and repletion into otherness and difference out of a will to give His plenitude. Thus Nature is imagined as having been founded on the will of the Creator; "desire produces reality."¹¹ But in the theology of creation it does so through the agency — the grace — of a divinely sovereign will, a will which excludes both the unrecuperated arbitrariness and strangeness of wild nature on the one hand, and on the other the autonomous participation of the creature in the production of the world. By this means createdness is, in the Judaeo-Christian tradition, inseparably linked to the idea of servitude, of a conditionality of the will; and yet the servants of the Creator must love freely and bear within themselves the image of their likeness to the Creator. The creature is the product of a differenced identity with the Creator, of a will defined as free only insofar as it loves and obeys. Both subject and sovereign posit themselves as freely, generously given — as loving in excess (though never really in contravention) of exchange. The refashioning of necessity — whether "natural" or *a posteriori*

social necessity — into choice and the simultaneous restriction of what there
actually is of choice to the absolute principle of a sovereign will are two
of the most powerful means whereby sovereignty makes love.[12]

In the Song of Songs, the Shulammite is nervous about her darkness
("Do not look down on me; a little dark I may be / because I am scorched
by the sun"), but the king, "a paragon among ten thousand," sees her as
perfect: "You are beautiful, my dearest, / beautiful without a flaw." The
Song of Songs celebrates the power of love to mirror extraordinariness;
and yet it is the Shulammite whose darkness is turned into flawlessness
by the king's "power of alteration," in this case, the power of his love. *The
Masque of Blacknesse* and *The Masque of Beautie*, composed by Ben Jonson for Queen Anne, emphasize this kingly power of alteration at the expense of dialectic. Movement and what Kristeva calls "expectancy" are given
only to the masquers, Ethiopian nymphs seeking confirmation of their
beauty, who find instead the English "SVNNE" and are thereby re-created:
his "light scientiall is, and (past mere nature) / Can salve the rude defects
of euery creature."[13] The resemblance of sovereign and subject is the result
of a redeemed, a magically transformed, difference. The Song of Songs
thus establishes the importance of marital metaphor to "supreme authority": for marriage, in the Judaeo-Christian tradition, is defined by its simultaneous suspension and preservation of inequality. And, as Henry
Ansgar Kelly explains, for St. Bernard there are no sweeter words to express the emotions of Word and soul than "bridegroom" and "bride." One
who loves perfectly has married: "There is clearly such an embrace where
two persons are of one will in their likes and dislikes. The two of them
become one spirit. No disparity between them can matter. Love recognizes
no reverence or respect for degree. It betrays and captures all other affections. . . . It is enough to be man and wife . . . no other bond is necessary:
'Sponsus et sponsa sunt; quam quaeris aliam inter sponsos necessitudinem
vel connexionem praeter amari et amare?'"[14] And yet for St. Bernard there
is no questioning the incommensurability of Word and soul. His theology
of love is perhaps the supreme mystical exemplification of the attempt to
sustain, in desire, a simultaneous equality and inequality of lover and
beloved.

In the Song of Songs, the king's special entitlement to the body of the
world — which is to say, materially speaking, his wealth — is prepared for
through an eroticization of the world's body. As in later pastoral, an affective expansionism is put into place.[15] The body of the world is ensouled
with the soul of a lover, the lover's soul embodied with the body of the
world. And the king is posited as one who loves: the body of the world
is borrowed to substantiate the king's love for his people, his free *choice*

of them, their election, absurd because beyond merit, beyond exchange.[16] Just so in St. Bernard's commentary on the Song of Songs, the love of the Shulammite for Solomon, hence of the soul for God, cannot be economized: "Pure love is not mercenary, does not draw its strength from hope, nor does it suffer injury from lack of hope. Such is the love proper to a bride; this is what a bride is, whoever she is; the possessions and hope of a bride are a single love: 'Sponsae hic est, quia haec sponsa est, quaecumque est; sponsae res et spes unus est amor.'"[17] Aspiration, inequities of distribution, differences of power, wealth, race, sex, disappear into the infinite lack of mirrored yearning; the Shulammite may work in the vineyards or among the flocks, but the king-in-disguise is also a shepherd. Aspiration is managed by images of fulfillment, and the limits set to aspiration are idealized and re-represented as freedom. The sovereign risks exposure in order to achieve an appearance of intimacy, of reciprocity—of what Bourdieu calls the "*symbolic* violence" of elective relations.[18] Thus the involuntary elements of the subject's surrender to the monarch's power of alteration, through an apparent exchange of confidences, can be refashioned as free, as willed—in short, as love.

One of the most important challenges facing the king is, then, the management of the desires he brings into being. The careful management of the creative power of desire is crucial to the art of sovereign love; for, when subjects aspire to creativity, they are aspiring to something other than belief in the superreality of a supreme authority. Thus the divine or monarchical "artifact," supreme authority, might be imagined not as the creation but as the creator of human ingenuity; the hypostatizing of productivity into an absolute principle would set limits to the openness and contingency of human making. In order to capture the vitality and urgency of aspiration, the sovereign is posited not only as the supreme object of the subject's desire but also as beyond reach.

This dialectic of accessibility and inaccessibility has been analyzed by Victor Turner as an opposition between two different, but nonetheless (in Turner's argument) complementary, ways of experiencing and organizing social phenomena: "communitas," on the one hand, and "hierarchy" or "structure" on the other. "Communitas" privileges totality, homogeneity, equality, unity, identity; "hierarchy" privileges differences of rank, heterogeneity, inequality, difference.[19] Hierarchy tries, in Turner's account, to set communion apart and thereby to make use of it in the conscription of aspiration and creativity. Communitarian ritual creates and expresses affective unities—like "nation," "people"—that seem larger, more inclusive, than structural specifications like "dynasty," "lineage," "estates." Though "liminal" groups — that is, groups (women, for example) largely excluded from official structures of power and wealth — may threaten, in fact or in fantasy, the interior unity of families, lineages, classes, they can serve also to embody principles of wholeness and unity, because the very outsideness of the liminal to particularized hierarchical interests can make the liminal seem "above" or "beyond" such interests.[20] The sovereign, in contrast, must represent not only the apex of "structure"; he must also represent the "total community," its "territory" and its "resources."[21] But this paradoxicality gives to the sovereign a particular kind of liminality and thus a potentially dangerous but also potentially powerful intimacy with other liminal entities — "foreign" women, prodigies (twins, dark sisters).

In Turner's analysis, communitarian experience serves paradoxically to "purify" hierarchy of its brutalities — through, for example, the subject's free exercise of "plain speech" or through the sovereign's humility, as when James IV would return each year to Holyrood before the end of Lent to distribute alms to his bedesmen on Skire Thursday. "There were as many of them as he was years old, and each . . . received a penny for each year of the King's life."[22] Communitarian experience thereby helps to obscure constraint. We might think of it as one of the means by which power makes love: it is the (ritual) refashioning of captivation as an experience of freedom, a remaking of the subject to enable identification with, and idealization of, an authority experienced as liberating and unifying rather than repressive and divisive; and a suspending of statuses to which the subject might aspire, of futures into which the subject might project his or her efforts.[23] As just such a redemption of the difference between sovereign and subject, or creator and created, communitarian experience can do essential work for sovereign love; it is a way of securing desire for hierarchy. It becomes a means whereby the resources that have been excluded or "liminalized" by particular structures — resources of risk, danger, newness, unthinkability — can be recovered for those structures. To the extent that the goal of communitarian "purification" is the "rebirth of structure," then, we can understand the functionality of such resurrections: the "thinkable" owes its life — its capacity to be experienced as alive, as well as its capacity for futurity — to its intrication with the "unthinkable."[24] The affective power of undifferentiating union thus plays its part in cultural negotiations between catastrophic change at one extreme and immobility at the other — death in all its forms.

Turner's analysis of the Ashanti *Apo* ritual suggests that queens may at certain times have a particularly intense relation to communitarian experience: The Queen Mother is present on the last day of the *Apo* ritual, which is held — just before the new year begins — by a river in the open air. The chief is excluded, and the ritual emphasizes "the universal aspects of Ashanti culture."[25] Pauline Stafford's work on early medieval European queenship also suggests that queens sometimes offer communitarian solutions to problems of sovereignty; by managing patronage, early medieval queens preserved "the essential distance and impartiality of royalty" and thus "provided for the charisma of royalty itself."[26] Kristeva notes that in the sixth-century church of Santa Maria Antiqua in Rome, Mary Regina "is called upon to represent supreme earthly power" and in so doing becomes the bearer of an "opulent infringement to Christian idealism."[27] And Louis Montrose has proposed that Elizabeth I's "sex" may have helped her in "combining intimacy and benignity with authoritarianism."[28] Thus one role a queen may sometimes be asked to play is enabling the prince's disembodiment, his difference from his subjects, by herself taking on "his" presence, immediacy, accessibility.

Still, a queen, whether regnant or consort, may need to maintain some heterogeneity, some distance from the body, in order to shape aspiration around her image; the association with splendid beauty negotiates these paradoxical demands, as in the masques of *Blacknesse* and *Beautie*, when the errant materiality of the Ethiopian nymphs turns into the "redeemed" diversity of the Elements of Beauty, and the splendor of the queen and her ladies at last shines forth.[29] The queen's beauty signifies that she is set-apart, peerless; at the same time, her beauty keeps her in the realm of the senses. Thus the association, in turn, of beauty and queenship with a discourse of virtue is also essential to the art of queenship. Insofar as virtue provides a hidden, inaccessible interior for the magnificent surface of beauty, the question of whether the queen is both beautiful and virtuous is a way of posing the question of queenship: how is it to make accessible the body of sovereignty, so that it may be "loved in the flesh," while limiting its circulation, preserving its rare, indeed its extraordinary, character? In the case of Mary Regina, for example, the Marian body is perfect not only in its constitution of a surface but also in its accessibility to God; it offers a *redeemed* openness as well as closedness. In *The Meroure of Wyssdome*, written in the late fifteenth century for James IV of Scotland, John of Ireland writes of Mary that "Sche is the schip closit benethe and opin aboue, for hire mynd and entencioune was closit to all erdlie thingis and plesaunce. Sche was opin aboue to resaue all hevinly licht, all wertu & grace. Jn this hevinly schip þe sone of god, jhesus, put all his precius tresoure of hevinly riches."[30] Mary is figured as a superlative remaking of the interior of the female body for belief, a remaking which requires both the inviolacy of boundary and the openness of bonds. Absolute fidelity and uniqueness on the one hand and absolute lovableness on the other are for the queen played out in her relation to sovereignty, which she possesses but to which she is also, unless she is regnant, to some degree subject.[31] The subject's heart, too, is to be chained to the king's with what Elizabeth I called "a most straight tye of affections."[32] "My beloved is mine and I am his"; "I am my beloved's, his longing is all for me"; "there is one alone, my dove, my perfect one": as the Song of Songs suggests, the queen exemplifies the impossible identification of the subject with the king.[33]

In Ireland's account of the Virgin Mary, her reliability makes her a good place to keep treasure; she is both supremely gifted and supremely given. Queens, partly because of their power of patronage, are often identified with the fecundity of the gift. Most queens marry into their sovereignty and thus share with the gift the quality of coming to an "inside" from an "outside" and of bearing something of the "outside" with them. As such, they represent a distance — real and symbolic — that has, ideally, been traversed. The queen's power to alter identity can serve purposes like unification; this is one reason why wedding pageantry often stresses communitarian themes.[34] For example, the epithalamium sung at the wedding of Princess Margaret of Scotland to King Eric of Norway at Bergen in 1281 associates the success of the bride's perilous journey and the lighting of the torch of peace with unanimity, community, the overflowing of boundaries: "With one accord the nation breaks into her praise"; "The regions of the world rejoice on every side"; "To her is highest reverence paid by high and low."[35] The trajectory of the nymphs in the masques of *Blacknesse* and *Beautie*, too, has something of the epithalamium about it, of the bride's "emergence . . . out of the shadows of girlhood" into "new or prodigious light"—an emergence which often "entails," as Nohrnberg remarks of Spenser's use of "the epiphany of the triumphant virago," "the securing of devotion."[36]

To emerge into the light of womanhood, then, is to take on a power of alteration; hence its paradoxical association with themes of masculinity. When the power of queens to transgress gender roles — "everyday reality"—is celebrated, though, it is often because everyday reality is in danger. An Italian *vita* of James III's queen, Margaret of Denmark, contrasted James's "tyranny" with her virtues, which have a communitarian quality: "She was most gentle, forbearing and devoted, and extremely religious. She was . . . most gracious to anyone in trouble; never sparing in favours to her peoples. . . . She never refrained from granting . . . sympathetic audiences. . . . She was much more loved and revered by the people than was the King, since she possessed more aptitude than he for ruling the Kingdom; she governed the people and the state with justice and integrity, as though she were a Numa Pompilius."[37] In this fascinating document, "female" virtues of modesty and forbearance magically modulate into masculine virtues of rule; sovereign love is rescued from the wreck of James

Fig. 6. Margaret of Denmark, Queen of Scotland. Trinity Altarpiece, attributed to Hugo Van der Goes. Reproduced by permission of Her Majesty the Queen. (On loan to the National Gallery of Scotland. Photograph provided by the National Gallery of Scotland.)

III's unpopularity by his queen, who — in a final "overturning" of roles — is said to have been poisoned. In her Italian *vita*, at any rate, Margaret of Denmark exemplifies the power of queenship to "purify" hierarchy of its brutalities, to make "absolute authority the more attractive as it appear[s] removed from paternal sternness."[38]

Of the best-known communitarian heroine of the later Middle Ages — Joan of Arc — Jean Gerson wrote in *De quadam puella* that "it is congruent with the Scriptures that God should have made blessed salvation manifest to the peoples and the kingdoms of the world *per fragilem sexum et innocentum aetatem*."[39] Joan was devoted to the reinstatement of the French monarchy (threatened by accusations of Charles's illegitimacy) and the identification of the monarchy's triumph as a sign of the "election" of the French as God's chosen people; the fractures of fifteenth-century French politics were badly in need of sovereign love. Regarding a later "epiphany of the triumphant virago," Winfried Schleiner notes the close connection between descriptions of Elizabeth as an Amazon and the Armada conflict; he mentions a Latin ode which comments, "A woman triumphs over a man, indeed over a mighty one," and mentions also the commemorative coin celebrating the English victory, which "bore the Virgilian tag '*Dux Foemina Facti*'": "A woman was conductor of the fact." Thus the English victory over Spain was consciously celebrated as the victory of a woman.[40] At stake in the art of the Armada, as in the biblical metaphors of the story of Joan of Arc, is the larger wholeness of the community — its invulnerability to wounding, to perforation, to invasion, whether from without or from within.

In the debates on gynecocracy, too, some writers invoked God's power to work miracles as justification for female rule; others saw female rule as plague, as monstrous and prodigious. Both interpretations saw female rule as an overturning of the normal course of history.[41] Thus the emphasis on unanimity often characteristic of the queenly art of rule may, depending on historical and cultural circumstances, be talismanic or even deliberately provocative of the very power of change against which it also defends. When "exchanged" in marriage, queens are, as Stafford points out, "the greatest of gifts"; but by that very token they can be the most threatening of gifts, most capable of changing that to which they are given.[42] As the story of Troy suggests — in which Venus "gives" Helen to Paris — the ambiguity of the gift is likely to come to the forefront when the queen's foreignness becomes a source of unease and her fidelity is questioned. The foreignness of queens — which compounds the liminality of their femaleness — heightens the stakes of sovereign paradoxicality.[43] The distance of queens from their subjects, as well as their intimacy with their subjects, will as often as not begin in and may readily take on an aura of dubiousness, danger, even crisis. Thus to the queen is attributed a specially frightening power to alter identities, and the crime of which she is most frequently accused, other than adultery, is witchcraft (in Jonson's *Masque of Queenes*, the antimasque is one of witches).[44] In extraordinary cases queens are enemies; but even ordinarily they are "representatives of rival families," "personifications of old grievances."[45] And queenly power is itself likely to be a contradictory compound of what Bourdieu calls "official" and "unofficial" power — of secrecy and publicity, of "private negotiations" and public decrees.[46] Thus, since the queen is likely to be considered in some sense a "masculine" woman as well as exemplary of Woman, her art of rule is likely to be riskier and more complicated than that of the king — especially since she is often asked to take on risk and complexity for the king.[47]

The paradoxicality of sovereignty, then, is in the case of queens given a critical, too often literally a life-and-death, consequentiality (the history of queens in Europe is a history of far greater vulnerability to failure than that of kings). For queens are not only unlike their subjects in that they are queens but are frequently unlike them in that they are foreigners and are unlike the bearers of official power in that they are women; and they are like their subjects not only in that they are human but also in that, unless they are regnant, they owe fidelity and must dedicate their creativity, their bodies as well as their hearts, to the king. The often intense association of queens with questions of division and unity, discontinuity and continuity, suggests that the role of queens in historical agency and experience may in fact be more critical and less purely ornamental than has traditionally been supposed. The art of queenship, for example, appears to have been even more difficult to negotiate in the later Middle Ages than was true earlier in the period. JoAnn McNamara and Suzanne Wemple have argued, at any rate, that the xenophobia of the later Middle Ages found it increasingly difficult to tolerate the foreignness of queens.[48] Margaret Tudor married James IV of Scotland fifteen years after James III's pursuit of a policy of peace with England was alleged as justification for his overthrow. And the question of gynecocracy exacerbated the problem of foreignness even further, by opening up the possibility that, for example, Spaniards and Scots might rule England, or a Frenchwoman (Mary of Guise) rule Scotland. Succession problems made anxieties about national identity especially fervid.

The best-known of these troubled successions to historians of England is of course the long history of the Tudor dynasty's failure to achieve anything remotely resembling primogeniture and its reliance, as a result, on two female "princes," one of whom was half Spanish and had married a Spaniard, the other of whom had been declared illegitimate by her father. It is less well known, but more significant for our purposes, that throughout the fifteenth and early sixteenth centuries in Scotland a series of mishaps produced not so much orderly succession as a succession of lengthy minorities, when Scotland had to wait for its seventeen-month-old or six-year-old kings to grow up and had to endure the political intricacies of regencies. With the exception of Rosalind Marshall, historians of fifteenth-century Scotland have largely failed to appreciate the significance of the fact that the minorities threw queens into situations both of heightened opportunity and peril and gave them a leading role in the rule of Scotland.[49] The history of that role remains to be written, but the framework of events at least is fairly clear.

As is well known to scholars of *The Kingis Quair,* James I met Joan Beaufort during his eighteen-year imprisonment in England, and it seems that their engagement improved his situation and hastened the willingness of the English to arrange his release.[50] After James I's murder in 1437, Queen Joan governed the country in association with the fifth earl of Douglas and the chancellor, Bishop Cameron of Glasgow. The government lasted two years, after which time, Donaldson suggests, the queen's marriage to Sir James Stewart of Lorne and the rise to power of the Livingstons seem to have brought an end to her effective power. After her marriage, the queen lost custody of the king.[51] James II married Mary of Gueldres on 3 July 1449. On Monday, 23 September 1449, there was a mass arrest of Livingstons; two members of the Livingston family who controlled significant parts of Mary of Gueldres's marriage portion were executed, and the day after, the marriage portion was confirmed by Parliament. In these events, writes Donaldson, "it may even be possible to detect the hand of the new Queen."[52] When her husband was killed by exploding artillery in 1460, Mary of Gueldres took over the administration of the country and managed with some success the complexity of Scotland's foreign affairs during the time of the English War of the Roses. According to Donaldson, however, an alliance with Hepburn of Hailes and an ensuing attempt to "gain control of the young King's person . . . discredited [her], in much the same way as Joan Beaufort had been by her marriage with Stewart of Lorne."[53] Mary of Gueldres died in 1463, and the death of Bishop Kennedy, who had succeeded her, in 1465, left the young king vulnerable to the machinations of the Boyds. James III married Margaret of Denmark in July 1469, and, as his parents had done with the Livingstons, he used the occasion of his marriage to ruin the Boyds. Margaret also played an important role in the crisis of 1482.[54]

It is perhaps not wise to draw conclusions from this admittedly bare chronology, but some preliminary considerations emerge that are at least worth registering, partly in light of their importance to Margaret Tudor's story. In the earlier fifteenth century, Scotland's queens were aristocratic women, but not princesses, before their marriages: Mary of Gueldres's father was the duke of Gueldres; Joan Beaufort's, the earl of Somerset. In the later fifteenth and early sixteenth centuries, Scotland's queens were royal princesses: Margaret of Denmark came from a country with a longstanding tradition of amity with Scotland, and Margaret Tudor came from a country with a longstanding tradition of enmity with Scotland (Margaret Tudor's marriage to James IV was negotiated in circumstances quite different from those surrounding the marriage of Joan Beaufort to James I; and Margaret's status as a royal princess considerably raised the stakes involved in her marriage, since it was undoubtedly clear to all concerned that any issue from the marriage would have strong claims to the throne of England). Whether royal princesses or not, though, the foreignness of Scotland's queens does not seem to have prevented the country from turning to them in time of need; at the same time, their liminality posed clearly felt dangers during those times of need, since remarriage or factional alliance seems often to have called their fidelity to national interests into question and to have put an end to their official practice of powers of regency and to their control of the heir.

These considerations broke out with special force during the minority of James V. The structural complexities of Margaret Tudor's position during the minority proved almost impossible to negotiate, and small wonder. She was the widow of James IV; mother of James V, likely heir to the throne of England if Henry VIII were to have difficulties producing an heir of his own; and sister of Henry VIII, whose army killed her very popular husband. The contradictions of this position have not been much appreciated by historians, who have instead applied to Margaret the character flaws associated historically with queens — nastiness, selfishness, fickleness — and accordingly have interpreted her actions as narrowly self-interested and therefore somehow categorically different from the selfless, high-minded pursuit of Scotland's best interests presumably displayed by her powerful male rivals.[55] The possibility that Margaret may herself have attempted on occasion to remain loyal to Scotland's interests as well as to her own, while enduring continual harassment at the hands of her brother — who essentially sought to make Margaret into an agent for English interests — has not often been mentioned. Scholars have underestimated the extent of her influence in Scottish politics — complained of constantly by Henry VIII himself — and the extent to which, as an English outsider, she was distrusted by the Scottish nobility, some of whom began intriguing against her immediately upon James IV's death.[56] Had she been possessed of the talents of Elizabeth I, Margaret would still have faced enormous difficulties in exercising power during the minority of her son.

Thus, in Margaret's case, scholars have tended to replicate rather than to address the difficulties of queenship. Donaldson, commenting on the similarities between Margaret's situation and those of Joan Beaufort and Mary of Gueldres, writes: "But Margaret Tudor differed from those earlier Queens in two ways, for she was the sister of the reigning King of England and she was conspicuously unstable in her affections. Indeed, her matrimonial adventures came near to rivalling those of her brother, Henry VIII. . . . This was the woman who, in terms of James IV's will, was tutrix to her son as long as she remained a widow, and therefore head of the government."[57] Henry VIII himself leveled similar accusations at his sister; he repeatedly, ironically, and without any apparent sense of contradiction, accused Margaret of deceitfulness and of making herself "a shame and disgrace to all her family," because she tried to divorce a man—Archibald Douglas, sixth earl of Angus, whom she had married in 1514—favored by Henry for his apparent friendliness to English interests.[58] Donaldson's rhetoric—"this was the woman"—seems designed to make us feel the folly of anyone's giving power to Margaret (why her husband, who knew her well, did so in his will—apparently against custom—remains a mystery).[59] But Margaret's "matrimonial adventures" hardly come near "rivalling those of her brother." None of her three husbands died by her writ. Moreover, some degree of matrimonial adventurism was standard practice for the day—even, when one recalls the examples of Joan Beaufort and Mary of Gueldres, not altogether unusual for fifteenth-century Scottish queens.[60] Margaret seems to have incurred displeasure largely because, despite the fact that she was a woman, she refused to retire gracefully from the pursuit of power. Margaret complained to her brother about Lord Dacre, warden of the march—a man deeply involved in Anglo-Scottish "diplomacy" during the time of the minority and therefore deeply involved in Henry's attempts to subordinate Margaret's interests to his own: "Also I complain to the King my brother of what my Lord Dacre does and says to my hurt, for he says to Scottish folk, 'that he marvels that *they will let any woman* have authority, and specially ME.' Quilk words should come of others, not of Englishmen. For, the more honor I get, England will have the more; and such words as these may do me mickle ill."[61] Margaret also seems to have incurred displeasure because, in pursuing authority, she was willing to change course. Many other queens, for reasons already discussed, have had to be more changeful, more "unofficial," in pursuing power than kings — Margaret herself wrote angrily to her brother of Angus's ill treatment of her, saying "As to my part, your Grace sal find no fault, but I am a *vhaman* [woman], and may do little but by friends." And queens have also often had to bear the symbolic charge of changefulness.[62] Though we must keep in mind that very little is known about the participation of Scotland's late medieval queens in ruling the country during times of comparative tranquillity, it remains striking that those queens — and above all, Margaret, the Tudor princess — should emerge with special force, both in scholarly writing and apparently also in fact, at moments of crisis, of "passage," when rulers were marrying, dying, or being born, coming into or losing their power; when aristocratic fortunes were made and unmade; at moments when change made way for both ambition and failure, gain and loss.

6

Legalized Passion:
The Idea of Marriage

> I am the Husband, and all the whole Isle is my lawful Wife; I am the Head, and it
> is my Body; I am the Shepherd, and it is my flocke.
> — James VI of Scotland and I of England

THE power of marriage to create lasting bonds and thereby new configurations of personhood — to create unities where before there were differences — is a power much admired by sovereigns.[1] Thus marriage, a ritual empowered partly by love's incapacity to imagine itself as ending, serves, in coronation ritual, to make "indissoluble" the bond between subject and sovereign. Because of their shared concern with the creation of unities and of distinctions, sovereignty and marriage can articulate for each other the concept of a relation of enduring obligation; but this relation is understood as enduring and obligatory because it is based on choice: on consensual love. The question of the will, and of the bodily freedom and expansiveness associated with it, is crucial both to marriage and sovereignty because the bonds of love which must link sovereign to subject, husband to wife, must appear to be freely undertaken.

For queens, the link between marriage and sovereignty is especially intense, since it is usually by means of the former that they achieve the latter.[2] Through marriage the queen is anointed, set apart from other women, at once made and recognized as unique; it is also through marriage that she becomes part of the "people" she will rule, which in many cases she will come to symbolize partly because of the aura of strangeness that never completely leaves her. It is partly for these reasons that the queen becomes the paradigm of the difficult alchemy whereby the subject, hence at times the nation, becomes sovereign — capable, that is, of the consensual activity that will, paradoxically, bind subject and nation to the king. Woman, subject, nation must in relation to the king be both sovereign Subject and object, both capable of choice and bound, made captive, by consent.[3] The kind of bond sought between sovereigns and their subjects will thus not necessarily be experienced as the kind of bond enjoyed by the owner of a possession, that is, by someone fixed "securely," at least in his mind, in the position of sovereign Subject, capable of enjoying the object of his possession. Rather, it is the kind of bond that involves, and risks, a mixture of difference and sameness, equality and inequality; it is the kind of bond that seeks love, that must have an answer, and hence must take place between beings capable of answering, hence capable of sovereignty, hence distinguishable from each other, at least for those moments when questions and answers are articulated. Though the safety of the sovereign's rights of possession in woman, subject, nation, may be what is finally at stake, sovereignty stands to lose but also to gain most if this relation is experienced subjectively, in the form of fidelity; that is, if a relation of social and economic "necessity" is refigured as volitional.[4] By such means the experience of devotion to a sovereign is imagined as devotion to the sovereign experience of love; the Subject acquires, through love, the very "inner life" necessary to allegiance.[5]

Mary Regina is, for the Middle Ages, the most important figuration of queen as faithful and loving bride, bride as volitional queen.[6] In the iconography of her Coronation, for example at Laon Cathedral, she appears as Queen of Heaven and as the New Jerusalem, "coming down from God out of heaven, prepared as a bride adorned for her husband."[7] The Assumption of the Virgin is frequently linked with her Coronation and glorification at the right hand of her Son; her special body, her special death, her figuration as queen and as bride are all ways of figuring her set-apartness, in icons that stage the "moment of royal choice."[8] Hence the motif of greeting and imagery from the Song of Songs are prominent in treatments of the Virgin. In Jacobus de Voragine's *Golden Legend,* the heavenly reception of the Virgin is made analogous to that of the Shulammite: Christ calls to himself his mother's soul, bringing her body from the tomb, "'Come from Libanus, my spouse, come from Libanus. Come: thou shalt be crowned!' and she responded, 'Behold, I come, for in the head of the book it is written of me that I should do Thy will, O my God; for my spirit hath rejoiced in God my Saviour. . . .' 'Come my chosen one, and I shall place thee upon my throne for I have desired thy beauty!' and she answered, 'My heart is ready, O Lord, my heart is ready!'"[9] The emphasis throughout these iconographic and discursive developments is on the transformative power of choice: on Mary's sovereignty as the result of election and hence of recognition, greeting, calling. In the passage from de Voragine, to be called, greeted, chosen, named, is to be hailed both as submissive and as sovereign: the spouse will find her crown, her status as sovereign Subject, in doing the will of her God, in fulfilling what is written of her. The readiness of her heart is like the readiness of her body to leave, move, come: the will moves freely, joyfully, *because* it does the will of God.

As the theology of the Annunciation also makes clear, the Virgin embodies consent: the making-available of the interior, the making-over of private desire (one consents *to* something or someone). What she consents to, in particular, is her very chosenness. In his remarks on the Annunciation in *The Meroure of Wyssdome*, John of Ireland explains that Christ chose the Virgin "oure all vthire and jn hire put his hail empleseire . . . for hire gret wertu and humilite."[10] Through her supreme consent to having been supremely chosen, she becomes what Scarry calls a "redistributive site where equalities and inequalities cross over"—where the activity of choice crosses over into the passivity of being chosen, will crosses over into obedience, Subject into subject.[11] As such, the Virgin is paradigmatic of secular queenship; the readiness of her movements and the passivity of her passion find their analogues in the bridal progresses of queens.

Marriage too is a site of crossover, between change and fixity, identity and difference, freedom and constraint, pleasure and sacrifice. As a version of the sensuous ideality of sovereign love, marriage is, in Kristeva's words, "legalized passion."[12] The medieval Church for the most part understood marriage as consisting of the act of consent itself.[13] The free exercise of the will implied in consent takes, in the canon law of marriage, the form of a binding vow, *per verba de praesenti*, the words of which are necessary because, as Scanlan explains, "they constituted the *form* of the sacrament, or, according to [other theologians] . . . , its *matter*."[14] In sacramental marriage, the exercise of choice generates constraint. But the consensual character of marriage is understood as giving it a power of freedom, even at times of transgression. In Thomas Usk's *Testament of Love* we find that "consent of two hearts alone maketh the fastening of the knot. Neither law of kind nor man's law determineth . . . but only accord between these two."[15] And in the *Ludus Coventriae* "Betrothal of Mary," the obligation to marry enjoined by the Old Testament is portrayed as a repressive law against which Mary will rebel, a resistance sanctified by her higher choice of that which is absolutely worthy of choice.[16]

In such texts, marriage is indeed a legalized passion. And it is a unification of what nevertheless remains separate. It is an activity of identification, whereby differences are brought into relation with one another and in the theology and ritual of marriage are made one—one person, one will, though mysteriously still two souls.[17] Usk writes in the *Testa-*

ment of Love that through marriages made in Love's presence "two that wern firste in a litel maner discordaunt, hygher that oon and lower that other, ben made evenliche in gree to stonde."[18] As noted earlier, in the Judaeo-Christian tradition marriage is defined by its simultaneous suspension and preservation of inequality; this is partly why it draws upon the excitement of transgression, confrontation, violence, even as it presents itself in opposition to discord and celebrates the values of peace, harmony, unity.[19] For sovereignty, the importance of the marriage metaphor lies in its power to express bonds between differences as intense — as important, as necessary to preserve — as that between native and foreigner, male and female, body and head, sovereign and subject.[20] The legal fiction of the king's two bodies is in fact intimately linked to the legal fiction of marriage as its conceptual obverse; each creates a fictive body, the one a multiplication of a singularity, the other a unification of a multiplicity.[21] Thus marriage and sovereignty function as two sites — one on the level of the family, the other on the level of the state — in which body and will constrict and extend.

In the Old Testament as in the later Christian theology of grace, the freedom that must seem to generate political and familial bonds is elaborated to the extent that God's love must be understood as based not even on merit but on the gift, on an arbitrary principle of choice. God's love, that is, must be the expression of the absolute unconditionality of the will of supreme authority — so that the love given by supreme authority cannot seem to be constrained even by a constraint so benign as the just deserving of the beloved. Because it is an attempt to imagine an absolute purity of choice, this radically unconstrained loving proper to God helps to position supreme authority as Creator, insofar as to choose is to originate: the concept of choice is difficult to separate from the concept of beginning, as our metaphors of crossroads, gateways, and thresholds would suggest — metaphors important in the rituals of marriage — and as the importance of love in the theology of creation would likewise attest.[22]

Marriage urges the crossing of thresholds, union with new worlds, the refiguration and extension of bonds and loyalties. And to begin anew is so often understood as a way of becoming a creator, even of recalling the original creation. The creative significance of the threshold moment is intensified in marriage because, as a rite of passage, marriage signifies the onset of maturity, in the form of the capacity to produce new life, literally to become a creator.[23] Precisely because of the adventurousness of marriage — the "exogamous impulse," the desire to go beyond boundaries — marriage can pose a threat to the stability of social and political structures.[24] It is, of course, crucial to all forms of authority that the disruptive potential of beginning, of creativity — the vitality of change, of transfiguring and being transfigured, of being made new, of love, or more cruelly of pain — be used to substantiate belief in authority. To choose to create must be to serve God's creativity.

The linking of marriage to paradise has accordingly been an important way of returning originary acts of choice to their origin. Marriage is seen as a form of closeness to an original, divine source, as a perfection of identification with supreme authority — whereby the will is free, because it makes the right choices, because it obeys, believes, is open to God. Thus the statutes of the thirteenth-century Scottish synods note that matrimony, "known to have been instituted in Paradise by God Himself, . . . is, as regards its origin, the first among the Sacraments."[25] The fourteenth-century canonist John Andreae (d. 1348), commentator on the *Decretals of Gregory IX,* gives as one reason "for the pre-eminence of the sacrament of matrimony" "the time when it was instituted, in the beginning of the world."[26] In Alain de Lille's *De planctu naturae* and *Anticlaudianus,* Natura argues that marriage repairs the fallen will and restores the couple to paradise, to likeness and intimacy not only with each other but also with the divine. For Alain de Lille, marriage becomes a way of recovering — at a distance — the immediacy, the nearness, the embodiment of divinity.

Both intimacy and strangeness are essential to the bonds of love. Supreme authority depends upon their interplay to create the subject's devoted allegiance. In sovereign love, intimacy and strangeness must each be made as intense as possible, but this very intensity poses dangers. Excessive familiarity between sovereign and subject is at times imagined as incest; and yet to come as close to incest as possible is one means whereby supreme authority can impassion the law. Another such means is through the embrace of strangeness, though it is as dangerous to mingle with the unfamiliar as with the familiar; in the myth of the Fall, it is through the embrace of strangeness that the subject loses paradisal intimacy, exchanging the samenesses of marital and devotional love for that form of outsideness which is secret, hidden, forbidden. Miracle plays of the Annunciation present God's union with Mary as mysterious, hidden — in Wakefield, Gabriel explains the actions of the "Holy Gost" as a "prevaté" (l. 125) — but at the same time the plays are anxious to distinguish God's workings from illicit, secret love.[27] A willingness to risk the dangers of privacy — its openness to unsanctioned intrusion — for the sake of its affective and ideological power is present also in the doubleness of the medieval Church's insistence on the power of consent to make marriage and its simultaneous reprobation of the clandestine marriages that were thereby to some extent legitimized. The sacramentality of consent permitted, if it did not approve, a delectation of privacy and risk that threatened the hold of family and lordship over sexuality but could nonetheless be identified, however marginally, with the law.[28] As John Andreae explains, "People often marry clandestinely, for, as Solomon says in Proverbs 9, 'Stolen waters are sweeter, and hidden bread is more pleasant.'"[29]

One of supreme authority's richest and most vulnerable thresholds is thus the one which transforms an unknown, hidden interiority into a shared secret, so that intimacy and strangeness or, in Bourdieu's terms, "integration" and "alliance," "security" and "adventure," may be experienced as mutually compatible.[30] The mystery of the Annunciation — when the human mingles with the divine, supreme authority takes on the risk of human flesh, and the human voice speaks its consent to this union — makes absolute the extraordinariness of uniting differences, makes absolute sovereignty's extraordinary entitlement to unions that dazzle with their strangeness or indeed with their intimacy.[31] Celebrating at once communitarian and structural experience, the Annunciation thereby makes absolute the redemptive claims of extraordinary political marriages, since it is through the union of God and Mary — the moment of God's most intimate intersection with the human body — that humanity is restored to paradise, its original creation reenacted.[32] Though, owing to the incommensurability of the participants, the absurdity, scandalousness, and impropriety of such a union challenge belief, these qualities nonetheless can also empower belief and seek not cancellation but legitimation through evocations of redemptive identity: God's union with Mary is anomalous and unexpected, but it is also a repetition, a return to origins, to deep familiarity; it brings together those ordinarily kept apart for their unlikeness, but those thus mysteriously brought together are after all Creator and creature, Father and daughter.[33] The Annunciation is the apotheosis of the mysterious confluence of pleasure and law figured in marriage, and as such, it is the apotheosis of the willed, free, and loving bond between supreme authority and the human body. By yoking extreme otherness in the extreme intimacy of the flesh, the Annunciation substantiates the reality of that supreme power through which the subject will seek the exhilarating conviction of its own being.[34]

John of Ireland's remarks on the Annunciation in his *Meroure of Wyssdome* try to substantiate belief in the Annunciation and the Incarnation by evoking the pleasures of intimacy and secret knowledge. Thus Ireland explains that while the king of heaven has made himself a noble palace to live in, that is the world, the "gret chaumere of rest, quiet and plesaunce, quhare he likit best and was maist sacret, was [the] . . . haly lady & virgin [Mary]."[35] The moment when divinity embodies itself is imagined as a moment of supreme innerness and repose, indeed of sexual bliss.[36] Moreover, Ireland writes, "This angell enterit jn þe lady and virgin jn hire sacret chaumere, and quhen all was closit and stekit, for, þocht sche closit hire chaumere to men quhen sche passit to prayere and contemplacioune, jt was ay opin to god and his angellis."[37] Remarkably, Ireland goes on to warn ladies to eschew "worldly plesance" in the form not only of the company of strange men, but also that of kinsmen and friends, because "gret perell js . . . to be allane with þame jn sacret placis and tyme."[38] For Ireland, Gabriel's visit both is and is not such a "perell"; he imagines the Annunciation as a paradisal moment in which secrecy, intimacy, and pleasure are neither perversely adventurous nor incestuous, but rather secure — secured from the world, closed off to it, but open to mystery, otherness, extraordinariness. This complex of repudiation and receptivity, openness and closedness, is repeated in Ireland's treatment of the Virgin's consent and the pleasure which results from it: she makes herself into the secret place of God's pleasure by becoming his "humyll chaumerere, and seruand. . . . In all things j me conforme to his haly will and plesaunce. . . . humely j consent þarto."[39] Mary's humble consent, moreover, gave her "gret powere and strenthe," whence she was able to conceive "hire blist sone without doloure; sche had gret and merwalus dilectacioune and plesaunce in þat, baithe naturall and spirituale."[40] Ireland's treatment of the Annunciation is an attempt to recuperate the experience of intimacy by linking it, rather than opposing it, to the creation of newness, to vitality: to exogamous rather than incestuous impulses. He celebrates Mary as "this virginale wame and hevinly paradice" because, for him, paradise *is* an experience of crossover, of dissolution, wherein consent *is* humble servitude, the hidden *is* the open, the law *is* joy — even a sexual joy. And his commentary shows how deeply the identificatory power of marriage — its capacity to undo distinctions, to equal the unequal, with respect to human and divine, male and female — is bound up with the function of marriage as a site of pleasure and of law, sexual desire and procreative labor, adventure and security.

7

Active Stars: The Wedding of Margaret Tudor and James IV

> Listen, my daughter, hear my words and consider them: forget your own people and your father's house; and, when the king desires your beauty, remember that he is your lord.
>
> — Psalm 45:10-11

JOHN of Ireland's commentary on one of the most extraordinary unions to have been imagined in Judaeo-Christian culture was part of his contribution to the *Speculum principiis* genre. He wrote at a time when the ambitions of Scottish kings were growing with regard to marriage prospects and the accompanying political and diplomatic advantages — when Scottish monarchs were increasingly able to contemplate the powers and possibilities of the arts of peace.[1] Ireland was by no means the only late medieval Scottish writer to make the link between sovereignty and love.

Through his description of the marriage of Eneas (Aeneas) and Lavinia in the "Thirteenth Book" of the *Eneados*, his translation of Virgil's *Aeneid*, Gavin Douglas provides us with a poetic treatise on the honorable arts of peace and with a "mirror" of the extraordinary marriage of Scotland's own sovereigns, Margaret Tudor and James IV.[2] In order to redeem the fallen city of Rome, what is required is the fulfillment of Latinus's "consideratioun and hys sworn band, / The wedlok promist"; "eternall peax" depends upon the full observation of the law, of the obligation incurred by political and personal betrothal alike.[3] Moreover, the narrative frame of betrothal allows the authentication anew of Eneas's entitlement to Lavinia; his emergence as sovereign lover is made consonant with his emergence as beloved and loving sovereign.

Thus ambassadors sent to Aeneas by Latinus repudiate Turnus completely and assert Eneas's "choiceness":

> Now lat that ilk rahatour [Turnus] wend in hy
> The blak hellis biggyngis to vissy,
> Vndir the drery deip flude Acheron;
> Lat hym go sers, sen he is thiddir gone,
> Other ostis or barganis in his rage,
> And als ane other maner of mariage.
> Thou, fer bettir, and gret deill worthiar
> To bair the riall ceptre, and to be ayr,
> Succeid to realm and heritage sall.
>
> (p. 201, ll. 7–15)

It is clear that Eneas must be chosen, because he has proven his extraordinariness, the difference that can make him king. But the fact that Eneas must await Latinus's invitation and that the Italians must await Eneas's assent in turn indicate the importance of the movements of will in the constitution of sovereignty. There is no choice other than Eneas; yet choice must be experienced as such. At this fragile inaugural moment, this imaginative threshold, there must be desire, invitation, assent: but to choose is to be at the origin of a destiny, to be open to commitment, inexorability, dynasty. *Because* Eneas's marriage represents his distinctiveness, then, it will also represent his capacity to effect union: "All, with a voce and haill assent at accord, / Desyris the as for thair prince and lord" (p. 202, ll. 1–2).

The risks of extraordinary marriage — of distant alliance, of adventure — are partly the result of the strangeness, even the enmity, of new allies and partly the result of the number of interests and people involved. In sovereign marriage, both the difficulties posed by distance and difference and the honor produced by and through the willingness to risk distance and difference are exacerbated to the greatest possible degree. The communitarian pageant of "beleif and traste" with which Douglas chooses to close the *Eneados* is thus itself the final epic exploit — this time an exploit of marital and political union — in the foundational work of empire. "Cum entyr in our weirly wallis stowt" (p. 202, l. 20), Drances invites Eneas; the absolute security of "haly peax" and "etern concord" (p. 203, ll. 11–12) will be the culmination of Eneas's great adventure, a closure — an enclosure — which will permit perpetual re-creation, new life. And when Drances finishes his oration, "all the remanent / Intill a voce sammyn gayf thair consent" (p. 202, ll. 23–24): we witness the adventurous creation of a new people through the power of alteration of the "voce sammyn," the words of mutual consent which, in marriage as in the polity, bring union into being through their binding power.

Marriage in the *Eneados* is thus fundamentally reparative, re-creative. Douglas describes the joy of "the pepill Ausonyane" at the wedding of Eneas and Lavinia in an extended pastoral simile which describes the emergence of the land from obscurity into brightness.[4] Like the land, like the people, "The fair fresch Lauinia the may" emerges "schynand in hir ryall array" (p. 209, ll. 29–32). The embrace of risk, of vulnerability – of expense, new life, visibility, the opening up of inside to outside – is everywhere in evidence at this marriage: Eneas gives Latinus the great gold cup which Priam had earlier given to Anchises; to Lavinia he gives Andromache's "precyus wedis" and the collar she was "wont to were in maiste pompe and delyte, / Quhill that the Troian weilfar stud abuife" (p. 210, l. 31; p. 211, ll. 6–7). The critical nature of the early stages of creation – expressed in themes of presumption, generational strife – are recalled as well in the stories told at the wedding feast: "Quhou vmquhile Saturn, fleand his sonnis brand / Lurkit and dwelt in Italy the land" (p. 214, ll. 5–6).[5] But we are also told that Saturn made the Italians "conveyn, / And gaif thame lawis and statutis, and full beyne / Tawcht thame to grub the wynis, and al the art / To eyr, and saw the cornys, and 30k the cart" (p. 214, ll. 9–12). The risks of world-building are great – no less than the loss of empire, or of divinity – but, Douglas assures us, if faith is kept, if choice crosses over into commitment, the result will be security as well as adventure, the solidity of the material as well as the breathlessness of visionary experience. The new "toune" will be founded even as the old city is saved; Venus will appear to prophesy the greatness of Eneas's race through the excellence of its material enclosures – "O happy cite, and weill fortunat wall" (p. 218, l. 27) – and then will crown this vision of security with Eneas's transfiguration, with a dazzling image of the body now absolutely free of matter, now absolutely free in movement.[6]

The "Thirteenth Book" of Douglas's *Eneados* is about imagining and making the future. It was written at a time when prophecies of perpetual empire through the mingling of enemy blood could scarcely have been read or heard or written without thought of the growing tension between James IV and Henry VIII, at a time, therefore, when James IV's visionary designs on the world were becoming at once most grand and most vulnerable.[7] Douglas's poem was completed not long before the disastrous battle of Flodden – Edinburgh's response to which, it will be recalled, was the building of the Flodden Wall – and the resulting collapse both of Scotland's hopes for greatness under the rule of James IV and of the policy of alliance with England which had inspired the tentative and unsuccessful diplomatic initiatives of James III and which were taken up again in emboldened fashion in the reign of James IV. The cornerstone of the alliance was the marriage between James and Margaret Tudor.

In 1502 the Peace of Glasgow – the first treaty of "perpetual" peace between Scotland and England since 1328 — was concluded with the treaty of marriage between Margaret and James. The peace was sealed — and indeed lasted until Henry VII's death in 1509 — by the spectacular ceremonies of the coronation and wedding in 1503.[8] These events inaugurated a period of roughly a quarter century during which brother and sister Tudors ruled both England and Scotland: "From 1509 until 1516 James's queen [Margaret] was Henry [VIII]'s heir presumptive," a fact which she seems to have celebrated by giving "her second son, Arthur (born in 1509 only to die in 1510) the name once borne by Henry VIII's elder brother, a name that was 'British' rather than Scottish or English."[9]

Yet despite these interesting consequences, historians have temporized with respect to the long-term significance of the Peace of Glasgow and the marriage that crowned it; given that conflict between Scotland and England continued drearily and sometimes violently throughout the rest of the sixteenth century, it has been tempting to regard the alliance as superficial or short-lived in its effects and to ignore the possibility that the imaginative work performed by it may have refigured the future despite, or perhaps even because of, unintended or scattered effects.[10] Though it is clear that both hindsight and contemporary politics were at work in the weight given to the marriage of James IV and Margaret Tudor by a number of later commentators, it is worth remembering that Bishop Leslie (who supported the succession of Mary Stuart to the throne of England), relates in his *Historie of Scotland* that some of Henry VII's English counselors opposed the marriage alliance because it could someday put a Scottish king on the throne of England; they were persuaded when Henry argued that if Margaret succeeded to the throne, England would profit rather than lose by it, for "the les cumis to the incres of the mair, Scotland wil cum till Jngland, and nocht Jngland to Scotland."[11]

Given, too, that James IV's father, James III, had long pursued rapprochement with England, the alliance might also seem less surprising an idea than it might otherwise have done. But James III's failure to make a pro-English policy popular with his nobility was one of the chief disasters of his difficult reign; and it is worthy of note that his son, who rebelled against him, eventually adopted rather than rejected the policy of peace with England that must have seemed, at the time at any rate, to have helped cost his father his throne.[12] However useful an alliance between England and Scotland might have seemed to judicious counselors like Bishop Elphinstone, it cannot have failed to present the appearance of enormous risk — a risk for which James IV's well-documented encouragement of a self-conscious Scottish nationalism might well be read as talismanic.[13] A thoroughgoing transformation of Scotland's relationship to the outside world must have seemed to have been at stake, for the alliance put on hold, if it did not rupture, ties of loyalty to France that were practically immemorial, however uneven, at times, in practice. It also linked two kingdoms whose enmity was as longstanding and well guarded, even as well loved, as it is possible for an enmity to be.[14]

Extraordinary marriage — the kind of marriage that makes and therefore risks prestige — is, Bourdieu argues, an effect of distance; and the distances that had to be crossed in order to bring about the Peace of Glasgow were considerable. That the marriage was extraordinary indeed was probably not lost on contemporaries. Henry VII's sense of his daughter's potential destiny may explain why Margaret's baptism was celebrated on St. Andrew's Day, November 30, and why her christening took place in the church near Westminster Abbey dedicated, according to Strickland, to St. Margaret, queen of Scotland.[15] Henry VII's elaborate and exhaustive preparations for the wedding may also have included a gift of the Book of Hours in which St. Margaret — who, as Buchanan points out, "had also been reared as an English princess" — figures prominently.[16] The identification of Margaret Tudor with her extraordinary predecessor may, moreover, have had some lasting power for Margaret's, and Scotland's, understanding of her role; St. Margaret, for centuries a potent icon in the mythic and material making of Scotland, received important attention in the late fifteenth and early sixteenth centuries, a development for which Margaret Tudor may have been partly responsible.[17] According to Buchanan, Margaret, worried about her fertility, acquired the *sark* (shirt) of St. Margaret, "an important relic" whose "timely discovery" "was considered an excellent omen for the sixteenth-century queen." James V was born not long afterward.[18]

The wedding preparations ongoing in Scotland in 1502 included not only arrangements for Margaret's reception in the south and for the tourneying that was to play an important part in the wedding festivities but also the wardrobing of the entire court, hangings for Margaret's bed of state, the making of her crown, the refurbishing of royal residences, and the building of an entirely new palace in Edinburgh — Holyrood — for the occasion.[19] "Even the prodigal King," writes Mackie, "became alarmed at the costliness of the preparations for the marriage. He resolved to rectify his financial position, not by cutting down his expenditure, but by discovering the philosopher's stone."[20] It was indeed at this time that James IV's extensive patronage of alchemical research began; the pages of the Treasurer's Accounts are littered with disbursements for "quinta essentia."[21] According to Macfarlane, moreover, the accounts suggest that the wedding, by Scottish standards outrageously expensive, inaugurated a new fi-

Fig. 7. Margaret Tudor, Queen of Scotland, from her Book of Hours. Photo from the Picture Archives of the Austrian National Library, Vienna. Codex Vindobonensis 1897, fol. 243 verso.

nancial expansionism which was to continue throughout the rest of James's reign.[22]

One of the purposes of the court festival is to represent the economic power of the prince as a form of supernatural intervention, indeed a kind of alchemy, a "power of alteration"; and James's new interest in alchemy, his new embrace of expensive display, suggest that a powerful sense of change, of new vigor, had come upon the monarch of Scotland. The festivities for his wedding were likely considered innovative, since nothing like them had been seen in Scotland before.[23] The festivities exploited extraordinary marriage as a means of articulating the ambitions of sovereignty and as a means of giving sovereignty its purchase on ambition: on newness, vitality, movement. Though marriage and sovereignty have at many times and in many ways been closely linked, it nonetheless seems to have been the case that, on the occasion of Margaret's wedding, Tudor and Stewart ambitions with respect to European politics and anxieties with respect to domestic unity worked in concert to produce an apotheosis of union as the source of communal honor. What is most distinctive about these festivities, furthermore, is not their intense exaltation of acts of union per se, but rather their exaltation of the changefulness, the transformative power, of acts of union.

It is easy enough to point to the real and apparent obstacles to the triumph of union at this time. Though the very newness of the Tudor dynasty — the changefulness it embodied — was in fact a potential source of the vitality, the conviction, needed to certify Henry VII's claim to the throne, it was more obviously also a source of anxiety. For Henry, the threat of fragmentation took the form of Ireland and of his own northern magnates; Buchanan notes that Margaret's bridal tour of the north of England was particularly intensive, and the north was the part of the country "where there had been most disaffection for the new monarchy."[24] For James IV, the threat of fragmentation took the form of Gaelic Scotland and the Lordship of the Isles, and of the powerful southern magnates who formed his chief political base and were most able to do him harm. Significantly, given that James IV's two greatest festivals were his marriage to an English princess and his tournament of the wild knight and the black lady, Ferguson has argued that "one of the most significant consequences of the English wars was the resurgence of Gaelic Scotland and the way in which the Lordship of the Isles gave it political as well as cultural expression. All this was symptomatic of a wider malaise whereby by the end of the fourteenth century whole regions of Scotland were falling under the sway of overmighty subjects."[25] Lordship on the borders of Scotland had depended for centuries on repeated, mimetic acts of border violence; a lasting peace might thus pacify lordship in more ways than one but might, of course, as had happened with James III, enrage it. What would become of retaliation, of that apparently remunerative allegiance of the plunderer to the past? What futuristic economy, both of honor and of wealth, would succeed it? Would union in fact produce enough honor for "all"? Or would "all" so refigure difference that, as in Henry VII's formulation to his council and as in marital law, "the les [would come] to the incres of the mair?" Would Scotland end by becoming the bride, not the husband, of England?

The treaty of 1502 thus linked two kings aware of the vulnerability of borderlines both within their kingdoms and without, who were willing to risk focus on those very borderlines in order to uphold for their kingdoms a powerful image of union, an image of the power of sovereignty to effect an extraordinary uniting of differences, an image, in fact, of sovereignty as constituted through its power so to alter. They strove to achieve at once, in a fashion and to a degree extraordinary in the history of relations between the two countries, both "integration" (security, sameness, the cohesion of the social order at any given time and throughout time) and "alliance" (adventure, difference, the expansion and transformation of the social order at any given time and throughout time). Henry and James strove, in fact, to make these two often contradictory goals coincide, so that the one would seem to depend completely on the other. It is not a simple matter to make daring and safety, or aspiration and contentment, or the integrity and permeability of borders, into simultaneous experiences, particularly when the enemy with whom one is risking one's safety, or, perhaps even more important, the enemy with respect to whom one is giving up one's power to take risks, is in fact the "auld" enemy. But since Henry and James were asking their borders to give up the pursuit of a long-familiar economy of honor based on hazard, it makes sense that they would seek to affirm the honor of risking identity through union and taking a chance on security.[26]

The quality of "exploit," of "prowess," which Bourdieu attributes to extraordinary marriage, is expressed not only in the tourneying with which the marriage celebrations were punctuated throughout—a reminder that marriage and war function as two aspects of the sovereign power of alteration, however often they are represented as opposites—but also in the statement that begins John Younge, Somerset Herald's, description of Margaret's journey to Scotland.[27]

Younge writes:

To the Exaltation of Noblesse shal be rehersed in thys littyl Treatys the Honor of the right noble Departinge owte of the Realme of Inglaund, of the right high and mighty, and the right excellent Princesse Margaret, by the Grace of God, Quene of Scotland. Also to th'Entent to comfort the Herts of Age for to here it, and to gyffe Coraige to the Yong to do thereafter in such Case to come: For sens the Hour of the said Departing, to the End of her Voyage, shal be written the Names of the Noblesse, after thyr Dignityz, Astats, and Degrees, that in this conveying were ordeined. The Gentylls after thyr Byrth, and the Meaner after thyr Place, and so of the others that shal be, to th' Entent that Ichon in his Right may be worshiped: For such valiant Spyrits desire after ther Deservyng, to have thereof Law[d]e, since all ther Thoughts have ben to doe Things to the Pleasure of the King, and to the Honor of her Majesty. Wherfor of ther Geftys and Maners during the sayd Voyage, togeder with those of them that apon the Marchers of the Lordschips shal be founden, as well Spiritualls and Temporalls, thorough the said Realme of Inglaund, till the Comyng of the Intryng of the Realme of Scotland, . . . and since after, of the Nobles Dyds that to the sayd Realme shal be doon, and of the Mettyngs in suche Forme ye shall knowe, unto the extreame Conclusion of the [marriage] betwix the King of the Scotts and the sayd Quene. In Hop that the same bee concluded, made, and solempnized, to the Lawde of God, and of the two Realmes, and bee to the Pleasur of all Christyns. (265)

Margaret's departure, says Younge, itself has "Honor": through a grandeur of movement, through expansive narrative reach ("unto the extreame Conclusion") and inclusiveness ("The Gentylls after thyr Byrth, and the Meaner after thyr Place"), Margaret's "Departinge" expresses that extraordinariness which is the sovereign form of honor. Through its expansiveness, moreover, the Departinge infuses structure ("after thyr Byrth," "after thyr Place") with communitas; the "Noblesse" of Margaret's movements is brought out by the vastness and variety of her entourage — those who accompany her, those who greet her at the borders, "Spiritualls" as well as "Temporalls." The exemplary function of the Departinge must be located here — in its melding together of hierarchy and communitas, of heterogeneity and homogeneity, so that the "excellent" — the very best — can be made representative, inclusive. By its very unusualness, this marriage will conjoin "all"; all have a part to play, the honor of all is at stake, all shall participate in the "Lawde" of "the two Realmes," of God. Younge's narrative itself shall "bee to the Pleasur of all Christyns" and will inspirit the future — the "Yong" — with the "Coraige . . . to do thereafter in such Case to come." Political marriages, as Bourdieu notes, cannot be repeated, because the alliance is devalued if it is common; but Margaret's Departinge imagines a capacity for self-transformation, for self-extension which — because it is the Departinge of such an excellent princess — extends, in turn, not only to her people but also to the people "to come." The daring of her journey is, and will be, their daring.

That daring is recapitulated by the narrative reach of Younge's account, a reach achieved not so much through the actual length of the work — it is not very long — but through the continuous elaboration of beginnings and endings, meetings and greetings, departures and farewells, whereby the "distance symbolic of prestige" is given amplitude, play. Thus, for example, among the "Fellyship" that attended Margaret from Colieweston, where the Departinge began, were "the Lords Marquis of Dorset, the Lord of Derby, Constable of Inglaund, and the Earl of Essex; the which conveyd her by the Space of one Mylle, and after they toke Licence in kissing her. And with them retorned many Noblemen to the sayd Coleweston" (266). Movement is temporalized, time is made into movement; timing and gesture are the essence of this pageant, because through them loyalties are shifted, bonds loosened and tied, differences confronted and conjoined, distances crossed. Borders are intensely articulated: at specially important points, such as the crossing into Scotland, Margaret exchanges her palfrey for her litter, the means and gestures of conveyance themselves richly elaborated and decorated. The crossing into Scotland is given a detailed and lengthy description — it is specially important to know who greets Margaret there (the archbishop of Glasgow) and who leaves her there (the earl of Northumberland).[28] It is always noted how far citizens have emerged from their places of residence in order to greet Margaret; distance is calibrated with respect to boundaries, placement and displacement.[29] The movements of the inhabitants of the places visited by Margaret embody greeting's habit, in welcoming, of first reaching out, displacing itself. Margaret's mobility thus seeks union through the acquisition of knowledge: parts of the country seem to emerge from anonymity to join for a time in the awareness of the entourage that represents and is crossing through the whole, before returning, transformed, to homes now more securely in synechdochal relation to the "communitas" of the realm.[30]

In extraordinary marriage as in the tournament and the aristocratic funeral, the heralds preside over the dangerous crossings, the confrontations, that create honor: with the earl of Northumberland, for example, "Northumberland Harault," "arayed of his said Liveray of Velvet, berring hys Cotte, sens the mettyng tyll to hys Departyng, thorough all the Entryng and Yssue of good Townes and Citez" (272). And of course there is Somerset Herald himself, author of the *Fyancells.* In Younge's treatise, transition is ritualized to a degree as extraordinary as are the risks involved; the *Fyancells* dedicates itself to the celebration of rupture, discontinuity, change (without which honor could not enact itself), even as it dedicates itself to the celebration of the continuity and identity wherein honor, once tested, argues that it has always resided. Younge's narrative moves between vulnerability and invulnerability, risk and protection. Watching over the ebb and flow of particular persons and places in the *Fyancells* is rhythm itself: in different places, the same kinds of places (bridges, gates), the same kinds of gestures (kissing the cross), the same responses ("it was a fayr Sight for to se") are repeated. The multitudes themselves appear regularly, in each place, in "so grett Nombre." To come out, to come forward, to greet, is to consent to be bonded. But to do these things is also to risk the lime-light; the multitudes are articulated and, like lordship, given borderlines to cross and confront, only joining in greeting rather than in combat. And to be further named, to emerge from the multitudinousness of many places, "many Lordes," "so grett Nombre," is given in the *Fyancells* something of the same force as the emergence of the warrior from the misty clouds of the troops into single combat, as the emergence of the bride — a movement anticipated repeatedly, insistently, throughout the royal progress — from obscurity into brilliant splendor, "cronned with a varey ryche Cronne of Gold garnished with Pierrery and Perles" (292). The epiphanic emergence of warrior and bride are made to coincide in the consensual poetics of the *Fyancells.*

At Colieweston, then, Henry VII made Margaret "to bee convayed vary noblely out of his sayd Realme; as more playnly shal be here folowing remembred, toward the right high and mighty and right excellent Prince Jamys, by the Grace of God, Kyng of Scotys, in following the good Luffe, fraternall Dilleccion, and Intelligence of Maryage betwix hym and the saide Quene" (265–66). As in the Song of Songs, it is love that issues in move-ment in the *Fyancells;* the Departinge is constituted through the place-ments and displacements, embodyings and disembodyings, of sovereign love. Roy Strong remarks that the royal entry was "the most public" of all forms of spectacle.[31] This publicity — this unusual accessibility of sover-eign, on the one hand, and massed populace on the other — is enhanced when royal entry is associated (as it so often was) with royal marriage. But while Margaret's progress is accordingly inclusive and ritualized, its purpose, again, is the delectation of parting and change — of breaking with the past, of entering a new life, a new world, and, for James as well as for Margaret, of the onset of a newly potent maturity, an official sexual-ity and fertility.

That, in Scotland, marriage marked a change not just in the life of a king but in his power to practice rule is suggested by the experience of James IV's own father, James III, who, during his minority, took the occa-sion of his marriage to free himself from the clutches of the powerful Boyd family.[32] James IV had achieved adulthood and was in full possession of his powers at the time of his marriage, but the transformation wrought by the marriage in his habits of expenditure and display seems, as we have noted, to indicate a new reach, a new expansiveness, for the Crown. This new expansiveness is also displayed in the marriage celebrations themselves, the ritual of holding state immediately after the wedding, and James's belting of forty-one knights and creation of three new earls (Arran, Montrose, and Glencairn) in the queen's honor.[33] Moreover, James's many and notorious promiscuities appear to have caused and perhaps made him vulnerable to domestic political conflict and intrigue; what was needed was "distant," glorious marriage and the legitimate heirs produced thereby. James did not, like Henry VII, have before him the task of certifying a new dynasty; he nonetheless had "to set his own [dynastic] house in order," though he never renounced his unofficial lovers.[34]

And while the marriage of James and Margaret made transition extraordinarily public, in doing so it made public intimacy itself. James and Margaret emerge as newly, extraordinarily, visible, but one aspect of this emergence is precisely their entitlement to obscurity and privacy. Most obviously, the moment when James and Margaret actually make love is, in Younge's narrative, unrepresentable — though at the same time Younge draws attention both to it and to its unrepresentability. He writes of the wedding night: "After the Soupper, the Nyght approched, therfor ychon withdrew hym to his Lodgyng for to take hys Rest, and the Kinge had the Qwene aparte, and they went togeder. God by his Grace will hold them in long Prosperitye. At Even grett Numbre of Fyers wer maid thorough the Towne of Edenbowrgh" (296).[35] The next day Younge remarks: "Touchynge the Qwene I say nothinge, for that sam Day I saw her not, bot I understand that sche was in good Helth and Mere" (297). Clearly at stake in such allusiveness is the protection of the paradoxicality through which sovereignty tries to construct itself, in this case for the voyeuristic gaze of the spectator: sovereignty must be at once divinized and also fully human; it is disembodied at one of its moments of intense embodiment. But the patterning of publicity with intimacy runs throughout the *Fyancells*, and one of its chief artists in this regard, Younge would have us believe, is the king himself.

At the first meeting of Margaret and James, which took place in Dalkeith during a four-day lull before the entry into Edinburgh, the king and queen "maid grett Reverences the one to the tother, his Hed being bare, and they kyssed togeder, and in lykwys kyssed the Ladyes, and others also. And he in especiall welcomed th Erle of Surrey varey hertly" (283). But this spectacle of generalized greeting is immediately succeeded by a moment of apparent privacy, a moment that appears to be chosen, unscripted, unregulated, which therefore has as one of its purposes the singling out of the chosen ones: "Then the Quene and he went asyd and commoned to-

geder by long Space" (283). They are, of course, being watched; it is a theatricalization of set-apartness. But while Younge will tell us how they looked
and what seemed to be going on ("She held good Manere, and he bare
heded during the Tym, and many Courteysyes passed" [283]), he will not,
apparently because he cannot, give us details. At this moment when they
first appear together before us, they seem to disappear, and their disappearance is meant to arouse our voyeuristic curiosity.

On the next day, the king makes what Buchanan describes as a "surprise visit": the queen had lost her horses in a stable fire the night before,
and a retinue including the archbishops of York and Glasgow, the bishop
of Durham, the earl of Surrey, and the earl of Bothwell set out "Att foure
of the Clok, after Dynner," to meet the king, who was coming to comfort
the queen (283). But "the Kynge flyinge as the Bird that syks hyr Pray,
tuke other Waye, and cam prively to the said Castell, and entred within
the Chammer with a small Company, wher he founde the Qwene playinge
at the Cardes. At the Entrynge, the Qwene avaunced hyr toward hym in
receyvinge hym varey gladly, and of Good Wyll kyssyng hym, and after
he gaffe Salut to the Ladyes and Company presente" (284). Orchestrated
and unspontaneous though this flight of the sovereign's desire may have
been — weighed down by the conventionality, the repetition, of *fin'amors* —
the point of the king's gesture and of the simile that accompanies it is
partly to surprise, to leaven the expected with the unexpected, however
expected, in turn, his so doing. Through such gestures — gestures which
at once transgress and celebrate the expected — the king must try to authenticate his desire, to authenticate himself as sovereign lover.[36] The movements of James's body as described in the *Fyancells* remind us, too, that
James was a notoriously restless, energetic, peripatetic king: after he
leaves the queen, he "went to hys Horse, on whom he did lepe, without
puttynge the Fowt within the Sterrop" (a feat which he will perform again
during the course of the celebrations). "And the sayd Horse was a right
fayr Courser, and incontynent the King sported, follow who myght" (284).
We are asked to feel an urgency, rapidity, unpredictability in his movements, his headlong love. We are to feel a vibrancy in his comings and
goings, a vitality in his capacity to appear and disappear: the certainty
of his passionate being through its very uncertainty. Were it not so, he
could not seem to love in a supremely honorable way; he could not prove
himself as supreme in "Coraige," as sovereign lover.

The progress into Edinburgh thus has as one of its chief purposes the
provision of a space and time for courtship. James must court Margaret
because consent — which includes the possibility that the beloved may not
choose to love in return — provides for marriage the element of chance on

which honor depends. The rituals of royal courtship thus resemble the tournament in this respect too: chance, art, timing, effort, risk, and adventure must be inscribed within them, the more so as the outcome is secure, predetermined. That this is so is, once again, indicated by the importance of tourneying within the marriage celebrations themselves, in particular by the tournament which interrupts the progress on its way to Edinburgh — in which a knight "by Avantur" robs another knight of his lady, and James intervenes, in the role played by Theseus in "The Knight's Tale," to settle their differences (288). Significantly, the issue of their conflict, as the wronged knight presents it, is the power of "Owtrage" to break secure bonds: "they did well ther Devor, tyll that the Kynge cam hymselfe, the Qwene behynd hym, crying Paix, and caused them for to be departed. After this the King called them before hym, and demaunded them the Cause of ther Difference. The Caller sayd, Syre, he hath taken from me my Lady Paramour, whereof I was insurte of hyr by Faith. The Defender answered, Syre, I schall defend me ageynst hym apon thys Cas: Then sayd the Kynge to the sayd Defender, brynge youre Frends, and ye schall be appoynted a Day for to agre you (288).[37] "Whereof I was insurte of hyr by Faith": the point of this pageant is, in part, to reintroduce — in a preordained way — the vulnerability of faith, the effort needed to sustain and create it. The pageant is a reminder of the createdness of the bonds which sovereign marriage must at the same time portray as destined, inevitable, absolute. It reminds us that in love as in war it is not always easy to distinguish oneself in a way clear enough to take on the form of absolute certainty of extraordinariness; and thus it seeks to remind us of how that power of alteration — in this case, that power of distinction — which is violence, can seem to dwell within that power of alteration known as courtship. The use of violence to distinguish the lover is reworked in this pageant, as it is in Chaucer's "Knight's Tale," in *The Parliament of Fowls,* and in Dunbar's *The Thrissill and the Rois.* In James's wedding tournament the sovereign emerges as he who is supremely entitled to his bride, and therefore as he who can exert the power of distinction over other aristocratic lovers. But just before leaving that wild woodland space in which, this pageant asserts, anything could happen — in which courtship might fail, or bonds be broken — for the paradise into which Edinburgh has been transformed, Discord, and its power to unmake superreality, has been recalled. It has been recalled because sovereign love, as a work of honor, needs to be embattled. Through such means, an activity is found for aspiration: that is, the activity of honor — the reward being, not chunks of territory or plundered livestock, but the love and faith of woman.[38]

Finally, in the *Fyancells,* courtship provides for a complex play of communitarian and structural pleasures and persuasions, in which the king's refusals to take precedence over Margaret put distinction at risk — seeming, like his other courtship gestures, to depart from precedent but at the same time displaying his power to effect union, to overcome the difference of his subjects. By such means are inequalities re-presented as equalities. After the royal entry, the king and queen go to the abbey of Holyrood; the archbishop of St. Andrews gives the king a relic to kiss, but he insists that Margaret kiss it first. The king refuses to kneel down first, "bot both togeder"; afterward, "the King transported himself to the Pallais, thorough the Clostre, holdynge allwayes the Qwene by the Body, . . . tyll he had brought hyr within her Chammer" (290). At the banquet after the wedding, the king desires the heralds first to cry the largesse of the queen; "And because there was noe more then three Cotts of Armes of Inglaund, the Kyng wold not suffer more thenne thre of his awne." Finally, the king refuses altogether to have his largesse cried, "saying, that it souffysed to cry hers" (295). Moreover, the very fact that James had Margaret crowned at the time of her entry may itself be striking evidence of the risks he was willing to take in celebrating the strength of royal ambition and choice.[39] Through such means we are asked to believe that the powerful love of the Scottish king for his English queen has overcome the differences between them: "Wear me as a seal upon your heart, / as a seal upon your arm; / for love is strong as death." At stake, however, is the domestication of England by Scotland. Margaret's differences — her Englishness, her femaleness — are represented as re-formed, through the identificatory power of love, for the power of Scotland's identity.

The power of alteration that was at work in the Edinburgh pageants for the royal entry was likely to have been, in fact if not in fantasy, at least as much that of the burgh as that of the king and the court. Pitscottie writes that the queen was received "with gret reverence and honouris in all the borrowis tounis of scotland quhan that scho maid hir entres evirie ane according to thair estait maid hir sic bankattin feirceis and playes that nevir siclykk was seine in the realme of scotland for the entres of na queine that was resawit afoirtyme in scotland and speciallie Edinburghe stiruilling Sanctandrois Dundie Sanct Johnestoun aberdeine glaskow linlythgow."[40] The Edinburgh pageants are, to my knowledge, the only ones for which a description survives, though we might well consider Margaret's reception at Aberdeen in 1511 as part of a continuing effort to strengthen the bond between the queen and her new country.[41] We have already noted Aberdeen's recognition of Edinburgh's preeminence in the matter of pageantry, and Edinburgh probably played a specially important role in the

country's celebration of the wedding. But though the marriage contract
was entered in Edinburgh's records, as indeed it apparently was "in all the
mes bukis of the contree," little is known of Edinburgh's preparations, and
even less is known of those who participated in planning, staging, and
acting in the entry pageants.[42]

We can reconstruct a few facts about the town's role in the wedding festivities in general from the Treasurer's Accounts, because the court's own
preparations in Edinburgh as well as Stirling were particularly extensive
and engaged the residents of the town, some of whom were also members
of the court. For example, Patrick Haliburton, made burgess and guild-
brother of the burgh gratis in January 1500, was reimbursed for a gold
chain which the king took from him and gave to "the Lady Gilfort of
England." James Homyll, merchant-burgess of Edinburgh, was paid four
shillings "for lynyng of the arres clathes," and another entry records that,
at the king's command, ten pounds were spent robing William Homyll in
cloth provided by "his brodir James Homyll."[43] Two of Edinburgh's most
prominent citizens—Alexander Lauder, provost of Edinburgh, who was
knighted by James in 1504, and William Todrik, one of the bailies—seem
to have been involved in financing and provisioning the building of Holyrood Palace undertaken just before the wedding.[44]

These items suggest close mutual involvement of Edinburgh and James's
court in the period before the marriage, but when the Treasurer's Accounts
take notice of the town's activities, they of course do so from the standpoint of the court and thus document cooperation without offering an
overall context within which to evaluate cooperation. And though these
records point to a number of different kinds of familiarity between town
and Crown, they portray Edinburgh's role chiefly as that of a purveyor
of goods and financial services. Though the "Johne Broun, masoun," who
"com fra Faukland to wirk in Halyrudhous" in 1502–3 may be the Joannes
Broun mentioned in Edinburgh's assise list of 1495, the reference to Falkland lessens the possibility, as does the fact that the former Broun was
a member of a craft. It is conceivable that the "Jok Steil" who was fetched
from Edinburgh "to the King" in October 1501 was the "John Steill" mentioned as "Kirkmaster" in the Taylors' Seal of Cause and thus may have
had some responsibilities for preparing garments for the royal entry or
other festivities.[45] We cannot conclude from the accounts the extent to
which the townspeople may have planned and worked alongside court
servants and the king himself in readying Scotland for the wedding; and
of course the accounts do not report independent activities on the part
of the burgh with respect to the royal entry or anything else concerned
with the wedding.

During the time of busy excitation preceding the wedding, a messenger

was sent "to pas to Edinburgh to fech the Provest and Bailyeis to the King";
a little later, a man went to Edinburgh "with writing of the Kingis to the
provost and bailʒeis of Edinburgh."⁴⁶ These messages may have concerned
preparations for the royal entry; the king's many messages to those who
were to meet the queen on her way to Dalkeith suggest at least the possibility that James had wished to consult the burgesses of the town regarding Margaret's reception.⁴⁷ But much other business besides preparing for
the entry itself was being transacted at the time, not least the work on
Holyrood. The only item in the Treasurer's Accounts that seems definitely
to link court and town with respect to the entry pageants records payment
"to Johne of Burgownis wif, for iiij elne plesance and tua elne double kirsp,
quhilk wes tane to the grathing of the madin the day the quene com in
Edinburgh": the "madin" might refer to the pageant of the marriage of the
Virgin which formed part of the festivities for the royal entry.⁴⁸ If it does,
then the picture it suggests of Edinburgh's role in the imagining and ar-
tificing of the entry pageants is a profitable though not particularly active
one, since the court seems to have been responsible for paying for the
maiden's costume, perhaps also for designing and making it. But the entry
in the burgh records "For the byrth of our King" in February 1506/7 demonstrates at least that the burgh officers did provide for marshaling the
townspeople on appropriate festive occasions and must have done so at
the time of the wedding: "The provest baillies and counsall hes ordanit
the seriandis to pas throw the toun and charge euery honest man mer-
chand and craftsmen that they have ilkane ane new tortys reddy, and pas
in thair best aray to the abbay with the provest and baillies quhen God
sall provyde the Quene to be deliuerit, and that ilk man be reddy to sett
furth thair fyre quhane thai sall be chargit be the bell."⁴⁹

The scarcity of documentary evidence on the town's preparations is not
surprising given the scarcity of documentary evidence in general from this
time; but this scarcity materially underscores the fact that, however much
the municipal artistry and labor of a royal entry was meant to participate
in the creation of "un sentiment de communion entre les membres d'une
ville ou d'une nation," the pageantry of such entries — and Edinburgh is
a case in point — often represents the town's own wealth and prosperity
as the product of a sovereign power of alteration.⁵⁰ For example, the York
pageant prepared for Henry VII in 1486 foregrounds the dependence of
the city's paradisal richness on the sovereign's creativity, thereby offering
the city to the sovereign as an other to love and be loved by. At the gate
of the city of York, Anglo explains, was the first pageant,

"craftely conceyved . . . in maner of a heven, of grete joy and angelicall armony."
Beneath this celestial roof it had been arranged to have a world "desolate [that is
devoid of inhabitants], full of treys and floures," in which was contrived: "a roiall

rich rede rose convaide by viace, unto the which rose shall appeyre another rich white rose, unto whome so being togedre all other floures shall lowte and evidently yeve suffrantie, shewing the rose to be the principall of all floures, as witnesh Barthilmow, and therupon shall come fro a cloude a crowne covering the roses."⁵¹

After this act of homage, "it was arranged that the 'desolate' world should be filled with a city and its inhabitants. The founder of York, called Ebrank, was to greet the King and present him with the keys of the city. . . . His appearance emphasized the purport of the mechanical display in the pageant: the world is desolate, but the union of the roses causes a city, York, to emerge with its populace." The celebration of loyalty — "this Citie of old and pure affeccion / Gladdith and injoith your high grace and commyng, / With oon concent, knowing you ther Sufferaine and King" — concludes with a pageant of the Assumption in which the Virgin Mary tells Henry that the city, "as a place pleasing [to her] . . , is to be trusted."⁵² It is understandable that, on Henry VII's first progress through the troubled waters of the north, such pageantry should foreground loyalty, trust, the kingly superreality (in the form of the supremacy of the rose) which loyalty in fact creates, the king's role in creating a city and a people, the origination of the city in a prelapsarian act of homage. However ancient a city York is, it depends upon a primordial act of consent in which, once again, the sovereign is chosen because he must be chosen — his supremacy is beyond all doubt. The delicacy of Henry's position at this time merely brings out these themes in a specially forceful and direct way.

But even at times when the legitimacy of dynasty was less in doubt — and James IV had, after all, the task of convincing Scotland to love an English princess — the association of city with paradise seems often to have the purpose of re-presenting the city's capacity to create itself through its arts and artistry as the product of sovereign "grace" — as gift. Younge describes Edinburgh at the time of the entry as "in many Places haunged with Tapissery, the Howses and Wyndowes war full of Lordes, Ladyes, Gentylwomen, and Gentylmen, and in the Streytts war soe grett Multitude of People without Nombre, that it was a fayr Thynge to se. The wich People war varey glad of the Commynge of the sayd Qwene: And in the Churches of the sayd Towne Bells range for Myrthe" (291). The city makes a spectacle of itself for the king and queen; it beautifies itself, it rejoices, it presents its multitudes, its populace, as a manifestation of Scotland's collective creative power to "deliver" Margaret into paradise. The city makes a kind of reparation, and reparation is, in one way or another, the theme that links the pageants of the royal entry, which began, according to Younge,

At the Entryng of the said Towne [where] was maid a Yatt of Wood painted, with Two Towrells, and a Windowe in the Midds. In the wich Towrells was, at the Windowes, revested Angells syngyng joyously for the Comynge of so noble a Lady; and at the sayd middle Windowe was in lyk wys an Angell presenting the Kees to the said Qwene.

Within the Towne ny to the said Yatt came in Processyon the College of the Perysche of Seint Gilles, rychly revested, with the Arme of that Seint; the wiche was presented to the Kynge for to kysse; wherof he did as before [that is, gave Margaret precedence], and began to synge *Te Deum Laudamus.*

In the Mydds of the Towne was a Crosse, new painted, and ny to that same a Fontayne, castynge forth of Wyn, and ychon drank that wold.[53]

Edinburgh's tapestries and cleanness and festively dressed crowds are a revesting of the material city mirrored in the city's representation of itself, upon James's and Margaret's entry, as a heavenly place, in its display of the relics that signify its blessedness, in its magical fountains pouring forth wine. The angels may, moreover, have sung the words of the poem by Dunbar known as "Now fayre, fayrest off every fayre":

> Now fayre, fayrest off every fayre,
> Princes most plesant and preclare,
> The lustyest one alyve that byne,
> Welcum of Scotland to be Quene![54]

As is true also of the York pageant, sovereignty here is presented as paradisally pleasurable: bodily vibrancy, aliveness, sensuality are the means whereby sovereignty can be distinguished ("The lustyest one alyve that byne").[55] But they are also the grounds for—they explicate—the community's desire for her; she has been singled out as "fayrest," her beauty—in anticipation of the pageant of the Judgment of Paris—legitimating the community's choice. In the last stanza, she becomes "the floure of oure delyte!" (l. 14); and, adumbrating the pageants of the Virgin, "Oure secrete rejoysyng frome the sone beme" (l. 15). Both "secrete" and a communal possession, Margaret is welcomed within the paradisal space of Edinburgh as herself an enactment of a sensuous ideality; at song's end, no longer a "Younge tender plant of pulcritud" (l. 5), but an embodiment, a sensualization, of delight whose choiceness and chosenness take the community into retreat behind the threshold of intimacy ("Oure secrete rejoysyng frome the sone beme"). At the threshold of her inclusion into the community of Scotland—for this is the significance of her reception in Edinburgh, Scotland's preeminent town—we find that she is already inside, so interiorized as to be incandescent, thereby so special that she belongs to everyone. For she is, as queen, finally an effect of feeling, of "rejoysyng."

The song "Now fayre, fayrest off every fayre" is the only text that can be connected even speculatively with the Edinburgh pageants. Of the other pageants, therefore, we can say little beyond trying to establish the range of meanings on which they might have drawn. The subjects chosen — the Judgment of Paris, the Salutation and Marriage of the Virgin, and the Four Virtues — seem, at first glance, to have little in common. But as we have already suggested, reparation is an important concern in each, as is the related issue of choice. We have argued that Scotland, in undertaking a marriage with England, itself had to choose to break with its past and revise its hopes for the future; in both the Judgment of Paris and the Salutation and Marriage of the Virgin, the question of historical redemption hinges on an extraordinarily consequential choice. And as we shall see, the pageant of the Virtues also addresses the anxieties of crossroads, of starting over.

The Judgment of Paris

Of the pageant of the Judgment of Paris, John Younge tells us only that it was placed near the freshly painted cross "in the Mydds of the Towne," where was also located the "fontayne, castynge forth of Wyn": "Ny to that Crosse was a Scarfawst maid, wher was represented Paris and the Three Deessys, with Mercure, that gaffe hym th Apyll of Gold, for to gyffe to the most fayre of the Thre, wiche he gave to Venus" (289).[56] He also notes elsewhere that in the chamber in which Margaret held state following her bridal Mass, the "Hangynge" represented the "Ystory of Troy Towne" (295). The Judgment of Paris seems to have been a theme considered specially relevant to queens. As is true also of the Four Virtues, its appearance among the Edinburgh pageants is an early instance of what was to become an important theme in pageantry.[57] A Judgment, composed by Nicholas Udall, appeared among the pageants for Anne Boleyn's entry into London in 1533.[58] In it, Paris explains that he believes Venus to be the most beautiful: "But suddenly he espies a fourth lady, Queen Anne, who is yet more worthy of victory for in her are united riches, wit and beauty, 'Whiche are but sundrie qualities in you three.' Nevertheless, he concludes, the golden apple is too insignificant a prize for her worthiness — 'to symple a reward a thousand fold.'" For Queen Anne there will be a better reward, one which cannot be conferred by Paris nor "geven here in this place"; as Anne leaves, a "ballad was sung repeating *ad nauseam* that the Queen, who united 'passing beautie,' 'chastitee,' 'high degree' and 'gret riches,' was truly peerless and that: 'The golden ball / Of price but small, / haue venus shall, / the fair goddesse, / Because it was / To lowe and bare / ffor your good grace / And worthynes.'"[59] The Judgment was also used frequently to compliment Queen Elizabeth; John Reeves notes, among numerous other examples, the wedding masque attended by Elizabeth which was performed at Bermondsey to celebrate the marriage of Francis Radcliffe to Thomas Mildmay, in which the "poet-presenter" (Thomas Pound) is instructed by Venus to confer the apple given her by Paris on the bride, the "fairest where she goes." The poet complies, but only after protesting repeatedly that there is one "'fayrere nowe in place,' whose radiant beams would make the brightest star seem pale."[60] George Peele's *Arraignment of Paris* likewise flatters Elizabeth by presenting her with the contested apple.[61]

Margaret Ehrhart, in *The Judgment of the Trojan Prince Paris in Medieval Literature*, remarks that "the sixteenth century brought a striking shift in applications for the Judgment. The theme . . . most commonly . . . served . . . as a device for the flattery of ladies. . . . but in the thirteenth, fourteenth, and even fifteenth centuries, all but a few references to the Judgment came too heavily laden with allegorical freight to allow the comparison to pass as a compliment."[62] The Judgment is an extremely complex tradition, and, once again, we have no text for the Edinburgh pageant and hence no ability to guess which aspects of the tradition it was most interested in or in what way, if at all, the pageant was used directly to compliment Margaret. It is possible that the Edinburgh pageant used the Judgment of Paris as a negative example of a mistaken choice, a false gift. More likely, it was used to pay a compliment of the kind featured in the pageants mentioned above. But while Ehrhart is certainly right to suggest that medieval traditions of the Judgment were critical of the choice that brought on the Fall of Troy, the discontinuities between medieval and Renaissance treatments of the theme should not be overemphasized — nor should the consciousness of Renaissance writers of the need to rewrite the Judgment be underemphasized.

Ehrhart herself notes that when the Judgment began to be used in medieval literature, first by Latin poets of the eleventh century, it suggested to Godfrey of Reims "graceful compliments"; his *Satyra de Quadam Pella Virgine* anticipates the flattery of later treatments by arguing that if the lady whom the poem compliments had accompanied the three goddesses to the Judgment, she would have won the prize.[63] Conversely, the Italian humanist Convenenvole da Prato, a teacher of Petrarch's, draws on medieval associations of the goddesses with witchcraft in a poem included in the *Panegyricus* for King Robert of Naples: Pallas refers to Venus as "That Medea"; Venus, seducing Paris, says, sotto voce, "It will not happen that I will be grateful to you, truthful with a true gift" (Ehrhart notes that Medea was "famed in medieval tradition as a witch").[64]

In Benoit de St. Maure's *Roman de Troie*, the mystery of the goddesses is presented in a slightly different, though related, way. Paris is led to the site of the Judgment by a stag that eludes him, leaving him separated from his hunting party; the motif, writes Ehrhart, "corresponds to an episode, found in early Irish literature, which Rachel Bromwich has identified as a dynasty myth: 'the intended ruler was set apart from his companions (in the stories he is separated from them in the hunt, either by nightfall or by a magic mist), and would inevitably and in spite of deceptive appearances, come together with the goddess representing his appointed territory.'"[65] As will be true of James IV's tournament of the wild knight and the black lady, it is a question of whether sovereignty, and the woman who represents her, will show herself "in the end beautiful," or whether her beauty will prove to be deceptively fascinating, her gift treacherous. In this sense the Judgment might be seen as a test of the young man's right to rule; the Judgment overturns the hierarchy of divine and human, presents the mystery of the goddess's need and choice of a mere mortal, in order to sanctify the mortal man's power to choose.[66] The Judgment is a test, too, of whether the goddess is a witch, or whether her powers of alteration are sanctified, for life rather than for death. Thus in Peele's *Arraignment*, Elizabeth is both sovereign and queen, and her beauty has a paradisal power of alteration; but according to Henry Lesnick, Peele has not forgotten medieval interpretations — for example, the *Ovide Moralisé*, which links the Judgment with the fall of Adam and Eve, above all with "the fall of Everyman, the individual reenactment of our first parents' sin."[67] Lesnick writes: "The nature of the myth upon which the earlier [tragic] action is based and the paradisal quality of Elizabeth's realm, strongly suggest the Biblical account of man's fall and restoration. . . . Offering the apple to Elizabeth, is obvious flattery but the more significant flattery is seen in presenting Elizabeth as a descendant of Priam and the ruler of the 'second Troy,' restorer of the paradisal harmony of Mt. Ida and, by implication, Christ-like redeemer of Trojan progeny."[68] The pageants for Elizabeth and Anne discussed above also use the Judgment to suggest that the present queen (Anne, Elizabeth) is an improvement over past history, a better — indeed the best — choice. Like the *Arraignment* and the *Roman de Troie*, they find in the Judgment a narrative movement which foregrounds choice, designation, appellation as the means whereby mystification struggles to emerge into the clarity of status.

    J. C. Nohrnberg argues a connection between the three goddesses of the Judgment and the Graces, the latter of whom appear in book 6 of *The Faerie Queene*.[69] "Spenser's formulation makes the ideal beauty the one composed of the parts of different beautiful women"; on Acidale, the fourth Grace is endowed with many graces and eludes the kind of analysis undertaken by "partial Paris," who "discriminates among the goddesses' gifts and beauties."[70] In Jonson's *The Masque of Beautie*, the Elements of Beauty anatomize the "sundry parts" of Beauty, thus recalling the diversification of the one into the many that attends the moment of creation and thus pointing to the creator's power of continuous production. The Elements of Beauty are linked, in the concepts that inspire them, with the Graces: the one turns into the many, thus imaging the unfolding of ideality in materiality; but the many are but aspects of the one, folding materiality and change back into ideality and eternity of form. Beauty is the visualization of a set-apartness, a chosenness that is nonetheless inclusive. Giordano Bruno, commenting on the Judgment of Paris, remarks that the lover "compares his object, which contains and unites the qualities, characteristics and species of beauty to other objects which can only offer one, and besides, each one distributed among diverse individuals." Of the different "species of beauty" of the three goddesses, he adds that "with respect to the qualities which predominate in her, each goddess appears sovereign and outweighs her rivals."[71] Thus the Judgment's concern with beauty could be interpreted as a way of addressing the paradox of exclusive inclusivity and hence, in Bruno's account, the loving discrimination, through which the idea of sovereignty is constituted.

Whether the treatment of the Judgment is medieval or Renaissance, then, the problem of choice may be paramount. One of the most important classical interpretations of the Judgment, further elaborated in the Middle Ages, was the notion of the Judgment as a choice between three lives: Juno was associated with riches and power and hence with the active life; Pallas, with the contemplative life; and Venus, with the voluptuous life.[72] Themes of maturation and choice also characterize a number of late medieval treatments of the Judgment. For example, the *Espinette amoureuse* of Jean Froissart, the anonymous *Echecs amoureux*, and Lydgate's "rehandling" of the latter poem in *Reason and Sensuality* all feature youthful narrators who set out on the road of life and, confronted with the three goddesses, choose Venus, that is, love. Scottish works in this tradition include Douglas's *The Palice of Honour; The Kingis Quair*, a love allegory probably written by James I of Scotland, which subjects its youthful ruler to the instruction of Venus and Minerva in the art of true love; Dunbar's *The Goldyn Targe*, a poem closely related to Lydgate's *Reason and Sensuality*, which includes, among other pagan gods and goddesses, Venus, Juno, "Pallas and prudent Minerva," and presents the issue of choice in the form of a battle between "Resoun" and "Venus."[73] These works' use of the Judgment in treating the crisis of "passage" is also found in Spenser's book 6, which Nohrnberg associates with adolescence and whose hero Nohrnberg associates with Paris: "The pressure on the adolescent to focus on a choice of occupation makes itself felt in Book VI. . . . Calidore's sojourn among the shepherds . . . implies a choice of 'lives.'"[74] Thus late medieval love allegory and its development in the Renaissance suggest a further relevance of the Judgment of Paris to the pageantry of extraordinary marriage, in the form of the Judgment's capacity to foreground the critical onset of sexuality, hence to foreground the danger and risk of choice.

The Judgment is concerned with peerlessness, uniqueness, heterogeneity, and hence structure or status; it is likewise concerned to explicate peerlessness as a richness rather than an impoverishment of being. The Judgment brings out the danger of choice, the critical character of commitment: in choosing, some paths are closed to us, only one way is opened. Many interpretations of the Judgment suggest in one way or another that making the best choice, whether of virtue or of a woman, will involve gain, not loss. Choice, then, is represented as potentially reparative — for the promiscuous James, choice may cross over into commitment and lose nothing and noone thereby — and to speak of enrichment in this context would not be merely to use a figure of speech: exchanges of gifts thread their way through the Judgment and the traditions that surround and impinge on it (the gift of the apple, the gift of Helen, the queen as gift), and the Judgment thus becomes a way of meditating upon the adventurousness of choice in extraordinary marriage — the risks undertaken in accepting the gifts of strangers, the potential for catastrophic loss that is the obverse of the potential for paradisal gain. The Judgment suggests that one of the sovereign's powers of alteration must be the ability to judge the gift, to see through its allure if it is false, to recognize its beauty if it is true. This is his "exploit," his honor. If he wins his "aventure," he will win prosperity, increase, new life, a new golden age for his land and his people; discord (promiscuity) will no longer wend its way through (the king's) history but be forever banished. Sovereign choice will abolish rivalry. The queen, in turn, will triumph in the contestation of honor that takes the form of "rival beauties." Through the king's choice of her, she stands forth — emerges splendidly — as everything. The Judgment thus enables the presentation of reparation as well as loss: to choose the queen is not really to sacrifice, for no one can compare with her.

The Marriage of the Virgin

Younge reports that in the same scaffold that represented the Judgment of Paris "was represented also the Salutacion of Gabriell to the Virgyne, in sayinge *Ave gratia*, and sens after, the Sollempnizacion of the varey Maryage betwix the said Vierge and Joseph." Though no Scottish miracle plays survived the Reformation, they were performed, and we may at least guess that an Edinburgh audience would have been familiar with the kind of material represented for us by the York, Wakefield, and *Ludus Coventriae* plays discussed earlier.[75] Enough, perhaps, has been said in the previous chapter about the Marian literature to indicate its importance to the celebration of extraordinary marriage; the present discussion will merely elaborate a few points already mentioned.

There is an appropriateness to the Edinburgh pageants' placement of the Judgment of Paris and the Salutation and Marriage of the Virgin on the same scaffold. These pageants foreground the consequentiality of making a choice in determining the destructive or redemptive course of history. They correspondingly represent the intermingling of human and divine as an effect of choice. In the Salutation, as in the Judgment, hierarchy is mysteriously overturned, the divine revealing its need of the human, its dependence on human judgment; the human deciding not only for itself but also for the divine, in a moment of at least apparent freedom. It is possible that the Edinburgh placement of the two pageants was meant to oppose them, in effect reminding the populace of the devastating consequences of a wrongful union—of a politics of rape and rapine—in contrast with the salvific consequences of a rightful union, rightful not least because of its daring and apparent absurdity. Moreover, the crisscrossing of gender roles between these pageants—in the case of the Judgment, a divine woman is chosen by a mortal man; in the case of the Salutation, a mortal woman is chosen by a divine man—multiplies the unsettling effect of the unions of opposites represented within the pageants and thus creates a mobile array of potential identifications, an array further extended in the Marriage's yoking of Mary's youth with Joseph's age and in Joseph's surrogacy for the divine husband. The result is a complex of positions that would allow the easing of Scotland's anxieties about domestication and even feminization, so that, for example, if the Judgment served as antitype, the nation could perhaps, like Israel, experience itself as bride, identifying with the foreign Margaret and agreeing, in effect, to serve the purposes of its ruler and its God not only without shame but also with the honor of a compensatory identification with absolute sovereignty (subject, but therefore Subject). If the Judgment served explicitly or implicitly as praise for Margaret, however, Scotland could imagine itself having the power, because of its choiceness—that is, Paris's special fame as judge—to choose a supplicating goddess; and it could imagine itself not as joined to a strange and powerful woman but as served by a peerless handmaiden. In any case, the effect of the pageants' multiplication of opposites is as profoundly talismanic as it is exciting and unsettling. Through such means, Scotland's risk in marrying England might be mystified, the historical consequentiality of such a risk at once exaggerated and defused, at once made heroic and made secure.

The power of the story of the Salutation to assert the virtue of belief in the unbelievable, of trust in the mysterious — specifically of trust in mysterious unions of incommensurables, unions that promise, against all expectation and previous experience, a resanctification of history — is of obvious importance to a celebration of entry, a celebration that sought to address Scotland's anxieties about the "inglorious arts of peace" and foreigners bearing gifts and therefore sought to persuade the Scots that they might put credence in the promises of mysterious strangers without fearing for their identity and honor.[76] Thus the Edinburgh pageant of the Salutation and Marriage of the Virgin would, like the York play of the Annunciation, have associated the Virgin's consent not just with love of God but with the intense form of love that is belief: with Mary's ability to believe and especially her ability to believe in God's creativity, his power to create, in time, a great "people." In the York Annunciation Mary begins with doubts regarding God's miraculous capacity to transcend human reproduction: "Howe sulde it be, I the praye, / That I sulde consayve a childe" (ll. 168–69). After the angel's explanation she says:

> Of Goddis will I holde me payde;
> I love my lorde with herte dere,
> The grace that he has for me layde.
> Goddis handmayden, lo! me here,
> To his wille all redy grayd;
> Be done to me of all manere,
> Thurgh thy worde als thou hast saide.
>   (ll. 184–90)

The truth of the angel's speech, in which Mary readily trusts, becomes a version of the authenticity and hence the creative power of the Word. The Wakefield Annunciation also associates concepts of love, belief, consent, and sovereignty with willing surrender to the Lord's power of alteration: that is, through this vertiginous surrender to the unbelievable promises of mysterious strangers, Mary becomes servant, willing to fulfill the Word in her body, but also sovereign. Gabriel greets Mary as "qwene" "Of all virgins" (l. 80). When Mary consents, she says

> I lofe my Lord all-weldand;
> I am his madyn at his hand,
> .   .   .   .
> I trow bodword that thou me bring
> Be done to me in all thing
> As thou has told.[77]

In the mystery plays, the problem of incommensurability — the problem, in effect, of extraordinary marriage — is addressed in the form of an explicit preoccupation both with scandal and with credulity: Joseph must accept the scandal of his own union and of that of the Holy Spirit with Mary, in contrast with an implied audience of doubters unwilling to believe in miraculous pregnancies. Mary is herself, of course, the product of God's intervention in human reproduction — in *Ludus Coventriae*, she explains that God sent her parents "both seed *and* flowre" in her conception (ll. 63–64). The heraldic imagery of the thistle and the rose in Margaret and James's marriage celebrations stressed particularly the theme of union; on a more ambitious scale, the York play of the Annunciation glosses the image of dew falling from heaven, from which "the erthe sall sprede and sprynge / A seede" (ll. 42–43), as the union of Mary with the Holy Spirit and thereby the making of peace and accord between divinity and humanity:

> The dewe to the gode Halygaste
> May be remeved in mannes mynde;
> The erthe unto the mayden chaste
> Bycause sho comes of erthely kynde
> . . . .
> All this sall ordan thanne,
> That mennes pees and accorde
> To make with erthely manne.
> (ll. 48–51, 70–72)

Since, once again, marriage unites and suspends differences, its power thereby to produce peace and life is always a power for change; the exclusive association of marriage with peace and nature, moreover, belies both its power of agency and its artificiality as an act of (apparent) choice, of "culture."[78] Insistence on the peacefulness and naturalness of marriage — always at its height in "extraordinary marriage" — can, paradoxically, allay anxieties about the power of marriage to pacify, to change and create by imposing order on chaos. It can allay them by presenting the violence of pacification and civilization as pleasure, as repetition. The complexity and intimacy of the relations between peace and violence, civilization and nature, that constitute marriage are expressed not only in the stories of the Annunciation and the Marriage of the Virgin but also, in somewhat different form, in the myth of the marriage of Peleus and Thetis, the story which sets off the chain of events that includes the Judgment of Paris and the Trojan War.[79] The Edinburgh pageant of the Salutation and Marriage of the Virgin, yoked to the Judgment of Paris, enjoined upon its audience a preference for supernature, for the interventionist power of intention and choice — a power recoded, as the concept of a heraldic plant might suggest, as superlatively natural — while permitting a covert nostalgia and mourning for the "natural" in the sense of the habitual, that is, the habitual violence of the past, the familiar ease of being "fallen," and thus for the continuity of past with present, rather than the miraculous transformation of how things have "always" been. The Edinburgh pageants are at some level deeply aware, despite their conservation of royal power, that, just as much in its acts of peace as in its acts of war, sovereignty pursues an "active star" and separates itself and its subjects from the past.[80] The pageant of the Virtues takes up again the theme of sacrifice more explicitly from the standpoint of the sovereign.

The Four Virtues

"More fourther" on from the scaffold on which the Judgment of Paris and the Salutation and Marriage of the Virgin were staged, Younge tells us,

was of new maid One other Yatt, apon the wiche was in Sieges the iiij Vertuz. Theys is to weytt, *Justice,* holdynge in hyr right Haunde a Swerde all naked, and in the t'other a Pair of Ballaunces, and she had under hyr Feet the Kyng Nero: *Force,* armed, holdyng in hyr Haund a Shafte, and under hyr Feete was Holofernes, all armed: *Temperance,* holdyng in hyr Haund a Bitt of an Horse, and under hyr Feete was Epicurus: *Prudence,* holdynge in hyr Haunde a Syerge, and under hyr Sardenapalus. With thos war Tabretts that playd merrily, whill the noble Company past thorough. Under was a Licorne and a Greyhound, that held a Difference of one Chardon florysched, and a Red Rose entrelassed. (289–90)

Though the Four Virtues were, as Anglo puts it, "an ancient iconographic tradition" — having appeared, for example, as bridesmaids to Philology in *Marriage of Mercury and Philology* — the Edinburgh pageant is an early instance of their use in civic pageantry.[81] Anne Boleyn's coronation pageant of 1533 featured a pageant of the Four Virtues as well as the Judgment of Paris; the Four Virtues "addressed the Queen in turn, promising never to leave her, 'but to be aydyng and comfortyng her.'"[82] Elizabeth I's entry into London in 1559 included an illustration of her descent in the form of "a vast rose tree of the houses of York and Lancaster," as well as a pageant of the Virtues defeating their relevant Vices and a pageant showing "a withered and a flourishing landscape to typify a good and bad commonwealth."[83] The use of the Virtues in pageantry is a development of the *Speculum principiis* tradition, for the Virtues were linked consistently, as Elizabeth's pageant itself suggests, with good government. Elizabeth "had herself painted wearing a robe embroidered with eyes and ears to symbolize the vigilance of the royal Justice."[84] Samuel Chew notes that "icono-graphically, the antithesis of Justice is Tyranny" and cites the Edinburgh pageant as an instance of the use of the antithesis between Justice and Tyr-anny as "a cautionary 'mirror for magistrates.'"[85] Chapter 22 of John of Salisbury's *Policraticus* argued "That Without Prudence and Watchfulness No Magistrate Can Remain in Safety and Vigor, and That a Common-wealth Does Not Flourish Whose Head is Enfeebled."[86] John Higgins, a continuator of *The Mirror for Magistrates*, links the Four Virtues together: Of Justice he writes, "If she be not constant, which is the gift of Fortitude, nor equal in discerning right from wrong, wherein is Prudence, nor use proportion in judgement and sentence, which pertaineth to Temperance, she can never be called Equitie or Justice, but Fraude, Deceit."[87]

The spectacular form of the *Speculum principiis* implies—as in Anne Boleyn's pageant—that the Virtues are, or will be, embodied in the prince being celebrated. As Roy Strong writes, "the fête enabled the ruler and his court to assimilate themselves momentarily to their heroic exemplars. For a time they actually became the 'ideas' of which they were but terrestrial reflections."[88] Bourdieu also stresses the importance of impersonation to the "exercise of gentle violence": "Authority, charisma, grace . . . are al-ways seen as a property of the person. . . . The illusion implied by per-sonal fidelity—that the object is the source of the feelings responsible for the particular representation of the object—is not entirely an illusion; the 'grace' which gratitude recognizes is indeed, as Hobbes observes, the recog-nition of an '*antecedent grace.*'" Bourdieu argues that the "'great' are those who can least afford to take liberties with the official norms"; "the price to be paid for their value is conformity to the values of the group." "The system is such that the dominant agents have a vested interest in virtue; they can accumulate political power only by paying a *personal* price, and not simply by redistributing their goods and money; they must have the 'virtues' of their power because the only basis of their power is 'virtue.'"[89] In this formulation of the homogeneity of "dominant agents," Bourdieu takes too little account of their equally pressing need for heterogeneity and, indeed, of the heterogeneous aspects of the very perfection of homoge-neity demanded of the great. That is, greatness involves the exacerbation of the alienating effects of becoming "civilized," of assuming social iden-tity—in Lacanian terms, the sacrifice of "being" to "meaning." This exacer-bation, displayed in part through the alienated form of the Virtues' con-quest of their "relevant" vices, provides opportunities for the heroization of greatness and for the delectation of its specially arduous forms of loss. Thus the virtue of the sovereign may be understood as a heroic repudia-tion, but equally as heroically sacrificial (Henry V, Aeneas) or as the product of a tragic discipline (Lear). In any case lamentation for the price of greatness – the cruelties or blindness of higher destiny – will not necessarily and inevitably constitute critique but may just as readily invite, from subjects, a mournful pride in the travail it takes to rule them.

In official pageantry, the Virtues signify the difficult transactions of heterogeneity and homogeneity that sovereignty demands; in order to be of extraordinary value to the culture of which it is a part, sovereignty must exemplify communal values to an extraordinary degree, and to take up the identity of sovereign greatness will be, correspondingly, an extraordinary task. A discipline, an ascesis, is required of the ruler. The use of abstractions like Virtues in secular pageantry thus enables the embodiments and disembodiments of sovereign love. Just as plays of the Annunciation represent an extraordinary intermingling of flesh and ideality – and a preservation, at the same time, of the boundaries between them – so the secular pageant enacts the metaphoricity of the princely body, a metaphoricity which has at least a double value. That is, through this metaphoricity the princely body arrogates to itself a full panoply of abstractions, so that the "natural" body of the prince can at special moments actually be figured as transfigured, as the body politic; but through this same metaphoricity the prince "cuts off" vice, is therefore understood as always in relation to vice, and seems to undergo his duress. Marriage, to the degree that it ritualizes a social transformation of personhood, becomes an opportunity to glorify both the gains and the losses ascribed to such transformation. Edinburgh stages a pageant of the Virtues triumphing over their Vices; James himself makes a special effort at the time of the wedding to acquire devotional and theological works.[90] In Dunbar's *The Thrissill and the Rois*, Nature demands that James IV give up his unofficial sexuality; *The Thrissill and the Rois* makes clear that, in embodying virtue, in choosing the best of all flowers – Margaret – something will and must be sacrificed – all other flowers, which when compared with Margaret seem but weeds. Marriage and virtue share the crossover between freedom and constraint, sacrifice and pleasure.

Thus in the theology of virtue, choosing and willing are of paramount importance; when one is virtuous, the will is repaired, made new, so that the choice of the good becomes a "deep-rooted condition," a "habit," but a habit which enables and enlarges the purposes of the will.[91] Virtue is understood as the means by which aspiration is defined and realized; as reparative of the Fall, virtue is the means to (officially sanctioned) creative activity; in Thomistic thought, each of the four cardinal virtues is opposed to one of four "wounds of nature."[92] Thus, for example, Thomistic teaching on temperance saw the "sensory perceptions and feelings man has generically in common with the animals" as "subsumed in the singleness of his substance under the seeing of meaning and the making of choices, and so become specifically human, *rationale per participationem*" (NCE 13:986). Though temperance is, more than any other virtue, betwixt and between, all the virtues are imagined to be enacted at crossroads; their interdependence, insofar as they become habitual, is thought to enable us to cross thresholds and make choices without being engulfed by crisis. It would be fair to say that moral theology proposes to guide us through life in large part by articulating and managing the changefulness of life, so that our entitlement to the designation "human," our entry into the human community, is figured as a willed transformation enacted through the exercise of a paradoxically fundamental power of choice and may be figured as a willed (but, paradoxically, bestial) failure of will.

In the later Middle Ages and the Renaissance, the idea of virtue was — as Jonson's *The Masque of Queenes* suggests — inseparable from the idea of honor. The anonymous *Enseignement de Vraie Noblesse* (ca. 1440) stresses "prudence, justice, continence, and *force* that some call *magnanimité*" as the means both to fame and to salvation; force, in the form of "physical courage and fearlessness," is "considered a talisman against the horrors of war," against its chaos and constant inconstancies, fortunes and misfortunes.[93] The Virtues arm the ideal body against the passions and vulnerability of the natural body, and thus are presented as guiding us through threatening, risky, extraordinary changes of life. Hence they are included in pageants for extraordinary marriage and are associated in the Edinburgh pageants with the Judgment of Paris and the Annunciation. It is useful, moreover, to recall that the Edinburgh pageant of the Virtues involved a prominent heraldic display of the thistle and the rose: "Under was a Licorne and a Greyhound, that held a Difference of one Chardon florysched, and a Red Rose entrelassed." The culminating spectacle in the Edinburgh pageants linked the heroism of virtue, the travail of the great in their paradoxical quest for a supremely communal identity, with the question that was of paramount importance to the marriage of James and Margaret: the question of national identity. As Priscilla Bawcutt notes, "the Thistle symbolises the duty of a king to guard his people effectively and to protect them from invasion."[94] The association of the Virtues with the thistle and the rose suggests the Virtues' talismanic power with respect to the perils of greatness: Scotland could be assured that, by repudiating the violence of the past, by opening and risking its borders, it would, surprisingly, triumph over its enemies. It is appropriate that, a century later, when James VI of Scotland, newly crowned James I of England, entered his new capital city of London, the four Virtues were paired with the four kingdoms of Britain — England, Ireland, Scotland, and France — a device called by an arch illustration "Cozmoz Neoz," "New World."[95] When an English queen enters Scotland, when a Scottish king enters England, the world is, indeed, potentially newer; and while these entry pageants present change as renovation, as return to paradisal beginnings, they also attempt to remake rulers, to "cast the kingdoms old / Into another mould."[96]

8

Speaking of Love: *The Parliament of Fowls, The Kingis Quair,* and *The Thrissill and the Rois*

BEFORE proceeding to discussion of *The Thrissill and the Rois*, the poem apparently written by Dunbar for the occasion of the wedding of Margaret Tudor and James IV, it will be helpful to establish a comparative context by first considering Chaucer's *The Parliament of Fowls,* an important source for both *The Kingis Quair* and *The Thrissill and the Rois;* the unique ending to the text of the *Parliament* found in the Bodleian's late fifteenth-century manuscript Selden Arch B. 24, the only surviving Chaucerian miscellany of Scottish provenance; and *The Kingis Quair* itself, a love-allegory which incorporates important motifs from the tradition of the Judgment of Paris and which is likewise preserved in Selden Arch B. 24.[1]

The love-vision in Chaucer's *Parliament of Fowls* largely consists of a love-debate between three of the "foules of ravyne" (l. 323) present at the Parliament called by Nature, aristocratic eagles (one is "royal") all suing for the hand of a lovely young female, or "formel," eagle.[2] Each of the male eagles speaks a lyric declaration of love in furthering his claim; other, less noble birds — seed-eaters and worm-eaters — also gathered at the Parliament to find mates, witness this lyric contest, while Nature personified sits in judgment. The eagles' debate attempts to establish sovereignty — sovereignty in love — through a discourse which admits rivalry and private desire. Sovereignty must be earned through the truth of one's discourse; the lyric of avowal — the lyric that enunciates the truth of the Subject's desire — is therefore the genre that mediates argument. The motifs of the complaint express a bid for power in the form of the authenticity, the certainty, of the lover's devotion; that certainty is in turn proclaimed through the lover's capacity for privation.

The royal tersel beseeches the formel eagle

> of merci and of grace,
> As she that is my lady sovereyne;
> Or let me deye present in this place.
> For certes, longe may I nat lyve in payne,
> For in myn herte is korven every veyne.
>
> (ll. 421–25)

Through the gap of yearning which separates lover and beloved, the lover constitutes the beloved as herself "sovereyne." Yearning creates the interiority, the subjective space, in which the sovereign in turn emerges as such because of his desire, because of the movement of his will. His desire is given space and mobility through the movement of yearning and is given the authenticity of flesh through pain: "For in myn herte is korven every veyne." The image, by bringing together lack — in the form of the cut — and the materiality of the body, turns the vibrant heart of flesh into an articulated space for the movement of the will. The tropes of complaint celebrate absence, lack, negativity; they disfigure the beauty and strength through which the aristocracy in general, and the sovereign in particular, must be imagined, yet in doing so they encode the quintessentially courtly claim to the sovereignty of love and thereby bring out the dependence of sovereignty upon lack as well as fullness. Suffering from what styles itself as real illness — as somatic disorder — the unnamed *finamen* is both a body and a voice — a voice whose authenticity depends upon the striations and suffering of its body — and hence is a site wherein the voice of the sovereign and the body of the subject are brought together, through self-inflicted suffering. The lover is sovereign because he chooses his pain, and that quality of his pain that seems to be inflicted from the outside — by the absence of the beloved — serves only, in the end, to certify his desire: the beloved, as ideal, as inaccessible, is constructed as such by the will of the lover.

But as body transformed by lack, by negativity, the lover is unrecognizable, unnamed; the voice of the *finamen* utters its own unworthiness to speak, loudly proclaims its inability to speak of itself, appeals to a symptomatology of lack — even of a lack of identity — to authenticate its sincerity. At the moment when the sovereignty — the certain being — of the loving subject is proclaimed through its love, its identity is obscured. The sovereign lover, though "royal," must finally await recognition by the beloved to be recognized as such — as unlike others, supreme. He must, like the wild knight in James IV's tournament, emerge from obscurity and anonymity because he must be recognized to have been extraordinary, superreal, all along; yet his extraordinariness must emerge as a function of a mutuality of desire, to free love from the taint of obligation, expectation, exchange. In this recognition by the beloved, there will be — enabled by the "tact," the mystifying modesty, of the sovereign's disguise as one of a field of striving supplicants — the response of freedom, love elected, uncoerced, reciprocal: the formel eagle would have her "choys al fre" (l. 649).

If it is pure choice, in the absence of any expectation of reward, that enables the sovereign to emerge as such, then, Chaucer's poem suggests, it will be the incapacity for purity of choice that will identify the realm of bestial nature and of the lower classes, whose bodies are insufficiently striated by the absolute pain of longing, whose voices are thereby inauthentic, and whose time is thereby short. As in Altieri's *Li Nuptiali,* human love is distinguished from that of the beasts by its capacity for "sacrifice," for an absoluteness of dedication to one's choice that signifies itself as such by its unconcern for anything else: this one exists for and through that other by choosing it endlessly, "longingly."[3] The rhetoric of absence enables, in *The Parliament of Fowls,* the endlessness of complaint, its inscription of a closure forever deferred; Chaucer's poem narrates this deferral by emphasizing the length of the eagles' complaint. The dreamer remarks:

> Of al my lyf, syn that day I was born,
> So gentil ple in love or other thyng
> Ne herde nevere no man me beforn —
> Who that hadde leyser and connyng
> For to reherse hire chere and hire spekyng;
> And from the morwe gan this speche laste
> Tyl dounward went the sonne wonder faste.
>
> (ll. 484–90)

The courtly complaint is valuable because it wastes time. It spends time magnificently; the economy of complaint is that of aristocratic display.[4] It encodes aristocratic leisure, *otium* — surplus time, a form of wealth — by refusing to economize time. The absurdity of yearning thus has economic and temporal forms: the "social efficacy" of time, Bourdieu writes, is "never more potent than when nothing *but* time is going on."[5] If "what distinguishes the gift from mere 'fair exchange' is the labour devoted to *form*," and if form necessitates the ability to occupy time with style and gesture, then an elaboration of endlessness and an endlessness of elaboration is how the sovereign lover pursues his freedom and masks — lays down, graciously — his coercive power. It is, moreover, through such means that the sovereign lover transforms the moment of choice into an eternal bond.[6]

In contrast with this temporality of splendid privation — in which nothing is expected, exchanged, demanded, in which there is nothing but want-ing — *The Parliament of Fowls* presents the urgency of the commoner, who spends time only to make time, whose avian (subhuman, nonaristocratic) desires brook no deferral. The lower-class body of desire cannot wait: it is unfree, impelled, lacking in the interior space of lack inhabited by the will. The reaction of the lower-class birds of the Parliament to the eagles' "gentil ple in love" is therefore a plea for closure: "Have don, and lat us wende! / . . . / Whan shal youre cursede pletynge have an ende?" (ll. 492, 495). The ignoble subjection of lower-class desire to a temporality of ex-change (courtship as investment in the future) is insisted on by the "gentil" birds: "Thy kynde is of so low a wrechednesse / That what love is, thow canst nouther seen ne gesse" (ll. 601–2). Ignorance is the epistemological form of insentience, of matter unaware of itself, unawakened into subjec-tivity: only the "gentil" birds possess a certain knowledge of the experience of love, and only they experience its paradoxically painful vitality.

The sovereign lover possesses a special body capable of deferral and lack; it can endure, because it so chooses, and its endurance is the mark of its special aliveness, its power of alteration over its own flesh. Because it de-sires, it lives beyond the limits of mortality, in contrast with the kind of "wormes corupcioun" (l. 614) represented by uncourtly birds like the cuckoo and the duck — who, again, cannot wait, and whose impatient discourse, as one of the "gentils" remarks, comes "Out of the donghil" (l. 597). Bodily exigency — the mortal body, the body subject to time — is projected onto the lower classes, giving them a language that is barely language, unauthori-tative, as close to the body as possible: scatological. The sovereign lover's endless complaint, his body of perpetual desire, appropriates negativity and loss to elaborate a sempiternal order of privation, a condition that transcends history and the bourgeois time of the clock. The body of the sovereign lover alone feels the pain of continual desire, the pain of a desire so special that the body can be imagined as dying of that pain, for that desire. It is a body that can endure a special kind of death, unknown to the commons, a body subject to a kind of mortality that, like the sacrifice of martyrdom, transcends temporal exigency. And since it is only worth dying for that which is most precious in life, dying for love paradoxically marks the body of the sovereign lover as intensely alive.

This special body that can "die by love" is manifested through a discourse akin to that of hysteria, a readable symptomatology of yearning. The manifestation of these bodily tropes of longing authenticates the desire of the subject; the subject can appeal to the physical tracings of woe and suffering on his body as evidence of — in both senses of the word — his pas-sion. But, unlike the hysteric, the sovereign lover can speak his pain; and his ability to reinscribe the ailing figurations of the body in discourse — to make body and voice coincide — will be the source of the authenticity of his passionate style. The point, however, at which body and voice, ideality and materiality, coincide is a delicate one. If the body is not present in this passionate figuration, but only represented by it, then the sincerity of the passionate complaint may be undermined, so that the statement My heart is breaking becomes just a figure of speech. The corpus of the text figures the absence of the body; the movement into discourse threatens the sovereign lover's power of alteration, his power to make body and voice coincide, hence threatening his heterogeneity, his priority. The impotence of a bodiless rhetoric appears simultaneously with the figure of the rival and the rival's appropriation of the sovereign lover's discourse; it may be impossible, then, to pierce the sovereign lover's disguise, to recognize the special certainty of his being, his difference from other men.[7] In the lyric poetry of the earlier Middle Ages, the slide in signification which threatens to empty the lover's lyricism of bodily meaning results in an intensification of tropes of passion until the lyric subjects the speaker to an erotics of masochistic torment.[8] The more exquisite and incurable the pain, the greater the claim of the *finamen* to authenticity. But the risk of thus appropriating pain for certitude is great, for the final paradox of this negative discourse of power can only be imagined as the extinction of the subject of desire: a chosen extinction, hence an image of absolute freedom. The aristocratic power of injury is inflicted on itself, yet at that very moment it puts an end to yearning. The seriousness of this risk will produce, in Dunbar's poem, an attempt to protect the boundaries of body and voice, and an attempt — through a poetics of marriage rather than of desire — to produce "new life," rather than death.

For in Chaucer's poem the endlessness of yearning produces its own impasse: it preserves the sovereign lover but permits the intrusion of rivalry, of failures of cognition and recognition. Deferral — actual postponement — is thus used in *The Parliament of Fowls* to narrate impasse, articulating endlessness with the promise of a future "moment of royal choice." Chaucer expresses the impasse to which the body of negativity brings aristocratic power through the rival lyricism of his three eagles. The "royal" tercel — of the three eagles the "Most of estat, of blod the gentilleste" (l. 550) — is given priority (he speaks first), a lyric of special beauty, and Nature's voice for his election. Nature explains to the formel eagle, "If I were Resoun, thanne wolde I / Conseyle yow the royal tercel take" (ll. 632–33). The poem thus establishes a connection between sovereignty and literary authority: monarchy might neither wish nor need to argue its claims in order to emerge triumphant from debate. The sovereign text tries to authenticate itself through a rhetoric in which the subject *is* sovereign, and the desire of the sovereign is equated with "commune profit," so that all is folded into the one, communitas into structure. Ideally, the moment when the sovereign articulates his truthful desire is a pacifying, civilizing moment: it resolves disagreement, puts an end to old habits of violence, to wildness. Yet the lyricism of the sovereign subject never conclusively emerges from anonymity in Chaucer's poem; the birds of the Parliament, even the "gentil terslet," have difficulty distinguishing between the rival utterances of the three eagles:

> Ful hard were it to preve by resoun
> Who loveth best this gentil formel heere;
> For everych hath swich replicacioun
> That non by skilles may be brought adoun.
>
> (ll. 534–37)

The length of the eagles' complaints is thus further overdetermined: it expresses paralysis as much as splendid expense. The "replicacioun" of the body of negativity brings out the aggressivity of the mirror image, the alienation which threatens to undo identifications with images of power.

And yet the risks taken by sovereignty in this poem make identification possible: *The Parliament of Fowls* negotiates the difficult relation of a sovereign to its aristocracy—negotiates, that is, a particular kind of likeness within which a particular difference (sovereign heterogeneity) must emerge. "Common profit" will depend upon how this relation is negotiated: whether the sovereign will emerge as such, or whether his anonymity will be destructive. The relation is negotiated by liminality—a royal eagle whose superior authenticity is nonetheless left to await the recognizant choice of the formel eagle; a decision deferred. The communitarian elements in the poem—the eruption of baseborn locutions like "Ye queke" (l. 594), the anonymity of the lovers, the formel eagle's freedom of choice, the extent to which "structure" must lay down its distinction to achieve a "common" purpose (the birds must all await the outcome of the eagles' contention)—serve structure, but with considerable delicacy and at the risk, as we have indicated, of uncontrolled aspiration, the social form of desire. If sovereignty is to authenticate itself in this poem, it must do so through a pluralized discourse; and though we are assured of the return of occasion, the eventuality of choice and therefore of commitment, by the formel's agreement with Nature and by the circularity of the roundel which closes the poem—"Now welcome, somer, with thy sonne softe" (l. 680)—the overall effect of the poem is nonetheless stippled by disquiet, by passion. The royal eagle does not fully emerge from "replicacioun," and through the formel's indecision, the end of the poem figures choice only in its absolute purity: disengaged from respects of fortune, from cognizance, from reason, it is mysterious, unrationalized, even arbitrary. *The Parliament of Fowls* reads sovereign love as adventurous: as exploit, the more so in the delicacy of its inconclusion. The dependence of sovereign love on the formel eagle's consent is actually the measure of the extraordinary quality of the love of supreme authority, its privileged "willingness" to risk unusual alliances, to attempt the crossing of perilous bounds into uncharted territory, to solicit the heart of a foreigner — of an unknowing and unknown woman. The poem's daring version of sovereign love would have been even more suspenseful if the *Parliament* allegorized actual negotiations for the wedding of Richard II and Anne of Bohemia, at a time, it will be recalled, when distrust of alien queens was comparatively high.[9] Chaucer's poem is, then, close in spirit to the *Fyancells'* portrayal of James IV's courtship of Margaret Tudor, "flyinge as the Bird that syks hyr Pray," even though James's courtship took place within the context of a sworn agreement. Both the Selden manuscript version of the *Parliament* and Dunbar's *The Thrissill and the Rois* largely eschew adventurism and — as seems to have been the case also with James IV's tournament and Dunbar's tournament poetry — suggest how the patronized poet (or scribe) will sometimes take on, or be given, the task of conserving power, homogeneity, and reason for a sovereign identified with pleasure. *The Kingis Quair,* on the other hand, will show how too much real-life adventure might make a sovereign long for the legalization of passion.

The Selden Arch B. 24 manuscript is itself — along with the "Thirteenth Book" of Gavin Douglas's *Eneados,* the Edinburgh pageants for Margaret and James's wedding, and *The Thrissill and the Rois* — an important contribution to the arts of marriage in late medieval Scotland. It is thought to have been written for Henry, Lord Sinclair, whose kinsmen were important participants in James IV's wedding; and Roderick Lyall has suggested "that the occasion for the gathering together for this collection of love poems was the marriage of Lord Sinclair to Margaret Hepburn, which took place some time before December 4th, 1489."[10] The manuscript's text of *The Parliament of Fowls* features an ending unattested, to my knowledge, in any other version of the poem. The ending which it offers is consistent with the idea that the manuscript was prepared for a marriage and points in interesting ways to Dunbar's own revisionist concerns in *The Thrissill and the Rois.* As we have already suggested, the harmonious circularities of the roundel that closes the Parliament in Chaucer's poem are not fully earned by the preceding narrative; its welcome to summer and its celebration of the passing of winter offer a closure of fertility — of "new life" — that is only obliquely resonant with the reading of sovereign love undertaken in the poem. By welcoming new life, the roundel — as would be consistent with an interest in the meaning of *betrothal* — celebrates the return of occasion, of the moment, and gives the poem's deferral of choice the strength of promise, even of expectation, which is as far as the *Parliament* will go in crossing over from choice to commitment. The Selden text of the *Parliament* similarly, but with greater intensity, recodes the risks taken by sovereign lyricism in Chaucer's poem: whereas the *Parliament* can only anticipate the rite of passage, the Selden text denudes it of its changefulness. In this ending, Nature offers no freedom of choice to the formel eagle. Instead, a peacock intervenes and recommends that the royal eagle win his lady; then, he says, each other bird may choose his own mate, never to change his lady for a new. Nature agrees with the peacock, saying that she does not wish the Parliament to be delayed by debate any longer. The birds fly off with their mates to their respective haunts; the text closes with a circular return to the beginning of the poem and a still-reading dreamer.

This new ending responds to the questions raised in the *Parliament* by certifying the lyricism of the noblest eagle of them all. The Selden text of the *Parliament* argues that the sovereign eagle's poem — his utterance of the truth of his desire — is able to distinguish him from, to set him above, all others and therefore is able to pacify, to civilize, to bring his people into a future of peace and prosperity. The Selden text further affirms the "sincerity" of the beautiful formality of the sovereign speaker by silencing other voices: the formel eagle, in particular, is erased from this text, so that the reciprocity of choice which stands as the central mystery of Chaucer's poem gives way to a sense of inevitability. In the Selden text the sovereign will be loved *because* of something, because he is sovereign. Circularity replaces dialectic as the mode by which coercion and exchange, enemies to the freedom of love, are made to disappear.[11] *The Kingis Quair* — like Dunbar's *The Thrissill and the Rois* — also celebrates this understanding of choice: choice as a bond that, in marriage as in rule, is strong enough to re-create personhood and thereby to make constraint into freedom.

The Kingis Quair was probably written by James I of Scotland (r. 1406–37) "about the time of his . . . marriage to Joan Beaufort in 1424."[12] Like Boethius's *Consolation of Philosophy*, which the poet of the *Quair* mentions at the beginning of the poem, the *Quair* is about vicissitudes of fortune, freedom and constraint, dependence and independence. James I languished in captivity for eighteen years because his imprisonment served England's interests and the interests of those governing Scotland in his absence. His love for Joan Beaufort — and, according to John Parsons, the intercession of Henry V's bride Katherine of Valois — hastened his release, probably because the resulting alliance might continue to bear fruit for a Lancastrian England in need of potential allies.[13] But James's dependence on such considerations for the freedom that allowed him at last to exercise his sovereignty is nowhere to be found in the *Quair*; the *Quair* instead celebrates the narrator's heaven-sanctioned love for Joan Beaufort as the power that released him from his prison and encouraged him to take hold once again of the wheel of change. James thus takes about as far as he can the tendency of Boethian prison literature to substitute the authority of the sovereign self for the constraints of "iron bars." Inner governance, and fidelity to a higher power, displaces English control of the young king's will; James's task both as sovereign and as subject was clearly to contend with how much of England there was, not only surrounding him but also within him.[14] Thus the poem's narrator is instructed in his quest for a more kindly Fortune by both Venus, goddess of love, and Minerva, goddess of reason; and the *Quair* shares with other love allegories that treat the Judgment of Paris more fully a concern with the reparation of the will, with the perils as well as the opportunities of those critical moments in which desire awakens.[15]

The *Quair* is a rich conspectus of the art of sovereign love.[16] It tells the story of the process by which the prince becomes a poet of love; his entitlement to marital bliss, which depends upon his proper understanding of the creation (and on which in turn depends his culminating identification with the Creator who has given him "lyf"), is inseparably bound up with the freedom that will allow him to return home and exercise his sovereignty. His adventure becomes his security ("sekirnes"), his doubts certainties. By the end of the poem his vision and his desire have been reconciled with

> the fatall influence
> Causit from hevyn, quhare powar is commytt
> Of gouirnance, by the magnificence
> Of him that hiest in the hevin sitt;
> To quhame we thank, that all oure lyf hath writt,
> Quho coutht it red, agone syne mony a ȝere
> Hich in the hevynnis figure circulere.[17]

Desire and the law, captivity and freedom, are harmonized; choice in *The Kingis Quair* provokes crisis but is also the means to its resolution. The narrator will have a guide for the "aventure" of his life; his earthly beloved can steer him, provided that his love is also steered by God. The element of risk, of the future's uncertainty, is strongly emphasized in the poem,

partly through its lengthy and vertiginous description of Fortune's wheel:
"And vnderneth the quhele sawe I there / An vgly pit, depe as ony helle";
"So mony I sawe that than clymben wold, / And failit foting"; "And sum
were that . . . / . . . to clymbe thair corage was no more" (sts. 162-64).
Partly, therefore, uncertainty is stressed through the courage clearly required for the narrator to ask for Fortune's help ("sche clepit me by
name, / And therwith apon kneis gan I fall," st. 166), partly through the
humor and the force with which she finally takes him "by the ere" (st. 172);
but all this adventuresomeness is part of a "lyf" that has been written "agone
syne mony a yere / Hich in the hevynnis figure circulere," and the poem
itself thus circles back to its first line.

The onset of desire in the *Quair* is at times full of torment and grief —
"Wofullest wicht and subiect vnto peyne" (st. 68) — and the lover vacillates
for a while between despair and hope. But the onset of desire in the *Quair*
also marks the beginning of a reparative and consolatory strategy. The
Quair's Venus, accordingly, is truly a legalized passion: an astronomical
deity, part of the orderly workings of God's Providence, intermediary for
— rather than rival of — Minerva. Not surprisingly, then, for the *Quair*-
poet, freedom means commitment: "sudaynly my hert become hir thrall /
For euer of free wyll" (st. 41). "Sudaynly" the *Quair*-poet makes up for
lost time and finds release in thralldom. Equally "sudaynly," after a period
of "Bewailling myn infortune and my chance" — the reference to Troilus
is clear — "my wit, my contenance, / My hert, my will, my nature and
my mynd, / Was changit clene ryght in anothir kynd" (st. 45). In contrast to Douglas's dreamer in *The Palice of Honour,* who fears that Venus
"suld throw hir subtillyte / In till sym bysnyng best transfigurit me," the
Quair-poet welcomes metamorphosis through the power of his "hertis
quene."[18] With the exception of the *Quair*'s habit of lingering on and
repeating the moment of conversion — it is both difficult and wonderful
for prisoners to awaken to their freedom — the luxuriant delay of the *Parliament* (and of lovers like Troilus who prove their truth through perpetual
yearning) has no place in this captive's poem, a poem which authorizes
love not so much through love's ability to yearn forever as through its
eagerness to get on with it. In Chaucer's poem, the birds are all too ready
to sing, and keep on singing; the *Quair*-poet's near-hysteria at the "Slug-
gart" nightingale's delay in singing makes the conventional *Natureingang*
into a sweetly funny but deeply appropriate plea for the beginning of loving speech.[19] In the *Quair,* the alternative to despair is a time either cosmological, absolutely secure in its patience, or a time urgent with effort.

The *Quair*-poet thus must prove the strength of his will, must be tested
and examined, and here again the poem offers effort, uncertain outcomes;

Venus says she will not send him on to Reason unless he is sincerely and fully committed to his choice. Minerva, too, has to test the narrator, because it is so difficult to tell lovers who "mene wele" from those who are "variant" (st. 137): "Opyn thy hert therefore and lat me se." And there follows the narrator's lyric declaration of the "kynde" of his "loving"—the *Quair*'s analogue to the speeches of the three eagle-lovers in Chaucer's *Parliament*.[20] In contrast with the *Parliament*, though, the *Quair*-poet's lyric is conclusive; this is a lover who has had far too much of "variance," who can hardly wait for—who ardently seeks—"sekirness." Thus Minerva's instruction in the art of Christian love discriminates, once and for all time, the true lover from the false: "Ground thou thy werk therefore vpon the stone, / And thy desire sall forthward with the gone" (st. 131). In Chaucer's *Parliament*, Nature remarks to the formel eagle, "If I were Resoun, thanne wolde I / Conseyle yow the royal tercel take" (ll. 632–33). James I's Minerva, being Reason, knows how to identify a sovereign lover.

Moreover, no troublesome rivalries emerge. The Judgment of Paris is not fully present in the *Quair* precisely for this reason, and the scene in the *Quair* which recalls that of Palamon and Arcite's first sight of Emelye, and their first falling-out, takes place inside the *Quair*-poet's head; rivalry is subsumed by a perplexity capable of clarification.[21] Nor are there questions about the consent of the beloved: the *Quair*-poet's "hertis quene" remains a completely silent vision of "Beautee eneuch to mak a world to dote" (st. 47). The phrasing is characteristically ambitious.[22] And though the voices of women of power are heard in Venus, Minerva, and Fortune (the latter is the most forbidding of the three and is the structural replacement for Juno, the female ruler in the Judgment trio), they are as much forces in the *Quair*-poet's internal quest for order as they are forces for order in the universe. Even Fortune falls into line; thus if Joan Beaufort had any power to leave James in prison by refusing his suit, or Katherine of Valois by refusing intercession, such dire possibilities have been completely rewritten by this revisionist poem. The English "hertis quene" is an agent for change, even for crisis, but this time for a crisis that will free the king rather than jail him. When his heart suddenly becomes her thrall "For euer, of free wyll," it is, he tells us, because "of manace / There was no takyn in hir suete face" (st. 41). The anxiety of English as well as of queenly influence emerges in the final stanza of the *Quair*, which commends the book to "my maisteris dere, / Gowere and Chaucere, that on the steppis sat / Of rethorike quhill thai were lyvand here, / Superlatiue as poetis laureate / In moralitee and eloquence ornate" (st. 197). This address is conventional enough, but it is still a careful negotiation of James's sense of indebtedness to English culture and his desire to suc-

ceed in its superlatives. *The Kingis Quair* is very much the king's book;
it celebrates an ultimately certain choice, the authority of sovereign love
and of the sovereign word, and it has no time left for the delectation of
obstacles.

The *Quair*'s celebration of legalized passion was the obverse of James
I's passion for legalism; Nicholson writes of his reign that "nothing was
too momentous or too inconsequential to escape legislation."[23] James I's
impatient and "masterful" style of rule was to a large extent inspired by
the wish to do for Scotland and its sovereign what centralized administration had done for England, perhaps also by the wish to be in England's
place — in the place of the master of fate, rather than that of the helpless
victim of fortune.[24] The law truly was the form of James I's desire, the
best-loved instrument of his ambition — the means by which he tried to
write his fate, and the means by which he tempted it.[25] Nicholson writes:
"The swing of the pendulum from the laissez-faire of the Albany gover-
norship to the authoritarian totalitarianism of James's personal rule was
too violent to go unchecked."[26] James was "before" his time partly because
he had lost so much time; his exercise of power was both intensely ordered
and futuristic. As would later be true of James III, James I's tragedy was
one of innovation; and he was brutally murdered by eight nobles who
apparently felt that such newfangled ideas as his plans for an English-
style parliament were in fact part of an assault on baronial freedom. His
"authoritarian totalitarianism" did not succeed in pacifying the habit of
violence.

Dunbar's *The Thrissill and the Rois* begins with a sleeping dreamer, thus
marking its relation to the dream-vision genre of *The Parliament of Fowls.*
But Chaucer's poem begins by musing on the mysteries of literary history
and the meaning of the "Drem of Scipioun"; the dream is inaugurated by
the textual "other" through the presence of "Affrican."[27] Dunbar's poem,
in contrast, makes no mention of the past, of previous writers, of "olde
bokes," or of a desire — Chaucer's dreamer cannot quite find what he is
looking for in his "olde bokes" — that is unmet. Dunbar's dreamer has a
different problem; at first, he desires nothing at all. *The Thrissill and
the Rois* will reject the space of yearning for an eternalized temporality,
which — recalling Chaucer's roundel — banishes both the literary past and
the variable weather of earlier spring months. The "variand windis" of
March are already past (l. 1). Variance, disorder, conflict — the explosive
power of the "union of contraries" — are already recuperated, distant. Belatedness, then, puts Dunbar's poem in a position already past the fear-

fulness of beginnings and endings: it is now the month ruled by "lusty May, that muddir is of flouris" (l. 4).

And May herself — the literary convention of the springtime opening, here personified as a figure of sovereign power — appears by the dreamer's bed to make a demand. Dunbar, like the *Quair*-poet, owed a great deal to his English queen, and May will require him to "discryve" Margaret.[28]

> Slugird, scho said, Awalk annone for schame,
> And in my honour sum thing thow go wryt;
> The lork hes done the mirry day proclame
> To rais up luvaris with confort and delyt;
> 3it nocht incress thy curage to indyt,
> Quhois hairt sum tyme hes glaid and blissfull bene,
> Sangis to mak undir the levis grene.
>
>   (ll. 22–28)

However paradisal the setting, then, Dunbar's poem gives us a moment in which problems of creativity and createdness, freedom and constraint, desire and obligation, abound. The springtime opening created and re-created by so many poets appears here not as a construct but as a super-real authority, with the power to oblige; poetic creativity crosses over into "convention," and the poet becomes the creature, the servant, of his own imaginings. The problem, according to May, is one of desire: once the poet wanted to make "Sangis . . . undir the levis grene," once desire coincided with expectation, devotion, with "honoring" the sovereign. Now, so disconnected is it from fulfillment, so empty the space in which it floats, that the dreamer seems in a state of lassitude.

The poet is subjected, as Lacan might say, to the desire of the other; the poem, likewise, will be a text whose narrative course is defined by the desire of the other, specifically by the desire to use the language of the poet to serve the other's meanings. Dunbar, like Foullis in the *Strena*, is subjected to a discipline whereby his own voice becomes an instrument for the discourse of sovereignty: the poem which follows, then, is an "observance" (l. 37). It fulfills a duty, performs a service, answers a demand; and as subjected to the desire of the other, it is subject to the time of the other. One must, to begin with, write an occasional poem "for" and "by" the occasion.[29] Moreover, the connection between spectacular poetry and "service" is made early on in Dunbar's own definition of the purpose of the *Thrissill*: "to discryve the Ros of most plesance," Margaret Tudor (l. 39). The term *discryve* brings together the ideas of writing down, delineating, and picturing with (from the verb *descry*) ideas of proclaiming, making known, announcing as a herald. Dunbar's poem is, in effect, a heraldic proclamation whose spectacular figurations of the sovereign text meet the desire of the other; like Lacan's Hamlet, Dunbar's dreamer "wears another man's colors."[30] Hence he experiences lassitude, the empty space of his own desire.

But from this state May would "Awalk" — awake — the dreamer, in a moment analogous to the awakening of human sentience and consciousness in Eden (and to the awakening of the *Quair*-poet's own desire). Beginning, in Dunbar's poem, is imagined as a rite of passage in the form of (re)birth, of being (re)created as a desiring, free creator by the sovereign demand that authorizes, rather than "shatters," his "self-transformation into a separate verbal or material form."[31] The poet's subjection to the desire of the other will be read as the creation of a creativity, as a freedom. This, too, is enjoined upon him by the dictates of sovereign love. For the poet must rewrite the demand as his own desire, his own promise, his own free gift. The poem in service transfigures its captivity, represents itself as a freely dedicated presentation copy. The structure of *The Thrissill and the Rois* is that of the demand transfigured as freedom, as gift to the sovereign, as "beginning" with the choice of the subject: even when — perhaps especially when — the desire of subject and sovereign are so closely identified, the response of love must still be decipherable.

Dunbar's first response to May's demand is a rivalrous one, in the form of an alternate representation:

> Quhairto, quod I, Sall I uprys at morrow,
> For in this May few birdis herd I sing?
> Thai haif moir caus to weip and plane thair sorrow,
> Thy air it is nocht holsum nor benyng;
> Lord Eolus dois in thy sessone ring;
> So busteous ar the blastis of his horne,
> Amang thy bewis to walk I haif forborne.
>
> (ll. 29–35)

Dunbar's complaint brings out what Lacan would think of as the alienation of being by meaning and language: the springtime convention, the written text, accords not with the experienced physical reality of the Scottish spring, even in May. *May* is just a name, whose relevance to the body's certain discomforts is achieved only by insistence and imposition. *May*, that is, is inauthentic, disembodied, lacking in certainty, mere "voice"; the voice of the dreamer, on the other hand, speaks with the authority of discomfort, speaks from the body, in a bid for the coincidence of these commonly polarized terms.

Dunbar's presumption is not answered through discussion or debate, but through a repetition of the demand:

> With that this lady sobirly did smyll
> And said, Uprys and do thy observance;
> Thow did promyt in Mayis lusty quhyle
> For to discryve the Ros of most plesance.
> Go se the birdis how thay sing and dance,
> Illumynit our with orient skyis brycht.
>
> (ll. 36–41)

Once the demand has been accepted, the rhetorical springtime opening will triumphantly transfigure the landscape by generating a garden in decorous fulfillment of May's language, "most dulce and redolent": "The purpour sone with tendir bemys reid / In orient bricht as angell did appeir" (ll. 50–51). Dunbar gives poetic language a power of alteration: his solution to the gap that opens between signified and signifier in the lyricism of Chaucer's *Parliament*, and in the grumbling observations of his own dreamer, is to distance language from body and world in order to inhabit and experience both in language. Language will acquire a power of alteration through its formal beauty, the interior elaborations of its style; as spectacular, it claims a vitality, a certitude, precisely through its power to re-represent the world, to create what C. S. Lewis called a "world of beautiful forms".[32] May's demand transforms disagreement into marvelous scenic display; the rich description of the "purpour sone" appearing "bricht as angell" (ll. 50–51) pictorializes the power of Dunbar's ambitious vernacular. The eloquence of the poet bespeaks national triumph: in the Old Testament, it will be recalled, God's power of alteration is exercised over land as well as people, originally through his creative Word; Dunbar, the newly created and creative poet, will create and enter a Scottish paradise of words, once his antimasque is over, thus revivifying both land and people — nation — through his power to "discryve."[33] Time, too, is transfigured in this eternal garden, this image of immutable union, not "variance," between past and present: the birds simply do sing and dance, and the authority of Dunbar's earlier, bleaker description is now so weak as not even to require rationalization. Dunbar's spectacular aureation tries to give to language a glorious, incorruptible body, a body that has transcended "the body of this death": it is a sensuous ideality rather than an idealized sensuality.

Essential to the scenic shift from antimasque to masque is, as we have argued, the restructuration of the poet's desire according to the demand of the sovereign other. The demand itself — the gap between the desire of the subject and the sovereign — must be transfigured. May accomplishes this through an insistence on psychic continuity, creating an interior space in which accession to the demand may be experienced as the coincidence of the subject with himself. At first May demands only that the poet make past and present agree by behaving as he used to do — that is, by making the "sangis" he was "sum tyme" happy to create (ll. 27–28). But after Dunbar's rebellious outbreak, May responds with a more powerful strategy, rewriting her own demand as the promise made by the poet himself: "Thow did promyt in Mayis lusty quhyle / For to discryve the Ros of most plesance" (ll. 38–39). The promise erases difference, establishes identity, conceals the economies of mediation: to promise is to demand of oneself. Herein lies Dunbar's authenticity as poet: in being asked to fulfill his own promise, he is being asked to make good his word with his words, to become what he once intended, to be faithful to his bond. He will write as a loyal subject. The poem, then, transforms an unmet demand into a fulfilled promise; and as a fulfilled promise, the poem is at one with its occasion: the fulfillment of a promise to marry. Dunbar's dreamer has caviled, grumbled, disagreed, so that although, from this point on, the poet *is* spoken, resubjected to tradition — the timeless relevance of poetic language — we may, once again, delight in the moment and movement of his consent.

Once difference has been rewritten as identity, the "blisfull soune" of birds can be heard in the poem, the garden can be described, and Nature's parliament begins:

> Dame Nature gaif ane inhibitioun thair
> To fers Neptunus and Eolus the bawld
> Nocht to perturb the wattir nor the air,
> And that no schouris scharp nor blastis cawld
> Effray suld flouris nor fowlis on the fold;
> Scho bad eik Juno, goddes of the sky,
> That scho the hevin suld keip amene and dry.
>   (ll. 64–70)

The presence of Nature in a poem about the birth of creativity is unsurprising, since Natura had, by this time, a long history in meditations on the origins of life.[34] The very "personification" of Nature is important to our argument: as a "person," rather than an amalgamation of wild natural forces, she represents the introduction of concepts of will and intention to the process of creation.[35] As just such a mediating figure — bringing together a willed creativity with the insentient opacity of matter — she figures the union of ideality and materiality, the creativity of the bond between them. The universe is vivified through creative unification of opposites. In both the classical and medieval traditions, she is *pronuba* of marriages.[36] Nature is the imagined possibility of bondedness between body and soul, form and matter, immutable and mutable, creator and created, male and female. A figure of universal communitas, she is frequently identified with the whole, as the mother of "all."[37] To conceive of Nature as the principle of generation — "art is thine," says the tenth Orphic hymn to Physis — to the point at which she must herself be thought of as a product of her own artistry is, of course, to accord her a vast power of alteration. Christianity required that Nature be understood, not as a rival to the Creator, but as vice-gerent in the sublunary world. Economou notes that early "Christian writers and apologists reacted to and vigorously combated . . . Natura."[38] Writers like William of Conches and Alain de Lille made her apologize for herself: of God, in the *De planctu naturae*, she says, "His operation is simple, my operation is multifold; His work is sufficient, my work is deficient; His work is marvelous, my work is mutable; He cannot be born, I was born; He is the maker, I was made; He is the creator of my work, I am the work of the creator. He works from nothing, I beg from another. He works by His divine will, I work under His name."[39] We are reminded that to serve is to be restricted not only in will but also in creativity; it is to be created, derivative. Creation, on the other hand, goes hand in hand with governance — with the extension of will through the world. The notion of Nature as servant to divine creativity enabled the annexation of her productive and reproductive powers by a God who could thereby maintain distance from materiality and reserve for himself the disembodiment of an inscrutable but certain intention; it enabled, too, the communitarian celebration of a unified creation, of bonds that created unities, while preserving hierarchy. It is comprehensible, then, that such a figure should preside over a poem whose subject is the creativity of servant and sovereign.

For, as a communitarian figure, Dunbar's Nature is well folded into structure. Dunbar's Nature is characterized neither by the sensuous materiality of Physis ("Heav'nly, abundant, venerable queen, / In ev'ry part of thy dominions seen") nor by her divine remoteness ("To all things common, and in all things known, / Yet incommunicable and alone"). She is present, but primarily through her powers of verbal command over the presence and absence of her subjects. In Dunbar's poem, Nature's creativity, like that of the poet, proceeds by means of language. Through "inhibitioun" (official prohibition) she forbids the presence, in the transfigured space of the ceremonial, of "Eolus the bawld" — that figure whose "blastis" the poet complained of earlier in his antimasque negation of "fresche May." That Eolus — the representative in this poem of rival weather, "variand windis" —

must be twice condemned to nonmanifestation suggests the antipathy of this poem to wild, uncultivated, uncontrollable, changeful nature — to nature, that is, as opposed to scenery.[40] Dunbar's Nature is an attenuated materiality indeed, and her queenship is a sign, paradoxically, of her service to a distant and distancing ideality. When Nature calls her Parliament — "Scho ordand eik that every bird and beist / Befoir hir hienes suld annone compeir" (ll. 71–72) — "All present wer in twynkling of an e." The performative power of Nature's language — its power over all that might be thought to resist language, over the need of natural bodies to move through space and exist in time, and its transformation of a wish into a law that speaks for all ("All present wer") — is expressed through the harmonizing of origins and ends written by apocalyptic closure.[41]

In the realm of Dunbar's Nature, the poles of life are pressed very hard indeed; the poem's elaboration of its origins and its sudden evocation of the Last Judgment make the poem, in at least this restricted sense, over almost before it begins. The poem thereby politicizes the Pauline promise of renewal:

Behold, I show you a mystery: We shall not all sleep, but we shall all be changed, in a moment, in the twinkling of an eye, at the last trump: for the trumpet shall sound, and the dead shall be raised incorruptible, and we shall be changed. For this corruptible must put on incorruption, and this mortal must put on immortality. So when this corruptible shall have put on incorruption, and this mortal shall have put on immortality, then shall be brought to pass the saying that is written, Death is swallowed up in victory. O death, where is thy sting? O grave, where is thy victory? (I Corinthians 15:51–55, KJV)

The spectacular figuration of Dunbar's poem eternalizes the body of power by signifying its power of alteration, its triumph over death, its transcendence of human necessity and "nature." Transfiguration — "turning into glorious form" — intercedes between the ephemeral occasion and eternity not by the promise of return, as in Chaucer, but by tracing figures "situated neither in time or space."[42] Transfiguration, moreover, addresses the risks of change brought out in transitions, in the crossing of thresholds, rites of passage. We are, in effect, being assured that marriage to an English princess will not corrupt — not make mortal, subject to time — the incorruptible body of Scottish sovereignty. Transfiguration takes place "in twynkling of an e"; it is the change that negates change. And we are being assured that the "confrontation between worlds," between opposed states, implicit in the notion of passage, will issue, precisely, in union and identity: "All present wer."

Eolus figures not only "variand windis" but also the possibility of variance within the body politic and within the unity of persons enjoined by marriage. In the passage in which Nature banishes him, he appears in the company of Juno and Neptune, forming thereby the terrible trio that attempts to thwart the *translatio imperii,* the founding of Rome in the ashes of Troy and Rome's eventual ascendance over rival Carthage – a triumph which must be sealed by Aeneas's "extraordinary" marriage to Lavinia. *The Thrissill and the Rois* celebrates, through the marriage of James IV and Margaret Tudor (the marriage which eventually produced James I and the union of the Crowns) an imperial destiny, to which no threat can be brooked – not the dangers of James IV's own sexual adventurism, not the mystery, the difficulty, the risk of an alien bride.[43]

Nature's Parliament does not permit the "variance" of debate; most of the poem is spoken by her, and she speaks for all. Whereas Chaucer's female eagle speaks for herself, the *Thrissill* lets the Rose be spoken for: the identity of her desire with that of the sovereign, indeed with that of "common profit," is assumed. Nature addresses the Rose not with an interrogative, as in Chaucer, but with an imperative: "Cum, blowme of joy, with jemis to be cround, / For our the laif thy bewty is renownd" (ll. 153–54). The diction recalls the Song of Songs and its emphasis on the movement of desire; the Rose, the alien bride, will come, will arrive, through the movement of her consent. But it is only through her willingness to present herself that we can decipher her desire; it is not spoken, and unlike the Shulammite, she will be a desiring subject only insofar as her will has been merged with that of the community.

Perhaps even more striking is that the king, too, does not speak; sovereign desire – the will that defines the subject in its freedom – is folded into the "all," the "all" for which Nature, the very principle of bondedness, is the communitarian spokeswoman. By the same token, however, the "all" is folded into a perfect unity of identification, a merging of structure and communitas, of which the obverse is the nearly complete erasure of yearning, of the motions of the will, decipherable, again, only in the willingness of "all," including the Rose, to arrive, come, be present when called: to be "hailed," and thus to give a kind of body to the poem's assertion of the power of "voice," of language. Meaning is not alienated from being; to be is joyfully to present oneself as signifier, to respond to one's name. Arrival and presence are among the poem's chief ways of "embodying," of substantiating, its figures "situated in neither time nor space." The sovereign himself, then, need not strive to emerge from anonymity to achieve recognition: he need only appear. The unusual modesty and passivity, therefore, which characterizes Dunbar's king and queen, is the result of the poem's particular solution to the problem of responsive love that besets sovereignty in general: the solution, that is, of reducing choice to arrival and presence. Only through the commitments made by presence do we understand that consent has been given.

Dunbar's treatment of Chaucer's three eagles also reveals the poet's determination to avoid the *Parliament*'s poetics of yearning. The three eagles are displaced by three symbols of James IV: the royal lion (justice), the eagle (liberality), and the thistle (strength). The rivalry, the specular aggressivity brought out by yearning in the *Parliament*, is recuperated in Dunbar's poem by a kind of Trinitarian structure: the many are folded into the one, difference is seen as a richness, a multiplication of the certain being of power. The king's triple sovereignty, moreover, takes up the motif of the three estates, present in Dunbar's poem in the form of beasts, birds, and flowers: the tripartite structure of the body politic is mirrored in the triplicity of the monarch. Inequalities are at once recalled and erased in the bond created by the mirror. The sovereign sees, in the locus of the other, a representation of himself; in this perfection of identity he is his own other.[44] Dunbar's poem celebrates that aspect of the power of alteration which is the power of predication, of metaphor: heterogeneity and homogeneity are thus reconciled at one stroke; the sovereign cannot be "substituted" for, since, in the realm of metaphor, he "is," uniquely, multiple. Dunbar's triplication of sovereignty thus tries to assert a fullness of being in and through the very "irreality" of the monarch, his entitlement to a surplus figuration, a richness of imagination.

Thus the "Lyone, gretast of degre, / Was callit thair, and he most fair to sene" (ll. 87–88): Dunbar calls attention to the beauty of the heraldic *image* of the king.

> This awfull beist full terrible wes of cheir,
> Persing of luke and stout of countenance,
> Rycht strong of corpis, of fassoun fair but feir,
> Lusty of schaip, lycht of deliverance,
> Reid of his cullour as is the ruby glance:
> On field of gold he stude full mychtely
> With flour delycis sirculit lustely.
>
>   (ll. 92–98)

This stanza describes the royal arms of Scotland, the lion rampant; the perfection of the royal body, the fullness of its being — its life — is expressed in a heraldic symbol which links James IV to the greatness of his dynasty, to sovereignty in perpetuity. Here, "gretast of degre" has no difficulty — in contrast with Chaucer's poem — in pressing his claims to sovereignty; Nature crowns him "king of beistis" with the "dyademe full deir / Off radyous stonis" (ll. 101-2) and instructs him in the exercise of justice. Moreover, in this ceremony of identity, the crowning of the sovereign is greeted with immediate acceptance and rejoicing by all his subjects: "All kynd of beistis" (l. 114) pledge their loyalty. This rhetoric of inclusiveness is insistently replicated in the coronation of three kings — one for the beasts, one for the birds, and one for the "flouris that grew on feild" (l. 127).[45] The triplication of the sovereign body and the symbolization of that body — which in this text attests the power of that body in signification — present to us the magnificence, the excess, the wealth of the sovereign's being. He is indeed a sensualized ideality: his is the sensuality of the image, and it is through this kind of sensuality that the loving bond with the nation will be effected.

The representation of the sovereign's body through heraldic signifiers thus tries, as we have indicated, to resolve the problems raised in Chaucer's text by the representation of the body of the sovereign lover in the discourse of passionate complaint. The body of death, of the "gentil herte," is no longer body, but sensualized image: not pain, but the beauty of art, will be used to substantiate belief in and devotion to sovereignty. Speech does not need to authenticate its desire by refiguring a symptomatology; there is no danger that the subject's self-representation in discourse will be accused of insincerity, because the sovereign subject does not exist, in Dunbar's poem, outside discourse. In *The Thrissill and the Rois* the bodies of the sovereign *are* symbols; or, the symbols *are* the three bodies of the king. In the fictional locus of this poem, a ruby lion "actually" stands on a field, not of "flouris," but of gold. This is an embodied signifier, a signifier that tries to be at one with the signified by erasing the distinction between them.[46] The poem, once again, refuses yearning — absence — in favor of presence, appropriately enough, for this is a poem not of protestations and promises, of *sponsalia per verba de futuro*, but a poem of marriage, *sponsalia per verba de praesenti* — in the words of which inhere its sacramental power of alteration.

Thus in Dunbar's wedding poem the sovereign's triplicity assures his heterogeneity; he is the sovereign lover, he has no erotic rivals, he claims priority over the virgin body of the female. He only may be chosen, because to choose him is to choose life and being; he is all that can be chosen. Marriage to him signifies this inevitability of choice — choice is now unimaginable except in relation to him, both for queen and for nation. it is useful to recall at this point Lucas de Penna's analogies: "Just as Christ joined to himself an alien-born as his spouse, the Church of the Gentiles . . . so has the Prince joined to himself as his *sponsa* the state, which is not his." The king's relation to the state is here expressed as a marital union which recuperates the alienated ("not his") and the alien: the "alien-born" bride, the alien name (*allotrios*) of metaphor and of the female, is caught up in the identities formed by marriage.[47] The *sponsa*, the "Inglisch" Rose, thus enters Dunbar's text as, once again, virginally present for king and for nation; she has not even had to be fought for, and her alienness has been erased through the fundamental fact of her arrival.

In the closing stanzas of *The Thrissill and the Rois*, Dunbar's power of "turning into glorious form" is engaged in fulfilling the promise to "discryve" the Rose, Margaret of England. "Reid and quhyt" do not belong merely to the beauty of the *donna* of the love-lyric; they are "michty cullouris twane" (l. 172), and Margaret is the beloved not of the isolated and anonymous subject of the lyric, but, through her marriage to the sovereign, of dynasty and of nation, as is appropriate to a poem whose links with Margaret's royal entry must have been very close indeed. In this eternalized locus of national ambition (in which Scotland, in effect, domesticates England), the Rose serves as the heraldic equivalent of the Virgin Mary, as the female term in the display of superreal personhood. The diction describing her is unmistakably that of lyric celebration of the Virgin, itself saturated with images from the Song of Songs. She is

> Aboif the lilly illustare of lynnage,
> Fro the stok ryell rysing fresche and ȝing,
> But ony spot or macull doing spring.
> (ll. 150–52)

Margaret's coronation, too, is a "moment of royal choice," identified, as in the iconography of Mary Regina, with nuptial choice — however much, in Dunbar's poem, the subject that chooses is pluralized and the moment of choice is folded into commitment. The heraldic body of the "Inglisch" Rose, to be crowned queen of Scotland, is written by Dunbar in the lyric tropes which graced the most disembodied and yet perfectly bodied female of all time, the "place palestrall / Of peirles pulcritud."[48] In the apocalyptic moment of Dunbar's poem, Margaret appears with something of the force of the New Jerusalem, a spotless virgin, as Marina Warner puts it, "free of all of the taint and strife of all that has gone on before." Sovereign love, in *The Thrissill and the Rois*, demands an exclusivity of choice, a virginity that precludes rivalry, "variance"; the purity of the Rose's appearance, of her arrival, reminds us, too, that the Virgin was herself not only the perfect choice but also the perfection of consent. She appears, then, simply *as* beautiful, not as "in the end beautiful."[49] The queen's epithalamic "emergence into glorious light" merges the rite of passage, of change, with the moment of her appearance.

The hymn of praise which greets the coronation of the Rose, and which closes the body of the poem, is the grand finale of the power of sovereign love to work its alchemy of identifications.

> Than all the birdis song with voce on hicht,
> Quhois mirthfull soun wes mervelus to heir:
> The mavys song, Haill Rois most riche and richt.
> . · . · . · . · . · . · . · . · . · .
> Quhois pretius vertew is imperiall.
>
> (ll. 162–64, 168)

> The merle scho sang, Haill Rois of most delyt.
> . · . · . · . · . · . · . · . · . ·
> The lark scho song, Haill Rois both reid and quhyt.
> . · . · . · . · . · . · . · . · . ·
> The nychtingaill song, Haill Naturis suffragene.
>
> (ll. 169, 171, 173)

> The commoun voce uprais of birdis small
> Apone this wys: O blissit be the hour
> That thow wes chosin to be our principall;
> Welcome to be our princes of honour,
> Our perle, our plesans and our paramour,
> Our peax, our play, our plane felicite:
> Chryst the conserf frome all adversite.
>
> (ll. 176–82)

Whereas Chaucer's poem closes with a roundel, a secular lyric, Dunbar's closes with an elaborate hymn sung in parts by a full choir. In this choral display of a communitas purged of all threat to structure through the perfection of their mutual enfoldment, the birds can now speak as a communal *subject* because they speak as a *communal* subject; their song is the only instance of direct discourse in Nature's Parliament other than that of Nature herself. They celebrate their joy over the choice of the Rose as their "principall" in a poetry of identity, marked by repetition and "riche array." They sing in their "own" voice—as subject, as "person"—but sing in unanimity; gone is specular rivalry, lyric combat. They have the authenticity of the "all." The "commoun voce . . . of birdis small," moreover, never interrupts the poetry of sovereign love with lower-class humor and wry pragmatic observations, as in Chaucer, but is left undifferentiated as a voice speaking its glad subjection for an entire stanza: here is the response of love, the poem's most fully elaborated moment of consent to being bound, made possible through the collectivization of the consenting and loving subject. And it is, it must be stressed, through the arrival and celebration of the queen—whose capacity to signify both "variance" and "larger unities," whose identification with communitarian concepts like "nation" we have insisted on—that this vocal manifestation of the bonds of love takes place.

The poem, however, does not quite end like this; the poet goes on, in the final stanza, to tell us how

> Than all the birdis song with sic a schout
> That I annone awoilk quhair that I lay,
> And with a braid I turnyt me about
> To se this court, bot all wer went away.
> Than up I lenyt, halflingis in affrey,
> And thus I wret, as 3e haif hard to forrow,
> Of lusty May upone the nynte morrow.
>
> (ll. 183–89)

The ending is modeled on the final stanza of Chaucer's *Parliament*, which follows immediately upon the singing of the roundel:

> And with the shoutyng, whan the song was do
> That foules maden at here flyght awey,
> I wok, and other bokes tok me to,
> To rede upon, and yit I rede alwey.
> I hope, ywis, to rede so som day
> That I shal mete som thyng for to fare
> The bet, and thus to rede I nyl nat spare.
>
> (ll. 693–99)

In Dunbar's stanza we see a poet "halflingis in affrey" writing down a vanished dream; in Chaucer's, an unperturbed dreamer still reading, still hoping "to fare / The bet." The discontinuities of rhythm in Dunbar's stanza are sharply felt by comparison; the diction of the stanza is equally, with its colloquial monosyllables, a rude awakening from the graceful spectacular of the Rose's coronation. Closure, in Dunbar's poem, brings on discomfort: "And with a braid I turnyt me about." The cause of this discomfort is precisely the univocity of the birds singing in full chorus, the "mirthfull soun" which becomes a "schout." (In Chaucer's poem, it is not the singing of the roundel itself that awakens the dreamer, but the "shoutyng" "That foules maden at here flyght awey.") Dunbar's rewriting of the song itself as a source of rupture and pain seems to be an instance of poetic disquiet, of displeasure with his own insistent harmonies. The univocity of identity deafens; the poem is silenced by its own phonic power. The eloquence, the power of "turning into glorious form" conferred earlier upon the vernacular patriot-poet through his acceptance of creatureliness, ends not with the leisured assurance of return as in Chaucer's roundel, but with the abruptness of shock.

It is a strange moment, but whatever Dunbar may have meant by it, and however surprising it may seem even against the background of the many enigmatic endings of medieval dream-visions, it is nonetheless decipherable in the context of the poem's attitude toward the embodiments and disembodiments of sovereign love. As we have argued, from the moment of the creation of the dreamer's desire through its identification with the sovereign will of the poem, the text insists on the power of its fictionality, on its deployment of fantastic signifers (heraldic lions, bellicose thistles) — on the power to imagine and thereby to move beyond the ephemerae of real occasion. But this attempt to substantiate the superreality of courtly ceremonial through its irreality is purchased, again, at the price of a radical discarnation. At the end of Dunbar's poem, the superreal collapses into the irreal; and the strong separation Dunbar makes between "the body of this death" and the "world of beautiful forms" is fully brought out in the contrast between the somatic unpleasure of the dreamer's last moments and the abrupt passing of the ceremonial's perhaps vain show. It is almost as if Nature's Parliament had appeared only to disappear: the poem's claims about the simple fact of presence are vitiated by the striking rapidity with which its pageantry can be made absent. The poem ends, that is, by returning us to the "variance" between real or waking world and the world of dream and poetry, with which the poem began. Lewis reminds us that aureate terms "are in language what the gorgeous armours of tournament were in life."[50] In choosing "appearing," rather than pain and violence, as the source of sovereignty's authenticity, Dunbar has perhaps inadvertently stressed the fictitiousness of "distinction"— its dependence on illusion. The problem, brought out in Chaucer's poem, of the sovereign's relation to others, in particular to his aristocracy and his consort, has been transfigured in *The Thrissill and the Rois*, but not solved.

We might take Dunbar's last two lines — "And thus I wret, as ȝe haif hard to forrow, / Of lusty May upone the nynte morrow"— as an attempt to confer upon spectacle the substantiality of the artifact; the work of imagination becomes a "work." But the overall effect of the ending, I think, does not support such a reading. The paradisal rhetoric of the transfigured "body" of the poem can give us the pleasure of art, but the power of this fantastic body is finally given, not the substance of the artifact, but the insubstantiality of dream. We might, too, imagine that the monarch's possession of a natural body is marked by Nature's possession of the sovereign voice; but Nature is a perfected, Edenic Scotland, hostile to, rather than responsible for, "the body of this death." In *The Thrissill and the Rois*, sovereignty purchases glory through disembodiment, and its price is the complete absence of royalty's natural body—a price revealed by the projection of textual dehiscence and bodily discomfort onto the poem's beginning and ending. The repressed obverse of the glory of beautiful form is the reminder that all flesh is grass; thus ends the poem which charts the sacrifice of the court poet's will.

The abrupt tone of the ending of *The Thrissill and the Rois* seems, in a way, even more mysterious if we consider that the early 1500s, the time of Margaret and James's wedding, seem to have been felicitous for Dunbar: the first payment of his pension is recorded in May 1501, and "promise of a church post had placed him on the first rung of the royal favour." "This must have been a time of bright hopes for Dunbar."[51] Dunbar was, more so than Chaucer, a court poet, in the sense that his involvement in the daily life of the royal court seems to have been both intimate and longstanding.[52] He was also a priest. From this last fact we might conclude that poems such as "Quhat is this Lyfe?" "This Warld unstabille," "All erdly Joy returnis in Pane," and so forth, represent another Dunbar, the priest and not the courtier. "Court life was burdensome at times to Dunbar," writes Baxter; "Dunbar distrusted the seeming stability of human life."[53]

Possibly, then, Dunbar was torn between the demands of the world of vanities and the demands of a better world. But it seems unsatisfactory to describe Dunbar's poetic career as an attempt to negotiate the competing claims of divine and earthly kingdoms, since his preoccupation with the vicissitudes of worldly variance is shared by many court poets never called to the priesthood. The courtier-priest "dichotomy" is a version of a dialectic deeply embedded *within* court life. Chaucer and the *Quair*-poet, to cite only those writers discussed in this chapter, were deeply influenced by Boethius; it need not surprise us that poets so closely concerned with worldly power, and so dependent on it, should be fascinated with its vulnerabilities. Common enough in court poetry are denials as well as admissions of dependence on worldly power. Not only in Dunbar's work do we find attempts to preserve independence by identifying with a power higher than that belonging to the kings of earth. Appeals to an ideal court, appeals which sustain and seem securely to reward the labor of the subject-poet's loyalty by creating a gap between ideal and real which the poet can obsessively traverse, transform his disappointment, grief, or sense of dishonor into the work of satire; hence, the subject-poet experiences pleasure in "exposing" the illusions, hence the mortality, of worldly power— its subjection to the "same" vicissitudes that rule the subject. Thus Dunbar's poems on Edinburgh reveal the splitting whose function it is to preserve the ideal from inward as well as outward aggression. The vanity and filth

of the world are to be found in the city; the court with its king is somewhere else — in paradise. And yet the "Dregy" is a parody.

What does seem to set Dunbar's poetry apart is the extent to which splitting informs his poetic attempts to negotiate the strengths and weaknesses
of worldly power. It is for this reason, I think, that he was not much given
to extended narrative, but rather more so to poetic genres capable of isolating single moods. Alternatives can be kept apart in different poems (ex-
cruciatingly "preclair" praise, the wild defamations of flyting). Dunbar can
write, in "Memento Homo quod cinis es," that

> Worthye Hector and Hercules,
> Forcye Achill and strong Sampsone,
> · · · · · · · · · · · · ·
> Hes playit thair pairtis, and all are gone
> At will of God that all thing steiris:
> Think, man, exceptioun thair is none
> *Sed tu in cinerem reverteris.*

And in "The Ballade of . . . lord Barnard Stewart lord of Aubigny" he can
compare Stewart to "feyrse Achill in furius hie curage, / O strong invin-
cible Hector undir scheild." Such "variance" is not, in Dunbar, a matter
only of different moods on different days and occasions, or of sensitivity
to particular genres, or of repetition of conventional examples under different but equally appropriate circumstances. Variance is in his diction:
the conventional alternations of lines like "Nixt efter joy aye cumis sor-
row" ("This Warld unstabille") and "Als schort ane joy for lestand hevynes"
("Quhat is this Lyfe?") reappear on the level of poetic structure. His "aureate"
language, whose ambitious claim to produce a transfigured world is put
forward in the vision of the *The Thrissill and the Rois,* is cut off when
the poet is rudely awakened into the realization that he is alone — "bot all
were went away." Another contrast with aureation is found in the comparatively simple rhetoric of the "Lament for the Makaris," a poem in which
repetition and death finally reduce the world to the size of Dunbar's trepi-
dation. As often as not, when Dunbar finds himself alone, cut off from
the world, he tells us that he is in pain; but it is also true that in the isolation of his voice he finds his independence from the world on which he
depends for his life and livelihood. Variance, finally, appears in Dunbar's
poetry in such a variety of forms — alternation, opposition, antagonism —
that it becomes the measure of the strength of Dunbar's engagement with
alternatives, as much as of his desire to keep them apart. Variance is the
heart of Dunbar's attempt to bear, with honor, his need of a world to
which he was not essential.

Tournament

9

A Royal Legend:
James IV and the Historians

In his *English Literature in the Sixteenth Century*, C. S. Lewis writes the following memorable account of James IV:

> Though patrons cannot create poets, and though James was no great patron, it is deeply appropriate that the court poetry which will mainly concern us in this chapter should have been written under such a king; for in him and in it alike, as also in the dress and architecture of the period, all that is bright, reckless, and fantastical in the late medieval tradition finds superb expression. He was primarily a knight, only secondarily and disastrously a king. . . . His very vices were chivalrous. . . . He was mercurial, wilful, restless, and inquisitive; much like Arthur himself. . . . The price was Flodden, and if he half killed Scotland he did it in character.[1]

This striking portrait of James IV presents us with a king whose supreme interest lies in his ability to express the "late medieval tradition." James is seen, and admired, for his power of representation; his age is fully accounted for in him, and he is fully accounted for in it.[2] So forcefully does James embody his age that even the poetry whose patronage he neglected comes to be identified with him, and "his very vices were chivalrous"; even, that is, what James lacked and the ways in which he failed — his delusiveness and self-destructiveness above all — become part of the completeness with which James exemplified his times. Conversely, James becomes a brilliant historical figure for Lewis not only because James embodies his age so superbly but also because the age he embodies is itself specially marked by transience and loss — "bright, reckless and fantastical," a heroism marked for death. Looked at another way, therefore, James is made strange, irreal by Lewis's way of looking at him — "fantastical," so far from being superreal as to be not fully in touch with reality. Though James exemplifies his era, he is distant from whatever was really real in it, and thus he is deeply identified not only with loss but also with destructiveness; when he "half killed Scotland he did it in character."

James is so superb an exemplar of the chivalric style of his era that, paradoxically, he must be compared, not with the other European princes of his day—with the perhaps equally bright and reckless Henry VIII, for example—but with the legendary King Arthur. Lewis's comparison perhaps unwittingly points to James's legendary power—in other words, that James, as Lewis understood him, was not so much an accurate representation of his age as he was a legendary figure. And James's legend, indeed, seems to share some important features with the legend of Arthur. Arthur had united Britain into greatness, replacing the lawless violence and fragmentation of the past with the chivalric amity of the Round Table, enabling Britain to conquer even the Saracens; and yet all was lost, finally, through weaknesses from "within"—a friend and a wife who deceived, a nephew who was also a son—failures of faith, sexual sin, excessive intimacies linked in turn to the resurgence of uncontrollable private violence. It seems also to have been James's intention to unite Scotland into greatness: shortly after his marriage to Margaret Tudor, he undertook the pacification of Gaelic Scotland and became increasingly involved in European diplomacy; this period of his reign culminated in his tournament of the wild knight and the black lady, held at about the time (in 1507 and again in 1508) that James seems to have begun thinking seriously about crusade. Making himself legendary—giving his reign the narrative shape of legend— was an important part of James IV's art of rule, and Arthur was an important name to James.[3]

The sixteenth-century historian John Leslie gives the following account of the summer of 1508:

This summer, the king, baith on fute and horse, bot in persone of a stranger, prouoiket to the singular combat mony, quha maist valʒeant war esteimet; and als we speik, ay brocht away the palme. . . . He was of sik corage, that quhom evir he hard maist commendet in vertuous and valʒeant actes, he intendet and kaist, him ay to follow, bot heiring of not ane in ancient antiquitie amang al his predecessouris, to quhom he wald be sa conforme as to King Arthur; remembreng of King Arthouris knychts, and thair forme desyreng to follow quha war knychtes of the round table, that time he wald be called a knycht of King Arthuris brocht vp in the wodis; his luk and gret grace in vanquissing his ennimis, his wicht spirit in onsetting, wil testifie mony a combat with sindrie french men, and men of diuerse natiounis, in . . . Ed^r [Edinburgh].[4]

Leslie's version of the tournament may not be an accurate description of its events; no contemporary record of the tournament, at least, makes any specific mention of King Arthur or his Round Table in connection either with the themes or the form of the tournament of the wild knight and the black lady. Leslie's account is nonetheless, like Lewis's, part of the making of James's legend — an activity that was put in train by James himself, for attaining the status of legend is one way in which sovereignty can seek immortality in the very form of history.

In 1509, the year after the tournament of the wild knight and the black lady was held for the last time, James and Margaret named their second son Arthur, "the name once borne by Henry VIII's eldest brother, a name that was 'British' rather than Scottish or English."[5] Nicholson comments that this gesture was "hardly tactful," given the nearness of James and Margaret's issue to the throne of England and given Henry VIII's failure rapidly to produce an heir. It is likely, then, that when James and Margaret named their son Arthur, they had in mind Arthur's power to unify, to transform petty division into grandeur of vision. It is likely, too, given the context of the pacification of the Highlands and the Isles, that they had in mind Arthur's fame as peacemaker in his own land, subduing the cruel rivalries of lesser nobles, as that king who brought chivalry into being by spiritualizing violence, explicating and elaborating its links to virtue and community, distinguishing between autonomous criminal violence and violence done "for" peace, thereby allowing knighthood to retain its manhood — its wildness — but also to lay claim to being the source of civilization. Through his futurism, his institution of a new order that set itself against incest, rape, and private violence, the legendary Arthur offered a means of distinguishing between criminal and knight. But because his kingship was also a fulfillment of destinal forces, the legendary Arthur offered a means of heroizing royal ambition — that is, the king's desire for and power to change. In making himself a legend, James IV seems to have presented himself as a redeemer of time; for example, Pedro de Ayala, the Spanish ambassador to James's court, reported of James that "rarely, even in joking, a word escapes him that is not the truth. He prides himself much upon it, and says it does not seem to him well for Kings to swear their treaties as they do now. The oath of a King should be his royal word, as was the case in bygone ages."[6] The truth of the king's word would restore the lost fullness of the past. But James's legend, like that of Arthur, has a strongly elegiac flavor: both kings meet disastrous ends and by doing so bring an end to a brilliant age; both kings, at least in legendary accounts, meet their ends because of dark forces working from within, in James's case at least because of a too-great eagerness for battle, a recklessness. Both men, in effect, are punished for their greatness, for reach that exceeded grasp. But James's death at Flodden played a crucial role in immortalizing him through history: Leslie records the persistence, in 1571, of reports that James was still alive and journeying in distant lands; R. L. Mackie comments in *King James IV* that "the persistence of the legend is simply the measure of his people's need of him."[7] Through the promise of his return, the legend of Arthur also offered the hope of miraculous intervention as a way of understanding the ambition of monarchs to force the past and the everyday into new molds, and the power of resistance to such efforts.

Thus violence and peace, friend and enemy, the named and the unnamed, inside and outside, could, as Fredric Jameson puts it, be "grasped as alternatives." Arthurian romance is a "symbolic answer to the perplexing question of how my enemy can be thought of as being *evil* (that is, as other than myself and marked by some absolute difference), when what is responsible for his being so characterized is quite simply the *identity* of his own conduct with mine, the which — points of honor, challenges, tests of strength — he reflects as in a mirror image."[8] The legendary Arthur became an important means of figuring the confusions of aristocratic identity, partly because of Arthur's own status as a British king; that is, for the many kings whose object it was to beat the surviving remnants of a former Britain into submission rather than to lead them into triumph, Arthur, in his legendary role as civilizing symbol of new monarchy, provided a bridge across which identifications could travel and thereby a talismanic power against the British enemy "within." That a power both of identifying and of elaborating distinctions between friend and enemy would have been of intense value to James makes sense not only in light of the intimate violence of his campaigns in Gaelic Scotland — campaigns that would have put in question who was friend, who was enemy; who was inside, who was outside — but also in light of James's rebellion against his father, James III, the consequence of which was James III's death in what Pitscottie called "batell intestine." James IV never attempted discovery or prosecution of his father's killers; and yet both chronicle accounts and contemporary records attest the zeal with which he personally pursued the administration of justice, riding to attend the justice ayres which his unpopular father had tried to leave to deputies. Though justice had been viewed, throughout the Middle Ages, as the most sacred duty of kingship — and thus we might simply see James IV as trying to be, or at least appear, a better king than was his father, despite their shared willingness to sell pardons — the circumstances of his assumption of power gave James a special motive for attempting so thoroughly to incarnate the principle of justice in his own person. That he may have been responsible in some way for the death of his father and his king, however, was again itself to become part of his legend; for example, there is a story that he wore an iron belt in penance for his role in his father's demise.[9] And his tournament of the wild knight and the black lady also recalled, rather than denied, the wildness of James's youth. In its drive both to recapture a lost past and to legitimate ambitions for the future, it is as characteristic of romance to bring the son to the father, the knight to the king, as it is to articulate relations between friends and enemies. In a host of different ways, James styled himself as a son — even Leslie's account of the tournament of the wild knight and the black lady presents James as a knight of Arthur's, not as Arthur himself — though as a son who would be what the father should have been. James sought to show that he was not a criminal; but at the same time he could be a somewhat tragic figure, filled (at least on occasion) with remorse and self-doubt. He could, in other words, be both a wild knight and a king, his power to compel aristocratic identifications considerably enhanced by his willingness to romance the story of his life. Moreover, James chose chivalric spectacle as one of his chief means of presenting his subjects — and his future — with his history; the remainder of this chapter will, through further discussion of the themes of James's historical tradition, suggest some of the ways in which spectacle enacts loss for sovereign legend.

Like Arthur, James has been associated with "newness" — freshness, youth, impetuosity, "new monarchy triumphant." He has also, like Arthur, been associated with the past, the lost idyll, belatedness (he is "late medieval"), outworn forms of war (his desire, as at Flodden, to fight in his own person, or to go on crusade), "the aureate age and its end."[10] It is his status as representation of a fantastical past, as well as his incarnation of the brightness and recklessness of youth, that gives James his historical efficacy in Lewis's text: this doubleness allows Lewis to locate, in James, not only the spirit of a "tradition" but also its evanescence. Lewis's sentimental regard for a vanished age and art embraces James for the clarity with which he recovers what has been lost but, again, makes James fictional by virtue of his status as a recovery. Lewis's own writing plays out this paradox, appealing simultaneously to loss and recovery, identity and difference — to the pleasures and pains of transition. The poetry which it is his purpose to discuss cannot really be identified with James, and yet, gloriously, it can; the king is not really a king, but a knight. James is "mercurial." "All" that is "fantastical" — everything, that is, that is nothing — finds "superb expression" in Lewis's passage. The ideal image is captivating, brilliant, larger than life; it also has no essence. It is everything we might attain; it is also everything we have lost. The contradiction is not only played out in Lewis's descriptive terms but also narrated. For James's brightness and recklessness — for his extravagance — "the price was Flodden." Splendid description—the rich multiplication of adjectives—gives way to the briefest of statements and turns into the story of how a prodigal life ended in a prodigal death. The illusion and the disillusion, the idyll and the loss, the hope and the disappointment, can be contained in a story about the price of exhibitionism.

R. L. Mackie, in his biography of James IV, considers the king's identification with Arthur an important motive in the crusading fever that seems, ultimately, to have led to the battle of Flodden. "Arthur's task—to war with the heathen—would be his task too. . . . For 'the Crusade against the Infidel,' to every other sovereign in Europe, to the Pope himself, a useful phrase in the jargon of diplomacy, was to James something far different: he saw himself in the near future, leading a great fleet to the shores of Palestine, and then, at the head of the united forces of Christendom, advancing, sword in hand, against the Turk."[11] Mackie's James IV "saw himself" playing a fantastic and romantic role as rescuer and liberator. And Mackie's own portrait of James as a "moonstruck romantic," a quixotic figure whose desire to liberate the Holy Land puts him at odds with the cynical realities of the new diplomacy, is more or less reproduced by Alan Macquarrie in *Scotland and the Crusades*. In Macquarrie's chapter "Castles in the Air," we find that whereas other "Christian princes" only paid "lip service" to the "crusading ideal," with James it became "something of an obsession": "Alone among the princes of Europe he took seriously the Ottoman threat, and was also genuinely concerned for the wellbeing of the Holy Land."[12] One wonders whether Macquarrie thinks it was fantastic to take the Ottoman threat "seriously"—or whether, as seems most likely, what was fantastic about James's seriousness was the "medieval" form it took. For we find that Macquarrie's James IV (rather like Lewis's) is a "medieval" king left "stranded" amid the Machiavellian princes of the Renaissance.[13] James seems, again, somehow behind the times, his ambitions unrealistic—a prince who comes to stand for the passing of the old order and hence for fantasy as opposed to the hard realities of the new order. Dreaming and grandiosity are banished to the medieval past; contemporaneity is equated with realism, as though, after 1500, ideal images—exemplars, like sovereigns—suddenly lost their power to produce new economic and political behavior.

Macquarrie's concession that "for a brief period in 1511 . . . a united crusade could [just possibly] have been organized" suggests the beginnings of an attempt to reimagine the legend of James IV in a more complex way.[14] So, too, does his remark that "subsequent interpretations of the events of the previous five years are bound to be coloured by the magnitude of the disaster of Flodden." In other words, historians trying to estimate James's policies and behavior in the years leading up to Flodden have tended to read those policies and behavior in the light of James's final, and disastrous, "chivalric" exploit.[15] But even the terms of Macquarrie's revised portrait valorize realism. If James is to be rescued from the charge of irrationality, it will not be accomplished by questioning the status of the reality to which the appeal is being made, or by taking an interest in the productive power of fantasy, but simply by finding James to have been a little more realistic than has hitherto been supposed.[16] And Macquarrie finally blames Flodden on James's poor generalship: "As long before as 1498 the Spaniard Pedro de Ayala had detected the tragic flaw in James's military ability: 'He is not a good captain, because he begins to fight before he has given his orders.' The irony of Flodden is that it resulted from an attempt by James to prove to the world that he was a great military leader — and the result was catastrophic."[17] Once again, grandiosity leads to failure. Macquarrie briefly distinguishes between the folly of James's crusading ambitions and the folly of Flodden but ends by conflating the two: Flodden, in the end, has the same function in Macquarrie's narrative as it does in Lewis's — to finish James off with dramatic brevity and to leave him trapped in the gap between what was and what might have been, between appearance and reality, to which Macquarrie gives the name "irony."

Mackie's account of Flodden similarly views the battle as the end result of James's desire to lead a crusading army and emphasizes the king's poor generalship. Mackie cites contemporary accounts of the battle that blame its failure on the king's rashness: and he notes how, in another confrontation of the heroic with the Machiavellian, Surrey's appeals to the "knight-errant" in James (Surrey, not Henry VIII, led the opposing English forces) may have manipulated the king into disadvantageous battle positions.[18] Echoing Ayala's earlier strictures, the instructions given in the name of the infant James V to Sir Andrew Brownhill, ambassador to Denmark, in 1514, explain how at Flodden "Our dearest father, made impatient by the very sight of the enemy, rushed too boldly on them."[19] This appeal to James's epic eagerness at the very sight of the enemy is, Mackie explains, "an excuse for, rather than an impartial exposition of the causes of the defeat"; but he argues nonetheless that "bad leadership" and *imperitia* ("lack of military skill") were in fact two of the main causes of the disaster at Flodden.[20]

Flodden itself, then, has helped to perpetuate certain ways of seeing James IV. Mackie's treatment of the king's efforts to develop a Scottish navy is a further case in point: Flodden shows the king up by showing how "the great fleet which had dazzled the imagination of friend and foe had still to be created"; the *Great Michael* and her five companions are "glittering toys."[21] The story of James IV, as told by Mackie, is that of an ideal fallen into illusionism and death: "And so, in these charnel-pits, ended the great Crusade."[22] Through his recklessness, James IV becomes, in historical narration, the defender who fails to protect. Not unlike the Arthurian legend itself, the story that ends in the charnel-pits of Flodden is about the desire for and the disappearance of greatness. The legend of Flodden is profoundly nostalgic, elegiac: as told even by modern Scottish historians, it is a story about ending, about the creation of a past.[23] Nicholson's concluding chapters present Flodden as a radical divide, a period between an aureate age of ambitious flamboyance, of grand and perhaps grandiose plans, and the disenchanted, troubled epoch that followed. In their collection of *The Poetry of the Stewart Court*, Joan Hughes and William Ransom describe James's reign as "'aureate' rather than 'golden' . . . because it is characterized by its tournaments, its splendour, its sense of ceremony . . . its display of kingly magnanimity and liberality rather than of kingly governance, by a sense of 'brukkilnes' which is epitomised by James's own 'crowded hour of glorious life.'"[24] The story of the aureate age and its end thereby suggests a periodicity rather different from that which informs the conceptualization of the Renaissance: the aureate age in Scotland has seemed not truly golden, its glitter false — as much a last hurrah as a brave new world, the final flush of beauty before the irretrievable fall from grace.

Because loss puts into question the reality of what was lost, it generates questions about the nature of the real.[25] Ontological anxiety, in the story of Scotland's aureate age, produces a fantastic figure indeed: Mackie's "moonstruck romantic, whose eyes were ever at the ends of the earth"; Lewis's "all that is bright, reckless, and fantastical"; more recently, Wormald's "unrealistic and ultimately pathetic figure, as events beyond his control overtook him."[26] The polarization of chivalric fantasy and "kingly governance" is at work in appeals to the theme of *imperitia* as in Lewis's idea of a knight "only secondarily and disastrously a king." James IV is, in this way of looking at him, a flash in the pan. His apotheosis as the hero dying young only serves to underscore his evanescence, his lack of staying power; James's "crowded hour of glorious life" is made the epitome of "brukkilnes." The image of James IV seems to transfix the onlooker with its brilliance, but the gaze which is thereby solicited seems to turn a bit baleful. James is, in the end, a vanity, a vain show, reduced to a gleam in the iconoclast's eye.

Our point, then, with respect to Lewis's picture of the "bright" and "fantastical" James is not so much that it is wrong but that it fails to analyze Lewis's own engagement with the retelling of legend and fails equally to consider the degree to which James himself was concerned to achieve the status of legend. James is, after all, something of a bright spot in the historical record. Whereas his father, James III, "remained a remote figure in Edinburgh, a ruler whom [his subjects] . . . never saw," James IV traveled constantly around his country, holding justice ayres, giving alms, hunting and hawking, making pilgrimages to the shrines of Scottish saints.[27] His behavior suggests a concern to make himself visible. And if, in Lewis's account, the king's public, spectacular qualities make him seem to hold nothing back — to have nothing in reserve — in this, too, James IV seems to have differed from his father. Whereas James III hoarded, for James IV having meant giving, just as being meant appearing. James III spent money on interiors and did little new building; James IV liked to spend money on things his subjects could see — his wedding, tournaments, public almsgiving, the construction of Holyrood Palace, of halls at Edinburgh and Stirling castles, of the chapel royal at Stirling, of the *Great Saint Michael*.[28] And he knew how to reward his supporters, something his father had difficulty bringing himself to do.[29] Giving is the economy of honor, and James was aware of its importance; gifts have a power of identification. Moreover, at least one contemporary account presents elements of the myth of James's excessive devotion to chivalry: Don Pedro de Ayala praises James for his liberality and stresses his rashness in war; James is "courageous, even more so than a king should be."[30] Leslie defends the "large liberalitie" of this "father of the cuntrie," arguing that James's habit — distasteful to Protestant restraint — of riding restlessly about the country was due to his eagerness to see justice done.[31] Pitscottie, following some verses of Sir David Lindsay's in his poem the *Testament of the Papingo* (1538), pictures James as the "leidstarne and lamp of liberallite" and praise the fame of his court, the kingly pastimes, the "Triumpheand turnamentis" that made James "the gloir of princlie gowerning."[32] These early sources see James much as C. S. Lewis saw him — resplendent with chivalric virtues, and flawed by chivalric vices.

For Pitscottie (via Lindsay) envisions a James who is tragic as well as splendid: "that prince in his triumpheand gloire / Destroyit was" by "his awin wilfull misgowernance." In Pitscottie's reflections on the fall of princes, James becomes a reflection whose very visibility is linked to its insubstantiality: "Thairfoir kingis mark in zour remembrance / Ane mirrour of thois mutabiliteis"; "princes willis" cannot stand against "fortoun." The lesson is that too much brilliance, too much of a desire for the limelight, can bring death. It is a version of the story of the hero as singular, conspicuous, light-struck — as *phaidimos*: "the man round whom the glory of the gods shines" is the object of the invidious gaze of gods and men.[33] Because glory attracts the gaze, death follows in its train; greatness cannot last. Pitscottie articulates the dilemma of greatness in this way: although James's splendid displays — his "Triumpheand turnamentis" — approve, rather than disprove, the glory of his "princlie gowerning" (in this Pitscottie sees more clearly than some modern historians), James sets himself too much apart from the counsels of men and is struck down. The dilemma is presented in the form of an exemplum, as a problem of the glorious man's will rather than of the gaze of the onlooker. Grandiosity and punishment are inextricably linked. We must ourselves, however, be aware that the story of the glorious man's fate is shaped as an effect of sight: the glorious man presents himself as an image for the gaze, and as such he must be looked at. The king must, as we have argued, negotiate a difficult paradox: he must be unlike — greater than — all others, but he must also be like all others. If he fails to maintain his representability, his link to the community, his failure will be redressed by the power of the community's gaze to see him as an illusion. What is more difficult to understand is how this very failure may itself become the stuff of legend.

The ambiguity of the historical tradition surrounding James IV — his greatness, his evanescence; his vitality, his self-destructiveness — is inspired in part by the romanticism that attends the production of sovereignty's historicity. James's legend suggests that sovereignty may, at least at times, have an intense relation to loss, both because of sovereignty's claim to restore the fullness of time and its involvement in the passage of time. Though the Tudor conception of the king's two bodies opposed the "natural" body of the king to the fictive "body politic" and made the former a matter of time — subject to decay, infirmity, sickness, old age, death, error — and the latter sempiternal, the natural body of the king also afforded opportunities for sovereignty to gain a hold on time itself and thereby upon those subjects who lived, while on earth, exclusively in it. Time is, we might say, too important for sovereigns to ignore it altogether in favor of sempiternity or even eternity, even if changelessness is the primary theme of sovereign narrative. Legends such as those of Arthur and James IV are almost by definition delectations, not denials, of the natural body, of the king's passage through time, of the king's relation to and experience of loss, even if such legends are ultimately devoted to the sovereign's power to redeem time. Legend has as its chief purpose the production of the values of immortality through, not against, a sense of history, and legend accomplishes this through the perpetuation of desire for the legendary figure and thus in part through emphasis on the fact of his loss — his passing away — as well as through the promise of his return. Legend is thus a work of sovereign love — it puts into play the "dynamic of flight and expectancy" and in doing so uses centuries, and death, and the promise of return to give sovereignty a hold on the vast duration of time. Thus the legends of

Arthur and of James IV tell stories of loss, and of a (forever) deferred reparation, so that desire for the legendary figure will make its way into the
future.

Moreover, though the sovereign's exemplary function demands a timeless relevance, sovereignty must, simply in order to be sovereignty, make
things happen and thus is bound up in particularities of time and place.
As ideal, the sovereign must be vitally contemporaneous, so that he is what
the subject "hopes" or "wishes" to be "now"; and this gives the sovereign
the futurity of the ideal, that function of the ideal or the exemplary which
is always to urge the subject into the future on the wings of an endless
aspiration. Thus even when the ideal represented by the sovereign is conceived as a recovery of past greatness, the sovereign offers to the subject
only the *hope* of recovering a lost potency and fullness (what once was,
and may be again). The relation to the ideal image purveyed by sovereignty therefore has a temporal structure and an historical efficacy, rather
like that outlined by Lacan in his study of the "mirror stage": the subject,
upon confronting the ideal image of the body as perfect, whole, organized,
while remaining in an experiential condition of fragmentation and weakness, is "precipitated" simultaneously into alienation from the ideal image
and aspiration toward it.[34] And in the intensity of his own relation to the
ideal image — in the king's own special sacrifice of "being" to "meaning" entailed in his assumption of the identity of sovereign — the king both attracts and models the paradoxical historicity and fixity of the relation to
the ideal. When, that is, the king tells the story of how he came to be king,
he tells the story of how he came to renounce fragmentation, violence,
error, in taking up identification with the ideal; thus narrated, the sovereign ideal itself is not so much the inimitable image of unmoving perfection, but the imitable action of the sacrifice involved in becoming "civilized," in accepting rule. The image is given narrative form.

James "identified" with his subjects — the glamorous impersonating the
ordinary — in a host of different ways. He was so successful that scholars
like Lewis continue to "see" him with an intensity and a nostalgic fervor
quite different from the ways in which other Scottish kings have been represented. Dunbar wrote that the king's "graciows countenance" was "In
ryches . . . sufficiance"; and James does seem to have given us a tradition
of looking, to have given by looking.[35] But the purpose of his magnificence was not to paralyze the waywardness of the world with the brilliance
of his look; it was, rather, to mobilize that waywardness. As we shall see
in the case of his tournament of the wild knight and the black lady, James
inscribed in a story of the historicity of his own personhood the story of
cultural loss and gain, mourning and reparation: by translating the force

of his ambitions into the story of the king's own emergence from wildness, James made the sacrifice of Gaelic Scotland's "freedom" — of its wild partiality — into the story of his own sacrifice for union and ideal identity, a sacrifice that would appear to be freely chosen — the result of quest, of willed effort — rather than one imposed by the totalizing exactions of the image. At the same time, James's own ambitions — both with respect to the subduing of Gaelic Scotland and with respect to his role in bringing about the downfall of his own father — become challenges that must be overcome in assuming kingship. In its own way, the tournament of the wild knight and the black lady becomes another site of "crossover" between freedom and constraint. It enabled James at least to attempt to transform "batell intestine" — the chaos of warfare against his "own" people — into an act of honor.

The extent to which the paradoxicality of kingship is "a matter of sight" and of the "form" of the king's body was familiar to James's contemporaries.[36] In *The Buke of the Governaunce of Princis,* Gilbert of the Haye's fifteenth-century translation of a French version of the *Secreta secretorum,* "Aristotle" advises Alexander that it is proper for the royal majesty always to be clad in the most "preciouse vestementis," "sa that he suld appere abone and before all otheris in knaulage of dignitee, sa that throu the nobilitee of him, his ornamentis and estate, all his contree war the mare prisit."[37] Aristotle adds that it is not appropriate for a king "tobe our familiare . . . and tharfore the peple of Ynde has a rycht noble custume as belangand thair king, for thai ordanyt that he suld never be sene bot anys in the ȝere, and that sulde be wele enarmyt at all poyntis kinglyke in company of mony notable lordis and princis."[38] These passages suggest that the king must solicit the gaze of his subjects: he is there to be seen. But he should be a rare, or at least not an over-familiar, sight: he is there to be seen as splendidly visible, as singularly conspicuous. The image he presents is designed to hypnotize, to compel collective fascination; he is such a splendid sight that he seems to look at us, to be both seen-by-all and all-seeing. He participates in what Lacan calls "the ambiguity of the jewel."[39] The "chieftain," as Tobin Siebers reminds us, is "dazzling and hypnotic"; "to look him in the face" is a hazardous enterprise.[40] It is, of course, not only the gaze of the king that makes him king; the gaze of the subject, as we have noted, is also necessary. The king's splendid visibility is produced by the desire to create an ideal difference that can then be identified with — by the desire to become great by participating in something greater.[41] The "something greater," the sovereign, is a creation. Insofar as the community desires identification with the ideal image of the king, it must participate in the creation of that ideal; and both community and king can therefore join in a communal mystification of the king's createdness.[42]

The king, then, cannot look "ordinary" or become a familiar sight; to do so would undermine the representation of difference that makes him king and might turn his similars into rivals. And yet, in order to maintain his link to the community, to be like other men, the king must risk allowing himself, his similarity, to be seen. This means that the king must continually risk display of the fact that his difference from other men — which makes him king — is itself a disguise. If he is a creation, he might also be that deceptive and unreliable form of creation, an illusion. For, while disguise — the mask of courtship or of war — may seem to make us superreal, larger than life, it can also seem to diminish us, to make us irreal. Disguise poses the question — the question posed, too, by Lacan's mirror stage — of whether one ever "is" what one appears to be, whether one can fully coincide with the image. To appear, in the end, might be simply to lose one's being, to become a fictive body, a passive reflection in another man's eye. In the *Iliad*, Hector abuses Diomedes by calling him a *"kakē glēnē . . . 'you poor doll' . . .* literally the pupil of the eye, glossed by Rufus Medicus as . . . 'the image in the eye,' and hence 'puppet' or 'girl.'"[43] To be seen — to become an image — can thus evoke feminization, mortification. It is with these evocations that the king flirts each time he makes a spectacle of himself. How can the king make his profound relation to the assumption of social identity — and the loss of "being" entailed thereby — into a strength rather than a weakness? How can he bring out the creative power of the image or even make the illusionism of the image work to his advantage?

The contradiction — potentially enabling as well as disabling — that informs the theatricalization of the king lies at the heart of many forms of public ornamentation. In *Horns of Honour*, Frederick Elworthy commented that in ancient times the "great importance of horns consisted" of their role "as potent protectors against the ever dreaded evil glance": "Not only were horns worn upon the head as objects intended to terrify the enemy and protect the wearer, but they were placed for the like purpose upon buildings and various inanimate objects."[44] The "intimate connection between the protective and the dignifying quality of horns" may itself help to explain a phenomenon that puzzled Elworthy: the "absolute reversal of meaning" which has marked the wearing of horns from a sign of honor to one of dishonor — specifically, to a sign of cuckoldry, of the failure of masculinity.[45] Cripps-Day also commented on the practice of decorating helmets with crests of cornets: in early Italian tournaments the horns adorned the helmet of a victorious knight, whereas "the defeated knight was deprived of them, and non-combatants could not wear them. Hence the Italian adage *'Tornare con le trombe nel sacco o scornato'*; the defeated knight was in fact designated as *scornato*." Cripps-Day, too, was puzzled by the conflation of horns of honor with the horns of the cuckold.[46] Thus the same image could, simultaneously and at varying times in its history, be used both to divert the gaze, to fix its evil on something else, and to solicit the gaze, to command and impress. At once aggressive and defensive, horrifying and horrified, the *fascinum* — the horn, the crest, the gorgon — images the ambivalence of seeing and being seen, the sense that those visible, visualizing performances that seem to confer identity are also the means by which identities — of person, gender, class — are undone. It is thus that symbols become weapons both for and against collective fascination.

The gaze that creates the king is risky not only because it creates him but also because it is potentially "accusatory"; the link between ideality and criminality is a close one.[47] The gaze that makes the difference that makes the king is projected onto the king, so that he seems to be all-seeing; similarly, the gaze that makes the difference that makes the criminal is projected onto the criminal, so that in the case of the "jettatore" (the "fascinator") he seems to have the evil eye, to see what should not be seen, to destroy or appropriate the objects of his gaze. Tobin Siebers argues that communal crisis erupts in societies that appoint different sources for "curses" and "cures" when the distinction between curse and cure collapses, but one aspect of the king's paradoxicality is that he is often conceived as a source both of cure and of curse; he assures prosperity, but he also has the power to destroy. Thus conceived, "curse" is an aspect of the king's legitimate power of alteration; but it must be distinguished from the violence of the common criminal, if the king is also to be conceived as the fount of justice.[48]

David Starkey has commented on the importance of "numinous powers" to the work of governance in late medieval and early modern kingship:

In the Middle Ages . . . [the] supernatural attributes [of kings] — as epitomised by touching for the king's evil — had provided the kings of England and France with a crucial weapon in their battle with the overweening pretensions of the papacy. . . . Revolutions or intended revolutions sought legitimacy by association with the divine: Henry IV's shaky title was reinforced by anointing him with an opportunely-rediscovered vial of oil that had been given by the Virgin to St. Thomas of Canterbury . . . Henry VII (another dubious usurper) elaborated both the ceremony of touching for the king's evil and that of the hallowing of cramp rings.[49]

There is some evidence that James IV was believed to have the healing touch; and though his right by blood to the throne of Scotland was not in doubt, his means of obtaining it, and some of his means of retaining it, had been forcefully interventionist. It is therefore not surprising that James might have taken pains to emphasize the king's "magical virtue" of "blessing," as a way of keeping his power to burn and destroy from being seen as criminality, as enmity to the community.[50] To ensure his association with blessing—and to ensure that his power to curse would be seen as divinely authorized, superreal, not as the autonomous and illegitimate violence of the private criminal—James IV, like many other medieval kings, practiced "distributive justice." It is in part within this context—that is, in its connection with justice—that the virtue of liberality, and James's concern to display it, must be understood.[51] Against the many crises in kingly economics that bedeviled the reign of James III, we should set James IV's reputation for liberality as an instrument, not a substitute for, governance: Leslie notes how "through fauour, luue and kyndnes, sindrie plesures and benefitis, he wan to hartis of his princis, that vehementlie tha war affected to him."[52] Ayala writes: "He gives alms liberally, but is a severe judge, especially in the case of murderers. . . . He said to me that his subjects serve him with their persons and goods, in just and unjust quarrels, exactly as he likes, and that, therefore, he does not think it right to begin any warlike undertaking without being himself the first in danger. His deeds are as good as his words. For this reason, and because he is a very humane prince, he is much loved."[53] In contrast with the notorious treacheries of his father, James IV's deeds are as good as his words. In contrast with his father's lack of enthusiasm for campaigning, James conducts his battles in person and is the first in danger because it is just to do so; and he is at one and the same time generous in almsgiving and a severe judge of murderers, powerful in his blessings and equally powerful in cursing (not being) the criminally violent. Thus James IV's ambitions, his conspiracy and warfare against his father, his warlike undertakings against, not with, his "own" people, might seem not to have tainted kingship with crime but to have restored it—to have given new life, not death, to the ideal of kingship betrayed, according to legend, by James III.

But though James could be a severe judge of murderers, rooting out and punishing an interior violence thereby revealed not to be his, he could also, as we have noted, risk not only leniency but also identification with wildness. Dunbar wrote in his "Epetaphe for Donald Oure":

> In vice most vicius he excellis
> That with the vice of tressone mellis;
> Thocht he remissioun
> Haif for prodissioun,
> Schame and susspissioun
> Ay with him dwellis.
> . . . .
> The murtherer ay murthour mais,
> And evir quhill he be slane he slais;
> Wyvis thus makis mokkis,

Spynnand on rokkis —
Ay rynnis the fox
Quhill he fute hais.[54]

Donald Oure (Gaelic *odhar,* dun, brown), or Dubh (black), illegitimate
heir to the forfeited Lordship of the Isles, was held at court in James's service but escaped in 1501. In 1503 he led a serious insurrection against the
king, and in 1505 he was defeated and imprisoned again.[55] Of the pacification of the Highlands and the Isles Pitscottie says (addressing James): "during thy tyme so iustice did prevaill / That the sawwage Iles trimbled for
terrour." But Mackenzie, in his edition of Dunbar's poems, remarks that
"the tone of the "Epetaphe" is unnecessarily malignant towards one who
had known no personal freedom save for the few years he was out against
the Government. He was partly the victim, partly the instrument of higher
powers."[56] Whether Dunbar's poem is one that would have pleased James
or reflected James's point of view is difficult to say; whether Dunbar's severity is the product of his "own" rigor or of the court poet's occasional
function of taking on "malignancy" for the king is also difficult to say. It
is clear, however, that Dunbar's poem attests the desire of some elements
in the court to construct a criminalized Gaelic "other" to the king. Dunbar
asserts that, though this thief, traitor, and murderer might be pardoned
for his crimes, he will always be a thief, traitor, and murderer, always a
danger, a fox, "odious as ane owle," "filthy . . . and fowle; / Horrible to
natour." It is, that is, in the unnatural nature of the traitor to be treacherous; his bestial identity is firmly fixed, apparently despite the king's power
of mercy. Dunbar almost seems to be warning the king, to disagree with
his policy of leniency, for James never sought the execution either of Donald Oure or of John, Lord of the Isles, whom James held in a rather com-
fortable captivity for many years.

The obduracy — the resistance to change, the absolute unwillingness to
convert — of the "nature" of the wild Scots was also a theme in John Major's *History of Greater Britain* (1521). Like Dunbar, Major invokes the
idea of nature to construct a perdurable, resistant difference of Highland
Scot from Lowland Scot.

Further, just as among the Scots we find two distinct tongues, so we likewise find
two different ways of life and conduct. For some are born in the forests and mountains of the north, and these we call men of the Highland, but the others men of
the Lowland. By foreigners the former are called Wild Scots, the latter householding Scots. . . . In dress, in the manner of their outward life, and in good
morals, . . . [the Wild Scots] come behind the householding Scots — yet they are
not less, but rather much more, prompt to fight; and this, both because they dwell

more towards the north, and because, born as they are in the mountains, and dwellers in forests, their very nature is more combative. It is, however, with the householding Scots that the government and direction of the kingdom is to be found, inasmuch as they understand better, or at least less ill than the others, the nature of a civil polity. One part of the Wild Scots . . . yield more willing obedience to the courts of law and the king. The other part . . . live upon others, and follow their own worthless and savage chief in all evil courses sooner than they will pursue an honest industry. They are full of mutual dissensions, and war rather than peace is their normal condition.[57]

Though there are some "good" Wild Scots — their goodness measured by their "willing obedience to the courts of law and the king" — the Wild Scots exemplify lawless violence, barbarism, an incapacity for civil society. Good Wild Scots, then, are comparatively "domesticated"; bad Wild Scots continue to pursue their own procedures of government and social organization, which is to say, from Major's point of view, no such procedures at all. They are creatures of the frontier, not "householding," part of wild nature, living in the forests; and whether they are good or bad, they all possess, as a result of their association with wild nature, a "combative nature." Major's distinction between good and bad Wild Scots is itself designed to protect his projection of lawless violence out of "civilized" Lowland Scots culture onto the Irish speakers of the north; that some Highland Scots had shown themselves to be permeable — capable of adopting the civilized ways of the South, of submitting to rule — could not be allowed to undermine the efficacy of the concept of "combative nature."

Though the Highlanders and Islanders may in fact have been, for reasons of economic and social organization, more prone to certain kinds of violence than the Lowlanders, Scots like Major could, through such geographical constructions, reassure themselves of the civilized nature of their own culture; indeed, they could identify their own culture with culture, their pacifications with peace, their brand of violence with the rule of law. Thus at the same time the enduring nature of the difference is insisted upon (the Wild Scots are not like the Lowland Scots), it also must (and paradoxically perhaps can, given that there are good Highland Scots) be erased (the Wild Scots must become "part" of Scotland, must be pacified). The power of Scottish civilization to alter wildness will thus be marked by the power of the lawless violence, the obdurate "combative nature," that is said to resist it. And thus, though the Highlands and the Isles were "troublesome," the elaborateness and urgency of the ideological illogic manifested in Major's passage seems somewhat incommensurate with the actual difficulties posed the Crown by Gaelic Scotland. One is reminded of Mackenzie's puzzlement at the "malignancy" in Dunbar's "Epetaphe," for the Scottish monarchy had during the fifteenth and early sixteenth century as much trouble with — to cite only one example — the powerful Douglas family and its repeated intrigues with England as it did with the north. William Ferguson, we recall, reminds us that the "resurgence of Gaelic Scotland" in the later fifteenth and early sixteenth centuries "was symptomatic of a wider malaise whereby by the end of the fourteenth century whole regions of Scotland were falling under the sway of over-mighty subjects."[58] Centuries-old habits of violence, and of resistance to monarchical rule, died hard everywhere in Scotland; but the south was able to construct an image of the violent north through which it could contemplate its "own" preference for civilization, its "own" grandeur of vision, rather than the failures of faith and divisiveness that on so many occasions broke out "within."

More will be said in subsequent chapters on the association of wildness with Gaelic Scotland; for now it is enough to say that, given the strong association of Gaelic "wildness" with natural violence by the civilization of which James should have been the acme, it is a measure of the risks he was willing to take that he jousted himself in the form of the wild knight. As we shall see, his identification with Gaelic Scotland ran deeper than we have yet had time and space to indicate; the paradox is that the "resurgence of Gaelic Scotland" also took the form of a king more fascinated by Gaelic culture than any other late medieval Scottish king, at the same time that both ideological and physical weaponry were being leveled at it with renewed and remarkable intensity. The opportunities, as well as the dangers, for James's legendary ambitions were accordingly considerable; in keeping with the prominently visual style of his reign, he sought in chivalric spectacle to make the most of wildness in telling the story of his life. During James's reign the glorification of chivalry became a veritable style of rule, a favorite way of becoming splendidly visible, of compelling identifications, of fascinating his "princis."[59] The risk, and the triumph, lay in the capacity of chivalrous spectacle to identify king and knight, different and similar — and in the capacity of chivalrous spectacle to enact the process of becoming, thereby to let flower the contradictions of the image, of being and appearing, plenitude and lack, what was once and what might again be. James seems at some level to have understood that chivalric spectacle itself tells a story of the relation of wildness to the ideal image: chivalric spectacle is in part "about" the confrontation of violence with form, the fear that form will pacify and ultimately effeminate, the nostalgia for an always-receding past of aristocratic freedom; chivalric spectacle tells the story of how the desire for lawlessness may be negotiated with honor, how ambition may be brought in relation to inherited status, effort brought in relation to essence. For however much the idea of aristocracy itself is predicated upon the idea of heritable and unchanging privilege, the aristocracy not only did change but also required constant change in order to assert its entitlement to privilege. The spectacular tournaments of the later Middle Ages were above all concerned with the endlessness of the aristocrat's need to prove his unalterable possession of honor — and therefore of his right to land and title and lady — by earning it all over again. Thus they were, in some sense, maturational rituals, and the allegories around which they came to be organized, sometimes explicitly, sometimes implicitly, try to tell the story of how wild youth takes possession of the field by discovering rather than losing its identity, by sacrificing and yet maintaining — for the story is and must be repeated — its relation to lawlessness. To turn the challenges of wild aristocratic aspiration — of the changefulness of those entitled to violence — into the story of his own life would thus become, in the tournament of the wild knight and the black lady, one of James's most cherished projects, one of his strongest bids for the identifying love of his noble subjects. The following two chapters discuss, respectively, the evidence for the cult of chivalry in late medieval Scotland — James's interest in chivalric spectacle helped to shape the tastes of his "age" but were by no means out of touch with its "realities" — and the history of tournament pageantry, especially its interconnections with the difficult play of the idea of honor. The final two chapters will explore how the figures of the wild knight and the black lady contributed to James IV's legendary art of rule.

10

Spectacle and Chivalry
in Late Medieval Scotland

THE richness and variety of pageantry in the reign of James IV has been emphasized by A. J. Mill, who writes: "Household minstrels, court 'makaris,' members of the royal retinue, wandering bards and jugglers, Clerks to the Chapel, bands of folk players from the town, professional jesters, all combined in the late fifteenth and early sixteenth centuries to make the Scottish Court a favourable nursing ground for dramatic activities. The idea that the masks of Mary Queen of Scots were delicate exotic products introduced from France in 1561 is untenable."[1] That these later masks and entertainments were indeed exotic is attested by a December 1561 event in which the French ambassador, M de Foys, and other lords "ran at the ring 'dysguised and appareled thone half lyke women, and thother lyke strayngers, in straynge maskinge garmentes.'"[2] The 1566 baptism of Prince James included Moors and "hieland wyld men," and in 1594 the revels for the baptism of Prince Henry at Stirling included a "maske" "in which the 'actors' were three Turks, three Christian Knights of Malta, and three Amazons."[3] The second day's pastime was to have featured beasts like griphons and dragons carrying their riders; a triumphal chariot was at one point drawn in so that it "appeared to be drawne in onely by the strength of a Moore."[4] The records dating from the time of James IV are not generous with circumstantial detail. With respect to tournaments, Mill notes that the records contain "many notices of 'hastiludia,' tourneys, running at the ring; but little is said as to disguises"; nonetheless, James's tournaments "attracted attention far beyond the bounds of Scotland."[5] The wild men, the fantastic beasts, the black lady, the great silk pavilion of the tournaments of 1507 and 1508 suggest that there began, during James IV's reign, a taste for visual splendor of a particular kind: for flamboyant, expensive, and carefully orchestrated court revelry. The tournaments of 1507 and 1508 were innovative in their use of "really elaborate allegorical themes."[6]

The festivities for the king's wedding to Margaret Tudor in 1503 were also elaborate and expensive, and much more spectacular in kind than the celebrations of royal weddings had been in the previous century. During Mary of Gueldres's bridal journey to Scotland in 1449, a "brilliant tourney" was held at Bruges; Jacques de Lalaing, a renowned Burgundian knight, won the honors.[7] He had also, in the previous year, jousted at Stirling in the presence of James II; Lalaing and two companions contended against two Douglases and Sir John Ross of Hawkhead.[8] But no "solemn" tournament seems to have been held in Scotland for the wedding celebrations of 1449. Matthieu d'Escouchy, castellan of Peronne for the duke of Burgundy, included in his *Chroniques* an account of the wedding that, as Dunlop puts it, stressed the "vivid contrast" between Scotland's "ambitions" and its "cultural standards," though d'Escouchy made note of the elaborate presentation of dishes at the banquet.[9] A painted and stuffed "figure" of a boar's head was brought in, surrounded with banners bearing the arms of Scotland's king and "seigneurs"; the stuffing was set on fire, much to the delight of the spectators. And then "on apporta une belle nef, laquelle avoit hunne, chasteau, masts, et les cordes qui estoient d'argent, le tout bien ouvré. Ensuite de quoy vint et marcha le comte d'Orquenay, avec quatre chevaliers, précédant."[10]

By the reign of James IV, court spectacular had gone beyond the elaborate arts of the banquet. James IV's wedding featured a dramatic tournament, an ambitious royal entry, and probably Dunbar's *The Thrissill and the Rois*. The poem is spectacular; and while we have no external evidence to suggest that it was performed to the accompaniment of dancing, costume, or "machinery," its poetics, as we have seen, are clearly those of the court masque — of shifting "scenes," visual astonishment, splendid "discryving." The same may be said of Dunbar's *The Goldyn Targe*, also an elaborate allegorical spectacle.[11] As Welsford wrote, Dunbar saw "nature" through the "medium" of courtly pageant; the artificiality of which his poetry has often been accused is an artifice that strives, like the masque, to empower illusion, to give evanescence an essence.[12] A number of his other poems attest both the strongly visual character of much of his writing and the court's interest in pageants and entertainments. "To Aberdein" describes the pageantry of the royal welcome staged by Aberdeen for Queen Margaret, the pageants for which included the Salutation, the Three Kings, and the Expulsion from Paradise. Twenty-four maidens sang and played on "timberallis"; and the Bruce "gart as roy cum rydand under croun, / Richt awfull, strang, and large of portratour." Dunbar's "Fasternis Even in Hell" presents a "dance" and pageant of the Seven Deadly Sins and a tournament "Betuix a telʒour and ane sowtar"; it may have been composed to accompany "the More taubronaris devis agane Fasteringis Evin" mentioned in the Treasurer's Accounts.[13] "Ane Blak Moir" blazons a black woman who may have been the black lady of the tournaments of 1507 and 1508. "The Ballade of Barnard Stewart lord of Aubigny" was composed for Stewart's last visit to Scotland, which took place at the time of the tournament of 1508. "Schir Thomas Norny" raises one of the court fools to the "dignity" of an "anterous knycht," who "quhar ever he went / At justing and at tornament / Evermor he wan the gre"; "He wanttis no thing bot bellis." "Ane Dance in the Quenis Chalmer" burlesques the balletic abilities of the court; another poem describes how, among the "Solistaris in Court," "sum singis, sum dances, sum tellis storyis, / Sum lait at evin bringis in the moryis."

The Treasurer's Accounts for James's reign also reveal the importance of pageant and revel in court life. The Dutch painter Piers, who arrived at court in 1505, was employed, along with Sir Thomas Galbraith, in preparing banners, standards and tabards for the tournaments of 1507 and 1508.[14] Galbraith also "illuminated books and documents for the king, notably the treaties of peace and marriage" of 1502 "and a great 'porteus' (breviary) for the king's chapel."[15] He was also paid for painting the "Mons clath," so it appears that the king's great gun was proudly decorated and starred in its own spectaculars: on 21 July 1497 Mons was brought forth from Edinburgh Castle "with minstrels playing before her 'doune the gait.'"[16] Alexander Chalmers helped to prepare the tabards and banners and made the wild beasts for James's tournaments.[17] He also painted "the kingis gret schip," the *Great Saint Michael;* numerous entries in the Treasurer's Accounts record his purchases of "bukis of gold" and "colouris" for work on "the kingis ymagery, pynsalis, and flaggis to the schippis."[18] And Chalmers was paid eight pounds for 140 "payntit armyis to the obsequijs of our souerane lord King James the ferd, quham God assolze," when a service was held in 1515 at St. Giles to commemorate the death of James IV at Flodden.[19]

The clerks of the chapel royal at Stirling—Sir Thomas Galbraith was one of their number—were regularly paid salaries of about twenty pounds per annum; the court's four Italian minstrels were paid almost as much.[20] "The six 'childir' or 'bairnis' of the Chapel appear . . . as the recipients of regular gratuities."[21] In 1492 Galbraith, John Goldsmith, and Crafurd, clerks to the chapel royal, sang a New Year "ballat" to the king; John Goldsmith was elected King of the Bean at Epiphany 1495/96, and again in 1501/2.[22] There were repeated expenditures for a wide variety of misrule celebrations—particularly for those having to do with the King of the Bean and the Abbot of Unreason — from the end of the fifteenth century; the duties of the Abbot of Unreason included organizing entertainments for the king. "St. Nicholas bishops from the Abbey and the 'hie toun' of Edinburgh received grants from the royal purse from 1473 till 1511"; and there are references in the accounts to Queens of the May.[23]

The king had mumming robes made for himself, so we know that the court participated in its own disguisings as well as patronized professional and municipal entertainments.[24] The court records show numerous payments to "gysaris," who seem at times to have danced, at times to have been involved in dramatic spectacle. "The 'thre gysaris that playit the play' at the Scottish court in August 1503 may have been . . . John English and his companions, who . . . acted a 'Moralite' at the time of the royal marriage."[25] Patrick Johnson, who seems also to have staged plays for James III, presented a play to the king and ambassadors from Spain in 1489.[26] The "More taubronaris devis agane Fasteringis Evin" took place in 1505. In 1506/7, "Wantonnes" and her companions are rewarded for singing; in 1511/12, there is an entry "to Gilleam, tabernar, for ane fars play to the King and Quenis Gracis in the Abbay, vj Franch crounis."[27] There is an entry for black silk "to be pointis to the capricht agane the Kingis passing to the Corpus Christi play"; James Dog was reimbursed for "girs" that he "laid doun . . . on Corpus Christi day, at the play, to the Kingis and Quenis chamires"; three pounds were spent on a "play coit to David Lindesay for the play playt in the King and Quenis presence in the Abbay."[28]

Dancing and music were regular features of court life: the records mention rich rewards to Spanish dancers; Pringill was paid to "be a precept of the Kingis, for a liffray to mak a dans again Vphaly day"; and there are rewards to "menstralis," "trumpatouris," "fithelars," "harpares," "lutares," "tawbronares," and "to the men that brocht in the morice dance, and to thair menstrales, in Strivelin."[29] The court festivities became more complex as a result of the king's marriage; in 1503/4, several entries for "daunsyng gere" suggest that the "Moris dans" in question was of the sophisticated and courtly variety.[30] On 3 January 1504 twenty-eight shillings went to Thomas Bosuell and Pate Sinclair (master of the king's wardrobe) "to by thaim daunsing gere"; on 5 January the same sum went to "Maister Johne" (the French alchemist, John Damien, afterward abbot of Tungland) "to by beltis for the Moris dans."[31] On the same night over five pounds were given "to the gysaris of the toun of Edinburgh"; on 7 January the large sum of over fourteen pounds was spent for red and blue taffeta for "daunsing cotis in Maister Johnis dans," more money for the "daunsaris hede gere," for "blew taffeti to the womanis goun in the said dance," and so forth.[32] The "More taubronaris devis" included twelve dancers, whose clothes cost over eight pounds. There were payments of nine pounds to "Monsure Lamote servitouris, that dansit ane moris to the King" and five pounds eight shillings "to Monsur Lamotis servitouris, that dansit ane uthir moris to the King and Quene."[33]

Though the tournaments of 1507 and 1508 were perhaps the most magnificent of James's spectacles, they were by no means isolated events; they were, rather, part of a pattern of elaborate and costly court revelry, including "moralites," "fars," "devis," moriscos, mumming, misrule celebrations at every turn in the calendar, and a number of tournaments of a less dramatic bent. In 1496 Perkin Warbeck, pretender to the English throne, was married to the king's cousin, Lady Catherine Gordon; the king seems to have held a tournament in honor of the event and to have jousted himself, for the accounts make provision not only for his attire but also for a "mittane" to ease his injured hand.[34] The Treasurer's Accounts for 25 May 1505 show a payment made "to the men that justit in the botes of Leith"; this may have been a water-tournament and seems to have been associated with the king's visit to a ship then being built in Leith harbor. The king dined on board, having ordered his silver plate and "verdours" to be transported to the ship for the purpose. Fourteen shillings were given on this occasion to William Merrymouth, a mariner known as King of the Sea, who was probably in command of the ship in question.[35] Such a tournament would have accorded well with James's own wish to be king of the sea.

The accounts for 26 November 1506 refer to preparations made for the "fechting of the Lord Hammiltoun and the Franch knyght."[36] Hamilton, created earl of Arran at the time of the king's wedding, was one of James's favorites; so was Hamilton's opponent, Antoine d'Arces, Lord of la Bastie, the "Franch knyght," who — like Bernard Stewart — had been involved in the Italian wars and who cultivated a reputation for chivalric exploits. His contemporary and compatriot Aymer du Rivail pictures him wandering through Europe, challenging all those "qui . . . étaient disposés à combattre à outrance. Partout il fut éconduit par les rois de ces pays, si ce n'est en Ecosse, où le cousin de Jacques IV joûta contre lui; mais Antoine d'Arces eut le dessus. Tel était l'amour qu'avait pour lui ce prince, que parfois il couchait dans la chambre royale."[37] Marc de Vulson, sieur de la Colombière — a French knight of Scottish descent — recounts in his *Le Vray Théâtre d'Honnevr* the "Emprise" of "Antoine d'Arces Seigneur de la Bastie en Dauphine, surnomme le Chevalier Blanc, & de trois autres Cheualiers ses Aydes, qui tous quatre par permission du Roy et de la Reine de France Anne de Bretagne, porterent au col vne escharpe blanche pour Emprise, & allerent visiter les Royaumes d'Angleterre, d'Espagne, d'Escosse & de Portugal."[38] Francisque Michel asserts that d'Arces was present at James's wedding, so his privileged position at the court may date from early in the decade — though, as Baxter notes, the records do not mention his presence in Scotland at the time of the ceremony.[39] The king gave him expensive gifts; d'Arces took to France the illuminated articles proclaiming the tournament of 1507. And though he may not have attended the 1507 tournament, he was certainly present when it was repeated in May 1508, and he traveled to France on a diplomatic mission for James shortly after Bernard Stewart's death in 1508.[40]

Lord Bernard Stewart was also present at the tournament of 1508, which appears to have been held in his honor. (Pitscottie makes him judge of the tournament in the king's place, so that the king himself could joust "onknawin" and "dissaguysed."[41]) Stewart's embassy to Scotland was meant to secure James's friendship for France at a time when tensions with England were high. In April 1508 Thomas Wolsey was in Edinburgh, reporting, "As to the renewal of the old league between Scotland and France, James says that as long as Henry treats him kindly, he will never break with him, nor renew the old league."[42] James wrote to Louis at the end of June 1508 to say that John Sellat — Stewart's colleague on the embassy — had convinced him that "there must be the same friendship for Louis on his part as Louis had shown to him, not only with letters and seals, but even more by his deeds, so that he may be seen to strengthen by his actions the treaty made by his ancestors."[43] Stewart's visit was thus an instance of James's increasing prominence in the "crusading diplomacy" and nationalist rivalries of Europe and marked a moment when — having recently consolidated his position in Gaelic Scotland — James's designs on the larger world were becoming increasingly elaborate. In 1509, "only a year" after Stewart's visit, Macdougall points out, "James IV and his queen would name their newborn son Arthur, a name recalling . . . the deceased brother of the new king of England" as well as the legendary King Arthur. By 1509, too, James was writing to Pope Julius II "that he would gladly shed his last drop of blood in the cause of Christendom."[44]

A kinsman of James's, Stewart was himself a sufficiently distinguished practitioner of chivalric politics to have served as a focal point for James's "devious" transactions of honor. Ian Ross writes that Stewart was "notable" for his chivalric conduct "amid the horrors of the Italian wars": "He was interested in the theory of statecraft and wrote or adapted a short treatise on the art of war, which was put in its final form by his secretary during [the 1508] . . . Scottish embassy."[45] If the tournament of 1508 did Stewart honor as well as impressing France and alarming England (not least by its celebration of James's ability to control his wild Scots), then it would, like many others of its day, have been a way of articulating national ambitions through the celebration of a chivalric ideal that in theory cut across national boundaries to create an aristocratic community. That this was a community of rivalry—that the aristocracy produced itself as a community in large part through rituals of rivalry—made tournaments all the more profound a way of registering the national bellicosities and class amities of late medieval and early modern Europe.

Dunbar's "Ballade of ane right noble victorius and myghty lord Barnard Stewart" was printed by Chepman and Myllar with the date 9 May 1508; the print lists Stewart's many titles and explains that the poem was "Compilit be Maistir William Dumbar at the said lordis cumyng to Edinburghe in Scotland send in ane ryght excellent embassat fra the said maist Crystin king to our maist souverane lord and victorius prince James the ferde kyng of Scottis."[46] At this time of a king's invoking the treaties of ancestors, the ancestral desire for pilgrimage and crusade, amid thoughts of redesigning the world of loyalties, Dunbar's poem catalogs Stewart's victories and the famous warriors of the past whose prowess Stewart reincarnates ("O feyrse Achill in furius hie curage"). Stewart exemplifies not only that honor is what it was in the past but also that it means what it says, for his

> knyghtli name so schynyng in clemence
> For wourthines in gold suld writtin be
> With glorie and honour, lawd and reverence.
>
> (ll. 94–96)

The "Ballade" was probably commissioned for presentation in a ceremony of welcome or at the tournament of 1508—though the preface in the Chepman and Myllar print may have been promotional, it hints at the poem's official character.

The "Elegy on Bernard Stewart," written after Stewart's death in June 1508, does not seem to have been published. It closes with a moving injunction to the "Scottis natioun": "Forȝett we nevir into our orisoun / To pray for him, the flour of chevelrie" (ll. 31–32). Stewart was buried at Blackfriars in Edinburgh; and though there is no external evidence to connect the "Elegy" with a public event, Dunbar's poem—like the depiction of the royal dirge in Margaret Tudor's Book of Hours—nevertheless turns loss into an occasion.[47] A knight's funeral was often a spectacular, the ritual culmination of the life of honor—the memorializing, the final theatrical manifestation, of a life ideally devoted to the risk of death, to an intentional relation with death.[48] Though Stewart died of illness, his last antagonist, in Dunbar's poem, is the "dragon dolorous"—a heroization of loss, the obverse of the grandeur of risk.

The aristocratic passion of and for chivalry was as strong in Scotland as elsewhere in medieval Europe. Though the first known armorial of Scottish provenance—that of Sir David Lindsay, Lyon Herald and author of *Ane Satyre of the Thrie Estaitis*—was not produced until the mid-sixteenth century, it is clear that in the fifteenth and early sixteenth centuries in Scotland a rich tradition of chivalric art and practice was developing.[49] James IV's art of rule was organized in particularly striking ways around the artfulness of chivalric practice; the following discussion attempts to map more completely the textual and imagistic fields within which James's art of rule was at work. James IV was by no means the only late medieval Scottish monarch to deploy chivalric motifs and heraldic symbolism in the production and representation of power; but he did so in distinctively thoroughgoing and spectacular ways.

His grandfather, James II, was extremely fond of warlike sports and made provision for jousting fields at Edinburgh.[50] The inventory of the imperial James III's treasure shows that he possessed the gold collars proper to the Danish Order of the Elephant and the French Order of St. Michael.[51] He adopted the thistle as his own personal badge and used it lavishly to ornament his household; it appears, too, as a motif in the Trinity Panels.[52] The motto of James III—*In my defens*—was first used on a gold medallion struck at Berwick in 1475; it subsequently became the motto of the royal arms of Scotland.[53] The royal arms appear in the Trinity Panels; and in the portrait of James IV in Margaret Tudor's Book of Hours, the altar-front shows the arms as developed by James III, with unicorn supporters and the crest of a lion sejant (fig. 5.). Margaret's arms are also pictured on her *prie-Dieu* (fig. 6.).[54] The portrait of James IV painted by Daniel Mytens includes an inscription of the motto *In my defens* and shows the royal unicorns, collared with crowns and chains, supporting the royal coat of arms.[55] In Margaret Tudor's Book of Hours a full plate is devoted to the depiction of James IV's achievement, in which the thistle and the marguerite make their appearance. The heraldic accuracy of the plate indicates that "the artist must have worked from a sketch sent him from the Scottish court, perhaps from James's own court painter, Thomas Galbraith."[56] We have already noted the work done by Piers, Galbraith, and Chalmers in painting shields and banners for the tournaments in 1507 and 1508 and Chalmers's work on James IV's funeral achievements; heraldic art was an important part of the production of the court painter.

Manuscript illuminators also had to be well versed in the symbolism of heraldry. The manuscript of the *Aeneid* that was possibly commissioned by James III contains a three-quarter-page miniature of Aeneas's arrival at Carthage; the royal arms are embedded in the surrounding floral bor-

der. The arms have been assigned to James III; and though this is not
proof of his connection with the manuscript, the inclusion of the arms
does mean that the book was executed for a Scottish owner.[57] In the Blackadder prayerbook—owned at one time by Alexander Stewart, archbishop
of St. Andrews and illegitimate son of James IV—armorial bearings are
illuminated on the first leaf; the Talbot Hours show, below an illumination of Mary Regina with the infant Jesus, armorial bearings and the inter-
woven initials IR set into a thistle design (the page is also bordered with
thistles).[58] The royal arms of Scotland appear in the Aberdeen Psalter just
after the calendar of saints begins.[59] Facing folio 1r in the early sixteenth-
century *Vitae Episcoporum Dunkeldensium* is a series of beautifully illuminated arms, again including the royal arms of Scotland.[60] The Herdmans-
ton Breviary—compiled much earlier (ca. 1300) than the works referred
to above, all of which date from the fifteenth or early sixteenth century—
contains a number of sketches of a chivalric and heraldic nature: drawings
of armor (fol. 85r), heraldic animals (86r, 96r), shields (306v, 334v), a
knight in tournament armor and a shield with arms (157v), a vizored knight
with shield (315v), and bearings of a shield with an elaborate crowned
crest (354v), which may indicate that the sketches are of a quite late date
(crests proper were a fifteenth-century development).[61] The late fifteenth-
century Makculloch manuscript is also strewn with some interesting heraldic
images: the initial of folio 12r, for example, is decorated with the mitred
shields of France and Scotland; the initial at folio 41r is decorated with
the royal arms of Scotland, including the motto *In my defens*, and with
other armorial bearings as well.[62] Particularly striking are the sketches at
folio 87v of a tournament *arbre*, hung with a shield bearing the royal arms
of Scotland, and at folio 136v of a soldier bearing a shield with a double
tressure. Inside it is a face in profile wearing an ermine crown, possibly
meant to represent James III. The Scottish aristocracy and clergy alike
thus took considerable pleasure in decorating their important books with
their own arms and motifs as well as with those of the royal house. It is
important to stress that these heraldic images were in fact images, not unlike portraits: distinctive combinations of meaningful visual motifs that
manifested identity.

    According to Stewart Cruden, a growing desire for heraldic art is also
characteristic of fifteenth-century Scottish interiors: "Heraldry, popular in
contemporary ecclesiastical work on vault bosses and buttresses, is exploited
over entrance doorways and on fireplace lintels."[63] The Borthwick buffet
features small shields "emblazoned in heraldic tinctures"; the vault was
"plastered and painted with allegorical scenes and motifs," the inscriptions
for which—"ye tempil of honour" and "ye tempil of religion"—have almost

completely disappeared.[64] Series of carved heraldic shields overhang the fireplaces at Elphinstone and Comlongon, both constructed, like Borthwick, in the mid–fifteenth century.[65] And both Holyrood and Falkland palaces, built chiefly during the course of the early sixteenth century, feature important heraldic sculpture.[66]

The literary evidence, too, suggests not only the growing popularity of heraldic motifs but also the increasing tendency to treat chivalric art discursively and theoretically. In *The Buke of the Howlat*, Richard Holland gives an elaborate description of the royal arms of Scotland. The "lyon" is pictured as

> Riche rampand as roy, ryke of array.
> Of pure gold was the ground, quhar the grym hovit,
> With dowble tressour about, flourit in fay,
> And flour delycis on loft, that mony leid lovit,
> Of gowliss sygnit and set, to schawe in assay;
> Our souerane of Scotland his armes to knawe,
> Quhilk sall be lord and ledar
> Our braid Brettane allquhar,
> As sanct Mergaretis air,
> And the signe schawe.[67]

The Buke of the Howlat is by no means a strongly royalist poem; it has been described as a "panegyric of the Douglases" and was written at a time (in the mid-1450s) when the Douglases were in conflict with Bishop Kennedy and the Crown.[68] But the "sign," strikingly, of empire over *all* of Britain is nonetheless to be read in the heraldic portraiture of the ideal king, the king as fictive body. In Dunbar's *The Thrissill and the Rois*, it will be recalled, the heraldic representation of the royal body is more complex—triplicate, in fact: the king is thistle, lion, and eagle. And whereas Holland's description implies narrative through prophecy of empire, Dunbar's triply represented king actually functions within an allegorical narrative. *The Goldyn Targe* also makes use of heraldic motifs, as the poem's title suggests: "Venus chevalry" assaults Reason and his "scheld of gold" and gains the field (ll. 193, 200). Court poets, as much as court painters, were involved in the production of heraldic art.

It will be recalled that the Chepman and Myllar print of Dunbar's "Ballade of . . . Barnard Stewart" is dated 9 May 1508, close to the time of James's tournament. All nine, in fact, of the Chepman and Myllar prints were issued in or about 1508, when the taste for chivalric spectacular was being amply indulged by James's court. The prints are thus an especially helpful index of the importance of courtly and chivalric art during James's reign. They included, in addition to Dunbar's "Ballade" and *The Goldyn Targe*, Lydgate's *Complaint of the Black Knight* (under the title of "The maying or disport of Chaucer"); *The porteous of nobleness* (20 April 1508, a translation of Alain Chartier's *Le breviaire des nobles*); *Eglamour*; and *Golagrus and Gawain*.[69]

Golagrus and Gawain, based on two episodes from *Percevalle le Gallois*, has been linked to *Lancelot of the Laik* because of its concern with the theme of homage.[70] The romance tells the story of Golagrus, whose castle has never had an overlord — a situation not to Arthur's liking. Gawain accordingly champions his king's desire to exact homage from Golagrus and must prove his chivalrous nature by pretending to be vanquished in jousting with Arthur's opponent. The romance, then, contains elements of disguise and of theater; Gawain must "act" as well as act. And it concerns royal expansionism — an expansionism achieved through the efforts of the loyal knight. The romance pits the isolate knight against the faithful vassal, the representative of aristocratic community, the courtier; but it thereby makes a space for risk and rivalry, for the proving of honor, at the same time that it identifies knightly exploits with monarchical government. The romance, in short, assures the pursuit of knightly honor while putting it to the service of kingship.

Lancelot of the Laik, associated by Janet Smith with the court of James IV but by other writers with James III, is a dream-vision poem containing a lengthy passage on royal duties.[71] Lancelot fights for Arthur disguised in red armor, and — as did James IV in his tournaments of 1507 and 1508 — also adopts the disguise of a black knight. *Lancelot* gives a central place to discourse of, about, and for monarchy, within a romance narrative of risk and disguise. Gilbert of the Haye's prose manuscript contains, in addition to *The Buke of the Governaunce of Princis*, *The Buke of the Law of Armys* (a translation of Honore Bonet's *Arbre des Batailles*) and *The Buke of the Ordre of Knychthede* (a translation of the anonymous fourteenth-century *Le Livre de l'Ordre de Chevalerie*).[72] Like *Lancelot of the Laik*, then, it brings questions of kingly governance together with knighthood, and at a number of points Haye reflects on the relations between the two: "For the honour of knychthede standis in that, that he be lufit, lovit, prisit, honourit, and doubtit, with the prince, lordis, and peple of the realme; for the honour of lordis and princis standis in the pluralitee of mony worshipfull and honourable knychtis."[73] For Haye, the honor of the knight is inseparable from the honor of the prince. This effort to harmonize knight and king was commissioned by the chancellor of James II, William Sinclair, earl of Orkney; but the surviving manuscript, traditionally dated in the mid–fifteenth century, is now thought to have been copied late in the 1480s. "The Sinclair family long maintained a tradition of patronage and scholarship"; it was at the suggestion of Henry, third lord Sinclair, "fader of bukis," that Gavin Douglas undertook his translation of the *Aeneid*.[74] The Sinclairs also continued their association with the royal court; Sir David Sinclair, for example, made James IV the executor of his will, which left *The Buk of Gud Maneris* — probably Caxton's edition — to Sir Magnus Harrode.[75]

The chivalric worship of heroes from classical antiquity — and of their more recent national avatars — was strong in Scotland. The Treasurer's Accounts for the reign of James IV record numerous payments to tale-tellers; and Blind Hary, one of the poets who benefited from James's patronage, composed *Schir William Wallace*, a poem that celebrates one of the chief heroes of the Wars of Independence.[76] Because of its "courtly" qualities, the poem has traditionally been contrasted with the "older epic spirit" of Barbour's *Bruce*.[77] But the epic was by no means dead; it was, rather, being retrained for a changing aristocracy. Stories of Alexander continued to be popular in the fifteenth century: *The Buik of the Most Noble and Valiant Conquerour Alexander the Grit* has been described as differing greatly from "chronicle-like accounts of Alexander's life and conquests"; "rather than an economical and fastmoving account of conquests centered around a superhuman hero," it is "a leisurely detailed narrative of individual performances both military and amorous."[78] *The Buik of . . . Alexander*'s preoccupation with single combats is striking and noteworthy for the play it thereby gives to the epic creation, through confrontation with the similar, of the honorable self. It consists in part of a rendition of the enormously chic "Les Voeux du Paon" ("The Avowis of Alexander"); the Scottish version of the French romance *Clariodus*, probably composed at the end of the fifteenth century, also contains an account of vows made to the peacock. Smith remarks of *Clariodus* that "whereas, in *Les Voeux du Paon*, the knights vow to accomplish deeds . . . in a real war, here the vows relate to a tournament and a marriage, and are little more than a courtly ceremonial. . . . The comparative insignificance of the vows seem to mark the romance as a late French treatment of the subject."[79] *Clariodus* is thus an instance of the intensification of the artfulness of chivalry — of the increasing abstraction and ritualization of chivalry — that has been thought by so many scholars (including Smith, as her belittling rhetoric suggests) to be a mark of its decadence and decline.[80]

The other part of *The Buik of . . . Alexander* is "The Forray of Gadderis"; like "Ane Ballet of the Nine Nobles," it emphasizes "hard feichthyngis" and conquest.[81] But it will not do to polarize overmuch epic and romance, martial vigor and courtliness; for the "Forray" tells the kind of story that lay behind many of the fictionalized *pas d'armes* of the fifteenth century. Like the *Chanson de Roland*, it is the story of a defense of a *pas* against overwhelming odds. It is also a story in which the theme of the *chevalier mesconnu*, likewise found in *Lancelot*, is central. Through the valiant figure of Pyrrus — whose identity is at first unknown and who is "scornit" for his "vnworthie" arms but who later reveals himself to be the nephew of Duke Emynedus — the "Forray" enacts the chivalric identification of nobility (blood) with nobility (virtue), bringing together the two motifs that late medieval tournament pageantry was most concerned to join: "The pure man that vnarmit was / Reid prekand stoutly throw the preis" (l. 1203–4). Pyrrus explains to Emynedus:

> I haue bene scornit this day greatlie
> For armour; louit mot God be,
> For now I have aneuch plentie!
> My father is of Archade.
>   (l. 1256–59)

Recognition — the cognition of identity — is thus linked, in the "Forray," to the restoration of armor (the aristocratic body's ideal image and "alienating armature") and of "arms," that is, family name; but Pyrrus must first "prove" himself before his likeness to his uncle can be identified.

The chivalric obsession with disguise is also important in *Roswall and Lillian*, a poem probably "written in the late fifteenth century in southern Scotland," which "survives in two early prints."[82] The poem treats a Three Days' Tournament: Roswall is sent away by his father for freeing prisoners and is betrayed by a false steward who assumes Roswall's identity; Roswall returns, calling himself Dissawar, and jousts in a tournament as a white knight, a black knight, and a red knight. As Jesse Weston notes, the Three Days' Tournament is often allied with the motif of the false claimant — the double-rival who claims to be the hero, the one who performed the hero's deeds, and who thus tries to steal the hero's identity.[83] The theme of disguise also appears in the popular *Rauf Coilʒear*, a poem mentioned by William Dunbar in the *Lament for the Makaris* and by Gavin Douglas in *The Palice of Honour*.[84] The king, who disguises his identity, dines one night with Rauf, a collier; the latter brings coal to the king's castle, realizes the king's true identity, and — against the objections of the courtiers — is made a knight. *Rauf Coilʒear* thus plays upon the intersection of the glamorous with the ordinary — on the theme of aspiration — that we have associated with the ideal function of the king and that so often finds expression in the chivalric motif of disguise.

King Hart, which has sometimes been attributed to Gavin Douglas and was probably written between 1501 and 1512, is another poem on a chivalric theme; in this allegory, the protagonist arrives at the Palace of Honour, gives himself up to worldly goods, fights in a tournament against the world, is beaten and forced to cry for mercy.[85] The poem attests the association of tournaments with *vanitas* prevalent in contemporary satires of the aristocracy; the tournament becomes a scene in which — as in book 1 of *The Faerie Queene* — anxieties about the nature of honor can be managed, and honor itself recoded. Gavin Douglas's *The Palice of Honour* (ca. 1501) is also, as its title indicates, a poem that explores the nature of honor, that tries to give this evanescent "virtue" an essence by identifying it with the architecture of the court. We will spend some time discussing it, because the poem brings together, in a spectacular manner, so many of the themes and motifs of the pageantry and literature associated with the reign of James IV. The poem was dedicated to James, and it may have inspired James's appointment of Douglas to the lucrative provostship of St. Giles.[86]

Priscilla Bawcutt comments: "The *Palice of Honour* seems to me very much a young man's poem. At one point the dreamer is addressed as "Galland" (1308). . . . There is an element of bravura about the poem, as if Douglas wished to show off newly acquired ideas and techniques."[87] We have, then, an image of a youth proudly "showing off" his new equipment. Douglas's "obtrusive" and "insistent" rhetoric is seen by Bawcutt as "bravura," a somewhat hollow show; youth and exhibitionism once again go together, as they do in the scholarly treatments of James IV that we explored in the previous chapter. While, then, Bawcutt clearly perceives the exhibitionism of the *Palice* — its desire to be seen, of which the obverse is the desire to see the "god armypotent" who rules the Court of Honour — Bawcutt does not examine either the nature of her own critical gaze or the dependence of the poetics of honor on exhibitionism, theatricalization, phenomenalization. My reading of the poem is greatly indebted to Bawcutt's very solid and interesting commentary but operates at the remove I have just outlined.

For Bawcutt's criticism of Douglas's inability to resolve "contradictions" in his "thought" ("His conception of Honour is more secular and this-worldly than perhaps he would admit, and not fully reconcilable with . . . Christian doctrines") likewise fails to consider that the contradiction between "worldly" honor and "spiritual" or "high" honor is the problematic that produces and constitutes the very concept of honor — not just Douglas's own "warlike" representation of the virtue.[88] The contradiction between the exteriority and materiality of honor (the need for honor to show off, to make an appearance, to "prove" something) and the interiority of honor as virtue (the need to locate an inner essence that will ground the appearances of honor) lies at the heart of the ideal image, the war mask — of "self-extension" through armature. Douglas thus attempts to tie together the notion of *virtue* as "moral excellence" and as "valour, courage" in his climactic vision of the Court of Honour — which is, in fact, not so much a vision as a blinding.[89]

> Schute was the dure; in at a boir I blent,
> Quhair I beheld the glaidest represent
> That euer in eirth I, wretchit Catiue, kend.
> ·   ·   ·   ·   ·   ·   ·   ·   ·   ·   ·   ·   ·   ·
> Enthronit sat ane God Omnipotent,
> On quhais glorious visage as I blent,
> In extasie be his brichtnes atanis
> He smote me doun and brissit all my banis.
> (ll. 1903ff.)

In this passage, the narrator's desire to see is styled as presumptuous, intrusive; he is a "wretchit Catiue," who cannot bear the brightness of the "represent" he peers at. The narrator looks in, believing himself to be unseen; but the brightness of the image is such that it seems to see, to detect him, beating him down so that he can look no longer. The passivity and activity of sight interchange with striking force in this blinding vision, so much so that we almost feel we are in the presence of a simultaneous voyeurism and exhibitionism; both the desire to see and the desire to be seen come together at this moment of direct perception of the ideal image. Douglas's version of Dante's inexpressibility *topos* represents the moment when the ideal is seen, and the onlooker is thereby catapulted at once into the aspiration and inadequacy that constitute identification. Thus, the excluded onlooker looks in and is seemingly punished for his presumption; but the greatness of the image, its power to "brissit . . . banis" — its power of alteration — remakes the onlooker through devastation. At the same time that we are reminded of the ideal's power of alteration over human flesh, though, we are also reminded of the immateriality of the ideal — Douglas uses the noun *represent*. The createdness of the ideal, its ficticity, is thus defended against with spectacular artillery: Douglas's own anxiety about his possible uncreation as a result of "being seen to see" is turned into a triumphant vision of the blinding power of the "jewel," the sovereign.

Bawcutt prefers the reading of the London edition (ca. 1553) of "God Omnipotent" as "god armypotent," and this indeed makes sense in light of the valorous chieftain to whom the poem is dedicated. Douglas's attempt to spiritualize honor legitimizes violence by making it a function of sight — of superreal brilliance and splendor. And his poem suggests that it is through the risk of mutilation that the subject of honor will recover plenitude, through its relation with the ideal. The Court of Honour asserts the clarity, the verticality of sovereign ideality and the risk involved in its approach (a foreshadowing of the risk involved in its internalization): it is, as Bawcutt says, "remote and difficult of access," "set upon a high mountain"; "it can be reached only after crossing a horrifying abyss."[90] But it is nonetheless "Pleneist with plesance like to Paradice" (l. 1413): *aula* includes *sinus*. The desire to recover protection and plenitude through a redemption of violence accounts for a number of the poem's metamorphoses.

For example, there is the shift, at the beginning of the poem, from a *locus amoenus* of "fragrant flouris" (l. 19) to a nightmare vision of a "laithlie flude" with fish that have become "grym monstures" (ll. 145, 148) — to a world, as Bawcutt puts it, "ruled by the caprice of Fortune."[91] The links with Chaucer's *House of Fame* — a poem that exposes the ficticity and contingency of reputation — are close indeed: Chaucer's House of Fame also asserts a remote and forbidding verticality, but the ground literally shifts — and, with the House of Rumour, disappears altogether — where women rule and are not ruled. Chaucer's poem works through an increasing spatial and physical unease — through vertigo and agoraphobia. But the integrity of the body is not, in Chaucer's poem, threatened for good *and* for ill to the degree that it is in Douglas's poem. Douglas makes explicit the problematic relation of body to image that is only implicit in *The House of Fame*; his ambitions — for plenty, power, splendor — are in accord with his enhanced sense of physical vulnerability. In the "Court Rethoricall" of Douglas's Muses is, then, to be found, not the shifting and uncertain ground of *The House of Fame*, but the "constant ground of famous storeis sweit," "the facound well Celestiall," "the Fontane and Originall / Quhairfra the well of Helicon dois fleit" (ll. 835ff.). Calliope — whose intercession saves Douglas from Venus — is the Muse of Heroic Poetry, of the "Kinglie stile . . . / Cleipit in Latine heroicus" (ll. 877–78). Douglas's language is thus the overflowing of a constant supply of plenty reinscribed into the space of violence: the body of the ground, of the woman, of the dreamer himself, is rescued from the threat of (feminine) caprice through the "Kinglie stile." And in the opening of the poem, Douglas, wandering in a "heuinly place" (l. 55), hears a voice singing in praise of May: "O May, thow Mirrour of soles, / Maternall Moneth, Lady and Maistres" (ll. 64–65). She is the

> verray ground till working of nature,
> Quhais hie curage and assucurit cure
> Causis the eirth his frutes till expres.
>   (ll. 69–71)

Lest we miss that the martial aspect of "curage" is being invoked alongside the maternal plenitude of May, the voice continues:

> In the is rute and augment of curage,
> In the enforces Martis vassalage,
> In the is amorous lufe and Harmonie
> With Incrementis fresche in lustie age.
>   (ll. 82–85)

The question, again, for Douglas, is whether the creative and destructive aspects of the power to alter can coexist in the "same" place or personage; hence it is a question about whether the ideal image can be preserved from the contradictions that beset Fortune (whom Douglas addresses after the paradise of the prologue is transformed into a desert) and that emerge also in Douglas's ambivalence toward Venus. Of Fortune he writes, "Now thair, now heir, now hie and now deuaillis / Now to, now fra, now law, now Magnifyis" (ll. 174–75). The sight of the unhappy lovers who have follow-ed Venus prompts him to a complaint, whose diction is reminiscent of the address of Fortune: "Bewaill this warldis frail vsteidfastnes" (l. 610).

The nightmare of groundlessness has to be faced and overcome before Douglas can attain either the Court Rethoricall or the Court of Honour. The scene that precedes his adoption by Calliope is a scene of detection, of being seen to see, of judgment, humiliation, exposure. Douglas has sworn to be Venus's "man"; he feasts his eyes on processions that pass be-fore him, led by Minerva, Diana, and Venus. Bawcutt writes: "It is strik-ing how different are the dreamer's reactions to these processions. Minerva and Diana excite in him chiefly curiosity and fear. By contrast, the court of Venus rouses powerful if conflicting emotions: he desires a glimpse long before it arrives, he lavishes hyperboles on its beauty and splendour, yet he then sings a 'ballat' highly critical of Venus. Minerva and Diana neither welcome him nor do him harm, but he becomes for a while disastrously involved with Venus."[92] It truly does seem as though seeing were the form of Douglas's desire in *The Palice of Honour* ("he desires a glimpse long before it arrives"). And the sight of the erotic woman ("he lavishes hyper-boles on its beauty and splendour") produces an unrationalized ambiva-lence. A poem that has as its *Paradiso* the apotheosis of exhibitionistic splendor in the form of its kingly "represent" has as its *Inferno* the detec-tion of intrusion and a trial for defamation—for disfiguration of the (femi-nine) icon to which one's loyalties have been pledged. Unless they are like Calliope—that is, linked to the "Kinglie style"—the powerful women in Douglas's poem are dangerous: they threaten violence (after he defames her court, Venus asks for his death). They threaten violence, paradoxically, because they are not "Kinglie." They are unreliable; they are not protective as they should be.

It is, again, chiefly Venus's mutability that provokes Douglas's "blasphemy." The punishment Douglas fears—more, he says, than death itself—is

> That Venus suld throw hir subtillitie
> In till sum bysyning beist transfigurat me
> As in a Beir, a Bair, ane Oule, ane Aip.
> I traistit sa for till haue bene mischaip
> That oft I wald my hand behald to se
> Gif it alterit, and oft my visage graip.
>
> (ll. 739–44)

If Douglas was "particularly impressed by book 11 of the *Metamorphoses*" it is because Ovidian shape-shifting terrorizes the integrity of the human form.[93] Douglas's nightmare is one of misrecognition: the decomposition and mutilation of the body is imaged as "misshapenness," as the transformation (and loss) of human shape. For the warrior, death comes by way of mutilation, triumph by way of an unbroken surface and possession of the "field" (though the marks of risk on the warrior's body are themselves proud signs of the capacity of the surface to reconstitute itself).[94] Douglas fears, specifically, that Venus (sensuality, love of women) will, Circe-like, change him into a beast. As MacCary puts it, "the hero seeks the primitive image of himself which the [sexualized, nonmaternal] woman . . . is responsible for destroying"; he notes that, in the *Iliad*, "the same verb *mignumi* [is] used both of sexual intercourse and martial engagement in the first ranks of men" but is also used of escape, retreat, assimilation into the crowd, disappearance into obscurity—the loss of the brilliant and outstanding image produced through single combat.[95]

The body of the woman, then, "forms" the body of the warrior insofar as sex is imagined as a martial engagement, whereby the warrior's body is shaped as an unbroken surface and instrument of penetration; but the body of the woman deforms the body of the warrior insofar as sex is imagined as a loss of surface and shape, an experience of obscurity and loss of identity. In the prologue, after he has heard the praise of May, Douglas tells us that "I raisit my visage, / Soir affrayit, half in ane frenesie" (ll. 89–90); but after he has asked Nature and May for help, he is so "desyit" that "all in till a fary / As feminine so feblit fell I doun" (ll. 107–8). In the dedication to James IV which appears at poem's end, Douglas describes himself as

thy pure leige vnleird;
Quhilk in the sicht of thy Magnificence,
Confidand in sa greit beneuolence
Proponis thus my vulgair Ignorance,
Maist humbillie with dew obedience
Beseikand oft thy michtie Excellence
Be grace to pardoun all sic variance
With sum bening respect of firme constance,
Remittand my pretendit negligence,
Thow quhais micht may humbill thing auance.
(ll. 2151–60)

The reconstitution of the poem's ground as Calliope is thus coincident with the rescue of the dreamer's heroic shape and language; the contradiction of *mignumi* is narrated as a movement from one pole of meaning to another. Cure, protection, maternity, are thus recovered, via the risk of deformation, for a heroic phenomenalization through violence: the body of the woman, *sinus*, serves *aula*.

The fear of the evanescence of worldly honor — its transience, its subjection to Fortune — sets off, in the *Palice*, a narrative structure whereby the risk of deformity is encountered and overcome. The contradiction between honor as reputation or reward (worldly honor) and honor as virtue (high honor) is thereby narrated as a displacement of one pole of meaning by the other, through a movement that is literally both upward and inward (toward the Court of Honour on its high marble mountain; through the eyes, into the chink whereby the god armypotent may be glimpsed). The inwardness and uprightness of honor tries to relocate *sinus* within *aula* in the culminating image of the "represent" of James IV, which puts an end to the metamorphics of narrative. The contradiction breaks out afresh, for honor demands a proving, a martial engagement, an exteriorizing action; it cannot afford to lose itself altogether in the innerness and obscurity of *sinus.* The image of the god armypotent as "represent" risks the "formal stagnation" of the image that Mulvey associates with the "to-be-looked-at-ness" of the woman in film.[96] The heroization of the "represent" is meant to recover image *for* action; the coincidence of *sinus* and *aula* in the Court of Honour is meant to reassure us that, in experiencing innerness, masculinity will be refound, and that ficticity, the elaboration of one's image, is a form of action.

In this sense the king is another version of Calliope; for it is finally the king and not the woman who becomes what Teresa de Lauretis calls the "narrative image" of woman — the woman as "reward" in the male hero's struggles through Oedipal narrative.[97] The martial innerness of the king, of the active represent, is the reward sought by the subject of honor. And it is appropriate to the king to whom Douglas's poem is dedicated — the "Maist gracious Prince, our souerane Iames the Feird" (l. 2145ff.) — that the contradiction implied in the term *chivalric spectacle* should make its last stand through a spectacular seeing of the blinding power of the image — the power of the image, that is, to do violence, to "brissit . . . banis" as well as any axe. To be seen is to risk deformity; but Douglas's poem "could almost serve as a blue-print for the real life 'padgeanes' that were then so popular in Scotland."[98] And the poem prays that James will be granted the "palme of victorie" and "Renoun of Chevalrie" that the king seems indeed to have urgently desired. *Honor* is a primal word; its senses are contradictory. In the late medieval tournament, the heraldic assertion of identity and the *chevalier mesconnu* collide and circle around each other. The following chapter will explore further the problematics of honor, and its relation to the "disguisings" and the disguises of the late medieval tournament.

11

Soft and Silken War

The connection between dress and war is not far to seek; your finest clothes are
those that you wear as soldiers.

—Virginia Woolf, *Three Guineas*

HISTORIANS of the medieval tournament have often told the story of the
tournament's increasing ritualization, artificiality, theatricality. The shift
from violence to ritual, reality to representation, is linked with the growing importance of women—as spectators, as queens of beauty, as participants in disguisings—to tournament display. It is linked also with a changing relation between the court and the field of combat. Welsford writes
that the tournament became "a grand public mummery; knights came to
the lists in all kinds of fantastic disguises; the challenges were couched
in terms of romantic gallantry, which furnished suggestion for the plots
of many later French and English masquerades."[1] Tournament becomes,
and produces, theater. Withington explains that "just as the sword dance
of the folk gave way to mumming, so the tournament of the court became
a 'soft and silken war.'"[2] In his view, tournament disguising "led to, or at
any rate stimulated," the masque. The court is imagined as a space that
manners the primitive and the violent: sword dances "give way" to mumming, tournament armor to women's clothing—to garments whose surfaces yield rather than repel. Once transformed, tournaments and folk
rituals may be seen to give rise to the masque—but only after they have
already been mannered. Nothing inherent in tourneying itself gives rise
to spectacle or to disguise.[3]

For Maurice Keen, medieval romance rather than masque is the chief
inspiration for the tournament's sophistication—though he is careful to
stress the "interplay of life and romance," the mutual dependence of romance with the "knightly world." This "interplay" adds to the tournament in the following way: "From the point of view that we have been

192

Fig. 8. "Jousting and Watching," from Margaret Tudor's Book of Hours. Photo from the Picture Archives of the Austrian National Library, Vienna. Codex Vindobonensis 1897, fol. 38 recto.

following until now, the hurly-burly of such engagements has presented a spectacle dominated by crude and sometimes extreme masculine violence. From the new angle of vision that the romance storytellers open for us, what we see now is a very different scene, in which colour and violence fuse together into the display of the male before the female."[4] If "crude and sometimes extreme masculine violence" takes the form of a "hurly-burly," then it would seem that masculine violence must itself be a spectacle; but in Keen's account the "angle of vision" shifts to a "different scene," one that adds "colour," and fuses it with violence. Color enters the picture only when the masks of love as well as of war are in play — when, that is, the woman appears to watch the hurly-burly. The woman appears, too, when the "interplay" of romance literature and the "knightly world" takes place; her role in the tournament is the result of the introduction of ficticity.

Keen tries not to polarize color and violence; in his history, one does not so much displace the other as add to it: "This additional courtly and amorous appeal of the tournament was one that could co-exist without difficulty with the other attractions we have been considering: the tourney's value as a training ground for war, its significance as an exercise in which great prizes could be won, and as a social gathering of a certain kind of elite. But it was capable of more elaborate development than they were, and in particular directions — those of ceremony, of theatre, and of what anthropologists call play."[5] The "particular directions" of "ceremony, of theatre," and of "play," are, then, to be associated with this "additional courtly and amorous appeal"; they coexist with, but are not "particular" to, hurly-burly, elite gatherings, the winning of prizes, or war. Masculine rivalry in all its forms is outside the space of theater — though, as Keen's own rhetoric again suggests, we do watch it. Pamela King's notion that as the tournament "moved towards masque, it also became more and more concerned with the battle for the unattainable lady" likewise associates theatricalization with a feminization of tournament narrative; her formulation suggests that prizes and women may be related in a more complex manner than the concept of "coexistence" would indicate.[6]

Scholars have also detected in the tournament "proper" — that is, aside from its relation to masque and mummery — a movement from war to the imitation of war. Whereas the rough and ready melee of the early tournament trained the aristocrat for real war — and was really violent — the carefully orchestrated joust, conducted with blunted weapons and elaborate regulations, seems to imprison the knight within gesture and meaning. Clephan writes that "tournaments generally tended to become milder as rules, regulations and limitations were enacted for their government."[7] The desire to display the power of violence rather than to exercise it is seen to motivate the development of the joust from the melee: Cripps-Day explains that "the just . . . began to be the more popular sport with the knight, because it enabled him to display his prowess more conspicuously than in the tourney."[8] The aristocratic body is remannered by the joust: once a practiced and trained body, a body of instrumentality, it becomes increasingly a dramatized and civilized body. The violence of the aristocratic body is caught up in and confined to meaning, even as the space in which it operates is redefined as scene rather than battleground. Malcolm Vale also believes that "the popularity of the joust in the fourteenth and fifteenth centuries may partly result from the fact that it offered greater opportunities for performing notable feats in public than did the collective *tournoi*."[9] Vale presents, in *War and Chivalry*, an exemplary critique of the scholarly tendency to associate tournaments with illusion and decadence; but in undermining the distinction between tournament and war, he is less interested in examining the theatricality of war than he is in asserting the tournament's continuing purchase on martial realities: "The stress laid upon one-to-one combat in the lists is matched by the emphasis on personal fame achieved by highly individualistic war-time behaviour."[10] Fantasy per se, in such formulations, is not powerful, thus not inherent in war.

Late medieval tournaments are seen increasingly to rely on mysterious, frequently allegorical plots, centered around the defense of a mythical "pass": mystery and allegoresis themselves seem to signify that representation, rather than fighting, has become the issue. For the marriage of Charles of Burgundy with Margaret of York in 1468, a great gilded fir tree, the *arbre d'or*, was erected in the Grande Place. The *tenants* holding the *pas* were the Chevaliers de L'Arbre d'Or; after the *venans* (the challengers) were disposed of in jousts, the chevaliers "then jousted . . . without touching each other; and the first day's proceedings finished with a banquet."[11] Sydney Anglo has traced the structuring of the late medieval *pas d'armes* around the *arbre* or the *perron* (a mound or, at times, a *colonne*) to "l'ancienne cérémonie du combat judiciaire par lequel on déterminait les droits de propriété": "Pareillement, quand des chevaliers entraient dans les lices et touchaient à l'écu pendant d'un arbre ou d'un perron, ils reproduisaient inconsciemment" these ancient ceremonies in which "tenure" would be decided.[12] The *perron* was a symbol of civic and local authority around which such combats would take place; and Anglo reports that "en 1467, après la défaite des Liégeois, Charles le Téméraire fit transporter le perron à Bruges et le fit élever sur la place du marché—à l'endroit même où, l'année suivante, un perron artificiel fut dressé avec un arbre pour le *Pas de l'Arbre*

d'Or."[13] Anglo traces the ceremony through a scene in *Yvain,* a romance
that appears to have had a powerful influence on tournament pageantry;
but though his own essay tries to recover the original meaning of the rite
of the *perron,* his *chevaliers* indulge in it, at best, unconsciously. The *perron* is an obscure fragment of an ancient ritual. And why "le *perron* n'ap-
paraît dans les tournois historiques qu'au milieu du xve siècle" is not explained.[14]

Keen remarks that the rite of the *perron* becomes "the acme of gesture
for gesture's sake, a truly empty rite indicative of concern with theatrical
effect rather than values." He continues: "There is . . . a connection between the expansion of the element of theatre in the *pas d'armes* and the
growing divorce between skill in joust and tourney and true military skill.
Theatre and décor as it were expanded to fill the gap left by the declining relevance of chivalrous sport to martial activity. . . . concern with
ritual gesture and imitation was becoming more obsessive."[15] The purpose
of Keen's book is ultimately to rescue late medieval chivalry from accusations of the inanition of its values; in this he largely succeeds, and his sym-
pathy for the extent to which ideals are truly motivating—truly productive—is moving. But in order to accomplish his purpose, he, like Malcolm
Vale, perpetuates the isolation of "value" from "theater" that informs the
histories he is trying to rewrite.

For many historians, indeed, the history of the late medieval tournament—like that of late medieval chivalry—is one of the collapse of vigor
into decadence, of a fall from reality into appearance. Ruth Huff Cline be-
queaths the kind of pageantry exemplified in the *Pas de l'Arbre d'Or* to
the Renaissance: the allegorical element in the tournament "has lost its [me-
dieval] seriousness of purpose and has become a mere plaything."[16] Arthur Ferguson, in *The Indian Summer of English Chivalry,* finds in the
tournament not so much the thoroughgoing inanition of value as a desperate last stand against irrelevance: "In the clash of arms alone . . . could
the illusion of reality be preserved."[17] For Huizinga, the tournament "filled
the place of the drama of a later age"; elements both of "mockery" and
of "sentimentality" enabled the "crying falsehood" of the "illusion of a high
and heroic life" to be borne.[18] And Cripps-Day writes that "when chivalry
is at last touched by the hand of decay, the tournament . . . survives to
carry on [chivalry's] . . . traditions under new forms, but with a florid extravagance which . . . dooms [the tournament] . . . to the trivial destiny
of the showy pageant."[19] For Cripps-Day, then, pageantry is both a sign
of "decay" and a fate which awaits mortal things; pageantry, in effect, dramatizes the mortification of chivalry. And it is, in particular, "florid extravagance"—conspicuous waste, an excess of gesture—that trivializes the

tournament, making of it a hollow show. The history of the tournament can thus be read as a history of representational excess, of a loss of substance or life which leads, inevitably, to the rococo. Feudalism declines, and aristocratic warfare goes with it—leaving behind a decadent and frivolous aristocracy, confined to the dramatization of its former glories.

The notion that violence disappeared at the end of the Middle Ages is of course, as Vale's study demonstrates, untenable. If warfare had been during the Middle Ages the "fate" rather than the "sport" of princes, it continued to be so in early modern Europe and even, according to Perry Anderson, found new life in new forms: the "zero-sum model of world trade" that treated the trade of the Dutch like the estates of the Moors "was derived from the zero-sum model of international politics which was inherent in its bellicism."[20] The loss that is being lamented in the histories which we have examined, then, is not so much the loss of violence per se, as the loss of a particular kind of violence—free, unruled, autonomous—to particular techniques of management: to the "civilizing," centralizing, and mechanizing of the warrior's aggressivity. What is being lamented is precisely the loss of a violence imagined as outside the space of the cultivated interior; violence, that is, "before" repression, rules, blunted weapons, politeness, order, sovereign control.[21] The court presents itself as that which civilizes violence and "nature," but this is a mystification, since "civilization" thus defined proceeds as much through unmaking as through making; the ascription of aggressivity to the realm of the natural has been mobilized in the legitimation of atrocity for as long as Western civilization can remember itself. But whether we imagine these ideological strategies as producing or gaining a hold on desire, they imply, precisely, the desire for "nature"—for, that is, a way out of the world that "man" has made. Historians of the tournament identify with the warrior and ascribe to him a purity of collision and confrontation, a full inhabiting of the body and a magical and legitimated motility—the loss of which they then lament. These lamentations thus find their place in a felt gap between the ideal and the real, between being and meaning; and they are themselves a way of closing that gap, through narratives that separate violence from theater by making the former appear to "give way to" (or be added to) the latter. It may be that the alienation from violence—from the real thing—being lamented in these histories is in part the result of the scholar's own voyeuristic exclusion, his own "feminization" as spectator; it is often the spectator who grieves over the onset of rules and the "fall" from uniform (imaged as "necessary") to costume.

We are now in a somewhat better position to understand why it is that James IV has been repeatedly associated with tournament pageantry; he has been seen to reign simultaneously over a heyday and a decline, his own "florid extravagance" giving expression simultaneously to vitality and emptiness. But while it is crucial for us to recognize the extent to which historical interpretations both of James IV and of the tournament itself are marked by common concerns, it is also necessary that we see some of the ways in which similar concerns shaped the art of the tournament. For while the readings of modern historians have been stamped by the ideology of realism — by the association of the later Middle Ages with fantasy, of chivalry with quixotic idealism, of aristocratic expenditure with poor but gallant economics, of display with mere appearance — both chivalric culture and the clerical culture with which it interacted developed discourses on the nature of reality and appearance which in turn helped to produce later readings of the tournament's function and history.[22] In the later Middle Ages, tournaments dramatized the mortification of chivalry; and this was itself a way of producing the aristocracy as the subject of history. Though concepts of "archaism" and "decline" have an historical efficacy particular to the modern scholarly texts we have been examining, the production of aristocratic violence and of the honorable subject was, in the Middle Ages, a simultaneously delicate and arduous occupation of a relation between ideality and the body, between a remembered past of greatness and the work of its reproduction.

The tournament had important connections with the ideal and practice of crusade. The complex relation of Western chivalry to the Eastern threat continually made the function of secular lordship problematic throughout the Middle Ages. It was the knight's chief duty to defend the faith — to uphold the rightness and sameness of Western Christendom against the threat of the Eastern other. The knight was in this sense the preeminent guardian of the boundaries of the Christian body; its integrity and purity were his responsibility. Tournaments were closely involved with the organization of and recruitment for crusades. If the tournament "trained the knight for war, his war-dream was the Crusade"; and it was the tournament "which was held to do honour to the home-coming crusader."[23] The tournament was a festival of honor, a ceremonial setting for the recognition of and competition for honor; and the ideal of crusade was a crucial means in the production of the ideology and practices of honor. The kind of tournament called a Round Table was also sometimes called the Pas de Saladin, in honor of the half-legendary exploits of Richard I and Saladin; Richard himself appears to have been the first English king to license tournaments.[24] Much later, the crusading spirit continued to be appealed to in a wide variety of chivalric texts and performances. The "Proclamation, whereby Six Gentlemen challenged all comers at the Just-Roiall for the marriage of Richard, duke of York, with Anne Mowbray, daughter to the duke of Norfolk," explains that the exercise of arms on "high dayes of honor" is an ancient, "laudable and noble custome of this Martiall and trivmphant Realme," meant to "enable nobles to the deserving of Chivalrie, by the which our mother holy Church is defended, Kinge and Princes served, Realmes and Countreyes kept and mainteyned in Justice and peace."[25] On 8 October 1518 the marriage agreement of the Dauphin and the Lady Mary was celebrated with a tournament and disguising: "In the Hall there was erected a rock, on top of which were a lady with a dolphin in her lap, and also five trees bearing the arms of Church, Empire, Spain, France, England, in token that these Powers were leagued together against the Turk. Ten knights came out of a cave, fought a tourney and returned."[26] And at the beginning of the "Articles de l'Emprinse du Chevalier Sauvage à la Dame noire," in Vulson's *Science Heroiqve* — the articles, that is, for James IV's tournament of the wild knight and the black lady — it is explained that the exercise of arms is "aux Chevaliers plus loüable ledit exercice, & principalement au service de Dieu à l'encontre des Infidelles, non seulement permis, mais meritoire."[27] The connection, that is, between tournament and the practice of arms for war — a connection repeatedly asserted by historians of the tournament — was in part a way of legitimating tournament pleasures, so long as the war in question was crusade. And the evocation of crusade enjoined upon the knight the perpetual repetition of a glorious past.

But the attempt to link tournament and crusade was not without its difficulties, and the failure to re-create ancient triumphs became an important motif in complaints against the aristocracy. Gilbert of the Haye, in *The Buke of the Law of Armys*, laments that "we se how amang kingis and princis and temporale lordis thare is rysin sa grete discensiouns discordis and weris that the brethir of the fayth — as nobles men that wont was to be werreyouris to defend the kirk rycht are now rysyn agane the commouns."[28] Aggressivity is turned inward, the body of the realm dismembered; the "true" enemy is forgotten. Crusade thus becomes a means of projecting aggressivity, of locating conflict not in the class structure of medieval society nor, for that matter, in territorial and economic "imperative," but in a global religious competition. But tournaments manifested a contradiction: they trained the knight for crusade, but they also made a spectacle of violence at home and celebrated rivalry for its own sake. The tournament was thus a site of abjection — it joined desire and repugnance, grief and joy. Dante put the tournament — its cruel laughter, its delight in dismemberment, its presentation of torture as play and weapon as plaything — in hell.[29]

The tournament thus earned considerable opprobrium from representatives of clerical culture. Innocent II condemned tournaments in the ninth canon of the Council of Clermont in 1130; "The ban was repeated by his successors over and over again, with increasing vehemence — and notable lack of effect — down to Clement V."[30] The chief complaints were extravagance — the waste of goods in display — and the equally prodigal and wanton loss of life. The Third Lateran Council's XX Canon proclaimed: "Felicis memoriae papae Innocentii et Eugenii praedecessorum nostrorum vestigiis inhaerentes, detestabiles illas nundinas velferias, quas vulgo torneamenta vocant, in quibus milites ex condicto venire solent, et ad ostentationem virium suarum et audaciae temere congrediuntur, unde mortes hominum et animarum pericula saepe proveniunt, fieri prohibemus."[31] The ideal of crusade offered the Church an ideological instrument whereby it could manage aristocratic violence and gain a purchase on honor; it should not be forgotten that Church and aristocracy were often difficult to distinguish. But precisely in order to create a sphere of values upon which its own distinct claims to power could be founded, the Church had to oppose an ethos in which the risking of life and the display of risk were of supreme importance. The tournament "positively fostered a cult of violence which was a stumbling block in the way of the mission which the Prince of Peace had entrusted to his vicars upon earth." At stake was not the instrumentality of violence, but the nature of its ideological legitimation; the tournament encouraged, not the pacification and mortification of the Christian subject, but the "tubulent spirit of secular knighthood."[32] The tournament, accordingly, became an image of nontranscendent risk — therefore, of emptiness.

It is above all the tournament's display of risk — its dramatization and valuation of risk for its own sake — that sermon literature inveighs against most strongly. Owst cites John Bromyard on the empty boasts of knights: "When they go in all their pride and splendour to the tournament and the joust, it is largely with a view to making topics for future conversation of a . . . [boasting] kind."[33] Despite his inflated appearance — his "pride and splendour" — the knight is made of words rather than deeds, language rather than action. He is a hollow show, a glittering toy:

Who . . . could praise any of them for strenuous battling with the enemy, or for their defence of country and Church, as Charlemagne, Roland, Oliver, and the other knights of antiquity are commended and praised? But rather for this — that they have a helmet of gold worth forty pounds, *ailettes* and other external insignia of the same style and even greater price; that so-and-so carried into the lists a huge square lance such as no one else carried, or could carry, and that he flung horse and rider to the ground; . . . or again, that so-and-so came to Parliament or to

the tournament with so many horse . . . they expose themselves in places and times
of peace and not of war; and to their friends, not to their enemies. Of what value
are arms adorned with gold, then, that only make the enemy bolder . . . what praise
is it that such are glorious and seek praise in prohibited deeds of arms, as in tournaments and the like, while in deeds of virtue, such as in just wars and in defence
of their own country, they are timorous, cowardly and fugitive, allowing the enemy
to devastate the land?[34]

These knights fail to fashion themselves on the basis of noble exemplars; rather than reproducing an illustrious past, they allow themselves
to be distracted by a kind of vain contemporaneity, by current fashions.
They value, at great price, "external insignia"; they display a kind of idolatry, a carnality, a refusal of transcendence, a fetishizing of the material
that accompanies the grotesqueries of competitive display, as lances become huger and huger, as retinues become likewise tumescent, as "arms
adorned with gold" become increasingly functionless. There is no interior
to this knight, no valuation of interiority; he values, solely, how he appears to others. Whereas, moreover, the knight should be a guardian of
boundaries, this knight exposes himself not to the enemy but to his friend.
He is caught up, again, in abjection—an exposure of the self to the other,
but to an other that is somehow the same (a "friend"). This knight represents, therefore, a kind of phenomenological crisis: a present without a
past, an outside without an inside, whose armor is his decoration and
whose enemies are his friends. This kind of knight delights in an "imaginary sense of heroism in battles which [he] actually would not dare to
enter or witness": he has fallen from reality into appearance, into the scene
of fantasy. He is, in short, not all there. A disappointment in the promise
of protection offered by power is perhaps at stake in these criticisms: the
knight fails to protect, to defend; he incites and wreaks violence, where
he should prevent it; he plays games instead of attending to serious business; he is, we might almost say, the abandoning father, who insists on
behaving like an adolescent son. Finally, the loss being lamented by Bromyard is the loss of a sustainable borderline—of a "clear positionality" of
good and evil, same and different, protector and assailant.

One aristocratic response to the abjection of appearance was the allegorization of chivalric materiality that has so often been accused of triviality
and frivolity. The elaboration of meaning in the display of risk functions
as a defense against the reduction of violence to "mere" gesture, costume
to an idolatry of the material. The allegory of the *pas d'armes* is a means
of reenacting the meaningfulness of violence, of recapturing both interiority and exteriority—both "principle" and the enemy. The spiritualization
of chivalry that took place in the later Middle Ages thus needs to be un-

derstood as inseparable from — not antithetical to — chivalric display. The relation is suggested in *Sir Gawain and the Green Knight*: the poem recoils from the rich description — the stiff, exteriorized allegoresis — of Gawain's armor and goes in search of the esoteric and earned symbolism of the green girdle, which is at last adopted as an exteriorized and trivialized badge by the court. The renewal of meaning is a perpetual production. But the search for meaning is enacted through the medium of virtuoso display, in a fantastic space which turns out not to be the outside of court so much as the inside; Gawain never gets out of the theater of gesture, and it is within that space that the revivification of chivalric symbol and the relegitimation of the aristocratic experience of violence and risk must take place. Throughout *Sir Gawain and the Green Knight*, as in *The Palice of Honour*, the poet desires to see; and the court is tried for its visibility.

The ideal of crusade structured knighthood within a particular phenomenology of identity and difference that positively mandated its own reenactment in the scene of chivalric fantasy; the dramatic enactment of the enemy enabled, for the aristocracy, the articulation of crucial psychosocial boundaries even as it re-created abjection on the level of theater. The spiritualization of chivalry was a means of consolidating and elaborating the place of the warrior (globally, within Western Christendom, but also within more particularized spaces), of giving him locus and meaning in interior space when the Church insisted on his legitimation exclusively in relationship to a radically other, outside-space, enemy. That this inevitably involved the warrior in the abjection of display does not alter the fact that a spiritualized chivalry allowed the aristocracy to shape its relations to clerical culture as well as vice-versa.

The sixth chapter of Gilbert of the Haye's *The Buke of Knychthede* makes clear the importance of the structuration of boundaries between inner and outer space in the ideological legitimation of knighthood:

Now declaris the doctour, that as the preste quhilk in the mess sayand has syndry habitis and habilliamentis, quhilkis ilkane has a syndry significacioun, as is acordand to thair office and order, and that office of preste and office of knycht has sa grete affinitee and alliance togeder. For quhy? that rycht as office of preste has certane thingis that pertenis to the ordre, and ilkane has a certane significacioun, sa has the order of knychthede: for ilke thing pertenand till his ordre has a certane significacioun, be the quhilkis is signifyit the noblesse of the order of knychthede.[35]

For Haye, the "affinitee" of priest and knight depends upon meaning; and in particular, it is the "significacioun" of "habitis" and "habilliamentis" that links the two. The order of knighthood is distinguishable as an order precisely by its possession of "certane thingis," of particular material and exterior marks — of particular ways of appearing — that signify "noblesse."

Knighthood is thus constituted as such through a determinate relationship between the seen and the unseen, and the following passage is accordingly an allegorization of the knight's armor:

> Item, chapellat of stele . . . is gevin to the knycht, in takenyng of drede of schame and repruf. For a knycht suld be schamefull as a maydin dredand repruf. . . . For rycht, as drede and schamefulnes, gerris a persone cast doune the hede, and luke to the erde, sa dois the stelin hat the knycht cast doune his eyne. And rycht as the stelyn hat kepis the knychtis hede, quhilk is the hyast membre, and maist principale of his persone, sa kepis drede of schame the knychtis honour, that is the hyast poynt of his ordre, and maist principale poynt of all.[36]

The allegorization of the "habilliamentis" of knighthood is, in effect, a legitimation of display, a return of the fetishized materiality of knighthood — Bromyard's "external insignia" — to transcendence. Knighthood is, then, a particular style of transcendence — a particular way of looking, of dressing, a particular kind of motility that is subject to the transcendence of "takenyng." So, there are "properteis . . . [that] pertenis till a knycht as to the habilnes of his corps." "Knychtis suld be wele ryddin, and in ʒouthede lere tobe wele ryddin on destrellis and courseris, till haunte justis and tournaymentis"; but "rycht sa is thare othir proprieteis pertenand to the saule."[37] The knight, once again, is distinguished by a special kind of outwardness, by special techniques of the body, one of which is the ability to ride in tournaments; but "rycht sa" he is distinguished by a special kind of inwardness. The need to confer an inside upon an outside — to allegorize armor, to link, through endless parallelism, the virtues of the knightly body with virtues of the soul — shapes, at every turn, the form and content of *The Buke of Knychthede.*

It is crucial for us to recognize the extent to which this discourse of interiority is a response to the ideological aggressions of clerical culture; but it is also an appropriation of clerical ideological practices for knighthood's own attempt to consolidate itself as "class" and as subject of history. The contradictions inherent in the concepts of honor and nobility made knighthood both vulnerable to and capable of meeting the challenge of clerical idealism. For the conferring of "inwardness" which we have seen in *The Buke of Knychthede* articulates boundaries between the inside and the outside of knighthood precisely so that the inside and outside thus produced may be "reconciled." And what this further suggests is that the obligation on the part of the knight to inhabit a space of transcendent nobility is in fact matched by his obligation to appear, materially, as noble.

From one point of view, then, the knight must cultivate interiority; but from another point of view he must cultivate exteriority. The knight is predicated as that man who possesses a particular kind of self which is always manifest, always engaged with that which is beyond its boundaries; he is also predicated as possessing a particular exterior which is always internalized, always engaged with a world within. The boundaries between the honorable self and its exterior are made to appear in order to disappear; and the disappearance is mediated through the positing of an immediate, unproblematic fullness of translation between word and deed, appearance and reality. The obligation to appear as what one is produces, in aristocratic culture, the idea of a self that exists through its appearances.

For all knycht is oblist at all powere to honour his persone; first to be wele cled in his persone, syne to be wele horssit, and syne wele enarmyt and harnest in his habilliament, and alssua aw nobily to be servit of noble personis, that is to say, personis vertuous, sen all nobilnesse presupponis vertu. But 3it mekle mare but comparisoun is he behaldyn till honour him self with noblesse of curage, for the quhilk noblesse of curage he beris that hye and noble order of knychthede, the quhilk alssua is defoulit and dishonourit quhen a knycht levis vertu of curage. . . . And thus sen knycht has in his hert a noble duelling place for the vertues and noblesse of curage.[38]

The passage explains that to be noble, one must look noble and be served by "noble personis." The quality of nobility inheres in the appearance of nobility, and the individual is defined as noble by the quality of the persons with whom he associates; nobility becomes a self-referential system. But, the passage goes on to say, the knight is "3it mekle mare but comparisoun" obliged to "honour him self with noblesse of curage," indeed to keep "in his hert a noble duelling place" for *curage;* the interiority of nobility is at least as important as its exteriority, if not more so. Indeed, Haye remarks that knights are honored for their hatred of vice and love of virtue, "and nocht for othir cause."

But Haye's rhetoric implies a contradiction: the order of knighthood is *"defoulit . . . quhen a knycht levis vertu of curage."* The term *defoulit* reintroduces forcibly the materiality of knighthood in the form of its vulnerability to pollution. And in one small clause both the contradiction and its resolution break forth: "that is to say, personis vertuous, sen all nobilnesse presupponis vertu." Nobleness simply presupposes virtue.[39] The contradiction — which runs throughout *The Buke of Knychthede* — is resolved by declaring the identity of exterior and interior virtue.

"Honor" enacts a problematic of the construction of the self through the image: through the way in which, as in Lacan's mirror stage, the image one develops of oneself — of one's body — is constructed by the way in which one is seen.[40] Honor becomes a way of expressing the self's need to be seen in order to constitute itself as self; the paradox of a self that must be seen, and hence must appear for — must dramatize itself to — an other in order to exist as self, is inherent in the concept of honor. The very need to be recognized, to be *seen* as what one is in order to *be*, involves the subject in a perpetual loss of being. To be seen is to be appropriated; as Lacan would put it, it is to become a "signifier" in "the discourse of the other." To take on a name, a title, is to be identified by and for the other. An honorable identity must perpetually be resignified, must perpetually be extorted from others, because it can never be signified without being simultaneously appropriated. The need to confer "inwardness" upon the honorable subject — the need to merge honor (virtue) with honor (title, trappings, precedence) — is a response to the perpetual emptying-out of the self in the drama of recognition which honor entails.

The problem is exacerbated when *honor,* in the sense of rank or office, is hereditary; when, precisely, the subject's need to achieve recognition confronts the need to assume a coincidence of the two senses of *honor.*

If honor establishes status, the converse is also true, and where status is ascribed by birth, honour derives not only from individual reputation but from antecedence. . . . The well-born are assumed to possess by inheritance the appropriate character and sentiments . . . but when it is asserted they do not . . . the concept of honour faces an ambiguity which can only be resolved by an appeal to some tribunal, the "fount of honour": public opinion, the monarch, or the ordeal of the judicial combat which implied a direct appeal to God.[41]

Honor thus raises the problem of "the facts and processes of recognition: how, on what grounds and by whom is the claim to honour recognized?" For the man of honor to admit "that his honour = precedence is not synonymous with his honour = virtue . . . would be to admit himself dishonoured. For him there is only one concept, his honour."[42] But the man of honor must, perpetually, dramatize the singleness of the concept — must show his honor (precedence) which he possesses is synonymous with his honor (virtue). The tournament was, for the warrior aristocracy of the Middle Ages, a scene wherein the drama of recognition — the coincidence of reality and appearance — could be enacted. If "simply to appear" at a tournament "was in itself a demonstration of a man's right to mingle in an elite society" — of a man's (hereditary) right to put in an appearance so that his appearance could be recognized as an essence — then it was precisely this right that the tournament itself was designed to "prove."[43]

In Gilbert of the Haye's *Buke of Knychthede,* the aristocratic body and

its "habilliamentis" signify the knight's honor; the decorated body of the
knight is a site wherein the coincidence of exteriority and inner virtue is
pictured for the gaze. The decorated body itself becomes a border, but the
kind of border on which is played out the identity of that which lies on
either side. Hence the notion, expressed in Haye, that honor can be "defoulit"; hence "the intimate relation between honour and the physical person."[44] The drama of recognition entails an *agon* simultaneously of the
body and of the gaze. The body must be offended and must be seen to
be offended; and there is a way in which—as we have noted—to be seen
is to be offended. Disfiguration of the body effaces the marks that signify the coincidence of honor and virtue. Violence is the medium through
which the honorable self, in its struggle to extort its own glorious image
from the face and look of the other, must constitute itself.

The honorable self must seem in order to be; it demands simultaneously
that the other reflect its image back to itself and that the other not appropriate that image by *becoming* it (hence stealing the essence from the
appearance). The honorable self is thus constituted through its relation
to the double; it demands and refuses the double. The honorable self is
always poised between finding itself through an image seen by and in the
other and losing itself by finding itself outside itself. The friend, in effect,
is the double that reflects back the image of honor without stealing it. The
enemy steals the image. But the boundary between the two is completely
unstable. The enemy, in other words, is the self when it is found outside
the self, hence the need for interiority as well as exteriority. Interiority appears to resist the alienation and death that accompany discovery of the
double and that lie behind the reflection.[45]

Even as the honorable self is constituted through violence, it is also constituted through nostalgia. If honor is its own vindication—if it is essen-
tialized, for example, as hereditary—then the vindication of honor is the
repeated recovery of an original essence, or, to be more precise, of the restoration of an original image. Nostalgia means, in part, that the honorable self's desire for the interior essence of honor must be pursued to the
death.[46] As the legend of James IV itself suggests, honor is therefore in-
herently self-destructive as well as destructive of others. The perpetual
need to assert honor as an interior essence thus produces the *meaning* of
a life, as well as cathecting its apparency; the life of a knight, if well lived,
becomes a perfect representation, and its end—the death of the knight—a
crowning and spectacular image of the validation of the honorable self
through violence. The identity and continuity of the honorable self with
its exterior images find expression in the worship of death and the worship of the past: the life of a knight is always an imitation of a past model,

a Roland or a Lancelot, because it is the knight's double imperative to confer interiority upon an exteriority — to make self out of the nonself — and
to confer exteriority upon interiority, to make nonself out of the self. At
the same time, though, the honorable self's need to prove itself, to strive
for approximation of the image, catapults it into the future, into ambition. The play between self and nonself, past and future, is the matrix for
the "biography of the perfect knight."[47]

To disguise oneself, then, at a tournament, either as a *chevalier mesconnu* or as Arthur, is to act out the acting-out inherent in the life of honor.
The disguise of the unknown knight is a way, paradoxically, of proving
that honor is its own vindication. "Plain arms" — tinctured but otherwise
unmarked shields — are, according to Brault, "a favourite device in Arthurian
literature used whenever an author needs to disguise a character or involve
him in a case of mistaken identity." The association of plain arms with
the uncouth Perceval is probably, Brault argues, "the reason why thirteenth-
century Arthurian romances frequently ascribe plain arms to unproven
knights (*chevaliers nouveaus*)."[48] The use of plain arms was particularly
connected with the motif of the Three Days' Tournament, in which a knight
jousts for a period of three days, wearing on each day a different color.
We have noted that the Three Days' Tournament is often linked to the motif
of the false claimant, the rival who claims to be the hero; it also has links
with the *Bel Inconnu* poems, in which the (unknown) knight is flouted
by a proud lady until she is confuted by his deeds of valor.[49] The Three
Days' Tournament thus vindicates, through the motif of disguise, the notion that honor is its own vindication; it dramatizes identity by breaking
up and then restoring the boundary between friend and foe, same and other.

Brault has commented on the quality of mystery attached to the black,
green, and red knights who "are forever emerging from the forest to challenge the heroes of Arthurian romances. These mysterious adversaries are
often evil-doers and the urge to give sinister connotations to their arms
is well-nigh irresistible. On the other hand, when the knights turn out to
be friends or relatives, the tendency is to turn to Celtic myth or Christian
ritual for an appropriate interpretation."[50] Plain arms represent, at least
in part, the difficulty of such interpretation, the challenge posed to attempts
to fix the play of honor, to recognize who is friend or foe so that honor
itself can be recognized. For the difficulty of interpreting these uncanny
figures is not a problem exclusive to modern scholarship; it is the problem
that *produces* the *chevalier mesconnu*.[51]

The disguised knight is often the protagonist of romance as well as the
challenger. Princes, too, adopt the disguise of the *chevalier mesconnu*. The
desire of knight and king, in romance and in tournament, to efface iden-

tity, is produced by the desire to prove the uncontestability of identity.[52] Moreover, the problem of recognition and nonrecognition — the problem of honor — continues to be dealt with not only through, as Jameson argues, a repositioning of evil in the realm of the black arts but also through the production of a theoretical discourse on the interiority of knighthood; through the tournament itself, as a way of producing class amity by means of rivalry; and above all, through disguise, "disguising," spectacles of identity mistaken and affirmed.[53] Tournament theater enabled the friend to function as the enemy, and this was in turn essential to the production of the subject of honor. For the subject of honor — the warrior — requires the extortion of recognition from the "similar." To this extent, were the enemy truly "other," his defeat would scarcely serve to validate honor. The similarity of the enemy is as essential to his function in the psychic economy of honor as is his difference. The class consciousness of the medieval nobility was consolidated through the *production* of what Jameson calls the "perplexing question of how my enemy can be thought of as being *evil* . . . when what is responsible for his being so characterized is . . . the *identity* of his own conduct with mine."[54]

As Lacan points out, the mask — the disguise — is itself a weapon both in love and in war. When we grimace at our opponents or unfurl our best feathers before our lovers, we are creating images of ourselves. We create these masks, these doubles, in order to make ourselves seen in an extraordinary way: in order to fascinate, or to ward off fascination. To make either war or love is to appear more brilliant, more terrible, than usual. By doubling himself, by pitting image against image, the knight proves his existence as knight, thus acquiring recognition, a name, an identity. War is theater — it is not outside the space of theater. And the tournament makes theater out of the theater of war and the drama of recognition and misrecognition inherent in it. It "brings out" the theatricality of war — spacing out bodies, elaborating the moment of confrontation, ritualizing gesture — in order to fix, *for* the gaze, those moments of fascination — of the giving and receiving, the solicitation and destruction, of the gaze — that give the knight his identity. The tournament thus preoccupies itself with disguise and identity, anonymity and fame; hence its paradoxical delight in, and dependency on, both *chevaliers mesconnus* and the elaborate art of the blazon.

The tournament is, as we have noted, a ritual that enacts the pursuit of the ideal image. In the tournament, the gaze is fully caught up in the staging and framing of human form and formlessness, within articulated structures that are themselves the spatial coordinations of the image. Both the power of the image to double the self—to make it larger than life—and the alienation brought out by the disjunction between image and being (the lived experience of the body) are enacted in those moments of "formal stagnation" that unleash the aggressivity of the gaze in the confrontation of warrior with warrior.[55] Lacan explains that when the infant assumes his "specular" image—when he sees himself in the mirror—the "I" is situated "in a fictional direction"; "the total form of the body by which the subject anticipates in a mirage the maturation of his power is given to him only as *Gestalt*, . . . in an exteriority."[56] The form of the subject's anticipated power "appears to him above all in a contrasting size . . . that fixes it and in a symmetry that inverts it, in contrast with the turbulent movements that the subject feels are animating him." There is thus, for the subject, an image of futurity, of power, of grandness, totality, symmetry—of "form" itself—but the image is exterior, alienated from the subject's own bodily experience of fragmentation and "organic insufficiency."[57]

The difficult relation in the project of honor between the "mental permanence of the I" and its "alienating destination"—between essence and effort, being and becoming honorable—is illuminated further by Lacan's stress on the inseparability of the *formative* (productive) power of objectifying identifications from the "fictional direction" they give to the "I." The specular image is formative precisely because of the discordance it establishes between the reality of the subject and the maturation of his power. The fantastic image of what the subject "is" projects the subject into his history even as the relation of the image to becoming is oblique (because fantastic). Change is simultaneously obscured and instantiated by the alienating form of the image. Thus the subject seeks to create a relation between an interiority and the exteriority of the image; the creation of this relation is the creation of his history. The image, too, is linked with the "question of the meaning of beauty as both formative and erogenic."[58] The tournament provides a space for the fantastic simultaneity of being and becoming. Through the aestheticization and magnification of male costume, through the function of the lady as image of beauty, through the symmetry of the "field," through the homology between lady and field as the goal of violent effort, the tournament enables the acting-out of the formative and erogenic role of beauty in a warrior culture: its role in the enabling of identifications, its vindication of the simultaneity of aspiration and goal.[59]

Through images of the fragmented body—against which the effort to consolidate and defend an articulated space (a *pas*, a castle) positions itself—the tournament both forms formlessness and deforms form.[60] The

attempt to reform "organic insufficiency" through spectacular efforts of becoming what one is thrusts the later medieval tournament into narratives
involving grotesquerie, transitivism, transvestism, and the possession of
beauty incarnate. Images of visceral persecution abound not only in the
spectacle of the field of the fallen but also in the fragmentation and
reconstitution of the body in heraldic blazon. As is attested by the black
lady of James's tournament (and Dunbar's parodic blazon of "My ladye
with the mekle lippis"), the discarnation and incarnation of beauty is central to tournament drama.

To emerge as victor from the chaos of the fragmented body is to be given
the prize of gilded armor or the right to choose the queen of the tournament. Both beauty and the look of recognition — in this context they are
inseparable — must be won from the rival-double, whose foundation is the
exteriorized image of the self. Transitivist rivalry enacts the aggressivity
of identification: the other with whom one identifies is also the other with
whom one must compete.[61] And the ground, the field, over which one struggles is again figured as the lady.[62] The lady's body is further translated
into the spatial symmetry of the image of fullness and completion, whereby
the promise of plenitude — in the form of "victory" over the rival — is restored. The body of the woman, as the "ground" of aspiration, can ultimately be caught up in the geometry of the father — and precipitated in
the "form" of the lady. Thus the body of the lady may be imagined as the
originary space both of aggressivity and of plenitude; the gaze of the lady
can either seem to project back to the subject the desired image of fullness
and completion, or instantiate alienation — hence the easy slippage, in the
talismanic function of images, from protection to danger and back again.
It is as much the gaze of the woman as what we see (or do not see) in
her that prefigures both fullness (safety, protection) and lack (danger, cas-
tration, mutilation). The talismanic images of heraldry enact the displacement of terror, chaos, mutilation by the mirror's lure of a totalized and perfected body, by the lure of protection; and heralds preside, as we have noted,
over the boundaries of chivalric life — its *rites de passage*, its entry to the
field of competition, its marriages, its funerals, its losses and its gains.

The tournament is a drama that stages the subject's recovery of the field
of the woman's body through the defeat of the mirror's dangers — the dangers of the relation to the rival-double. The tournament attempts to control the uncontrollable anxiety of being surrounded by doubles — "friends"
— through a reconstitution of them as defeatable rivals and through the
elaboration of ever more powerful talismanic images. Because the psychic
economy of the tournament is structured through rivalrous identifications,
it is capable of precipitating the identification with the ideal that promises

closure to transitivist violence, just as, in Douglas's poem, it offers closure to the destabilization of the masculine body caused by excessive intimacy with the feminine. Writes Lacan: "The pacifying function of the ego ideal, the connection between its libidinal normativity and . . . cultural normativity [has been] bound up from the dawn of history with the *imago* of the father."[63]

The tournament can thus enact an identificatory reshaping of the subject that promises an end to the endlessness of the violent phenomenalization of the honorable subject by placing the subject in the space of an anticipatory or synecdochal relation to the ideal. The fixation inaugurated by the ideal, moreover, permits the pacifying, infantilizing, indeed feminizing effects of putting an end to violence to be mediated through forms of identification with the rival. The tournament can thus enact a transition from rivalry and the space of the woman's body to the geometric rule of the father in which the lady appears as figure: territorial ambition is thus managed through the creation of symbolic land and eroticized through the image of an (attainable, winnable) beauty. In Chaucer's "Knight's Tale," Palamon and Arcite attempt to fight their way out of the woods — out of wildness — through the violence of the doubles; but no closure can be reached until Theseus's architectural, geometric, and ritualistic interventions permit the constitution of a stadium, a tournament, a form — a form that remains a "mirror" but has nonetheless been invested with the "pacifying function" of the ideal.

The transition from the space of female wildness to the civilized realm of the sovereign — in which, once again, the lady is winnable as symbolic reward — is implied in the *pas* of the Femme Sauvage of Anthony, bastard of Burgundy, which took place in 1470: "his 'Champion of the Joyous Quest' had been cured of wounds by the *Femme Sauvage* as he left the land of *Enfance* for that of *Jeunesse,* and entered the lists surrounded by a troop of her 'wild women.'"[64] Claude de Vauldray "called himself 'le Compaignon de la Joyeuse Queste' and his mistress 'Dame Sauvaige,' and allegorized his adventure in the following manner": "Vray est que ledit entrepreneur, pour sa première bonne adventure, se partist, n'a pas grammrent, du riche royaume d'Enfance, et entra en ung pays gasté, maigre et stérile, que on appele Jonesse."[65] Welsford, too, notes that "the performance of the wild men who jumped out of a rock and danced a morisco before Gaston de Foix is called a 'mystère d'enfans sauvages'"; the motif of the *sauvage* is repeatedly associated with infancy or childhood in the disguisings of the later medieval period.[66] The stories of Perceval (who is brought up in the woods by his mother) and of Degare (whose name means "almost lost it is" and who is brought up in a woodland hermitage) suggest the

association of plain arms and the *chevalier nouveau* with wildness, infancy, the space of the mother.[67] And Vulson, interestingly, says that the
"tres-haut, tres-excellent & ancien exercice d'armes" is "mere & nourrice de
vertus."[68] Though recognition can be accomplished through confrontation
with the rival-double en route — that is, still in the woods — arms and identity are not fully established until the arrival at court, the exposure to the
judgment of the king. Still, it is crucial to see that the vogue for primi-
tivism and for the *sauvage* in late medieval romance and tournament pageantry — of which James IV's tournament of the wild knight is an instance —
must be understood in the context of resistance to, as well as acceptance
of, the pacifying function of the ideal image, the sovereign — in the context
of narrativities not only of maturation and aspiration but also of a "regressive" resistance to the king's powers of identification. Such stories demonstrate that the knight, while supremely loyal, supremely civilized, is yet
empowered by the forces of wildness; they are in him because he has overcome them.

The tournament is, as we have explained, a means of extorting recognition from the male "similar." The struggle to fascinate — and to defend
against fascination — is a struggle to reduce the similar to the mortified and
feminized image in the eye of the subject. But in deploying a fascinating
image — in making himself larger than life — the knightly subject opens himself up to the very mortification and feminization that he tried to defend
against. The knight is to "win" the woman; he is not to be a woman or
to live with women as he did before he became a knight. The tournament
is a scene in which chivalric culture acts out the choice — the taking up — of
"masculinity." The tournament thus serves crucial homosocial functions
in the later Middle Ages. It brings men together but allows them to constitute themselves as "men," who fight for and who are watched by women.
The "lady" thus enters the tournament — as spectator, as prize — in part to
signify the masculinity of the knight, to defend against the feminizing effects of the identification and rivalry with the similar and against the lure
of wildness itself. The lady dramatizes the masculinity of the warrior by
being what he is not and by watching his effort from another place. The
struggle to fascinate involved in male display is thus bound up, through
the question of the "truth" of the image one presents, in the question of
how the subject comes to be gendered.

Knighthood seems, then, by its nature, to generate the effeminate or
feminized double; for in the accusatory gaze of medieval estates satire and
sermon literature effeminacy is always associated with the aristocracy. The
lamentable tendency of knights to overvalue their armor — to dress up, like
women — and to "go in all their pride and splendour to the tournament and

the joust" instead of battling with the enemy is clearly linked in the literature of complaint with wantonness and effeminacy, a branch of the sin
of sloth "myche noryssched in lordys courtys."[69] Effeminacy is "whan a
man delitith him in softe clothing, in nesche bedding; he most ofte be
waische, ofte bathid, ofte kempt and kerchevid and cherschid so tendirli."[70]
Effeminacy is when a man allows himself to be tended like a baby, when
he wears women's clothing, when he cares about his appearance. Nobles,
too, were always needing new fashions (James IV himself indulged the
fashion of wearing the new big sleeves at court): "they devise some new
piece of foppery to make men gaze at them in wonderment anew," so that
the attempt to amaze — to fascinate others through one's visual splendor —
is here seen to redound on the subject.[71] At work in these satires is a kind
of insistence on seeing, as costume, clothing that the sumptuary laws tried
to designate as proper to the office of rule. A preacher in the early fourteenth century finds in the victories of Scotland over a decadent English
knighthood the fulfillment of a certain prophecy concerning the sin of
varietas vestium which would inevitably bring national disaster in its train.[72]
Owst links this sermon with the story of how the Scots, at about the same
time, pinned upon the church doors of St. Peter in Stangate in York an
insolent verse mocking the current foppishness of Englishmen in beards
and attire, a variation of which is to be found in a later sermonbook:

> Long berdes hertles
> Streyte cotes graceles
> Peyntet hodes wytles
> Longe tepetes redles
> Partie hosen thryftles
> Makeyt this world laweless.[73]

But the association of effeminacy and sloth was not only a feature of
homiletic satire. Caxton's preface to *The Book of the Ordre of Chyvalry;
or, Knyghthoode* (1484) remarks: "O ye knights of England, where is the
custom and usage of noble chivalry that was used in those days? . . . read
the noble volumes of St. Graal, of Lancelot, of Galaad. . . . And look in
latter days of the noble acts sith the conquest, as in King Richard's days,
Coeur du Lyon. . . . Read Froissart. . . . Alas! what do ye, but sleep and
take ease, and are all disordered from chivalry?"[74] Nobles, take note; read
books, else you will lose your manhood. John Lydgate, in the *Secrees of
Old Philisoffres,* writes:

> It is in erthe oon the moste pereilous thyng,
> A prynce to been off his condicioun
> Effemynat, his wittis enclynyng,

Be fals desir off fleshli mocioun,
To put himself vnder subieccioun,
And thralle his resoun, tresour most precious,
To onleeful lustis, hatful and lecherous.
.   .   .   .
There is the sentence ful pleynli in menyng:
Where women haue the dominacioun
To holde the reyne, ther hookis out castyng,
That sensualitie ha[ue] iurediccioun
.   .   .   .
It taketh from men ther cleernesse off seyng.[75]

As in Douglas's *Palice of Honour,* if women are not properly ruled by men, the result is a lapse into a blinding interiority, the loss of the power of vision.

David Lindsay's *Ane Satyre of the Thrie Estaitis* — written in the mid-sixteenth century — deals explicitly with the problem of effeminacy, regression, and the failure to "see through" appearances.[76] His Majesty the Baby, "King Humanity" ("I have been to this day / *Tanquam tabula rasa,* / Ready for good and ill," 1.170–72) is beguiled by courtiers (Wantonness, Solace, Placebo), by Lady Sensuality, and finally by the vices of Flattery, Falset, and Deceit into living a life of wasteful display and sexual laxity (Solace urges the king "sa lang as ye want a wife, / Sir, tak your pleasure!" 1.322–23). The play thus associates promiscuity with an infantile aristocracy unwilling to give up its narcissism, incapable of reform or maturity (hence the deferral of marriage) until it interiorizes divine justice and hangs or banishes its seducers. Divine Correction awakens the prodigal youth with "Get up, Sir King, ye have sleepit eneuch / Into the arms of Lady Sensual!" (1.1195–96). Though he admits that "Princes may sometime seek solace / With mirth and lawful merriness, / Their spirits to rejose" (1.1316–18), the overall means of managing excess, illusion, and women in this play is repression. The play clearly links deception with sloth, the company of women, the prodigality of youth and of the aristocracy; and as in *The Thrissill and the Rois,* reform of the body of the realm — signified by the gift of a "gay garmoun" (2.2279ff.) to a transfigured John the Common-Weal — is predicated on the reform of the private or "natural" body of the monarch. The redemption of appearance from merely theatrical illusion, from disguise — Flattery advises his fellow vices that "We mon turn our claiths" (1.594) and dresses up as the "freir" Devotion — is thus coterminous in the play with a maturation imagined as dependent on the displacement of the (erotic) woman from the narrative and on the "finding" (through interiorization) of masculine authority. The play thus enacts a wish that the king grow up and act like a father — that is, start incarnating justice instead of indulging in pleasure. In *Ane Satyre of the Thrie Estaitis* change is figured as a utopian restoration of image to essence (John's "gay garmoun") through the destruction of scapegoats and through models of repudiation. "Maturation" takes place through the interiorization of paternal authority, the principle of discrimination itself; though reform is attendant upon the recovery of narcissism through images of bodily perfection — John's "gay garmoun" is after all a kind of transvestiture, insofar as it recovers the absent body of Lady Sensuality — the play wants to get rid of the woman herself, so that she does not, in the end, "change" King Humanitie at all.

If the image itself is imagined to unleash a mortification — if being seen is to risk fascination in the very attempt to fascinate — then it is scarcely surprising that transvestiture should appear in tournament drama. Travesty, in the tournament, is one means by which the risk of feminization involved in display is at once approached and avoided, enjoyed and refused. An English chronicler writing during the reign of Edward III reported that

In those days arose a great rumour and clamour among the people, that whenever there was a tournament there came a great concourse of ladies of the most costly and beautiful, but not of the best of the kingdom, sometimes forty or fifty in number, as if they were a part of the tournament, in diverse and wonderful male apparel, in parti-coloured tunics with short caps and bands wound cordwise round their heads, and girdles bound with gold and silver, and daggers in pouches across their body; and then they proceeded on chosen coursers to the place of tourney, and so expended and wasted their goods and vexed their bodies with scurrilous wantonness that the murmurs of the people sounded everywhere; but they neither feared God nor blushed at the chaste voice of the people.[77]

Promiscuity, display, prodigality are associated with the monstrous image of women dressed as men. Cripps-Day cites a miniature from a manuscript in the British Museum that shows the arrival of "courtesans in male attire riding with lances and shields on horses richly caparisoned."[78] And Ulrich von Lichtenstein — a master of disguise — went about tourneying in drag, wearing long golden hair, dressed as Frau Venus. In a picture of Ulrich that appears in the Manasseh Codex, a figure of Venus herself perches atop his helmet, holding a flaming torch in one hand and a red arrow in the other.[79] In his guise as Frau Venus, Ulrich was acting out the possibility that chivalry was merely a vain show in which the actors were all really women, that the spectacles meant to stage the identity of a knight as knight only turned him into a girl. Travesty and transvestiture in tournament pageantry enact the *identity* of "martial engagement" with sexual intercourse and the identity of sexual intercourse with the loss of identity, action and vision in the slothful space of interiority. As in *Ane Satyre of the Thrie Estaitis*, "mingling" with women effeminates because it can be imagined as becoming woman.

The question, too, of whether the war mask — armor, achievements, escutcheons — empowers the ideal image or merely serves to make apparent the subject's alienation from the image is the question that produces the efflorescence and aesthetics of heraldic forms in the later Middle Ages. For the preoccupation with disguise is doubled by the preoccupation with identity; the *chevalier mesconnu*, as we have noted, is doubled by the elaboration of the art of blazon. The role of heraldry in aestheticizing the instruments of war must be understood as a means of dramatizing the honorable subject's attempt to capture an identity and a sex through the deployment of fascinating images. Thus the discourse of honor insists upon the efficacy of heraldic images in distinguishing true knights from false. For Haye, "takyn of armes to bere is gevin the knycht in his schelde, or in his cote of armes, or othir wayis, sa that he be knawin and kend in bataill be otheris; sa that gif he dois wele he suld have honore and worschip, and if he dois evill he suld have dishonor and disworchip."[80] It is hoped, once again, that an exterior image will enable the phenomenalization of an inner reality. Through the phenomenalization of interiority, same and other — friend and enemy — can be distinguished from each other. David Lindsay explains in his *Armorial* that "ȝe armis of ȝame quhilkis bene foirfaltit and banisit for crymes of lese maieste and vtheris enormiteis ar interit and registrat in ȝis . . . buik and put in memory alsweill as ȝe armis of ȝam [quhilk] . . . hes bene euir haill and trew" so that posterity will learn from their bad example.[81] The anxiety about reality that permeates the discourses of chivalry — the question of where evil is to be located, of who is friend and who is enemy — is an anxiety of the borderline, which is so often anxiety about protection and danger. Heraldry tries to split "primal images" — images that can signify both protection and danger. Marks of evil or savagery are projected onto, appropriated from, and turned against the other; wild men and frightening beasts take their place as supporters on noble achievements and come alive in tournament pageantry.

Chivalrous costume becomes a means whereby the knightly subject can displace — recover and repress — his ambivalent relation to the body of the woman, attempting to stabilize the doubleness of protection and danger. The body of the woman, in its dystonic form of chaos and threat, is projected off and reappropriated through the vast panoply of heraldic display. Dressing up enacts the anticipatory and identificatory relation to the ideal that empowers tournament drama, and it serves the wish for protection by relocating omnipotence in an exteriorized and formed materiality. Dressing up marks the tournament as a site open to the dramatization of risk, in which the apotropaic function of fear is developed in the place of paralyzing anxiety.

If "arms were regarded as the *alter ego* of their owner," the later Middle Ages is the period during which this "alter ego" was given a symbolic elaboration well in excess of any function of recognition — well in excess, that is, of the job of identifying individuals on the field of battle.[82] Brault remarks that in the fifteenth century heraldry "entered into a phase marked by unnecessary elaborateness and hermeticism"; it is precisely this quality of the "unnecessary" in heraldic symbolism that marks the importance of aesthetic form in the dramatization of knightly identity.[83] Rather than simply borrowing a "necessary" form of identification from the battlefield, tournaments themselves may have been originally responsible for the practice of painting knightly devices on shields.[84] By about 1360 shields were no longer used in battle, but only in tournaments. Plate armor developed by the fifteenth century, as did crests far more elaborate and symbolic in nature than the earlier fans painted with arms; crests also were used almost exclusively in jousting and tournaments. Mantling — the attachment of drapery to the helmet — was "in real use originally very simple, but in late heraldic art it is often drawn in wildly flowing shapes."[85] If crests were feathered, then later artists carried the feathering down into the mantling. Supporters were a development of the later Middle Ages, as were standards — "a wonderfully ostentatious means of displaying" the increasingly popular badges and crests.[86] Arms were also painted on surcoats and horse-trappers, possibly before the thirteenth century but certainly by the mid-fourteenth century. That "costume" seems so often to mark out the space of theater and illusion — and is often projected onto women, so that only women and not men are "seen" to be dressed up — is the difficult double of the desire to fascinate, to assume a grand size, the blinding power of a spectacle that will "brissit . . . banis."[87] The wish to see costume as "necessary," as "official" and hence functional or traditional, is a wish to recuperate effeminacy through the power of visibility, to keep the woman under rule, to recover and control the woman through the image one projects of oneself.

If the later Middle Ages was the time when the function of beauty was allowed to flower in tournament costume and pageantry, then it was also the time of the monarchy's determined appropriation of the tournament for its own spectacular purposes. When the "warrior" gives a command performance for the gaze of the king, the theatricality of war is made, finally, into the explicit theater of spectacle. The prince, too, tries to capture the tournament's potential for an identificatory reshaping toward the end of aggressivity — for, that is, a pacification of his knights. The monarch can thus stage himself as the source of peace and plenty; at the close of one of the tournaments staged for her entertainment, Elizabeth's knights presented an olive branch "signifieing the humble-hearted submission of the foure foster children of Desire," "in token of her triumphant peace and of their peaceable servitude," craving only the gift of "some token to those knights which maie be judged to have doone best in each kind of weapon."[88] But he can also enact himself as the ideal of knighthood; king identifies with knight, and knight identifies with king. In the later Middle Ages monarchs accordingly used the tournament as a means of managing the opportunities it afforded for sedition and misrule. Du Cange writes that "at times tournaments and justs have been prohibited temporarily on account of some great solemn fête, in the fear that great lords, seigneurs and knights would prefer to show their skill at these contests, and absent themselves from the ceremonies which would consequently have suffered in their impressiveness."[89] The rivalry of the similars is brought into the space of the geometric ideal and of "resolution"; the knight comes to fight before the gaze of the king and to be judged for his prowess. The aristocratic *agon* of recognition is included within a royal drama of identification — and is made a spectacle of, and for, the king.

The later medieval "solemn" tournament is staged, explicitly, by and for the prince. It is linked, as Keen argues, to the romance, in which the son's quest for the father — and away from infancy and his mother — is so important a narrative structure: thus "at a tournament at Rennes in the XIV century Du Guesclin, the 'unknown knight,' finds himself justing with his father."[90] We have already referred to the maturational thematics of tournaments and romances that impel the unknown toward the power of the prince to identify him, to give him arms. Once again the woman, too, appears in tournament drama, as spectator, as queen of beauty, as the promised reward for the hero's struggles. Her separation from the subject can be solicited because of the promise that she will be there waiting for him once he has completed his task — that she will function as the "narrative image" of his quest. The king stages the "solemn" tournament as a means, simultaneously, of allowing and controlling rivalry.

The ideological plasticity of the contradiction between essence and effort — inheritance and proof of merit — helps to structure the tournament. The solemn tournament makes a space for social mobility without undoing inheritance. It allows the warrior to prove himself and to be rewarded for his efforts, but in an anticipatory or synecdochal space — as the son "finds" the father, is "identified" by the father, proves himself a worthy "successor" to the father. And when the king wins, he proves himself to be both son and father, knight and king, deserving and inheriting, meritorious and dynastic. The logic of honor, in a sense, produces the king. Insofar as it attempts to fix the play of honor, monarchy both stabilizes recognition and destabilizes the process of vindicating honor as its own vindication. The monarch himself, too, becomes a symbol of the abjection of recognition — of how the need to be recognized, to vindicate one's honor, makes the man of honor depend upon the gaze of the other.

Gilbert of the Haye explains that "quhen a baroun banneroll has mony knychtis under him, thai aw to diffend thair lordis landis, and his lyf, and his honore. For the honor of knychthede standis in that, that he be lufit, lovit, prisit, honorit, and doubtit, with the prince, lordis, and peple of the realme; for the honor of lordis and princis standis in the pluralitee of mony worschipfull and honorable knychtis."[91] Here, honor is defined as the value placed upon the knight by the prince — the knight's honor is, simply, how much he is honored by the prince. The prince thus becomes the privileged other whose gaze confers recognition, interiority, identity. It is the king's gaze that "proves" a knight simultaneously an aristocrat and a man. But the king's honor is inseparable from those of his knights. That the knight's honor is a reflex of the king's honor which is in turn a reflex of the knight's honor is a hall of mirrors that both mystifies and brings out the ficticity — the createdness — of honor.

For thare is nouthir Emperoure, na king, that can na may in his regne governe all his subditis but help of his knychtis. Bot the King of Glore can wele allane, but othir power, na of his awin vertu and majestee, can and may governe and reugle all this erde, and all the hevin, at his awin plesaunce, the quhilk is ane anerly God allane in Trinitee and Unitee. And tharfor wald he nocht that only knycht allane mycht mak a knycht that suld governe all the knychtis of this warld bot he allane; and tharfore ordanyt he in this warld mony of knychtis to be, that his magestee may the better be knawin, and that kingis and princis suld mak officeris under thame of knychtis. And forthy dois a king or a prince grete wrang to the order of knychthede quhen he makis othir sereffis, baillies, or provostis of othir lawlyar men na knychtis.[92]

Knights make knights who make knights; the king is a knight who makes knights upon whom he must then depend in governing knights. There is no privileged gaze or source of being to solve the paradox of achieved essentialism, except for God, who is "ane anerly God allane" — the only principle capable of creating the knight who will make all the other knights. The Creator, then, is evoked as a mystification of the createdness, not only of knighthood but also of the "knight who makes knights" — that is, the king.

Or, trying for an interior rather than an exterior transcendence, Haye sets out the following piece of logic: "And, tharfore, sulde a knycht dispise all vicis, and lufe all vertues; for the quhilkis, all knychtis ar honorit, and nocht for othir cause, and all prince, king, lord, or baroun, that honoris knychthede, outhir in court or in counsale . . . he honoris himself."[93] Haye needs to fix the play of recognition so that either an exterior or an interior source can be provided for the mysterious element of honor that underwrites both knighthood and monarchy. In this passage, honor as virtue — honor as achieved interiority, as a quality of soul capable of elaboration — "recognizes" the king as honorable when the king in turn recognizes the honor for what it is. Simply to recognize honor when one sees it, then, is to be honorable; honor inheres in the capacity to recognize, and be recognized for, honor. Once again, honor moves perpetually between transcendence and self-referentiality; looked at one way, honor is, simply, its own referent.

And though the discourse of honor moves away from this self-reference toward transcendence, it also moves toward it: the contradiction allows the identification of king and knight. As Pitt-Rivers explains, "the idea that the honor of the group resides in its head was fundamental to the conception of aristocracy and assured the fidelity through the oath of the liegeman to his lord; the inferior in such a relationship participated in the honor of his chief and was therefore interested in defending it."[94] But the "vicarious glory of the noble's servant" — becoming great by participating in something greater — is no more vicarious than that of the noble himself, or of the king whom he in turn serves; it is precisely this unending vicariousness, this createdness without origin, that makes glory both communal and theatrical. The theatricality of honor is bound up with its communality, with identities that are constructed as identifications. And if the concept of honor must simultaneously be constructed as a transcendence and deconstructed as such — if, in short, honor is founded in part on its own lack of foundations — the concept of authority is subject to a similar ambiguity. Pitt-Rivers writes that "the political significance of the sacred is that it arbitrates questions of value. . . . Authority as political power claims always to be moral authority, and the word therefore enjoys the same duality as honour from the moment that the legitimacy of the use of force is disputed. It cannot admit that its actions are devoid of legitimacy."[95] In order to be legitimate, authority must appeal to a transcendence that is also an inherence; the right to authority depends precisely on the assumption of that right. Authority is contestable only if its incontestability is assumed; and its incontestability makes it incapable, finally, of proving itself. Moreover, the moral quality that must be an aspect of authority redoubles the ambiguity; those in authority must "earn" their position by being morally deserving, but at the same time their morality is beyond question by virtue of the position they occupy. The morality of the ruler likewise mirrors the morality of the ruled; and so authority itself becomes its own deconstruction.

If honor, then, is constituted phenomenologically in and through absurdity, then, as Feuerbach puts it in a different context, the illusion becomes the sacred: the theatricalization of the monarch-as-knight becomes central to the simultaneous sanctity and absurdity of his creation as the possessor of the gaze that creates the honor of others.[96] The honor of the knight and the honor of the king are mutual creations; this is, as we have stated, what makes honor communal. But the ficticity of knightly honor is exacerbated in kingship; for if the aristocrat is created thereby as different from the commoner, the king is thereby created as different from the aristocrat—as unique. (In Haye, the king is the privileged reflection of the eye of divine majesty.) The king, then, "cannot be dishonored. What he *is* guarantees the evaluation of his actions."[97] The monarch, therefore, can vindicate his honor only in the theater of honor—only by representing it in spectacle. Posited as a difference, the honor of the monarch cannot be constituted through the violent acting-out of the doubles. This is not to put aristocratic violence outside the space of theater; it is to put aristocratic violence in the space of an open-ended theater, whose open-endedness, in the case of the monarch, must be scripted. Hence illusions are made that represent the king as the winner—whether the winner be figured as the paternal judge of the efforts of others or as the supreme knight, who cannot help but win. When the citizens of London throw dice with Richard II—dice loaded in the king's favor—it becomes clear that the phenomenalization of the honorable self through risk will be subjected to a further kind of dramatization.[98] The exchange of the gaze must be seen by the spectator, now, to have had an inevitable outcome; and this restructuring of the narrative of combat is one of the most profound effects wrought by the presence of monarchy in the fields of honor. When Henry II is killed in the lists by his opponent's failure to lower his splintered lance quickly enough, the man who killed him is allowed by Catherine de Medici to live for fifteen years—and is then executed. The remarkable regularity with which Henry VIII wins his tournaments and the consummate skill which James IV is reported to have displayed in his tournament of the wild knight and the black lady further suggest the extent to which the king must exemplify, with a difference, the coincidence of authority and ability. In the case of the king, honor derives "an *ought* from an *is*"; the king wins

the tournament.[99] The ficticity of honor means that honor — like the king —
is the creation of a communal suspension of disbelief. For

the notion, common in all the languages of Europe, that honour is susceptible of
"defilement" or "stains" of which it requires to be purified entitles us to mark a
resemblance to the customs of primitive societies whose chiefs are the object of
prohibitions similar to those which circumscribe the man of honour. The early
anthropologists might well, in fact, have translated the word *mana* as *honour,* at
least in the contexts in which it referred to persons, and noted that the Polynesian
victor who acquired the *mana* of his slain foe by taking his name was behaving
rather like the conquering kings of the hymn ["Conquering kings their titles take /
From the foes they captive make"].[100]

Another look at the the tournament drama staged by James IV for his
wedding in 1503 will help us to consolidate some of the points we have
been pursuing in this chapter. Just before the entry into Edinburgh, according to Somerset Herald,

was a Pavillon, wherof cam owt a Knyght on Horsbak, armed at all Peces, havyng
hys Lady Paramour that barre his Horne. And by Avantur, ther cam an other also
armed, that cam to hym, and robbed from hym hys sayd Lady, and at the absent-
ing blew the said Horne, wherby the said Knyght understude hym, and tourned
after hym, and said to hym, wherfor hast thou this doon? He answerd hym, what
will you say therto? — I say, that I will pryve apon thee, that thou hast doon Owtrage
to me. The tother demaunded hym if he was armed? He said ye, well then, said
th'other, preve the a Man, and doo thy Devoir.[101]

They fought and "maid a varey fayr Torney";

and they did well ther Devor, tyll that the Kynge cam hymselfe, the Qwene behynd hym, crying Paix, and caused them for to be departed. After this the King
called them before hym, and demaunded them the Cause of ther Difference. The
Caller sayd, Syre, he hath taken from me my Lady Paramour, wherof I was insurte
of hyr by Faith. The Defender answered, Syre, I schall defend me ageynst hym
apon thys Cas. Then sayd the kynge to the sayd Defender, brynge youre Frends,
and ye schall be appoynted a Day for to agre you. Wheroff they thaunked hym,
and so every Men departed them for to drawe toward the said Towne. The Names
of thos war Sir Patryk Hamilton . . . and Patryk Synklar . . . and ther was com
grett Multitude of People for to se thys.[102]

The tournament represents precisely the kind of "mimic warfare" which
so many historians of chivalry have considered to be a mark of decadence,
of the fall from reality into appearance. Though there is, of course, fighting in this scene, it is, precisely, a scene; in fact it is the scene of that fantasy which lies at the center of late chivalric art. Specifically, the scene

stages the enactment of honor, played out over the possession of the woman; and honor is elaborated through a ritual of gestures and language, a ritual which includes the athleticism of the joust but which goes quite beyond it. To act, to enact one's identity through a formalized *agon*, is to stage oneself as a knight and, even more fundamentally, as a man: "preve the a Man, and doo thy Devoir." The drama suggests, in fact, that warfare is a performance art; it brings out a theatricalization which, in the terms of chivalric fantasy, is inherent in the art of war. And the art of war is here specified as a joust: that is, the scene of aristocratic discord in which the king wishes to stage himself as the bringer of peace, is eroticized and strikingly individualized, in the sense that the scene of chivalric romance can be said to stage an erotics of the phenomenalization of the self. The king presides over the staging of aristocratic identity through the acts of honor and presides, furthermore, over the way in which this staging of identity articulates gender. We are watching knighthood perform its honor as a specifically masculine enterprise: "preve the a Man." The knight, in fighting over the female, proves that he is not a female. And we are watching the king and his courtiers as actors in a drama of the king's devising: the message is that the king presides over the articulation of knightly identity and thereby presides over the dramatic space of the court; his courtiers enact his drama, which is a drama that makes them, simultaneously, mere actors and real men. Honor becomes a matter of the king's theater.

James's tournament thus conflates two scenes in "The Knight's Tale": the scene in which Palamon and Arcite are discovered fighting in the wood by Theseus, and the tournament scene itself, which figures the monarch's attempt to restore order to aristocratic rivalry through the creation of a ritual space large and elaborate enough to contain that rivalry. James IV stages himself as a Theseus "always already" in control of the rivalry inherent in the chivalric phenomenalization of identity through his very control of dramatic space; thus, he stages himself as the source simultaneously of peace and of power. It is as though the *agon* itself becomes defined as the antimasque element which must be expelled by the king's masque; these courtiers only pretend to be agonistic, outside, in the woods of romance. Really they are courtly insiders, in the space of the same, identified with the king. What is further signified is the specialness of a particular kind of dramatic space: the romance encounter in the woods, which must be reincluded in the space of monarchy before the king enters his city. This appeal to "a scene common in the old romances" suggests the king's own sensitivity to chivalric nostalgia, to the rivalries of youth: the space of the mother and of the doubles must be ruled by power, but it is given its due.[103] The king, moreover, signifies himself as the foundation of aristocratic identity — as the person who settles difference — for spectators, and especially for one very privileged spectator-actress — his English queen, Margaret Tudor. In this sense, then, his activity as a dramatist mirrors that of the knight within his drama — to "preve the a Man." The tournament drama itself is his own sexual display. The tournament drama thus articulates for us the monarch's recovery of agonistic display through its inscription within a specifically monarchical poetics of spectacularity which figures the king simultaneously as the source of identity and the master of illusion.

12

The Wild Knight

JAMES IV's tournament of the wild knight and the black lady appears, from the records of the lord high treasurer, to have been held first in June 1507 and then again, with yet more grandeur, in May 1508.[1] The articles of jousting for the tournament—sent out, according to Pitscottie, to France, England, and Denmark—were themselves elaborate and expensive: the accounts list "tua quaris gold to illummyn the articules send in France for the justing of the wild knycht for the blak lady," and Sir Johne Ramsay was paid "for the writing of the articules that the Franch knycht hed in France for the justing."[2] Thus the articles were probably taken to France by Antoine d'Arces, Lord of la Bastie.

In *Le Vray Théâtre d'Honnevr*, Vulson identifies the "Cheualier Sauuage à la Dame noire" for whom Marchmont Herald published the articles with "Antoine d'Arces Seigneur de la Bastie, surnommé le Cheualier Blanc, auec ses aydes; car les articles portent qu'ils estoient armez de blanc, & ceux qui scauent la vie de ce genereux Cheualier Dauphinois, seront asseurement de mon opinion, puis que son Histoire porte qu'il fut long temps en Escosse, ayme du Roy et de la Reine, & que sa vertu luy acquit en ce Royaume plusieurs enuieux."[3] That the knights were to wear white—the articles in *La Science Heroiqve* give "et premierement, commenceront lesdites armes à cheval armé à blanc à six courses de lance en lice"—is supported in a rather muddled way by Pitscottie, who reports that soon after Bernard Stewart came to Scotland "he causit the kingis graice to set ane gret justing and turnament at Edinburgh in halyrudhous of the dait I^m v^e fyve zeiris and the said justing and turnament to stand the spaice of xl dayis. . . . thair come money gentilmen out of ingland france and denmark. Amang the rest thair come ane knycht and ane lady callit the quyht rois."[4] But while, as we have noted, it is clear that d'Arces was in Scotland at the time of the 1508 tournament, it is probable that he was still in France when the 1507 tournament was held. Moreover, judging by the Treasurer's

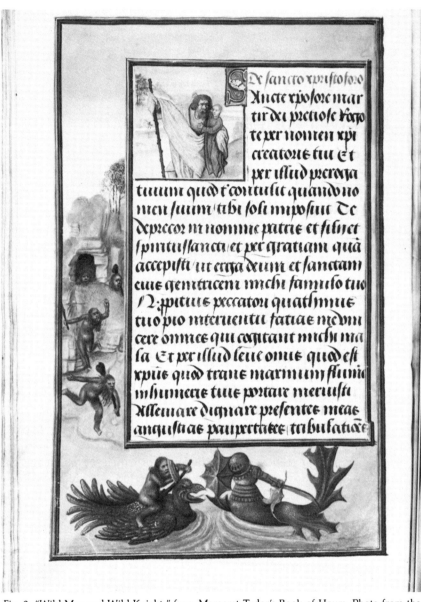

Fig. 9. "Wild Men and Wild Knight," from Margaret Tudor's Book of Hours. Photo from the Picture Archives of the Austrian National Library, Vienna. Codex Vindobonensis 1897, fol. 49 verso.

Accounts, and indeed by the articles printed in Vulson's text, the theme of the tournament seems to have been well in hand before foreign knights would have begun to appear on the scene. The inspiration for the tournament likely originated, then, in the Scottish court, though d'Arces could still have influenced its conception. While white was d'Arces's tincture and seems, from the articles, to have been a thematic color in the tournament — perhaps, as Pitscottie suggests, to contrast with the darkness of the black lady and the wild knight — d'Arces is an unlikely candidate for the Cheualier Sauvage. As we shall see, the chronicle accounts consistently assign the role to James himself, and the records of the tournament expenses indicate that he was armed in black.

The editor of the Treasurer's Accounts demotes d'Arces even further, suggesting that the articles for the tournament "were published in Edinburgh by the king's own herald Marchmont, and that the opportunity was taken of another herald going abroad at any rate with the news of the Prince's birth to send the articles of jousting with him to the countries to which he was despatched."[5] The records, however, seem fairly clear on the subject of the "Franch knycht's" responsibility for the articles. That "Blewmantill, now callit Rothsey," was despatched to announce the news of Prince James's birth in February 1507 does not preclude d'Arces's having taken the articles to France when he left Scotland in January of that year. But the connection with the prince's birth is nonetheless of some interest: it may be that the 1507 tournament was conceived in part as a celebration of the new prince. The tournament's themes of aspiration and maturation at least would accord with such an occasion; the birth of a son might well have inspired James to stage a tournament dramatizing his own quest for recognition.

Vulson's text of the articles of jousting provides us with a richly imagined portrait of the tournaments of 1507 and 1508 — and a number of Vulson's details are corroborated by the contemporary records. The articles state that "Lesquelles Armes se feront en cedit Royaume & ville d'Edinbourg dedans le Camp de Souvenir, lequel sera entre le chasteau nommé des Pucelles, & le Pavillon Secret, & dedans ledit Camp sera l'arbre d'Esperance, lequel croist au jardin de Patience, portant feuïlles de plaisance, la fleur de noblesse, & le fruit d'honneur."[6] The Treasurer's Accounts list payments for "xxxvij peris to the tree of esperance," which cost over three pounds. Over five pounds were spent on "ij^c platis to be leifis to the tree"; "xviij dosan of leifis' to the tre of esperance, and sex dosan flouris to the samyn" cost over seven pounds. Further expenses for wire and nails are listed for what was undoubtedly a spectacular tournament *arbre*.[7]

One of the largest expenditures for cloth was for 160 ells of Flemish taffeta, "quhit, ʒallo, purpur, grene, and gray"; these colors also appear prominently in the tournament rituals, for "au bas dudit arbre seront attachez par l'espace de cinq semaines cinq Escus, l'vn aprés l'autre de différentes couleurs, en chacune semaine vn, dont le premier sera blanc, le second gris, le tiers vert, le quart de pourpre, & le cinquiéme d'or; ausquels & à chacun desdits Escus aura vne lettre d'or, couronnée du nom dudit Chevalier Sauvaige & de sa Dame, ensemble desdits Chevaliers, & pareillement de leurs Dames, laquelle lettre est cy-dessus mise par signature."[8] The accounts mention "the gret heich pailʒoun for the feild" and at least one other "small pailʒoun"; the "gret pailʒoun" was covered with white and green taffeta, bought in London for the purpose.[9] Flemish taffeta was used lavishly in the construction of the "chair triumphale for the blak lady," which was adorned with "flouris" made of taffeta; and she wore a gown of damask "flourit with gold."[10] Her "tua ladyis" wore gowns of green Flemish taffeta bordered with yellow taffeta; her "squeris" wore white English damask.[11]

The lackeys to the wild knight wore doublets of velvet and cloth-of-gold, yellow and black hose, and yellow and black bonnets.[12] The wild knight would presumably also have been accompanied by the "wildmen" mentioned in the accounts as wearing "hert hornes and gayt skinnis"; the editor of the accounts suggests that they may have ridden on dragons made of feathers and canvas, for the accounts mention saddles and reins for the "bestis" and two "Estland burdis" sacrificed "to be weyngis to the bestis."[13] The accounts also mention the preparation of shields, banners, and all the other accoutrements of heraldic display; wild men and "bestis" were by this time also familiar motifs in heraldic art. The evidence suggests, then, that the tournament of the wild knight and the black lady was an extravagant and spectacular tournament disguising, starring a mysterious protagonist and an equally mysterious lady and set in an allegorized "scene." The tournament scene played in the woods outside Edinburgh for James's wedding has been brought, in effect, inside the court and has been costumed, scripted, and staged with "magnificent" care and deliberation.

The articles published by Vulson consist largely of the expected list of the kinds of fighting to be done, on horse and on foot, described in the highly formulaic style characteristic of heraldic discourse at this time. Violence, in the late medieval tournament, is scripted with as much deliberation and care as are its narratives. The armored style of the articles of jousting represents the violent concourse of aristocratic bodies as a repetitive series of isolated "Items," for example: "Item, d'autres à cheval sans lice en harnois de guerre, armé à blanc depuis la teste jusques aux pieds, sans estre cramponée, guindé, ny attaché par autant de courses de lance à fer emolu."[14] Through the ritualization and stylistic isolation of violence, the articles articulate the scene of violence, making it visible, forming its genres, elaborating the art of the similar so that lance meets lance, axe meets axe. In the articles, different things do not touch; they thus defend against bodily chaos, against the jumble of mutilation. The assurance of a purity of scenic confrontation between similars brings together pain and beauty, gives form to the pursuit of form and deformation: it provides for risk (without which the image cannot be affirmed) and for protection (the armored preservation of the fascinating image). Moreover, by anticipating – by planning with deliberate care – the events of the tournament, the articles intend and time and seriate violence, making vulnerability into the activity of forethought.

The generation by the articles of a predestined series of gestures and the tournament's enactment, in turn, of a series of gestures that have already been thought, is linked, moreover, to the narrativity both of "The Knight's Tale" and James's wedding tournament – with the arrest of the unplanned, the contingent, the accidental, and its reformation in the space of ritual. Forethought, Otto Fenichel suggests, enables the production of a sense of "right" behavior through the fulfillment of ideals and "execution" to the "letter"; it is a form of protection, of the fantasy of a protective fate.[15] The ascription of "destination" to violence – its emplotment – is a way of providing for both violence and peace, for the contingency of violence and an essentializing closure (the man who wins, wins neither because of chance nor simply because of prowess, but because of who he "is" – which is another way of saying that he is favored by the gods). The tournament, then, dramatizes trial, which is itself a form of repetition, of the recurrence of the same or of identity: the honor of the knight is proven to be an essence, and while fate appears to try the knight, fate is itself on trial. The tournament thus promises both contingency (necessary to risk) and closure; each movement of the articles of jousting closes with a ritual gesture: "Et si celuy qui la requerra faut à rompre sur son compagnon en celle ditte course, sera tenu envoyer vne verge d'or, à la Dame de celuy à qui le cas ne sera advenu, & se rendre à la mercy du meffait qui luy est survenu."[16]

In "The Knight's Tale" too the tournament is clearly established to permit an outcome that will distinguish between similars; the narrative of the tournament, which may or may not be thematized in an explicit narrative, is an instrument crucial to monarchical management (not repression) of aristocratic violence. "The Knight's Tale" suggests that tournament ritual is played out under the eye of a protective (and potentially destructive) authority – another feature of the tournament that opens it to the pacifying function of the ideal.[17] The emphasis placed by the articles on "le vouloir & congé de tres-haut tres-excellent & tres-puissant Prince le Roy des Escossois" attests to this, as does the articles' mention of the "plaisir & volonté des Iuges & Dames" to which the contending knights are repeatedly to refer.[18] Whether we imagine this structure as satisfying or as producing a desire, the desire at stake is that of submitting to judgment even in the moment of triumph — of becoming great by identifying with something greater. And when the king jousts himself, the peacemaker acts in a space deliberately destabilized in order to prove his power of protection.

The setting, moreover, for the tournament of the wild knight and the black lady constructs that field of aspiration which refigures bodily fragmentation and chaos. I will quote again the articles' description of the setting: "Lesquelles Armes se feront en cedit Royaume & ville d'Edinbourg dedans le Camp de Souvenir, lequel sera entre le chasteau nommé des Pucelles, & le Pavillion Secret, & dedans ledit Camp sera l'arbre d'Esperance, lequel croist au jardin de Patience, portant feuïlles de plaisance, la fleur de noblesse, & le fruit d'honneur."[19] The articles also mention that "seront tenus les venants, venir droit audit Arbre le premier jour d'Aoust, que les Armes commenceront, & toucheront audit Escu blanc gardé de la Dame noire, accompagnée de Sauvages, trompettes, & tous instruments; Et là seront avec ladite Dame les Roys d'armes & Héraults qui là seront, comme pour les recevoir en declairant avec quelles armes ils veulent fournir, & delivrer leur Escu armoyé de leurs Armes & timbré de leur timbre, ensemble leur nom & surnom, afin qu'ils foient receus chacun en leur rang."[20]

The explicit quality of the allegory of the Tree of Esperance, that grows in the Garden of Patience, bearing the fruit of honor, attempts to phenomenalize an interiority for the tournament field, to make manifest a significance that might otherwise be hidden. This explicit allegoresis has as its purpose revelation: the production of a meaning for lushly material signifiers. Though explicit allegory — emblematics — is a favored (not to say belabored) semiosis in the later Middle Ages and the Renaissance, its functionality in and specificity to a class discourse of honor needs to be stressed again. For the explicitness of the allegory is itself thematized: patience and hope bear the fruit of honor. To make known, to stage, to gloss, is to produce the relationship between being and image that involves both the aspiration to and the ficticity of form.

The explicit allegoresis of this tournament thus exteriorizes and shapes an interiority, a *hortus conclusus.* One of the functions of the image is to restore plenitude; and the paradisal quality of the tournament setting (flowers, trees, fruits and gardens) marks this recovery. Flowers, trees, fruits, and gardens are, however, denatured through their very allegorization;

they are abstracted and named (the tree is one of "Esperance"), just as, in the Garden of Eden, only certain trees were given names (Knowledge of Good and Evil, Immortality) to signify their special role in a narrative of aspiration, their status as marks of transition from an inclusion in and union with nature to the world that "man" must make.

Obscurity—which is the "field" of man's endeavors to phenomenalize himself—thus makes its appearance in the tournament, through the pointing of explicit allegory to the inexplicit interior ("le Pavillon Secret"), and through the presence of the disguised figure of the black lady, who presides over the explicit and formalized rituals of heraldic recognition that the knights must endure in order to enter the field of aspiration. The black lady is the portress of mystery, who, along with the heralds—those who proclaim, publish, make known—awaits the arrival of the knight. The ceremonies of entry juxtapose the known with the unknown, disguise with revelation. The woman appears in order to disappear at the moment when the knight stages his identity, because she is simultaneously recovered and transcended at the moment when the knight proves himself a man. The black lady—her color is linked to obscurity, the mystery of the unknown knight, in contrast with the whiteness of the *venans*—is thus a visualization (insofar as she is costumed, spectacled, given a "to-be-looked-at-ness") of the threat posed to man's vision by interiority.[21] To emerge from this space—from the hiddenness that is an estranged familiarity—is to become a man and to lose a home. To revisit this space, and to recreate one's departure from it, is to revisit one's own creation.

The accounts of the tournament of the wild knight and the black lady given by the historians Pitscottie, Leslie, and Drummond place the tournament itself within a narrative framework structured according to the phenomenology of disguise and revelation, visibility and invisibility. Pitscottie writes that, after the tournament was first proclaimed, "the king gart set the haill justing and callit the samyn the turnament of the black knicht and the black lady and maid Monsieur Deobanie iudge in the said turnament and justing and set him in his awin plaice and seit royall becaus the king iustit him selff dissaguysed onknawin and he was callit the blak knicht." When the tournament was over, according to Pitscottie, the judge and the heralds gave the king "the degrie of that turnament that he vsed all kynd of turnament maist manlie and knichtlyk of ony that was thair at that tyme." The king then made a great show of rewarding those other knights who had distinguished themselves; he gave them gold and silver weapons, to be kept "in memorie for the kingis honour and thair glorie in tymes cuming that thair posteritie might sie eftir quhat nummer thai haue beine and how thay vsit thame sellffis to the kingis graice thair maisteris pleasour and to the adwancment of thair awin honour."[22] Leslie, it will be recalled, gives the following account of the summer of 1508:

This summer, the king, baith on fute and horse, bot in persone of a stranger, prouoiket to the singular combat mony, quha maist valʒeant war esteimet; and als we speik, ay brocht away the palme, ay bure the bel, and ay wan the victorie. He was of sik corage, that quhom evir he hard maist commendet in vertuous and valʒeant actes, he intendet and kaist, him ay to follow, bot heiring of not ane in ancient antiquitie amang al his predecessouris, to quhom he wald be sa conforme as to King Arthur; remembreng of King Arthuris knychts, and thair forme desyreng to follow quha war knychtes of the round table, that tyme he wald be called a knycht of King Arthuris brocht vp in the wodis; his luk and gret grace in vanquissing his ennimis, his wicht spirit in onsetting, wil testifie mony a combat with sindrie french men, and men of diuerse natiounis, in . . . Ed[r] [Edinburgh].[23]

Another version of Leslie's text reads: "thair wes gret atturnementis and justinge in Edinburch, be ane quha callit himself the wyld knycht, and ranconterit be the frenshe men, with counterfutting of the round tabill of King Arthour of Jngland. This wild knycht was the king himself, quha wes vailyeannt in armeis, and could very weill exerce the same."[24] William Drummond of Hawthornden — who mistakenly associates the tournament of the wild knight and the black lady with James's wedding and appears also to have conflated the 1507 and 1508 tournaments with an earlier joust between d'Arces and Hamilton — says that

solemn Days were kept at Court for Banqueting, Masks and Revelling, Barriers and Tilting proclaimed. Challenges were given out in the Name of the *Savage Knight* (who was the King himself) and Rewards designed to the Victors. Old King *Arthur*, with his Knights of the Round-Table were here brought upon the Lists. The Fame of this Marriage had drawn many foreign Gentlemen to the Court. Amongst others came Monsieur *Darcy*, naming himself *Le Sieur de la Beaute*, who tried Barriers with the Lord *Hamilton*, after they had tilted with grinding Spears. Some of the Savage Knight's Company (who were robust High-land Men) he giving Way unto them, smarted really in these feigned Conflicts, with Targets and Two-handed Swords to the Musick of their Bag-pipes, fighting as in a true Battel, to the Admiration of the *English* and *French*, who had never seen Men so ambitious of Wounds and prodigal of Blood in sport. All were magnificently entertain'd by the King, and with honourable Largesses and Rewards of their Valour, licensed to return Home.[25]

There are, then, some differences among the chronicle accounts of the tournament. Pitscottie does not mention Arthur or the wild knight but calls him instead the "black" knight; the Treasurer's Accounts, however, quite clearly refer to the "allocayis [lackeys] to the wild knycht."[26] On this point Leslie and Drummond agree: there was a "knycht of King Arthuris brocht vp in the wodis" (Leslie) or a "Savage Knight" (Drummond); Leslie and Drummond agree that this wild knight was the king himself, and Pitscottie concurs that the king "iustit him selff dissaguysed onknawin." It is, of course, the business of the chronicler to glorify kingship as much as possible, and the legend of James IV's devotion to chivalry was, as we have seen, already well formed by the time Pitscottie and Leslie were writing in the later sixteenth century (Drummond wrote in the seventeenth century). These accounts are thus distanced in time from the tournament by nearly a century or more, and they are botched and muddled in some significant ways. Pitscottie gets the date wrong, and Drummond conflates nearly every one of James's important tournament spectacles. But these accounts nonetheless suggest, in their outlines, a clear "tradition" that James himself jousted as the wild knight.

When we turn to the Treasurer's Accounts for their testimony on the matter of the king's role in the tournament, we find that the wild knight is mentioned only three times in entries that describe the outfitting of his lackeys.[27] The wild knight is not identified as the king in these entries, nor is the king associated with the wild knight elsewhere in the accounts. But the black lady is not identified either, and thus we can speculate that the wild knight and the black lady did not need to be identified—and did not chance to be identified—simply because everyone knew who they were. This does not prove that the king was the wild knight; it simply means that the accounts' failure to identify him as such is not definitive.

The entries in the Treasurer's Accounts do suggest the king's active participation in the tournaments of 1507 and 1508. Black and yellow or gold seem to have been his chief colors at the tournament, colors which may link him to the "allocayis to the wild knycht" (who, it will be recalled, wore doublets of velvet and cloth-of-gold, black and yellow hose, and black and yellow bonnets): there are entries for three ells of "blak satin to be ane armying doublat to the King," for half an ell of "blak satin to be foresleffis for the Kingis harnes doublat"; other entries mention black damask for the king's "cote" sleeves, yellow cloth for the king's hose, and a yellow taffeta hood.[28] Black is not a color that appears elsewhere in connection with the tournament's materials, save for the black gloves and sleeves worn by the black lady.

It is also clear that extensive preparations were made for the king's arming both in 1507 and 1508. Fourteen pounds were spent on a clasp of gold for the king's "pissan" (gorget).[29] There are entries "for ane buklar" and "ane scheith" to the king, for "armyng spuris," for swords and daggers; numerous items record work done on the king's swords, spearheads, and har-

ness.[30] There are also entries "for tua battale axes gilt and ane armyng
sword with hilt and plomet gilt"; "for iiij gilt dagaris deliverit to the King
at divers tymes"; "for gilting of the plaitis of the harnes sadil and graving
tharof"; and "for ane steil mais gilt, with ane dagar in it."[31] Whether these
last were intended for the king's use in the tournament or were among the
weapons "of fyne gold or of siluir or than doubill ovir gilt" mentioned by
Pitscottie as prizes for the tournament — or both — is not possible to say;
the accounts do record that "ane chenȝe of the Kingis to mak speris, gluffis
of plait, and prises for the feld" was given to be worked by "Matho Auchlek,"
so it is at least clear that the king intended to reward the contenders with
metallic splendor.[32]

It is possible that the expense and effort put into arms and saddlery for
the king was intended merely to help him project the appearance of a power-
fully and splendidly accoutred warrior. The editor of the accounts — whose
capacity for visualization is elsewhere truly impressive — admits defeat on
the subject of James's own costume: "It is difficult to say," he writes, "exactly how the king was attired in his capacity of the wild knight." An entry of 8s. 4d. for a pair of gilt buckles and a pair of silver horns for the
king may have meant that the king wore horns, as did the wild men.[33]
But this particular pair of silver horns may simply have been the everyday
"horns" worn on the ends of points and laces, and indeed their purchase
along with something so relatively mundane as gilt buckles suggests that
they may not have been destined for elaborate headgear. But that the king's
appearance may not have been in any way bizarre has a particular theatrical significance that will be discussed shortly. The evidence points securely
to James's active participation in the tournament and points — albeit more
tentatively — to his association with the colors of the wild knight. And if
he did joust, he did so not without precedent; for we know that he jousted
in the tournament held to honor the marriage of Perkin Warbeck to Lady
Catherine Gordon.

The wild knight was, as we have noted, probably accompanied by the
"wildmen" mentioned in the accounts as wearing "hert hornes and gayt
skinnis." The editor of the accounts is probably correct to suggest that
they may have ridden the harnessed and winged "bestis," for Richard Bernheimer reports that one of the most striking of the wild man's traits is his
mastery over animals; his steeds are bears and lions, serpents and dragons.[34] The wild man appears in virtually every form of pageantry, every
form of the visual and literary arts, in virtually every social context, at
one time or another throughout the Middle Ages. This "ubiquity," Bernheimer writes, "must be regarded as a sign that he represented a major,
if unacknowledged, trend of thought"; for corresponding to this ubiquity

is the marginality with which the figure is often treated. He appears on house signs, chimneys, love-caskets and saddles.[35] In heraldic art he is usually a supporter; his role in pageantry seems often to have been a secondary one, accompanying or pulling pageant machinery or serving as a torchbearer.[36] The wild man is thus a liminal figure: he appears on borders and edges; he guards limits; he ushers in and out; he shows, or makes, the way.

Henry VIII's tournament of 1510 — which featured the king himself and three other challengers calling themselves "Les quater Chivalers de la forrest salvigne" — included a pageant that brought the challengers into the hall at Westminster.[37] It was made like a forest, drawn by a golden antelope, and led in by "certayne men appareiled like wilde men, or woodhouses, their bodies, heddes, faces, handes and legges, covered with grene Silke flosshed." This pageant — like the troop of wild men in James's tournament — illustrates the "supporting" role so often given to the carnivalesque — to the grotesque — in court disguisings. But Henry VIII's tournament — again, like that of its predecessor, James's tournament — also puts wildness into the foreground. For Henry's wild men lead in a pageant wagon bearing four knights of the wild forest, who are indeed agonists in the king's tournament. Marginality moves into the privileged space of tournament narrative; the possibility of movement between margin and center is evoked when a horde of fuzzy wild men support with their antics the articulate motility of a chivalrous wild knight. Plain arms, the *chevalier nouveau* — Perceval, and Degare ("almost lost it is") — emerge from the same forest space as does the wild man.

Bernheimer suggests that the notion of the wild man responds and is due to a "persistent psychological urge" to "give external expression and symbolically valid form to the impulses of reckless physical self-assertion which are hidden in all of us, but are normally kept under control."[38] The wild man is "a creature on the border line between beast and man," who occupies a "curiously ambiguous and ill-defined position in God's creation" — a characteristic drawn on by Dunbar in his disfiguring portrait of Donald Oure.[39] But this ambiguity, not surprisingly, gave the figure of the wild man at least a double valence: Bernheimer suggests that in the Middle Ages wildness represented not only a threat to civilization and its conventions — a "task" and a trial for the knight — but also a temptation.[40] That interest in wild-man iconography, particularly in its courtly forms, took an upturn at the end of the fourteenth century makes sense when we consider the simultaneous elaboration, toward the close of the Middle Ages, of discourses of courtesy and civility. He is, at least in his late medieval manifestation, the product of court culture's intense preoccupation with the mannering of the body and its perhaps equally intense nostalgia for the bodily "freedom" thus sacrificed.[41]

As a representation of what cannot be accounted for by prevailing codifications of "knowledge" about human beings (such as the Great Chain of Being) — as what is "left out," for good or ill, by "civilization" and yet seems as much to emerge from within it as to dwell outside it, and hence as an image of the troubling instability of the distinction between the human and the bestial, the civilized and the natural — the wild man gives "symbolically valid *form*" to "impulses," to the body without restraint. Moreover, precisely as a "figure," the wild man gives bodily image to what cannot be seen by means of such categorical distinctions. Moreover, his embodiment of the mourned body of freedom — of the uncivilized human body, of an ungoverned aggressivity and sexuality — gives his image a narrative power; the wild man is a nostalgic figure, who embodies the idea that somewhere was (and may still be) a being wild and free of the totalizing impositions of the ideal image. To conceptualize the wild man is in part to fear and to defend against the threat he poses to convention and conceptualization itself — he is, in this capacity, a talismanic figure. But even the talisman defends by making use of what it fears; since however much the ideal image lays claim to totality and perfection, it nonetheless seems to demand a deracination of the "lived experience of the body," to conceptualize the wild man is also to wish for reintegration with the very chaos one has sacrificed in the name of unity. To imagine him is thus, once again, to revisit, at least in fantasy, the scene of one's own creation as fully human, and therefore the scene of lost "nature."

Talismans reverse fascinating images — images that have the power to paralyze the onlooker through terror (or beauty) — into apotropaic images. The talisman turns passivity into activity, vulnerability into aggression: the image that seems to lure the subject into his own, or his culture's, past or potential wildness, returns as the blinding power of the subject's gaze.[42] Hence the wild man was popular as a supporter in heraldry, which may have given rise to his use as squire or lackey in tournaments.[43] And in his role as "supporter," the figure of the wild man lends himself to the representation of subjection. In an example that is of particular relevance to the tournament of the wild knight and the black lady, Bernheimer suggests that the presence of the wild man in the armorial shield of the Swedish province of Lapland may be due to "the existence within its borders of a primitive people whose appearance and mode of life must have seemed 'wild' to their Germanic neighbors." The wild man could serve as an image of wildness or nature "harnessed" through the rule of the sovereign, who is the embodiment of civilization, of the human, and who wields a power of alteration over nature. Accordingly, the wild man could serve as an explication of domination in strange lands (of adventure, conquest, exploration) as well as at home. Felipe Fernández-Armesto, in *Before Columbus*, also notes that "the traditional heraldic wild man on the scutcheon of one conqueror of the Canaries became assimilated to primitive Canarians."[44] The archaic, the primitive, will thus seem rooted in the ruler who is, at the same time, civility and contemporaneity itself; the ruler thus doubles his power of substantiation by mannering the body and reclaiming the wild supplement constructed thereby. To stage oneself, fashionably, as a wild knight is the theatrical representation of the ruler's own multiplicity with respect both to the codifications of the Great Chain of Being and to the categories of history.

The semic multiplicity of the wild man thus offered the imagination rich possibilities for the simultaneous grasping of "alternatives" otherwise kept rigorously apart. James IV, as we have already suggested, had special needs in this regard, and Ranald Nicholson has noted the double quality of James IV's approach to Gaelic Scotland: if Pedro de Ayala is to be believed, James spoke Gaelic, and the king "rewarded players of the clarshach and even Highland bards."[45] Moreover, the Highlands seem to have become, for James, a special place of bodily freedom, as well as of the penitential bodily discipline that may have been meant, at least in part, to remind James of the death of his father: "Hunts in Glenartney and Glenfinglas, together with many other expeditions, military, devotional and amorous, made him more closely acquainted than his predecessors with many regions of the Highlands and Isles. Yet the Gaelic regions were more than ever regarded as the abode of outlandish folk whose restlessness offended the majesty of the new monarchy. Almost simultaneously, though by no means in cooperation, Henry VII undertook the subjugation of Ireland and James IV began the daunting of the Isles."[46] Thus while James IV may have spoken Gaelic, it is also true, as William Ferguson notes, that "after the forfeiture of the Lordship of the Isles in 1493 the Stewart kings tried to suppress Gaelic in the belief that it fostered barbarism and fomented disorder."[47] Indeed there was, as we have already had occasion to note, disorder in the Highlands and the Isles at the beginning of the sixteenth century, owing in large part to the uprising of Donald Oure ("brown," "dun"), or Dubh ("black") — the bastard traitor on whom Dunbar turned his talismanic mirror in the "Epetaphe for Donald Oure" and whose colors James seems, so to speak, to have worn in his tournament of the wild knight and the black lady. Ferguson, we recall, links the "resurgence of Gaelic Scotland and the way in which the Lordship of the Isles gave it political as well as cultural expression" not only to the "wider malaise whereby by the end of the fourteenth century whole regions of Scotland were falling under the sway of over-mighty subjects" but also to the related problem of the longstanding enmity with England: it was "one of the most significant consequences of the English wars."[48] Thus in a number of important respects the tournament of the wild knight and the black lady engaged the same issues that were of importance in the marriage of James and Margaret; even though the tournament was more centrally preoccupied with the problem of intimate violence, of the foreigner within, and the marriage with the problem of the foreigner without, both marriage and tournament took place in the context of a whole array of challenges to and possibilities for the formation of national identity. The Scottish "wildmen" of the later fifteenth and early sixteenth centuries brought out the problem and the opportunity of rivalry within and between national boundaries, and between sovereign and (aristocratic) subject.

The problem was, again, conceived in terms of the boundary between barbarity and civilization. A discourse of "wildness" and a policy of "benign" interventionism were produced by Lowlands commentators on doings in the north and west: "The rising of Donald Dubh had elicited from the parliament of March 1504 an unwonted show of concern for the betterment of government in the Highlands and the Isles, where 'the pepill ar almaist gane wilde.'"[49] "Summonses for treason [also] proliferated" after 1504; provisions were made for the administration of royal justice, and "the troubled regions were to be purged of the remnants of ancient Celtic law and be ruled by the king's laws and by 'nane othir lawis.'"[50] The Church was already being used in the pacification of the "troubled regions": In Argyll "a bishop with local connections . . . was succeeded in 1497 by a Lowlander, David Hamilton; since he served among 'wild people' he received royal grants to strengthen his hand."[51] The Papal Bull of 10 February 1494 that authorized the founding of the new university of Aberdeen noted that the "university intended to cater for those parts of the kingdom 'separated from the rest . . . by arms of the sea and very high mountains, in which dwell men rude, ignorant of letters, and almost barbarous.'"[52] And in 1510 John Campbell, bishop of the Isles, "was succeeded by the king's treasurer, George Hepburn, member of that favoured Lowland kin"; the king "petitioned the pope that the new bishop might hold Arbroath and Iona *in commendam,* so that 'his authority and nobility of race may bind that uncivilized people in devotion to the church.'"[53]

James's attempt to pacify the Highlands and the Isles took place, then, not only through the force of arms but also through the deployment of a rhetoric of civilization and wildness that marked out, in effect, the racial supremacy of Lowland blood—that, in Major's terms, distinguished between "combative nature" and natures capable of rule – and equated legal and cultural pluralism with the "greit abusioune of [royal] justice."[54] At the same time, the king romanced the Highlands, as his hart-hunting, his own restless travels in those restless lands, and his tournament of the wild knight attest. Drummond's picture of "Some of the Savage Knight's Company (who were robust High-land Men) he giving Way unto them, smarted really in these feigned Conflicts, with Targets and Two-handed Swords to the Musick of their Bag-pipes, fighting as in a true Battel" is perhaps a garbled relic of the wild knight's troupe of wild men, who would likely not have resembled quite so closely the Highlander of a later century's imagination. But that James's wild men would have been linked, in his mind and the minds of his courtiers, with the wild Scots of the north is beyond question. And Drummond's picture remains a telling one, since it indicates how some of the cruel policies of later centuries were being prepared for at the close of the Middle Ages, through the expansionism of the Lowland powers that had fought under the banner of James IV in his rebellion against his father and had continued to form the basis of his political support throughout his reign. The Lowlands "discovered," ideologically speaking, the wildness of the north at the moment of its own attempts at consolidation.

Telling, too, is the coincidence of the first run of James's tournament with the final triumphs of James's policy in the "troubled regions." "The last stronghold of the insurgents," Torquil McLeod's castle of Stornoway, had fallen by October 1506, and "by August of 1507 Donald Dubh was safely warded in Stirling Castle."[55] James IV thus might well have had reason to celebrate, as Nicholson comments that "from 1507 until the end of the reign an illusory peace settled upon the Highlands and Isles. . . . The MacDonalds . . . had disappeared as overmighty subjects."[56] The question of how "overmighty" the MacDonalds really were, compared at least with other overmighty subjects within the Lowlands themselves and compared with overmighty enemies outside Scotland, remains somewhat unsettled; for the intensity of the monarchy's cultural as well as political and military pacification program seems, again, to accord as much with Lowland culture's need to purify itself of wildness and as much with its own ambitious designs on an impoverished, decentralized, and culturally diverse nation facing an "overmighty" neighbor on its borders as it does with the degree of Gaelic Scotland's troublesomeness. To represent that troublesomeness as so dangerous as to be rooted in a nature that must be rooted out is once again to represent aggressive ambition as an act of peace and is to represent the power of alteration that accomplishes such a peace as strong indeed – strong enough, perhaps, to make over a nation in its own image, though James's achievements in Gaelic Scotland were not long lasting.[57]

It is characteristic of James that his mode of dealing with the Highlands should include not only repressive and totalizing strategies ("nane othir lawis") but also talismanic identifications and compromise figures: the king forfeits the Lord of the Isles but disguises himself as his dark double, the wild knight. The wild men of his tournament were, after all, adorned not in elaborately artificed costumes — not in "grene silke flosshed" — but in goat skins and harts' horns. The disjunction between the literally outlandish quality of their apparel and the apparent restraint of James's own appearance as the wild knight suggests the complex conjunction, in James's spectacular artistry, of subjection and identification.

In dressing up as the wild knight James revisits his own creation through his emergence from a wild interiority; and he also revisits his creation as king, through his emergence from the "troubled regions" of his own rebellion, the taint of parricide and regicide. Though destined for the crown by birth, his father had suspected him of the capacity for treachery which Dunbar, John Major, and many others designated as inherent to wildness. James's rebellion against his father seems to have been brought on by signs of his father's preference for his younger brother, and though James may have felt himself to have been averting a potential injustice to himself by taking up arms, he nonetheless — in this more like Mordred than Arthur — ended by fulfilling in some way the suspicions of his father. His tournament atones for his rebellion, by making one and making good both the great king and the criminal. And the tournament, too, is a form of mourning; it is a way of taking leave of the joys of a violent, rebellious, wild past, by marking them *as* past: as the forest from which he has emerged. But the tournament is also a means of inclusion: for the knight is still a wild one, a "stranger" knight, as Leslie calls him, who wears the disguise that marks his phenomenological ambiguity, his indeterminacy; and his lady is the "black" lady of mystery, who presides over the crossroads of identity and anonymity, openness and secrecy. Thus it is James's identification simultaneously with a similarity and a difference that is at stake in his tournament. The wild men are like, but also unlike, the wild knight: they measure the aspiration to transformation, to the assumption of "recognizable" human form. Just so, James's own wildness — his rebellion, his promiscuity, his restlessness, in short his reluctance to stay in one place or time — is imagined as redeemed through the civilizing process also represented by James's political rhetoric as the heart of royal policy. The figure of the wild man becomes a means to represent the domestication of the body politic and the body of the monarch — both the natural and the

fictive body of kingship. Through talismanic reversal, strangeness is recovered and redeployed as already within, and already behind, the subject of honor. That which terrifies or tempts — the archaic, the wild — is
split off so that it may return as protective, contemporary.

The figure of the wild man thus generates a narrative of rejuvenation
and revitalization, in which the old can become the new, the father refound in the son. The wild man takes on an expiatory function in a spectacle that undoes the crime that made James king; the king is "protected,"
not threatened, by his own wildness. The undoing sought by the representation of reform is, again, talismanic in purpose: the fear of danger, the
desire for protection, produce motifs of emergence from obscurity, of
disguise and unknown identity. So the legendary narrative also suggests
that greatness cannot be muffled; alone, in the wasteland (the dystonic form
of the forest), the "true" king will emerge, and the truthfulness of his claim
to be extraordinary will be seen in a spectacle staged for the community
of similars. Pitscottie's account of the tournament stresses the king's
emergence from the field not only as victor but also as final judge and giver
of gifts; in making one and making good wildness and kingship, so the
tournament of the wild knight and the black lady presents the doubtful,
anonymous knight as the principle of justice in its power both to give and
to take away. The tournament of the wild knight and the black lady enacts
the identity of the king with the unnamed, the outsider. The double of
the king — the potential rival — is thus revealed to be the same as the king.
The wild knight proves himself to be the rightful king through his outstanding prowess; he turns out already to be king, to be rightful. Essence
and effort, inheritance and combat, are made one.

James's tournament thus comes down on the side of the son whose secret identity is that he is already the father, the true father; he has the
power to identify himself. As such, he is, in a sense, self-created; he has
revisited the scene of his exclusion and triumphed through the power of
legendary narrative to enact a kind of immortality in time. Identity must
be revealed at the right place and time — the concern expressed in Dunbar's
The Thrissill and the Rois over reform of the king's promiscuity likewise
both questions and asserts the king's willingness to be placed, timed, and
identified — so that the king may finish his narrative of aspiration and
assume the ideal image of the body of kingship. The reform of promiscuity and aggressivity thus promises the resolution of maturational crisis;
Shakespeare's Hal charts something of the same course. And just as Shakespeare's Hal models, though with a more rigid repudiation of wildness —
one which brings out the ambiguity of pacification with respect to the
prince's own intimates — the sacrificial reorganization of the body politic

for the sake of imperial greatness, James's tournament of the wild knight
and the black lady may have been designed in part to precipitate as much
of Scotland as possible into James's larger designs on the outside world,
to identify rivalrous interests with his own grand visions.[58] For James—
both wild knight and king—reveals himself as king to his subjects but does
not thereby cease being a knight. The king is the best and strongest knight;
the anonymous, obscure knight can become a magnanimous king. The
tournament thus promises mobility and rewards aspiration while reserv-
ing, for kingship, full responsibility for the pains, as well as the pleasures,
of shifting shape.

But it remains true, despite the pains thus taken, that there are possibly
irreducible risks in such display. James's tournament takes greater risks than
does the masque; the king wears a costume, impersonates, makes an effort.
Instead of having to be the unmoving eye of the sun, the figure that banishes Proteus or, in *The Masque of Blacknesse*, reforms the imperfections
of Ethiopian nymphs, James himself is protean, and the changes of maturation are wrought within him even though they are wrought, finally, by
the power of his identity. His emergence as king through a maturational
and revelatory narrative is accomplished through a series of inclusions that
treat disguises, not as appearances to be discarded or as imperfections to
be perfected, but as forms of identity in their own right. The narrative
of the tournament of the wild knight and the black lady is thus both a
protection and a dare: the king, in effect, dares the eye of the spectator
to see his disguises as "nothing but" disguises.

To some extent, James retreats from this challenge. The Treasurer's Accounts do not suggest that James's costume was in any way bizarre. His
elegant difference from the animallike appearance of his troupe of wild
men proposes his identity with them as well as his subjection of them;
the transformation of wildness into civilization is not accomplished entirely through the story of his own person, but rather through an ascend-
ing and descending series of compromise figures. And as we shall see in
the following chapter, the black lady functions in part as a *divertissement*,
a lure for the gaze who is, like an antimasque, projected off in a spectacular disappearing act. The wild knight's mysteriousness attracts the curiosity of the spectator, and his identity becomes the question of the day; but
it turns out that he is not so much seen as seeing. Moreover, by effecting,
through his role as aspirant, a talismanic identification with the gaze of
those who would be king, the troubling possibility of twinship—that the
king might be like other men, and therefore that other men might be like
the king—is defused through the coincidence of identity and revelation:
the aspirant knight was the king all along, and thus the aristocracy can

come to understand how the king can emerge from within their ranks and yet be categorically different from them. The king thus enacts for them their hope of recognition, but he reserves the power of recognition for himself, and as unique, only he can recognize himself, can confer the gaze that distinguishes him from all others.

Finally the tournament plays its sacrifices out as pleasure; it delights in the moment at which disguise and identity, otherness and sameness, obscurity and brilliance, meet. The story of the wild knight is a story about becoming visible, phenomenalizing the self, "making" oneself "into" one's images; it is a dramatization of self-dramatization that comes down finally on the side of the creativity, rather than the deceptiveness, of legends. As such it both thematizes and celebrates the theatricality inherent in tournament drama. While one strand of the tournament's artistry suggests that its point is the recovery of the king's power to see, rather than to be seen, this other strand suggests that the point of the tournament is the king's theatricality. The "king" is a fiction; the pleasure of the ideal is precisely the pleasure of art, of making something out of nothing. Insofar as the ideal is a fiction, it is open to freedom and change. But this daring rehabilitation of the ficticity of the image is for the king alone, and its obverse — the loss of being, evanescence — will not be forgotten. For only if both lack and fullness, destruction and creation, are at work in the story of the king will that story become a legend.

13

The Black Lady

Thou still abidest so entirely one,
That we may know thy blackness is a spark
Of light inaccessible, and alone
Our darkness which can make us think it dark.
                                        — Edward, Lord Herbert of Cherbury

In *Male Fantasies*, Klaus Theweleit argues that the body of woman has served as territory of desire in place of the body of the earth, the latter of which is withheld; the earth's body has been figured as the body of infinite womanhood, which has in turn been figured as the "utopian site of an absence of lack" and therefore as an instrument whereby the movement of lack in desire has been perpetuated.[1] The affective fusion of woman with nation or land or people enables an eroticization of aspiration: the woman's status as fantasy provides an affective displacement of ambitious designs on the body of the world. Beauty, once again, has a "formative" and "erogenic" power; it forms desire into desire for perfect form and therefore has a "civilizing" efficacy whereby wildness — "free," unruled aggressivity, sexuality, greed, ambition — may be ruled, and yet appropriated. "With the expansion of the European world, which followed in the wake of exploration by seafaring adventurers," Theweleit writes, the images of the queen and of the Blessed Virgin Mary "were supplemented by images of women from other continents — the black slave woman, the woman of the almond eyes. . . . Collectively, these images began to construct the body that would constitute a mysterious goal for men whose desires were armed for an imminent voyage, a body that was to be more enticing than all the rest of the world put together."[2] Both queen and black lady are captivating images, whereby the freedom of "historical deterritorialization" is recuperated for authority, and authority may, once again, be experienced as liberating. The king himself can be just such an image; but the extent to which embodiment and visibility threaten to unmake as well as to make sovereignty can, as we have shown, be defused if the queen takes on this challenge for the king. In the masques of *Blacknesse* and of *Beautie*, the queen, disguised as an Ethiopian nymph, takes on the quest for the king, bringing the mysteries of other lands to Albion, bringing the voyage, and the goal, to the English Sun. In *Blacknesse* and *Beautie*, the dream of imperial power creates and then borrows the exoticism of gendered and racial and geographic otherness to exacerbate both its own mysteriousness and its own accessibility, and thus pictures the subjugation of the body of the world by the monarch as the desire of strangeness for the principle of identity. Sovereign love, through the image of the black lady, works its magic, its "dynamic of flight and expectancy," through geography — when oceans and deserts are crossed or when rivers (like Niger in *Blacknesse*) change course. Blackness can function for sovereign love as an intensification of outsideness: it signifies worlds to be conquered, both the exterior world of the body of the earth and the interior world of love and faith. The black lady poses a double challenge: Can her foreignness as well as her femaleness be domesticated? What are the limits of the sovereign power of alteration, over land, over subject bodies?

Thus the association, during the Middle Ages and the Renaissance, of blackness with both beauty and ugliness, both of soul and of body, is more a complex of related conceptions than an array of diverse perceptions. Blackness and beauty may be split off from each other, thus imaging conflict between the grotesque and the well formed, wildness and civilization, the unknown and the known, mystery and intelligibility.[3] Black beauty itself offers an image of wildness and civilization reconciled, wherein the gaze of the onlooker penetrates through appearances to see the beauty within or recognizes that black beauty — often, in the Renaissance, figured specifically as an unchanging beauty — signifies beauty, "brightness," of soul. In either case, moral whiteness is found within blackness; and in either case, the white gaze presents itself as overcoming a challenge to its sight, as uncovering a mystery, whether the challenge is located in the appearance of blackness or in white perception: "alone / Our darkness which can make us think it dark."[4] Though the Renaissance was fond of asserting that its capacity to appreciate black beauty distinguished it from "the old age," similar understandings of blackness and its relation to beauty were available during the Middle Ages.[5] Wolfram von Eschenbach's *Parzival* (ca. 1197–98), for example, amply illustrates the complexity of the white gaze's determination to see goodness as whiteness, thereby to overcome obscurity, wherever it looks; in *Parzival*, these issues take the form of a problem of belief, of Christianity versus the "heathen," appropriate to the spirit of crusade.

In *Parzival*, Belacane is the queen of Zazamanc, probably in Africa, a country inhabited by black Moors. Gahmuret, the white knight, gains an audience with her, and she falls in love with him instantly: "The great queen's eyes caused her grievous pain when they beheld the Angevin, who, being of Love's color, unlocked her heart whether she wished it or not."[6] They sit down to converse, and the narrator comments: "If there is anything brighter than daylight—the queen in no way resembled it. A woman's manner she did have, and was on other counts worthy of a knight, but she was unlike a dewy rose; her complexion was black of hue" (14). In place of the expected blazon, an antiblazon—a contrast which we will see again in Dunbar's poem "Ane Blak Moir"—precedes the conversation in which Belacane is established as one who, like the black lady of James's tournament, tests the identity of knights; for the issue between Gahmuret and Belacane is "whether he could be my friend," that is, whether he could act as her chivalrous protector. The testing of Gahmuret's identity is mirrored in the testing of Belacane's identity. Through sacramental intervention, she becomes beautiful: "Gahmuret reflected how she was a heathen, and yet never did more womanly loyalty glide into a woman's heart. Her innocence was a pure baptism, as was also the rain that wet her, that flood which flowed from her eyes down upon the furs about her bosom" (17). Through Belacane's self-baptism, the blackness of her body is made into an inessential exterior, her skin displaced by images of a redeemed nature; and it is at this moment that "between the two there sprang up a genuine desire" (18), that Belacane is constituted as a proper object of desire for the white knight.

Gahmuret eventually tires of his Dido—for his adventures in Africa, like those of Aeneas, are a preliminary testing ground for his final destiny in Europe: "The lady's protectiveness held a tight bit on me, so that I could not get to knightly action" (51). He escapes from this devouring interiority, leaving Belacane pregnant with their child and leaving a note saying, "Lady, if you will receive baptism, you may yet win me back" (32). Belacane's self-baptism loses its sacramental efficacy when it is time for the white knight to leave; later on, back in Europe, when the Lady Herzeloyde claims his love, the shifty Gahmuret—who, like James IV in his promiscuous youth, resists being placed and timed—explains that he already has a wife. But Herzeloyde insists, "You should renounce the Moorish woman for my love's sake. The sacrament of baptism has superior power. Therefore give up your heathenry and love me by our religion's law" (53). Thus Belacane, at one time both heathen and baptized, erotic and saintly, is reread in time and then split in two; only in the space of knightly errancy, when whiteness courts blackness, can these contradictions be allowed to stand. When whiteness has had its way with blackness, black innocence is revealed to have no real sacramental power, no power of alteration or re-creation, against the efficacy of white religion. *Parzival* urges a maturation based on renunciation, but what is renounced can nevertheless be enjoyed by the white knight without punishment precisely because a linear maturational or developmental structure is employed. Thus *Parzival* finally models an early instance of the colonialist's, in the form of the adventurer's, dilemma: how to enjoy and to profit from the resources of foreign lands without thereby losing one's identity. *Parzival* assures its audience that it may venture outside Christendom, penetrate the mysteries of foreign lands, find "value" there without fear of losing home and without fear that home will lose its unchallengable identity with virtue. Thus can a Christian knight make his way in the world: Gahmuret's ambitions are formed through his choice of a true religion and a true lady. *Parzival* thus suggests an important correction to Theweleit's formulation: the body of the earth is sometimes not so much withheld as dangled before us. Though the conventions of adventure literature most often depict the desire for travel as spontaneous and free, at times of crusade and of conquest subjects, even whole populations, must be mobilized for adventure in foreign lands.[7]

When, in the fifteenth century, Africans began to appear in Europe in significant numbers, strategies for their domestication were thus already in place, through the experience of crusade, travel literature and romance, the rhetorical tradition, popular drama, court disguisings. Rhetorical tradition associated blackness with ugliness and churlishness; countless representations linked devilry with blackness (miracle-play devils wore vizards or were painted black).[8] Face-blackening was an important feature of early disguisings and dramas and of later folk-plays and processions: Chambers cites the Turkish knight, one of the combatants in the (late) Cheshire mummers' play, who is referred to as a "black Morocco dog."[9] A play put on in Roxburghshire is reported as including "Gysarts" dressed in shrouds with faces painted black or blue, who perform a tragedy sometimes called "Galatian" or "Alexander of Macedon."[10] In the courtly morisco or morris-dance, face-blackening was also employed.[11] There are, moreover, numerous examples of the association of the morisco and Moors with wildness. The famous "Bal des Ardents" of 1393 — in which Charles VI of France and five of his lords, disguised as *hommes sauvages*, were mistakenly set ablaze by the duke of Orléans — was, according to Welsford, "probably a morisco, for it was accompanied by *'choreas saracenicas,'*" a Latin translation of "moorish dances."[12] The pageantry for the marriage, in 1502, of Lucrezia Borgia to Alfonso, the eldest son of Duke Ercole d'Este, featured a morisco of Moors with flaming tapers in their mouths and a dance of *sauvages* "contending for the possession of a lady."[13] A king of Moors, too, appears in a pageant of the London drapers in 1522, and the accounts for the pageant list payments "to John Wakelyn, for playing the king of the Moors, (the company finding him his apparell, his stage, and his wyld fire)." Because he carried wild fire, Withington suggests that he "may, perhaps, have taken the place of the wild-man on this occasion"; in pageantry, torch-bearers and crowd-clearers were at times Moors, at times wild men.[14] Moors also began to appear as supporters in heraldic art at about the same time as wild men. It is clear, then, that *sauvages* and Moors performed some of the same talismanic and "supportive" functions in European pageantry—and featured in similar anthropological fantasies.

Africa and Asia had long been "known" to medieval Europe through the Alexander tradition, through authorities like Pliny and Herodotus, Solinus and Martianus Capella, writers like Bacon and Dante and Mandeville, and through crusaders' tales.[15] These sources represented Africa and India as places full of marvels and "monstrous prodigies"; commenting on the "fantastic exuberance" of the "surrealistic anthropology" of the medieval literature on India, Le Goff writes that the Indian Ocean was "a mental horizon, the exotic fantasy of the medieval West, the place where its dreams freed themselves from repression." Its dreams of riches were "the psychological repercussions of the . . . structure of medieval trade"; dog-headed men and cyclopes allowed a "poor and limited world" to form for itself "an extravagant combinatoric dream of disquieting juxtapositions and concatenations," a "vision of a world where a different kind of life was lived," unrestrained or perverse in its libidinal ways.[16] Le Goff adds that "the Celtic world was another oneiric horizon for the medieval West," and indeed the two often merged: "Indian myths invaded the Arthurian legend."[17] Wild men—figures of the "lost" world of European and Celtic paganism—were part of the medieval way of dreaming; they found their way into far-off lands and offered a means of imagining the faraway. Pliny had described the Choromandri of India as hirsute *silvestres*; Herodotus referred to wild men and women in western Libya.[18] An eleventh-century English manuscript on the marvels of the East shows a cannibal wild man in India.[19] The Prester John tradition mentions *homines agrestes*, wild men, along with fauns, satyrs, and pygmies.[20] In *Le Livre des merveilles*, a composite volume of the early fifteenth century containing travel accounts of Marco Polo and Mandeville, giants are rendered as wild men, "satyrs as wild men with horns."[21] In the Alexander manuscripts, the "various hairy creatures of the romance are usually portrayed as conventional wild-men"; wild men in animal skins or costumes made of artificial leaves, lint, or tow dance their way through the margins of the fourteenth-century *Roman d'Alexandre* bought by Richard Wydeville, father of Elizabeth, in 1466.[22] That wild and black people could occupy the same oneiric space is also attested by a fifteenth-century Swiss tapestry that shows "hairy wild men assailing blackamoors, including a black king and queen."[23]

The "surrealistic anthropology" of the medieval literature on India and Africa exemplifies, then, the doubleness of the ideal of beauty: its "formative" or productive power — its power to propel the body into a history of formation — and its power to alienate the body, to "produce" it as grotesque, excessive or insufficient, chaotic. It produces at once aspiration to perfection of form and a distancing from sensuality and materiality; it is both enticing and humiliating. Hence, "ironically," Le Goff notes, the monsters of the East "often served as screens between man and the riches he glimpsed, dreamed of, and desired."[24] Thus Alexander quested for marvels because the narrative structure of aspiration itself permitted the alienated recovery of the grotesque and the exotic. Medieval dreams of the East made and unmade the body, turned it inside out and upside down, because the figures thus created seemed to represent a startling materiality that could not be emptied out by the familiarizations or perfections of conventional forms. In this sense they were child's play, dreams of an exuberant and grotesque body and motility wishfully unsculpted by the need to signify for the ideal, dreams, then, that seemed to put the body beyond the humiliation of "organic insufficiency," that allowed the subjectivity of medieval Europe to consider its smallness in the pigmy or its clumsiness in the giant. They were dreams that allowed the medieval subject to reinclude the grotesque through its externalization — to revisit the imagos of the fragmented body and constitute them as manifoldness rather than lack.

But Le Goff's argument, like Theweleit's, tends to assume the spontaneity of the desires that give rise to these dreams. Insofar as these dreams were compensatory for the poverty of material well-being in the West, they had the effect of withholding the body of the earth from the aspirant through concentration on the form of the human body, thereby making home fantastically acceptable; but insofar as they enticed desire, they also had the potential to mobilize for exploration and conquest those who might otherwise have preferred to stay at home, to protect what they had rather than risk losing everything. Not all Westerners merely glimpsed, or fantasized, the riches of the trade in luxury goods; the heterogeneity of the aristocracy was deliberately signified by its indulgence in material pleasure, its excessive display and conspicuous consumption of silk and spices — its participation, in effect, in the sensuality and materiality imagined as proper to faraway places. In this sense, the gown and "chair triumphall" of the black lady in James's tournament — though the materials were from

London and Flanders — was a costume that figured the command of an ultimately "foreign" luxury, as much as if she had been dressed in turbans,
feathers, and wigs. The close connection between bodily, sartorial, and
political re-formation during the later Middle Ages and the Renaissance —
as, for example, John the Commonweal's "gay garmoun" in Lindsay's *Ane
Satyre of the Thrie Estaitis* — thus recognizes the degree of wildness within
civilized courts but also brings out the extent to which that wildness was
the product of civil society's intense stratification of access to the body
of the earth and its increasingly ambitious designs upon it.[25]

For if pageantry, like travel literature, allowed European culture vicari-
ously to experience danger as novelty or exoticism or splendid apparel,
pageantry could likewise lead Europe into danger. Felipe Fernandez-
Armesto's work in *Before Columbus* reminds us that foreign adventurism
was a material reality of the later Middle Ages, not just an "oneiric" experience. The Portuguese slave trade indirectly brought black women to Scotland, one of whom may have been the black lady of James's tournament,
and James's interest in building a navy was such that Macdougall calls it
a "royal obsession."[26] Moreover, just as the Highlands and Isles, as well
as England, were a longstanding thorn in the side of the Scottish monarchy, so "for Europe, Islam was a lasting trauma"; and it should not be
forgotten that 1507–8 were years not only to celebrate James's successes
in the "troubled regions" but also to begin thinking about warfare against
the "Turk." Mackie writes: "Arthur's task — to war with the heathen — would
be his task too. It was perhaps as a dedication to this task that he sent
Robert Barton, shipmaster — and, some said, pirate — to offer a costly ship
of silver at the shrine of his patron saint at Compostella in Spain." Barton was reimbursed for the silver ship on 2 May 1508.[27] Moreover, the
Bartons — Robert and his brothers John and Andrew, "shipmasters of Leith,"
who, as Mackie says, stood high in James's favor and were closely involved
with the king's naval ambitions — were also probably responsible for the
presence of black women, "More lassis," in James's court.[28] The "More lassis" seem to have arrived at James's court because of the Barton's attacks
on Portuguese shipping; the Portuguese were "deeply involved in the African slave trade by this time," and in 1496 James granted John Barton letters
of marque against the Portuguese to redress an attack by a Portuguese
squadron. As we shall see, the black lady of James's tournament may or
may not have been one of the "More lassis"; but the tournament is unques-
tionably a response to the arrival of blackness within James's court — not
long after the arrival of the Tudor Rose, Margaret, and James's struggles
with the wild men of Gaelic Scotland — as well as to James's interest in
"war with the heathen," and war with the English, outside. James's two

most magnificent tournaments, then, were given at a moment of crossover from "domestic" to "foreign" conquest, a moment when the enticements and anxieties of a transgressive expansionism, a movement beyond borders, were sharply on the rise.[29] And like that of the wild man, the figure of the Moor would serve a variety of talismanic functions, providing protection from danger and preventing protection from becoming dangerously safe.[30]

We need to understand more fully how the category of "woman" functions with respect to the categories of "blackness" and "wildness." In 1446 at Saumur René d'Anjou came to his Emprise de la Gueule du Dragon "Armé d'armes toutes noires" "because of his country's misfortunes" and the "recent death of his queen."[31] His tournament linked blackness — disguise, anonymity — and national misfortune with the death of the queen, hence linked identity with national prosperity and the presence of the queen. In the Thornton manuscript of *Thomas of Erceldoune*, Thomas meets a "lady bryghte" who turns black after he lies with her seven times:

> Thomas stode vpe in þat stede,
> and he by helde þat lady gaye;
> Hir hare it hange all over hir hede,
> Hir eghne semede owte, þat are were graye,
> and alle the riche clothynge was a waye,
> þat he by fore sawe in þat stede,
> hir a schanke blake, hir oþer graye,
> And all hir body lyke the lede.
> Thomas laye & saw þat syghte,
> Vndir nethe þat grenewod tree.
> þan said Thomas, "allas, allas,
> In fayþ, þis es a dullful syghte.
> How art þou fadyde þus in þe face,
> þat schane by fore als þ sonne so bryght."[32]

Much later, after an interlude at the castle of the changeful lady's jealous husband (she has by now been restored to her former brightness), Thomas insists that she tell a "ferly." She begins to tell stories of important battles in Scottish history and to prophesy:

> þer sall a lorde come to þat werre,
> þat sall be of full grete renownne,
> And in his Banere sall he bere,
> Triste it wele, a rede lyone.
> (ll. 577–80)

The encounter between Thomas and the lady occurs at "Eldone tre" (l. 84), that is, Eildon in the Roxburghshire hills; Erceldoune is probably to be identified with Earlston in Berwickshire. The story is, then, associated with the borders — an appropriate setting for concerns about sovereignty and the well-being of the nation and for prophecies featuring the royal arms of Scotland, the "alter-ego" and heraldic image of the monarch. In *The Awntyrs of Arthure at the Tern Wathelyne*, which follows immediately after *Thomas* in the Thornton manuscript, Gawane and Gaynoure (Guinevere) rest "vndir a lorrere"; a storm breaks out, and the ghost of Gaynoure's mother appears to them from purgatory to prophesy the death of Arthur and to warn the living against sexual sin: "Bare was hir body and blake to the bone."[33] In both these works, prophecy is linked to sexual crime, to infidelity, betrayal from "within"; to disfiguration or metamorphosis, and to blackness; to the fortunes of the kingdom, played out across the changing body of the woman.

Wild women were often conceived to be shape-changers. Bernheimer notes that the most persistent and most revealing trait common to wild women is their sexuality: they crave the love of mortal men, and in pursuit of their obsession they change into glamorous young creatures when they meet a likely prospect. Bernheimer summarizes: "The wild woman is thus a libidinous hag . . . a witch."[34] In these versions of female wildness, beauty is an illusion; "behind" its insubstantial form lies the grotesquerie of the unruled female body, here in its terrifying aspect, its devouring intentions with respect to manhood. Blackness and beauty combine only in the form of a malignant deception, and to penetrate the mystery of the glamorous young creature's identity is for a mortal man to lose his identity. Moreover, such stories of wild women, like the stories of *Thomas of Erceldoune* and *The Awntyrs of Arthure*, are about extraordinarily risky unions and remind us that queens — always outsiders, so often foreigners — were easily distrusted, their mysteriousness easily imagined as secret intrigue, witchcraft, hidden poison working its way through the natural or the body politic. But, being liminal figures — such as the wild people also were — queens could be identified with "land," "people," "nation," their liminality serving the very principle of identity — of the invulnerability rather than the vulnerability of the body of the realm. Queens themselves, then, are talismanic; they are a potential threat — a foreign body let in through open and even decorated gates, capable of causing internal torment — turned into an aegis of protection, a banner under which to ride against the enemy (hence, the *divina virago*).

Thus another context we might invoke for our understanding of the woman who changes shape is the tradition of the Loathly Bride or the Lady of the Land, who, as Ananda K. Coomaraswamy puts it, is the "Spirit of Sovereignty" who "appears in her form of beauty only to those who deserve her" and whose transfiguration thereby figures the hero's acquisition of the "right to rule."[35] Michael J. Enright, who has studied James VI's "marriage metaphor" ("I am the Husband, and all the whole Isle is my lawful Wife") in the context of Irish sovereignty tales, notes that in one of these a loathly goddess — who is transformed into a beautiful maiden — tells Niall of the Nine Hostages: "As at first thou hast seen me ugly, brutish, loathly but in the end beautiful, even so is royal rule. Without fierce conflict it may not be won; but in the end, he that is king shows comely and nobly forth."[36] Just as in the story of Belacane, the testing of Niall's identity as rightful king is mirrored in the testing of the goddess's identity; just as in the Judgment of Paris, the right choice would bring peace and life to the nation, the wrong choice violence and devastation. The ambiguous lady "stands for" intimate violence, internecine strife, as much as she stands for a threat from without; and we might say that the queen is potentially also a "black," wild, foreign woman, who, when she stands by the rightful king, demonstrates that he has earned her through his efforts because of his kingly essence, thus assuring both the triumph of greatness and the well-being of the whole body of the realm. This is also the function of the lady in the tournament and explains the importance of her gaze, her spectatorship; in her look, once again, is mirrored the choice of the right knight. The Manasseh Codex contains a picture of women watching a tournament spectacle. They look down upon contending knights below — one of whom is being armed by his lady — and point exaggeratedly with big, long fingers at each other and at the "male display" taking place before them: they are both pointed at and pointing.[37] They both look and are looked at — the structure of the gaze in tournament pageantry is in this sense reciprocal — because their beauty is the mirror in which honor recognizes itself, their mystery the mystery through which identity constitutes itself, just as blackness is the obscurity through which the white gaze finds itself to be perceptive, capable of penetrating appearances.

The "ground" of the woman's body — the change that takes place on it — figures conflict over sovereignty; the rivals, once again, pursue, in Lacan's words, their "deleterious dominance" over her "sacred regions." But she is a way of imagining a conflict whose outcome is nonetheless predetermined ("he that *is* king"); she is herself a sign of and a means to the protections of "fate," the reconciliation of effort and essence, whereby narrative and risk play out an anterior destiny. Her dark potentiality, her capacity to betray, and the corresponding danger posed by rivals to the sovereign subject, are thus represented, through a kind of undoing, as merely apparent. The aging, loathly woman who desires sovereignty over her husband in "The Wife of Bath's Tale"; the unstable Venus of the Judgment of Paris, whose gift might not be a true gift; the blackened purgatorial ghost of *The Awntyrs of Arthure,* once beautiful but terribly transformed through sexual corruption and infidelity; and indeed, the wanton bride Israel might all be "in the end beautiful" when fidelity to the right man, a willingness to be ruled by him, are revealed. Thus sovereign love ends in "marriage" through the legends of the king's struggles in claiming his rightful inheritance. As in James's tournament, the wild past of kingship meets its match just at the right time.[38] James's tournament thus represents the power of the sovereign to transform the land, his subjects, the woman, himself: the wasteland is recovered through the well-ruled (well-signified) allegorical garden; wild men become civilized knights; that which was brutish and black will become "in the end beautiful" as the rose Dunbar celebrates in his marriage poem for the king. Through the proving of James's right to be king, the foreign queen proves that she, too, can be trusted.

The late medieval tournament produced the lady as both audience and actress, spectator and spectacle. As the above discussion suggests, the knight must see his own reflection in the mirror of the woman's gaze; if he sees something other than the integrity of form with which he seeks to identify, then her look will be dangerous rather than protective.[39] The gaze is a function of distance from the body, a way of making meaning about bodies; when it collapses, the organized body of the knight collapses too, or metamorphoses.[40] An active looking on the part of the lady — that is, a gaze of difference rather than a gaze that reflects identity — threatens to make her into a man, thus a potential rival, a danger, ultimately, to rightful rule. The "great concourse of ladies of the most costly and beautiful, but not of the best of the kingdom," who, in mid–fourteenth-century England, dressed "as if they were a part of the tournament, in diverse and wonderful male apparel" — thus scandalizing the "chaste voice of the people" — were acting out the masculinity of the female spectator. The role of the female spectator is complex: she is rightfully, virtuously, masculinized insofar as her identity mirrors the identity of masculine honor — as masculine, Heroic Virtue is associated with Bel-Anna in Jonson's *Masque of Queenes* — but there is a danger that she may become too masculine, just as Jonson's Valasca killed her husband and instituted a nation of Amazons. The knight wants his lady to be like Douglas's Calliope in *The Palice of Honour,* a promise of phallic interiority for the male; he does not want the lady actually to wield the weapon.

The black lady was one of the most splendid visual effects of James's tournament. Twenty-four ells of Flemish taffeta went into the making of her "chair triumphale," which was adorned with "flouris" likewise made of taffeta.[41] Over six ells of damask "flourit with gold" went into the making of a very costly "goun for the blak lady," which was bordered with yellow and green Flemish taffeta.[42] She wore black leather gloves and sleeves, and above them, sleeves of "plesance."[43] Her "tua ladyis" wore gowns of green Flemish taffeta bordered with yellow taffeta; her "squeris" wore white damask from England.[44] While the Treasurer's Accounts clearly report the black lady's decoration with floral motifs, they give no other indication of how the materials that went into her costume were shaped; they do not, that is, suggest an attempt to achieve the kind of "Ethiopian" effects sought in later Renaissance pageantry, such as Jonson's *Masque of Blacknesse.* It therefore seems likely that the black lady of James's tournament was meant to represent blackness and wildness in the form of a splendid court lady, rather than a splendid court lady in the form of blackness.

Of the black lady's role in the tournament, little is known. The articles printed in Vulson suggest, as we noted earlier, that, accompanied by wild men and heralds, she presided over the ceremonies of entry. The "chair triumphale" mentioned in the Treasurer's Accounts was probably mobile rather than stationary; she may have ridden in style to the great "bancat" that, according to Pitscottie, followed the tournament and was the occasion for a number of interludes: "betuix everie seruice thair was ane phairs or ane play sum be speikin sum be craft of Igramancie quhilk causit men to sie thingis aper quhilk was nocht. And so at the hennest bancat pheirs and play vpone the thrid day thair come ane clwdd out of the rwffe of the hall as appeirit to men and opnit and cleikkit vp the blak lady in presence of thame all that scho was no moir seine."[45] Though there is no substantial evidence for this dramatic exit in the Treasurer's Accounts, one item of 1508 records the expenses "for bukkilling and grathing of Martin and the blak lady agane the bancat"; so it appears that a banquet actually took place and was attended by the black lady — possible evidence for her spectacular role on this occasion.[46]

Dunbar's "Ane Blak Moir" may have been composed for the same occasion. The poem reads as follows:

> Lang heff I maed of ladyes quhytt;
> Nou of ane blak I will indytt
> That landet furth of the last schippis;
> Quhou fain wald I descryve perfytt
> My ladye with the mekle lippis:
>
> Quhou schou is tute mowitt lyk ane aep
> And lyk a gangarall onto graep,

And quhou hir schort catt nois up skippis,
And quhou schou schynes lyk ony saep,
My ladye with the mekle lippis.

.   .   .   .

Quhai for hir saek with speir and scheld
Preiffis maest mychttelye in the feld
Sall kis and withe hir go in grippis,
And fra thyne furth hir luff sall weld —
My ladye with the mekle lippis.

And quhai in felde receaves schaem
And tynis thair his knychtlie naem
Sall cum behind and kis hir hippis
And nevir to uther confort claem:
My ladye with the mekle lippis.[47]

Dunbar's poem, then, parodies at once the blazon ("Lang heff I maed of ladyes quhytt"), the *donna* ("My ladye with the mekle lippis") and the tournament: the winner of this competition gets to kiss her lips; he who "receaves schaem" and loses his "knychtlie naem" gets to kiss her "hippis" (a euphemism for "ass"). Dunbar does his best to discarnate beauty. So much for the image of knightly fame; so much for the look, which ends in the bung-hole of the "real" produced by the emptying-out of glory into vain-glory.[48] If the queen — the white lady — is potentially also "black," Dunbar seems to agree, but with a vengeance.

It is not possible to determine for certain whether Dunbar's poem "reflected" the court's view of the black lady of James's tournament or satirized it. It is also not possible to determine whether the poem was written before, for, or after the tournament. Hence it is not possible to determine, on the basis of Dunbar's poem, whether the black lady of the tournament was in fact one of the "More lassis" living in James's court, or whether the black lady of the tournament was a white lady presented as a black lady, and Dunbar was inspired to write his poem upon imagining what a tournament whose lady was really black would be like. The Treasurer's Accounts give an entry "for ane pair of blak sleffis and gluffis to [the black lady] . . . of blak seymys leder," materials often used at this time in costuming whites as Moors.[49] Perhaps, then, the black lady was not black. Had she been, black sleeves and gloves would not have been necessary to signify her blackness. She might possibly have been Queen Margaret herself; but the queen is not mentioned in any of the Treasurer's Accounts that itemize expenditures for the black lady, and while these records are similarly silent on the subject of the king's identity as the wild knight, the many details regarding his dress and armor at least, as we have argued, point strongly toward it.

Laing seems to have been largely responsible for linking Dunbar's poem with James's tournament and with the presence of black women at court. He proposed, apparently without firm evidence, that two African women, Elen and Margaret, were brought to Scotland by the Bartons and baptized in 1504 (the accounts mention only one "More las" as having been "cristinit" at that time, and do not name names).[50] Laing remarks, "That Dunbar's poem was occasioned by either of them, might be doubted, as the description seems far more applicable to a person well advanced in years. Yet the allusion in the fourth verse to the contention that was to take place 'with speir and scheild,' seems to favour such a notion, as a tournament in honour of the Queen's Black Lady, Elen More, or Black Ellen, as she is variously styled, was held in June 1507 with great splendour."[51] Unfortunately the accounts do not connect the black lady of the tournament with Elen More or Black Ellen. And the editorial tradition has displayed some reserve on this question. James Paterson hesitates about some of Laing's conclusions: "Although [Dunbar] wrote of a tournament in [a blackamoor's] . . . honour, it is not necessary that such an affair should actually have taken place."[52] Mackay, too, notes that in Dunbar's poem the black woman is said to have "landet furth of the last schippis"; if the poem, then, refers to the "More lassis" of 1504, it would be, Mackay says, "poetic license" to describe them thus in 1507 or 1508.[53] But despite these difficulties, Mackay and, one year later, Schipper agreed upon the likelihood of Laing's conclusions.[54] More recently, Baxter has been perhaps more noncommittal than the early editors: he regards Dunbar's poem as having been "evidently written on the eve" of either the 1507 or 1508 tournament, but describes Laing's identification of the black lady with one of the "More lassis" of 1504 or with the Black Ellen of 1511–13 as "without justification." He repeats earlier hesitations about the "last schippis" and says that "the black lady of the tournaments is not named." He then adds: "There is, of course, no reason why the same negress should have acted at both tournaments."[55] One wonders why no one has yet suggested that Dunbar's poem may not have been about a black woman at all.[56] But this is perhaps an uncertainty not worthy of proliferation.

The possibilities, then, are these: Dunbar wrote a poem about an imaginary black woman and an imaginary tournament; Dunbar wrote a poem about one of the black women at court and an imaginary tournament; Dunbar imagined the white woman who played the black lady in the tournament as an actual black woman, examples being before his eyes (in other

words, a poem about an imaginary black woman and an actual tournament); Dunbar wrote a poem about one of the black women at court who
played the black lady of the tournament. Dunbar may have written the
poem before the tournament, in which case it may have inspired the idea
for the tournament; he may have written it for the tournament; he may
have written it after the tournament, in which case it is difficult to believe
that he was not himself inspired by the tournament, it having been no-
ticeable. Since we have a poem by Dunbar on the subject of a black woman
and a tournament and since we have a tournament of a wild knight and
a black lady, it may seem simplest to argue that the black lady of the tournament was a black woman. The black people at James's court were often
involved in entertainments, and this may lend some support to the view
that Dunbar's poem was written about the tournament of 1507 or 1508.
At least it can be said that there are clear connections between the themes
and the visual strategies of tournament and poem.

The question of the tonality of the black lady of James's tournament
is thus an extremely complex one, partly because we cannot say for sure
whether the black lady was a black woman and partly because we cannot,
as noted earlier, say for sure whether Dunbar's poem reflected taste or
satirized it. The editor of the Treasurer's Accounts — who agrees that the
black lady was "probably one of the 'Moor lasses' . . . that 'lady with the
meikle lippis' of whom the poet Dunbar sings" — thinks that "there was an
odd strain of unconventionality in the character of James. That he, the
very pattern of a Paladin of chivalry, should set up an absolute negress
at a tournament, if not exactly as the Queen of Beauty, at least as the one
whose excellencies were to be defended at the sword's point, seems well-
nigh incredible."[57] Perhaps it seemed more incredible at the turn of our
own century than it did in the early sixteenth century. But if we are to
take Dunbar's poem as a satire of James's taste, whether the black lady
was a white woman disguised as a black lady or was in fact a black woman,
his reservations may not have been unusual, at least if contemporary reaction to *The Masque of Blacknesse* is any guide. Dudley Carleton wrote
that "the presentation of the maske at the first drawing of the trauers was
very fayre, and theyr apparel rich, but too light and curtisan-like; Theyr
black faces, and hands wch were painted and bare vp to the elbowes, was
a very lothsome sight, and I am sory that strangers should see owr court
so strangely disguised."[58]

Tom Scott associates the foul tone of Dunbar's poem with "the barbarity of . . . [a] court . . . apparent, not only in the fact of the cruel enslav-
ing of a negress as an object of amusement, but in the fact that Dunbar
could write such a poem about her for a court audience. It is brutally in-

human and insensitive."[59] Paul Edwards has defended Dunbar, and the court, by arguing that "the Scots were not engaged in the slave trade, and far from having the status of slaves at court, the Black people seem to have enjoyed popularity, and as much freedom as other court servants."[60] The term *court servant* is, however, itself an ambiguous one — it could range in referents from kitchen help to messengers, heralds, court jesters, minstrels, dramatists, clerks, and perhaps even to Dunbar himself, who "was granted a royal pension of ten pounds in 1500" — a third as much as what was spent on the black lady's gown — of twenty pounds by 1507, and of a "most preclair" eighty pounds, at last, in 1510.[61] Dunbar was somewhat in the habit of vilifying his rivals and counterparts; how, then, to measure the distance between a reasonably wellborn and well-paid native white male benefice-seeker and a black woman whose status may have ranged from exotic sign of the monarch's naval reach to grotesque, from "the latest novelty of fashionable society" to well-beloved lady-in-waiting of the queen?[62] Dunbar's poem, perhaps, tries to defend a distance between himself and this woman and charts thereby the common space of their servitude. Perhaps the gifts they received were not always so different.

But fundamental issues remain, despite the continuing mystery of the black lady's identity. Whether she was the queen or one of the "More lassis," she can be described as a way of turning the female spectator — and hence the danger of active, phallic looking on the part of the woman — into spectacle. The female spectator is herself brought into the field of vision by becoming part of a tournament disguising: she presides, as we have noted, over the ceremonies of entry; she is paraded around in a "chair triumphall"; she is richly (and brightly) dressed; and she becomes (if we follow Pitscottie's account of the banquet) a spectacular escape artist. Thus the woman who threatens to look is made to disappear. Her disappearance is the culmination — not the end-point — of her spectacularity; for the role of the tournament lady is to be seen only when what one sees in her is one's own reflection. In other words, the very spectacularity of her image is meant to make her look. To reshape the woman into the mirror image is, then, to reshape one's own beauty on the field of her body. It is, once again, to rule her, to turn her into the "field" over which one fights to prove one's sovereignty — one's right to rule.

It is, then, to prove one's own capacity to transform through the power of the sovereign gaze — to see beauty in blackness, to see the knight in the woman. James's sovereignty asserts itself through a presentation of blackness, obscurity, mystery, made visible and bright through the king's own power to "spectacle" her — to dress her up in damask. The contrast between

the black lady's blackness, then, and the brightness of her costume figures the reach of the king's own artistry — and hence figures the legitimacy
of the wild knight's kingship. In the end — after the king's costuming is
done — blackness is beautiful; in the end, too, he who *is* king shows comely
forth. His beauty and legitimacy are reflected in the beauty of the image
he creates. And the disappearance of this beauty perhaps marks the transcendence of the ideal image he has created: too good for earth, she van-
ishes into the heavens.

In this reading, Dunbar's poem is, in one way, closely related to James's
artistry; his poem argues the dependence of the woman's beauty on the
male gaze — he can give it, or he can take it away, and the changefulness
of the image will thus be a function of his own power of perception, not
of the woman's own power to deceive. When he takes his gaze away — the
brightness of "ladyes quhytt" — beauty discarnates, leaving behind the gross
and deformed, the loathly lady. Dunbar's antiblazon thus defends against
the danger of the female spectator precisely by turning her into the "form-
less" body that would otherwise be fearful. To this extent, then, the joke
is on the white lady too — on her supposed centrality to the tournament,
as the queen over whom men fight. Precisely by making the black lady
a spectacle at the center of tournament doings, the centrality of the lady
to the art of the male aristocrat is treated as a mystification and sent back
to the margins. The dirty joke is thus iconoclastic with respect to the blazon proper; with respect to the convention that it is the woman for whom
the man fights; and with respect to tournament itself, to the heroism of
men who fight for something that is weaponless. But it should be stressed
that, in so doing, Dunbar's poem does not constitute a thoughtful critique
of the mystifications of courtly literature; rather, it uses critique to disem-
power the lady. For while it is in some sense true that the centrality of
the lady is both a fiction and a dilemma for the warrior — why fight for
something you would not wish to be — it is also true that black ladies,
foreign queens, even black court servants (insofar as they represented,
however domesticated, the heathen to be overcome — and the Moor lass,
like Belacane, was christened) were dangerous, even if that danger is conceived only as the power of the woman's look to imply the effeminacy of
the knight. Dunbar's antiblazon thus reconstitutes the homosocial function of the tournament even as it parodies the manly efforts of knights;
that is, the poem reconstitutes the propriety of the gaze to masculinity,
by offering a dirty joke. Dunbar's poem domesticates, through humor, the
absence of essence and of its coincidence with appearance that the knight
is afraid of finding at the end of his effortful removal of obstacles.

What the eye sees first in this poem is the black woman's grotesque materiality, her toadiness and apishness, her animality. Only later do we see her clothing, her "reche apparrall," that which marks the human body as human and civilized. By seeing her "for what she is," Dunbar is slaying monsters; the quest is played out on the level of the poet's gaze. In seeing the black lady thus, Dunbar alienates her body from the clothes that adorn it; she is denuded of her claim to humanity and culture. And the poet's power to denude is the reverse of his power to transfigure. Once again the body of the woman becomes both field of battle and obstacle to be overcome. The "threat," once again, "is to man's vision."[63]

> Quhai for hir saek with speir and scheld
> Preiffis maest mychttelye in the feld
> Sall kis and withe hir go in grippis,
> And fra thyne furth hir luff sall weld —
> My ladye with the mekle lippis.
>
> (ll. 16–20)

The victor will suffer something like the fate of the knight in "The Wife of Bath's Tale," had his loathly lady not undergone transfiguration; but Dunbar can mock the dangers of extraordinary unions.

> And quhai in felde receaves schaem
> And tynis thair his knychtlie naem
> Sall cum behind and kis hir hippis
> And nevir to uther confort claem:
> My ladye with the mekle lippis.
>
> (ll. 21–25)

Dunbar asserts the power of his own vision to see the truth, as against the hapless blindness of these knights who undergo "fierce conflict" in the field. In the rivalry between poet and knight, it is the poet who wins — who claims his ability to see, not so much the true image of beauty as the false one. The visibility of the tournament queen — she is at first visible to all — thus comes under the exclusive control of the gaze of the poet, in the sense that he gets to see her as she "really" is. Hence he begins his poem with a detached stance — the pluralization of "ladyes quhytt" is itself hostile to the tradition of idealized description — and implies syntactically that there may not be much difference between ladies white and ladies black. This means that Dunbar needs no woman — despite the fact of his dependence on the patronage of his white queen — because his rewards lie in the pleasures of his own gaze, in its capacity to see clearly. The black lady becomes, through the antiblazon, the unrewarding reward of a poem that appears to demystify quest and knightly "aventure," only to move it to another level — that of the poem's capacity to "descryve."

Dunbar's poem, then, serves the gaze of the king — sees as the monarch *should* see. It is the poetic manifestation of the sovereign's mastery of illusion. He sees the king as he thinks the king should like to be seen — which is to say that, while the king's gaze is everywhere, he is not himself to be seen in any embarrassing way. While inviting the king, and anyone else who might enjoy his poem, to be entertained by the spectacle he has made of the black woman, Dunbar in effect demands that the king relinquish the desire to associate with wild animals and thus prove himself to be ideal. Dunbar gives and takes the pleasure of iconoclasm — the idol is broken through the power of his vision — but the libidinal energy poured into this destruction finally serves, precisely, a strictness of vision. The pleasures of this poem — its scopophilic demystifications, its serving-up of the grotesque, its humiliation of the body — might finally be described as the pleasures of combat with another man's vision — that man who sees beauty in blackness, who is willing to be "fooled," and, worse, who is willing to be a fool.

Pitscottie, as we have noted, concludes his version of the tournament with an optical illusion; and he remarks that this "igramantic" feat is performed "for the kingis pleasour," so that tournament, in effect, turns into masque. It is, at last, the sovereign who is seen to be the master of illusion. If it is the king's role to appear out of obscurity as the patron of illusion — who can make men see things that are not — then it is the black lady's role to disappear into obscurity, to become illusory; the transcendence of the image created by the king is thus pushed to the point of a pure ficticity. The wild knight's task, we could say, is thus not fully complete even after he has demonstrated his prowess at the tournament; it is not complete until the obstacles to his "vision" have been overcome and his power of perception is revealed to be triumphant. This may, finally, be why — as seems likely — the queen herself was not the black lady, for her disappearance is so fantastic a measure of the king's power of perception — and hence of his power to domesticate foreignness — that it removes her altogether, an undesirable implication, for a host of reasons, with respect to an actual queen. Even though Queen Anne, in the masques of *Blacknesse* and of *Beautie*, was willing to submit her imperfections to the radiant eye of the English Sun, finally to emerge in the transcendent form of an Element of Beauty, her purpose in these masques seems partly to have been, precisely, to refuse to disappear altogether, to insist that James admire her. In the later masque, at any rate, only the charms of Night (in *Beautie*) and of the witches (who vanish without a trace in *Queenes*) are revealed to be completely without efficacy. And in *Parzival*, the evanescence of Belacane's sacramental power of innocence underscores the authority of Herzeloyde's pronouncements with respect to the superior power of white Christian baptism. Queen Anne, too, was only temporarily Ethiopian. It seems most reasonable to suggest, then, that the black lady was the queen's double, her antimasque — not only in the sense of refiguring, as tournament queen, the role of the real foreign queen in mirroring the legitimacy of the king but also in the sense of figuring the absolute disappearance of the queen's mystery, so that the real queen could remain, purged of ambiguity, a veritable icon of trust. Once again, the message is that adventure may be risked without loss of home; and if an English princess could become a faithful queen of Scotland, then engagement with heathenism might remove it altogether from the face of the earth.

We could argue, then, that the black lady is thus a diversion for the gaze; she takes on the feminizing, mortifying consequences of being seen and thus settles the question of whether, by displaying himself in his own tournament, the king has made a spectacle of himself. The tournament of the wild knight and the black lady would thus be preoccupied with the desire to exhibit and extend oneself and the fear of so doing; and this makes sense in light of James's efforts to make himself into a legendary figure. The black lady thus serves also as a displaced, feminized version of the king — as a double and opposite: he, a white man dressed in black; she, a black woman (or a white woman dressed as a black woman) dressed in brilliance. Insofar as she is created as an image of the consequences of being seen, when she is expelled, the consequences of being seen go with her. Thus James can make his spectacularity into story — into the story, again, of how his powers of perception overcame mystery; this he could not do all by himself.

There is, however, a further possibility, one that seems to be defended against in Dunbar's poem: in doubling himself with the black lady, James was asserting outright an identity with her. Neither the wildness nor the blackness nor indeed the femaleness of the king need be hidden away, in contradistinction to the case of Louis XIV. Despite the common concerns of the later masque with James's tournament, it would be unwise to let the masque's formulations of the subjection of blackness to royal powers of beautification influence overmuch how James's tournament should be read. *The Masque of Blacknesse*, for example, was apparently inspired in part by an Italian tournament held at Florence in 1579 for the wedding of Francesco de' Medici and Bianca Capello. "A theatre was erected in the courtyard of the Pitti Palace; the scene was a loggia overlooking the sea realistically painted with waves that seemed to move, break on the rocks, and leave a fringe of foam. Three Persian knights put forth a challenge that Persian beauties were superior to all others in the world. The challenge was accepted by masquers and knights in triumphal cars, one of which was of mother of pearl containing two queen-like ladies, Europe and Africa, with their knights."[64] The open war, rivalry, and eroticism of this tournament is transformed in *Blacknesse* into a fantasy of domestication so intense as to be almost incestuous; the beauties seeking confirmation of their beauty are championed by their father, find a new creator in the eye of the English Sun — who does not impersonate anyone besides himself and need not fight, or move, at all, in order to conquer worlds. The beauties do not so much win out over other women as turn into improved versions of themselves. The spirit of the masque, then, is in important respects not in keeping with the spirit of the tournament. Correspondingly, even though James's tournament of the wild knight and the black lady asserts the power of James's perception and his readiness for rule, it also asserts, in a way the later masque does not, the power of his pleasures — of which his self-theatricalization, and thereby his commonality with mystery, is not the least.

Mary Ann Doane writes: "It is understandable that women would want to be men. . . . What is not understandable . . . is why a woman might flaunt her femininity, produce herself as an excess of femininity, in other words, foreground the masquerade." Masquerade, she argues, is "not as recuperable as transvestism precisely because it constitutes an acknowledgement that it is femininity itself which is constructed as mask — as the decorative layer which conceals a non-identity."[65] What seems most scandalous in the masquerade is the inhabiting of something that isn't there, the "being" of something "else." The masquerade bespeaks both the illusory and the productive power of ficticity, the inseparability of our identities with our createdness. The black lady, by doubling the categories of "woman" (who is always "costumed," "made up") and "blackness" ("obscurity," "nonidentity"), by being the central human spectacle of this tournament, and even, perhaps, by disappearing — the final visualization of her own evanescence — is made to act out ficticity itself as the ground of being. In producing her this way and in pairing himself with her, the power James asserts most exuberantly in his tournament is the imperial power of self-creation, and hence the imperial power of remaking the body and gaze of the captive and captivated subject, that goes into the making of a legend. That some members of his court — Dunbar, for example — might have found this assertion disturbing would not be surprising, since it threatens to unking the king — to make his superreality irreal — at the very moment that the king is asserting his readiness for crusade, his sobriety, his capacity to judge the excellence of his knights. But then other members of his court may have understood the extent to which such an assertion is precisely an assertion of the king's power to constitute ficticity as a mode of self-dramatizing pleasure and *thereby* a mode of self-legitimizing rule.

Abbreviations

Notes

Select Bibliography

Index

Abbreviations

APS	*The Acts of Parliament of Scotland*. Ed. T. Thompson and C. Innes, 12 vols. Edinburgh, 1814–75.
Burgh Convention Records	*Records of the Convention of the Royal Burghs of Scotland, with Extracts from Other Records Relating to the Affairs of the Burghs of Scotland, 1295–1597*, vol. 1. Ed. Sir James D. Marwick. Edinburgh: William Paterson, for the Convention of Royal Burghs, 1866.
Cal. Docs. Scot.	*Calendar of Documents Relating to Scotland, 1108–1509, preserved in Her Majesty's Public Record Office, London.* Ed. Joseph Bain. Edinburgh: H.M. General Register House, 1881–88.
Charters, Edinburgh	*Charters and Other Documents Relating to the City of Edinburgh, A.D. 1145–1540.* Ed. Sir James D. Marwick. Edinburgh: Scottish Burgh Records Society, 1871.
Edinburgh Burgh Recs.	*Extracts from the Records of the Burgh of Edinburgh, 1403–1589*, 4 vols. ed. Sir James D. Marwick. Edinburgh: Scottish Burgh Records Society, 1869–82.
ER	*Rotuli Scaccarii regum scotorum: The Exchequer Rolls of Scotland*, 23 vols. Edinburgh: H.M. Register House, 1878–1908.
LHTA	*Compota thesaurariorum regum Scotorum, Accounts of the Lord High Treasurer of Scotland*, 12 vols. Edinburgh: H.M. General Register House, 1877–1916.
NCE	*New Catholic Encyclopedia.*
NLS	National Library of Scotland.
Pitscottie, *Historie of Scotland*	Robert Lindesay of Pitscottie, *The Historie and Cronicles of Scotland from the Slauchter of King James the First to the Ane thousand fyve hundreith thrie scoir fyftein zeir.* Ed. Æ J. G. Mackay. Edinburgh: William Blackwood and Sons, for the Scottish Text Society, 1899–1911.
RMS	*Registrum Magni Sigilli Regum Scotorum: The Register of the Great Seal of Scotland, 1424–1513*, vol. 2. Ed. Sir James Balfour-Paul. Edinburgh: H.M. General Register House, 1882.
RSS	*Registrum Secreti Sigilli Regum Scotorum: The Register of the Privy Seal of Scotland.* Ed. M. Livingstone et al. Edinburgh, 1908–.

Notes

Introduction

1 Domna C. Stanton, *The Aristocrat as Art: A Study of the Honnête Homme and the Dandy in Seventeenth- and Nineteenth-Century French Literature* (New York: Columbia University Press, 1980), 3.

2 Elaine Scarry, *The Body in Pain: The Making and Unmaking of the World* (New York: Oxford University Press, 1985), discusses the "unrecoverable" createdness of the superreal, of institutions whose contingent human origin is, at least within the context of a particular culture and a particular moment, hidden from view (312).

3 Julia Kristeva's commentary on the Song of Songs in *Tales of Love*, trans. Leon S. Roudiez (New York: Columbia University Press, 1987), has been helpful to me in my attempts to understand the reasons why "supreme authority" might seek links with volatility, undependability, mortality.

4 See Pierre Bourdieu, *Outline of a Theory of Practice*, trans. Richard Nice (Cambridge: Cambridge University Press, 1977, on the "institutionally organized and guaranteed misrecognition" which is the basis of gift exchange and of all the "symbolic labour intended to transmute, by the sincere fiction of a disinterested exchange, the inevitable, and inevitably interested relations imposed by kinship, neighborhood or work, into elective relations of reciprocity" (171).

Chapter 1. Imagining the City

1 Royal burghs were those burghs whose charters of privileges originated from the Crown and whose privileges, in actuality, tended to be more extensive than were those of the burghs of barony or the ecclesiastical burghs (for example, in the area of monopolies of foreign trade). Andrew Gibb and Ronan Paddison, "The Rise and Fall of Burghal Monopolies in Scotland: The Case of the North East," *Scottish Geographical Magazine* 99 (1983): 130–40, discusses the monopolistic practices of the royal burghs and the competition they entered into with other types of burghs.

2 See Edward W. Said's contrast between a notion of beginning as "dynastic, bound to sources and origins, mimetic," and as fraternity, complementarity, adjacency, break, in *Beginnings: Intention and Method* (Baltimore: Johns Hopkins University Press, 1975), 66.

3 For a review of different theories of the origins of Scottish towns, see Ian H. Adams, *The Making of Urban Scotland* (London: Croom Helm; Montreal: McGill-Queen's

University Press, 1978). See also George Gordon and Brian Dicks, eds., *Scottish Urban History* (Aberdeen: Aberdeen University Press, 1983), especially "Prolegomena," 1–22, and Dicks's essay "The Scottish Medieval Town: A Search for Origins," 23–51. See Henri Pirenne, *Medieval Cities: Their Origins and the Revival of Trade*, trans. Frank D. Halsey (Princeton: Princeton University Press, 1925), and the collection of essays edited by Rodney Hilton in *The Transition from Feudalism to Capitalism* (NLB, 1976; rpt., London: Verso Editions, 1978; rpt., 1984), essential reading for anyone interested in the debate on merchant capital (hence, towns) and its role in the transition from feudalism to capitalism. The definition of these two "modes of production" are, needless to say, as problematic within Marxist theory as without. A provocative theoretical treatment is Barry Hindess and Paul Q. Hirst, *Pre-Capitalist Modes of Production* (London: Routledge and Kegan Paul, 1975).

 4 See Gordon and Dicks, eds., *Scottish Urban History*, 2, and Dicks, "Scottish Medieval Town," 26. The documentary debut of the burghs has startled many historians: Mackenzie, for example, described the burghs as "sudden in the record." William Mackay Mackenzie, *The Scottish Burghs: An Expanded Version of the Rhind Lectures in Archaeology for 1945* (Edinburgh: Oliver and Boyd, 1949), 3.

 5 R. G. Rodger, "The Evolution of Scottish Town Planning," in Gordon and Dicks, eds., *Scottish Urban History*, 73. See Colin McWilliam, *Scottish Townscape*, (London: William Collins Sons, 1975), 34: "These burghs were 'planned' insofar as their layouts were the result of deliberate decisions by the first burgesses and their successors." See also Adams, *Making of Urban Scotland*, 31. Of the common layout of an axial market street leading from the castle (Edinburgh's Lawnmarket), Mackenzie argues that, though simple, it was "the outcome of deliberate planning and execution" (*Scottish Burghs*, 58).

 6 N. P. Brooks and G. Whittington, "Planning and Growth in the Medieval Scottish Burgh: The Example of St. Andrews," *Transactions of the Institute of British Geographers*, n. s. 2 (1977): 291–92.

 7 "The Growth of Edinburgh," in *The Book of the Old Edinburgh Club* (Edinburgh: T. and A. Constable, for the Old Edinburgh Club, 1908), 369.

 8 The site "led to the placing of the town on the high ridge as near as possible to the defences"; "the plan . . . can be closely compared with those of Elgin, St. Andrews, Haddington and many others, all of them showing the same regular arrangement." "Growth of Edinburgh," 374, and fig. 5.

 9 McWilliam, *Scottish Townscape*, 34; Rodger, "Evolution of Scottish Town Planning," 74.

10 Rodger, "Evolution of Scottish Town Planning," 72. Mackenzie, too, wrote that "The key-word to the burgh is creation, not growth" (*Scottish Burghs*, 14). For a review of the different theories of the origins of Scottish towns, see Adams, *Making of Urban Scotland*, 20.

11 Mackenzie, *Scottish Burghs*, 2–3.

12 "Growth of Edinburgh," 354.

13 Dicks, "Scottish Medieval Town," 48.

14 Ibid., 27–28. See also p. 23 for Dicks's review of the debate on medieval town origins between "supporters of legal origins on the one hand and those of economic origins on the other."

15 Ibid., 25. Dicks describes the tendency of earlier historians to explain significant developments in Scotland by way of "innovations" originating "south of the border."

16 Ranald Nicholson, *Scotland: The Later Middle Ages*, vol. 2 of *The Edinburgh History of Scotland* (New York: Barnes and Noble; Edinburgh: Oliver and Boyd, 1974), 14–15.

17 Archibald A. M. Duncan, *Scotland: The Making of the Kingdom*, vol. 1 of *The Edinburgh History of Scotland* (New York: Barnes and Noble; Edinburgh: Oliver and Boyd, 1978), 475; cited by Dicks, "Scottish Medieval Town," 27.

18 Mackenzie, *Scottish Burghs*, 97; Gordon and Dicks, eds., *Scottish Urban History*, 4.

19 See Nicholson, *Scotland*, 17, on the burghs' increasing separation from the rest of the population.

20 Rodney Hilton, "Capitalism — What's in a Name?" in Hilton, ed., *Transition from Feudalism to Capitalism*, 157.

21 Gibb and Paddison, "Rise and Fall of Burghal Monopolies," 136–37.

22 See Mackenzie, *Scottish Burghs*, 144. See also p. 86 for the Crown's interest in business matters.

23 John Merrington, "Town and Country in the Transition to Capitalism," in Hilton, ed., *Transition from Feudalism to Capitalism*, 177–78; Perry Anderson, *Lineages of the Absolutist State* (NLB, 1974; rpt., London: Verso Editions, 1979), 22–23.

24 Hindess and Hirst, *Pre-Capitalist Modes of Production*, 263.

25 *The Acts of Parliament of Scotland*, ed. T. Thompson and C. Innes, 12 vols. (Edinburgh, 1814–75); hereinafter cited as *APS*.

26 Nicholson, *Scotland*, 389–90, citing *APS* 2:50; *APS* 2:46–47, chaps. 9 and 10; 50, chap. 22.

27 Nicholson, *Scotland*, 390.

28 Ibid., 390–91, citing *APS* 2:50, chap. 20.

29 Ibid., 564.

30 Fredric Jameson, *The Political Unconscious: Narrative as a Socially Symbolic Act* (Ithaca: Cornell University Press, 1981), 97.

31 See Bourdieu, *Outline of a Theory of Practice*, which links "the emergence of a field of discussion"— of a culture's inclusion and discussion of competing opinions — with "the development of cities": "This is because the concentration of different ethnic and/or professional groups in the same space, with in particular the overthrow of spatial and temporal frameworks, favours the confrontation of different cultural traditions" (233 n. 16). Bourdieu thus links the city to "crisis, which, in breaking the immediate fit between . . . subjective structures and . . . objective structures, destroys self-evidence practically" (168–69). In other words, it destroys what we take for granted and makes its arbitrariness apparent. See also his discussion of "genesis amnesia" (79).

32 See Scarry, *Body in Pain*, in which Scarry links the "unequivocally negative connotations to city-dwelling" in the Old Testament (Babel, Sodom and Gomorrah, the destruction of Jericho) to the Old Testament's prohibition of "human acts of building, making, creating, working" (221). The narrative of Revelation is itself organized around the vision of the destruction of Babylon and its replacement by the New Jerusalem.

33 In the psychoanalytic literature on "borderline" cases — which involve disturbances in subject-object relations and in the differentiation between mother and child — "splitting" is one of the most important defense mechanisms. By splitting off the aggressive from the libidinal impulses, splitting protects the "good" mother from the "bad," i.e., from the dangers threatened by (internal) aggression. See Edward R.

Shapiro, "The Psychodynamics and Developmental Psychology of the Borderline Patient: A Review of the Literature," *The American Journal of Psychiatry* 135 (1978): 1307. On "abjection," see Julia Kristeva, *Powers of Horror: An Essay on Abjection*, trans. Leon S. Roudiez (New York: Columbia University Press, 1982), in which the experience of abjection is explained as follows: "It is . . . not lack of cleanliness or health that causes abjection but what disturbs identity, system, order. What does not respect borders, positions, rules. The in-between, the ambiguous, the composite" (4). Abjection, in Kristeva's thought, is particularly brought out through the collapse of subject-object distinctions and hence is important in the relation of the child to the figure of the mother. The dissolution of distinction is also crucial to René Girard's understanding of the plague: "The distinctiveness of the plague is that it ultimately destroys all forms of distinctiveness. The plague overcomes all obstacles, disregards all frontiers." See Girard, "The Plague in Literature and Myth," *Texas Studies in Literature and Language* 15 (1974): 834. Scarry also discusses how the "dissolution of the boundary between inside and outside" is one of the most important aspects of physical pain (*Body in Pain*, 53).

34 Ned Lukacher, *Primal Scenes: Literature, Philosophy, Psychoanalysis* (Ithaca: Cornell University Press, 1986), 39. Lukacher uses the term *primal scene* to refer to "an intertextual event that displaces the notion of the event from the ground of ontology." He states, "Rather than signifying the child's observation of sexual intercourse, the primal scene comes to signify an ontologically undecidable intertextual event that is situated in the differential space between historical memory and imaginative construction" (24). Lukacher bases much of his reading of the primal scene on the ontologically uncertain status of the primal scene in Freud's case history of the Wolf-Man; the primal scene — the "origin" of the Wolf-Man's neurosis — could never be "remembered" by the Wolf-Man, and yet Freud's reconstruction of the scene has the truth-status of an interpretive construction — an imaginative creation.

35 Kenneth Burke, *The Rhetoric of Religion: Studies in Logology* (Berkeley: University of California Press, 1970), 126.

36 I will quote from one passage at length to give a sense of the richness of Burke's reading of the infantile strand in the *Confessions*: "At first, [Augustine] . . . says, all he 'knew' (*noram*) was how to suck (*sugere*), to rest (*adquiescere*) and to cry (*flere*). The term 'fill,' that in the opening invocation had been applied to God (in His plenitude filling all Creation) is here applied literally to the milk that filled the breasts (*ubera implebant*) of the women who had nursed him (I, VI). . . . A similar bridge between infancy and adult motivation is also explicitly supplied by a parallel he draws between the 'consolations' of God's mercies (*consolationes miserationum tuarum*) and the 'consolations' of human milk (*consolationes lactis humani*). . . . In the opening invocation of Book IV, when deriding Manichaean views on food and holiness, he speaks of himself as sucking God's milk and eating of Him as a food that does not perish. Characteristically, when speaking of the Word made flesh (VII, xviii), he calls it a food whereby God's Wisdom (*sapientia*) might give milk (*lactesceret*) to our infancy" (*Rhetoric of Religion*, 66).

37 It might be said that whereas in the *Confessions* Augustine tries to work out absolute reunion with maternal love, in *The City of God* he tries to work out, through a penitential subjection to God, an identification with the paternal judge. See, for example, the passage beginning" even now God judges, and has judged from the beginning of human history," in which Augustine celebrates the omnipresence of

judgment in the workings of salvation history, including especially the principle of discrimination and its ability to separate the deserving from the undeserving. Saint Augustine, *The City of God*, trans. Marcus Dods, vol. 2 of *The Works of Aurelius Augustine, Bishop of Hippo* (Edinburgh: T. and T. Clark, 1871), xx, 345. Thus categories — boundaries, distinctions — are absolutely restored. In Augustine, the fixing of responsibility through injurious punishment is essential to the substantiation of belief. See Scarry, *Body in Pain*, for an account of how the "vibrancy," "incontestable reality," "certainty" of pain "can be appropriated away from the body and presented as the attributes of something else," something that lacks this kind of material certainty — such as a cultural construct or belief (13–14).

38 Burke, *Rhetoric of Religion*, 126.

39 Ibid., 122, 141, 165.

40 William Kerrigan has concentrated more intently than most psychoanalytic critics on the relations between the primal scene and the question of origins. His work has the advantage — in contrast with Lukacher's — of retaining a sensitivity to the ontological crisis provoked by the primal scene without displacing issues of sexuality and the cultural construction of gender. He argues that, through the primal scene, the child mourns the loss of the fantasized parent — the loss of absolute protection, of union with the All — and encounters the contingency of the child's own being. The meaning of the primal scene, in Kerrigan's terms, is the "mourned passing of the narcissistic ego" — of fantasies of union, of omnipotence — "translated into the love, jealousy, and terror of the oedipus complex." The primal scene is a blow to narcissism not only because it means that the mother is "not-with" the child or that, instead of being the source of all things, she is instead a part and participant of desire but also because "the image of parental intercourse . . . foretells the end of narcissism in the knowledge of contingency and createdness: the imaginer is as nothing before the fully revealed meaning of his image — there in the image, he *was not*. . . . An awesome revelation of one's nothingness must somehow be countered." Seeing becomes a way of including oneself in the scene from which one has been excluded; the figure of the paternal gaze as benign can function as a defense against — or, in Kerrigan's analysis of Milton, as a triumph over — the implications of the primal scene. See William Kerrigan, *The Sacred Complex: On the Psychogenesis of "Paradise Lost"* (Cambridge: Harvard University Press, 1983), 164–67.

41 See Leah Sinanoglou [Marcus], "The Christ Child as Sacrifice: A Medieval Tradition and the Corpus Christi Plays," *Speculum* 48 (1973): 498.

42 Philippe Ariès, *Centuries of Childhood: A Social History of Family Life*, trans. Robert Baldick (New York: Vintage Books, 1962), 26: "The idea of childhood was bound up with the idea of dependence: the words 'sons,' 'varlets' and 'boys' were also words in the vocabulary of feudal subordination. One could leave childhood only by leaving the state of dependence, or at least the lower degrees of dependence." See also Jean-Louis Flandrin, *Families in Former Times: Kinship, Household and Sexuality*, trans. Richard Southern (Cambridge: Cambridge University Press, 1979), for the premodern use of the word *family* to refer to "an assemblage of co-residents who were not necessarily linked by ties of blood or marriage" (4) and for information on the dependence of servants and the importance of service in the education of children (64). The structure of the medieval *maison* — the well-to-do household — made for particularly intense relations between nurturance and the discipline of violence. In the *maison*, the symbolic domination of the "gift"

coexisted with overt violence; this was the matrix of the inseparability, for the aristocracy and those who lived within it, of familial, political, and economic dependence.

The elision of production as an ideological strategy has been explored by Raymond Williams in *The Country and the City* (New York: Oxford University Press, 1973). He stresses the significance of Christianity's elision of a "charity of production" in favor of a "community of consumption," so that the feast — rather than the labor that produces it — becomes the dominant symbol of Christian togetherness (30–32). In the medieval *maison*, consumption and reproduction are merged in the banquet's function as expression of the lord's magnanimity and of the strength of his community.

43 See Dicks, "Scottish Medieval Town," 26–27.

44 See Burke, *Rhetoric of Religion*, on the language of Genesis: "The possibility of a 'Fall' is implied in the idea of the Creation, insofar as the Creation was a kind of 'divisiveness,' since it set up different categories of things which could be variously at odds with one another and which accordingly lack the proto-Edenic simplicity of absolute unity" (174).

45 Gilles Deleuze and Félix Guattari write that capitalism "haunts all societies . . . as the nightmare and the anxious foreboding of what might result from the decoding of flows." Deleuze and Guattari, *Anti-Oedipus: Capitalism and Schizophrenia*, trans. Robert Hurley, Mark Seem, and Helen R. Lane (Minneapolis: University of Minnesota Press, 1983), 144.

46 All citations to Dunbar's poetry are taken from James Kinsley, ed., *The Poems of William Dunbar* (Oxford: Clarendon Press, 1979).

47 Joanne S. Norman, "Thematic Implications of Parody in William Dunbar's 'Dregy,'" in Roderick J. Lyall and Felicity Riddy, eds., *Proceedings of the Third International Conference on Scottish Language and Literature (Medieval and Renaissance)* (Glasgow: William Culross and Sons, 1981), 349. See also, in the same volume, Elizabeth Archibald, "William Dunbar and the Medieval Tradition of Parody," 328–44.

48 Norman, "Thematic Implications of Parody," 346.

49 Ibid., 347. On the king's iron belt, see also Thomas Dickson, Sir James Balfour-Paul, and C. T. Innes, eds., *Compota thesaurariorum regum Scotorum, Accounts of the Lord High Treasurer of Scotland*, 12 vols. (Edinburgh: H. M. General Register House, 1877–1916) 3: cii–civ; hereinafter cited as *LHTA*.

50 Burke, *Rhetoric of Religion*, 201.

51 See Jeremy W. R. Whitehand and Khan Alauddin, "The Town Plans of Scotland: Some Preliminary Considerations," *Scottish Geographical Magazine* 85 (1969): 114. The phenomenon is remarked upon by nearly every historian of Edinburgh.

52 Otto Fenichel, *The Psychoanalytic Theory of Neurosis* (New York: W. W. Norton and Co., 1945), 281; Marcel Mauss, *The Gift: Forms and Functions of Exchange in Archaic Societies*, trans. Ian Cunnison (Glencoe, Ill.: Free Press, 1954), 9.

53 Mauss, *Gift*, 93 n. 25.

54 Ibid.

Chapter 2. Edinburgh's Story

1 At the beginning of the century, Edinburgh produced 1,168 pounds for the Great Customs; its closest rival, then Dundee, produced only 660 pounds. For the period

July 1455 to October 1466, the export duties from fourteen burghs totalled slightly over 3,029 pounds; Edinburgh answered for slightly more than 1,908 pounds. In 1478-79 the Great Customs from over twenty burghs came to 3,887 and a bit; almost half was from Edinburgh. The gross receipts from the Great Customs during the reign of James IV averaged 3,000 pounds a year; of that, Edinburgh contributed 2,000 pounds, and Aberdeen, "its nearest rival," 500 pounds. See Nicholson, *Scotland,* 391, 439, 565, and map C.

Jennifer M. Brown [Wormald] has argued that the kings of Scotland "could not, even if they [had] wanted, aim at anything like the degree of centralization of the governments of England and France, nor begin to build up power at the centre at the expense of power in the localities." Brown, "The Exercise of Power," in Jennifer M. Brown, ed., *Scottish Society in the Fifteenth Century* (New York: St. Martin's Press, 1977). 35. Her essay successfully challenges unthinking comparisons of the power of the Scottish Crown with that of its neighbors and demonstrates the fluidity of the Crown's reliance on a wide variety of local and regional powers and interests in the work of governing. But the revisionist urgency of her essay has swung too far in the opposite direction. A number of the Scottish kings of the fifteenth and sixteenth centuries "wanted" some degree of centralization, however hapless in practice their efforts may have been; and they tried to pursue it.

2 *LHTA* 1:lvii-lviii, and nn. 5, 6. On Thomas of Yare see Sir James D. Marwick, ed., *Charters and Other Documents Relating to the City of Edinburgh,* A.D. *1143-1540* (Edinburgh: Scottish Burgh Records Society, 1871), 152, 157, 166; hereinafter cited as *Charters, Edinburgh.*

3 *LHTA* 1:53, 69.

4 *Charters, Edinburgh* 41:119-20, 2 January 1463/64. Only an abstract of the charter is given.

5 For other reasons, though, the period from 1464 to 1468 was comparatively benign to Scottish commerce with England; twenty-four licenses for access to English markets were issued. See S. G. E. Lythe, "Economic Life," in Brown, ed., *Scottish Society in the Fifteenth Century,* 76-77.

6 Norman Macdougall, *James III: A Political Study* (Edinburgh: John Donald, 1982), 116; citing *Rotuli Scotiae in Turri Londinensi et in Domo capitulari Westmonasteriensi Asservati,* ed. T. H. Horne, vol. 2 (1819), 446-47, and Joseph Bain, ed., *Calendar of Documents Relating to Scotland, 1108-1509, preserved in Her Majesty's Public Record Office, London,* vol. 4 (Edinburgh: H. M. General Register House, 1881-88), nos. 1417, 1418 (hereinafter cited as *Cal. Docs. Scot.*).

7 Geoffrey Stell, "Architecture: The Changing Needs of Society," in Brown, ed., *Scottish Society in the Fifteenth-Century,* 169. See also McWilliam, *Scottish Townscape,* 42.

8 Stell, "Architecture," 168-69.

9 *Charters, Edinburgh* 34:79-80. As much as possible, I have preserved the dating forms (e.g., 1454/55) as given in the sources.

10 Sir James D. Marwick, ed., *Extracts from the Records of the Burgh of Edinburgh, 1403-1589,* 4 vols. (Edinburgh: Scottish Burgh Records Society, 1869-82), 1:9, 12 January 1450/51; 1:30, 15 October 1475. Hereinafter cited as *Edinburgh Burgh Recs.*

11 *Edinburgh Burgh Recs.* 1:122, 15 May 1509.

12 *Charters, Edinburgh,* 42-45:120-33; and I. A. Cameron's calendar of papal supplications to Rome (the relevant entries have not been published but may be consulted at the University of Glasgow), 22 February 1468, 12 March 1468, 30 April

1470. See also 30 May 1438 for record of an indulgence describing Edinburgh as the most populous of all Scottish towns.

13 Sir James D. Marwick, ed., *Records of the Convention of the Royal Burghs of Scotland, with Extracts from Other Records Relating to the Affairs of the Burghs of Scotland, 1295–1597,* vol. 1 (Edinburgh: William Paterson, for the Convention of Royal Burghs, 1866), xi; hereinafter cited as *Burgh Convention Records.* For a study of the convention, see Theodora Pagan, *The Convention of the Royal Burghs of Scotland* (Glasgow: University Press, for the Convention of Royal Burghs of Scotland, 1926).

14 *Burgh Convention Records,* 542. See *Charters, Edinburgh* 33:76–78, for an entry into the burgh record of Letters Patent under the Great Seal, 5 November 1454, appointing the Court of the Parliament of the Four Burghs to be held at Edinburgh yearly.

15 Macdougall, *James III,* 303.

16 One glance at *LHTA* 1:50, will suffice to indicate the busyness of the king's many messengers; for example, to David Rudman "ix Maij, passande to Glasgew with lettres vndir the signete for certane clerkis to cum to Edinburgh, . . . vij s."

17 Macdougall, *James III,* 304. *LHTA* 1:xvi, and appendix to preface, no. 3, ccxcvi ff., "The Bombards"; *LHTA* 1:ccxvi ff. and 4:lxiii ff., on artillery. Artillery is connected with Edinburgh from the earliest entries in the accounts. See *LHTA* 1:48, for reference to "William goldsmyth that makis the gun"; see *LHTA* 1:54, for evidence of the making of artillery at Edinburgh. *LHTA* 1:ccxx, explains that workshops were in the "werkhous" in Edinburgh Castle, at the abbey of Holyrood, and at the King's Werk at Leith. On the *Great Michael,* see Lythe, "Economic Life," 74. Adams, *Making of Urban Scotland,* notes that "Edinburgh's pre-eminence over other burghs was marked, for coins minted there have survived for fifteen of the eighteen reigns of the Scottish monarchy since David I" (41).

18 Macdougall, *James III,* 303. See also Macdougall on the king's evident pride and "close personal interest" in Restalrig, which was founded and constructed in the years 1485–87, and on the possibility that the king may have been planning to use the revenues from the suspension of Coldingham Priory to endow the foundation of Restalrig as the new chapel royal (231).

19 But see Roderick J. Lyall, "The Court as a Cultural Centre," *History Today* 34 (1984): 30, on James's copy of *Mandeville's Travels* and the possibility that James commissioned "the royal copy of the *Aeneid,* now Edinburgh University Library MS 195." Lyall also discusses the king's patronage of men like Archibald White-law (Latin secretary to the king, humanist, commentator on canon law); William Scheves (trusted servant of the Crown, archbishop of St. Andrews in 1479, bibliophile, with interests in theology and in Flemish art); Dr. John Ireland (theologian, author of *The Meroure of Wyssdome*). See also John MacQueen, "The Literature of Fifteenth-Century Scotland," in Brown, ed., *Scottish Society in the Fifteenth Century,* 193–94, regarding James's manuscript commissions and Archibald Whitelaw's considerable Latin learning. Macdougall, in *James III,* reviews Ireland's career and concludes that Ireland's "patronage by the King in the last years of the reign provides the only striking example of James III as a devotee of the arts" (196).

20 Macdougall, *James III,* 306, quoting W. Croft Dickinson, *Scotland from the Earliest Times to 1603,* rev. and ed. Archibald A. M. Duncan, 3d ed. (Oxford: Clarendon Press, 1977), 224; Macdougall, *James III,* 299, 306, 97–98. See also Nicholson, *Scotland,* 483–84, on James's "high-flown view of royal authority." An act of Par-

liament of 1469 "affirmed that James possessed 'ful jurisdictioune and fre impire within his realme,' and might therefore create notaries public (hitherto the prerogative of the pope and emperor); henceforth notaries created by the emperor were to have no authority within Scotland." In Parliament in April 1478 "a clerk was accused of 'treasonable usurpacioune' for having legitimated a bastard 'in the name and authorite of the emperoure, contrare to oure souverain lordis croune and majeste riale.'" See *APS* 2:95, chap. 6, and p. 115.

21 Sir James D. Marwick, *The History of the Collegiate Church and Hospital of the Holy Trinity and the Trinity Hospital, Edinburgh, 1460–1661* (Edinburgh: Scottish Burgh Records Society, 1911), 19–20.

22 Sir James D. Marwick, ed., *Charters and Documents Relating to the Collegiate Church and Hospital of the Holy Trinity and the Trinity Hospital, Edinburgh, A.D. 1460–1661* (Edinburgh: Scottish Burgh Record Society, 1871), chap. 5, p. 39. On the organ(s), see Marwick, *History of the Collegiate Church and Hospital*, 23 n. 1. The reference is to John Stuart et al., eds., *Rotuli Scaccarii regum scotorum: The Exchequer Rolls of Scotland*, 23 vols. (Edinburgh: H. M. General Register House, 1878–1908), 7:502; hereinafter cited as *ER*. On the altarpiece, see Colin Thompson and Lorne Campbell, *Hugo van der Goes and the Trinity Panels in Edinburgh* (Edinburgh: Trustees of the National Galleries of Scotland, 1974), 42.

23 Thompson and Campbell, *Hugo van der Goes*, 69–70.

24 Ibid., 76, 80.

25 Macdougall, *James III*, 307. With respect to James IV's own penitential artistry, it is striking how much the image of the Trinity in the Book of Hours probably given by James to Margaret Tudor (fig. 4) resembles the Trinity panel image. See pp. 306–7 n. 16 below.

26 Thompson and Campbell, *Hugo van der Goes*, cites Panofsky to the effect that by this time gold leaf was rarely used, and then chiefly for the representation of "unreal" or "unearthly" things (74; citing Erwin Panofsky, *Early Netherlandish Painting: Its Origins and Character*, vol. 1 [Cambridge: Harvard University Press, 1953], 336).

27 Thompson and Campbell, *Hugo van der Goes*, 54ff.

28 Ibid., 32; Nicholson, *Scotland*, 577, quoting David McRoberts, "Notes on Scoto-Flemish Artistic Contacts," *Innes Review* 10 (1959): 92 n. 6; Macdougall, *James III*, 98. See Ian Halley Stewart, *The Scottish Coinage*, 2d ed. (London: Spink and Son, 1967), 67.

29 Thompson and Campbell, *Hugo van der Goes*, 11.

30 Ibid., 32, citing *APS* 2:102.

31 *LHTA* 1:cclxx, 328–29.

32 *Edinburgh Burgh Recs.* 1:24, 20 March 1468, letter of advice to the burgh of Aberdeen regarding a question of inheritance.

33 See Anna Jean Mill, *Mediaeval Plays in Scotland* (Edinburgh: William Blackwood and Sons, 1924; rpt., New York: Benjamin Blom, 1969), 100; citing *Extracts from the Council Register of the Burgh of Aberdeen, 1398–1625*, 2 vols. (Aberdeen: Spalding Club Publications, 1839–70), 158.

34 Mill, *Mediaeval Plays in Scotland*, 72, citing *LHTA* 2:229, 438; *LHTA* 1:ccxlvi–ccxlvii.

35 R. Pitcairn, *Criminal Trials and Other Proceedings before the High Court of Justiciary in Scotland, from A.D. MCCCCLXXXVIII to A.D. MDCXXIV*, vol. 1 (Edinburgh: William Tait; London: Longman, Rees, Orme, Brown, Green, and Longman, 1883), 1:84, 7 December 1512.

36 J. D. Mackie and G. S. Pryde, *The Estate of the Burgesses in the Scots Parliament and its Relation to the Convention of Royal Burghs* (St. Andrews: W. C. Henderson and Son, 1923), 3–4.

37 Albert Mackie, *Scottish Pageantry* (London: Hutchison and Co., 1967), 218.

38 Nicholson, *Scotland*, 450, 563.

39 *Edinburgh Burgh Recs.* 1:34–36, letter of 3 October 1477.

40 Macdougall, *James III*, 304.

41 Ibid., citing *The Acts of the Lords of Council in Civil Causes*, ed. T. Thompson et al. (Edinburgh, 1839, 1918), 81–118 passim.

42 Pitcairn, *Criminal Trials*, 78.

43 Rosalind K. Marshall, *Virgins and Viragos: A History of Women in Scotland from 1080 to 1980* (London: Collins, 1983), 50. Isabel Williamson's prominence is recorded in the tacks of lands and annual rents for the burgh, 1480–81; she paid four pounds rent on the sixth booth, north side of the Tolbooth, the most expensive level of rent going. *Edinburgh Burgh Recs.* 1:39.

44 *Edinburgh Burgh Recs.* 1:39, 31, 40.

45 Macdougall, *James III*, 146, citing *Registrum Magni Sigilli Regum Scotorum: The Register of the Great Seal of Scotland, 1424–1513*, vol. 2, ed. Sir James Balfour-Paul (Edinburgh: H. M. General Register House, 1882), no. 1563. Hereinafter cited as *RMS*.

46 Macdougall, *James III*, 255, 261.

47 Nicholson, *Scotland*, 592.

48 Charles B. Boog Watson, ed., *Roll of Edinburgh Burgesses and Guild-Brethren, 1406–1700* (Edinburgh: Scottish Record Society, 1929), 535.

49 Nicholson, *Scotland*, 441, citing *ER* 8:lx. See *LHTA* 1:lxi–lxii, for discussion of the king's carvel in the charge of John Barton.

50 *Charters, Edinburgh*, pp. 199–204, no. 64, under the Great Seal, Stirling, 9 March 1510/11.

51 Nicholson, *Scotland*, 441.

52 Ibid., 440.

53 Ibid., 441, citing *RMS* 2, no. 1266, and *ER* 8:lix.

54 Robert Renwick, ed., *Ancient Laws and Customs of the Burghs of Scotland*, Vol. 2, *A.D. 1424–1707* (Edinburgh: Scottish Burgh Records Society, 1910), 30, from the Parliament held at Edinburgh, 31 January 1466.

55 Lythe, "Economic Life", 83.

56 Nicholson, *Scotland*, 440.

57 *LHTA* 1:ccxc–ccxci; *ER* 12:565, no. 332.

58 *LHTA* 1:ccxc–ccxci; *ER* 13:367, nos. 344, 358.

59 Michael Lynch, *Edinburgh and the Reformation* (Edinburgh: John Donald, 1981), 2, 3. See also Whitehand and Alauddin, "Town Plans of Scotland," 114, and Adams, *Making of Urban Scotland*, 33–35.

60 "Growth of Edinburgh," 389–90. See Adams, *Making of Urban Scotland*, 38, figure 2.4, for a sketch of medieval Edinburgh and its walls. See *Charters, Edinburgh*, pp. 134–35, no. 47, for the letter by King James III under the Privy Seal, charging the inhabitants of Edinburgh to assist in fortifying the town (28 April 1472). The charter is by no means temperate in its insistence; if anyone withdraws or removes the "fortressing" of the town, it is enjoined "that . . . thair gudis be arrestit . . . and that . . . thai . . . be deseryset for alwais of the fredome of the said Burgh."

61 *Burgh Convention Records*, vi; citing *APS* 2:179, chap. 17.

Chapter 3. Exchanges of Faith: James III and the Crisis of 1482

1 Macdougall, *James III*, 158.

2 Ibid., 161. Macdougall links James's hoarding with his policies of currency devaluation, as part of James's new policy of enrichment of the Crown in the 1470s — a response to being "acutely embarrassed" with respect to financial resources (301).

3 Ibid., 161-62.

4 Ibid., 171, 129-30; citing *RMS*, no. 1446, and *APS* 2:126.

5 Sometime before 1476 the uncles were granted a remission for this crime, and in the Parliament of March 1482 the remission was renewed. The king's remissions were not known for their permanence. See Macdougall, *James III*, 151-52, citing *APS* 2:138.

6 Macdougall, *James III*, 166, citing *ER* 9:219; Macdougall, 83-84.

7 For the terms of the Treaty of Fotheringhay, see Macdougall, *James III*, 153, citing PRO Scots Doc. E 39/92 (38), and *Cal. Docs. Scot.*, no. 1476.

8 This is Nicholson's way of phrasing James's grandiosity (*Scotland*, 483).

9 Nicholson puts it rather mildly and constructively by saying that James III "notably developed the concept of treason" (ibid., 498).

10 In addition to the issue of the "black money," the king's attempt to appropriate the revenues of Coldingham Priory for the chapel royal — a move that did as much as anything else to bring about his ultimate downfall — is a good example of the king's avarice, particularly since he may have been planning to move the chapel royal to Restalrig, near Edinburgh. See Macdougall, *James III*, 236-39, on the role played by Coldingham in the crisis of 1488; see p. 231 on the "coincidence" that the king's supplication to make Restalrig into a collegiate church was registered "little over a week after the pope's suppression of Coldingham and the reallocation of the priory's revenues to the chapel royal." Scotland's monarchs, always in need of fresh revenues, had throughout the fifteenth century used forfeiture and other "grasping" methods to improve the Crown's finances; but James III seems to have had a special fondness for strategies of enrichment, one that brought ideological crisis in its train.

11 While the role of the familiars in the rebellion at Lauder has clearly been overemphasized in chronicle accounts of the event, the familiars were also a significant theme in James III's reign. See Nicholson, *Scotland*, 502, and Macdougall, *James III*, 163, 190, for the histories of some of the men thus favored by the king — including one Thomas Preston, who "may have been a well-to-do Edinburgh merchant burgess" and was hanged at Lauder. Norman Macdougall, "The Sources: A Reappraisal of the Legend," in Brown, ed., *Scottish Society in the Fifteenth Century*, 10-32, is an essential discussion of the ideological biases of the stories that grew up around the question of James III's familiars.

12 James's clearly marked and, as it was to prove, fatal preference for his second son during the latter years of his reign is a further instance. His eldest son, the adolescent duke of Rothesay, was perhaps simply too much to bear. He was next in line to the throne, and he was nearing the age of fifteen; therefore, he could not be trusted. See Macdougall, *James III*, 237-38.

13 Macdougall comments that "the concern of both major factions to secure Edinburgh castle underlines its importance as the repository of the records and the hub of the king's administration." Ibid., 174.

14 *Charters, Edinburgh*, pp. 146-47, no. 51.

15 *Charters, Edinburgh,* pp. 148–54, no. 52. There is, however, no record of payments being made to Edward.

16 Macdougall, *James III,* 170–71, citing John Leslie, *The History of Scotland, from the Death of King James I in the Year MCCCCXXXVI to the Year MDLXI, by John Leslie, Bishop of Ross* (Edinburgh: Bannatyne Club, 1830), 49–50.

17 *Charters, Edinburgh,* pp. 154–56, no. 53.

18 Macdougall, *James III,* 165–66, citing *RMS,* no. 1418.

19 Nicholson, *Scotland,* 512–13, citing *APS* 12:31–33.

20 Gordon Donaldson, *Scotland: James V to James VII,* vol. 3 of *The Edinburgh History of Scotland* (Edinburgh: Oliver and Boyd, 1965; rpt., New York: Frederick A. Praeger, 1966), explains how Edinburgh's preeminence in the sixteenth century made its provostship vulnerable to the political factionalism between the Douglases and the Hamiltons. "The provost of Edinburgh was a Douglas in 1513, 1517, and 1519 and a Hamilton in 1515 and 1518" (11). But the displacement of local candidates for the provostship by members of powerful aristocratic families seems to have begun much earlier and suggests, again, Edinburgh's growing importance to national politics.

21 *Edinburgh Burgh Recs.* 1:266. See the entry for 8 August 1487: "The quhilk day a richt nobill michty Patrick Lord Hales my Lord Provost, chosin of this burgh for this yeir to cum . . . hes with the consent of the baillies and counsale and a pairt of the community of this burgh chosin James Creichtoun of Felde to be his depute and president vnder him indurand his will" (52).

22 Hailes was made master of the household and given charge of the shires of Kirkcudbright and Wigtown, as well as Lothian and Merse "jointly with Alexander Home," another well-rewarded supporter ("instigator" is probably more accurate). In less than a year Hailes became "Constable of Edinburgh Castle and Governor of the Duke of Ross the king's brother"; "sheriff-Principal of Edinburgh, collector of the king's rents and casualties from the shires of Edinburgh, Haddington, Kirkcudbright, and Wigtown"; "Steward of Kirkcudbright, Keeper of the Castles of Threave and Lochmaben, Warden of the West and Middle Marches." He became great admiral of the realm, and ultimately the earl of Bothwell. Other Hepburns appeared as household officers — keeper of the privy seal, for example — and as clerk of Council and Register (William Hepburn). See *LHTA* 1:lxix–lxx and n. 1; Macdougall, *James III,* 243.

23 Macdougall, *James III,* 243, citing *ER* 9:433.

24 *Edinburgh Burgh Recs.* 1:298. On Alexander's relation to Patrick, see Sir James Balfour-Paul, ed., *The Scots Peerage* (Edinburgh: David Douglas, 1904–14), 2:141–52.

25 Macdougall, *James III,* 243.

26 *Edinburgh Burgh Recs.* 1:47–48.

27 *Charters, Edinburgh,* p. 157, no. 54; p. 165, no. 55.

28 Walter Bertram, provost of Edinburgh during the time of the siege, was also "granted an annual pension of £40 payable during the lifetime of himself and his wife." See Nicholson, *Scotland,* 509, citing *ER* 9:219–20, and *RMS* 2: no. 1829.

29 *Charters, Edinburgh,* p. 164, no. 54.

30 Macdougall, *James III,* 172.

31 The Court of the Parliament of the Four Burghs — which was succeeded by the Convention of Royal Burghs — "decided questions involving the usages of Burghs, and

the rights and privileges of burgesses" and legislated regarding "such matters as the principles of moveable succession." See *Burgh Convention Records*, xi.

32 Nicholson, *Scotland*, 452.

33 On imitative desire, and the complex relations between rival and model which it sets in train, see Girard, "Plague in Literature and Myth": "The divinity this desire is trying to capture never fails, sooner or later, to appear as the divinity of someone else, as the exclusive privilege of a model after whom the hero must pattern not only his behavior but his very desires, insofar as these are directed toward objects. . . . To imitate the desires of someone else is to turn this someone else into a rival as well as a model" (836–37).

34 Aside from the detailing of the privileges themselves, the language of both charters is substantially the same. For ease of reference I will cite *Charters, Edinburgh,* no. 54, as Charter 54.

35 Charter 54, pp. 157–58: "fidem legalitatem amorem et beneuolenciam cordialeque seruicium que dilecti et fideles nostri officiarii moderni Burgi nostri de Edinburghe subscripti . . . jam nobis prouide prestiterunt cum carissimo fratre nostro Alexandro duce Albanie comite Marchie ac de Mar et Garviauche domino Vallis Anandie at Mannie, et nostram de carceribus ex Castro nostro de Edinburghe liberando personam in quo contra nostre voluntatis libitum fuimus detenti, suas personas grauibus vite opponendo periculis dictum castrum cum dicto fratre nostro obsidendo, ex quo insultu nostra jam persona Regia libertate gaudet."

36 Charter 54, p. 157: "Cum ad beneuolencie officium spectare dinoscitur vt hijs plurimum tribuamus a quibus plurimum diligimur nullus humanitatis actus magis necessarius: hinc est quod nos alta mente considerantes fidem legalitatem amorem. . . ."

37 Charter 54, p. 158.

38 See Bourdieu, *Outline of a Theory of Practice,* on the effects of urbanization. It results, he argues, "in the collapse of the collectively maintained collective fiction of the religion of honour. *Trust* is replaced by *credit*" (239 n. 62).

39 Charter 54, p. 161.

40 See *Charters, Edinburgh,* pp. 120–33, nos. 42–45; and Cameron's calendar of papal supplications to Rome (the relevant entries have not yet been published but may be consulted at the University of Glasgow) for 22 February and 12 March 1468, and 30 April 1470, for record of James III's support of St. Giles's erection to collegiate status.

41 See Mauss, *Gift,* 9.

42 Macdougall, *James III,* 237, citing *APS* 2:181.

43 Macdougall, *James III,* 248–50, citing *APS* 2:210.

44 Re the Court of the Parliament of the Four Burghs, see *Burgh Convention Records,* vi. On the burgh customs, see Macdougall, *James III,* 245, citing *ER* 10:57.

45 Robert Lindesay of Pitscottie, *The Historie and Cronicles of Scotland from the Slauchter of King James the First to the Ane thousand fyve hundreith thrie scoir fyftein zeir,* ed. Æ. J. G. Mackay, vol. 1 (Edinburgh: William Blackwood and Sons, for the Scottish Text Society, 1899), p. 212, ll. 19–21. The editor points out that the verses are taken from Sir David Lindsay's *The Testament and Complaynt of the Papingo;* see *The Poetical Works of David Lindsay,* ed. David Laing, vol. 1 (Edinburgh: W. Paterson, 1879), p. 77, ll. 444ff. On the king's movements between Edinburgh and the north, and his concern for his worldly goods, see Macdougall,

James III, 241, 254, citing *ER* 10:82, and *LHTA* 1:85–87; see also Nicholson, *Scotland*, 527–29.

Chapter 4. God's Own Hand: The Poetry of James Foullis

1 Watson, ed., *Roll of Edinburgh Burgesses and Guild-Brethren*, 144. In October 1541 the king appointed Davidson "searcher" of English merchants, ships, and goods arriving in Scotland without sufficient conduct. In 1542 he was granted the tavern and booth that had formerly belonged to Walter Chepman, who, with Andro Myllar (and James IV), had begun Scottish printing in 1507. See Robert Dickson and John Philip Edmond, *Annals of Scottish Printing: From the Introduction of the Art in 1507 to the Beginning of the Seventeenth Century* (Cambridge, Eng.: MacMillan and Bowes, 1890), 105–6.

2 The reverse of the title page of the *Actis* records "the copie of the kingis grace licence and privilege granted to [our lovit] Thomas Davidson, prentar, from Imprenting of his gracis actis of Parliament," and specifies that Davidson was chosen by the lord clerk register. Dickson and Edmond comment that "this evidently placed him in the position of king's printer" (105). Davidson also used a woodcut of the royal arms of Scotland, perhaps designed by Sir David Lindsay. See Dickson and Edmond, *Annals of Scottish Printing*, 123, 105, 109, 135.

3 The title page reads, "AD SERENISSImum Scotorum Regem Iacobum Quintum de suscepto Regni Regimine a diis feliciter ominato STRENA"; the colophon at the end of the print reads, "Impressum Ediburgi apud Thomam Dauidson." The print is in the British Museum; a facsimile of it, with a translation (spirited but not very precise) by Archdeacon Wrangham, is printed in *The Bannatyne Miscellany [Containing Original Papers and Tracts, Chiefly Relating to the History and Literature of Scotland]*, ed. W. Scott, D. Laing, and T. Thomson, vol. 2 (Edinburgh, 1836; rpt., New York: AMS Press, 1973), 5ff.; J. IJsewijn and D. F. S. Thomson have edited the poem in "The Latin Poems of Jacobus Follisius or James Foullis of Edinburgh," *Humanistica Lovaniensia* 24 (1975): 135–37. I would like to take this opportunity to thank Matthew Glendenning and Lori Berger for their work in preparing the translations of Foullis's poetry used herein.

4 Dickson and Edmond, *Annals of Scottish Printing*, 122; *Bannatyne Miscellany* 2:3–4. John Durkan, in "The Beginnings of Humanism in Scotland," *Innes Review* 4 (1953), suggests 1525 (8 n. 16). IJsewijn and Thomson accept 1528 ("Latin Poems," 151). At a much later date Foullis "was chosen with Adam Otterburn and David Lyndsay to compose a French welcome to the new queen"; see Durkan, 8–9, and no. 18, citing Mill, *Mediaeval Plays in Scotland*, 180; *Edinburgh Burgh Recs.* 2:89–91, 17 July 1538.

5 Durkan, in "Beginnings of Humanism," remarks that Foullis "may be the unknown author of the poem *Strena* published in Edinburgh on the occasion of James V's assumption of power" (8).

6 Rev. A. W. Cornelius Hallen, ed., *The Account Book of Sir John Foulis of Ravelston, 1671–1707*, (Edinburgh: T. and A. Constable, 1894), xiv. (Sir John was a descendant of James Foullis.) Foullis's *Carmina* contains an epigram in honor of Sir James Henryson; see Durkan, "Beginnings of Humanism," 8.

7 J. A. Hamilton, "Sir James Foulis," *Dictionary of National Biography*, ed. Leslie Stephen, vol. 20 (New York: Macmillan and Co.; London: Smith, Elder and Co.,

1889), 70; John MacQueen, "Some Aspects of the Early Renaissance in Scotland," *Forum for Modern Language Studies* 3 (1967): 207.

8   The dating is John Durkan's; see Durkan, "The Cultural Background in Sixteenth-Century Scotland," in David McRoberts, ed., *Essays on the Scottish Reformation, 1513–1625* (Glasgow: Burns, 1962), 290, and Durkan, "Beginnings of Humanism," 7–9. See also Marron, "Foulis, (Jacques)," *Biographie Universelle: Ancienne et Moderne*, (Paris: Ch. Delagrave, 1854–65), 14:500. IJsewijn and Thomson date the *Carmina* print as 1512 ("Latin Poems," 103–4). See also John B. Dillon, "Some Passages in the *Carmina* of James Foullis of Edinburgh," *Studies in Scottish Literature* 14 (1979): 187–95. Thanks to John Durkan, a copy of the *Carmina* is now in the National Library of Scotland.

9   John Kirkpatrick, ed. "The Scottish Nation in the University of Orléans, 1336–1538," in *Miscellany of the Scottish History Society*, vol. 2 (Edinburgh: Edinburgh University Press, 1904), 55–56, 64. Kirkpatrick gives information on the Scottish nation at Orléans and extracts from "The Book of the Scottish Nation" with translation appended.

10   See Scarry, *Body in Pain*, 19, 29ff., 45ff.

11   Girard, "Plague in Literature and Myth," 834, 849.

12   Scarry, in *Body in Pain*, argues that in the Hebrew Scriptures God the Creator has voice; humans have bodies. To transgress this distribution — either by embodying the Creator or by giving voice to the human — is to undermine the structure of belief and bring on the readjustments of injurious punishment (181). Her analysis of torture contends that the reduction of self and world to body which is effected through pain is also accompanied by the destruction of the victim's voice; the goal of the torturer, the reason for his endless questions, is to be all voice, to be radically disembodied, free from the constraints — the mortality and vulnerability — of the human body.

13   The closing passage reads as follows: "Lumina iam sistant lachrymas; compesce sonoros, / Musula, singultus; fletibus ora vacent. / Singula si fleres livente cadavera tabo, / Que misere extremum tacta obiere diem, / Pluribus esset opus, quam lucent sidera, linguis, / Quam ludat vitreo squammea turba mari, / Gramina quot gignit tellus, quot volvit arenas / Pontus, habet vernas cedua silva comas; / Ora tibi valido si tot clamore sonarent / Pulsaretque tuam iusta querela lyram; / Nec satis efferres damnose incommoda pestis, / Nec pareret finem longa querela suum. / Turgida continuo maculares lumina fletu, / Lassarent vocem verba canora tuam. / Pone igitur questus gemebundi pectoris altos, / Et sit pacato purior aura Deo." (The light already puts an end to tears; Muse, stifle your noisy sobs; the shores may be free from tears. If you weep for every livid, decaying corpse — for things that, once touched, move wretchedly on to the last day — this would be a task for many tongues: for more tongues than the stars that shine; than the scaly crowd that plays in the glassy sea; than the blades of grass that spring from the earth; than the grains of sand turned around in the sea; than the green grass of the forest. If, so many times, the shores resounded for you with a strong clamor, and a just complaint plucked your lyre, you could not spread widely enough [the truth of] the disasters of the plague's destruction; nor would a long complaint help to hasten its end. You may [only] defile eyes swollen with continual crying, and melodious words may [only] exhaust your voice. Put aside, therefore, the profound complaints of the heart's lamenting, and may heaven be purer, with a peaceful God). (481–96).

The text of the *Calamitose* used here is taken from IJsewijn and Thomson, "Latin Poems," 108–22.

14   Scarry links the plague of Exodus 12 to this "shattering of the reluctant human surface and repossession of the interior": "The fragility of the human interior and the absolute surrender of that interior . . . *is itself belief*—the endowing of the most concrete and intimate parts of oneself with an objectified referent" (*Body in Pain*, 204).

15   Girard discusses contagion in "Plague in Literature and Myth," 836.

16   Geoffrey H. Hartman, "The Voice of the Shuttle: Language from the Point of View of Literature," in *Beyond Formalism: Literary Essays, 1958–1970* (New Haven: Yale University Press, 1970), argues that "Human life, like a poetical figure, is an indeterminate middle between overspecified poles always threatening to collapse it. . . . In human history there are periods of condensation . . . where the religious spirit seems to push man up tight against the poles of existence. Middles become suspect; mediations almost impossible" (348). Hartman's essay does not adequately stress or investigate the extent to which these "overspecified poles" are themselves a product of the human imagination.

17   Cf. Girard on the mythical guilt of the scapegoat, "Plague in Literature and Myth," 841.

18   On the superreal body, see Scarry, *Body in Pain*, 57.

19   Nicholson, *Scotland*, 564; see *Edinburgh Burgh Recs.* 1:71, 22 September 1497, "Ane grandgore act."

20   *Edinburgh Burgh Recs.* 1:74, 17 November 1498; see also 76–77, 27 April 1499 and following; 84–85, 14 October 1500.

21   The translation of the *Carmen elegum* is taken from "Extracts from the Book of the Scottish Nation," in Kirkpatrick, ed., "The Scottish Nation," which also contains a version of the Latin text; see 83 and 97. The text of the *Carmen elegum* used here is taken from IJsewijn and Thomson, "Latin Poems," 134–35.

22   *Jussive* has the sense of "ordering"; the jussive subjunctive is a more polite way of expressing a command than is an imperative proper. We could describe it rather loosely as a mediation of imperative and optative moods.

23   In "Plague in Literature and Myth," Girard remarks that "in cases of massive contamination, the victims are helpless, not necessarily because they remain passive but because whatever they do proves ineffective or makes the situation worse" (836).

24   The *Calamitose* is also crisscrossed with references to the fall of Troy and to the *Aeneid*. See ll. 59–82, 213–14, 376, in IJsewijn and Thomson, "Latin Poems," for examples.

25   It may be of interest in this connection that the title page of the *Strena* is the earliest instance of the use of roman type in Scotland. See Dickson and Edmond, *Annals of Scottish Printing*, 122.

26   See Scarry, *Body in Pain*, on the torturer's "swelling sense of territory" (36). "The torturer's growing sense of self is carried outward on the prisoner's swelling pain"; "it is not the pain but the regime that is incontestably real" (56). My purpose is to draw an analogy between—not to equate—Foullis's art with the art of the torturer.

27   Henryson's death is noted in IJsewijn and Thomson, "Latin Poems," 140.

28   The crisis is exemplified by Edinburgh's long travail in building the fortification known as the Flodden Wall (see The Royal Commission on the Ancient Monuments of Scotland, *An Inventory of the Ancient and Historical Monuments of the*

City of Edinburgh, with the Thirteenth Report of the Commission [Edinburgh: His Majesty's Stationery Office, 1951], lxiv); by the persistence of reports, as late as the 1570s, that James was still alive and journeying in distant lands (see R. L. Mackie, *King James IV of Scotland: A Brief Survey of His Life and Times* [Edinburgh: Oliver and Boyd, 1958], 268, referring to John Leslie, *History of Scotland* (1830); John Leslie, *De origine, moribus et rebus gestis Scotorum libri decem*, 1675 ed., 96 Scottish, 349 Latin); by the long years of civil strife that ensued after James's death; and by the elegiac writing Flodden still prompts from Scotland's historians (see, for example, the closing passage of Nicholson, *Scotland*, which quotes from the *Carmen elegum* [606]).

29   Donaldson, *Scotland*, 35, citing *Acts of the Lords of Council in Public Affairs, 1501–54: Selections from the Acta Dominorum Concilii*, ed. Robert Kerr Hannay (Edinburgh: H. M. General Register House, 1932), 97, 121, and *Edinburgh Burgh Recs.* 1:192, 196. James Hamilton, the first earl of Arran, was next in line to the throne after John, duke of Albany and heir-presumptive, who had for a time governed Scotland but then returned to France, leaving behind a commission of regency which included Arran and Angus. Archibald "Bell-the-Cat" Douglas, fifth earl of Angus, has traditionally been held responsible for controlling James III in the crisis of 1482. Macdougall, in *James III*, describes him as a "chronic rebel" but minimizes his role in 1482 (166–67). Margaret Tudor, widow of James IV and the Queen Mother, had been appointed tutrix to her sons and given, along with a council, powers of regency; these were withdrawn when she married Archibald Douglas, sixth earl of Angus and grandson of "Bell-the-Cat" Douglas. She later became estranged from him, eventually cooperated with Arran, and finally arranged for the release of her son from the Douglases' control. My discussion of the events of James V's minority is at all points heavily indebted to Donaldson's third chapter, "Albany, Arran and Angus," 31–42.

30   Donaldson, *Scotland*, 38–40 (on James's erections to power), and 39 (on Edinburgh), citing *Edinburgh Burgh Recs.* 1:221.

31   Donaldson, *Scotland*, 39–41.

32   The *Strena* may have been commissioned for a royal welcome. Davidson's later printing of Gavin Douglas's "The Palice of Honour" — Douglas had been active in pursuing the interests of the Douglases and was imprisoned during Albany's regency — may have been of factional significance, though it seems unlikely.

33   All citations are to IJsewijn's and Thomson's edition of the *Strena*, in their edition of the *Carmina* ("Latin Poems," 135–37).

34   Girard, "Plague in Literature and Myth," 837, 839.

35   See Scarry, *Body in Pain*, on the weakness of the human voice in the Old Testament: "God is their voice; they have none separate from him. Repeatedly, any capacity for self-transformation into a separate verbal or material form is shattered" (200).

36   As the logic of Mauss's *The Gift* would imply, the Creator — and, in the human realm, the king — must be the supreme giver, for giving is an act of power. To accept the gifts of the king is to eat his "food," his materialized honor; it is to be incorporated by him, hence to allow the surface of the body to be penetrated by him so that its interior can be ritually rededicated to him. Mauss stresses the strong association of the gift with nourishment (84 n. 10; 105 n. 142). Mauss also finds, in the cultures he studies, a contrast between the gift as an aristocratic form of exchange (*kula* among the Trobrianders), conducted in the spirit of etiquette and

generosity, and the "straightforward exchange of useful goods" (*gimwali* among the Trobrianders), conducted in the spirit of immediate gain and "distinguished by most tenacious bargaining on both sides, a procedure unworthy of the *kula*" (20). By deferring the immediacy of exchange, or by obscuring the relation of equivalence and obligation between one gift and the gift that returns the "favor," "aristocratic" exchange dreams of a nonreciprocity, an asymmetry, in giving; the asymmetry thus can be used to figure hierarchy and the relation between creator and creature. The creature "must" make return gifts to the creator (though, again, the obligation must be concealed), but his gifts can never hope to equal the creator's gift of his own life to him. Should they do so, of course, presumption is in the air.

37 Scarry, *Body in Pain*, 199, 189.
38 *Plaga* is a primal word to Foullis in the sense developed by Freud in his essay "The Antithetical Sense of Primal Words," in *On Creativity and the Unconscious: Papers on the Psychology of Art, Literature, Love, Religion*, ed. Benjamin Nelson (New York: Harper Torchbooks, 1958), 55–62.
39 See Burke, *Rhetoric of Religion*, 61, 119.

Chapter 5. Sovereign Love

1 Joan DeJean, *Literary Fortifications: Rousseau, Laclos, Sade* (Princeton: Princeton University Press, 1984), 30.
2 See Georges Bataille, "The Psychological Structure of Fascism," in *Visions of Excess: Selected Writings, 1927–1939*, ed. Allan Stoekl, trans. Allan Stoekl with Carl R. Lovitt and Donald M. Leslie, Jr. (Minneapolis: University of Minnesota Press, 1985), on sovereignty as a coordination of the "homogeneous" ("commensurability"; "productive . . . useful society") and the "heterogeneous" ("elements that are impossible to assimilate") (140). "Since the king is the object in which homogeneous society has found its reason for being, maintaining this relationship demands that he conduct himself in such a way that the *homogeneous* society can exist *for him*"; but the king must also constitute himself as "a single *heterogeneous* object" (147).
3 Themes of blackness and disguise appear also during the reign of James VI of Scotland, in *The Masque of Blacknesse* and in *Measure for Measure*. See n. 5 below, and C. H. Herford, Percy Simpson, and Evelyn Simpson, eds., *Ben Jonson*, vol. 7, *The Sad Shepherd, the Fall of Mortimer, and Masques and Entertainments* (Oxford: Clarendon Press, 1949), 169–80.
4 Captivity and torture are the sovereign's cruelest ways of signifying the subject's privation, by criminalizing it, and by seeming either to mimic it or to bring it out of hiding. Torture — and accusations of witchcraft — enact, in particular, the fiction that the privacy of the subject is *chosen* and is a form of obduracy against supreme authority. DeJean suggests that one meaning of the story of Louis XIV's twin brother and black sister is that the king can keep natural forces, prodigies of nature, under control — imprisoned, captive, involuntarily hidden (*Literary Fortifications*, 16). The king's entitlement to the body of the world is figured, not through the exuberant comparisons of the Song of Songs, but through a poetics of the repressed and its return. The king's entitlement to the body of the world is accomplished by figuring the world, and the subject, as a chaotic materiality in need of the rigors of order. In capturing such forces, he can appropriate the motive will of the body (whereby the deprivation of freedom bespeaks, albeit

in different form, the same power of alteration at stake in spectacular punishment) by radically altering the relation between will and body that has been formulated in the West as the essence of personhood. The enslavement of darkness thus, during the "Enlightenment," goes hand in hand with a desouling of the world's body. In contrast with the captive — the body without will — the king must represent the apotheosis of the voluntary; and the apotheosis of the voluntary is the identification of the king's will with the bodies of everything and everybody. With the power thus to "possess" the body of the subject and the world comes the power to constrain those bodies to one's will; thus the king is an enchanter, whose subjects' bodies always threaten to escape his control.

5 See J. W. Lever, ed., *Measure for Measure* (London: Methuen; Cambridge: Harvard University Press, 1965), whose section "The Disguised Ruler" discusses the modeling of Shakespeare's duke on James I (xliv–li). The motif of the king-in-disguise has been analyzed by Maurice Keen as the "misconception" of a "victimized agrarian class" and by Anne Barton as "a wistful, naive attitude toward . . . the relationship of subject and king" and "a nostalgic but false romanticism." Barton, "The King Disguised: Shakespeare's *Henry V* and the Comical History," in Joseph G. Price, ed., *The Triple Bond: Plays, Mainly Shakespearean, in Performance* (University Park: Pennsylvania State University Press, 1975), 97, 99. Barton discusses Maurice Keen, *The Outlaws of Medieval Legend* (London: Routledge and Kegan Paul, 1961), 156. But the motif is clearly also a powerful affective instrument in the hands of sovereigns willing to use it; Barton herself cites one of Henry VIII's disguisings, in which the monarch participated in a reenactment of Richard Coeur de Lion's feast with Robin Hood, and James IV's wild knight takes the bolder step of coalescing the figure of the Celtic outlaw with that of the king. Moreover, though disguisings of kings clearly can inculcate nostalgia and romanticism, they can for that very reason serve the advancement of new and perhaps unpopular initiatives.

6 Pitscottie, *Historie of Scotland*, 231.

7 The subject's "plain speech" is a sign of his diminished capacity for metaphor, for predication. Accordingly, it — like the openness of heart with which it is associated — is a sign of the subject's loyalty; but it also threatens to expose the failure of monarchical magic actually to transform bodies. In *The Queen's Two Bodies: Drama and the Elizabethan Succession* (London: Royal Historical Society, 1977), Marie Axton argues that the "king-as-common-man" plays were used to challenge Stewart claims regarding the magical powers of the king's body politic; the metaphoricity of James VI's and James I's proposals for union ("I am the Head, and it is my Body") was opposed by a Commons that persisted in seeing the Union "simply as the policy of a Scotsman called James." The settlement of the English succession turned on conflicting views of the legal standing of king and commoner. The Stewarts wanted an absolute discrimination; the Suffolk party did not. The "'King as common man' history plays follow this debate and form a distinct genre from 1561 to 1642; they are persistently anti-Stuart" (26). For Axton's discussion of James I's speech to his first Parliament on 22 March 1603/4 and her comparison with Elizabeth's handling of the metaphor of the body politic, see pp. 133–46. She also notes that the revels at Gray's Inn in the winter of 1566/67 literalized Elizabeth's metaphors by turning the mother and spouse of England into Jocasta (54).

8 My discussion of the Song of Songs is heavily indebted to Kristeva, *Tales of Love*, in which Kristeva points out that "as intersection of corporeal passion and idealization, love is undisputably the privileged experience for the blossoming of meta-

phor . . . as well as incarnation" (95). "Love is the time and space in which 'I' assumes the right to be extraordinary. Sovereign yet not individual" (5).

9 Kristeva, *Tales of Love*, 90.

10 See Bourdieu, *Outline of a Theory of Practice*, 171.

11 Deleuze and Guattari, *Anti-Oedipus*, 30. The misrecognition of the role played
by human desire in the production of the world is also an important issue both
in *Anti-Oedipus* and in Scarry, *Body in Pain*; see, for example, Scarry, p. 181:
"The scriptures can be understood as narratives about created objects that enable
the major created object, namely God, to describe the interior structure of all
making."

12 The gift, moreover, as Pierre Bourdieu points out, is one of the most important
forms of symbolic activity whereby obligations are refashioned as freedoms, and
autonomy refashioned as bond. The *différance* involved in gift exchange and circulation—the "style" of giving, which depends upon timing and therefore upon
deferral and delay—gives temporality, continuity to evanescent ties; but it also
makes a space for yearning, anticipation, uncertainty. (On "the temporal structure
of gift exchange," see Bourdieu, *Outline of a Theory of Practice*, 5–7, 194.) Just
so the materiality of the gift—the banquet, the civic welcome, the presentation
copy, the benefice—enables the production and substantiation of insubstantial ties;
but the gift is distinguished from the commodity by always meaning something
that cannot be fully expressed by the sheer materiality or market value of the object. If, as Mauss argued, the gift is always "possessed" by the "spirit of its giver,"
then the gift is always something other than what it appears to be and precipitates
the receiver into an openness of meaning. Thus "the mutual transference of personality" involved in gift exchange—which, in the case of sovereign and subject,
is not really "mutual"—remakes the subject for the sovereign by giving exchange
its affective power. (Arnold van Gennep, *The Rites of Passage*, trans. Monika B.
Vizedom and Gabrielle L. Caffee [Chicago: University of Chicago Press, 1960],
points out that rites of exchange usually occupy a central place in marriage ceremonies, because a "mutual transference of personality" is involved [30].) The gift
thus helps to produce the alchemy of identifications and differences that constitute
the relation of subject to sovereign, whereby inequalities are fashioned as reciproci-
ties that nonetheless depend on inequality for their affective power.

13 Herford, Simpson, and Simpson, eds., *Ben Jonson* 7:177, ll. 255–56.

14 Henry Ansgar Kelly, *Love and Marriage in the Age of Chaucer* (Ithaca: Cornell
University Press, 1975), 307, citing St. Bernard of Clairvaux, *Sermones super Cantica canticorum*, ed. J. Leclercq, C. H. Talbot, and H. M. Rochais, Éditiones cister-
cienses, *Opera* 1–2 (Rome, 1957–58), 83.3.

15 What Louis Adrian Montrose has described as Elizabeth's "pastorals of power" enabled a number of important magical transformations: of "the complex into the
simple"; of "public relations of power into intimate relationships of love"; of "an
expanding market economy of an age of gold into the maternal plenitude of the
Golden Age"; of the "powerlessness and compulsory physical labor of the peas-
ant . . . into a paradoxical experience of power, freedom, and ease." Montrose,
"'Eliza, Queen of shepheardes,' and the Pastoral of Power," *English Literary Renaissance* 10 (1980): 155, 157, 158.

16 Kristeva's reading of the Song of Songs stresses "the immediate love of God for
his people, a love that demands neither merit nor justification but is based on
preference and choice" (*Tales of Love*, 84).

17 Kelly, *Love and Marriage*, 307, citing *Sermones super Cantica canticorum*, 83.5.
18 Bourdieu, *Outline of a Theory of Practice*, 237 n. 47: "If acts of communication —
exchanges of gifts, challenges, or words — always bear within them a potential
conflict, it is because they always contain the possibility of domination. *Symbolic
violence* is that form of domination which, transcending the opposition usually
drawn between sense relations and power relations, communication and domination, is only exerted *through* the communication in which it is disguised."
19 Victor Turner, *The Ritual Process: Structure and Anti-Structure* (Aldine, 1969; rpt.,
Ithaca: Cornell University Press, 1977), 106–7. Turner's theoretical analysis in *The
Ritual Process* is problematic insofar as it proposes a totalization of culture within
which his distinction between communitarian and stratified experience is folded;
that is, his conception provides no account whatever of the problem of "resistance"
or of the related problem of how change takes place in cultures whose disruptive
and egalitarian energies are so completely absorbed by ritual. Mary Douglas's classic work *Purity and Danger* shares some of Turner's totalizing tendencies but gives
real agency to "impurity" and "danger," particularly with respect to cultural change:
she points out that a pure culture is a dead one and that cultures committed to
purity and aliveness must discover ways of making use of what they fear most.
Douglas, *Purity and Danger* (London: Routledge and Kegan Paul, 1966; London:
Ark Paperbacks, 1984), 161. Both her work and Turner's have the advantage of
suggesting how elites might gain, as they must if they are to survive, access to such
resources; the problem is, again, whether or not such resources are understood
to be utterly absorbed by elite appropriations. And their work further enables a
rethinking of the tendency — itself a reaction to historical narrative in which only
the "great" featured as agents — to assume that power expands primarily to perpetuate itself, therefore that its agency is inevitably conservative, opposed to change,
even in forms of imperial aggrandizement, and that therefore only revolutionary
segments of populations work toward "real" change. Such an approach in turn
absorbs any newness that might be produced by elite agency and fails to articulate
the possibility of multiple sources of change.
20 Turner associates the temporary liminality of ritual states with the structural liminality or "inferiority" of conquered groups — minorities, social deviants, foreigners, women. The "weak" are ritually powerful precisely because they are not the
norm; they are sacred with respect to the profane world of everyday, familiar, ordinary experience. They are, in other words, ritually powerful exactly insofar as
they are practically disempowered. Turner, *Ritual Process*, 99–100, 114, 166–68.
21 Turner makes the point with reference to Ndembu chieftains, who represent the
"tribal territory itself and all its resources" as well as the "apex" of tribal hierarchy.
Ibid., 98.
22 In one of Turner's examples, communitas is enacted in the *Kumukindyila* rite whereby
tribal members are allowed to advise, threaten, revile, and beat the chief-elect on
the night before his inauguration; it is a night in which the chief may be treated
like a slave (ibid., 100–102). It seems possible to view some instances of the "advice
to princes" tradition in medieval and Renaissance Europe as more cautious versions of the "use of plain speech" "to purify structure." Regarding James IV's bedesmen, see Mackie, *King James IV*, 124, citing *LHTA* 2:71, 78, 249, 259. Roy Strong
mentions the medieval Maundy Thursday ritual of washing the feet of the poor
in *Splendor at Court: Renaissance Spectacle and the Theater of Power* (Boston:
Houghton Mifflin, 1973), 21–22. The motif of kings (and queens) in disguise —

whereby, again, the sovereign is spoken to quite "plainly" and often subjected to physical abuse — is a further instance of the power of communitas to mystify status.

23 Cf. Kristeva's remarks, in her study of Celine, on the "attempt to substitute *another Law . . .* that would be absolute, full, and reassuring . . . for the constraining and frustrating symbolic one," for the deprivations and inequities that complicate identifications with authority in stratified social structures. Kristeva, *Powers of Horror,* 178.

24 On the rebirth of structure, see Turner, *Ritual Process,* 181.

25 The rites of the following day, New Year's Day, exclude not only the Queen Mother but all women; they take place inside the temple, where the chief prays alone. Thus (male) structure is "reborn" from (female) communitas. See ibid., 180–81.

26 Pauline Stafford, *Queens, Concubines, and Dowagers: The King's Wife in the Early Middle Ages* (Athens: University of Georgia Press, 1983), 99, 107. She notes the identification of the queen with hospitality and generosity (101) and discusses the association of royal women with spectacle and with wealth (108–9).

27 Kristeva, *Tales of Love,* 244: "Interestingly enough, it is [Mary Regina] . . . woman and mother, who is called upon to represent supreme earthly power. Christ is king but neither he nor his father are pictured wearing crowns, diadems, costly paraphernalia, and other external signs of abundant material goods. That opulent infringement to Christian idealism is centered on the Virgin Mother. Later, when she assumed the title of *Our Lady,* this would also be an analogy to the earthly power of the noble feudal lady of medieval courts."

28 Montrose argues that Elizabeth made use of "pastorals of power" because, "helped by her sex," they succeeded in "combining intimacy and benignity with authoritarianism" ("Eliza, Queene of shepheardes," 180). Montrose points to a larger cultural context for Elizabeth's artistry: he notes, for example, that Christian pastoral exploits the "tension between temporal hierarchy and spiritual communion" that is "woven into the fabric of traditional Europe's Christian culture." Though stratified among themselves, in relation to the Good Shepherd "*all* human creatures belong to a single flock of sheep" (162).

29 The Elements of Beauty adorn the "*seate of state, call'd the* throne of beautie, *erected*" (ll. 165–66) and represent the domestication and masculinization of the Ethiopian nymphs as the perfect achievement of form by matter. Despite the static quality of their presentation, their purpose is to give to the idea of beauty the sensuous plenitude of variety and thus to celebrate the king's power of alteration as vivifying and bountiful rather than imprisoning and mortifying. See Herford, Simpson, and Simpson, eds., *Ben Jonson* 7:181–94, for *The Masque of Beautie.*

30 John of Ireland, *The Meroure of Wyssdome . . . by Johannes de Irlandia,* ed. Charles Macpherson, vol. 1 (Edinburgh: William Blackwood and Sons, for the Scottish Text Society, 1926), 153.

31 Cf. the Old Testament's antithesis between the present faithlessness and wantonness of Yahweh's bride Israel with the lovely and perfectly loving bride of the future; see Marina Warner, *Alone of All Her Sex: The Myth and the Cult of the Virgin Mary* (New York: Alfred A. Knopf, 1976), 123–24.

32 Louis Montrose writes that when Thomas Arundell of Wardour returned from the continent in 1596 an earl of the Holy Empire, "the Queen of England expressed her displeasure in a pointed pastoral: 'Between Princes and their Subjects there is a most straight tye of affections. As chaste women ought not to cast their eye upon any other than their husbands, so neither ought subjects to cast their eyes

upon any other Prince.'" Montrose, "Eliza, Queene of shepheardes," 159, citing William Camden, *Annales; or, The History of the most Renowned and Victorious Princesse Elizabeth*, trans. R. N., 3d. ed. (London, 1635), 469.

33 In the Song of Songs, as in the Old Testament in general, jealous exclusivity expresses the fury of choice, the passionate certainty that this one *is* through being *for* that other. The set-apartness, the exclusivity of choice — of which perfect beauty is the signifier ("O fairest of women") — helps to give sovereign love its ontological certitude, the certainty of the one, of only this one, for the other. See J. C. Nohrnberg, *The Analogy of the Faerie Queene* (Princeton: Princeton University Press, 1976), 430: "Beauty . . . may be characterized as 'set apart.'" Yet though the Shulammite is "fairest of women," she is nervous about her darkness; the king belongs to her as intensely as she to him, yet her desire seems to strive after him more than his after her. The errancy, on the other hand, of the "wanton" bride of Israel is frowned upon, and Yahweh's fidelity never fails (see Warner, *Alone of All Her Sex*, 123).

34 Stafford suggests that "sympathetic identification and the exclusion of women from direct rivalry in the roles of men may create strong bonds between royal women and their sons or brothers the kings, and allow queens to become regents or chief counsellors in situations where kings have reason to fear other men" (*Queens, Concubines, and Dowagers*, 191).

35 Rev. John Beveridge, ed., "Two Scottish Thirteenth-Century Songs, with the Original Melodies, Recently Discovered in Sweden," *Proceedings of the Society of Antiquaries of Scotland* 73 (1939): 276–88. The translation of "The Marriage Ode" is on pp. 279–80.

36 Nohrnberg, *Analogy of the Faerie Queene*, 452. Nohrnberg's discussion of epithalamic motifs has been extremely helpful to me, in particular his comment on the "motif of trespass" involved in the "theme of crossing a sexual threshold" (450).

37 S. B. Chandler, "An Italian Life of Margaret, Queen of James III," *Scottish Historical Review* 32 (1953): 55.

38 Kristeva, *Tales of Love*, 245, speaking of Mary Regina. Stafford, *Queens, Concubines, and Dowagers*, notes that stories of saintly queens were often used during the early Middle Ages to illustrate the virtues of female rule (30–31). In the later Middle Ages, queens formed the largest category of women saints.

39 See Deborah Fraioli, "The Literary Image of Joan of Arc: Prior Influences," *Speculum* 56 (1981): 813, citing Dorothy Wayman, "The Chancellor and Jeanne d'Arc," *Franciscan Studies* 17 (1957): 273–305, which contains an edition of Gerson's *De quadam puella*; the quotation from Gerson is from Wayman, 299. Fraioli writes that "much of what Joan of Arc proclaimed agreed with a number of unorthodox medieval religious views which despite their irregularity appear to have been cherished by many of Joan's contemporaries. To the delight of everyone, Joan of Arc seemed to confirm that God would still intervene directly in human affairs, and this rekindled the treasured notion (possible in the context of the Old Testament but hard to reconcile with the New) that the French were God's chosen people. . . . Joan of Arc gave expression to many secretly harbored but unorthodox hopes, and in doing so she brought these hopes to the surface" (829). She brought them to the surface, however, in a way that supported belief in the *commensurability* of temporal and divine authority, so that God's power of alteration, of overturning — his power to express by force of miracle or plague his transcendence of human limitations, expectations, "reason" — is linked to monarchy, rather than sev-

ered from it. Still, the paradoxes — the transvestism, the maternal aggression, the weak strength, the meek boldness — of Joan's image finally proved to be too much, for certain authorities at least.

40 Winfried Schleiner, "*Divina virago:* Queen Elizabeth as an Amazon," *Studies in Philology* 75 (1978): 163-80.

41 The "conservative" position exemplified by Knox and, earlier in Scotland, by Sir David Lindsay, devoted itself to the preservation of the hierarchy of creation and of woman's subordinate place in it. For these writers, the female sovereign, by breaking "natural" law, is herself tyrannical and presumptuous; she aspires beyond the thinkable. Lindsay — who, as tutor to the young James V during the "troubles" of the minority, had been at odds with the Queen Mother, Margaret Tudor, and who later became an outspoken critic of James V's wife, Mary of Guise — argues against women's rule in *The Monarchie.* He explains that women should not be "manlye," nor men "womanlye"; the intentions of the Creator are invoked to prove that, by "kynde," men should "haue preheminens" and women be "vnder obediens." James E. Phillips, Jr., "The Background of Spenser's Attitude toward Women Rulers," *The Huntington Library Quarterly* 5 (1941-42): 7, citing Lindsay, *Ane Dialog betuix Experience and ane Courteour, off the Miserabyll Estait of the World [Dialog Concerning the Monarché],* ed. John Small (1883), p. 106, ll. 3234-40. See also Paula Louise Scalingi, "The Scepter or the Distaff: The Question of Female Sovereignty, 1516-1607," *The Historian* 41 (1978): 64, citing Lindsay, *The Monarchie* (1552), in *The Works of Schir David Lyndesay* (Edinburgh, 1574), 107-8. John Knox wrote, "For that Women reigneth above man, she hath obteined it by treason and conspiracie committed against God . . . [men] must studie to represse her inordinate pride and tyrannie." Constance Jordan, "Woman's Rule in Sixteenth-Century British Political Thought," *Renaissance Quarterly* 40 (1987): 434, citing Knox's *First Blast of the Trumpet against the Monstrous Regiment of Women.* Protestant literature on Mary Tudor resurrected the stories of evil queens used in the early Middle Ages, according to Stafford (*Queens, Concubines and Dowagers,* 30-31), to illustrate the dangers of female rule; see Scalingi, 67.

But female rule is understood by other writers as an instance of communitarian reversal. In 1554 Calvin wrote that since female government was "contrary to the legitimate course of nature, such governments ought to be reckoned among the visitations of God's anger. But even so, the grace of God sometimes displayed itself in an extraordinary way, since, as a reproach to the sloth of men, he raises up women, endowed not after the nature of men, but with a certain heroic spirit, as is seen in the illustrious example of Deborah." Calvin charts the movement of paradox from monstrosity to wonder; female rule, as a suspension of "the legitimate course of nature," can be understood as plague, but also as miracle. In either case, female rule becomes an attestation of God's power of alteration — his power to intervene directly in human affairs, to overthrow the "laws" of nature. See Phillips, "Background of Spenser's Attitude toward Women Rulers," 9, citing Calvin, *Corpus reformatorum,* xliii, 125 (translation from P. Hume Brown, *John Knox: A Biography,* vol. 1 [London: Adam and Charles Black, 1895], 228).

42 Stafford, *Queens, Concubines, and Dowagers,* 108.

43 Scarry, *Body in Pain,* notes that in the Old Testament "to be a foreigner . . . is . . . an extreme form of disbelief, a state of existing wholly outside the circle of faith" (202).

44 The witches are presented as particular enemies of clear, proper, public knowl-

edge; in *The Masque of Queenes* "envious Witchcraft" flees not at the entrance of
the queens themselves but at the sight of "masculine" or "Heroique" Virtue. Good
queens are understood to exemplify heroic virtue, but the apotropaic design of
the masque becomes clear when Bel-Anna's portrait succeeds that of Valasca, who,
"to redeeme her selfe, and her *sexe*, from the *tyranny* of Men, wch they liu'd
in, . . . led on the Women to the slaughter of theyr barbarous *Husbands*, and *Lords*."
Herford, Simpson, and Simpson, eds., *Ben Jonson* 7:312, ll. 646–51. Jonson's par-
enthetical qualification, in his portrait of Artemisia, that she waited until after her
husband was dead to eat him, also suggests that even good queens made Jonson
quite nervous, despite his insistence, in the antimasque, on the powerlessness of
the witches.

45 Stafford, in *Queens, Concubines, and Dowagers*, argues that the ideal of dynastic
unity, and of the queen's role in creating that unity, is one whose potency derives
in part from the reality of family tension: "As intruders who are suspect, wielding
power within the tensions and crosscurrents of the family but denied the expression of legitimate aggression, wives and queens are accused of domestic crimes,
of encompassing their ends by covert means, by plots, poison and witchcraft" (29,
46). Stafford cites the case of Queen Bertillia, who was accused of the "crimes of
Circe" and put to death ca. 911 (188). Evidence of a Renaissance concern with the
crimes of Circe may be found at the end of Machiavelli's *Discourses*, which focuses
on female poisoners and on conspiracies to murder husbands (Arlene W. Saxon-
house discusses Machiavelli's identification with such covert means of aggression —
learning, in his exile, lessons from weak women who have the power to subvert
because their strength is both covert and unexpected — in *Women in the History
of Political Thought: Ancient Greece to Machiavelli* [New York: Praeger, 1985],
165). Lucy Mair, *Marriage* (New York: Pica Press, 1972), 125–26, notes that in
patrilineal cultures the wife, as the outsider, often bears the "brunt of conflicts of
interest"; the wife is blamed for being quarrelsome and will be blamed for witchcraft if it is suspected.

46 Bourdieu's analysis of Kabyle culture points to a division of labor between the
official and the unofficial, which entrusts religion (public, solemn, official, collective) to men, and magic (secret, clandestine, private) to women; women possess
a certain *reality* of power, perform a certain *work* of power for the group, i.e.,
the work of intimate power, of private negotiations. "Women's interventions," however, are condemned "to a shameful, secret, or, at best, unofficial existence"; the
appearance of power must be left to men. Liminality is the fate of women whenever a culture tends to identify male interests as "official" or "group" interests, female interests as "unofficial" or "private" or "particular." The condition of liminality is one in which what Bourdieu calls "officializing strategies" — strategies enabling
the transmutation of "private, particular interests" into "disinterested, collective,
publicly avowable, legitimate interests" — will be largely denied to women but also one
in which the condition of "particularity" that results may be exploited in cultural
figurations of the "whole." See Bourdieu, *Outline of a Theory of Practice*, 40–41.
Queens are often associated with "women's interventions," with the intimacies and
intrigues of court life, with private negotiations; but queens may be called upon to
exercise and exemplify official power when kings must protect their inaccessibility.

47 Even the relation of queens to virtue was complicated by contradiction. Though
queens are associated in Jonson's *Masque of Queenes* with the figure of "masculine" Heroic Virtue, a number of classical, medieval, and Renaissance writers be-

lieved that women were as incapable of virtue as they were of honor or were not capable of the same virtues as men. Sometimes heroic virtues were reserved for men, and women conceded the semivirtues of shamefastness, chastity, modesty, best practiced in the home. But what of the virtues of princesses and queens? The problem was recognized and widely debated: queens were required to play what Ian Maclean calls a "public, promiscuous social rôle," yet in doing so they broke the bounds of the centuries-old tradition of the "good woman." Maclean, *The Renaissance Notion of Woman: A Study in the Fortunes of Scholasticism and Medical Science in European Intellectual Life* (Cambridge: Cambridge University Press, 1980), 49–66. Maclean notes that Tasso took a comparatively radical position on the question, by arguing that when heroic virtue and chastity conflict, princesses are obliged, because of their public responsibilities, to give up the latter, and comments: "The princess is, as it were, a man by virtue of her birth" (62). Queens were obliged not only to dress splendidly and to take part in courtly pastimes and banquets but also to acquire at least a rudimentary education and to exercise some degree of power — at a time when woman's relation to truth was at best unclear and the notion of her involvement in politics was met with what Maclean calls a "near unanimity [of] . . . distaste." As such, queens became a "point of contradiction," a "dislocation" in the "structure of thought" (60, 66).

48   JoAnn McNamara and Suzanne F. Wemple, in "Sanctity and Power: The Dual Pursuit of Medieval Women," in *Becoming Visible: Women in European History,* ed. Renate Bridenthal and Claudia Koontz (Boston: Houghton Mifflin, 1977), write that "by the fourteenth century, the position of royal ladies was . . . weakened by growing xenophobia. Queens normally were foreigners and often were cut off from their friends and retainers, who were suspected of pursuing inimical interests. During the Hundred Years' War, the 'foreign woman' frequently became the focus of popular discontent, a scapegoat for the follies of her husband as often as the victim of her own thwarted ambition." They cite Margaret of Anjou and Isabeau of Bavaria as particular examples (113–14). The comparison with the earlier Middle Ages is of course difficult,. though fascinating, since both periods are often linked with rapid change and are therefore especially interesting for queenship. In the later period, xenophobia and nationalism created particular problems for queens, but compared with the queens of the earlier Middle Ages they were somewhat better protected through the development of canon law of marriage. Stafford, however, considers institutional development also to have been detrimental to the exercise of queenship: "Removal of the succession question [i.e., the emergence of primogeniture] made [household] . . . politics less and less those of the family, where the queen had an obvious role, and more and more those of the kingdom, where she did not" (*Queens, Concubines, and Dowagers,* 196).

49   See Marshall, *Virgins and Viragos,* 45–46. James I of Scotland (r. 1406–37) was captured by the English during a sea voyage to France at the age of twelve and remained a prisoner in England until he was thirty, during which time the duke of Albany served as governor of Scotland and appears not to have pressed for the king's release. James I was assassinated when his son, James II (r. 1437–60), was only six years old. The Livingston family rose to power during his minority, and their fall, writes Gordon Donaldson, "was sudden and spectacular." Donaldson, *Scottish Kings* (London: B. T. Batsford, 1967; 2d ed., 1977), 81. James II was killed accidentally "as he watched the discharge of one of his beloved bombards" (95)

and was succeeded by his nine-year-old son, James III (r. 1460–1488), who fell during the later part of his minority into the hands of the Boyds and destroyed them when he married Margaret of Denmark in 1469. James III was overthrown by his son, James IV (r. 1488–1513) – or by a faction of discontented southern nobles, notably Humes and Hepburns, who were able to attach James IV to their interests – when the latter was just in his teens. James IV was killed at Flodden Field when his heir was only seventeen months old; the troubles of James V's minority have been discussed in the section "City."

50 Donaldson, *Scottish Kings*, 63–64.

51 Donaldson explains that "in May 1439 Cameron was replaced as chancellor by Sir William Crichton and in the following month Douglas died. Shortly afterwards the Queen married Sir James Stewart of Lorne. This marriage to a subject, and one not of the first rank, may have been thought to disqualify the Queen from any further part in government, and if she and her husband had any thought of seizing power they were thwarted by Sir Alexander Livingston, who arrested them and let them go only on condition that they were not to retain custody of the young King. Livingston and Chancellor Crichton for a time competed for the keeping of the King's person." (*Scottish Kings*, 80–81).

52 Donaldson, *Scottish Kings*, 82.

53 Ibid., 98.

54 Ibid., 100; Norman Macdougall, *James IV* (Edinburgh: John Donald, 1989), 6–10.

55 A brief but refreshingly thoughtful treatment of her situation as Queen Mother may, however, be found in Leslie J. Macfarlane, *William Elphinstone and the Kingdom of Scotland, 1431–1514: The Struggle for Order* (Aberdeen: Aberdeen University Press, 1985), 434–35. Patricia Hill Buchanan, *Margaret Tudor, Queen of Scots* (Edinburgh: Scottish Academic Press, 1985), avoids the excesses of Margaret-bashing but offers little new analysis of Margaret's attempts at rule. Agnes Strickland, *Lives of the Queens of Scotland and English Princesses Connected with the Regal Succession of Great Britain*, vol. 1 (New York: Harper, 1859), remains, despite Buchanan's book, Margaret's most serious scholarly biography, and in the work the suppositions of the Victorian bourgeoisie about the proper conduct of queens are strikingly evident. A useful analogy to the ways in which Margaret's position has been misperceived may be found in Christiane Klapisch-Zuber's excellent essay "The 'Cruel Mother': Maternity, Widowhood and Dowry in Florence in the Fourteenth and Fifteenth Century," pp. 117–31 in *Women, Family, and Ritual in Renaissance Italy*, trans. Lydia Cochrane (Chicago: University of Chicago Press, 1985). There, if a woman was widowed, her family of origin could force her to remarry; if she remarried, she had to leave the *casa* of her late husband and leave her children there as well. A literature accordingly developed in Florence on the subject of the cruelty and unnaturalness of mothers; but Klapisch-Zuber cites a contemporary dialogue in which one of the speakers, a woman, points out that the structure of the family is such that these mothers have no choice and often grieve a parting they are helpless to change. Some of these mothers may of course not have minded; Margaret Tudor may indeed have been a living exemplar of queenship's stereotypical vices. But such considerations cannot stand in place of analysis of a woman's particular social and historical circumstances.

56 W. Croft Dickinson usefully notes that when Margaret was named tutrix to her son, "it would appear that, almost at once, certain of the nobility sent secret letters

to France, to John, duke of Albany, inviting him to come to Scotland to take over
the regency." Dickinson, *Scotland from the Earliest Times to 1603*, rev. and ed.
Archibald A. M. Duncan, 3d ed. (Oxford: Clarendon Press, 1977), 300.

57 Donaldson, *Scottish Kings*, 148.

58 See Strickland, *Lives of the Queens*, 139–40, on Henry VIII's resentment of Margaret's foolish, evil, and shameless pursuit of a divorce from Angus.

59 Patricia Buchanan writes that the position of regent of Scotland, which James IV
granted to Margaret in his will, "was a somewhat unusual position to be granted
to a woman, since by custom the Regent was the one nearest in line to actual succession to the throne" (*Margaret Tudor*, 71).

60 Robert C. Palmer, in "Contexts of Marriage in Medieval England: Evidence from
the King's Court circa 1300," *Speculum* 59 (1984): 42–67, presents fascinating evidence from the plea rolls of the king's court to suggest that marriage "cases were
often part of a . . . complicated social reality" (43) and that "such transactions were
extremely varied. . . . It is . . . inadequate, when speaking of marital transactions,
to focus exclusively on dowry. . . . The focus should rather be on bargaining and
the respective positions of the families and the expectations of the parties" (56).
Margaret's supposed avarice and the flexibility of her approach to marital and financial negotiations loom a little less large in the context of common practices
of the day, even among the less privileged. To quote from only one of the many
cases cited by Palmer: In *Hog vs. Latton*, "Sibil had a very modest holding: thirteen
acres of arable, an acre of meadow, and rents of 12d annually. William de Latton
pledged his faith to her, so that they were validly married. Then, however, he proceeded to marry a different woman solemnly in church. Sibil could have claimed
him in ecclesiastical court, but seemingly considered herself well rid of him. She
would thereafter be suspect, however, since Latton might later claim her; she used
her lands to secure a second husband. She enfeoffed one Adam of her few acres;
Adam established himself in the land and then enfeoffed Robert Hog, who likewise established himself. Hog and Sibil then married. Thereafter, Latton's second
wife died; and he still considered Sibil an attractive enough mate. He claimed her
in ecclesiastical court and won: she was divorced from Hog, and her marriage to
Latton was solemnized. Thus possessed of Sibil, Latton ejected Hog, perhaps believing that the land was still Sibil's right — Sibil, after the divorce, would certainly
want to maintain that. Hog had nevertheless gained title to the land and could
not be thus casually thrown out. He recovered the land in court" (52–53). The cases
cited by Palmer are, of course, the cases that found their way into court, but there
are enough of them to suggest widespread creativity as well as confusion in marriage negotiations.

61 Quoted in Strickland, *Lives of the Queens*, 178. Debates over gynecocracy, and
more broadly, over the political role of women, were not just theoretical. It was
not unusual for late medieval and Renaissance queens to display explicit interest
in the question of female power. Scalingi, in "Scepter or the Distaff," notes that
Margaret Beaufort was an enthusiastic patroness of early English humanism, which
also often meant "feminist" views; she adds that "Catherine of Aragon and Catherine Parr did much to encourage this early feminist movement" (59 n. 1). Feminist
literature, of the kind represented by Thomas Elyot's *Defence of Good Women* (1540),
"was popular in court circles"; "the first edition of [*The Defence of Good Women*]
. . . was dedicated to Queen Anne of Cleves" (62).

62 Margaret's letter was written in July 1524, in the midst of the troubles of James

V's minority; see Strickland, *Lives of the Queens*, 176. For Bourdieu on the "condemning [of] women's interventions to a shameful, secret, or, at best, unofficial existence," see *Outline of a Theory of Practice*, 41; see also n. 46 above.

Chapter 6. Legalized Passion: The Idea of Marriage

1 Instances of the connection between sovereignty and marriage are many and well known. In late medieval and early modern France, coronation ritual was explicitly viewed as a wedding sacrament; see Charles T. Wood, "Queens, Queans, and Kingship," chap. 1 of *Joan of Arc and Richard III: Sex, Saints, and Government in the Middle Ages* (New York: Oxford University Press, 1988), and Ernst Kantorowicz's well-known classic, *The King's Two Bodies: A Study in Mediaeval Political Theology* (Princeton: Princeton University Press, 1957), 222–23. Kantorowicz cites the fourteenth-century Italian legal scholar Lucas de Penna's statement that as the man was head of the wife and Christ the head of the church, the wife being the body of the man and the Church the body of Christ, so the prince was head of the realm and the realm was the body of the prince (214–18, citing Lucas de Penna, *Commentaria in Tres Libros Codicis* [Lyon, 1597], 563). See Kantorowicz's section on "Corpus Reipublicae mysticum," *King's Two Bodies*, 207–32, which discusses a number of marriage metaphors in medieval and early modern political theory, including James VI of Scotland and I of England's famous speech to his first Parliament on 22 March 1603, which argued for the union of the kingdoms through the metaphor of marriage between sovereign and kingdom-bride. Kantorowicz cites James's speech as an exception to the rule that "in mediaeval England, the marriage metaphor seems to have been all but non-existent" (223), though Michael Enright has argued for Irish precedents; see Enright, "King James and His Island: An Archaic Kingship Belief?" *Scottish Historical Review* 55 (1976): 29–40. Elizabeth I's use of the indissolubility of the bonds of marriage to justify her single life should also be noted: "this . . . makes mee wonder, that you forget yourselues, the pledge of this alliance which I haue made with my Kingdome. (And therwithall, stretching out her hand, shee shewed them the Ring with which shee was giuen in marriage, and inaugurated to her Kingdome, in expresse and solemne terms.)" Axton, *Queen's Two Bodies*, 38, citing William Camden, *Annales* [London, 1625], 38). Late medieval wedding pageantry often draws on associations between marital and political bonds even when a fully developed marriage metaphor is not in evidence; thus union not merely within but between kingdoms was figured in the marriage ceremonies of Margaret Tudor and James IV of Scotland through the heraldic device of the interlaced thistle and rose. See John Younge (Somerset Herald), *The Fyancells of Margaret, eldest Daughter of King Henry VIIth to James King of Scotland: Together with her Departure from England, Journey into Scotland, her Reception and Marriage there, and the great Feasts held on that Account; Written by John Younge, Somerset Herald, who attended the said Princess on her Journey*, in John Leland, *De Rebus Britannicis Collectanea*, Tomus Tertius (London: Gvl. et Jo. Richardson, 1770), 290, 295. All citations to Younge, hereinafter cited as *Fyancells*, are taken from Leland's text. *Fyancells* is a somewhat misleading short title, since it refers only to one part of Younge's account of the rituals and festivities of Margaret's wedding, but since it is familiar to scholars of late medieval Scottish literature, I have chosen to retain it. I thank Gordon Kipling for drawing my attention to the difficulties both of Leland's text and of the College of Arms

MS of Younge's narrative (College of Arms MS 1st M.13); see Kipling's "Textual Introduction" in his edition *The Receyt of the Ladie Kateryne*, EETS o.s. no. 296 (London: Oxford University Press, 1990).

In turn, "ordinary" marriage ritual often draws on the imagery of sovereignty; van Gennep, *Rites of Passage*, notes that "marriage ceremonies often include details resembling aspects of enthronement" (141). Duncan MacGregor, ed. and trans., *The Rathen Manual* (Aberdeen: Aberdeen Ecclesiological Society, 1905), 39, provides for the use of the bridal pall, which did in fact feature in Margaret and James's wedding: after the *Te Deum* "two Prelatts helde the Cloth apon [James and Margaret] . . . durying the Remanent of the Masse" (Younge, *Fyancells*, 294).

2 Margaret Tudor was anointed during the celebration of her bridal Mass, "After wich the Kynge gaffe hyr the Septre in hyr Haund" (Younge, *Fyancells*, 294). In one of the London pageants for the reception of Catherine of Aragon in 1501, King Alphonso of Spain tells Catherine "Ye shall acchieve the dignytie of a quene, / By meane of Mariage in this noble land." Charles Lethbridge Kingsford, ed., *Chronicles of London* (Oxford: Clarendon Press, 1905), 241. Sydney Anglo discusses this entry in "The London Pageants for the Reception of Katharine of Aragon: November 1501," *Journal of the Warburg and Courtauld Institutes* 26 (1963): 53–89.

3 The meanings of the term *subject* bring out the very interchangeability of freedoms and constraints with which this chapter is concerned. One can be a *subject* in the sense of "one who is under the dominion of a monarch or reigning prince," "in the control or under the dominion of another"—that is, by definition unfree, not fully self-possessed, not sovereign. Or one can be a *subject* in the sense of "mind, as the 'subject' in which ideas inhere," "the self or ego," in other words, by definition self-possessed and, in effect, "sovereign" (definitions taken from the *OED*). The term *subject* is used in psychoanalysis, among other disciplines, as contrasting with *object*, and in such usage implies the capacity for intention, desire, activity—in short, will—in contradistinction to the object's passivity. In this part of our discussion, *Subject* refers to the latter understanding of the term, *subject* to the earlier sense of one under the dominion of another; elsewhere in this book, however, no attempt is made thus to distinguish them, either because it is assumed that the specific contexts are disambiguating or because both senses are wanted at once.

4 Thus in Kristeva's analysis of the Song of Songs, "the Sublime, regal one turns into God having an amorous dialogue with his beloved, the nation of Israel"; the Shulammite in turn submits, but as Subject, made equal through her love to the other's sovereignty. An entire "nation" can thereby imagine itself as the Shulammite chosen by God (*Tales of Love*, 95–100). Marina Warner notes that in the Old Testament the "wanton" bride Israel will be rewarded if she learns to return God's love of her with loyalty and faith. In Revelation the epithalamic motif of the emergence of the bride is used to transfigure wanton Israel into the New Jerusalem, a "pure, beautiful, spotless creation of God, free of all the taint and strife of all that has gone before," a harlot become virgin, and hence sign of the absolute priority of God, His power of alteration—her absolute choice of Him mirroring His choice of her, in turn signified by the perfection of her creatureliness. In the New Testament, the figure of marriage promises closure to the sometimes violent, sometimes harmonious "dance" of Jehovah and Israel, that constitutes the Old Testament account of sovereign love. See Warner, *Alone of All Her Sex*, 123–24.

5 Kristeva, *Tales of Love*, 94.
6 Pauline Stafford, writing on Queen Ælfthryth's friendship with Æthelwold at Winchester, notes that it was there that the iconography of Mary Regina "was elaborated in the late tenth century" and perhaps also the idea of queenly anointing. The ritual used for Ælfthryth's consecration was West Frankian and "bore the marks of its origin in the marriage ceremony"; anointing, like marriage, made the queen a "new woman" for the purposes of fertility, thus emphasizing and specifying the nature of her set-apartness from other women. Stafford, *Queens, Concubines, and Dowagers*, 127–34. For information on epithalamia to the Virgin, see Virginia Tufte, *The Poetry of Marriage: The Epithalamium in Europe and Its Development in England* (Los Angeles: Tinnon-Brown, 1970), 81–82.
7 Rosemary Muir-Wright, "The Iconography of the Coronation of the Virgin," in *Kingship*, ed. Emily Lyle (*Cosmos* 2 [1986]), 57, citing Revelation 21:2.
8 Muir-Wright, "Iconography," 56–57.
9 Ibid., 63, citing Jacobus de Voragine, *The Golden Legend*, trans. Granger Ryan and Helmut Ripperger (New York: Arno Press, 1969), 451.
10 John of Ireland, *Meroure of Wyssdome*, 151.
11 Scarry's phrase is taken from her unpublished lecture "Consent: Injury, Departure, Desire."
12 Kristeva, *Tales of Love*, 90, 227.
13 The act of consent was, according to Gratian, inseparable from love or "'marital affection,' a positive assent to the other person as a spouse." See Angela M. Lucas, *Women in the Middle Ages: Religion, Marriage and Letters* (New York: St. Martin's Press, 1983), 100, citing J. T. Noonan, Jr., "Marital Affection in the Canonists," *Studia Gratiana* 12 (1967): 489–99. James D. Scanlan, "Husband and Wife: Pre-Reformation Canon Law of Marriage of the Officials' Courts," in *An Introduction to Scottish Legal History* (Edinburgh: Robert Cunningham and Sons, 1958), discusses the development of the canonical rule that the consent of both parties was the essence of marriage ('Nuptias consensus non concubitus facit,' chap. 30, 10.4.1) on pp. 69–74. Just before Margaret Tudor's marriage to James IV by proxy in England, the archbishop of Glasgow "demanded and sperred the . . . Princesse, Whither shee were content without Compulsion, and of her free Will? Then she answered, If it please my Lord and Father the King, and my Lady my Mother the Queene. Then the King shewed her, that it was his Will and Pleasure: And then shee had the Kinges and the Queenes Blessings" (Younge, *Fyancells*, 261). In this ritual the movement of the royal virgin's will is barely traceable, so gracious and so immediate is her identification of her will with the pleasure of her parents; and yet traceable it must be.
14 Scanlan, "Husband and Wife," 72, citing *Summa Theologica*, Supplementum Tertiae Partis, question 45, article 2. *Sponsalia per verba de futuro* vowed the couple's intention to be married in future; *sponsalia per verba de praesenti* was marriage proper, the fulfillment of a promise. See also John Dowden, *The Medieval Church in Scotland: Its Constitution, Organisation and Law* (Glasgow: James MacLehose and Sons, 1910), 251. The theology of the twelfth century established the supremacy of indissolubility, the *stabilitas* of marriage which Hildebert of Lavardin regarded as constituting "the very foundation of the sacrament, since it is the sign of a sacred thing (*signum sacrae rei*)." Cited by Georges Duby in *Medieval Marriage: Two Models from Twelfth-Century France*, trans. Elborg Foster (Baltimore: Johns Hopkins University Press, 1978), 64; see also Scanlan, 70. The principle of

the indissolubility of marriage was supported by its interpretation as symbol of Christ's union with the Church; one of the prayers in the *Rathen Manual* gives "O God, Who hast consecrated the marriage bond of such an excellent mystery, that by the covenant of matrimony Thou mightest signify the Mystic Union of Christ and the Church" (MacGregor, ed., *Rathen Manual*, 40).

15 Thomas Usk, *The Testament of Love*, 1.9, in W. W. Skeat, ed., *Chaucerian and Other Pieces*, supplement to *The Complete Works of Geoffrey Chaucer* (Oxford, 1897); cited by Kelly, *Love and Marriage*, 290.

16 The play begins with "Abysakar episcopus" warning the populace that "þe lawe of god byddyth this sawe / þat at xiiij ȝere of age / Euery damesel what so sche be / to þe Encrese of more plente" (ll. 8–11). Joachim says to Anne "A-ȝen þe lawe may we not do" (l. 24), and they take Mary to the temple; but she explains, "A-ȝens þe lawe wyl I nevyr be / but mannys ffelachep xal nevyr folwe me / . . . / Whan þat I was to þe temple brought / and offerde up to god Above / ther hestyd I as myn hert thought / to serve my god with hertyly love" (ll. 36–37, 66–69). Joseph tells the same story in the Wakefield Annunciation, ll. 228–45.

17 The form for the crying of banns just before the marriage service is given in a manuscript in the York Minster Library as "Frendys, yᵉ cawse of our commynge at yⁱˢ tyme es for yᵉ worthy sacrament off Matrimone, the qwylk es for to cupyll two persons in one wyll, ayere of yam gowernynge one sawle." Cited by MacGregor, *Rathen Manual*, 33–34 n. 6. The manuscript is in the Fothergill Collection. The York Manual gives "for to couple and to knyt these two bodyes togyder, . . . that they be from this tyme forth, but one body and two soules."

18 Usk, *Testament of Love*, 1.9, 40–41; cited by Kelly, *Love and Marriage*, 67. The power of love to transform difference is a central theme in the mystical tradition; Richard Rolle asks, "What else is love . . . but the transformation of affection into the thing loved? . . . Everyone becomes like that which he loves." Kelly, *Love and Marriage*, 314, citing Margaret Deanesly, ed., *The Incendium amoris of Richard Rolle of Hampole* (Manchester: Manchester University Press, 1915), chap. 17, pp. 194–95.

19 See Mair, *Marriage*, 109, on the dramatization in marriage ritual of "tension between the old kin ties and the new." Christiane Klapisch-Zuber, "An Ethnology of Marriage in the Age of Humanism," in *Women, Family, and Ritual in Renaissance Italy*, 254–56, discusses Marco Antonio Altieri's *Li nuptiali* (ca. 1500), ed. E. Narducci (Rome, 1873); in Altieri, peace and marriage, violence and rape, are "opposed," but his interpretation of ritual everywhere suggests the ease with which these oppositions are undone. In Bourdieu, *Outline of a Theory of Practice*, violence is found within marriage itself; in Kabyle society, the opening rite of the marriage season, homologous with the initial rite of plowing, was meant "to exorcize the threat contained in the coming together of male and female, fire and water, sky and earth, ploughshare and furrow, in acts of inevitable sacrilege" (45).

20 Lucas de Penna, it will be recalled, writes that "just as Christ joined to himself an alien-born as his spouse, the Church of Gentiles . . . , so has the Prince joined to himself as his *sponsa* the state, which is not his." Kantorowicz, *King's Two Bodies*, 216, citing Lucas de Penna, *Commentaria*, 563.

21 See Kantorowicz, *King's Two Bodies*, 7, quoting Plowden, *Commentaries or Reports*, 212a, on the king's "Body mortal, subject to all Infirmities that come by Nature or Accident," and his "Body that cannot be seen or handled, consisting of

Policy and Government." That marriage is a "mystery" is brought out by the apparent inconsistency between the gospel and the epistle for the bridal Mass in the Roman Rite. In the former (Matthew 19:3–6), Christ says, "a man shall leave his father and his mother, and be made one with his wife; and the two shall become one flesh. It follows that they are no longer two individuals: they are one flesh"; the latter (Ephesians 5:22–23) enjoins, "Wives, be subject to your husbands as to the Lord; for the man is the head of the woman, just as Christ also is the head of the Church." G. Campbell Paton, writing on the *ius mariti* as it is developed in the medieval Scottish law code *Regiam Majestatem*, explains that "on marriage the husband acquired power over the person of his wife, who was considered to have no legal *persona*. As ruler of the house he had the control of her person and conduct." Paton, "Husband and Wife: Property Rights and Relationships," in *Introduction to Scottish Legal History*, 99. In legal theory, the "sinking of [the wife's] . . . person in the husband" is, again, the obverse of the extension of the sovereign's person through the body of the realm (101). The legal development of both marriage and sovereignty involved the intense scrutiny of relations between personhood and property, the fluidity *and* fixity of which relations were of the utmost importance; the theory of the king's two bodies was itself worked out partly in relation to questions about the inalienability of the "fisc" (the crown's property, as opposed to the personal property of the king as a private person). See Paton, 100–101, on the wife's property rights. The Scottish law code *Regiam Majestatem and Quoniam Attachiamenta*, ed. and trans. Right Hon. Lord Cooper (Edinburgh: J. Skinner and Co., 1947), Bk. 2, chap. 16, pp. 120, 126; Bk. 2, chap. 17, pp. 30–31; and Bk. 2, chap. 36, pp. 148–49, lists a number of restrictions on the married woman's power to dispose of property. Lynda Boose has drawn my attention to a ritual form specified in the *Rathen Manual* that emphasizes the role of property in legal transformations of personhood: "If the bridegroom endowed the bride with land, she went down on her knees beside him and kissed his right foot, while he instantly raised her up" (MacGregor, ed., *Rathen Manual*, 36 n. 1).

22 The ease with which gateways are opened is an important aspect of royal marriage entries; in Catherine of Aragon's entry into London, Policy speaks from his castle: "Who openeth these gates? What! opened they alone? / What meaneth this? O! now I se wele why. / The bright Sterre of Spayn, Esperus, on them Shone, / Whos goodly Beamys hath persed mightely / Through this Castell to bryng this good Lady, / Whos prosperous comyng shall right ioyfull be / Both vnto noblesse, vertu, and vnto me" (Kingsford, ed., *Chronicles of London*, 237). See also Priscilla Bawcutt, "Dunbar's Use of the Symbolic Lion and Thistle," in *Kingship*, ed. Lyle (*Cosmos* 2 [1986]), 94, on the importance of gateways in royal entries, including that of Margaret Tudor into Edinburgh, and in Dunbar's *The Thrissill and the Rois*. The Virgin Mary's power to open and close is also prominent in John of Ireland's treatment of the Annunciation in *Meroure of Wyssdome*, 154, 168.

23 Nohrnberg, *Analogy of the Faerie Queene*, explains the transgressive power of the onset of maturity, of "sexual awakening involving Oedipal fantasies," of "adopting a sexual role and goal that will lead to one's replacing one's own parent" (445). That is, the onset of maturity is always presumptuous to the extent that it involves the recognition of the mortality of one's own creators and of one's own power of creation.

24 Lynda E. Boose, "The Father and the Bride in Shakespeare," *PMLA* 97 (1982): 340.

25 Dowden, *Medieval Church*, 253, citing *Concilia Scotiae: Statuta Ecclesiae Scoti-*

canae, ed. Joseph Robertson, vol. 2 (Bannatyne Club, 1866), 36 (hereinafter cited as *SES*).

26 Kelly, *Love and Marriage,* 257, referring to John Andreae, *Novella* on *Decretales of Gregorii IX* (X) 4.15.7 (Litterae) v. instituter (4.51.[6]). Theologians of marriage argued that "marriage was first established in the garden of Eden for the purpose of multiplying the human race" and served "as a remedy for the sexual concupiscence that was one of the consequences of the fall" (Kelly, 246–47). One of the prayers in the *Rathen Manual* reads, "Almighty and everlasting God, who by His own might united our first parents Adam and Eve; Himself sanctify and bless your bodies, and join you in a fellowship and love of true affection" (MacGregor, ed., *Rathen Manual,* 37). In Catherine of Aragon's entry into London, "the ffader of heven" says: "I am begynnynge and ende, that made eche creature / Myself and for myself, but man specially, / Both male and female, made after myn owne figure; / Whom I ioyned to-gidre in Matrymony, / And that in Paradise, declaryng opynly, / That men shall weddyng in my chirch solempnyse / ffigured and syngnyfied by the erthely paradise" (Kingsford, ed., *Chronicles of London,* 245).

27 David Bevington, ed., *Medieval Drama* (Boston: Houghton Mifflin, 1975), 356–67; all citations of the Wakefield Annunciation are taken from this edition. When Joseph returns from working in the country to find Mary pregnant, she responds to his accusations with "Yee, God he knowys all my doing" (l. 215). Joseph knows that he himself is not responsible for Mary's pregnancy because "Passed I am all prevay play" (l. 168).

28 Kelly, *Love and Marriage,* refers to Boccaccio's *Decameron* 10.8, in which Tito comments that some might object, "not to him as a husband, but to the manner in which he became a husband — secretly and furtively, without the knowledge of friend or relative. He admits that this frequently happens, and he speaks of those women who have taken husbands against the will of their fathers" (185). Kelly comments on "the stunning ease with which marriage could be made. It was supposed to be licensed; but, at bottom, it need not be. The authorities were fighting a losing battle in their efforts to keep marriage public and aboveboard" (201). The statutes of the Scottish synods of the thirteenth century insist that marriages must be performed in the presence of priest and witnesses "Since matrimony is known to have been instituted in Paradise by God Himself" (Dowden, *Medieval Church,* 253, citing *SES,* 36). Another medieval Scottish statute on clandestine marriage insists that the nuptial benediction "should be given, not in private chapels, nor at night (*in tenebris*), but solemnly and openly in . . . parish churches" (Dowden, *Medieval Church,* 256, citing *SES,* 68). See also Scanlan, "Husband and Wife," 73, on the issue of clandestine marriages.

29 Kelly, *Love and Marriage,* 58, citing John Andreae, on X 4.3, "Saepe etenim clandestine contrahuntur, testante Solomone, Prover. 9: 'Aquae furtivae dulciores sunt, et panis absconditus suavior.'"

30 Bourdieu contrasts the two values "all marriages seek to 'maximize'": "the integration of the minimal unit and its security" versus "alliance and prestige, that is, opening up to the outside world, towards strangers. The choice between fission and fusion, the inside and the outside, security and adventure, is posed anew with each marriage" (*Outline of a Theory of Practice,* 57).

31 Though "extraordinary marriage" — Bourdieu's term for prestigious, risky, and expensive marriage alliances between distant groups, usually undertaken only by the politically ambitious or prominent — was of course an aristocratic practice in

the Middle Ages, Georges Duby has clarified the "strong tendency toward endogamy" in medieval France: "Families frequently felt that a marriage between cousins could be used to reunite . . . scattered portions of inheritances. . . . while marriage remained forbidden within the house itself and within the close family group, the notion of incest came to lose all rigor beyond the third degree of kinship" (Duby, *Medieval Marriage*, 8). And though marriage "within the house itself and within the close family group" was not permitted, incest was nonetheless a central practice and sign of seigneurial power; see Duby's chapter "Incest, Bigamy and Divorce among Kings and Nobles."

32   The miracle plays of the Annunciation make this connection explicit: the York play sets Mary's consent to the Incarnation in the context of the loss and recovery of Paradise: "Lord God, grete mervell es to mene / Howe man was made withouten mysse / And sette whare he sulde ever have bene— / With-outen bale, bidand in blisse. / And howe he lost that comforth clene, / And was putte oute fro Paradys / . . . / Tille God graunted tham grace / Of helpe als he hadde hyght." R. George Thomas, ed., *Ten Miracle Plays* (London: Edward Arnold, 1966), 65–73, ll. 1–6, 11–12; all citations of the York Annunciation are taken from this edition. Both the York and Wakefield Annunciations begin their rebeginnings by recalling the original creation, and Wakefield puts particular emphasis on Mary's role in the reparation of the image of God in man. In the latter, God explains: "Sithen I have mayde all thing of noght, / And Adam with my handys hath wroght, / Like to min[e] image, att my devise, / And giffen him joy in paradise / To won therin, as that I wend, / To that he did that I defend— / Then I him put out of that place— / Bot yit, I myn, I hight him grace" (ll. 1–8).

33   It is interesting to note in this connection Rosemary Muir-Wright's observation that "the veneration of the Virgin reached new heights" in the later fifteenth century with Sixtus IV's "formal institution in 1476 of an Office and Mass for the Feast of the Immaculate Conception. As the doctrinal arguments concerning the latter increased, so the image of the Coronation became widespread. . . . In the fact of such controversy regarding the moment of Mary's sanctification and its import, the earlier iconography of the Coronation, in stressing the nuptial element in the glorification ritual, might have seemed confusing. . . . The Sponsa imagery is now superseded by that of the image of the Daughter of God. Mary is crowned by God the Father" ("Iconography," 74).

34   For an interesting essay on the Annunciation as a "legal fiction" and on its continuity with Jewish traditions on divine intervention in human generation, see J. Duncan M. Derrett, "Virgin Birth in the Gospels," *Man* 6 (1971): 289–93, esp. 289–90.

35   John of Ireland, *Meroure of Wyssdome*, 99. Ireland also compares "occult and sacret operacioune of þe haly spreit" to the way in which "þe wattir, be occult operacioune generit within the Erd, procedis jn Riueris and fludis for gret jncressinge of herbis, treis and all vthire thingis" (151). The day of Gabriel's coming to Mary was, he explains, "nocht expremyt in þe euuangell, for his fyrst cummyne was occult & secret; bot it was þe xxv day of marche, jn þe faire tyme vernale, for in that tyme þe waurld was creat. Tharfor conuenient was, þat jn þe sammyne tyme of the ȝere jt suld be restorit and recretit." He adds: "Alsua þat tyme js mare dissolute, and men mare jnclinit to volupte and plesaunce, and þarfor þe blist sone of god come and halowit þat tyme be his blist jncarnacioune" (128).

36   The supreme interiority of the Annunciation is stressed in a different way in the

York Annunciation: Mary says of the angel's greeting, "What maner of halsyng is this / Thus prevely comes to me; / For in myn herte a thoght it is, / The tokenyng that I here see" (ll. 147–50).

37 John of Ireland, *Meroure of Wyssdome*, 131.
38 Ibid., 137.
39 Ibid.
40 Ibid., 138.

Chapter 7. Active Stars: The Wedding of Margaret Tudor and James IV

1 Macdougall, *James IV*, notes that Ireland — James III's "confessor, counsellor and diplomat in the 1480's" — originally intended *The Meroure of Wyssdome* for James III but, because of James III's death in 1488, presented it to James IV in 1490 in an effort to "find royal patronage" (86). Ireland "may . . . have had a hand in James's upbringing" (284).

2 The *Eneados* was, as Priscilla Bawcutt notes, finished on 22 July 1513, shortly before the death of James IV at Flodden on 9 September 1513. The work was dedicated to his kinsman Henry, Lord Sinclair. The "Thirteenth Book" is a translation of Maphaeus Vegius's *Supplementum*. Priscilla Bawcutt, *Gavin Douglas: A Critical Study* (Edinburgh: Edinburgh University Press, 1976), 10, 92, 104.

3 Gavin Douglas, *Eneados*, in *The Poetical Works of Gavin Douglas*, ed. John Small, vol. 4 (Edinburgh: William Paterson, 1874), p. 197, ll. 21–22; p. 198, l. 25. All subsequent citations to the *Eneados* are taken from this edition.

4 "Lyke as, quhen the gret ithand weit or rayne, / From the clowdis furth ʒet our all the plane, / Haldis the husbandis idill aganys thair will, / Lang with his crukit beyme the plewch lyis still; / Syne, gif brycht Tytan list do schaw his face, / And with swift curs far furth a large space / Dois each hys stedis and his giltyn chayr, / And kythis hys goldyn bemys in the ayr, / Makand the hevynnis fayr, cleyr, and scheyne, / The weddir smowt, and firmament serene; / The landwart hynys than, baith man and boy, / For the soft sessoun ourflowis full of joy, / And athir otheris gan exhort in hy / To go to laubour of thair husbandry" (p. 208, ll. 23–24; p. 209, ll. 1–12).

5 See Scarry, *Body in Pain*, on problems "in the relation between maker and made thing that [carry] . . . us back to the original moment of making" (182).

6 Venus washes Eneas's body clean of "All that was mortale or corruptibill thyng"; his soul is then borne above the air "Amyd the starnys" (p. 222, ll. 13, 18).

7 Henry VIII might well have appeared, from Scotland's point of view, an English Turnus, who had perversely been allowed to succeed a Latinus-like Henry VII. Latinus's role as peacemaker and oath-keeper is constantly emphasized in Douglas's poem. See, for example, p. 202, ll. 11–17, in which the ambassadors explain to Eneas that Latinus "Hes only this beleif and traste . . . / That he hys douchter may do wed with the, / Quhilk of kyn, successioun, and lynnage, / Be that ilk souerane band of mariage, / Of Troian and Italian blude discend / Sall childryng furth bryng, quhill the warldis end / Perpetualy to ryng in hie empyre."

8 A full account of the progress north is found in Younge, *Fyancells*; Buchanan, *Margaret Tudor*, gives an extended account of the wedding festivities at 11–34, Strickland, *Lives of the Queens*, at 12–62; see also Mackie's chapter "The Thistle and the Rose" in *King James IV*, 90ff.

9 Nicholson, *Scotland*. He notes that, in the early sixteenth century, "the ques-

tion of the royal succession in both England and Scotland must have contributed to the nervousness of their rulers" and adds that Margaret's choice of the name Arthur was "hardly tactful. . . . On 10 April 1512 James's confidence, and Henry's irritation, must have been increased when Queen Margaret at last gave birth to a son (the future James V) who escaped infant mortality to inherit his mother's potential claim to the English crown" (595).

10   Nicholson comments that "James's far-reaching diplomacy . . . and his own role as peace-maker . . . [gave] Scotland increasing weight in European politics. . . . From the time of James's marriage until the death of his father-in-law, Scotland had no serious foreign foe and many apparent friends" (*Scotland*, 556). Nicholson sees the accession of the "egocentric teenager" Henry VIII as a disruption of this time of prosperity (595), made irreparable by Flodden ("the disaster was not retrieved," 606). Nicholson is in substantial agreement with Mackie's view in *King James IV*: Mackie writes: "James was now the son-in-law of Henry VII, and the heir, twice removed, to the crown of England. Already, having brought his kingdom to comparative peace and . . . prosperity, he had begun to play a part in European affairs. . . . But his realm was only comparatively peaceful" (113). Flodden irreparably dashes Scotland's futuristic visions: "And so, in these charnel-pits, ended the great Crusade" (269). William Ferguson, in *Scotland's Relations with England: A Survey to 1707* (Edinburgh: John Donald, 1977), remarks of the 1502 treaty and subsequent marriage that "it looked as if the age-old enmity between England and Scotland had at last worked itself out" (40); but after Flodden "[a] period of slow, uncertain and spasmodic rapprochement between England and Scotland was resumed" (41).

Norman Macdougall, in *James IV*, argues that the treaty of 1502 has been overpraised "as the beginning of a new and more realistic Anglo-Scottish relationship" (248). While Macdougall is right to stress the brittleness of the alliance and the atmosphere of suspicion and "mistrust" that still prevailed from 1502 onward, the very difficulty of the alliance, and the history of "Anglophobia" preceding the period of the alliance, are exactly what made the alliance a daring and terribly risky one. It is true that, as Macdougall writes, "it cannot be said that the treaty of 1502 was occasioned by any spontaneous outburst of Anglo-Scottish amity" (249), but I do not find the historical literature arguing that position. If, as Macdougall argues, the alliance of 1474 "may be regarded as the forerunner of the much more famous treaty of perpetual peace of 1502" and signaled "an important shift of emphasis in Scottish foreign policy," then 1502 may be assumed to mark at least a shift of similar importance ("Foreign Relations: England and France," in Brown, ed., *Scottish Society in the Fifteenth Century*, 109–10; see also n. 12 below).

11   John Leslie, *The Historie of Scotland Wrytten first in Latin by the Most Reuerend and Worthy Jhone Leslie Bishop of Rosse and Translated in Scottish by Father James Dalrymple*, ed. E. G. Cody and William Murison (Edinburgh: William Blackwood and Sons, 1890), Bk. 8, pp. 117–18. Ferguson, *Scotland's Relations with England*, discusses the speech and uses it as evidence for the seriousness of Henry VII's intentions for peace (40). Leslie adds that history—in the form of James V, son to Margaret and James IV—has shown that King Henry that day "spak and foirtald as verilie appeires be a spirit of prophesie." Bacon was no less enthusiastic. Commenting on the public rejoicing which took place at the announcement of Margaret's marriage to James, Francis Bacon detected "a secret instinct and inspiring (which many times runneth not only in the hearts of princes, but in the pulse and

veins of people) touching the happiness thereby to ensue in time to come." Bacon, *History of the Reign of King Henry VII*, in *Works*, ed. James Spedding, Robert Leslie Ellis, and Douglas Denon Heath (London, 1858), 6:216, cited in Mackie, *King James IV*, 98. See Mackie, *King James IV*, 97, and Kingsford, ed., *Chronicles of London*, 255, on the festivities in London after the announcement of the betrothal. "In Joyyng wherof *Te Deum* was there solempnely songen. And in the after none folowyng In dyuers places of the Citie were greate ffires to the number of x or xij. And at euery ffyre an hoggeshed of wyne Cowched, the which in tyme of the ffires brenning was drunkyn of such as wold; the which wyne was not long in drynkyng" (Kingsford, ed., *Chronicles of London*, 255).

12 Ferguson, *Scotland's Relations with England*, discusses James III's "shrewd, if premature [and unpopular], conclusion that . . . a durable peace with England had much to recommend it" (39–40). Norman Macdougall suggests that "widespread resistance north of Forth to payment of the 1501 tax" levied by James IV might be explained by the unpopularity of "the projected alliance with Henry VII. . . . as recently as 1496–7, James IV's wars with England had to some extent harnessed a popular reaction to [James III's pro-English] diplomacy; and Pedro de Ayala was in no doubt that King James had made [peace] . . . in 1497 'against the wishes of the majority in his Kingdom.'" Macdougall, *James IV*, 149, citing G. A. Bergenroth, ed., *Calendar of Letters, Despatches and State Papers relating to the negotiations between England and Spain*, vol. 1 (London, 1862), no. 210.

13 Nicholson argues for the "nationalist aim" of many of the cultural and technological activities of James IV and his contemporaries and includes among these Bishop Elphinstone's *Aberdeen Breviary*, which featured Scottish saints and was published by the new Scottish Chepman and Myllar press in 1509 and 1510 (*Scotland*, 592). Macfarlane discusses the marriage of James and Margaret and the pro-English Bishop Elphinstone's perspective on it in *William Elphinstone*: "James IV was fundamentally committed to his father's main policy of forging a lasting peace with England; a policy which seemed at last to come to fruition" with the marriage alliance. Again, the accession of Henry VIII "was to put an end to this run of good fortune" (426).

14 The terms of the 1502 treaty include provisions for extradition in the case of treason: "Neither of the kings aforesaid nor any of their heirs and successors shall in any way receive or allow to be received by their subjects any rebels, traitors or refugees suspected, reputed or convicted of the crime of treason." Provision is also made for the kings' obligations to come to each other's assistance in case of invasion. See Gordon Donaldson, ed., *Scottish Historical Documents* (Edinburgh: Scottish Academic Press, 1974), 93–94.

15 Mackie remarks that Henry VII did "all that he could to make his subjects sensible of the greatness of [Margaret's] . . . destiny" (*King James IV*, 105). On Margaret's baptism and christening, see Strickland, *Lives of the Queens*, 2–3. Strickland cites no sources, but speculates that "Henry VII and his sagacious mother . . . arranged all these coincidences for the purpose of conciliating the national predilections of the Scotch."

16 Buchanan, *Margaret Tudor*, 16. See Leslie J. Macfarlane's discussion of the Book of Hours (Austrian National Library, Codex Vindobonensis 1897) in "The Book of Hours of James IV and Margaret Tudor," *Innes Review* 11 (1961); it was, he says, "almost certainly a gift to Margaret Tudor on the occasion of her marriage to James IV" (3). He notes at 6–7 evidence that the book may have been commissioned by Henry VII rather than James IV, "but whether the gift came from Henry

or from James, one thing is certain: the artists commissioned for the work had a considerable and accurate knowledge of Scottish and English heraldry at their disposal. A study of James IV's coat of arms and other insignia, for example, shows it to be so accurate that it could only have been done from sketches already prepared by someone at the Scottish Court" (8). The emblems which decorate the manuscript throughout (the IM monogram tied with love knots, and the intertwined thistle and daisy) are similar to those painted by Sir Thomas Galbraith on the border of James's ratification of marriage contract, 17 December 1502, in the Public Record Office (PRO E/39/81), London. Macfarlane, "Book of Hours," 5, citing *LHTA* 2:350: "Item, [the xi day of December], to Schir Thomas Gabreth to pas to Edinburgh to illumyn the trewis and the conjunct infeftment, to by gold and to his expens, . . . lix s̄." Macfarlane identifies the artists of the Book of Hours as Gerard Horenbout of Ghent and Simon, eldest son of Alexander Bening (18); the atelier which produced the MS was strongly influenced by the work of Hugo van der Goes (16–17), and the picture of James IV at prayer (24v) has affinities with the portrait of James III in the Trinity Altarpiece. The Royal Arms are at fol. 14v; the picture of Margaret Tudor at prayer is at 243v (see figs. 2, 5, 6). It is surprising that, at least so far as the contemporary records suggest, no pageant of St. Margaret was included in Margaret Tudor's entry into Edinburgh, such as had greeted Catherine of Aragon in her entry into London in 1501. See Anglo, "London Pageants," 56–58, and Kingsford, ed., *Chronicles of London,* 234–36. A pageant of St. Margaret met Margaret of Anjou in her entry to London in 1445; see Robert Withington, *English Pageantry:* 148, and Sydney Anglo, *Spectacle, Pageantry, and Early Tudor Policy* (Oxford: Clarendon Press, 1969), 54–56.

17 Bishop Elphinstone's *Aberdeen Breviary,* as Macfarlane notes, deliberately highlighted "the importance of national saints like Andrew, Ninian, Columba and Queen Margaret" (*William Elphinstone,* 244). James Foullis wrote a Sapphic ode in praise of St. Margaret; for an edition, see IJsewijn and Thomson, "Latin Poems," 123–26. IJsewijn and Thomson comment that "it may be noticed that when Foullis was writing it, another Margaret (Tudor) was queen of Scotland" (144).

18 Buchanan, *Margaret Tudor,* 57.

19 Mackie notes that "the anxiety of each monarch that his own—and his neighbour's—subjects should be fully aware of the importance of the occasion" is attested in the Treasurer's Accounts, which show, for example, that "as early as September of the previous year [1501] messengers had been despatched from Edinburgh to warn the gentlemen of the southern shires to provide themselves with festal attire 'agane the marriage.' In the Castle . . . fifteen armourers . . . were now hard at work. The armourers came from France; from Middleburg in Flanders came merchants bringing with them the chairs of state, the tapestries, the silver plate, velvets, satins, damasks, taffetas, furs, and cloth of gold, which the King had commissioned them to buy in Bruges. The plate, the chairs, and the tapestries, including 'ane pece of Hercules, ane pece of Marcus Corianus, tua pecis of Susanna sewit togiddir, ane covir for ane bed of Susanna, ane pece of Salamon' were destined for his new palace of Holyroodhouse, where he was even now hurrying on the construction of a chapel and a forework or barbican. To the plenishing of the palace, too, went some of the velvet and cloth of gold. Red and 'purple-blue' velvet, costing £369, was used for the hangings of the Queen's chamber, seventy-seven and a quarter ells of cloth of gold, costing £386.5.0 were required for the canopy and curtains of her bed of state; there was cloth of gold to the value of more than

£200 in each of the canopies of state provided for herself and her husband, and for fourteen cushions, some of blue and red velvet, some of crimson and cloth of gold, the Treasurer had to disburse £172.7.0. But most of the rich stuffs went to adorn the persons of the King and the members of his household. The King, for example, had provided himself with two gowns of cloth of gold lined with fur, each costing more than £600; of his eleven pages five were to wear with their new tawny satin doublets and crimson hose coats half of cloth of gold and half of blue velvet, and six coats of blue damask or of blue velvet only; his master cook was presented with a gown of velvet lined with fur, a doublet of crimson satin, and black hose, and his horse was caparisoned with cloth of gold at a cost of £63." Mackie, *King James IV,* 102–3. A fuller summary may be found in *LHTA* 2:liii–lxxiii.

20 Mackie, *King James IV,* 103.

21 The items on alchemy are summarized in *LHTA* 2:lxxiii–lxxix. James IV's interest in alchemy has not often enough been appreciated as an aspect of his interest in scientific experimentation in general, nor has the significance of its link to his marriage and the alliance with England. For example, of John Damien, who seems to have become chief alchemist at James's court (see *LHTA* 2:lxxvi–lxxviii), Wormald writes: "The question has been asked whether it is possible that the attempt by James IV's protegé, John Damien de Falcusis, abbot of Tongland, to fly from the battlements of Stirling castle is an echo of the world of Leonardo da Vinci. Such was the interest in what was happening in Europe that the answer may well be yes, although it then has to be admitted that nothing more typifies the prosaic nature of Scottish society; Damien neither flew nor died a dramatic death, but dropped gracelessly down into a midden, from which he picked himself up and complained that he had been cheated, for the feathers of hens which 'covet the myddyng and not the skyis' had been infiltrated into the wings of eagles' feathers which should have borne him aloft. Yet Damien's farcical leap into the limelight hardly does justice to the sheer exuberance of Scottish cultural and intellectual life in the late fifteenth and early sixteenth centuries." Jenny Wormald, *Court, Kirk, and Community: Scotland, 1470–1625* (London: Edward Arnold, 1981) 56. It is true that Dunbar's own satiric treatment of John Damien (see "Ane Ballat of the Fenyeit Freir of Tungland," Kinsley, ed., *Dunbar,* no. 161) suggests a desire on the part at least of one contemporary to deflate alchemical pretensions; and the tradition of commentary which Wormald here exemplifies may also have been inspired partly by the increasing distrust of alchemy and of "superstition" in general in the early modern period (see criticisms of Damien in Leslie, *Historie of Scotland* [1890], 124–25) and of witchcraft. Still, while James IV may never have found the philosopher's stone and Damien may never have flown, the transformation, at the time of the wedding, of Edinburgh into a paradise full of figures from Christian and Greek mythology hardly exemplifies "the prosaic nature of Scottish society."

22 Macfarlane writes of James's "constant and remorseless" demands for "fiscal innovations" that "it all began with his wedding to Margaret Tudor in 1503, when £6,125 was spent on the festivities alone between 7 August and 6 September, out of the total annual expenditure of £11,412. . . . By the end of his reign his household expenses had doubled. . . . This was the price he was prepared to pay to court the popularity of his subjects, and take his rightful place, as he thought, among the monarchs and princes of Europe" (*William Elphinstone,* 419). Macdougall's chapter "Money and Power" (*James IV,* 146–69) also stresses the link between James

IV's marriage and his financial needs and ambitions; Macdougall notes the expenses of "the quest for an alliance and a foreign bride" in the early years of James's reign and describes Margaret's dowry as "the greatest single financial windfall of the reign" (147). "But the King, increasingly committed to his naval programmes, to meeting the costs of war in the Isles in 1504-6, and to the renovation or rebuilding of royal castles and palaces – not to mention the 'one-off' expense of a lavish wedding . . . began to treat [Margaret's dowry payments] . . . as normal revenue. After 1505, when the . . . payments ceased, James IV required urgently to find further sources of income" (155).

23 Roy Strong's comments on the court festival seem apposite: "In the court festival the Renaissance belief in man's ability to control his own destiny and harness the natural resources of the universe find their [sic] most extreme assertion. . . . they celebrate man's total comprehension of the laws of nature" (*Splendor at Court*, 76).

On the question of the innovativeness of the Edinburgh pageants, Withington writes that "mythological characters do not appear in English pageants before the sixteenth century, and then – to use a Celticism – they are found in Scotland. *The Judgment of Paris* welcomed the daughter of Henry VII to Edinburgh in 1503; and twenty years later Udall used the same theme in welcoming Anne Boleyn to London. We shall see that this became a very important element in pageantry; I suggest it came to England from France, through Scotland" (*English Pageantry*, 81). Neither the wedding of James II in 1449 to Mary of Gueldres nor of James III to Margaret of Denmark involved elaborate pageantry. Gordon Kipling's forthcoming book on medieval royal entries documents the rich history and shared conventions of such celebrations; but while the Edinburgh pageants of 1503 are clearly part of a tradition, there is also an ambitiousness to them that requires analysis. (I thank Kipling for providing me with a copy of his fifth chapter "Assumpt Aboue the Heuenly Ierarchie.")

24 Buchanan, *Margaret Tudor*, 18. Buchanan's supposition is supported by the particular attention given to the role played by the earl of Northumberland in conducting Margaret through the north, and to her stay in York, by the *Fyancells*. She was accompanied throughout the entire journey by a large entourage led by the earl and countess of Surrey; a number of dignitaries met her on her way, not all of whom continued on to Edinburgh. The riskiness of the confrontations of extraordinary marriage is well illustrated by the fact that the earl of Surrey also led the forces of Margaret's brother against James at Flodden.

25 Ferguson, *Scotland's Relations with England*, 34–35. In "Foreign Relations," Macdougall discusses those "victorious rebels" who, upon the death of James III at Sauchieburn in 1488, declared that the king had been responsible for "the inbringing of Inglissmen to the perpetuale subieccione of the realm" (111, citing *APS* 2:210). He also criticizes the discarding of James III's policy of rapprochement with England "in favour of a reversion to dubious foreign adventures by the young James IV" (111). It makes sense that the rebels' need to unify Scotland and certify James IV's right to the throne would take the form of linking James III to the old enemy, particularly since James IV depended so heavily on the support of southern magnates in his bid for the throne. Macfarlane, *William Elphinstone*, emphasizes the role of James's marriage to Margaret in quelling, at least for a time, "the restless Anglophobia of some of his Border magnates" and in helping James to establish "a united kingdom" (235).

26 Macdougall, in *James IV*, notes "the perennial difficulty of keeping the peace on
    the borders, where violent infringements of the treaty were part of life, and part
    also of the normal give-and-take of Scottish diplomacy" (256). He also notes the
    symbolism of James's leading, in August and early September 1504, a large host
    to the West March to join Lord Dacre, the English warden, in a "punitive raid on
    Eskdale" (251).

27 That the king himself may have jousted after the wedding is suggested by the num-
    bers of entries in the Treasurer's Accounts for "harnessingis for the King," "ane
    armyng sword," "ane lang riding suord," "ane gilt dagar deliverit to the King," and
    so forth (*LHTA* 2:206–7).

28 Tufte, *Poetry of Marriage*, notes that "a car of some kind . . . had long been a fea-
    ture of pagan epithalamia as a conveyance for the bride in procession or for Venus
    en route to weddings," and the chariot returns in the medieval epithalamium as
    transportation for Brides of the Church and other Christian dignitaries (78). Younge's
    Fyancells give the following account: at Colieweston, "the Qwene was richly drest,
    mounted upon a faire Palfrey, and before her rode Sir Davy Owen, during all the
    sayd Voyage, richly appoynted. Thre Fotemen wer allwayes ny hyr varey honestly
    appoynted, and had in their Jaketts browdered Portecollys. After her was convayed
    in Hand by a Gentlemen, one Palfrey vary richly drest, till that Sir Thomas Wor-
    teley came to hyr, the wich was ordonned Master of hyr Hors, and who from hens-
    forth fullfilled the Office abouff sayde. Next after was convayed by two Fotemen
    arayd as the others, one varey riche Lytere borne by two faire Coursers varey nobly
    drest. In the wich Litere the sayd Qwene was borne in the Intryng of the goods
    Townes, or otherways to her good Playsur. Then came the Ladyes mounted upon
    fayre Pallefrays, Many Sqyers before them, and non others. Of the wich was a
    fair Sight, and nobly they were beseene. Following came a Char richly drest, with
    six fayre Horsys leyd and convayd by thre Men, in the wich were iiij Ladyes, last-
    inge the sayd Voyage" (267). For the crossing into Scotland, see 279–82.

29 A number of persons in Margaret's entourage went with her all the way to Scot-
    land, some even remaining there with her, but many went only part of the way,
    and many joined her at points along the way. Her master of horse, Sir Thomas
    Worteley, for example, joined her three miles before "Sirowsby (a Manayr of
    the . . . Archbyshop of Yorke) . . . compayned of his Folks in his Liveray, . . . to
    the Nomber of xxv Horsys" (Younge, *Fyancells*, 269). The earl of Kent and the
    lords of Strange, Hastings, and Willoughby, were among those who conveyed Mar-
    garet as far as York (266). Representatives of places — sheriffs, burgesses, proces-
    sions of religious — met her outside their towns and abbeys, sometimes at gates
    and at bridges; at Grantham, for example, "Halfe Way before hyr came Sir Robert
    Dymock, Knight, Sheriff of the County of Lincoln, honestly accompayned of xxx
    Horses well arayd of his Liveray, and salved the Quene, holdyng a whyt Rod in
    his Haund, the wich hee bered before hyr, lastyng the sayd County of Lyncoln,
    as the other Sheriffs did here afterward in their Counties" (268).

30 "The XIth Day of the sayd Monneth the sayd Quene departed from Newerke, hyr
    noble Trayne befor hyr from better to better rychly drest; and the sayd Bally, Bour-
    ges, and Habitaunts conveyed her out of their Franchises, and ther they toke ther
    Leve" (Younge, *Fyancells*, 269).

31 Strong, *Splendor at Court*, 23.

32 Marfarlane, *William Elphinstone*, explains that James III's authority was restricted
    by the Boyds and their followers, who "seized him after the Exchequer Audit at

Linlithgow in July 1466 and kept him in Edinburgh until his marriage to Margaret . . . of Denmark . . . in July 1469" (155). Nicholson points out, "When the vessels that had brought James III's bride to Scotland anchored in the Forth, the ship of the Earl of Arran had been boarded by the Lady Mary, who bore her husband such tidings of her brother the king that Arran hoisted sail and sped back to Denmark with his wife. His precaution was well justified: when parliament met in Edinburgh in November 1469 its members not only witnessed the queen's coronation but heard charges of treason against the Boyds" (Scotland, 418).

33   Nicholson, Scotland, 554.

34   Mackie, King James IV, 94. Mackie has stressed in his account of the wedding the difficulties posed by James's sexual adventurism: an earlier mistress poisoned, a "brood of illegitimate children," another mistress secluded at Darnaway (100, 94). Dunbar's The Thrissill and the Rois apparently refers to James's promiscuity as well; Nature counsels the thistle to put the rose above all others (see below, chap. 8). Buchanan, Margaret Tudor, 37–38, reports the story that James had contemplated marrying one of his earliest mistresses, Lady Margaret Drummond; Margaret Drummond died a little over a year before James's wedding to Margaret, poisoned "along with her two sisters" possibly "by the Kennedys, the family of James's next mistress, Lady Jane Bothwell," to whom by the time of the wedding James had given Darnaway Castle as a residence. Pedro de Ayala writes: "When he [James IV] was a minor he was instigated by those who held the government to do some dishonourable things. They favoured his love intrigues with their relatives, in order to keep him in their subjection. As soon as he came of age, and understood his duties, he gave up these intrigues. When I arrived, he was keeping a lady with great state in a castle. He visited her from time to time. Afterwards he sent her to the house of her father, who is a knight, and married her. He did the same with another lady, by whom he had a son. It may be about a year since he gave up, so at least it is believed, his lovemaking, as well from fear of God as from fear of scandal in this world, which is thought very much of here. I can say with truth that he esteems himself as much as though he were lord of the world." P. Hume Brown, Early Travellers in Scotland (Edinburgh: D. Douglas, 1891), 41. Ayala seems to have been trying to present James to the Spanish court in a flattering light; but still it is interesting to note his association of James's love "intrigues" with youth and with his "subjection" to others. When he possesses himself fully, is fully sovereign, he renounces them (though in fact he did not).

35   Douglas does likewise in the "Thirteenth Book" of the Eneados; of the wedding night of Eneas and Lavinia, he writes, "Bot for to telling quhou with torch lycht / Thai went to chalmer, and syne to bed at nycht, / Myne author list na mensioun tharof draw: / Na mair will I, for sik thingis bene knaw; / All ar expert, eftir new mariage, / On the first nycht quhat suld be the subcharge" (ll. 15–20).

36   Buchanan writes, in Margaret Tudor, that the king's surprise visit was "not . . . entirely spontaneous. . . . All chivalric romances told how the eager monarch and his retinue would go disguised as a hunting party and intercept the path of his intended" (23).

   Discussing an epithalamium addressed to the Virgin Mary by Conrad of Hirschau, Tufte notes that "there is a suggestion of the personification which produced the fantastic bird courts of the medieval love paradise" (Poetry of Marriage, 83). Birds were an important part of the epithalamic tradition, partly because of the doves of Venus in the pagan epithalamium and partly because of the Song of Songs.

37 It is not clear from the *Fyancells* whether the conclusion of this pageant was to become the subject of one of the later jousts in Edinburgh. The two knights involved were Patrick Hamilton and Patrick Sinclair, and they are mentioned as among those who jousted after the wedding (see Younge, *Fyancells,* 298), but the plot of their initial encounter is not mentioned again.

38 The episode of the hart-hunting which takes place at the same time as the tournament likewise seems to stage, for the "grett Multitude of People" that had come to see the entourage before its entry into Edinburgh, the need to interleave peace with danger: "A Mylle from Dacquick [Dalkeith] the Kynge sent to the Qwene, by a Gentylman, a grett tame Hart for to have a Corse; bot because the Kynge was ny, the Erle of Surrey answerd, that the said Hert should be brought ageyn toward the Kynge, that they myght both be at the said Course, and so it was doon" (Young, *Fyancells,* 286–87). "Half a Mylle from thens [the meadow in which the tournament took place] was the said Hert, the wich the Kynge caused to be losed, and put a Greyhond after hym that maid a fayr Course; bot the said Hert wanne the Towne, and went to hys Repayre" (289).

39 Apparently it was not unusual for princes to delay coronation of spouses until well after their entries, often until first pregnancy, particularly if the marriage were a dangerous one (Gordon Kipling, personal communication). In Scotland, however, there were precedents for the early coronation of royal brides; Nicholson notes that Mary of Gueldres, married to James II in 1449 in Holyrood Abbey, "was crowned shortly afterwards" (*Scotland,* 348).

40 Pitscottie, *Historie of Scotland,* chap. 9, p. 240. Buchanan notes that James and Margaret undertook their first long journey together in September 1503; Linlithgow, one of Margaret's dower houses (as was Stirling), was their first stop (*Margaret Tudor,* 43).

41 Dunbar's poem "To Aberdein" ("Blyth Aberdeane, thow beriall of all tounis") describes a reception of Margaret there in 1511: she was greeted by the burgesses of the town; four men bore a pall of velvet above her head; artillery was shot; pageants included a Salutation of the Virgin, the Three Kings, the expulsion of Adam and Eve from paradise, and one celebrating the Stewart dynasty and featuring "the Bruce that evir was bold in stour" (Kinsley, ed., *Dunbar,* pp. 135–37, no. 48). The 1511 pageants at Aberdeen were more traditionally medieval in theme than were the Edinburgh pageants of 1503. Gordon Kipling argues that the Aberdeen show, with its pageants of the Expulsion from Paradise and of the "dreidful" Bruce, "suggests the possibility of hostility toward the queen, as if the city wanted to limit severely the queen's role and influence in the kingdom . . . at a time of increasing Anglo-Scottish tension" ("Assumpt Aboue the Heuenly Ierarchie"). Kipling's analysis helpfully points out the potential for ambiguity in such pageantry, but tends too readily to view queens' entries as monovocal lessons teaching queens the dangers of presumption.

42 *LHTA* 2:347, referring to the "Erle of Bothuiles band." For the marriage contract, see *Edinburgh Burgh Recs.* 1:93–94, 25 January 1501/2.

43 *LHTA* 2:401, 390, 313. Watson, ed., *Roll of Edinburgh Burgesses and Guild-Brethren,* 259, lists a James Homyll as merchant-burgess and son and heir of father on 8 December 1500, and a James Homyll again as burgess and heir of father for January 1500/1501. The James Homyll mentioned in the Treasurer's Accounts was likely a merchant-burgess, as reference is made to six dozen Flemish "lang silkin pointis" and a Flemish "pair of pantonis of wellus" "brocht hame by James Homyll" (*LHTA*

2:212). A number of other town-dwellers are mentioned in the Treasurer's Accounts at the time preparatory to the wedding. William Foular, probably the William Fouller listed as merchant-burgess in January 1500/1501 (Watson, 191) provided books for the king and "glasses" (*LHTA* 2:359, 365). Andrew Myllar, later of the Chepman and Myllar press, did likewise; Walter Chepman was dressed by the royal treasury in five ells of English cloth at the cost of eight pounds and ten shillings (*LHTA* 2:364, 313). William Hoppar sold a chest for the king's wardrobe (*LHTA* 2:391; Watson, 260). Thomas Ramsay provided six "gret sadilles" costing eighteen pounds (*LHTA* 2:207; Watson, 413). Robert Rind, burgess and member of the town council, provided "ane hat to the King" (*LHTA* 2:212; *Edinburgh Burgh Recs.* 1:63, 89, 107). John Stewart sold taffeta for traverses for both the king and queen (*LHTA* 2:213); Watson, 472, lists two different John Stewarts, a guild-brother entered on 7 December 1493 and a merchant-burgess entered at the request of William Elphinstone, bishop of Aberdeen, on 8 December 1500.

44 *LHTA* 2:270, refers to entries for "sums received" from Lauder "to the werk of Halyrudhous"; "William Tothrik, burges of Edinburgh," is recorded as having been paid the large sum of just over thirty-one pounds for "rachteris . . . to the werk of Halyrudhous" (274). References to Lauder and Todrik can be found in *Edinburgh Burgh Recs.* 1:271–72. George Corntoun also seems to have been involved in provisioning the work at Holyrood (see *LHTA* 2:276, 280); a George Cornentoun the younger, "indweller" of Leith, got into trouble in 1493 for not paying dues to Edinburgh (*Charters, Edinburgh* 1:172, no. 56, 28 October 1493).

45 Brown is mentioned in *LHTA* 2:271, 272. It is difficult to trace crafts, since they were mentioned by name in the burgess rolls only for a special reason. For Jok Steill, see *LHTA* 2:122; the Taylors' Seal of Cause is dated 26 August 1500 (*Edinburgh Burgh Recs.* 1:82).

46 *LHTA* 2:344, 355. The first payment is recorded for 9 October 1502; the second for 13 January 1502. The Treasurer's Accounts refer, after the wedding was over, "to the cartaris of Leith brocht the Quenis gere to Edinburgh fra Dalketh" (386); "to vj men that bure the Inglis coffir fra the Abbay to the Castell of Edinburgh" (386); "to the cartaris of Leith for carying away of the Inglismennis gere" (388); again "to the cartaris of Leith that brocht the Inglis Thesauraris chareot to Linlithqw fra Edinburgh" (397). But none of these entries refer to labor performed for the Edinburgh pageants themselves.

47 For example, "to Beg, to pas with the Kingis lettrez to the Erle of Mortoun and the Maister of Angus to warne thair ladyis agayne the cummyng of the Quene" (*LHTA* 2:379); on the same page, "to David Tempilman to pas in the Westland, to warne of the ladyis for the cummyng of the Quene," and "to Beg, to pas with the Kingis lettrez to warne the Countess Marschell and the Lady Glammys for the Quenis cummyng."

48 "Jhone of Burgoune" is mentioned in *Edinburgh Burgh Recs.* 1:79, as having served on the assise of April 1500; for the reference to the "madin," see *LHTA* 2:391.

49 *Edinburgh Burgh Recs.* 1:111.

50 See Jean Jacquot, ed., *Les Fêtes de la Renaissance* (Paris: Centre National de la Recherche Scientifique, 1961), 15. Jacquot's introduction to this collection raises the question of "la fonction des arts dans un société comme moyen de communion entre ses membres et de participation à des mythes, à des croyances qui renforcent les institutions et contribuent à leur assurer une continuité" (10). "Toute fête princière a deux aspects: la réjouissance publique à laquelle le peuple s'associe, qui

se déroule dans la rue, sous la forme d'un cortège; la réjouissance réservée aux privilégiés, qui se déroule dans un palais, son parc ou ses jardins" (10–11). Royal entries "supposent la participation de toute une cité à la réception d'un monarque. Et lorsqu'il s'agit d'une capitale, c'est toute la nation que la cité est censée représenter. . . . Le pouvoir monarchique se donne en spectacle à la cité; la cité se donne en spectacle au souverain – et à elle-même car elle prend alors conscience de son unité, de son harmonie dans la diversité des responsabilités, des rangs, des professions. Les sentiments de fidélité et de protection, l'idée de concorde nécessaire au travail pacifique et à la prospérité ne s'expriment pas seulement dans un cortège solennel aux costumes éclatants et accompagné de musique, mais par des décors, des tableaux vivants commentés par des devises ou des discours" (11). The question of "d'ou vient l'initiative premiere, et comment s'organise une collaboration entre les representants des pouvoirs publics et les diverses categories d'artistes employes" (13) is indeed an interesting one, but unfortunately in the case of Edinburgh it is also an exceedingly difficult one. If Dunbar's *The Thrissill and the Rois* was presented at the time of the wedding, it probably was part of the "rejouissance réservée aux privilégiés, qui se déroule dans un palais, son parc ou ses jardins" and not part of the royal entry itself. Dunbar may have been the author of the poem "Now fayre, fayrest off every fayre," which Mackie suggests may have been sung by the angels that greeted Margaret at the Edinburgh gate (Mackie, *King James IV,* 109), but both the authorship of the poem and its place in the wedding festivities are uncertain. Its comparative simplicity may indicate its appropriateness for a progress, however. The poem is discussed at p. 109.

51 Anglo, *Spectacle,* 23–24, citing *York Civic Records,* ed. Angelo Raine, vol. 1 ([printed for the] Yorkshire Archaeological Society, 1939), 156. Anglo notes the affinities of the York pageant with *The Thrissill and the Rois;* see also Bawcutt, "Dunbar's Use of the Symbolic Lion and Thistle," 84. Anglo comments that "the word *lowte* signifies the act of stooping or making obeisance – an idea repeated in William Dunbar's *The Thistle and the Rose* where all flowers acknowledge the supremacy of the rose" (24). The source of the rose symbol cited is Bartholomaeus Anglicus's *De Proprietatibus Rerum.*

52 Anglo, *Spectacle,* 23–24.

53 The full description of the Edinburgh pageants is in Younge, *Fyancells,* 289–90.

54 William Mackay Mackenzie, ed., *The Poems of William Dunbar* (Edinburgh: Porpoise Press, 1932), pp. 178–79, no. 89, ll. 1–4. Mackenzie's note, following Laing, remarks that "above the words [in the manuscript] are the notes of a musical setting, but only of one of several parts and that part not the melody" (231). The poem continues:

> Younge tender plant of pulcritud,
> Descendyd of Imperyalle blude;
> Freshe fragrant floure of fayrehede shene,
> Welcum of Scotland to be Quene!
>
> Swet lusty lusum lady clere,
> Most myghty kyngis dochter dere,
> Borne of a princes most serene,
> Welcum of Scotland to be Quene!

Welcum the Rose bothe rede and whyte,
Welcum the floure of oure delyte!
Oure secrete rejoysyng frome the sone beme,
Welcum of Scotland to be Quene;
Welcum of Scotlande to be Quene!

55 Anglo notes that in Bartholomaeus Anglicus's *De Proprietatibus Rerum*, on which
    the creators of the York pageant relied, the chapter on the rose says: "Among alle
    floures of the worlde the floure of the rose is cheyf and beeryth the pryce. And
    therfore ofte the cheyf partye of man: the heed is crownyd wyth floure of roses
    as Plinius sayth. And by cause of vertues and swete smelle and sauour, for by
    fayrnesse they fede the syghte: and playseth the smelle by odour, and the towche
    by nesshe and softe handlynge" (*Spectacle*, 24, citing Trevisa's translation, Lib. XVII,
    cxxxvi [Westminster: Wynkyn de Worde, c. 1495]).

56 Withington, *English Pageantry*, 169, notes that Young's phrasing ("Deessys," "Mer-
    cure") may indicate a French origin for the pageant but may also simply be French
    forms natural to a herald.

57 Withington, *English Pageantry*, 169, says that it is first used in Margaret's 1503
    progress, but Anglo notes an earlier instance in 1496, for Joanna of Castile's entry
    into Brussels. Anglo, *Spectacle*, 255, citing Max Herrmann, *Forschungen zur
    deutschen Theatergeschichte des Mittelalters und der Renaissance* (Berlin: Weid-
    man, 1914), 391.

58 See Anglo, *Spectacle*, 255–56, for discussion of this pageant in Anne's entry, and
    John D. Reeves, "The Judgment of Paris as a Device of Tudor Flattery," *Notes and
    Queries* 199 (1954): 7.

59 Anglo, *Spectacle*, 256. This is not among Anglo's favorite pageants, owing to what
    he considers to be its repetitious emphasis on Anne's peerlessness, its vulgar obses-
    sion with her fertility, and its lack of the kind of learning displayed by the pag-
    eants for Catherine of Aragon's entry. The show is in fact an extremely interesting
    one, partly for these very reasons; like the York pageant for Henry VII, it is very
    close to the bone, for not only was Anne's claim to queenship weak and the need
    for an heir strong but Henry had only recently declared England an empire and
    broken from the Church of Rome. Moreover, Anglo seems to understand neither
    the import of the show's struggle to create belief in the peerlessness of a queen
    who had recently replaced a once-peerless predecessor, nor the function of repeti-
    tion in assisting such a crisis of belief.

60 Reeves, "Judgment of Paris," 7–8. Other instances include John Lyly's Latin poem
    "Iouis Elizabeth" in *Euphues and his England*, in which Elizabeth sums up the quali-
    ties of Juno, Minerva, and Venus (8); and George Kirbye's 1601 madrigal in honor
    of Queen Elizabeth: "Her apple Venus yields as best befitting / A Queen beloved
    most dearly" (printed as no. 20 in Thomas Morley's *Madrigales: the Triumphes
    of Oriana*, ll. 3–4; Reeves, "Judgment of Paris," 11, citing Edmund H. Fellowes,
    ed., *English Madrigal Verse, 1588–1632*, 2d ed. [Oxford: Clarendon Press, 1929],
    150).

61 Henry G. Lesnick, "The Structural Significance of Myth and Flattery in Peele's *Ar-
    raignment of Paris*," *Studies in Philology* 65 (1968): 169.

62 Margaret J. Ehrhart, *The Judgment of the Trojan Prince Paris in Medieval Litera-
    ture* (Philadelphia: University of Pennsylvania Press, 1987), 195.

63 Ibid., 174–75.

64 Ibid., 180–83. For Convenenvole, Paris's judgment forsakes "brilliance of light" and "ancestral good" for the pit of filth that is Venus; Convenenvole's language is full of images of poison and decay. An example of the association of Medea with witchcraft is Guido de Columnis's *Historia Destructionis Troiae*, which makes the Judgment occur on Friday, a day of bad luck; at noon, "traditionally the time of day when demonic influence was at its greatest"; and on 24 June, the summer solstice, St. John the Baptist's Day, when witches were believed to come abroad. Guido's goddesses are also nude, and nudity, Ehrhart says, was also traditionally associated with witches. Guido implies that Paris "places his trust in a devilish delusion, and thus the stage is set for the fall of Troy" (49).

65 Ibid., 41–42, citing Rachel Bromwich, "Celtic Dynastic Themes and the Breton Lays," *Études Celtiques* 9 (1961): 453.

66 Gordon Kipling's discussion of the 1503 pageants stresses the Edinburgh Judgment's greater interest "in Paris' choice (as an analogy of the king's choice of bride) than in the queen's good qualities. . . . Paris' choice of Venus [is linked] with God's choosing of Mary to be his mother and bride" ("Assumpt Aboue the Heuenly Ierarchie"). For the phrase "in the end beautiful," see p. 255.

67 Ehrhart, *Judgment*, 92.

68 Lesnick, "Myth and Flattery," 169.

69 Nohrnberg, *Analogy of the Faerie Queene*, 722–23 nn. 142–43; in n. 143 Nohrnberg cites material on Elizabeth as the fourth Grace, including Spenser's "Aprill" in *The Shepheardes Calendar*. He also notes the inclusion of a pageant of the Graces along with the pageant of the Judgment in Anne Boleyn's entry into London. He notes, too, Spenser's attribution of his life, in the seventy-fourth *Amoretti*, "to three women: his mother, his sovereign, and his wife. They have given him 'guifts of body, fortune and of mind.' These ought," says Nohrnberg, "to be the gifts of the three goddesses, but in fact Spenser calls his benefactors the three graces" (723). "A comparison of Paris' three goddesses to the three Graces is . . . plausible iconography" (469).

70 "Diuine resemblance, beauty soueraine rare, / Firme Chastity, that spight ne blemish dare; / All which she with such courtesie doth grace / That all her peres cannot with her compare" (6.10.27; Nohrnberg, *Analogy of the Faerie Queene*, 728).

71 Bruno writes: "Now it happens that here there are three species of beauty, although all three are found in each of the three goddesses; for Venus is not deficient in wisdom and majesty, and Juno is not wanting in beauty and wisdom any more than Athena is wanting in majesty and beauty. Nevertheless, in each of the three goddesses one of these qualities happens to surpass the others and for that reason is considered proper to her." Nohrnberg, *Analogy of the Faerie Queene*, 469, citing Giordano Bruno, *Heroic Frenzies*, I.v.11, trans. Paul Eugene Memmo (Chapel Hill: University of North Carolina Press, 1964), 167f.

72 Ehrhart cites Hyginus's *Fabulae* as an important source for this tradition and mentions also the work of the Stoic Chrysippos; the contrasts between the three goddesses could be reduced to a contrast between Pallas and Venus, virtue and pleasure (*Judgment*, 5–6, 15–16). The *Mythologies* of Fabius Planciades Fulgentius, a Latin Christian writer of the fifth and sixth centuries, opens with a treatment of the Judgment that is critical of both the active and the voluptuous life (*Judgment*, 23–25).

73 *The Kingis Quair* is discussed at greater length in chap. 8; Lydgate's *Temple of Glass* is one of its chief sources. See Ehrhart, *Judgment*, 14–16, on the theme of

the "choice among three modes of life" in classical allegoresis; for the *Espinette amoureuse,* see pp. 149–50. Ehrhart also establishes the importance of the Judgment of Paris to the *Speculum principiis* tradition and to the literature of honor and chivalry; see her discussion of the *Echecs amoureux* (117, 151–54) and of Christine de Pisan's *Epitre d'Othéa* (117–21). Both in the *Echecs amoureux* and Lydgate's *Reson and Sensuallyte* Nature figures as an important personage, as she will in *The Thrissill and the Rois;* see Ehrhart, 157–61. Ehrhart notes the indebtedness of the presentation of Nature in the *Echecs amoureux* to Alain de Lille's *De planctu naturae* and to the *Roman de la Rose.*

74 Nohrnberg, *Analogy of The Faerie Queene,* 671; for Calidore's relation to Paris, see 722–23 nn. 142–43.

75 Mill, *Mediaeval Plays in Scotland,* 71–74, discusses the evidence for Corpus Christi plays in Edinburgh.

76 Quotation from Andrew Marvell, "An Horatian Ode upon Cromwell's Return from Ireland," in *The Complete Poems,* ed. Elizabeth Story Donno (Harmondsworth, Eng.: Penguin Books, 1972), l. 10.

77 Wakefield Annunciation, ll. 143–48. In the Wakefield play, as well as in the *Ludus Coventriae* play of "The Betrothal of Mary," Joseph's consent is also of importance, both in bringing about his marriage to Mary and in consenting to continuance of the marriage after he discovers that she is with child. He must overcome his reservations about his age: "I haue be maydon evyr *and* evyr more wele ben / I chaungyd not ȝet of all my long lyff / *and* now to be maryed sum man wold wen / it is a straunge thynge / An old man to take a ȝonge wyff" (*Ludus Coventriae,* ll. 179–82). Joseph's resistance to change, like his tarrying behind in the presentation of his rod ("I xal a-byde be-hynde preuyly / now wolde god I were at hom in my cote / I am aschamyd to be seyn veryly" [ll. 200–202]), is a form of obduracy; his reluctance to mingle youth with age is a version of his incredulity, in the Wakefield play, regarding the possibility that Mary's pregnancy might be the result of angelic visitation: "A hevenly thing, forsothe, is he, / And she is erthly; this may not be" (ll. 296–97). In Wakefield, Joseph is at the opposite end of the reproductive spectrum from God's superreal creativity: "I am old, sothly to say. / Passed I am all prevay play; / The gams fro me ar gane. / It is ill cowpled, of youth and elde, / I wote well, for I am unwelde; / Som othere has she tane" (ll. 167–72). Joseph's creaturely consent to divine "alteration" makes possible the flowering of his rod, and in Wakefield, his belief in the Annunciation becomes the ground for the enduring force of his marriage to Mary: "He that may both lowse and binde, / And every mis amend, / Leyn me grace, powere, and might / My wife and hir swete yong wight / To kepe, to my lifys ende" (ll. 369–73).

78 "Uniting . . . [entails] sacrilegious violence, which breaks the natural order of things to impose on them the counter-natural order which defines culture." Bourdieu, *Outline of a Theory of Practice,* 127.

79 In a remark intriguing with respect to *The Parliament of Fowls* and Dunbar's *The Thrissill and the Rois,* Bourdieu notes that the meal of blood-alliance "proclaims the specifically human (i.e., male) order of the oath of loyalty against nostalgia for the struggle of all against all, . . . embodied in the jackal (or woman, the source of division) and his sacrilegious cunning. Like the natural world, within whose domesticated fertility lie the only half-tamed forces of a wild nature (those embodied and exploited by the old witch), the social order sprung from the oath which

tears the assembly of men from the disorder of individual interests remains haunted by consciously repressed nostalgia for the state of nature" (*Outline of a Theory of Practice*, 136).

80 Marvell, "Horatian Ode," l. 12.

81 Anglo, *Spectacle*, 355. Anglo notes that "it was in the pageants for Elizabeth that the notion was fully developed, with Virtues pertinent to the contemporary English situation trampling upon equally relevant Vices. This last conceit had not hitherto been employed in English pageantry – though it was an ancient iconographic tradition, and had made an interesting appearance in Edinburgh in 1503" (355). Withington, *English Pageantry*, notes a 1427 mumming of Lydgate's which included "dame *fortune* dame *prudence* / dame *rightwysnesse* / and dame *ffortitudo*" (107; Add. MS 29729, fol. 140); the Virtues also appeared in Margaret of Anjou's 1456 entry at Coventry (149), and Prudence spoke to Henry VII in his 1486 entry into Bristol (160). Emile Mâle discusses the representation of Prudence at Paris, Chartres, Auxerre, and Amiens in *The Gothic Image: Religious Art in France of the Thirteenth Century*, trans. Dora Nussey (New York: Harper and Row, 1972), 120; Fortitude is discussed at 121–22. In these representations the Virtues are linked with their Vices (Fortitude with Cowardice, Prudence with Folly). He gives a brief summary of the history of the Four Virtues in Christian thought at 110–11. On *The Marriage of Mercury and Philology*, see Tufte, *Poetry of Marriage*, 70; Discord and Sedition must be expelled, and Philology raised to the level of a deity, before Jove decides to permit the marriage.

82 Anglo, *Spectacle*, 257, citing Edward Hall, *The Union of the two noble and illustre Famelies of Lancastre and Yorke*, ed. Henry Ellis (London, 1809), 801. See also Withington, *English Pageantry*, 184 n. 4.

83 Strong, *Splendor at Court*, 25.

84 Samuel C. Chew, *The Virtues Reconciled: An Iconographic Study* (Toronto: University of Toronto Press, 1947), 93, 143 n. 72: "The 'Rainbow' portrait of Queen Elizabeth at Hatfield, attributed by some authorities to Federigo Zuccaro and by others to Marcus Gheeraerts the Elder. It is reproduced in E. M. Tenison, *Elizabethan England*, III (1933), Frontispiece, and less satisfactorily in *The Connoisseur*, CXVIII (1944), 73, fig. 6.–The fact that Jealousy may wear a robe painted all over with eyes and ears . . . exemplifies the shifting, interpenetration, and overlapping of symbols." (On Jealousy, Chew cites Cesare Ripa, *Iconologia* [Padua, 1630], 285–86.) It is an interesting conjunction, since we have already had occasion to note the importance of jealous exclusivity to sovereign love in general and to Elizabeth's deployment of it in particular; the jealous love of superreality for its people is often connected with acts of retribution for infidelity or, in its secular form, treason.

85 Chew, *Virtues Reconciled*, 99–100.

86 John of Salisbury, *Policraticus*, trans. D. W. Robertson, Jr., in *The Literature of Medieval England* (New York: McGraw-Hill, 1970), 218.

87 Chew, *Virtues Reconciled*, 96, citing John Higgins, "To the Nobilitie, and all other in office," prefixed to *The First parte of the Mirour for Magistrates* (1574), Sig. *iiij.

88 Strong, *Splendor at Court*, 76.

89 See Bourdieu, *Outline of a Theory of Practice*, 192–94.

90 *LHTA* 2:359, notes the acquisition of the following: "Missale et Breviarium de usu Rome; Strabo de scitu orbis; Racionale divinorum officiorum; Conclusiones Sancti Pauli; Sermones Domini in monte; Ars moriendi; Stimulus amoris in Deum; Manu-

ale pro ecclesia de Strivelin; Holcatis; Dorbellis; pro Fratribus de Strivelin," at a cost of over five pounds. These books, then, appear to have been a gift in whole or in part to the Observantine Friary at Stirling, a favorite retreat of James's. The Treasurer's Accounts also list the acquisition of "Decretum magnum; Decretales; Sextus cum Clementinis; Scotus super quatuor libris Sententiarum; Quartum Scoti; Opera Gersonis in tribus voluminibus; Viaticum," at a cost of ten pounds (364). The library of James IV is described by John Durkan and Anthony Ross as conservative with respect to the changing "climate of thought" in early sixteenth-century Scotland. Durkan and Ross, *Early Scottish Libraries* (Glasgow: Burns, 1961), 20.

91 *New Catholic Encyclopedia* 14:705 s.v. "Virtue." This encyclopedia is cited hereinafter as *NCE*.

92 Nohrnberg, *Analogy of the Faerie Queene*, 319, citing Aquinas, *Summa Theologica*, Pt. II, 1st Pt., q. 85, art. 3; and q. 61, art. 2. The concept of creativity is important to atonement theology because of the creative power of the will, i.e., of desire. Thus the will must be perfected by justice in order to pursue goods that transcend the partial goods of self or nature (see *NCE* 14:705). Prudence is understood as an empowering of truth through action (*NCE* 11:927); fortitude enables the will through constancy (*NCE* 5:1034).

93 Malcolm Vale, *War and Chivalry: Warfare and Aristocratic Culture in England, France and Burgundy at the End of the Middle Ages* (London: Duckworth, 1981), 25–26, citing Bibliothèque Royale, Brussels MS 11,047, fol. 9v. Vale's chapter "The Literature of Honour and Virtue" summarizes the literature. (The Virtues, and particularly Fortitude, continued throughout the later Middle Ages and the Renaissance to play the role in the definition and spiritualization of chivalry present earlier in the figuration of Fortitude on the doorways at Paris and Amiens, and in the south porch at Chartres; see Mâle, *Gothic Image*, 121–22). The *Instruction d'un Jeune Prince* explains that *force* can mean "magnanimity, boldness of heart or force of courage" (Vale, 25, citing Ghilebert de Lannoy, *Oeuvres*, ed. C. T. Potvin [Louvain, 1878], 354). In the *Instruction*, force (magnanimity, bravery) is considered to be the most important of the cardinal virtues in war; it "is the fourth of the virtues that one must greatly honour, for princes and knights of high repute never performed enterprises nor bold deeds of arms worthy of memory without its accompaniment, aid and comfort. This force of courage, or bravery, belongs especially to princes and knights, for by its nature they are armed for everything that can happen: encounters with lance, bombard, cannon, storm at sea, harshness of winter, or heat of the sun. . . . the shedding of his own, or others' blood cannot dismay or frighten him; death seems a small penalty to endure in order to gain honour and great renown." Vale's comment that "physical courage and fearlessness are thus considered a talisman against the horrors of war" refers to this passage. (Vale, 26, citing Lannoy, 356–57: "Magnanimité est le iiiie des vertus que on doit moult honnourer, car princes ne chevaliers de haulte renommée ne firent oncques entreprinse ne vaillance en armes dignes de mémoire sans sa compaignie, aide et confort. Ceste vertu, selon nostre langaige, vault autant à dire que force de courage ou hardement, qui appartient espéciallement aux princes et chevaliers, car de sa nature elle est resconfortée de tout ce qui poet advenir: recontrée de lance, bombarde, canon, tourment de mer, dureté d'yver, chaleur de soleil . . . l'effusion du sang, de lui ne d'aultres, ne le poet esbahir ne doubter; la mort luy samble petite paine à endurer, pour acquérir honneur et bonne renommée.") The pairing of the Virtues with their opposing Vices is a talismanic structure.

94   Bawcutt, "Dunbar's Use of the Symbolic Lion and Thistle," 90.
95   Withington, *English Pageantry*, 225, and n. 2; the pageant was presented by Zeal.
96   Marvell, "Horatian Ode," ll. 35–36.

Chapter 8. Speaking of Love: *The Parliament of Fowls, The Kingis Quair,* and *The Thrissill and the Rois*

1   See Lyall, "Court as a Cultural Centre," 29; and Lyall's discussion of the Selden MS in "Books and Book Owners in Fifteenth-Century Scotland," in *Book Production and Publishing in Britain, 1375–1475,* ed. Jeremy Griffiths and Derek Pearsall (Cambridge: Cambridge University Press, 1989), 250–52. I discuss the MS in my chapter "Chaucer and the *Kingis Quair:* The Pleasures of Imitation," in Louise Fradenburg, "The Scottish Chaucer: Studies in Fifteenth-Century Reception," Ph.D. diss., University of Virginia, 1982, pp. 109–20. Aage Brusendorff notes that the twenty stanzas that follow the colophon "Incipit oratio galfridi chauncer" (actually, Hoccleve's "Mother of God") in the Advocates Library MS of *The Meroure of Wyssdome* (18.2.28, fol. 112) are the same as those included in the Selden MS, there also attributed to Chaucer, and adds that Ireland's copy "is possibly a mere transcript of the Selden MS." Brusendorff, *The Chaucer Tradition* (London: Oxford University Press, 1925), 436–37.

2   All citations to *The Parliament of Fowls* are taken from *The Riverside Chaucer,* ed. Larry D. Benson (Boston: Houghton Mifflin, 1987).

3   Klapisch-Zuber, "Ethnology of Marriage," 256, citing Altieri, *Li Nuptiali,* 45–46.

4   See Paul Zumthor, "The Great Game of Rhetoric," *New Literary History* 12 (1981): 493, on the "emblematizing of appearances" in the court: "Wealth is diffused in expenditure."

5   Bourdieu, *Outline of a Theory of Practice,* 7.

6   Ibid., 194. Bourdieu speaks of strategies designed to transform "the impersonal relationships of commercial transactions, which have neither past nor future, into lasting relationships of reciprocity" (186).

7   The poetry of the troubadours is preoccupied with the problem of insincerity, which is inseparable from the problem of the rival — of being distinguished from other, false lovers. In "Non es meravelha s'eu chan," Bernart de Ventadorn laments: "Ai Deus! car se fosson trian / d'entrels faus li fin amador, / e·lh lauzenger e·lh trichador / portesson corns el fron denan!" ("Ah, God! if only true lovers / stood out from the false; / if all those slanderers and frauds / had horns on their heads.") The poet goes on to explain that "Cant eu la vei, be m'es parven / als olhs, al vis, a la color" ("Whenever I see her, you can see it in me, / in my eyes, my look, my color"). See Frederick Goldin, ed. and trans., *Lyrics of the Troubadours and Trouvères: An Anthology and a History* (Garden City, N.Y.: Anchor Press/Doubleday, 1973), pt. 1, pp. 126–29, no. 21, ll. 33–36, 41–42.

8   For example, Thibaut de Champagne, "De bone amor vient seance et bonté," who imagines arousal as an incurable wound: "Li cous fu granz, il ne fet qu'enpoirier, / . . . . / Se de sa main i daignoit adeser, / bien en porroit le coup mortel oster / a tout le fust, dont j'ai grant desirrier; / mès la pointe du fer n'en puet sachier, / qu'ele bruisa dedenz au cop doner." ("The wound was great and can only get worse, / . . . / If she deigns to touch it with her hand, / she would take away that mortal wound — / at least the shaft, which I greatly want. / But she cannot draw out

the iron point, / for that broke off inside my heart when the arrow struck.") Goldin, ed., *Lyrics,* pp. 454–57, pt. 2, no. 31, ll. 33, 36–40.

9 See Benson, ed., *Riverside Chaucer,* 384, on the argument "that the poem concerns the negotiations in 1380 for the betrothal of Richard II to Anne of Bohemia, with Anne represented by the formel eagle and her three suitors (Richard II, Charles of France, and Friedrich of Meissen) by the three tercels. . . . such theories cannot be proven. . . . we know by historical hindsight that Anne did choose the royal tercel, Richard. But when Chaucer wrote this poem (assuming the theory is valid), he could not be sure she would do so."

10 Lyall, "Court as a Cultural Centre," 29. Lyall refers to Sinclair's marriage and the "clear thematic focus" of the MS in "Books and Book Owners" (252). In addition to Patrick Sinclair, who, as we have noted, jousted in James's wedding tournaments, the Treasurer's Accounts mention funds provided "to William Sinclair, to pas in France to by him clathes and harnes agane the mariage" (*LHTA* 2:359).

11 In distinguishing between a single and a plural sovereign, Preston King, in *The Ideology of Order: A Comparative Analysis of Jean Bodin and Thomas Hobbes* (London: George Allen and Unwin, 1974), stresses that the single sovereign's "word" is alone "regarded as legally final" (28); he cites Jean Bodin, *Les six livres de la Republique* (1576), to the effect that the sovereign speaks for all, "touchant tous les subiects en general" (129 n. 2). "Procedurally, an individual sovereign is not required to consult others to issue a directive. A collectivity, by contrast, simply in order to know its own mind, has to accept the indispensability of some form of public communication known as *debate*" (30). It is interesting to recall that the Commons of the English Parliament of 1621 — James I's first Parliament in seven years — responded to James's threats to restrict their privileges with a protestation (18 December 1621) that insisted specifically on "their right to consider and debate a wide range of 'arduous and urgent affairs.' This was the protestation . . . that the king himself tore up, followed by the dissolution of parliament, the imprisonment of five parliamentary leaders and the banishment of others from England" (62).

12 Matthew P. McDiarmid discusses the question of the authorship of *The Kingis Quair* in his edition of *The Kingis Quair of James Stewart* (Totowa, N.J.: Rowman and Littlefield, 1973), 28–48; all citations to the poem will be taken from this edition. The heading to the poem in the Selden MS is "Heireftir followis the quair Maid be / King James of scotland the first / Callit the kingis quair and / Maid quhen his Maiestie wes In / Ingland" (cited in McDiarmid, 5). The names of various members of the Sinclair family have been written into the MS (see J. T. T. Brown, *The Authorship of the Kingis Quair: A New Criticism* [Glasgow: James MacLehose and Sons, 1896], 77, for a full listing of these names), prompting McDiarmid to conclude that a Sinclair rather than one of the scribes wrote the heading (5). Henry Sinclair's grandmother was a sister of James I, his aunt the wife of one of James III's brothers. See Alexander Lawson, ed., *The Kingis Quair and the Quare of Jelusy* (London: Adam and Charles Black, 1910), lii. This closeness of kinship does not prove James I's authorship, and if the heading to the *Quair* were written by one of the later Sinclairs, Henry himself might never have set eyes on it. Still, the Sinclairs' connection with the royal family might lend credence to the heading, and there remains the testimony of the manuscript's second scribe, who wrote the colophon that follows the *Quair*: "Quod Jacobus primus scotorum rex Illustrissimus" (fol. 211).

The first scribe, James Gray, served as secretary to William Schevez and James Stewart, brother of James IV, both archbishops of St. Andrews; Gray was vicar of Hailes in 1490. MacQueen, "Literature of Fifteenth-Century Scotland," 201. Henry Sinclair's wife, Margaret Hepburn, was the daughter of Adam, second lord Hailes, and thus, as Lawson puts it, Gray "had a certain personal relation to his patron" (lii). Between 1485 and 1490, Gray copied Gilbert Haye's translations for the Sinclair family; Henry Sinclair's grandfather, William, first lord Sinclair, had commissioned Haye's translations of the *Arbre des Batailles*, *Le Livre de l'Ordre de Chevalerie*, and the French rendering of the *Secreta secretorum* that was to become *The Buke of the Governaunce of Princis* (MacQueen, 197, 201).

At least it can be said that James's authorship was a Sinclair family tradition; and their right to take a personal interest in the poem was based not only upon the bonds of kinship but also upon the fact that "it was their ancestor, the Earl of Orkney, who had 'the cure' of Prince James when he made his fateful voyage" to France and was intercepted and captured by the English (McDiarmid, 5).

13   Parsons writes: "The association of coronation [of queens] and intercession was translated into royal gesture, for . . . English queens interceded for pardons from the kings at the time of their coronations. . . . on 23 February 1421, Katherine of Valois induced Henry V to free the long-imprisoned King James of Scotland." John C. Parsons, "Esther's Eclipse?: Appeal and Intercession in Thirteenth-Century England," unpublished paper, 11.

14   The question of how, and how much, English culture influenced James has been a somewhat vexed question; historical tradition, from Bower's *Scotichronicon* to Balfour-Melville (James's most thorough modern biographer) has it that Henry IV took care with James's education and that James had ample opportunity to experience what cultural graces were available at the Lancastrian court. McDiarmid is less sure: "English sources . . . are silent about this enlightened treatment of the captive." See E. W. M. Balfour-Melville, *James I, King of Scots: 1406–1437* (London: Methuen, 1936), 52–53, citing Bower, *Scotichronicon*, xvi, 28, 30; Donaldson, *Scottish Kings*, 60; and McDiarmid, ed., *Kingis Quair*, 42. Of James I's reading material while he was in prison, we know that the University of Paris sent him, in 1414, the *Epistola Consolatoria*, described by Balfour-Melville as a "turgid document" which assures "James of the heartfelt condolence of the writers in his hateful captivity, but reminds him that adversity is a better teacher than prosperity. . . . This leads up to the real object of the letter — the request that James will bring Scotland over from the side of Benedict XIII to accept the decisions of the Council of Pisa." Balfour-Melville, 60, referring to *Chartularium Universitatis Parisiensis*, ed. H. Denifle and A. Chatelain (Paris, 1889–97), iv. 285. Such a letter might well have sparked the *Quair's* insistence that philosophical reflections on the nature of Fortune be tested through personal experience.

Still, James was present at the wedding of Henry V and Katherine of France in the cathedral of Troyes; he returned to London for Katherine's coronation and the ensuing state progress. Henry V knighted him on St. George's Day of the following year (23 April 1421) and made him a member of the Order of the Garter; when Henry V died in France, James accompanied the funeral cortege from Rouen to Westminster. After his captivity he engaged actively in English trade. See Nicholson, *Scotland*, 250–52, 290.

15   According to Nohrnberg, we recall, marriage, as a rite of maturation, brings out the problem of presumption, of displacing one's origins and originators, in con-

nection with the advent of sexuality; see Nohrnberg, *Analogy of the Faerie Queene*, 445. Diana's complaint in the *Echecs amoureux* is reminiscent of Nature's: "Once . . . her wood was full of gods and men, but all has changed on account of Venus, who, because of what Jupiter did to Saturn, has drawn everyone to her side. . . . She is alluding to the fable of Venus's birth from Saturn's severed genitals, thrown into the sea by his son Jupiter, marking the end of the golden age. At least as old as Ovid is a link between the end of the golden age and the end of sexual innocence. Now chastity, justice, faith, and truth have fled, she says, and no one lives a virtuous life, but all strive after pleasure." Ehrhart, *Judgment*, 162.

16   In *The Kingis Quair*, the narrator, unable to sleep, picks up Boethius's *Consolation of Philosophy*, a book which reminds him of his own earlier experiences of misfortune. He decides to describe those experiences – how, when a boy, he set out on a journey to France, was captured by an English ship, and spent eighteen years in exile and imprisonment. One day during his imprisonment, he looks down from his tower room into a beautiful springtime garden, in which the birds are singing of love. He then sees his future wife come into the garden; she is superlatively beautiful, and the sight of her makes him feel his imprisonment more keenly, for he cannot love freely. But in a vision he ascends to the House of Venus; she counsels hope and tells him he must learn to serve Love patiently and properly, under the guidance of Minerva, the goddess of Reason. Reason tells him that his love must be reconciled with wisdom, must be a Christian rather than an appetitive love; he must declare that he intends marriage, and upon his doing so, Reason says she will help him make use of Fortune. He then finds himself in an earthly paradise; he is able to feel joy and to delight in God's creation, now that Venus and Minerva have helped him to see it properly. He seeks out Fortune's tower; she explains to him that "Though thy begynnyng hath bene retrograde" (st. 170), he will be able to change course. He steps on her upward wheel but then starts out of his vision when she raps him on the ear while warning him to make good use of the rest of his life. Awakened, he is assailed again by doubts; he prays for reassurance, and divine grace sends to him a turtledove bearing "kalendis of confort" (st. 177). He then recounts how bliss came to him through marriage, speaks of the faults of his book – upon which his queen will have mercy – and recommends it to Gower and Chaucer, "Ane eke thair saulis vnto the blisse of hevin." My summary relies on the more extended summary to be found in McDiarmid, ed., *Kingis Quair*, 50–55.

17   Stanza 196. Though the image of the "hevynnis figure circulere" – with which the poem also begins – could have been inspired by many different sources (among them, the roundel in Chaucer's *Parliament*), it is interesting to speculate that the attention given by this poem to celestial phenomena may have been encouraged by the pageantry of Henry V and Katherine of France's wedding, which James attended. Nicholson, *Scotland*, 250. The pageantry for that occasion included "'immensae staturae gigantes, artificii mirabilis,' who were made to bow as the queen passed; there were lions, whose eyes could roll – 'leoninas effigies, oculorum motibus'; the apostles, martyrs, and confessors reappeared; there were choruses of virgins, who sang beautiful songs; the conduits ran wine; boys were dressed up as angels; and there were pageants. One recalls the last one of the 1415 entry [after Agincourt] – 'illac tronos, coelum simulantes emperium angelorum psallencium ierarchiis, fulgore mirabili radiare stuperes.'" Withington, *English Pageantry*, 137–38, citing Charles Lethbridge Kingsford, *Henry V* (London, 1901), 344; Thomas de

Elmham, *Vita et Gesta Henrici Quinti,* ed. Thomas Hearne (Oxford, 1727), 297–98; T. Walsingham, *Historia Anglicana,* ed. H. T. Riley, vol. 2 (London, 1863), 336; Benjamin Williams, ed., *Gesta Henrici Quinti* (London: English Historical Society, 1850), 147.

18 Gavin Douglas, *The Palice of Honour,* in Priscilla J. Bawcutt, ed., *The Shorter Poems of Gavin Douglas* (Edinburgh: William Blackwood for the Scottish Text Society, 1967), ll. 739–40.

19 The *Quair*-poet's plea lasts for seven stanzas before the bird begins to sing, "And to the notis of the philomene / Quhilkis sche sang, the ditee there I maid / Direct to hir that was my hertis quene, / Withoutin quhom no songis may me glade" (st. 62). The pleading stanzas are among the most beautiful in the poem — for example,

> O lytill wrecche, allace, maist thou noght se
> Quho commyth yond? Is it now tyme to wring?
> Quhat sory thoght is fallin vpon thee?
> Opyn thy throte — hastow no lest to sing?
> Allace, sen thou of resoun had felyng,
> Now, suete bird, say ones to me "pepe."
> I dee for wo, me think tho gynnis slepe.
>
> (st. 57)

20
> "Madame," quod I, "sen it is 30ur plesance
> That I declare the kynd of my loving,
> Treuely and gude, withoutin variance,
> I lufe that floure abufe all othir thing,
> And wold bene he that to hir worschipping
> Myght ought auaile, be him that starf on rude,
> And nouthir spare for trauaile, lyf nor gude!"
>
> (st. 139)

21 For example, "And in my hede I drewe ryght hastily, / And eft-sones I lent it forth ageyne / And saw hir walk, that verray womanly, / With no wight mo, bot onely wommen tueyne. / Than gan I studye in myself and seyne: / 'A, suete, ar ye a warldly creature, / Or hevinly thing in liknesse of nature?'" (st. 42).

22 Her description is in stanzas 46–51. The fixing of beauty's power of "variance" through cosmological images is fully developed in *The Masque of Beautie:* during the delay between the staging of *Blacknesse* and its sequel, *Beautie,* the Ethiopian nymphs were trapped by the evil charms of Night on a "seate: that seate which was, before, / Thought stray'ing, vncerteyne, floting to each shore," but which, upon their acquisition of the Elements of Beauty, is "fixed," and "*beauties* perfect *throne* / Now made peculiar to this place alone" (ll. 382–83, 86–87). This throne "still is seene / To turne vnto the motion of the World; / Wherein they sit, and are, like Heauen, whirl'd / About the Earth" (ll. 128–31).

23 Nicholson, in *Scotland,* 305, writes of "the articles which James presented to the parliament of 1424 that initiated the new order": "Incongruously intermingled with those that were to bring revolutionary political changes were others that ordered the destruction of rooks' nests and of all fish weirs in tidal waters." From the very beginning of his reign, James's parliaments poured forth legislation on a scale wholly unprecedented in Scotland. Nicholson concludes that it was "James's large legislative output [that] brought the beginnings of a real statutory law" to Scotland (310). These energetic legislative practices were probably modeled on those of England,

one of the most intensively governed nations in Europe at the time; and James imitated English practice in letter as well as in spirit, for example, by legislating in 1424 that each shire was to send to Parliament two or more wise men, who were to be chosen at the head court of the shire, with full powers from the shire "to heir treit ande finally to determyn." Together the commissioners of all the shires were to choose a "common spekar." Balfour-Melville, *James I*, 47–48, citing *APS* 2:15, chap. 2.

24 The term *masterful* is from Nicholson, *Scotland*, 325.

25 Nicholson writes that "from the very outset of his personal rule James had been well aware of the risks he ran. There was an element of fatalism in his vow . . . 'If God grant me life [and aid, even the life of a dog, throughout all the realm I will make the key keep the castle and the bracken bush the cow].' He had even prepared for the worst by an act of 1428 that required oaths of fealty to be sworn to the queen, and by a similar act of 1435." Nicholson, *Scotland*, 320.

26 Nicholson, *Scotland*, 320.

27 In particular, the dream is represented as generated by the gaps in the ancestral text: the dreamer, after reading his old book, goes to bed "Fulfyld of thought and busy hevynesse; / For bothe I hadde thyng which that I nolde, / And ek I nadde that thyng that I wolde" (ll. 89–91). Chaucer's poem is therefore located in the space of that which is unsaid by the other; it is the attempt to represent a desire effaced by the precursor.

28 Margaret Tudor's patronage was important to Dunbar, and he wrote several poems for her, including "Ane Dance in the Quenis Chalmer" (Kinsley, ed., *Dunbar*, no. 28), and "To the Quene" (no. 49), a poem without "title or ascription in the Bannatyne MS," writes Kinsley (329), but "for subject and author, Margaret and Dunbar are strong candidates." "To the Quene" may have been written after the death of James IV at Flodden: "O fair sweit blossum, now in bewty flouris, / Unfaidit bayth of cullour and vertew; / Thy nobill lord that deid hes done devoir, / Faid nocht with weping thy vissage fair of hew" (ll. 33–36). Dunbar's "To the King" (Kinsley, no. 25) is a "begging-poem" asking James IV to accept Margaret's petition on Dunbar's behalf; it uses the refrain "God gif ʒe war Johne Thomsounis man!" (*Johne Thomsounis man* is glossed by Kinsley as "a fellow who yields to the wishes of his wife" [299]). Margaret was also a patron of Gavin Douglas until her marriage with Archibald Douglas broke down; see Bawcutt, *Gavin Douglas*, 12–14, 17–18.

29 Lacan would argue that the subjection to the desire of the other is always a feature of the subject of language. But in court poetry, when the other is the sovereign, subjection to the demand is emphasized; private desire ideally does not exist apart from the desire of the sovereign. See Lacan's discussion of the other in "Function and Field of Speech and Language in Psychoanalysis," in *Écrits: A Selection*, trans. Alan Sheridan (New York: W. W. Norton and Co., 1977), 30–113; and Jacques Lacan, "Desire and the Interpretation of Desire in *Hamlet*," *Yale French Studies* 55–56 (1977): 11–52. See also my article "The Manciple's Servant Tongue: Politics and Poetry in *The Canterbury Tales*," *English Literary History* 52 (1985): 85–118, for a fuller discussion of Lacanian theory in relation to the production of courtly poetry.

30 Lacan, "Desire in *Hamlet*," 29.

31 Scarry, *Body in Pain*, 200.

32 See C. S. Lewis, *English Literature in the Sixteenth Century Excluding Drama* (Oxford: Clarendon Press, 1954), 91–92. Dunbar's rhetoric of transfiguration — in which

his "aureate" terms play a central role — has been mistaken by many critics for mere
decor, a mistake which replicates the anxieties about illusion to be found within
Dunbar's poetry. Even Denton Fox, one of his admirers, explains that Dunbar's
poetry "is a poetry of surfaces — precise, static, and two-dimensional" ("The Scottish Chaucerians," in *Chaucer and Chaucerians: Critical Studies in Middle English
Literature*, ed. D. S. Brewer [University, Ala.: University of Alabama Press, 1966],
186). Dunbar's surface brilliance, his "intense preoccupation with craft" *is* his meaning, insofar as he is thought to have one; Lois A. Ebin, "The Theme of Poetry
in Dunbar's 'Goldyn Targe,'" *Chaucer Review* 7 (1972): 148. P. M. Kean argues
against modern critics' concentration on the "artificiality" of the aureate style; she
suggests that "diction of this kind is part of a widespread movement to increase
the capabilities of the English language" (*Chaucer and the Making of English Poetry*, vol. 2, *The Art of Narrative* [London: Routledge and Kegan Paul, 1972],
226-27). Chaucer's own term *enlumynyng* seems to Kean to have meant "to cast
lustre on the whole of Italy" or "to shed an illuminating light, an enlightening ra-
diance over" (232-33); the "influence" rained down from the stars became the influence of a truly stellar poet. The term *aureate* itself was probably coined by Lydgate
(Kean, 226) and seems to have been used to refer both to poetic style and inspiration. Dunbar's use of aureate language in *The Thrissill and the Rois*, a poem about
the wedding of an English princess to a Scottish king, seems significant given Dunbar's ambitions as a poet writing in the English tongue.

33 The effect of the contrast between Dunbar's earlier description of Eolus's "busteous
    . . . blastis" and the "dulce and redolent garden" into which he then enters is analo-
    gous to the magical shifts of scenery in Jonsonian masque.

34 See George D. Economou, *The Goddess Natura in Medieval Literature* (Cambridge:
    Harvard University Press, 1972).

35 Ibid., 22: "Providence expresses creative activity through matter."

36 Economou, *Goddess Natura*, 48-49. The narrator of Alain de Lille's *De planctu
    naturae* addresses her as "bond and steadfast knot of the world," "uniting all things
    in stability with concord's knot and with the bond of peace, marry[ing] the heav-
    ens to earth." Economou, *Goddess Natura*, 80-81, citing Alain de Lille, *De planctu
    naturae*, ed. Thomas Wright, vol. 2 of *The Anglo-Latin Satirical Poets and Epi-
    grammatists* (Wiesbaden: Kraus, 1964), 458.

37 The tenth Orphic hymn celebrates her as "Nature, all-parent, ancient and divine, /
    O much mechanic mother, art is thine; / Heav'nly, abundant, venerable queen, /
    In ev'ry part of thy dominions seen"; "Finite and infinite alike you shine; / To all
    things common, and in all things known, / Yet incommunicable and alone. / With-
    out a father of thy wondrous frame, / Thyself the father whence thy essence came."
    She is "bond connective of the earth and skies. / Leader, life-bearing queen, all
    various nam'd, / And for commanding grace and beauty fam'd." Economou, *God-
    dess Natura*, 40, citing *The Mystical Hymns of Orpheus*, trans. Thomas Taylor
    (London, 1896), 29-33.

38 Economou, *Goddess Natura*, 42.

39 Ibid., 79, citing de Lille, *De planctu naturae*, 455. According to William of Conches,
    "these are called works of nature that are made by nature in subservience to God"
    (Economou, 35-36, citing J. M. Parent, *La doctrine de la création dans l'école de
    Chartres* [Ottawa, 1938], 128). St. Ambrose, in the *Hexaemeron*, argued that since
    it was God who created nature, it is God who gives her her law; likewise the sun,
    a part of nature, formerly worshipped as Sol, has no creative power in itself. Na-

tura says, "Indeed, the sun is good, but as one that serves, not as one that commands; good as one that assists my fecundity, but not as one that creates; good
as nourisher of my fruits, but not as their maker . . . Standing by me, it praises
the Creator, it sings a hymn to our Lord God" (Economou, 56–57, citing Saint Am-
brose, *Hexaemeron*, ed. J. P. Migne, *Patrologia Latina* XIV [Paris, 1866], 202).

40 I owe this distinction to Richard Corum.

41 Nature sends the "swyfte ro," the "restles suallow," and the "yarrow, / Quhilk did
furth swirk als swift as ony arrow" (ll. 78, 80, 83–84) to collect the beasts, birds,
and flowers; she uses, that is, the powers of nature to command its obedience. Its
responsiveness, however, is rendered as magically prompt.

42 See *OED*, s.v. "transfiguration," especially the entry from Wyclif; Zumthor, "Great
Game of Rhetoric," 495.

43 This is one reason for Nature's warning to the sexually adventurous James IV to
"hald non udir flour in sic denty / As the fresche Ros of cullour reid and quhyt"
(ll. 141–42). The perfections of the Rose enjoin a perfection of choice, of commitment; Didos threaten the purity of the dynastic body. Nature's function as adviser
is evidence of her communitarian status in the poem. On the poem's assertion of
Scotland's imperial destiny, Bawcutt, in "Dunbar's Use of the Symbolic Lion and
Thistle," notes that "Dunbar's stress on the act of crowning might indeed be linked
with James IV's adoption at about this time of the arched or imperial crown in
the royal arms" (93).

44 As Hamlet says of Laertes, "his semblable is his mirror, and who else would trace
him, his umbrage, nothing more" (5.2.18–19). The triplicity of Dunbar's monarch
should be compared with the more customary image of the monarch as the "head"
of the body politic, with the estates representing other parts of the body.

45 Bawcutt, in "Dunbar's Use of the Symbolic Lion and Thistle," notes that the motto
parcere prostratis applied to the lion — "Qhois noble yre is *parcere prostratis*" (l.
119) — was a maxim belonging to the *Speculum principiis* tradition and was regularly
linked with the virtue of clemency, which distinguished good rulers from tyrants
(84–88). Thus at the moment of the lion's coronation — the ritual which makes him
a "new man," distinguishes him from all others — the sovereign is identified with
communitarian concerns, through his care for the "weak." At the moment he is
"created" king, not only through coronation but also through the recognition of
others — the other beasts "maid him homege and fewte" (l. 117) — we are reminded
that he must return the favor, but in such a way that the dependence of sovereignty
on such exchanges is obscured. Bawcutt also notes that Dunbar was the first Scottish poet to make use of the heraldic image of the thistle, which was a "personal
badge of the Scottish king" — James III made extensive use of it, as well as James
IV — but "the thistle, like the rose or the fleur de lys, rapidly also became a national
badge", signifying "warlike readiness to defend oneself or one's country," "the duty
of a king to guard his people effectively and to protect them from invasion" (90).
Bawcutt notes the previously "adverse" association with the thistle, which "figures
in God's curse on mankind — 'thorns and thistles shall it [i.e., the ground] bring
forth to thee,'" and "regularly symbolizes unfruitfulness and disorder" (90). The
thistle thus exemplifies the apotropaic function of much heraldic symbolism, in
this case the appropriation of wild nature in the protection of culture and "country." In *The Thrissill and the Rois*, as in the Song of Songs, the "nation" celebrates
itself through sovereign love; Bawcutt suggests that the poem's emphasis on coronation, which may, as noted above, have been linked to James IV's new use of the

imperial crown in the royal arms, was also inspired by the Song of Songs 4:7–8: "Macula non est in te. . . . Veni . . . sponsa mea . . . veni coronaberis" (93–94). And though Bawcutt stresses that to emphasize, in a poem about the wedding of a Scottish king and an English princess, the fact that "the Scots associated the danger of invasion primarily with England" would be "discourteous" (92–93), it is clear that the "extraordinariness," the riskiness, of marriage with the English enemy is registered by *The Thrissill and the Rois* precisely through the care the poem takes to defend against the mystery of the foreigner, that form of "disbelief" which, in Dunbar's poem, is converted to devotion to Scotland's national symbols.

46 In Lacanian terms, this is the "signifier of power, of potency." Lacan, "Desire in *Hamlet*," 51.

47 The Aristotelian concept of *allotrios* is opposed to *kurion*, the "ordinary"—that which is "in general use in a country." See Paul Ricoeur, *The Rule of Metaphor: Multi-Disciplinary Studies of the Creation of Meaning in Language*, trans. Robert Czerny with Kathleen McLaughlin and John Costello, S.J. (Toronto: University of Toronto Press, 1977), 18–19.

48 From Dunbar's "Ane Ballat of Our Lady," ll. 73–74. He refers to the Virgin as the "ros virginall" (l. 79) and as "the ros Mary, flour of flouris" (l. 4) in "Rorate celi desuper."

49 On beauty and the transformative power of the sovereign, see chaps. 11 and 13, below.

50 Lewis, *English Literature in the Sixteenth Century*, 75–76.

51 J. W. Baxter, *William Dunbar: A Biographical Study* (Edinburgh: Oliver and Boyd, 1952), 93–94. Baxter discusses Dunbar's court career, pensions, and petitionary poetry at some length, notably in the chapters "Ane Courtman" (93–112) and "In Court Our Lang" (119–32).

52 Paul Strohm, *Social Chaucer* (Cambridge: Harvard University Press, 1989), is an excellent account of Chaucer's relation to court society; Strohm demonstrates that being a "court poet" can mean many different things and that Chaucer's relation to the court, and to his own circle within it, changed many times during his life. On the former question, Strohm writes: "All [the chamber knights, merchants like Nicholas Brembre, "urban intellectuals" like Thomas Usk] were king's men, but Chaucer and his associates managed to be king's men in a less rushed, less greedy, more circumspect, and more thoughtful way" (40). The distinction is highly problematic but points in its own interesting way to the intensity with which courtly careers seem to bring out the question of the self's sovereignty—i.e., of the careerist's excessive dependence on others or of his or her self-seeking, forms of malaise which seem inimical to honor.

53 Baxter, *William Dunbar*, 133, 137; on Dunbar's priesthood, 123.

Chapter 9. A Royal Legend: James IV and the Historians

1 Lewis, *English Literature in the Sixteenth Century*, 66.

2 Jonathan Goldberg's statements on the theatricality of public life in the Jacobean court—there is "no privacy that is not . . . also displayed, re-presented" elsewhere—suggest, in a different context, the same demand for the king's representative fullness, i.e., that nothing should be held back. Goldberg, "'Upon a publike stage': The Royal Gaze and Jacobean Theater," in David M. Bergeron, ed., *Research Opportunities in Renaissance Drama* 24 (1981): 17–18.

3 This book was in production before I was able to consult Macdougall's fine analy-

sis "The Legend and the King," in *James IV*, 282–312. I have not been able to take his work into account as fully as I would wish, but he and I are in substantial agreement on a number of important points. Macdougall notes, for example, that "a great deal of post-Flodden writing about James IV is rooted firmly in the *Speculum principiis* tradition; and it has exercised an enormous influence on historians down to the present day" (289). Macdougall also stresses James's talent for governing—his capacity to inspire "purpose, drive, unanimity [in] . . . the political community" (309), to inspire loyalty among the magnates with whom he consulted widely and regularly, as well as in the "vast array" of workers engaged in his many projects (308). James, in Macdougall's portrait, possessed the "elusive factor of charisma": James "appeared infinitely more approachable, infinitely more aware of his duties, than his father. He showed an instinctive grasp of the essentials of Scottish kingship, of the need above all to lead by example" (308). What Macdougall himself calls "the legend of Flodden" (289), however, is not altogether absent from his portrait of James, for example in the elegiac tones of his final pages: "He failed only at the very end"; "Scottish national self-confidence was lost for the remainder of the century" (309). Macdougall's chief interest in this chapter is to restore substance to the image of James IV—to demonstrate that James was neither foolhardy nor romantic, but rather in nearly all respects a remarkably able king. Macdougall is also unconcerned with the ways in which James IV's Arthurian solicitations of "unanimity" may themselves have helped to produce the legend of his vulnerable magnificence.

4   Leslie, *Historie of Scotland* (1890), 2:128. Another version of Leslie's text gives the following account: "thair wes gret atturnementis and justinge in Edinburch, be ane quha callit himself the wyld knycht, and ranconterit be the frenshe men, with counterfutting of the round tabill of King Arthour of Jngland. This wild knycht was the king himself, quha wes vailyeannt in armeis, and could very weill exerce the same." John Leslie, *History of Scotland* (1830), 128.

5   Nicholson, *Scotland*, 595.

6   Ayala, in Brown, *Early Travellers*, 40–41.

7   Mackie, *King James IV*, 268, citing Leslie, *History of Scotland* (1830); John Leslie, *De origine, moribus et rebus gestis Scotorum libri decum*, 1675 ed., 96 Scottish, 349 Latin.

8   Jameson, "Magical Narratives," *Political Unconscious*, 118. Jameson argues that the romance must be understood as a rewriting of the positionality of good and evil implied by the *chansons de geste*, a positionality conditioned by the "social and spatial isolation" and anarchic brigandage of the period preceding the twelfth century. But when, in the twelfth century, "civilization" reconstitutes itself and the feudal nobility develops a class consciousness and ideology, a contradiction arises between "the older positional notion of good and evil" and an "emergent class solidarity." Jameson thus argues that romance treats as contemporaneous opposites —good knight, bad knight; unknown knight, known knight—differences that were actually historical and thus is a genre that responds to actual changes in the situation of the European aristocracy. I would suggest in turn that the romance narrates contemporaneous ambiguities as temporal alternatives, so that the difficulty of distinguishing between friend and enemy, same and different, hence just and unjust violence, can be eased through historical explanation: once barbarism, now civilization; once violence, now peace.

9   See *LHTA* 3:250 for a reference to "the kingis irn belt."

10 "New Monarchy Triumphant" and "The Aureate Age and its End" are the titles of Nicholson's chapters on James IV in *Scotland;* they suggest a narrative trajectory also very similar to that of the *Morte d'Arthur.*

11 Mackie, *King James IV,* 201–2.

12 Alan Macquarrie, *Scotland and the Crusades, 1095–1560* (Edinburgh: John Donald, 1985), 108–9.

13 Macquarrie temporizes: "James's ideals were 'medieval' rather than 'renaissance'; but it is doubtful if either designation has much real value except as a label of convenience" (*Scotland and the Crusades,* 112). Still, Renaissance historiography has left its mark on Macquarrie's own narrative. He notes that crusade was a "declining fashion" in the sixteenth century; that "when Erasmus published his criticism of warfare against the Turk (1529) he sent a copy," and a dedicatory letter to Hector Boece, a historian brought to Aberdeen by Bishop Elphinstone, "who had himself been an opponent of the policies which led James IV to Flodden." Macquarrie, 113, citing Desiderius Erasmus, *Opus Epistolarum,* ed. P. S. Allen and H. M. Allen (Oxford, 1906–48), 8:372–77; and John Durkan, "Early Humanism and King's College," *Aberdeen University Review* 163 (1980): 259–79. The ideological grounds of the humanist distaste for crusade Macquarrie leaves unexamined, and his account seems haunted by the sense that there is something self-evidently more real about Machiavellianism than there is about the crusading spirit, as though, once again, medieval crusading kings were never motivated by interests and as though, after the Middle Ages, kings did not continue to crusade in different ways. After the Middle Ages crusade may have been redeployed as archaism, mercantilism, nationalism; during the Middle Ages, it may have been a form of economic and cultural imperialism — a practice of "survival" — deployed as recovery of the past, and hence "regressive" in its orientation of desire, though not, precisely, an "archaism." See Perry Anderson, for example, on the "surface 'modernity'" and "subterranean archaism" of the "new" monarchy, and on its "swollen memory of the mediaeval functions of war" (*Lineages of the Absolutist State,* 29, 33).

14 Macquarrie, *Scotland and the Crusades,* 112.

15 Ibid., 112.

16 In the same way, Nicholson argues that James was "never blind to his own interests" (*Scotland,* 595). These views are in fact a useful corrective to the idea of James as a "moonstruck romantic" but ultimately display the same distrust of the king's legend-making as do Mackie's.

17 Macquarrie, *Scotland and the Crusades,* 112.

18 Mackie, *King James IV,* 253.

19 Ibid., 273, citing *Epistolae Jacobi Quarti, Jacobi Quinti & Mariae Regum Scotorum . . . ab anno 1505 ad annum 1545,* vol. 1 (Edinburgh, 1722), 187–88.

20 Mackie, *King James IV,* 273–74.

21 Ibid., 242, 274.

22 Ibid., 269.

23 Ranald Nicholson closes his book with a quotation from Foullis's *Carmen elegum:* "Love James the Fourth, O Scotland, with whose aid / Auspicious Fame will thee to heaven exalt." He comments: "Flodden saw the end both of James IV and heavenly exaltation. Sometimes in the past the Scots had suffered a reverse as great as that of 1513 and had quickly recovered; they did not regard Flodden as an irretrievable disaster; but the disaster was not retrieved" (*Scotland,* 606).

24 Joan Hughes and William S. Ransom, *The Poetry of the Stewart Court* (Canberra: Australian National University Press, 1982), 5.

25 Jacques Lacan refers to the "hole in the real" brought on by loss in "Desire in *Hamlet*," 37–38.

26 Mackie, *King James IV*, 201; Wormald, *Court, Kirk, and Community*, 7.

27 Macdougall, *James III*, 304.

28 James III does seem to have spent a great deal on household "furnishings" and treasure, and on clothing: "The king's outlay on clothes and personal accoutrements was surpassed only by that of the queen, and amounted in 1473-4 to £639 0s. 5d. An extravagant court ill suited 'a barane land . . . fertile of folk, with great scantnes of fude' that was racked by famine, inflation and feud" (Nicholson, *Scotland*, 483, citing *LHTA* 1:13-28, and *Liber Pluscardensis*, ed. Felix J. H. Skene, vol. 1 [Edinburgh: W. Paterson, 1877], 392-400), though it seems to have better suited the Scotland of James IV, which was not vastly more prosperous.

29 See Leslie, *History of Scotland* 8:ciiii, 107, on James's "large liberalitie."

30 Ayala, in Brown, *Early Travellers*, 39–49.

31 Leslie, *History of Scotland* 8:ciiii, 107.

32 Pitscottie, "Ane Exclamatioun of James the Fourt And Quhat He was in His Lyf Tyme, How he was Exteimit," in *Historie of Scotland* 277-78. The following citations to Pitscottie are from this text. These verses are taken from Lindsay's poem, in *The Poetical Works of David Lindsay*, ed. David Laing, p. 79, ll. 486ff.

33 W. Thomas MacCary, *Childlike Achilles: Ontogeny and Phylogeny in the Iliad* (New York: Columbia University Press, 1982), 31.

34 Lacan, *Écrits*, 4.

35 Kinsley, ed., *Dunbar*, p. 71, no. 20, ll. 25-26.

36 As Goldberg puts it with respect to Renaissance kingship: "Although all 'gazingly behold' the king, his gaze is of a different nature. His eye is bent on all, seeing as God sees. Sovereignty is a matter of sight" ("Royal Gaze," 19). Recently, some studies of the problems of identity raised by "theatricalization" have emerged that share some of my concerns in this chapter — for example, Laura Levine, "Men in Women's Clothing: Anti-Theatricality and Effeminization from 1579 to 1642," *Criticism* 28 (1986): 121-43, and Katharine Eisaman Maus, "Horns of Dilemma: Jealousy, Gender, and Spectatorship in English Renaissance Drama," *English Literary History* 54 (1987): 561-83. Neither essay, though, is concerned with the issues of historicity brought out by the spectacled image, nor with the extent to which theatricalization can usefully be understood in the context of the ideology of honor.

37 J. H. Stevenson, ed., *Gilbert of the Haye's Prose Manuscript* (A.D. 1456), vol. 2, *The Buke of Knychthede and The Buke of the Governaunce of Princis* (Edinburgh: William Blackwood and Sons, for the Scottish Text Society, 1914), 92. MacQueen explains that William, first lord Sinclair "requested Sir Gilbert Haye, 'maister in arte and bachilere in decreis,' a former chamberlain to Charles VII of France (1422–61) to translate from the French the *Arbre des Batailles* (*Buke of the Law of Armys*) of Honoré Bonet (c. 1340-c. 1410), the anonymous fourteenth-century *Le Livre de l'Ordre de Chevalerie* (*Buke of the Ordre of Knychthede*), later translated by Caxton, and *The Buke of the Governaunce of Princis*, based on a French rendering of the Latin *Secreta secretorum*, usually in the Middle Ages attributed to Aristotle. These were completed in 1456." Haye later made *The Buik of Alexander the Con-*

queror for Lord Erskine. MacQueen, "Literature of Fifteenth-Century Scotland," 197, 198.

38 Haye, *Governaunce of Princis*, 93.

39 Jacques Lacan, "Of the Gaze as *Objet Petit a*," in *The Four Fundamental Concepts of Psycho-Analysis*, ed. Jacques-Alain Miller, trans. Alan Sheridan (New York: W. W. Norton and Co., 1981), 96.

40 Tobin Siebers, *The Mirror of Medusa* (Berkeley: University of California Press, 1983), 136.

41 See Laura Mulvey, "Visual Pleasure and Narrative Cinema," *Screen* 16 (1975): 9–10, on the importance of the visibility of the human form to identification. Visual perception is one of the most important ways of enacting idealizing identifications, partly because of its ambiguous status: is sight merely a passive activity, whereby the eye receives images, or does it involve action by the eye on its environment? David C. Lindberg, "The Science of Optics," in Lindberg, ed., *Science in the Middle Ages* (Chicago: University of Chicago Press, 1978), notes that "the common premise of all ancient theories of vision was that there must be some form of contact between the object of vision and the visual organ, for only thus could an object stimulate or influence the visual power and be perceived" (339). Atomistic theory, which "argued that thin films of atoms depart from visible objects in all directions, . . . and enter the eye of an observer," can be called an "'intromission' theory of vision"; "the obvious alternative is an 'extramission' theory, in which radiation is sent out from the observer's eye to 'feel' the visible object" (339–40). The latter theory "was proposed by Euclid and further developed by the mathematician and astronomer Ptolemy" (340); "Aristotle's theory of vision might be called . . . 'mediumistic,' for contact between object and observer is established through the medium" (340). Lindberg's summary of visual theory in medieval Christendom — including Augustine's reception of "Plato's stress on the visual fire emanating from the observer's eye (coupled . . . with external illumination and light or fire from the observed object)" is at 349–54.

42 Siebers proposes a revision of Freud's myth in *Totem and Taboo:* the first "individual" was not, as Freud imagined, the epic poet, who created the epic hero "out of longing for the dead father"; he was, instead, the monarchical "fascinator," the primal father-leader upon whom is imposed the fascinating persona — the representation of difference — that distinguishes him from the many and places him at the center of the community (Siebers, *Mirror of Medusa*, 134).

43 MacCary, *Childlike Achilles*, 149.

44 Frederick Thomas Elworthy, *Horns of Honour and Other Studies in the By-Ways of Archaeology* (London: John Murray, 1900), 56.

45 See ibid., 51–52, on scorn.

46 Francis Henry Cripps-Day, *The History of the Tournament in England and in France* (London: Bernard Quaritch, 1918), 32–33 n. 2.

47 Siebers argues that the representation of identity as difference is the enactment of an "accusatory thought that creates gods" to be both idolized and despised; the accusatory gaze can appear in a variety of forms — Nemesis, the gorgon, public opinion. The idea of the "narcissist" and the "jettatore" are both accusatory and mystifying concepts: ways of isolating, through projection, the object of a curse, as though that object deserved to be isolated (*Mirror of Medusa*, 85, 80). The king is similarly isolated, but his power is conceived to be legitimate, directed toward the good of the community. Siebers reviews the anthropological literature on the

evil eye at 27–56; see also the essays in Clarence Maloney, ed., *The Evil Eye* (New York: Columbia University Press, 1976).

48 Michel Foucault, *Discipline and Punish: The Birth of the Prison*, trans. Alan Sheridan (New York: Pantheon Books, 1977), offers the following gloss on the king's fictive body: "Kantorowitz [*sic*] gives a remarkable analysis of 'The King's Body': a double body according to the juridical theology of the Middle Ages, since it involves not only the transitory element that is born and dies, but another that remains unchanged by time and is maintained as the physical yet intangible support of the kingdom; around this duality, which was originally close to the Christological model, are organized an iconography, a political theory of monarchy, legal mechanisms that distinguish between as well as link the person of the king and the demands of the Crown, and a whole ritual that reaches its height in the coronation, the funeral and the ceremonies of submission. At the opposite pole one might imagine placing the body of the condemned man; he, too, has his legal status; he gives rise to his own ceremonial and he calls forth a whole theoretical discourse, not in order to ground the 'surplus power' possessed by the person of the sovereign, but in order to code the 'lack of power' with which those subjected to punishment are marked. In the darkest region of the political field the condemned man represents the symmetrical, inverted figure of the king. We should analyse what might be called, in homage to Kantorowitz, 'the least body of the condemned man'" (28–29).

49 David Starkey, "Representation through Intimacy: A Study in the Symbolism of Monarchy and Court Office in Early Modern England," in Ivan Lewis, ed., *Symbols and Sentiments: Cross-Cultural Studies in Symbolism* (London: Academic Press, 1977), 194. Starkey begins the essay by remarking that "the appearance of Keith Thomas's *Religion and the Decline of Magic* has marked an epoch in the study of early-modern English history. It shows, irrefutably, that the men of that time . . . were soaked in the occult and the irrational. . . . No more will it be possible to push these aspects of the period into the margin. . . . From one point of view this has already been understood: thus Thomas himself stresses the propaganda value of the king's powers as a miraculous healer. . . . the actual instruments of government at the command of a miracle-working king are different from those available to a lounge-suited Prime Minister" (187). "English kingship, like other sacred monarchies, had a double face: the beneficent (the king as healer), and the terrifying (fear of the royal presence)" (193).

50 Starkey, "Representation through Intimacy," 194, citing J. G. Frazer, *The Golden Bough*, abridged ed. (Macmillan, 1963), 267. He also cites Richard Burney's sermons on the restoration of Charles II: "God has also seated the latitude of the power of kings, or the highest style of their prerogative in a *maledicere* [power of cursing] and a *benedicere* [power of blessing]" (*Kerdiston Doron*, printed by J. Redmayne, for the author [1660], 7–9). On James IV's healing touch see *LHTA* 4:lxxxii; three shillings were given "to ane pure barne that tuke the King by the hand" (on 30 April 1508). The editor asks: "May we see in this the Royal power of touching for scrofula?"

51 As R. C. Maclagan notes in his study of the evil eye in Scotland — where, it is said, envy could break the very stones — the giving of gifts is a powerful prophylactic against the evil eye: "The danger of refusing a request is great." Maclagan, *Evil Eye in the Western Highlands* (London: David Nutt, 1902), 48. Moreover, "a man who wishes to have everything for himself will do harm to whatever he sees," whereas

a good man to have dealings with is "a man that thinks highly of what belongs to himself, and would not exchange it with any man" (40–42). To avoid frightening others, one must appear to be complete, to lack nothing; to avoid the envy of others, one must be open-handed.

52 Leslie, *History of Scotland*, 8:ciiii, 107.

53 Ayala, in Brown, *Early Travellers*, 40–41. It is of course difficult to assess the "truth" of Ayala's claims; he seems to have been partial to James and to have worked to further an alliance between Scotland and Spain by presenting James's virtues in a flattering way to his masters at home. (Macdougall discusses Ayala's portrait of James in *James IV*, 282–87.) James seems to have worked tirelessly to incarnate the principle of justice in person, as against his father's attempts to delegate the practice of justice to deputies, and thus succeeded to a large extent in gaining the confidence of his subjects in this regard. Macdougall writes: "From beginning to end, James IV is to be found using the ayres to mete out summary justice for serious crimes. In many cases he might also grant remissions to make sizeable profits for the Crown, a custom for which his father had been much criticised in parliament, and for which he himself was mildly rebuked in 1504. But there was a world of difference between the remote, aloof James III amassing money from profits of justice without moving from Edinburgh in the process, and his energetic son, who . . . might be expected to appear very rapidly in any area in which unrest was likely to have damaging effects on Crown resources or prestige" (*James IV*, 304). Macdougall's comment registers both the extent to which James IV had to differ from his father in the financial practice of justice, and the extent to which he resembled him. James IV's remissions were plentiful.

54 Kinsley, ed., *Dunbar*, p. 107, no. 34, ll. 1–6, 43–48.

55 Ibid., 309, citing *LHTA* 1:273, 342, 380, 381, and 3:lxxxii, 415.

56 Kinsley, ed., *Dunbar*, 309, quoting Mackenzie, ed., *Dunbar*, 211.

57 Selection from John Major, *A History of Greater Britain* (Edinburgh: Scottish Historical Society, 1892), 30–31, 47–50, quoted in Donaldson, *Scottish Historical Documents*, 100–101. Katherine Simms, in her important book *From Kings to Warlords: The Changing Political Structure of Gaelic Ireland in the Later Middle Ages* (Woodbridge, Suffolk: Boydell Press, 1987), has pointed to the tendency of historians to view Gaelic culture as "static and timeless . . . surviving unaltered from the sixth century to the sixteenth" (10). Major appears to have been an early proponent of the obduracy of the Gaelic "nature."

58 Ferguson, *Scotland's Relations with England*, 34–35.

59 James IV, of course, was not alone among late medieval European princes in so doing, as Malcolm Vale's book *War and Chivalry* suggests; Vale's chapter "Orders of Chivalry in the Fifteenth Century" is particularly helpful in demonstrating the "political purpose and function" of "fifteenth century orders of chivalry," for example, in creating and cementing oaths of allegiance to sovereigns that appear to have been taken quite seriously (34). James II of Scotland was an important predecessor of James IV in terms of his reputation for chivalrous pursuits—his love of hunting and tournaments is cited in Nicholson, *Scotland*, 395–96. And James III himself participated in chivalric culture: during the crisis of 1482, for example, he sealed a letter with a signet ring "portraying a unicorn and bearing the legend 'Tout a Une'" (Macdougall, *James III*, 173), and the thistle, a royal emblem which was to become a national symbol, appears on some of James III's coinage (Bawcutt, "Dunbar's Use of the Symbolic Lion and Thistle," 89), as well as on the richly decorated

household goods inventoried after his death. But James III seems to have had little interest in tourneying, or in other forms of chivalric spectacle per se.

Chapter 10. Spectacle and Chivalry in Late Medieval Scotland

1 Mill, *Mediaeval Plays in Scotland*, 104.

2 Ibid., 53, citing Joseph Bain, ed., *Calendar of the State Papers relating to Scotland and Mary, Queen of Scots, 1547–1603*, vol. 1 (Edinburgh: H. M. General Register House, 1898), 576, no. 1049.

3 Mill, *Mediaeval Plays in Scotland*, 53–54, citing J. Nichols, *The Progresses of Queen Elizabeth*, vol. 3 (London, 1823).

4 Mill, *Mediaeval Plays in Scotland*, 54, 50; see also 50–51 n. 2.

5 Ibid., 53.

6 Pamela M. King, "Dunbar's *The Golden Targe*: A Chaucerian Masque," *Studies in Scottish Literature* 19 (1984): 121, citing Withington, *English Pageantry* 1:80–81. The statement, however, is perhaps a bit of an exaggeration, and King's reference to Withington is erroneous.

7 Annie I. Dunlop, *The Life and Times of James Kennedy, Bishop of St. Andrews* (Edinburgh: Oliver and Boyd, 1950), 100, citing Gilliodts van Severen, *Inventaire des Archives de la Ville de Bruges*, vol. 5 (Bruges: E. Gaillard, 1876), 498.

8 Dunlop, *James Kennedy*, 100, and n. 6, citing *Auchinleck Chronicle* (Edinburgh, 1819, 1877), 18, 40; *Extracta ex Variis Cronicis Scocie*, ed. W. B. D. D. Turnbull (Edinburgh: Abbotsford Club, 1842), 238; *Scotichronicon Joannis de Fordun*, ed. W. Goodall, vol. 2 (Edinburgh, 1759), 515; and cf. *Mémoires d'Olivier de la Marche*, ed. Henri Beaune and J. d'Arbaumont (Paris: Société de l'Histoire de France, 1883–88), 2:104–5.

9 Dunlop, *James Kennedy*, 102; her reference is to *Chronique de Mathieu d'Escouchy*, ed. G. du Fresne de Beaucourt, vol. 1 (Paris: Société de l'Histoire de France, 1863).

10 Mill, *Mediaeval Plays in Scotland*, 49 n. 5, citing *Chroniques de Mathieu de Coussy*, in Buchon, *Collection des chroniques nationales françaises*, 156.

11 See King, "*Golden Targe*": the poem "anticipates the flowering of the imitative spectacular artifice of Ben Jonson's masques" (128).

12 Enid Welsford, *The Court Masque: A Study in the Relationship between Poetry and the Revels* (Cambridge: Cambridge University Press, 1927), 74. King, "*Golden Targe*" reviews the scholarship on Dunbar's poem at 115–16.

13 Kinsley, ed., *Dunbar*, p. 150, no. 52; see *LHTA* 2:477, for a record of "the More taubronaris devis agane Fasteringis Evin." The "More taubronar" may have played "Mahoun," who orders the "dance / Off schrewis" to begin (ll. 6–7, in "Fasternis").

14 *LHTA* 3:xci; Mill, *Mediaeval Plays in Scotland*, 56–57.

15 Michael R. Apted and Susan Hannabuss, eds., *Painters in Scotland, 1301–1700: A Biographical Dictionary* (Edinburgh: Edina Press, 1978), 40–41, citing *LHTA* 2:lviii.

16 Apted and Hannabuss, eds., *Painters in Scotland*, 41, citing *LHTA* 1:351, clvi, 348.

17 Apted and Hannabuss, eds., *Painters in Scotland*, 33, citing *LHTA* 3:xcii, 189, 196, 201, 387, 394.

18 Apted and Hannabuss, eds., *Painters in Scotland*, 33, citing *LHTA* 4:lv, 295–96, 376, 399, 406, 409, 477–78.

19 Apted and Hannabuss, eds., *Painters in Scotland*, 33, citing *LHTA* 5:xxxiv, 26.

20 *LHTA* 3:lxxxix–xc.

21 Mill, *Mediaeval Plays in Scotland*, 57.

22 Ibid., 56, citing *LHTA* 1:184, 270; 2:131.

23 Ibid., 16, 18. For the "Quene of Maij at the Abbay ʒet," *LHTA* 3:195, 197; for Abbots of Unreason, 2:374, 320, 430; 3:127, and so on.

24 *LHTA* 3:249, for "vij elne Rowan gray to be ane mummyng goun to the King; . . . iiij li. xj s̄."

25 See *LHTA* 3:141, "to gysaris dansit [in] the Kingis chamir. . . . iiij li. xs̄." Mill, *Mediaeval Plays in Scotland*, 14–15, citing *LHTA* 2:387; Younge, *Fyancells*, 300.

26 *LHTA* 1:xcii, 118.

27 For the "More taubronaris devis," see *LHTA* 2:477; for "Wantonnes" see *LHTA* 3:372; for Gilleam, *LHTA* 4:330.

28 *LHTA* 2:229, 438; 4:313. The author (Sir) David Lindsay is referred to.

29 *LHTA* 1:179, "to the Spanʒeartis that dansyt before the King on the cawsay of Edinburgh before the Thesauraris lwgeing, xxx vnicornis . . . xxvij li" (this is a considerable sum). *LHTA* 1:232-33, 326-27; 2:135.

30 Welsford, *Court Masque*, notes that the morris or morisco dance, very popular in the fifteenth, sixteenth and seventeenth centuries, "appears both as a folk-dance and as a favourite dance at Court theatricals" (25). "At the French and Tudor courts the dancers sometimes appeared as 'fools' or 'wild men', i.e., sophisticated versions of the village grotesques" (26–27). The morisco itself was, Welsford hypothesizes, "originally a Moorish dance" introduced into the Spanish and Italian courts, "characterised by a peculiar step and . . . the jangling of bells" (29). The court morisco, unlike the village morris dance, was "absorbed" into plays and other revels and "in its developed form closely resembled the momerie or disguising." E. K. Chambers, in *The English Folk-Play* (Oxford: Clarendon Press, 1933), notes that "a *Moresca* or *Morisco* first appears in the fifteenth century among the dances used as *intermedii* in the courtly *ludi* of Italy, Burgundy, and France"; he speculates that traditional face-blackening, "rather than any real oriental origin, led to the notion that the dance was one of Moors, and gave it its name" (150–51). Whatever the origins of the morisco, however, it is clear from the Treasurer's Accounts that both "folk" and "sophisticated" versions of the morris took place at James's court; the identification, factual or fanciful, of the morisco with Moors is also interesting in light of the apparent involvement of "Moors" (such as the "More taubronar") in courtly entertainments.

31 *LHTA* 2:413–14.

32 *LHTA* 2:414.

33 *LHTA* 2:477; 4:399–400.

34 *LHTA* 1:cxxvii, cxxx–cxxxi, 257, 262–63.

35 *LHTA* 3:xvii, 141, 143.

36 *LHTA* 3:xli, 354.

37 *Aymari Rivalii Delphinatis . . . de Allobrogibus Libri novem*, Ludovicus Perrin, typographus Lugd. 1844, in 80, lib. IX, 547; cited by Francisque-Michel, *Les Ecossais en France, Les Français en Ecosse*, vol. 1 (London: Trübner and Co.; Edinburgh: Williams and Norgate, 1862), 304.

38 Marc de Vulson, *Le Vray Théâtre d'Honnevr et de Chevaleri Ov le Miroir Heroiqve de la Noblesse*, vol. 1 (Paris: Avgvstin Covrbe, 1648), 70.

39 Francisque-Michel, *Les Ecossais en France*, 303; Baxter, *William Dunbar*, 165, citing *LHTA* 3:412.

40 Baxter, *William Dunbar,* 165, citing *LHTA* 3:xli–xliii, 358, 312, 366, 365, 372, 412; 4:117, 124. That d'Arces was in Scotland at the time of the tournament of 1508 is attested also by one of James's letters, written in June of that year, to Anne, queen of France; he asks her to "please excuse the detention of Darces in Scotland, for which James is responsible, and promote his interests in France." Robert Kerr Hannay and R. L. Mackie, eds., *The Letters of James IV, 1505–1513* (Edinburgh: Edinburgh University Press, 1953), 178. See also Macdougall, *James IV,* 255.

41 Pitscottie, *Historie of Scotland,* 243.

42 Hannay and Mackie, eds., *Letters of James IV,* no. 171, p. 111. See Macdougall, *James IV,* 255: "An elaborate tournament was arranged in honour of the French," in contrast with the coolness and the "devious diplomatic technique" with which James had only just received Henry VII's ambassador, Thomas Wolsey, who was in Scotland in the spring of 1508 "to try to forestall the making of a Franco-Scottish treaty" (254).

43 Hannay and Mackie, eds., *Letters of James IV,* no. 178, p. 115.

44 Macdougall, *James IV,* 295, 203; he minimizes the connection with the legendary King Arthur but on no apparent grounds. James was thinking of pilgrimage to the Holy Land in March 1507, "moved," writes Macdougall, "by the prospect of being the first Scottish king to succeed in making a pilgrimage to Jerusalem. It had been the dying wish of his ancestor Robert Bruce." Macdougall's chapter "Piety and Politics" (196–222) offers a careful analysis of the role played by the idea of crusade in James's diplomatic maneuverings. On the connection with James's campaigns in Gaelic Scotland, Macdougall notes that in March 1507, while James was on pilgrimage to Whithorn, Hugh O'Donnell of Tyrone wrote to James "mentioning a report which had been circulating amongst his Irish enemies, that James had for some time been considering leaving Scotland on pilgrimage." O'Donnell's attempt "to embroil James in Irish feuds" is "significant, for in March 1507 the news of James's final victory over Donald Dubh and Torquil MacLeod was still very recent" (198).

45 Ian Simpson Ross, *William Dunbar* (Leiden: Brill, 1981), 71.

46 Kinsley, ed., *Dunbar,* 108. Jean-Jacques Blanchot has discussed the possibility that Dunbar may have served under Stewart in the Scottish Guard in France; see Blanchot, "William Dunbar in the Scottish Guard in France? An Examination of Historical Facts," in Lyall and Riddy, eds., *Proceedings of the Third International Conference on Scottish Language and Literature,* 315–27.

47 Macfarlane, "Book of Hours," 12. The plate of the royal dirge (fol. 141v) shows a coffin, nine mourners, six canons in choir-stalls: "Tabard, standard and banner, bearing the royal arms of Scotland, hang from the gallery, in their temporary position, to denote that the Dirge is being sung for a King of Scots. Small escutcheons on gallery and walls bear the saltire" (12, and see plate 7). Macfarlane speculates that "the artist wished to commemorate some particularly Scottish occasion, perhaps the obsequies of James III, who was buried at . . . Cambuskenneth" (12).

48 See Maurice Keen, *Chivalry* (New Haven: Yale University Press, 1984), 155, on the extensive treatment given in heraldic treatises to noble funerals: "hatchments to be displayed, candles stamped with the arms of all the dead man's lines of nobility to be burned, and . . . the rules that govern the display of his arms and his effigy on his tomb. If the noble way of life was expensive, so was the noble way of dying." Vale, *War and Chivalry,* discusses funerals, stressing their extravagance and religiosity (88–92, 94, 97).

49 David Lindsay's "Armorial," National Library of Scotland (NLS) MS Adv. 31.4.3.
    See Robert Brydall, *Art in Scotland: Its Origin and Progress* (Edinburgh: William
    Blackwood and Sons, 1889), 28–29, for discussion of armorials of the Scottish
    nobility.

50 *Charters, Edinburgh*, 36:82–83, 13 August 1456, grants to Edinburgh land between
    Cragingalt and the Leith road "for tournaments, sports and proper warlike deeds"
    ("pro tournamentis, jocis, et justis actibus bellicis ibidem").

51 *LHTA* 1:lxxii.

52 *LHTA* 1:lxxii–lxxiii, for "a bedcover of purple silk embroidered with thistles and
    a unicorn," and similar items.

53 Charles Burnett, "The Royal Plant Badge of Scottish Sovereigns," paper delivered
    at Traditional Cosmology Society Conference on Kingship, Edinburgh, 8–10 Au-
    gust 1985.

54 Macfarlane, "Book of Hours," pp. 10, 13, and plates 2, 3.

55 The portrait was painted either for James VI or Charles I and is recorded by Van
    der Doort in Charles I's collection as "done after an Auncient water cullored peece,"
    according to the Scottish National Portrait Gallery.

56 Macfarlane, "Book of Hours," p. 9, and see plate 1; MS fol. 14v.

57 Edinburgh University Library MS 195, fol. 65. Catherine R. Borland, *Catalogue
    of the Western Mediaeval Manuscripts in Edinburgh University Library* (Edinburgh:
    University of Edinburgh, 1916), 281–82; appendix 2, 326.

58 NLS Dep. 221, MS 1. The Blackadder prayerbook is NLS MS 10271.

59 NLS Adv. MS 18.8.14, fol. 25r.

60 NLS Adv. MS 34.5.4.

61 NLS Adv. MS 18.2.13A.

62 Edinburgh University Library MS 205; MacQueen briefly discusses the MS in "Lit-
    erature of Fifteenth-Century Scotland," 201.

63 Stewart Cruden, *The Scottish Castle*, 3d ed. (Edinburgh: Spurbooks, 1981,) 129,
    131.

64 Ibid., 134.

65 Ibid., 136, 140.

66 Ibid., 149, pl. 24.

67 Richard Holland, *The Buke of the Howlat*, in F. J. Amours, ed., *Scottish Allitera-
    tive Poems in Riming Stanzas* vol. 1 (Edinburgh: William Blackwood and Sons,
    1897), 59–60, ll. 368–77. For a reading, see Margaret A. Mackay, "Structure and
    Style in Richard Holland's *Buke of the Howlat*," in Lyall and Riddy, eds., *Proceed-
    ings of the Third International Conference on Scottish Language and Literature*,
    191–206.

68 Nicholson, *Scotland*, 367.

69 William Beattie, *The Chepman and Myllar Prints* (Edinburgh: Edinburgh Biblio-
    graphical Society, 1950), vii.

70 Robert W. Ackerman, "English Rimed and Prose Romances," in Roger Sherman
    Loomis, ed., *Arthurian Literature in the Middle Ages: A Collaborative History*
    (Oxford: Clarendon Press, 1959), 492.

71 *Lancelot of the Laik*, ed. Margaret Muriel Gray (Edinburgh: William Blackwood
    and Sons, for the Scottish Text Society, 1912). See Janet M. Smith, *The French
    Background of Middle Scots Literature* (Edinburgh: Oliver and Boyd, 1934), 23;
    Ackerman, "English Rimed and Prose Romances," 491–92; and Bertram Vogel,

"Secular Politics and the Date of *Lancelot of the Laik*," *Studies in Philology* 40 (1943): 4–5. Scholars have detected, in the hortatory tone of the poem's treatment of Arthur, an allegory of the troubles of James III's reign. See Roderick J. Lyall, "Politics and Poetry in Fifteenth and Sixteenth Century Scotland," *Scottish Literary Journal* 3 (1976): 5–29, on the difficulties of dating satiric literature in the later Middle Ages.

72 Stevenson, ed., *Gilbert of the Haye's Prose Manuscript*, vols. 1 and 2.

73 Haye, *The Buke of Knychthede*, in Stevenson, ed., *Gilbert of the Haye's Prose Manuscript* 2:51.

74 See MacQueen, "Literature of Fifteenth-Century Scotland," 197, citing Gavin Douglas, *Virgil's Aeneid Translated into Scottish Verse by Gavin Douglas, Bishop of Dunkeld*, ed. David F. C. Coldwell, vol. 2 (Edinburgh: Scottish Text Society, 1957), prologue to Bk. 1, l. 85. Sinclair also commissioned MS Selden Arch B. 24.

75 "The Testament of Sir Dauid Synclar of Swynbrocht Knyght," *The Bannatyne Miscellany*, vol. 3 (Edinburgh, 1855), 107. Sinclair was the third son of William, earl of Orkney and Caithness and chancellor to James II (105).

76 *LHTA* 1:176: "to Wallass that tellis the geistis to the King, xviij s̄"; 1:307, "to Watschod the tale tellare and Widderspune the tale tellare togidder, xviij s̄" ("Widderspune" was also a fowler). On Blind Hary, see *LHTA* 1:176, "to Blind Hary, xviij s̄"; see also 1:xcix–c, civ, 133, 174, 181, 184. *Wallace* has been edited by James Moir (Edinburgh: William Blackwood and Sons, 1885, 1886, 1889).

77 "The *Wallace* is far removed from the true epic tradition, and its author no doubt felt that a little modern romantic embellishment was necessary to give glamour and polish to his rough tale of war." Smith, *French Background*, 22–23.

78 John Barbour, *The Buik of the Most Noble and Valiant Conquerour Alexander the Grit*, ed. R. L. Graeme Ritchie, 4 vols. (Edinburgh: William Blackwood and Sons, 1921–29); R. M. Lumiansky, "Legends of Alexander the Great," in *A Manual of the Writings in Middle English, 1050–1500*, ed. J. Burke Severs (New Haven: Connecticut Academy of Arts and Sciences, 1967), 111. See also MacQueen, "Literature of Fifteenth-Century Scotland," 193, and 198 on Sir Gilbert Haye's composition of *The Buik of Alexander the Conquerour* for Lord Erskine, and the *Taymouth Alexander* (which has now been edited by the Scottish Text Society).

79 Smith, *French Background*, 25, citing *Clariodus* (Edinburgh: Maitland Club, 1830), Bk. 4, pp. 216–17, ll. 811–24.

80 The subject will be discussed more fully in the next chapter, but the titles alone of Johan Huizinga, *The Waning of the Middle Ages: A Study of the Forms of Life, Thought, and Art in France and the Netherlands in the Fourteenth and Fifteenth Centuries*, trans. F. Hopman (Harmondsworth, Eng.: Penguin Books, 1924; rpt. Pelican Books, 1972), and Arthur B. Ferguson, *The Indian Summer of English Chivalry: Studies in the Decline and Transformation of Chivalric Idealism* (Durham, N.C.: Duke University Press, 1960), illustrate the poetics of decline in treatments of late medieval chivalry.

81 Edinburgh University Library *Scotichronicon*, 186, fol. 343 (at fol. 345 there is a genealogical tree with portraits of Scotland's kings and queens from Malcolm Canmore and Margaret to James II); Borland, *Catalogue*, 273; and David Laing and John Small, eds., *Select Remains of the Ancient Popular and Romance Poetry of Scotland* (Edinburgh: William Blackwood and Sons, 1885), 186ff.

82 *Roswall and Lillian* (Edinburgh, 1775): black-letter print, 14 leaves, 846 lines (884

in Lengert's ed.). See Lillian Herland Hernstein, "Miscellaneous Romances," in Severs, ed., *Manual* 152.

83 For the importance of the Three Days' Tournament in romance literature and its connection not only with the false claimant but also with the motif of the "rescue [of the princess] and escape from the Otherworld," see Jesse L. Weston, *The Three Days' Tournament: A Study in Romance and Folk-Lore* (London: David Nutt, 1902), 23, 26ff.

84 Laing and Small, eds., *Select Remains*, 3–4; an edition appears in Amours, ed., *Scottish Alliterative Poems*, 82–114; facsimile ed. by Robert Lekpreuik (St. Andrews, 1572), ed. W. Beattie (Edinburgh, 1966). See also p. 74 above.

85 Bawcutt, *Gavin Douglas*, 48.

86 See Douglas, 1:viii; and Bawcutt, *Gavin Douglas*, 49. All citations to *The Palice of Honour* are taken from Bawcutt, ed., *Shorter Poems of Gavin Douglas*.

87 Bawcutt, *Gavin Douglas*, 67.

88 Ibid., 63.

89 Ibid., 62.

90 Ibid., 60.

91 Ibid., 53.

92 Ibid., 54.

93 Ibid., 59. Laura Mulvey's comments on "mainstream film" seem curiously apposite: "Scale, space, stories are all anthropomorphic. Here, curiosity and the wish to look intermingle with a fascination with likeness and recognition: the human face, the human body, the relationship between the human form and its surroundings, the visible presence of the person in the world" ("Visual Pleasure," 9).

94 We are reminded of Lacan's remarks on "the role of spatial symmetry in man's narcissistic structure"—the physical space in which the subject constitutes his "reality" (his "ground," as Douglas would put it)—and on "the extent to which the fear of death . . . is psychologically subordinate to the narcissistic fear of damage to one's own body." Lacan, "Aggressivity in Psychoanalysis," *Écrits*, 27–28.

95 MacCary, *Childlike Achilles*, 234, 222.

96 The woman's "visual presence tends to work against the development of a story line, to freeze the flow of action in moments of erotic contemplation" (Mulvey, "Visual Pleasure," 11). Lacan comments on the strangeness of the "faces of actors when a film is suddenly stopped in mid-action" ("Aggressivity in Psychoanalysis," *Écrits*, 17).

97 Teresa de Lauretis, "Desire in Narrative," in *Alice Doesn't: Feminism, Semiotics, Cinema* (Bloomington: Indiana University Press, 1984), 140. She borrows the term *narrative image* from Stephen Heath, *Questions of Cinema* (Bloomington: Indiana University Press, 1981), 121, 140.

98 Bawcutt, *Gavin Douglas*, 50.

Chapter 11. Soft and Silken War

1 Welsford, *Court Masque*, 65.

2 Withington, *English Pageantry*, 100.

3 Cripps-Day also notes that masques were frequently included in the feasts preceding and following the tournament; tournament disguisings, he proposes, developed from indoor disguisings, not, once again, from any theatrical potential in the tournament itself. Cripps-Day, *History of the Tournament*, 133 n. 3, citing Percy Simp-

son, "The Masque," in *Shakespeare's England*, vol. 2 (Oxford: Clarendon Press), 311, to the effect that "In very early tournaments the procession of the knights disguised came from the masque."

4   Keen, *Chivalry*, 92.

5   Ibid.

6   King, "*Golden Targe*," 125.

7   R. Coltman Clephan, *The Tournament: Its Periods and Phases* (London: Methuen 1919), 11.

8   Cripps-Day, *History of the Tournament*, 46–47.

9   Vale, *War and Chivalry*, 76.

10 Ibid., 78. See 63–65 for Vale's discussion of the scholarly tradition on tournaments; his introduction (1–12) is a cogent analysis (via commentary, in particular, on Huizinga's *The Waning of the Middle Ages* and *Homo Ludens*) of the ascription of irreality to chivalry. Vale, however, does not consider the possibility that what we might call the "illusionist" approach to tournaments is to some degree a defense against recognizing the fictional element in war. Juliet R. V. Barker's excellent book *The Tournament in England, 1100–1400* (Woodbridge, Suffolk: Boydell Press, 1986), similarly suggests that "the Tournament was much more than a game. . . . As a gathering in arms of professional soldiers it had great potential for manipulation" (1). Barker argues for "an intimate, important, and long lasting" connection between the tournament and war (43). Anne Middleton, "War by Other Means: Marriage and Chivalry in Chaucer," *Studies in the Age of Chaucer* 6 (1985): 119–33, also contains an important critique of the tendency "to think of late-medieval chivalry as making virtually *nothing but appearances*. Moreover, these appearances are defined as deceptive, evasions rather than expressions of the most important truths about this culture. . . . What is left out . . . is the possibility that social fictions may proclaim and enact cultural truths, 'making' them rather than replacing them" (119–20). There is considerable evidence, however, that anxieties about the ficticity of chivalry were prevalent in the later Middle Ages and not merely the result of the "vantage point just after the Great War" (119).

11 Clephan, *Tournament*, 78–79, citing *Mémoires d'Olivier de la Marche* 3, Liv. II, chap. 4, pp. 101ff.

12 Sydney Anglo, "L'Arbre de Chevalerie et le Perron dans les Tournois," in Jacquot, ed., *Les Fêtes de la Renaissance*, 298.

13 Ibid.

14 Anglo, "L'Arbre de Chevalerie," 291; on *Yvain*, 287–88, quoting Chrétien de Troyes, *Yvain: Le Chevalier au Lion*, text by Wendelin Foerster, ed. T. B. W. Reid (Manchester: Manchester University Press, 1942), ll. 380–428: "La fontainne verras, qui bout, / S'est ele plus froide que marbres. / Onbre le fet li plus biaus arbres, / Qu'onques poïst feire Nature. / An toz la fuelle li dure, / Qu'il ne la pert por nul iver, / Et s'i pant uns bacins de fer / A une si longue chaainne, / Qui dure jusqu'au la fontainne. / Lez la fontainne troveras / Un perron tel con tu verras, / (Je ne te sai a dire, quel, / Que je n'an vi onques nul tel), / Et d'autre part une chapele / Petite, mes ele est mout bele. / S'au bacin vians de l'eve prandre / Et dessor le perron espandre, / La verras une tel tanpeste, / Qu'an cest bois ne remandre beste." Kalogrenant easily finds the tree and the chapel but discovers that the *bassin* is of gold, and the *perron* "fu d'une esmeraude"; he throws a stone into the water, the tempest ensues, birds shout, and then the defending chevalier appears, furious at this disturbance in his garden.

15   Keen, *Chivalry*, 205, 206.
16   Ruth Huff Cline, "The Influence of Romances on Tournaments of the Middle Ages,"
     Speculum 20 (1945): 210.
17   Ferguson, *Indian Summer*, 17.
18   Huizinga, *Waning of the Middle Ages*, 77–78.
19   Cripps-Day, *History of the Tournament*, 9.
20   Anderson, *Lineages of the Absolutist State*, 37. Anderson suggests that the "typical
     medium of inter-feudal rivalry . . . was military and its structure was always po-
     tentially the zero-sum conflict of the battlefield, by which fixed quantities of ground
     were won or lost" (33, 31). He contrasts this rivalrous style with "inter-capitalist
     competition," in which the "normal medium . . . is economic," and the "structure
     . . . typically additive."
21   At a number of points in his discussion, Vale stresses the usefulness of chivalric
     ritual to princes in controlling the violence of their subjects. He writes that "the
     cash nexus was not enough to hold a man's allegiance, nor to prevent him from
     slipping into a rival camp. The crucial questions of loyalty and disloyalty, of fi-
     delity and *lèse-majesté*, were as much a part of the rationale and justification for
     orders of chivalry as they were for the treason trial and *lit-de-justice*" (*War and
     Chivalry*, 35–36). Commenting on the difficulty of "restraining the excessive zeal
     of participants in a *tournoi*" (a zeal often motivated by private feuds), he remarks
     that "the sovereignty of kings and princes had not yet entirely eliminated feudal
     independence or private feud among the fifteenth-century nobility. Without the
     tournament the inclination towards violence found in every medieval nobility might
     have erupted more often into open defiance and civil war" (87).
22   On the ideology of realism and its treatment of romance, see Fredric Jameson,
     "Beyond the Cave: Modernism and Modes of Production," in Paul Hernadi, ed.,
     The Horizons of Literature (Lincoln: University of Nebraska Press, 1982), 166–67.
23   Cripps-Day, *History of the Tournament*, 3–4, and n. 1; see also Keen, *Chivalry*,
     96–98.
24   Cripps-Day, *History of the Tournament*, 15, 17, 31.
25   Ibid., appendix 6: "Extracts from the Harleian MS 69."
26   Welsford, *Court Masque*, 125, citing Edward Hall, *Henry VIII*, in *The Lives of
     the Kings* (London: T. C. and E. C. Jack, 1904), 171, 172 (10th Yr.).
27   Marc de Vulson, *La Science Heroiqve, Traitant de la Noblesse, et de l'Origine des
     Armes* . . . (Paris: Sebastien Mabre-Cramoisy, 1669), 491.
28   Haye, *The Buke of the Law of Armys*, in Stevenson, ed., *Gilbert of the Haye's
     Prose Manuscript* 1:5.
29   Dante Alighieri, *Inferno*, vol. 1, ed. and trans. Charles S. Singleton (Princeton:
     Princeton University Press, 1970), 222–23, canto 22, ll. 1–12: "Io vidi già cavalier
     muover campo, / e cominciare stormo e far lor mostra, / e talvolta partir per loro
     scampo; / corridor vidi per la terra vostra, / o Aretini, e vidi gir gualdane, / fedir
     torneamenti e correr giostra; / quando con trombe, e quando con campane, / con
     tamburi e con cenni di castella, / e con cose nostrali e con istrane; / né già con
     sì diversa cennamella / cavalier vidi muover né pedoni, / né nave a segno di terra
     o di stella." ("Ere now have I seen horsemen moving camp, and beginning an as-
     sault and making their muster, and sometimes retiring to escape; I have seen cours-
     ers over your land, O Aretines, and I have seen the starting of raids, the onset
     of tournaments, and the running of jousts, now with trumpets and now with bells,
     with drums and castle-signals, with native things and foreign — but never to so

strange a pipe have I seen horsemen or footmen set forth, or ship by sign of land or star!")

30 Keen, *Chivalry*, 94, citing Charles-Joseph Hefele and Dom H. Leclercq, *Histoire des Conciles*, vol. 5 (Paris: Libraire Letouzey et Ane, 1912–13), pt. 1:688, 729, 825; pt. 2:1394, 1660.

31 Cripps-Day, *History of the Tournament*, 39, citing Hefele and Leclercq, *Histoire des Conciles*, vol. 7 (1872), 507.

32 Keen, *Chivalry*, 96.

33 G. R. Owst, *Literature and Pulpit in Medieval England: A Neglected Chapter in the History of English Letters and of the English People*, 2d ed. (Oxford: Basil Blackwell, 1961), 333–34, citing John Bromyard, *Summa Predicantium*, s.v. "Nobilitas."

34 Ibid.

35 Haye, *The Buke of Knychthede*, in Stevenson, ed., *Gilbert of the Haye's Prose Manuscript* 2:44.

36 Ibid., 45.

37 Ibid., 23.

38 Ibid., 69.

39 Vale, "The Literature of Honour and Virtue," *War and Chivalry*, 14–32, is an important introduction to the subject; the "emphasis on the qualities of 'true nobility'" which "pervades much of the didactic literature of honour and virtue" was to some extent stimulated by the challenges posed to the hereditary nobility of the later Middle Ages by "newly ennobled families" (20–21).

40 Lacan envisions the infant seeing itself in a mirror and, through its gazing at itself, functioning as other; the infant may also be imagined to respond to the image of itself reflected back to it in the gaze of the mother. See Lacan, "The Mirror Stage," *Écrits*, 2.

41 Julian Pitt-Rivers, "Honour and Social Status," in J. G. Peristiany, ed., *Honour and Shame: The Values of Mediterranean Society* (Chicago: University of Chicago Press, 1966), 23. Pitt-Rivers notes that once the monarchy no longer allowed the appeal to God through the ordeal of judicial combat, but "took on the entire responsibility of arbitrating the claims to honour," the courts of chivalry incurred the criticisms that arose from the conflicts inherent in the notion of honor (23). See Cripps-Day, *History of the Tournament*, 70, on judicial combat, courts of chivalry, and, as an illustration of Pitt-Rivers's point, on the criticisms levied at Richard II's Court of Chivalry.

42 Pitt-Rivers, "Honour and Social Status," 22, 37.

43 This quoted material is from Keen, *Chivalry*, 90.

44 Pitt-Rivers, "Honour and Social Status," 25.

45 See MacCary, *Childlike Achilles*, 226, on the "paradoxicality" of doubles in the "phenomenology of war" and of "the self."

46 See Keen, *Chivalry*, 250: "The life of honour has to be lived through to the end: the final seal of approbation on it is a sepulchral monument." For a late heraldic treatise devoted to sepulchral monuments, see 169: "This is the manner . . . how a man may know how a noble has lived and used his life and persevered to the end, when he is buried and his effigy is depicted on his tomb armed" (citing MS 21552, fols. 27–28, Bibliothèque Royale, Brussels).

47 See Huizinga, *Waning of the Middle Ages*, 69, 71.

48 Gerard J. Brault, *Early Blazon: Heraldic Terminology in the Twelfth and Thirteenth*

Centuries with Special Reference to Arthurian Literature (Oxford: Clarendon Press, 1972), 30; 30–31 n. 6, for a list of examples.

49   The Three Days' Tournament is discussed in Laura A. Hibbard, *Mediaeval Romance in England: A Study of the Sources and Analogues of the Non-Cyclic Metrical Romances* (New York: Oxford University Press, 1924), 152, 226, as well as in Weston, *Three Days' Tournament*. See also Dorothy E. Winters, "The Three Days Combat," Ph.D. diss., University of Chicago, 1939.

50   Brault, *Early Blazon*, 31.

51   Fredric Jameson, in arguing that the romance emerges as a result of the contradiction which arose during the twelfth century between the old "positionality" of good and evil that marked the *chansons de geste* and the "emergent class solidarity" of the feudal nobility, describes the romance as a "new kind of narrative, the 'story' of something like a semic evaporation"—in which the hostile and unknown knight at first "exudes that insolence which marks a fundamental refusal of recognition and stamps him as the bearer of the category of evil, up to the moment when, defeated and unmasked, he asks for mercy by *telling his name* . . . at which point, reinserted into the unity of the social class, he becomes one more knight among others and loses all his sinister unfamiliarity." Evil then must float off to create the romance realm of magic and sorcery. Jameson, "Magical Narratives" *Political Unconscious*, 118–19.

52   See Cripps-Day, *History of the Tournament*, 60–61; he refers to *Rychard Coer de Lion* (ca. 1261), ed. Henry Weber, *Metrical Romances*, vol. 2 (Edinburgh: George Ramsay and Co., 1810), p. 14, ll. 267–74: "Kyng Richard gan hym dysguyse / In a fal strange queyntyse. / He cam out of a valaye, / For to se of theyr playe, / As a knyght aventurous: / Hys atyre was orgulous: / Al togyder cole black / Was hys horse withoute lacke." Hibbard, in *Mediaeval Romance in England* (152), also discusses Richard's "successive disguises of black, red, and white"; he is disguised as a pilgrim on his first journey to the East. Rude speech takes place between Richard incognito and a minstrel, paralleled by the ballad stories of kings incognito (cf. *Rauf Coilȝear* for a Scottish example). The king's adoption of plain arms is thus a version of "the glamorous impersonating the ordinary"; James IV appears to have jousted in black in his tournament of the wild knight and the black lady. Examples from late medieval tournament pageantry are too numerous to mention, but see Welsford, *Court Masque*, 123, citing Hall, *Henry VIII*, 22–23 (2d Yr.), on Henry VIII's performance in 1510 as one of "Les quater Chivalers de la forrest salvigne."

53   Withington, *English Pageantry*, suggests that the knight's "habit of travelling incognito" gave rise to tournament disguising and masquerade (101).

54   Jameson, "Magical Narratives," *Political Unconscious*, 118. As Pitt-Rivers explains in "Honour and Social Status," there must be equality between the challenger and the challenged for honor to work; there is a difference between punishing impudence and avenging an affront (31).

55   Lacan, "Aggressivity in Psychoanalysis," *Écrits*, 17, on "feelings of persecution as phenomenological moments in social behaviour."

56   Lacan, "The Mirror Stage," *Écrits*, 2.

57   A forceful image of this kind of disjunction between ideality and flesh can be found in *Sir Gawain and the Green Knight*, in which Gawain's splendid armor becomes, on his journey, a torturing armature that freezes and imprisons the suffering flesh beneath.

58   Lacan, "The Mirror Stage," *Écrits*, 3.

59 On the symmetry of the field, see Lacan: "It is the subjective possibility of the mirror projection of [a spatial field] . . . into the field of the other that gives human space its originally 'geometrical' structure" ("Aggressivity in Psychoanalysis," *Écrits*, 27).

60 See Lacan, "The Mirror Stage," *Écrits*, 4–5.

61 If, according to Lacan, it is "by means of an identification with the other that [the child] . . . sees the whole gamut of reactions of bearing and display," it is "at this structural crossroads" that "the primordial coming together . . . is precipitated into aggressive competitiveness . . . from which develops the triad of others, the ego and the object" ("Aggressivity in Psychoanalysis," *Écrits*, 19).

62 For Lacan — as for Melanie Klein, whom he follows in this regard — it is the primordial *imago* of the mother's body in which "the *imagos* of the father and brothers (real or virtual), in which the voracious aggression of the subject himself, dispute their deleterious dominance over her sacred regions" ("Aggressivity in Psychoanalysis", *Écrits*, 20–21).

63 According to Lacan, "the Oedipal identification is that by which the subject transcends the aggressivity that is constitutive of the primary subjective individuation" ("Aggressivity in Psychoanalysis," *Écrits*, 23).

64 Keen, *Chivalry*, 204, citing Alice Planche, "Du turnoi au théâtre en Bourgogne: Le Pas de la Fontaine des Pleurs à Chalon-sur-Saône, 1449–50," *Le Moyen Age* 81 (1975): 102 nn. 27, 28.

65 Cline, "Influence of Romances on Tournaments," 210, citing *Traicté de la forme et devis comme on faict les tournois, par Olivier de la Marche*, ed. Bernard Prost (Paris: A. Barraud, 1878), 58.

66 Welsford, *Court Masque*, 58, citing H. Prunières, *Le Ballet de Cour en France avant Benserade et Lulli* (Paris: H. Laurens, 1914), 9.

67 Hibbard, *Medieval Romance in England*, 301, on Degare; Teresa de Lauretis, in "Desire in Narrative," discusses (following Propp in "Oedipus in the Light of Folklore") the forest as a "place of the hero's education," as a "female domain," instances of which appear in "hybrid forms" until the full flowering of patriarchy and the onset of narratives in which the son, who doesn't know the identity of the father, sets out in search of him (115). The story of Romulus and Remus is of particular interest to our discussion, since the space of the mother is so often associated with the rivalry of the doubles in tournament pageantry.

68 Vulson, *La Science Heroiqve*, 491.

69 Owst, *Literature and Pulpit*, 332–34, citing Bromyard, *Summa Predicantium*, s.v. "Nobilitas"; p. 412, citing *Jacob's Well: An English Treatise on the Cleansing of Man's Conscience*, ed. Arthur Brandeis, pt. 1 (London: Kegan Paul, Trench, Trübner, and Co., 1900), 104.

70 Owst, *Literature and Pulpit*, 411, n. 3; MS Bodleian Laud Misc. 23, fols. 33–34.

71 Owst, *Literature and Pulpit*, 408; Bromyard, *Summa Predicantium*, s.v. "Inconstantia." On James's fashions, see *LHTA* 1:clxxiv.

72 Owst, *Literature and Pulpit*, 130–31 n. 6, 406–7; MS Hereford Cathedral Library P. 5.2, fol. 105.

73 Owst, *Literature and Pulpit*, 406–7; MS Worcester Cathedral Library F. 10, fol. 238.

74 Cited in Cripps-Day, *History of the Tournament*, 92–93.

75 Robert Steele, ed., *Secrees of Old Philisoffres: A Version of the Secreta Secretorum* (London: Kegan Paul, Trench, Trübner and Co., 1894), ll. 1611–25.

76 David Lindsay, *A Satire of the Three Estates*, ed. Matthew McDiarmid (London:

Heinemann, 1967). All citations are taken from this edition. For a fine study of Lindsay's play, see Joanne Spencer Kantrowitz, *Dramatic Allegory: Lindsay's Ane Satyre of the Thrie Estaitis* (Lincoln: University of Nebraska Press, 1975).

77 Cripps-Day, *History of the Tournament*, 40, citing Green, *History of the English People* 1:456.

78 Cripps-Day, *History of the Tournament*, 40; B.M. MS Roy. 19, CI. Cf. also the account of a tournament in 1389: St. Palaye, *L'Ancienne Chevalerie* (1759), 2:68.

79 Keen, *Chivalry*, 92, and plates 18 and 27. In 1225 Ulrich also staged a scene reminiscent of the Three Days' Tournament: after a day of jousting, he decided to mystify the knights the next day by disappearing from the jousts and returning with himself, his horse, and eleven boys clothed all in green. See Winters, "Three Days Combat," 1–23; Ulrich von Lichtenstein, *Frauendienst*, ed. Reinhold Bechstein (Leipzig: F. A. Brockhaus, 1888), stanzas 1416, 1430, 1437, 1454, 1548, 1553; and Cline, "Influence of Romances on Tournaments," 204–11.

80 Haye, *The Buke of Knychthede*, in Stevenson, ed., *Gilbert of the Haye's Prose Manuscript* 2:51.

81 David Lindsay, *Armorial*, NLS MS Adv. 31.4.3, fol. 53r.

82 Rodney Dennys, *Heraldry and the Heralds* (London: Jonathan Cape, 1982), 24.

83 Brault, *Early Blazon*, 3. Vale, *War and Chivalry*, notes that in the later Middle Ages "coats [of arms] had become . . . much more difficult to recognise," stimulating reliance on "simpler methods of identification"; "the *devise*, or personal badge, was to some extent a reversion to the bolder heraldic signs of an earlier period" (96–97).

84 This is, at any rate, Dennys's argument; see *Heraldry*, 31.

85 Ibid., 42, 5.

86 Ibid., 7.

87 Virginia Woolf, *Three Guineas* (London: Hogarth Press, 1938), is a fascinating commentary on public regalia: "The fact that both sexes have a very marked though dissimilar love of dress seems to have escaped the notice of the dominant sex owing largely it must be supposed to the hypnotic power of dominance" (270–71 n. 16). See, especially, 207–8, on the connection between fascism and the "limelight": "The power to change and the power to grow, can only be preserved by obscurity."

88 Cripps-Day, *History of the Tournament*, 127–28, citing Holinshed's *Chronicles* (1586), 3:1321, and *Polyhymnia, describing the honourable Triumph at Tylt before her Majestie, printed at London by Richard Jhones, 1590, by George Peele, Maister of Artes in Oxforde*.

89 Cripps-Day, *History of the Tournament*, appendix 1, ix: *Dissertation VI. sur L'Histoire de Saint Louys par le Sire de Joinville*, by Charles Du Fresne, Seigneur Du Cange (1668).

90 Cripps-Day, *History of the Tournament*, 61, citing *Anciens Mémoires sur du Guesclin*, in M. Petitot, ed., *Collection complète de Mémoires relatifs à l'Histoire de France* 4:179.

91 Haye, *The Buke of Knychthede*, in Stevenson, ed., *Gilbert of the Haye's Prose Manuscript* 2:51.

92 Ibid., 21.

93 Ibid., 68.

94 Pitt-Rivers, "Honour and Social Status," 36.

95 Ibid., 37.

96 Feuerbach, preface to the 2d ed. of *The Essence of Christianity*, quoted in Guy Debord, *Society of the Spectacle* (Detroit: Black and Red, 1983), chap. 1.
97 Pitt-Rivers, "Honour and Social Status," 37.
98 Welsford, *Court Masque*, 39. The 1377 mumming for Richard II by the Commons of London included "8 or 10 arayed and with black vizardes"; they used a pair of dice "subtilly made that when ye prince shold caste he shold winne." Harleian MS 247, fol. 172v, printed in Edward Mound Thompson, ed., *Chronicon Angliae* (London: Longman and Co., 1874), lxxxii–iii. Stephen Orgel, *The Jonsonian Masque* (Cambridge: Harvard University Press, 1965), comments: "The fiction is that a game of chance is taking place, and the work thus contains adversaries and a central action. But chance has been defeated. . . . The sovereign wins, the masque says, because it is his nature to win" (19).
99 Pitt-Rivers, "Honour and Social Status," 38.
100 Ibid., 35.
101 Younge, *Fyancells*, 288.
102 Ibid.
103 The quotation is from Withington, *English Pageantry*, 96.

Chapter 12. The Wild Knight

1 The accounts for the tournament expenses are edited in *LHTA*, vols. 3 and 4; see 3:xlv ff., for discussion of the tournaments and their dates.
2 *LHTA* 3:365, 372; Lindesay of Pitscottie, *Historie of Scotland* 1:242: "the warneing and proclamatioun heirof was ane hundreith dayes befoir to the effectt that france ingland and denmark micht haue knawledge of the samyn."
3 Vulson, *Le Vray Théâtre d'Honnevr*, 271.
4 Vulson, *La Science Heroiqve*, 492; Pitscottie, *Historie of Scotland* 1:242.
5 *LHTA* 3:xlviii; the reference is to an entry "to Blewmantill, now callit Rothsey, for to pas in France, Spanze, and Portugall the Kingis erandis" (371).
6 Vulson, *La Science Heroiqve*, 491–92.
7 *LHTA* 3:394.
8 *LHTA* 3:256; Vulson, *La Science Heroiqve*, 492.
9 *LHTA* 3:259–60, 256–57.
10 *LHTA* 3:258–59.
11 Ibid.
12 Ibid.
13 *LHTA* 3:li, 385–86, 393–94, 397.
14 Vulson, *La Science Heroiqve*, 492.
15 Fenichel, *Psychoanalytic Theory of Neurosis*, 483.
16 Vulson, *La Science Heroiqve*, 492.
17 According to Fenichel, students of war neuroses have found infantilization characteristic of the "military situation": the "typical attitude of the soldier" is "an expectation of parental protection," which "may give place to a sudden and severe disappointment" (*Psychoanalytic Theory of Neurosis*, 122).
18 Vulson, *La Science Heroiqve*, 491–92.
19 Ibid.
20 Ibid., 493–94.
21 Lauretis, "Desire in Narrative," 110; Mulvey, "Visual Pleasure," 11.
22 Pitscottie, *Historie of Scotland* 1:242–44.

23 Leslie, *Historie of Scotland* (1890), 2:128.

24 The Scottish text of Leslie's work (as opposed to Dalrymple's translation) is printed in *History of Scotland* (1830).

25 William Drummond of Hawthornden, *The History of the Life and Reign of James the fourth, King of Scotland,* in *The Works of William Drummond of Hawthornden* (Edinburgh: James Watson, 1711), 69.

26 *LHTA* 3:258.

27 *LHTA* 3:258, 365 (1507); 4:63 (1508).

28 *LHTA* 3:261, 254–55. The king had other clothing prepared for the occasion of the tournament, including doublets – one of "tanne satin" (261), one of "satin crammesy" with gold borders (256) – and "cotes" made of satin crammesy, velvet, and cloth-of-gold (261).

29 *LHTA* 3:259.

30 *LHTA* 3:394–96; 4:121, for work done on the king's swords, spear heads, and harness in 1508.

31 *LHTA* 3:396.

32 Pitscottie, *Historie of Scotland* 243; *LHTA* 3:255.

33 *LHTA* 3:1

34 Richard Bernheimer, *Wild Men in the Middle Ages: A Study in Art, Sentiment, and Demonology* (Cambridge: Harvard University Press, 1952), 26–27.

35 Ibid., 2.

36 Withington, *English Pageantry,* 72ff. For wildmen as supporters, see, for example, the beautiful depiction of the arms of Jean de Malestroit, which shows a wild man and woman in a natural setting, carrying the armorial banners of Malestroit and his wife and supporting the helmet atop the shield, in *Chroniques des France,* Gaguin MS 1477, 1, Bibliothèque de l'Arsenal, Paris, reproduced in Ottfried Neubecker with J. P. Brooke-Little, *Heraldry: Sources, Symbols and Meaning* (New York: McGraw-Hill, 1976), 196–97. See also Withington, *English Pageantry,* 73–74 n. 5, on the use of wild men as heraldic supporters.

37 Welsford, *Court Masque,* 123, citing Hall, *Henry VIII,* 1:22–23 (2d Yr.).

38 Bernheimer, *Wild Men,* 3.

39 Ibid., 7, 6.

40 Ibid., 20.

41 The pairing of wild-man buffoon and wild knight in the tournaments of James IV and Henry VIII thus bespeaks a certain preoccupation both with motility and with its mannering. Norbert Elias expounds the case for late medieval society's development of civility – the "moderation of the affects" which he associates with the growing "importance of the courts as a social authority, a source of models of behavior" – in his trilogy *The Civilizing Process* (citations are from *Power and Civility,* trans. Edmund Jephcott [New York: Pantheon Books, 1982], 4–5). In light of the buffoonery often associated with the figure of the wild man, it is interesting to note Freud's point that humor has one of its deepest roots in the gap between the childish body's failures of control and the ideal image one must present of oneself in the "courts" of the adult world. See *Wit and Its Relation to the Unconscious,* in A. A. Brill, ed. and trans., *The Basic Writings of Sigmund Freud* (New York: Random House, 1938), 777: "When I speak of the exalted . . . I impose upon myself a dignified restriction, not much different than if I were coming into the presence of an illustrious personage, monarch, or prince of science"; and see pp.

777–78 for discussion of the human dependence on physical needs that Freud finds crucial to the comedy of unmasking and degradation.

42 The wild man differs from the *gorgoneion* insofar as, from the male point of view, he is created as a "similar" rather than as a "different" kind of threat; he gives expression to the internal contradiction of the warrior who seeks at the same time to exemplify the values of civilization.

43 See Bernheimer, *Wild Men*, 177–78, for the notion that the use of the wild man as a supporter was "talismanic," "based upon the thought that a creature as overwhelmingly strong as the wild man could surely be trusted to protect and defend the escutcheon." He argues that representations of wild men as supporters in heraldic art "antedate the recorded examples . . . at the jousts by more than fifty years" (178) and dates the first example of the wild man's use in the tournament at 1438 (215 n. 6). Earlier writers often reverse this causality, as for example Menestrier in *L'Art du Blason et l'Origine des Armoires* (1672): "Les supports d'hommes et de femmes sauvages, de Lions, de Griffons, d'Anges, et de Dieux de la fable, sont venus des Tournois, où l'on déguisoit des hommes de toutes ces manières pour leur faire porter les Escussons des Chevaliers, et pour leur faire garder les pas et les Ecus pendans" (175); cited by Cripps-Day, *History of the Tournament*, 2 n. 1.

44 Bernheimer, *Wild Men*, 177. See Felipe Fernández-Armesto, *Before Columbus: Exploration and Colonization from the Mediterranean to the Atlantic, 1229–1492* (Philadelphia: University of Pennsylvania Press, 1987). Fernández-Armesto adds that "the actual phrase 'wild men of the woods' . . . became a standard term for the natives" (241). The association of wildness and blackness is discussed in chapter 13, below.

45 Nicholson, *Scotland*, 541, citing Ayala, in Brown, *Early Travellers*, 9.

46 Nicholson, *Scotland*, 541.

47 Ferguson, *Scotland's Relations with England*, 46.

48 Ibid., 34–35.

49 Nicholson, *Scotland*, 546, quoting *APS* 2:249, chap. 3.

50 Nicholson, *Scotland*, 545, 547, citing *APS* 2:244, chap. 27.

51 Nicholson, *Scotland*, 547, citing *Registrum Secreti Sigilli Regum Scotorum: The Register of the Privy Seal of Scotland*, ed. M. Livingstone et al. (1908–), vol. 2, nos. 1196, 2369, 3208 (hereinafter cited as *RSS*).

52 Nicholson, *Scotland*, 587; *Facsimiles of the National Manuscripts of Scotland* (London, 1867–73), vol. 3, no. 8.

53 Nicholson, *Scotland*, 547; Mackie, *King James IV*, 158; D. E. R. Watt, ed., *Fasti Ecclesiae Scoticanae Medii Aevi* (St. Andrews: Fasti Committee, 1969), 207–8; *RSS* 1: no. 184; *RMS* 2: no. 3784; J. R. N. MacPhail, ed., *Highland Papers*, vol. 4 (Edinburgh: T. and A. Constable, for the Scottish History Society, 1934), 185.

54 Nicholson, *Scotland*, 546, citing *APS* 2:249, chap. 3.

55 Nicholson, *Scotland*, 546, citing *LHTA* 3:lxxxii.

56 Nicholson, *Scotland*, 547.

57 Nicholson, *Scotland*, notes that, despite James IV's successes, "whenever the crown . . . managed to 'beate downe the hornes of proude oppressours,' a power vacuum was created that the crown was usually unable to fill"; the peace of 1507 was "illusory" (547, quoting *The Basilicon Doron of James VI* [Scottish Text Society] 1:69).

58 We recall that, at the beginning of the "Articles de l'Emprinse du Chevalier Sauvage

a la Dame noire," in Vulson, *La Science Heroiqve,* it is explained that the exercise of arms is "aux Chevaliers plus loüable ledit exercise, & principalement au service de Dieu à l'encontre des Infidelles, non seulement permis, mais meritoire" (491).

Chapter 13. The Black Lady

1   Klaus Theweleit, *Male Fantasies,* vol. 1, *Women Floods Bodies History,* trans. Stephen Conway (Minneapolis: University of Minnesota Press, 1987), 299, 359.
2   Ibid., 296.
3   At least by the later sixteenth century, blackness of skin "was commonly equated with ugliness, lechery and wickedness in general." Paul Edwards and James Walvin, *Black Personalities in the Era of the Slave Trade* (London: Macmillan, 1983), 9; Paul Edwards, "Africans in Britain before 1560," unpublished MS, 4 (I am indebted to Dr. Edwards for providing me with a copy of his essay). See also Ruth Cowhig, "Blacks in English Renaissance Drama and the Role of Shakespeare's Othello," David Dabydeen, ed., *The Black Presence in English Literature* (Manchester: Manchester University Press, 1985), 1. Fernández-Armesto's chapter "The 'Discovery of Man,'" in *Before Columbus,* is a very important study of late medieval attitudes toward people of color (223–45).
4   Edward, Lord Herbert of Cherbury, "Sonnet of Black Beauty," ll. 13–14, in Hershel Baker, ed., *The Later Renaissance in England: Nondramatic Verse and Prose, 1600–1660* (Boston: Houghton Mifflin, 1975), 121; the title of the sonnet is annotated by the editor as meaning "Brunette." This sonnet celebrates the immutability of "Black beauty, which above that common light / Whose power can no colors here renew / But those which darkness can again subdue, / Dost still remain unvaried to the sight, / And like an object equal to the view, / Art neither chang'd with day, nor hid with night" (ll. 1–6). In *The Masque of Blacknesse,* Niger describes his daughters as "the first form'd dames of earth, / And in whose sparckling, and refulgent eyes, / The glorious *Sunne* did still delight to rise; / Though he (the best iudge, and most formall cause / Of all dames beauties) in their firme hiewes, / drawes / Signes of his feruent'st loue; and thereby shewes / That in their black, the perfectst beauty growes; / Since the fix't colour of their curled haire, / (Which is the highest grace of dames most faire) / No cares, no age can change; or there display / The fearefull tincture of abhorred *Gray:* / Since *Death* her selfe (her selfe being pale and blue) / Can neuer alter their most faithfull hiew" (ll. 138–50). Niger's perceptions, however, are ultimately questioned and reordered by the masque; his daughters may be the "first form'd dames of earth" but, if they are to attain true beauty, must nonetheless be recreated by the power of the English Sun, whose "light scientiall is, and (past mere nature) / Can salve the rude defects of euery creature" (ll. 255–56). All citations to *The Masque of Blacknesse* are from Herford, Simpson, and Simpson, eds., *Ben Jonson* 7:169–80.
5   Shakespeare's Sonnet 127: "In the old age black was not counted fair, / Or if it were it bore not beauty's name."
6   Wolfram von Eschenbach, *Parzival,* trans. Helen M. Mustard and Charles E. Passage (New York: Vintage Books, 1961), 14. All citations to *Parzival* are taken from this translation.
7   In a similar vein, Ruth Cowhig argues that "in Marlowe's *Tamburlaine the Great* . . . the three Moorish kings['] . . . main contribution to the play is in adding to the impression of power and conquest by emphasising the extent of Tamburlaine's

victories. . . . Marlowe's plays reflect the curiosity of his contemporaries about distant countries, and must have whetted the appetites of his audiences for war and conquest" ("Blacks in English Renaissance Drama," 2).

8   Chambers, *English Folk-Play*, 164; *The Mediaeval Stage*, 2 vols. (Oxford: Clarendon Press, 1903), 2:142, M. Lyle Spencer, *Corpus Christi Pageants in England* (New York: Baker and Taylor Co., 1911), 226. The 1377 mumming for Richard II put on by the Commons of London included "8 or 10 arayed and with black vizardes like deuils appearing nothing amiable seeming like legates." Harleian MS 247, printed in *Chronicon Angliae*; Welsford, *Court Masque*, 39.

9   The Turkish knight of the mummer's play also appears as the Black Prince of Paradise, Paradine, or Paladine, who is also "Morocco dog" or "Morocco King"; in north Somerset, the "Black Prince of Darkness." Chambers, *English Folk-Play*, 27–28. A prominent character in the medieval mummers' play was the "King of Egypt, who had a black face and who was accepted by tradition as the father of St. George" (22, 85).

10 David Buchan, ed., *Scottish Tradition: A Collection of Scottish Folk Literature* (London: Routledge and Kegan Paul, 1984), 213–14. My thanks to Dr. Emily Lyle — who was responsible for the fieldwork involved in collecting this material — for pointing out this reference to me.

11 Eldred Jones has suggested that the practice of blackening was transferred from civic and folk festivities to courtly disguisings in the sixteenth century. Jones, *Othello's Countrymen: The African in English Renaissance Drama* (London: Oxford University Press, 1965), 28.

12 Welsford, *Court Masque*, 43–44, citing *Religieux de Saint Denis*; and see 27 n. 1. The occasion was a wedding, for which Charles and his companions wore garments covered with pitch, onto which frayed linen was fixed; the over-curious duke of Orléans came too near with a torch. Two of the company died on the spot, two more after two days of agony, and Charles never recovered from the shock. Juvenal des Ursins called it "une feste . . . d'hommes sauvages enchaisnes, tous velus." Cf. Prunières, *Le Ballet de Cour*, 9; and Welsford, 3 and notes, citing *Religieux de Saint Denis*, tomus 2, chap. 16, p. 65; Buchon, ed., *Les Chroniques de Sire Jean Froissart*, vol. 3 (Panthéon Littéraire) Bk. 4, chap. 32, 177ff.; Juvenal des Ursins, *Histoire de Charles VI, Roi de France*, ed. Buchon, *Choix de Chroniques et Mémoires*, 378ff.

13 Welsford, *Court Masque*, 48–49, citing Buchon, ed., *Les Chroniques de Sire Jean Froissart*, vol. 3, Bk. 4, chap. 1, pp. 3ff; p. 58, citing Prunières, *Le Ballet de Cour*, 9; p. 89, citing Ferdinand Gregorovius, *Lucretia Borgia*, trans. John Leslie Garner (London: John Murray, 1904), 256–64.

14 Withington, *English Pageantry* 1:72 n. 3; William Herbert, *The History of the Twelve Great Livery Companies of London* (1837), 1:455. See also Jones, *Othello's Countrymen*, 29.

15 See Jones, *Othello's Countrymen*, 2ff., 8, 25, 126, for discussion of this background; and Jacques Le Goff, *Time, Work, and Culture in the Middle Ages*, trans. Arthur Goldhammer (Chicago: University of Chicago Press, 1980), 189–200. Le Goff cites Pliny, *Historia Naturalis* 7.2.21, "praecipue India Aethiopumque tractus miraculis scatent"; Solinus, *Collectanea rerum memorabilium*, ed. Theodor Mommsen, 2d ed. (Berlin: Weidmann, 1895); Martianus Capella, *De nuptiis Philologiae et Mercurii*, lib. vi. (p. 342 nn. 17–19). See Jones, 3, for Bacon, *The Opus Majus of Roger Bacon* 1:330ff., who quotes Pliny on the Troglodites and discusses the Garamantes, who, "free from marriage ties, live at random with women." The tradition seems

to have originated in Pliny and Solinus, through Martianus Capella, Isidore of Seville, and Rabanus Maurus, to Honorius of Autun and Vincent of Beauvais. Jones points out that the Ethiopian's blackness was "fairly common knowledge" in the Middle Ages, citing Chaucer's "Parson's Tale": "his flesh was blak as an Ethiopeen for heete." The reference to the Ethiopian's skin color in Jeremiah 13:23 "gave rise — through the emblem books — to the widely quoted proverb regarding the vain labour involved in 'washing an Ethiop white'" (5). On Alexander, see Armand Abel, *Le Roman d'Alexandre, légendaire médiéval* (Brussels: Office de Publicité, 1955); George Cary, *The Medieval Alexander* (Cambridge: Cambridge University Press, 1965); and D. J. A. Ross, *Alexander historiatus: A Guide to Medieval Illustrated Alexander Literature* (London: Warburg Institute, 1963). The notes to Le Goff's essay "The Medieval West and the Indian Ocean," in *Time, Work, and Culture,* are a bibliographical essay in themselves (341ff.).

16   Le Goff, *Time, Work, and Culture,* 195ff. See also Bernheimer, *Wild Men,* 106–7.

17   Le Goff, *Time, Work, and Culture,* 200, citing Roger Sherman Loomis, ed., *Arthurian Literature in the Middle Ages* (Oxford, 1959), 68–69, 130–31.

18   Bernheimer, *Wild Men,* 86–88, citing Pliny, *Historia Naturalis* 7.2.24; Herodotus, *Histories,* 4.91.

19   Bernheimer, *Wild Men,* figure 20.

20   See ibid., 92.

21   Ibid., 92 n. 22, 204; MS in Bibliothèque Nationale, Paris, M.F. 2810. See H. Omont, *Le Livre des Merveilles* (Paris, 1907), pl. 182, 189; and Morgan Library MS 461, fol. 41v.

22   An example of wild men in Alexander manuscripts may be found in an illustration in Harleian MS 4979 (ca. 1300) of the text of a chapter entitled "Coment Alexander trova un home sauvage et le fist ardoir pour ce que il navoit, point dentendement mais estoit ausi come une beste"; see Bernheimer, *Wild Men,* 92 and 204 n. 23, citing M. R. James, *The Romance of Alexander* (Oxford: Clarendon Press, 1933), facsimile of MS of 1338–44, Bodleian 264, fol. 36v, *Comment Alexander combata avec ieaundis,* and fols. 66v and 67r. See also Margaret Dean-Smith, "Folk-Play Origins of the English Masque," *Folk-Lore* 65 (1954): 84–85, for discussion of the Wydeville MS. Bernheimer notes the "widespread belief that wild men and women were black" (15 and n. 34). He comments that the romanciers "do not regard hairiness as a necessary symptom of wildness induced by insanity; they are satisfied with describing the victim's total disarray, or with letting him turn all black as a sign of his demoniac state." *Wigalois,* by Wirnt von Gravensberg (13th c.), describes a wild woman as "Diu was in einer varwe gar swarz, ruch als ein beer" ("She was of a black color and as rough as a bear" — with a flat nose, big teeth, and a twisted hunchback). *Wigalois,* ed. J. M. N. Kapteyn (Bonn: F. Klopp, 1926), vv. 6288, 6284; Bernheimer, 191–92 nn. 34, 38. In Hartmann von Aue's *Iwein,* "'unz daz der edel tore wart gelich einem môre in allem sînem lîbe'* — the noble fool became like a negro in all his body." Bernheimer, 192 n. 34; citing Aue, *Iwein, der Ritter mit dem Löwen,* ed. H. Naumann and H. Steinger (Leipzig, 1933), v. 3237.

23   Bernheimer, *Wild Men,* 147, citing Betty Kurth, *Die Deutschen Bildteppiche des Mittelalters* (Vienna: A. Schroll and Co., 1926), pls. 108, 114–19.

24   Le Goff, *Time, Work, and Culture,* 197.

25   It is not surprising, then, that masques of Moors and other "grotesques" were extremely popular with the young king Edward VI of England, but not at all during the bleak reign of Phillip and Mary; see Orgel, *Jonsonian Masque,* 84, citing

Chambers, *Mediaeval Stage* 1:406: By the time of Edward VI, masques "began to emphasize spectacle for its own sake and often turned into grotesquerie. . . . In 1551, 'the masks . . . were of apes and bagpipes, of cats, of Greek worthies, and of "medyoxes" ("double visaged, th'one syde lyke a man, th'other lyke death").' In this year Edward had revived the office of Lord of Misrule, . . . and conferred it on George Ferrers. Possibly it was his influence that resulted in the exoticism of the entertainments: we find masques of women as Moors . . . of Amazons, of covetous men with long noses and torchbearers with baboon faces, . . . and finally, eight days before the young king's death in 1553, what Ferrers described as a 'dronken maske.'" George Ferrers staged for Edward a masque of Moors in 1547, another "masque involving Moors on 6 January 1551, and a masque of female Moors at Christmas 1551." See Albert Feuillerat, ed., *Documents Relating to the Office of the Revels at Court in the Time of King Edward VI and Queen Mary* (London: David Nutt, 1914), 26–33, 48, 85; Jones, *Othello's Countrymen,* 30; Welsford, *Court Masque,* 145ff. The history of this shift enacts a split between the chaotic body and the demand for its reform. The 1594 revels in Scotland for the prince's baptism included a "maske" of Turks and Christian Knights of Malta: "The Abbot of Haly-rudhous, in woman's apparell tooke up the ring sindrie tymes. The Lord Hume, in Turkish raiment, the king himself, in his masking geir, with a white overthwart croce, the badge of the knights of the Holie Spirit, which was muche mislyked by good men" (cited in Mill, *Mediaeval Plays in Scotland,* 53–54 n. 2).

26 Fernández-Armesto notes the importance of "chivalry" in Portuguese expansionism in the Atlantic (*Before Columbus,* 185). See Macdougall's chapter "Royal Obsession," in *James IV* (223–46).

27 On the "lasting trauma" of Islam, see Edward W. Said, *Orientalism* (New York: Pantheon Books, 1978), 59. Mackie, *King James IV,* 201–2, citing *LHTA* 4:40–41: "The secund day of Maij [1508], payit to Robert Bertoun, quhilk he laid doun for ane schip of silvir weyand xxxj½ unce, quhilk he offerit for the King in Sanct James in Spanze." Mackie discusses the early history of James's maneuverings with regard to a crusade at 202–6. Macdougall criticizes Mackie's and others' "broadly accepted view of James's naivety" with respect to his desire for crusade but agrees that James "professed himself interested" in the idea (*James IV,* 201). Macdougall also notes that "the outworn crusading ideal had acquired new relevance in European diplomacy following the seizure of Constantinople by the Turks in 1453" (202); the Moors were driven from Spain in 1492 (203).

28 There is considerable evidence for the presence of blacks in James's court. Payment, for example, "is recorded in 1504 for the transport of the 'More lassis' from Dunfermline to Edinburgh," and later that year a "More las was cristinit." Edwards, "Africans in Britain before 1560," 6–7. See *LHTA* 2:465, 469; 3:182, 377, 388; 4:338, 62, 112, 139, for references to the "Moors" in James's court. See also Edwards and Walvin, *Black Personalities,* esp. 3–15, "Africans in Britain before the Eighteenth Century."

29 Edwards, "Africans in Britain before 1560," 6. Mackie, *King James IV,* discusses the Bartons' longstanding feud with Portugal at 207. Macdougall, in *James IV,* discusses the link between events in the Highlands and James's ideal of pilgrimage to the Holy Land (198), and the tournament ceremonies "as aggressive reminders of James IV's closeness to the English throne": "In the last analysis, . . . it was not simply the Scottish nobility, but James himself, who looked beyond the tournament to the reality of conflict with England" (295).

30 In the 1590s Elizabeth — who had staged, earlier in her reign, a masque of Moors and a masque of Barbarians — received an "embassy from the King of Morocco, along with the gift of a fine portrait of a Moorish nobleman," at the same time that she was issuing instructions to deport, on the grounds of dearth and heathenism, the "great number of Negroes and blackamoors which . . . are carried into this realm." See Jones, *Othello's Countrymen*, 10, 12, 49 n. 38; *Acts of Privy Council* 26 (1596–97): 16, 20–21; P. L. Hughes and J. F. Larkin, *Tudor Royal Proclamations, 1558–1603* (New Haven, 1969), 221; Edwards and Walvin, *Black Personalities*, 12–13. But at the Lord Mayors' show in 1617 the Grocers exhibited a King of the Moors, an island of spices, and blacks (mounted on griffins and camels) who distributed foreign fruits to the spectators. Edwards and Walvin, *Black Personalities*, 11, citing Charles Knight, ed., *London*, vol. 6 (London: Henry G. Bohn, 1851), 155. A foreign threat is domesticated and then becomes a domestic threat, re-represented as the gift of a portrait (the Moor in his ideal "form") and finally as a plenitude and manifoldness recovered through England's commercial power and available, not only to the aristocracy, but to the entire nation.

31 Jeanne de Laval, for whom the emprise was secretly arranged and who married René in 1455, presided over the tournament. Vulson, *Le Vray Théâtre d'Honnevr* 81; Cripps-Day, *History of the Tournament*, 87, 83, citing Menestrier, *L'Art du Blason*, 169; Theodore Quatrebarbes, *Oeuvres Choisies du Roi René* (Paris: Picard, 1849), 1:lxxvi; Antoine de Ruffi, *Histoire des Comtes de Provence*, 396.

32 Ingeborg Nixon, ed., *Thomas of Erceldoune* (Copenhagen: Akademisk Forlag, 1980), pt. 1, ll. 129–140, pp. 35–36. All citations to the poem are taken from this edition. Thanks to Dr. Emily Lyle for pointing out this reference to me. Nixon observes, interestingly, that in the romance *The Turk and Gawain* a Turk plays something like the role of the lady in *Thomas* (pt. 2, pp. 23–24).

33 Nixon, ed., *Thomas of Erceldoune*, pt. 2, p. 49; p. 2, p. 23, citing *Syr Gawayne*, ed. Sir Frederic Madden (Edinburgh: Bannatyne Club, 1839), 95ff.

34 Bernheimer, *Wild Men*, 34–36, and n. 28. A number of early glossaries give entries like "Lamia, holzmoia vel wildaz wip" (from a tenth-century Austrian glossary). Two glossaries of the twelfth century equate *holzwib* or *vvildiz wip* with *lamia* (35). Bernheimer also notes the various forms of *holzmove, -mowa, -muowa, -muevo, -muhwa, -mûa, -muoia, -miua, -moa* (collected in Hansen, *Quellen und Unterschungen Zur Geschichte des Hexenwahns und der Hexenverfolgung im Mittelalters* [Bonn, 1901], 618 and 649), related to the German *Muhme*. The form *Maia* survives in the carnival in the Vintschgau, the Tyrol, and "is there applied to the mask of a man dressed as a woman who sprinkles water on the spectators" (Bernheimer, 196 n. 49). Welsford, *Court Masque*, notes early modern derivations of *mommon, mommerie* from the Greek *mommo*, meaning "a mask," which is equated in the glossary of Hesychius with *mormo*, "a thing that frightens children" (33–34, citing Hesychius, *Lexicon* [Jena, 1861]). The Greek word means "'a child's bugbear, a frightening mask and an ugly female spirit' (sometimes identified with the child-slaughtering ogress Lamia)" (34, and n. 2). These etymologies are speculative. See Welsford, 14–15, 35 n. 3, for parallels between Perchta and Mormo, for the name Perchten applied both to maskers and to ghosts or demons, and for the custom of the ugly Perchten who wear black sheepskins and appear by night vs. the beautiful Perchten who wear no masks and appear by day, citing Frazer, *The Scapegoat* (London: MacMillan, 1913), 240–52. Perchta led the wild hunt, it appears, and Bernheimer notes that the wild man was sometimes used to frighten

children (23–24, 193 nn. 1 and 2). Cf. also Ovid's myth that Anna Perenna, "feminine impersonation of the year," tricked Mars by putting her old body "in the place of that of the goddess Minerva" (Bernheimer, 81; Watt, ed., *Fasti* 3:675).

35 Ananda K. Coomaraswamy, "On the Loathly Bride," *Speculum* 20 (1945): 393, 395, citing Jatis Chandra De, "Sidelights on the Hindu Conception of Sovereignty," in *The Cultural Heritage of India*, vol. 3 (Calcutta: Sri Ramakrishna Centenary Committee, 1937), 258. See also William Price Albrecht, *The Loathly Lady in "Thomas of Erceldoune"* (Aubuquerque: University of New Mexico Press, 1954), on the theme of "sovereignty desired by women."

36 Michael J. Enright, "King James and His Island: An Archaic Kingship Belief?" *Scottish Historical Review* 55 (1976): 37 n. 3. He refers to Charles Howard McIlwain, *The Political Works of James I* (Cambridge, 1918), 272, and to Alexander H. Krappe, "The Sovereignty of Erin," *American Journal of Philology* 63 (1942): 448–49. Krappe also suggests that since the epithet applied to Uthr Ben (Uther Pendragon) by Talieson is *arthu*, "black," there is "sound reason to revert to the etymology of the name *Arthur* proposed by Robert Briffault: Arthur is the Welsh *arthu*, composed of *ar* 'very' and *du* 'black.' Arthur would then be the Very Black One." See Briffault, *The Mothers: A Study of the Origins of Sentiments and Institutions* (London: G. Allen and Unwin, 1927), 432, and Krappe, "Arturus Cosmocrator," *Speculum* 20 (1945): 407, referring to William F. Skene, *The Four Ancient Books of Wales*, vol. 2 (Edinburgh: Edmonston and Douglas, 1868), 2:203–4. These etymologies, again, are speculative. On dynasty myths, see also p. 114, p. 316 n. 65.

37 Keen, *Chivalry*, plate 22; Universitätsbibliothek, Heidelberg.

38 See Coomaraswamy, "On the Loathly Bride," 396 n. 1, for a reference to Coomaraswamy, *Spiritual Authority and Temporal Power in the Indian Theory of Government* (New Haven: American Oriental Society, 1942), esp. nn. 26, 45: "Alike in government and marriage, the woman's is the power, and the man's the authority. By a tyrant or virago the feminine 'power' is abused; by legitimate king or true wife, exercised in accordance with justice."

39 See Mary Ann Doane, "Film and the Masquerade: Theorising the Female Spectator," *Screen* 23 (1982): 74–87.

40 Doane discusses the opposition between look and image, activity and passivity, in terms of "an opposition between proximity and distance in relation to the image. It is in this sense that the very logic behind the structure of the gaze demands a sexual division. . . . For the female spectator there is a certain over-presence of the image — she *is* the image"; "This body so close, so excessive, prevents the woman from assuming a position similar to the man's in relation to signifying systems. For she is haunted by the loss of a loss, the lack of that lack so essential for the realisation of the ideals of semiotic systems," i.e., the distance from the body that allows language and signification to take place. Ibid., 77–79.

41 *LHTA* 3:258.

42 *LHTA* 3:259; the cost of the materials for the black lady's gown was over twenty-nine pounds.

43 *LHTA* 3:259.

44 *LHTA* 3:259, 258. Green is, in Dunbar's *The Goldyn Targe*, associated with "Venus chevalry"—who wars against the golden shield of Reason. It is tempting to suggest that the dark lady's colors were themselves a double image — of, on the one hand, embodiment and enthrallment, and, on the other hand, the visual brightness that encodes the gaze's power to distance the body.

45 Pitscottie, *Historie of Scotland* 244.

46 See *LHTA* 4:129.

47 Kinsley, ed., *Dunbar*, p. 106, no. 33.

48 See Lacan, "Desire in *Hamlet*," 38.

49 *LHTA* 3:259. Thanks to Priscilla Bawcutt for pointing out to me the potential sig-
    nificance of this entry. Feuillerat, ed., *Revels at Court*, 85 lists for the 1551/52
    Christmas masques "one of moores wth black skallopes vpon tynsell . . . for ye
    making and garnishing wherof was . . . vysars lawne partelettes sleves gloves
    sarcenett of Dyverse Sortes." Jones, *Othello's Countrymen*, 29–30, cites Feuillerat,
    26–33, on the costuming of characters for Edward's Shrovetide masque of 1547,
    in which "blackening was effected through the use of black gloves, nether stock-
    ings, and face masks." See Jones, 28, on an entertainment attended by Henry VIII
    and the earl of Essex in 1510, in which six ladies appeared with their "faces, neckes,
    armes and handes covered with fyne plesaunce blacke . . . so that the same ladies
    semed to be nigrost or blacke Mores." Hall, *Henry VIII*, 15–17 (1st Yr.); also cited
    by Welsford, *Court Masque*, 126–27.

50 See Edwards, "Africans in Britain before 1560," n. 28, for an account of this problem.

51 David Laing, ed., *The Poems of William Dunbar*, vol. 2 (Edinburgh: Lang and
    Forbes, 1834), 306–8.

52 James Paterson, ed., *The Life and Poems of William Dunbar* (Edinburgh: William P.
    Nimmo and Simpkin Marshall and Co., 1860), 275.

53 Æ. J. G. Mackay, introduction to *The Poems of William Dunbar*, ed. John Small
    (Edinburgh: Scottish Text Society, 1893), 1:ciii.

54 Mackay writes that "the blackamore lady seems to have been one of the African
    girls captured in a Portuguese ship by one of the Bartons, and presented to the
    king, who had them baptised, under the names of Elen and Margaret. . . . A tour-
    nament was held in June 1507 in honour of Elen More, or Black Elen. . . . It has
    been doubted whether Dunbar's verses refer to the same sable beauty [because his
    poem describes the black woman as having "landet furth of the last schippis"] . . .
    but this is probably no more than a poetic licence as to time" (Small, ed., *Dunbar*
    1:cii–ciii). In Small, ed., *Dunbar* 3:286, note to l. 3, Mackay adds: "It is only a
    matter of probability to whom this poem was written." Schipper in essence repeats
    Mackay, adding that "the preparations for this ludicrous tournament, which must
    have formed part of the gossip of the court for some time, probably instigated
    our poet to express his own opinion on that strange kind of tournament shortly
    before it would come to pass"; he echoes earlier cautions regarding the dating of
    the poem. J. Schipper, ed., *The Poems of William Dunbar* (Vienna: Kaiserliche
    Akademie der Wissenschaften, 1894).

55 Baxter, *William Dunbar*, 166.

56 This is not quite as ludicrous a proposition as it may at first seem; the colophon
    "Quod Dunbar of ane blak moir," from which the poem derives its traditional
    title, is found in the Maitland Folio MS (ca. 1570) and cannot be presumed to
    be authorial. Moreover, the rhetoric of ugliness and churlishness in the Middle
    Ages often deployed "blackness" without specific reference to the category of race
    (though racial and rhetorical conceptions of blackness could crisscross with ease).
    In the *Roman de la Rose*, Danger is described as "Hairy and black"; Guillaume
    de Lorris and Jean de Meun, *The Romance of the Rose*, ed. Charles W. Dunn, trans.
    Harry W. Robbins (New York: E. P. Dutton and Co., 1962), section 13, p. 63,
    l. 69. Wild men, moors, churls like Danger, and loathly ladies like Dame Ragnell

were all part of the "literary tradition in the description of human ugliness and deformity" that went back to Thersites, through the Roman schools of rhetoric, and was partly conveyed to the later Middle Ages through the exotic monstrosities of the Alexander romances. See Bernheimer, *Wild Men*, 124–25.

57 *LHTA* 3:xlviii–xlix.
58 Carleton's letter is quoted in Herford, Simpson, and Simpson, eds., *Ben Jonson* 10:449.
59 Tom Scott, *Dunbar: A Critical Exposition of the Poems* (Edinburgh: Oliver and Boyd, 1966), 67.
60 Edwards, "Africans in Britain before 1560," 10.
61 Kinsley, ed., *Dunbar*, xiii. Baxter gives the date of the first payment of Dunbar's pension as 1501; see pp. 148, 328, 51.
62 The quotation is from Mackay, in Small, ed., *Dunbar*, liv.
63 de Lauretis, "Desire in Narrative," 110.
64 Welsford, *Court Masque*, 176–78. The tournament is described in M. Raffaello Gualterotti, *Feste nelle Nozze del Serenissimo Don Francesco Medici Gran Duca di Toscana: et della Sereniss. sua Consorte la Sig. Bianca Capello* (Florence, 1579), 13ff. Herford, Simpson, and Simpson, eds. *Ben Jonson* 7:450.
65 Doane, "Film and the Masquerade," 81.

Select Bibliography

The Acts of Parliament of Scotland. Edited by T. Thompson and C. Innes. 12 vols. Edinburgh, 1814–75.

Adams, Ian H. *The Making of Urban Scotland.* London: Croom Helm; Montreal: McGill-Queen's University Press, 1978.

Anderson, Perry. *Lineages of the Absolutist State.* NLB, 1974; rpt., London: Verso Editions, 1979.

Anglo, Sydney. "The London Pageants for the Reception of Katharine of Aragon: November 1501." *Journal of the Warburg and Courtauld Institutes* 26 (1963): 53–89.

Anglo, Sydney. *Spectacle, Pageantry, and Early Tudor Policy.* Oxford: Clarendon Press, 1969.

Apted, Michael R., and Susan Hannabuss, eds. *Painters in Scotland, 1301–1700: A Biographical Dictionary.* Edinburgh: Edina Press, 1978.

Axton, Marie. *The Queen's Two Bodies: Drama and the Elizabethan Succession.* London: Royal Historical Society, 1977.

Balfour-Melville, E. W. M. *James I, King of Scots: 1406–1437.* London: Methuen, 1936.

Bawcutt, Priscilla. "Dunbar's Use of the Symbolic Lion and Thistle." In *Kingship.* Edited by Emily Lyle. (*Cosmos* 2 [1986]: 83–97).

Bawcutt, Priscilla. *Gavin Douglas: A Critical Study.* Edinburgh: Edinburgh University Press, 1976.

Bawcutt, Priscilla, ed. *The Shorter Poems of Gavin Douglas.* Edinburgh: William Blackwood, 1967.

Baxter, J. W. *William Dunbar: A Biographical Study.* Edinburgh: Oliver and Boyd, 1952.

Bernheimer, Richard. *Wild Men in the Middle Ages: A Study in Art, Sentiment, and Demonology.* Cambridge: Harvard University Press, 1952.

Bevington, David, ed. *Medieval Drama.* Boston: Houghton Mifflin, 1975.

Bourdieu, Pierre. *Outline of a Theory of Practice.* Translated by Richard Nice. Cambridge: Cambridge University Press, 1977.

Brault, Gerard J. *Early Blazon: Heraldic Terminology in the Twelfth and Thirteenth Centuries with Special Reference to Arthurian Literature.* Oxford: Clarendon Press, 1972.

Brown, Jennifer M., ed. *Scottish Society in the Fifteenth Century.* New York: St. Martin's Press, 1977.

Brown, P. Hume. *Early Travellers in Scotland.* Edinburgh: D. Douglas, 1891.

Buchanan, Patricia Hill. *Margaret Tudor, Queen of Scots.* Edinburgh: Scottish Academic Press, 1985.

Burke, Kenneth. *The Rhetoric of Religion: Studies in Logology.* Berkeley: University of California Press, 1970.

Chew, Samuel C. *The Virtues Reconciled: An Iconographic Study.* Toronto: University of Toronto Press, 1947.

Clephan, R. Coltman. *The Tournament: Its Periods and Phases.* London: Methuen, 1919.

Cline, Ruth Huff. "The Influence of Romances on Tournaments of the Middle Ages." *Speculum* 20 (1945): 204–11.

Coomaraswamy, Ananda K. "On the Loathly Bride." *Speculum* 20 (1945): 391–404.

Cowhig, Ruth. "Blacks in English Renaissance Drama and the Role of Shakespeare's Othello." In David Dabydeen, ed., *The Black Presence in English Literature.* 1–25. Manchester: Manchester University Press, 1985.

Cripps-Day, Francis Henry. *The History of the Tournament in England and in France.* London: Bernard Quaritch, 1918.

Cruden, Stewart. *The Scottish Castle.* 3d ed. Edinburgh: Spurbooks, 1981.

Deleuze, Gilles, and Félix Guattari. *Anti-Oedipus: Capitalism and Schizophrenia.* Translated by Robert Hurley, Mark Seem, and Helen R. Lane. Minneapolis: University of Minnesota Press, 1983.

de Laurentis, Teresa. "Desire in Narrative." in *Alice Doesn't: Feminism, Semiotics, Cinema.* 103–57. Bloomington: Indiana University Press, 1984.

Dennys, Rodney. *Heraldry and the Heralds.* London: Jonathan Cape, 1982.

Dicks, Brian. "The Scottish Medieval Town: A Search for Origins." In Gordon and Dicks, eds. *Scottish Urban History.* 23–51.

Dickson, Robert, and John Philip Edmond. *Annals of Scottish Printing: From the Introduction of the Art in 1507 to the Beginning of the Seventeenth Century.* Cambridge, Eng.: MacMillan and Bowes, 1890.

Dickson, Thomas, Sir James Balfour-Paul, and C. T. Innes, eds. *Compota thesaurariorum regum Scotorum, Accounts of the Lord High Treasurer of Scotland.* 12 vols. Edinburgh: H. M. General Register House, 1877–1916.

Doane, Mary Ann. "Film and the Masquerade: Theorising the Female Spectator." *Screen* 23 (1982): 74–87.

Donaldson, Gordon. *Scotland: James V to James VII.* Vol. 3 of *The Edinburgh History of Scotland.* Edinburgh: Oliver and Boyd, 1965; rpt., New York: Frederick A. Praeger, 1966.

Donaldson, Gordon. *Scottish Kings.* London: B. T. Batsford, 1967; 2d ed., 1977.

Donaldson, Gordon, ed. *Scottish Historical Documents.* Edinburgh: Scottish Academic Press, 1974.

Douglas, Gavin. *The Poetical Works of Gavin Douglas.* Edited by John Small. Vol. 4. Edinburgh: William Paterson, 1874.

Douglas, Gavin. *The Shorter Poems of Gavin Douglas.* Edited by Priscilla J. Bawcutt. Edinburgh: William Blackwood, for the Scottish Text Society, 1967.

Dowden, John. *The Medieval Church in Scotland: Its Constitution, Organisation and Law.* Glasgow: James MacLehose and Sons, 1910.

Duby, Georges. *Medieval Marriage: Two Models from Twelfth-Century France.* Translated by Elborg Foster. Baltimore: Johns Hopkins University Press, 1978.

Dunbar, William. *The Poems of William Dunbar.* Edited by James Kinsley. Oxford: Clarendon Press, 1979.

Dunbar, William. *The Poems of William Dunbar.* Edited by William Mackay Mackenzie. Edinburgh: Porpoise Press, 1932.

Dunbar, William. *The Poems of William Dunbar.* Edited by J. Schipper. Vienna Kaiserliche Akademie der Wissenschaften, 1894.

Dunbar, William. *The Poems of William Dunbar.* Edited by John Small. Edinburgh: Scottish Text Society, 1893.

Dunlop, Annie I. *The Life and Times of James Kennedy, Bishop of St. Andrews.* Edinburgh: Oliver and Boyd, 1950.

Durkan, John. "The Beginnings of Humanism in Scotland," *Innes Review* 4 (1953): 5–24.

Economou, George D. *The Goddess Natura in Medieval Literature.* Cambridge: Harvard University Press, 1972.

Edwards, Paul, and James Walvin. *Black Personalities in the Era of the Slave Trade.* London: Macmillan, 1983.

Ehrhart, Margaret J. *The Judgment of the Trojan Prince Paris in Medieval Literature.* Philadelphia: University of Pennsylvania Press, 1987.

Enright, Michael J. "King James and His Island: An Archaic Kingship Belief?" *Scottish Historical Review* 55 (1976): 29–40.

Fenichel, Otto. *The Psychoanalytic Theory of Neurosis.* New York: W. W. Norton and Co., 1945.

Ferguson, Arthur B. *The Indian Summer of English Chivalry: Studies in the Decline and Transformation of Chivalric Idealism.* Durham, N.C.: Duke University Press, 1960.

Ferguson, William. *Scotland's Relations with England: A Survey to 1707.* Edinburgh: John Donald, 1977.

Fernández-Armesto, Felipe. *Before Columbus: Exploration and Colonization from the Mediterranean to the Atlantic, 1229–1492.* Philadelphia: University of Pennsylvania Press, 1987.

Feuillerat, Albert, ed. *Documents Relating to the Office of the Revels at Court in the Time of King Edward VI and Queen Mary.* London: David Nutt, 1914.

Fradenburg, Louise. "The Scottish Chaucer: Studies in Fifteenth-Century Reception." Ph.D. diss. University of Virginia, 1982.

Gennep, Arnold van. *The Rites of Passage.* Translated by Monika B. Vizedom and Gabrielle L. Caffee. Chicago: University of Chicago Press, 1960.

Gibb, Andrew, and Ronan Paddison. "The Rise and Fall of Burghal Monopolies in Scotland: The Case of the North East." *Scottish Geographical Magazine* 99 (1983): 130–40.

Girard, René. "The Plague in Literature and Myth." *Texas Studies in Literature and Language* 15 (1974): 833–50.

Goldberg, Jonathan. "'Upon a publike stage': The Royal Gaze and Jacobean Theater." In David M. Bergeron, ed., *Research Opportunities in Renaissance Drama* 24 (1981): 17–21.

Gordon, George, and Brian Dicks, eds. *Scottish Urban History.* Aberdeen: Aberdeen University Press, 1983.

"The Growth of Edinburgh." In *The Book of the Old Edinburgh Club.* Edinburgh: T. and A. Constable, for the Old Edinburgh Club, 1908.

Hall, Edward. *Henry VIII.* In *The Lives of the Kings.* London: T. C. and E. C. Jack, 1904.

Hannay, Robert Kerr, and R. L. Mackie, eds. *The Letters of James IV, 1505–1513.* Edinburgh: Edinburgh University Press, 1953.

Herford, C. H., Percy Simpson, and Evelyn Simpson, eds. *Ben Jonson.* 11 vols. Oxford: Clarendon Press, 1925–52.

Hilton, Rodney, ed. *The Transition from Feudalism to Capitalism.* NLB, 1976; rpt., London: Verso Editions, 1978; rpt. 1984.

Hindess, Barry, and Paul Q. Hirst. *Pre-Capitalist Modes of Production.* London: Routledge and Kegan Paul, 1975.

Huizinga, Johan. *The Waning of the Middle Ages: A Study of the Forms of Life, Thought, and Art in France and the Netherlands in the Fourteenth and Fifteenth Centuries.* Translated by F. Hopman. Harmondsworth, Eng.: Penguin Books, 1924; rpt., Pelican Books, 1972.

IJsewijn, J., and D. F. S. Thomson. "The Latin Poems of Jacobus Follisius or James Foullis of Edinburgh." *Humanistica Lovaniensia* 24 (1975): 102–52.

Ireland, John of. *The Meroure of Wyssdome . . . by Johannes de Irlandia.* Edited by Charles Macpherson. Vol. 1. Edinburgh: William Blackwood and Sons, for the Scottish Text Society, 1926.

Jacquot, Jean, ed. Les Fêtes de la Renaissance: Etudes réunies et présentées. Paris: Centre National de la Recherche Scientifique, 1961.

Jameson, Fredric. *The Political Unconscious: Narrative as a Socially Symbolic Act.* Ithaca: Cornell University Press, 1981.

Jones, Eldred. *Othello's Countrymen: The African in English Renaissance Drama.* London: Oxford University Press, 1965.

Kantorowicz, Ernst. *The King's Two Bodies: A Study in Mediaeval Political Theology.* Princeton: Princeton University Press, 1957.

Keen, Maurice. *Chivalry.* New Haven: Yale University Press, 1984.

Kelly, Henry Ansgar. *Love and Marriage in the Age of Chaucer.* Ithaca: Cornell University Press, 1975.

King, Pamela M. "Dunbar's *The Golden Targe*: A Chaucerian Masque." *Studies in Scottish Literature* 19 (1984): 115–31.

Kingsford, Charles Lethbridge, ed. *Chronicles of London.* Oxford: Clarendon Press, 1905.

Kinsley, James, ed. *The Poems of William Dunbar.* Oxford: Clarendon Press, 1979.

Kirkpatrick, John, ed. "The Scottish Nation in the University of Orléans, 1336–1538." In *Miscellany of the Scottish History Society,* vol. 2. Edinburgh: Edinburgh University Press, 1904.

Klapisch-Zuber, Christiane. *Women, Family, and Ritual in Renaissance Italy.* Translated by Lydia Cochrane. Chicago: University of Chicago Press, 1985.

Kristeva, Julia. *Powers of Horror: An Essay on Abjection.* Translated by Leon S. Roudiez. New York: Columbia University Press, 1982.

Kristeva, Julia. *Tales of Love.* Translated by Leon S. Roudiez. New York: Columbia University Press, 1987.

Lacan, Jacques. "Desire and the Interpretation of Desire in *Hamlet.*" *Yale French Studies* 55–56 (1977): 11–52.

Lacan, Jacques. *Écrits: A Selection.* Translated by Alan Sheridan. New York: W. W. Norton and Co., 1977.

Laing, David, ed. *The Poems of William Dunbar.* Vol. 2. Edinburgh: Lang and Forbes, 1834.

Laing, David, and John Small, eds. *Select Remains of the Ancient Popular and Romance Poetry of Scotland.* Edinburgh: William Blackwood and Sons, 1885.

Lawson, Alexander, ed. *The Kingis Quair and the Quare of Jelusy.* London: Adam and Charles Black, 1910.

Le Goff, Jacques. *Time, Work, and Culture in the Middle Ages.* Translated by Arthur Goldhammer. Chicago: University of Chicago Press, 1980.

Leslie, John. *The Historie of Scotland Wrytten first in Latin by the Most Reuerend and Worthy Jhone Leslie Bishop of Rosse and Translated in Scottish by Father James*

Dalrymple. Edited by E. G. Cody and William Murison. Edinburgh: William Blackwood and Sons, 1890.

Leslie, John. *The History of Scotland, from the Death of King James I in the Year MCCCCXXXVI to the Year MDLXI by John Leslie, Bishop of Ross*. Edinburgh: Bannatyne Club, 1830.

Lesnick, Henry G. "The Structural Significance of Myth and Flattery in Peele's *Arraignment of Paris*." *Studies in Philology* 65 (1968): 163–70.

Lewis, C. S. *English Literature in the Sixteenth Century Excluding Drama*. Oxford: Clarendon Press, 1954.

Lindsay, David. *A Satire of the Three Estates*. Edited by Matthew McDiarmid. London: Heinemann, 1967.

Lukacher, Ned. *Primal Scenes: Literature, Philosophy, Psychoanalysis*. Ithaca: Cornell University Press, 1986.

Lyall, Roderick J. "Books and Book Owners in Fifteenth-Century Scotland." In *Book Production and Publishing in Britain, 1375–1475*. Edited by Jeremy Griffiths and Derek Pearsall, 239–56. Cambridge: Cambridge University Press, 1989.

Lyall, Roderick J. "The Court as a Cultural Centre." *History Today* 34 (1984): 27–33.

Lyall, Roderick J., and Felicity Riddy, eds. *Proceedings of the Third International Conference on Scottish Language and Literature (Medieval and Renaissance)*. Glasgow: William Culross and Sons, 1981.

Lythe, S. G. E. "Economic Life." In Brown, ed., *Scottish Society in the Fifteenth Century*. 66–84.

MacCary, W. Thomas. *Childlike Achilles: Ontogeny and Phylogeny in the Iliad*. New York: Columbia University Press, 1982.

McDiarmid, Matthew P., ed. *The Kingis Quair of James Stewart*. Totowa, N.J.: Rowman and Littlefield, 1973.

Macdougall, Norman. *James III: A Political Study*. Edinburgh: John Donald, 1982.

Macdougall, Norman. *James IV*. Edinburgh: John Donald, 1989.

Macfarlane, Leslie J. "The Book of Hours of James IV and Margaret Tudor." *Innes Review* 11 (1961): 3–21.

Macfarlane, Leslie J. *William Elphinstone and the Kingdom of Scotland, 1431–1514: The Struggle for Order*. Aberdeen: Aberdeen University Press, 1985.

MacGregor, Duncan, ed. and trans. *The Rathen Manual*. Aberdeen: Aberdeen Ecclesiological Society, 1905.

Mackenzie, William Mackay. *The Scottish Burghs: An Expanded Version of the Rhind Lectures in Archaeology for 1945*. Edinburgh: Oliver and Boyd, 1949.

Mackenzie, William Mackay, ed. *The Poems of William Dunbar*. Edinburgh: Porpoise Press, 1932.

Mackie, R. L. *King James IV of Scotland: A Brief Survey of His Life and Times*. Edinburgh: Oliver and Boyd, 1958.

Macquarrie, Alan. *Scotland and the Crusades, 1095–1560*. Edinburgh: John Donald, 1985.

MacQueen, John. "The Literature of Fifteenth-Century Scotland." In Brown, ed., *Scottish Society in the Fifteenth Century*. 184–208.

McWilliam, Colin. *Scottish Townscape*. London: William Collins Sons, 1975.

Mair, Lucy. *Marriage*. New York: Pica Press, 1972.

Mâle, Emile. *The Gothic Image: Religious Art in France of the Thirteenth Century*. Translated by Dora Nussey. New York: Harper and Row, 1972.

Marshall, Rosalind K. *Virgins and Viragos: A History of Women in Scotland from 1080 to 1980.* London: Collins, 1983.

Marwick, Sir James D. *Charters and Other Documents Relating to the City of Edinburgh, A.D. 1143–1540.* Edinburgh: Scottish Burgh Records Society, 1871.

Marwick, Sir James D. *Extracts from the Records of the Burgh of Edinburgh, 1403–1589.* Edinburgh: Scottish Burgh Records Society, 1869–82.

Marwick, Sir James D. *The History of the Collegiate Church and Hospital of the Holy Trinity and the Trinity Hospital, Edinburgh, 1460–1661.* Edinburgh: Scottish Burgh Records Society, 1911.

Marwick, Sir James D., ed. *Records of the Convention of the Royal Burghs of Scotland, with Extracts from Other Records Relating to the Affairs of the Burghs of Scotland, 1295–1597.* Vol. 1. Edinburgh: William Paterson, for the Convention of Royal Burghs, 1866.

Mauss, Marcel. *The Gift: Forms and Functions of Exchange in Archaic Societies.* Translated by Ian Cunnison. Glencoe, Ill.: Free Press, 1954.

Mill, Anna Jean. *Mediaeval Plays in Scotland.* Edinburgh: William Blackwood and Sons, 1924; rpt., New York: Benjamin Blom, 1969.

Montrose, Louis Adrian. "'Eliza, Queen of shepheardes' and the Pastoral of Power." *English Literary Renaissance* 10 (1980): 153–82.

Mulvey, Laura. "Visual Pleasure and Narrative Cinema." *Screen* 16 (1975): 6–18.

Nicholson, Ranald. *Scotland: The Later Middle Ages.* Vol. 2 of *The Edinburgh History of Scotland.* New York: Barnes and Noble; Edinburgh: Oliver and Boyd, 1974.

Nixon, Ingeborg, ed. *Thomas of Erceldoune.* Copenhagen: Akademisk Forlag, 1980.

Nohrnberg, J. C. *The Analogy of the Faerie Queene.* Princeton: Princeton University Press, 1976.

Orgel, Stephen. *The Jonsonian Masque.* Cambridge: Harvard University Press, 1965.

Owst, G. R. *Literature and Pulpit in Medieval England: A Neglected Chapter in the History of English Letters and of the English People.* 2d ed. Oxford: Basil Blackwell, 1961.

Paterson, James, ed. *The Life and Poems of William Dunbar.* Edinburgh: William P. Nimmo and Simpkin Marshall and Co., 1860.

Paton, G. Campbell H. "Husband and Wife: Property Rights and Relationships." In *An Introduction to Scottish Legal History.* 99–115. Edinburgh: Robert Cunningham and Sons, 1958.

Pitcairn, R. *Criminal Trials and Other Proceedings before the High Court of Justiciary in Scotland, from A.D. MCCCCLXXXVIII to A.D. MDCXXIV.* Vol. 1. Edinburgh: William Tait; London: Longman, Rees, Orme, Brown, Green, and Longman, 1883.

Pitscottie, Robert Lindesay of. *The Historie and Cronicles of Scotland from the Slauchter of King James the First to the Ane thousand fyve hundreith thrie scoir fyftein zeir.* Edited by Æ. J. G. Mackay. Edinburgh: William Blackwood and Sons, for the Scottish Text Society, 1899.

Pitt-Rivers, Julian. "Honour and Social Status." In J. G. Peristiany, ed., *Honour and Shame: The Values of Mediterranean Society.* Chicago: University of Chicago Press, 1966.

Reeves, John D. "The Judgment of Paris as a Device of Tudor Flattery." *Notes and Queries* 199 (1954): 7–11.

Ross, Ian Simpson. *William Dunbar.* Leiden: Brill, 1981.

Scalingi, Paula Louise. "The Scepter or the Distaff: The Question of Female Sovereignty, 1516–1607." *The Historian* 41 (1978): 59–75.

Scanlan, James D. "Husband and Wife: Pre-Reformation Canon Law of Marriage of the Officials' Courts." In *An Introduction to Scottish Legal History*. Edinburgh: Robert Cunningham and Sons, 1958.

Scarry, Elaine. *The Body in Pain: The Making and Unmaking of the World*. New York: Oxford University Press, 1985.

Schipper, J., ed. *The Poems of William Dunbar*. Vienna: Kaiserliche Akademie der Wissenschaften, 1894.

Scott, Tom. *Dunbar: A Critical Exposition of the Poems*. Edinburgh: Oliver and Boyd, 1966.

Siebers, Tobin. *The Mirror of Medusa*. Berkeley: University of California Press, 1983.

Small, John, ed. *The Poems of William Dunbar*. Edinburgh: Scottish Text Society, 1893.

Small, John, ed. *The Poetical Works of Gavin Douglas*. Edinburgh: William Paterson, 1874.

Smith, Janet M. *The French Background of Middle Scots Literature*. Edinburgh: Oliver and Boyd, 1934.

Stafford, Pauline. *Queens, Concubines, and Dowagers: The King's Wife in the Early Middle Ages*. Athens: University of Georgia Press, 1983.

Starkey, David. "Representation through Intimacy: A Study in the Symbolism of Monarchy and Court Office in Early Modern England." In Ivan Lewis, ed., *Symbols and Sentiments: Cross-Cultural Studies in Symbolism*. London: Academic Press, 1977.

Stevenson, J. H., ed. *Gilbert of the Haye's Prose Manuscript (A.D. 1456)*. Vol. 2, *The Buke of Knychthede and The Buke of the Governaunce of Princis*. Edinburgh: William Blackwood and Sons, 1914.

Strickland, Agnes. *Lives of the Queens of Scotland and English Princesses Connected with the Regal Succession of Great Britain*. New York: Harper, 1859.

Strong, Roy. *Splendor at Court: Renaissance Spectacle and the Theater of Power*. Boston: Houghton Mifflin, 1973.

Stuart, J., et al. *Rotuli Scaccarii regum scotorum: The Exchequer Rolls of Scotland*. 23 vols. Edinburgh, 1878–1908.

Thomas, R. George, ed. *Ten Miracle Plays*. London: Edward Arnold, 1966.

Thompson, Colin, and Lorne Campbell. *Hugo van der Goes and the Trinity Panels in Edinburgh*. Edinburgh: Trustees of the National Gallery of Scotland, 1974.

Tufte, Virginia. *The Poetry of Marriage: The Epithalamium in Europe and Its Development in England*. Los Angeles: Tinnon-Brown, 1970.

Turner, Victor. *The Ritual Process: Structure and Anti-Structure*. Aldine, 1969; rpt., Ithaca: Cornell University Press, 1977.

Vale, Malcolm. *War and Chivalry: Warfare and Aristocratic Culture in England, France and Burgundy at the End of the Middle Ages*. London: Duckworth, 1981.

Vulson, Marc de. *La Science Heroiqve, Traitant de la Noblesse, et de l'Origine des Armes . . .* Paris: Sebastien Mabre-Cramoisy, 1669.

Vulson, Marc de. *Le Vray Théâtre d'Honnevr et de Chevaleri Ov le Miroir Heroiqve de la Noblesse*. Paris: Avgvstin Covrbe, 1648.

Warner, Marina. *Alone of All Her Sex: The Myth and the Cult of the Virgin Mary*. New York: Alfred A. Knopf, 1976.

Watson, Charles B. Boog, ed. *Roll of Edinburgh Burgesses and Guild-Brethren, 1406–1700*. Edinburgh: Scottish Record Society, 1929.

Watt, D. E. R., ed. *Fasti Ecclesiae Scoticanae Medii Aevi*. St. Andrews: Fasti Committee, 1969.

Welsford, Enid. *The Court Masque: A Study in the Relationship between Poetry and the Revels.* Cambridge: Cambridge University Press, 1927.

Weston, Jesse L. *The Three Days' Tournament: A Study in Romance and Folk-Lore.* London: David Nutt, 1902.

Whitehand, Jeremy W. R., and Khan Alauddin. "The Town Plans of Scotland: Some Preliminary Considerations." *Scottish Geographical Magazine* 85 (1969): 109–21.

Williams, Raymond. *The Country and the City.* New York: Oxford University Press, 1973.

Withington, R. *English Pageantry: An Historical Outline.* Vol. 1. Cambridge: Harvard University Press, 1918.

Wood, Charles T. *Joan of Arc and Richard III: Sex, Saints, and Government in the Middle Ages.* New York: Oxford University Press, 1988.

Wormald, Jenny. *Court, Kirk, and Community: Scotland, 1470–1625.* London: Edward Arnold, 1981.

Younge, John. *The Fyancells of Margaret, eldest Daughter of King Henry VIIth to James King of Scotland: Together with her Departure from England, Journey into Scotland, her Reception and Marriage there, and the great Feasts held on that Account; Written by John Younge, Somerset Herald, who attended the said Princess on her Journey.* In John Leland, *De Rebus Britannicis Collectanea.* Tomus Tertius. London: Gvl. et Jo. Richardson, 1770.

Zumthor, Paul. "The Great Game of Rhetoric." *New Literary History* 12 (1981): 493–508.

Index

Aberdeen (burgh of), 29, 173
Aberdeen Articles, 46
Aberdeen Breviary, 306n13, 307n17
Aberdeen Psalter, 180
abjection, 9, 199, 201, 202, 219, 272n33
accessibility, of sovereign, xiii, 70, 73
adventure: and security, 90, 93, 129, 131;
  literature of, 247; and marriage, in Bourdieu, 302n30
advice, to princes, 289n22
Aeneas, 55, 141, 246. *See also* Douglas,
  Eneados
Aeneid: and *Carmen elegum*, 55; manuscript commissioned by James III, 179–
  80, 276n19. *See also* Douglas, *Eneados*
Africa: as "known" to medieval Europe,
  248, 249
Africans: representations of, in Europe,
  247–48
aggression: and mother's body, 345n62. *See
  also* aggressivity
aggressivity, 197; and tournament, 197,
  218; in *Buke of the Law of Armys*, 199;
  and identification, 210, 345; and wild
  man, 236; and beauty, 244
Alain de Lille (poet), 139; *Anticlaudianus*,
  88; *De planctu naturae*, 88, 139, 317n73,
  326n36
Albany, Duke of. *See* Stewart, Alexander
alchemy, 95, 97, 288n12, 308n21
*Alexander, The Buik of. See Buik . . . of
  Alexander, The*
Alexander, MSS. of: and wild men, 248,
  249, 352n22
allegory: and tournament, 230–31
alliance, 98, 302n30; between Scotland and
  England, 305n10
alteration, power of, 92, 98, 104, 112, 126,
  139, 143, 287n4; and Creator, 59; in
  Strena, 60; and beauty, 112; and Judgment of Paris, 112; and sovereign, 114,

166, 167, 245; and language, 137, 142;
  and God, 137, 291n39, 298n4; in *Thrissill
  and Rois*, 140; in *Palice of Honour*, 186,
  188; in *Parzival*, 246–47
Amazons, in *Masque of Queenes*, 254
Andreae, John (14th-c. canonist), 88, 89
Anne, of Bohemia, Queen of England, 129,
  321n9
Anne, of Denmark, Queen of England, 72,
  113, 245, 262, 263
Anne Boleyn, Queen of England: 1533
  royal entry, 110, 118, 119, 309n23,
  315n59, 316n69
Annunciation, 86, 88, 303n34; and communitarian experience, 89; exogamous
  impulse in, 90; miracle plays of, 120,
  303n32; in Edinburgh pageants, 121;
  York play of, 116, 117, 303–4n36;
  Wakefield play of, 116, 300n16, 302n27,
  303n32, 317n77. *See also Ludus Coventriae*; Mary [Virgin, Regina]
antimasque, 79, 137, 139; and tournament
  of wild knight and black lady, 242; and
  Masque of Queenes, 293n44
Antoine d'Arces, Lord of la Bastie, 176–77,
  225, 227, 337n40
Aristotle: concept of *allotrios*, 328
armor: and tournament, 192, 201; in Bromyard, 201; in *Sir Gawain and the Green
  Knight*, 202, 344n57; in *Buke of Knychthede*, 203; and ideal image, 216; of James
  IV, for tournament of wild knight and
  black lady, 257
arms, 217, 218, 346n83; royal, of Scotland,
  179, 180, 181, 252; plain, 207, 212,
  344n52
Arthur, King, 337n44, 355n36; legend of,
  154, 155, 156, 248; in *Golagrus and Gawain*, 182; in *Lancelot of the Laik*, 182;
  and tournament of wild knight and
  black lady, 232, 240